Basic Dimensions in Conscious Thought

The Self and Socialization of Human Concerns

Psychocultural Research with the Thematic Apperception Test, Volume I

GEORGE A. DE VOS
AND ERIC DE VOS

ROWMAN & LITTLEFIELD PUBLISHERS, INC.
Lanham • Boulder • New York • Toronto • Oxford

ROWMAN & LITTLEFIELD PUBLISHERS, INC.

Published in the United States of America
by Rowman & Littlefield Publishers, Inc.
A wholly owned subsidiary of The Rowman & Littlefield Publishing Group, Inc.
4501 Forbes Boulevard, Suite 200, Lanham, Maryland 20706
www.rowmanlittlefield.com

PO Box 317
Oxford
OX2 9RU, UK

The Interpersonal Concerns Scoring System (ICSS) that is included as an Appendix in this volume is also available as a downloadable .pdf file, in a format suitable for research use. That downloadable file can be found at http://sunsite.berkeley.edu/Anthro/devos/depub_2000.html. At that page, select the button for the decade 2000 and then find the bibliographic listing for the volume's title. You will find the link to the .pdf file there.

British Library Cataloguing in Publication Information Available

Library of Congress Cataloging-in-Publication Data

Library of Congress Control Number: 2003113924

ISBN 0-7425-0002-0 (cloth : alk. paper)

Printed in the United States of America

™ The paper used in this publication meets the minimum requirements of American National Standard for Information Sciences—Permanence of Paper for Printed Library Materials, ANSI/NISO Z39.48-1992.

Table of Contents

TAT Research Participants

William Caudill, Ph.D. (Deceased)
: Social and Environmental Studies, National Institute of Mental Health, Bethesda, Maryland

Dorsh de Voe, Ph.D.
: Visiting Scholar, Anthropology Department, University of California, Berkeley, California

George A. De Vos, Ph.D.
: Emeritus Professor of Anthropology, University of California, Berkeley, California

Eric Steven De Vos, Ph.D.
: Professor of Psychology, Saginaw Valley State University, University Center, Michigan

David Ephrahim, Ph.D.
: Professor of Psychology, National University, Caracas, Venezuela

Emmit B. Evans, Ph.D.
: Lecturer, Political Science, California Polytechnic State University, San Luis, Obispo, California

Eun-Young Kim, Ph.D.
: Anthropologist

Robert Manlove, Ph.D.
: Emeritus Dean, Division of Science, City College of San Francisco, San Francisco, California

Eiji Murakami, Ph.D. (Deceased)
: Professor of Psychology, Department of Education, Nagoya National University, Nagoya, Japan

Leslie Rabkin, Ph.D.
: Chief Clinical Psychologist, Hawaiian School System, Kona, Hawaii

Nancy Scheper-Hughes, Ph.D.
: Professor of Anthropology, University of California, Berkeley, California

Carola Suárez-Orozco, Ph.D.
: Co-director, Harvard Immigration Project, Senior Research Associate and Lecturer in Human Development and Psychology at the Harvard Graduate School of Education, Cambridge, Massachusetts

Marcelo Suárez-Orozco, Ph.D.
: Victor S. Thomas Professor of Education, Harvard University Graduate School of Education, Cambridge, Massachusetts

Irina Todorova, Ph.D.
: Post Doctoral Fellow in Human Development and Psychology at the Harvard Graduate School of Education, Cambridge, Massachusetts

Cicero Emidio Vaz, Ph.D.
Professor of Psychology, Pontifical Catholic University, Rio Grande do sul, Porto Alegré, Brazil
Hiroshi Wagatsuma, Ph.D. (Deceased)
Professor of Anthropology, Tsukuba National University, Tsukuba, Japan

Preface

Volume I:

——This is my quest
To follow that star
no matter how hopeless
no matter how far——

The Impossible Dream

From *Man of La Mancha*
(J. Darein and M. Leigh)

You have in your hands the first volume in a two-volume series. The purposes of the two-volume work are fivefold:

First: In volume I we have presented in detail a system of coding categories that enables objective coding of the manifest content of thematic stories, or other verbal or narrative material that depicts both normative and deviant interpersonal concerns, in a manner that enables valid cross-cultural comparative research. The system was initially applied to materials obtained in Japan, 1953–1954. It has subsequently been developed over a period of forty-five years, largely through the efforts of the senior author, George De Vos, and his colleagues.

The system, which we call the Interpersonal Concerns Scoring System (ICSS), has been developed primarily from the analysis of spontaneous narratives given in response to the Thematic Apperception Test (TAT). It has also been used successfully on other types of material produced by methods such as sentence completion tests, problem situation tests, and interviews that evoke various forms of thematic stories or other forms of spontaneous answers.

Second: A major purpose for developing this system is to make possible types of interpretation that are based not only on what individuals actually say (i.e., the manifest content of responses) but also on a group-level assessment of what constitutes normative versus nonnormative responses. In sociological terms, the system is designed to enable quantification of the normative occurrence of collective or social representations within given social groups or cultures. By using this system, one can demonstrate that the TAT or other methods that evoke thematic responses, when quantified properly, can be used with considerable validity in doing systematic cross-cultural comparison of emic descriptions of interpersonal relationships. Some of these comparisons are illustrated in the present volume.

Categorization of data helps us avoid, to some degree, problems of interpretation. Too often, social scientists derive generalized interpretations directly from responses that may not be representative of the group being studied. This may lead to erroneous generalizations and superficial characterizations of a group. This type of direct or unmediated interpretation evades the responsibility for making some normative assessments, whether of within-group or between-group norms. If comparative or cross-cultural work is to be conducted systematically, some form of comparative quantification is necessary. The psychologist as well as the anthropologist or sociologist cannot avoid some commitment to objective assessment of the representative or normative nature of what is elicited from informants. In group research, interpretation should only follow upon some systematic categorization that reveals the normative differences between groups that constitute cultural variability.

Third: This system's sociological and cross-cultural comparative purpose is placed within a developmental-psychodynamic frame of reference that interrelates the coding categories. In developing the system of coding we have made recourse to an explicit psychodynamic approach to human thought and perception. We see, in the existence of culture-based patterning of experience, indications of culturally distinct generational continuities in the development of psychological functioning. We have tried to relate the categories of interpersonal concerns to relevant developmental mechanisms operative in human socialization.

The categories can be seen to reflect a progression of interpersonal concerns from infancy through adulthood that involve the internalization of sociocultural patterns including social or cultural representations of the social world within the individual. This is not simply a list of human concerns. Use of the scoring system can provide an objective basis for more psychodynamically oriented interpretive efforts to relate normative categories of interpersonal concerns to relevant developmental mechanisms and socialization processes.

Fourth: This system attempts to provide a comprehensive system for scoring the full range of manifest content produced by respondents, rather than scoring only those particular aspects of responses related to single-focused issues, be they concerns with achievement, or political issues of interpersonal dominance or control. The major categories of the system reflect psychological universals of interpersonal and self-directed social attitudes. Depending on the group and its broader social context, these attitudes are emphasized differently. But as universal categories of human concern, examples can generally be found in some form in every group studied as is illustrated amply in the present volume.

Fifth: The potentially exhaustive nature of the category system does not mean that it cannot be applied to very specific issues of investigation. In the present volume, we shall illustrate in several chapters taken from several selected past studies how the scoring of stories elicited by particular TAT stimuli can shed light on the relative saliency of a variety of specific themes. These themes range from the different status perceptions of husbands by Japanese women from two different villages, through the different perceptions of violence by American and Japanese delinquents, the concerns with competence in particular groups of youth, patterns of alienation characterizing the Korean ethnic minority in Japan, or difficulties of mother-son communication in Canadian students compared with samples of Venezuelans or Brazilians, etc.

The Two Volumes Are Organized in Three Parts

In Part I volume I, "Social Representations in Narrative Expression," we include a brief historical introduction to the use of the Thematic Apperception Test for narrative analysis, a discussion of the experiential self in society, and a preliminary delineation of the universal categories of purpose and emotion found in human experience.

Part II volume I, "The Interpersonal Concerns Scoring System: Expressive and Instrumental Categories," examines each of the expressive, or emotionally oriented, and then the instrumental or purpose-directed categories into which the system is divided. The scorings of these categories are briefly illustrated in each chapter. Note that Japanese and Korean illustrations are used contrastively throughout to highlight issues that are usually treated differently when Western cultures alone are used to generalize about psychological processes.

Part III volume II, "Narrative Analysis: Illustrative Research," contains chapters that are adapted from a number of previously published research reports as well as some unpublished material. These chapters illustrate how the system can help make sense of the human experience of self in relation to others, across a wide range of cultural contexts in Asia, Africa, and the Americas. They also exemplify the type of cross-cultural comparisons that can be made, based on responses to a number of the more commonly utilized Murray TAT cards.

A scoring manual, "Basic Interpersonal Concerns," is included as an appendix in each volume. It comprises the complete ICSS scoring categories and sub-categories.

A second appendix, "Illustrations of TAT Cards used in Japan, Kenya, and the Philippines," is also included in each volume. It contains the altered or additional TAT cards used for research in Japan, Kenya, and the Philippines, and should provide the reader with a clear image of various TAT stimuli discussed in the two volumes.

Acknowledgments

Editorial assistance provided by the senior author's wife, Suzanne, has much improved the readability of the manuscript. The senior author also wishes to express special appreciation for the able intellectual advice and editorial assistance provided by his son, Eric, who contributed many helpful suggestions over a period of years, making improvements to the scoring system and its theoretical relevance as it is now being published. Eric ultimately became substantially responsible for editing and co-authoring many portions of both volumes, and is co-author of the entirety of volume I. The senior author is most happy that Eric has chosen to assist as the junior author/editor of these volumes, and that he is now working with his own students to carry this system into the future.

The helpful suggestions of the senior author's students over the years have also been incorporated into versions of the scoring system as it approached its present form. Some of their own innovative work is represented in several of the illustrative chapters in volume II, and their research has informed much of the discussion throughout volume I.

Last, but not least, we want to thank Saun Strobel, technical secretary at Saginaw Valley State University. Her thorough expertise and her inimitable good nature (even while tackling tedious editorial tasks) has contributed greatly to the pleasure with which we are now able to publish this book.

George A. De Vos
Professor Emeritus of Anthropology
University of California at Berkeley

Eric S. De Vos
Professor of Psychology
Saginaw Valley State University

Introduction

The Thematic Apperception Test in Social Sciences Research: Historical and Methodological Considerations

The TAT as a Basis for Narrative and Thematic Analysis

The Thematic Apperception Test (TAT) is one among a variety of techniques for eliciting stories from informants. The method consists of presentation of a standard series of drawings that are printed on 8½-inch card stock, published originally by Harvard University Press. The drawings depict a variety of settings and situations; many include the presence of human figures and various objects. The complete Harvard-published set also includes a blank card, the presentation of which is accompanied by the same instructions as for the cards that have images on them. If the test is administered in accord with Murray's prescribed method, the informant is requested to tell a story about what is seen in each card as it is presented, including "what has led up to the event shown in the picture," "what is happening at the moment," what the people depicted in the picture "are feeling and thinking," and what is going to happen (Murray, 1943, 3, as cited in Cramer, 1996). Thus the informant is explicitly instructed to tell a story that has a time dimension as well as human "feeling and thinking" content to it. As a result, many of the responses provided by informants can legitimately be considered narratives, and it has been suggested that TAT responses can properly be studied with methods developed for more general use in narrative-structural and hermeneutical analyses (Cramer, 1996).

There is presently widespread interest among social scientists regarding the problems of understanding and interpretation, and there is an increased willingness to see lives and social-relational processes as texts that are amenable to the analytical and interpretive methods of the "human sciences" (Rabinow and Sullivan, 1979). It is clear that the TAT method as it is commonly used shares many strengths and weaknesses with the more general field of narrative and interpretive analysis. We concur with Cramer's assertion that the tradition of using the TAT to elicit stories can be seen as very clearly falling within this larger emerging tradition, although its historical origins predate the present widespread popularity of interpretive method in social sciences. The use of TAT-elicited narratives also predates the present popularity of the idea that human development can be seen as a writing and rewriting of our lives and selves, and the methodical studies of narrative in life span developmental psychology (Freeman, 1993; Josselson, 1996; McAdams, 1993).

Although Murray did not invent the use of pictures as stimuli for eliciting stories (Cramer, 1996), the TAT method, developed in collaboration with Christina Morgan, has become one of the most widely used assessment methods in clinical psychology. The first publication drawing attention to the specific method that is known as the Thematic Apperception Test appeared in 1935, in a paper by Christina Morgan and Henry A. Murray titled "A Method for Investigating Fantasies: The Thematic Apperception Test." In a 1937 paper, Murray also described the test, and the TAT is mentioned in Murray's 1938 volume *Explorations in Personality*.[1] Morgan and Murray believed that their method of using standard stimuli to elicit fantasies had a special capacity to activate the expression of personally relevant thematic concerns while at the same time bypassing psychological inhibitions about self-revelation. It was thought that this particular strength of the TAT was based on its capacity to selectively mobilize projective mechanisms (Cramer, 1996) by using indeterminate stimuli.

Although the pictures may set the stage for an informant's fantasy or story, by providing the gender and rough age of human figures, and by depicting the presence of objects, they do not explicitly provide additional thematic or narrative content. Indeed many objects and figures in various pictures are only vaguely depicted. What a given informant chooses to do with the pictorial content as it is transformed into a narrative form is based very substantially on the informant's perceptual-interpretive processes. These perceptual processes make use of the informant's personally and culturally derived internal representations, as well as their associated evaluative or affective tone. These together provide the basis for whatever meaning is invoked in the informant by the picture, the perceived saliency of people and objects, the categorization of people and objects, relationships between people or objects, the communicative dialog, or possible causal time-based sequences that might be anticipated, etc. Thus the individual informant's constellation of both culturally and idiosyncratically constructed readings of the pictures provides a substantial contribution to the resulting narrative and its thematic content. To the

[1]According to Cramer (1996), the extensive discussion of the TAT that is found in Chapter 7 of that book was written by Christina Morgan.

extent that the story is derived from these inner processes and not directly from the objective content of the pictures, the constructed narratives are legitimately considered to be projections. Hence the TAT, along with other tests (such as the Rorschach test which employs "meaningless" ink blots) that provide minimal predetermined basis for the informant's responses to standardized stimuli have become known as "projective tests."

As a further indication that the thematic content of stories elicited by the TAT derives from a projection of the individual informant's internal concerns, one can observe that the stories are often either autobiographical or clearly expressive of concerns or themes that are self-relevant for the individual. As was recognized by Murray and colleagues, the use of the TAT cards appears to reduce an informant's inhibitions about revealing self-relevant information. Because they are requested to tell a story about what they see in a picture, the story is not seen by the informant to be self-revelatory. As a result of this invocation of projective mechanisms, in some cases, an informant may even express attitudes or concerns that are not conscious, thus providing information to which the social scientist or clinician might otherwise not gain access.

In recognition of the clinical and research benefits of analyzing stories obtained as responses to a standardized set of pictures or drawings,[2] several other psychologists also developed a variety of tests of a related nature. Some of the better known tests to be put to clinical diagnostic work were "The Children's Apperception Test" (CAT) of Leopold Bellak, using animal figures (Bellak, 1954) and "The Blacky Test" of Gerald Blum which utilized drawings of a single black puppy in family situations (Blum, 1950).[3] Clinicians and researchers alike have believed that projective techniques provide important information about the informant's underlying personality. Both the Rorschach and the TAT (as well as some other projective tests) remain frequently used tests in clinical settings (Archer, Maruish, Imhof, and Piotrowski, 1991; Cramer, 1996).

---

[2]The exact procedure used in administering a set of pictures to subjects and the cards selected can differ somewhat depending on the context and the specific purpose of the examiner. See the manual of the standard series published by Harvard and the description of suggested procedures in the test situation found in Cramer (1996). In our own studies we used the method of introducing the cards to the subject described in the Harvard manual. We briefly describe the content of each of the cards for which we report results in context throughout the following chapters.

[3]For additional historical information on the development and use of the TAT, and subsequent use of projective tests, see Cramer (1996) and Morgan (1995).

Brief History and Rationale for Use of the TAT in Social Sciences

The usefulness of these (and other) psychological assessment techniques was not lost on anthropologists, some of whom in the 1940s and 1950s had become intrigued by the possibilities of making cross-cultural comparisons of "culture and personality." They therefore became attracted to the use of psychological instruments. For example, the Rorschach test, which was being widely used in clinical psychology, was also adopted by several investigators who were attempting research on modal personality structures in different cultural settings (see De Vos and Boyer, 1989). The so-called Murray set of TAT cards, published by Harvard University Press (Murray, 1943), became the most frequently employed thematic-narrative type of projective test to be used with any frequency outside of western cultural settings.

The cross-cultural use of TAT-style projective-thematic assessments has been characterized by three approaches:

(1) *Direct Application*. In a good number of instances, cards taken from the Harvard-published series were used without modification. There are obvious advantages of standardization of usage across diverse research samples and historical time (as well as potential disadvantages as indicated below). Yet, lest the reader develop an unduly rigid notion about the importance of the Harvard-published set, it should be noted that the pictures that came to comprise the published set were themselves selected from a variety of sources. Some cards used in Murray and Morgan's earlier research were eliminated in the course of their studies and others were added, often so as to elicit themes related to desired context, such as parent-child situations, etc. From the beginning, for example, there was interest in eliciting stories about achievement concerns. A particularly good card for eliciting these concerns is Card 1 of the published set. This card depicts a boy looking at a violin, and was adapted from an actual photograph of Yehudi Menuhin who had at that time become a recognized child prodigy. It is interesting to note that the image serves to elicit achievement themes in cultural settings where the person of Yehudi Menuhin is not known. The achievement-related possibilities of a violin are widely understood, even among Amazonian indigenous people.[4] Another card that commonly elicits achievement themes, as well as family-duty themes (Card 2) depicts a rural farm scene, and features a young woman with books in her arm, a man plowing, and a woman resting against a tree. This card was a rendering taken from a large mural that had been painted on the wall of a U.S. post office during depression years when the government was subsidizing art works with federal funds. Nevertheless, through some virtue of the artistic vision of its creator,

[4]See the later chapter on the Tukuna Indians in volume II.

the image of farm life remains compelling of rich fantasy for people in a wide variety of sociocultural settings.

(2) *Modification of Details*. Given the unavoidably culture-embedded origins of the published cards, some researchers were concerned about the issue of possible culture-based unfamiliarity with the human images on the cards, or about the lack of cultural relevance of the scenes depicted, or even about the presence of specific yet unknown cultural significances of objects or settings. This has led some to develop cards that were thematically similar to the standard cards, but that were more or less modified in regard to facial features and clothing. New cards were also sometimes added to the set, to depict situations seemingly more appropriate to the particular culture studied. For example, in our own research in Japan in the 1950s (De Vos, 1973b), and in keeping with the methods used by Murray to develop the initial set of cards, we used illustrations modified from images found in popular magazines and also some drawings by commissioned artists. However, we found no significant differences in themes elicited by the cards modified from the Harvard-published series. Subsequent to this experience we have felt more confident in the applicability of the standard cards, and this confidence has been supported over the course of more than forty years of cross-cultural use. The fact that there are culture-specific significances of objects and settings is not a handicap for comparative analysis. Indeed the cross-cultural comparison of TAT responses to standardized cards provides very clear evidence that such differences in perceptual-semiotic experiences do exist. That is, after all, one of the very aims of comparative analysis.

(3) *Special Cards to Elicit Particular Content*. In other studies, any attempt at direct cross-cultural comparison of themes was forsaken. Only the idea of evoking social or personal themes that reflect personality was kept. In some of these instances cards were developed that bore little resemblance to the type of drawings or interpersonal situations used in the Harvard University Press edition of the cards.

Although there are obvious advantages (as well as disadvantages) of standardized protocols to enable comparative analysis, no uniformity of approach or consensually recognized similarity of methods of analysis ensued from the general use of the TAT either among psychologists or anthropologists. Almost no one came to use a series of twenty cards in the fixed sequence, distinct sets for males and females, etc., as suggested in the manual that accompanies the published set (Cramer, 1996).

As an example of the prescribed administration procedures, Morgan and Murray thought that it was easier to identify with a figure of one's own sex and approximate age. They suggested some specific adult and child cards of both sexes to be used alternatively as part of the series. Their original distinction between cards with different gender applicability may have not been entirely off target in one sense, in that the cards often do elicit thematic material that can be considered gender-related. In fact, Worchel, Aaron, and Yates (1990) have found that cards originally designated as female-relevant do indeed elicit feminine-gendered concerns more frequently than do the cards originally designated as masculine-gendered. Yet this is found among both men and women. Thus what might be considered to be masculine-typic or feminine-typic themes (as defined in psycho-culturally constructed gender-categorical systems) may be elicited from *both* men and women, depending on the cards that are used. Moreover, in our own experience, men or women are sometimes found to feel psychologically freer to create a story that reveals a personally significant theme by using a figure of the other sex as the protagonist in the story.

It is well recognized that specific pictures serve as promptings toward certain kinds of thematic possibilities. The cards do indeed set the stage, as they are intended to do. Sensitivity to the theme-eliciting characteristics of the cards is appropriate, and where selected subsets of the Harvard-published version of the cards have been used, they have been chosen more in regard to the thematic material to be elicited than in regard to Murray's (1943) prescribed administration process. This fact that some cards are more useful than others in eliciting certain types of material has not been lost on clinicians or researchers who are often operating under very real time constraints.

Clinicians have used those cards from the Harvard series that they have found most useful for particular diagnostic interests, and there appears to be "agreement across clinicians working in different settings as to which are the most useful cards" (Cramer, 1996, 17). Researchers have also chosen cards that provide them with responses illustrative of whatever particular set of thematic issues are of greatest interest to them. This does not, however, contradict the projective nature of the informant's responses, but instead indicates that the researcher or clinician needs to give careful consideration to the choice of stimuli based on the particular thematic issues in which they are interested.

Among anthropologists, the use of the Harvard-published set has also varied. The TAT is among the preferred testing devices (where such devices are even used) for eliciting culturally relevant content, but anthropologists have usually limited the number of cards presented to between eight and twelve. Again, particular cards have been favored by anthropologists.

What is very apparent in the history of the use of the TAT is that Murray's (1938) original interests in trait-like lists of internal "needs" and external social "presses," and their interactions in the structure of a personality, have gone largely ignored. The cards took on a life of their own, far beyond their application in the development of Murray's theory of personality. Nevertheless, some particular motivational factors from among Murray's original list, such as the needs for achievement, power, or affiliation, did gain an ascendancy of research interest among psychologists and cross-cultural researchers for several decades (McClelland, 1987). Specific thematic concerns related to the individual's achievement motivation became a central focus of many of the nonclinically oriented research studies that utilized the TAT, both in the United States and elsewhere (McClelland, 1987).

In 1948, the senior author of the present volume, George De Vos, began his own detailed study of achievement motivation, as part of cross-cultural research that included the use of both the Rorschach and the TAT (Caudill and De Vos, 1956). De Vos had also gained experience with the use of the TAT while performing diagnostic work as a clinical psychologist. His first training with the cultural-analytic uses of the TAT was under the guidance of William E. Henry at the University of Chicago in 1947. By 1947, Henry had already begun to apply the test both to research in industrial psychology and as part of a comparative psycho-cultural study of American Indian child development (Henry, 1956).

Thus, De Vos was aware, early on, of a wide variety of research uses for projective techniques. In particular, he has personally found them useful as a technique for documenting the presence of themes within cultural groups as they respond to changing sociohistorical circumstances, for example, following processes such as modernization, migration, or acculturation. Additionally, in keeping with Henry's use in studying human development cross-culturally, De Vos was interested in using the TAT to identify age-related changes over life span developmental timeframes, particularly as they reflect developmental changes in social role-related identity or the interpersonal self.

Over the course of subsequent decades, De Vos and colleagues have made extensive use of the TAT in a wide variety of cultural settings, including use with multiple generations among immigrant populations and among varied age groups, as we will illustrate in the present chapter, and in the chapters of volume II. Although our interest did begin with an emphasis on achievement themes, our interests ultimately moved far beyond that initial focus, and our work became devoted to the broader analysis of fantasies, using systematic quantitative methods to categorize the full spectrum of basic interpersonal concerns one finds expressed in narrative productions. Our method for accomplishing this task is based, in part, on using the scoring system we present in the present volume.

Issues of Method in Comparative Psycho-Cultural Analysis

Despite the failure among both clinicians and researchers to establish uniformity of use, the TAT is clearly useful for both clinical-interpretive purposes as well as for more psychological-developmental explorations. These uses include the exploration of issues related to culture-based constructions of gender and age (Cramer, 1996). In Volume I we will illustrate that the usefulness of the TAT can be and has been extended substantially further in this direction, into an area of study that we have called "comparative psycho-cultural analysis," i.e., an exploration of social, cultural, and historical patterns as they are reflected in the stories elicited by the TAT when used in varied sociocultural groups. As we will discuss presently, this does require the application of methods that differ somewhat from the narrative-analytic and interpretive methods suggested by Cramer. In particular, we suggest and present a method for systematic notation of the manifest content of stories, prior to semiotic interpretation or critical analysis. This is to be used as a basis for, but not as a replacement for interpretation and contextualization, in comparative psycho-cultural analysis. Additionally, the type of contextualization that is required for psycho-cultural analysis is somewhat different from that which is needed for individual-focused narrative interpretation. Nevertheless, despite some differences in emphasis or focus, many of the issues pertaining to interpretation and understanding in narrative analysis more generally are equally important in psycho-cultural analysis.

The popularity of thematic analysis based on responses to projective tests such as the TAT is not accidental. This type of method differs substantially from much of mainstream psychology's methodology in a manner that makes it particularly well suited for the rich exploration of human concerns in varied cultural contexts or life-course situations. Projective-thematic methods for finding the relative strength of various personality characteristics (as they are found in the individual person) are the opposite of methods that rely on scales that measure the presence of traits depending on how a respondent completes a self-descriptive paper-and-pencil checklist where specific items are selected or rejected self-consciously. The TAT derives much of its strength from the fact that the informant is providing all the material, in his or her own words, and the responses are contextualized within the informant's own narrative framework (Cramer, 1996). In doing so, the informant is disclosing aspects of "self" without necessarily knowing that the self-produced narrative is actually a form of self-disclosure. This is therefore quite different from the widely used adjective-checklist style of personality assessment.

The TAT researcher is not limited to the presentation of an a priori set of responses that the informant is expected to own or disown consciously or self-reflectively. Additionally, and of great relevance for the field researcher, the researcher need not have undergone what is often a prohibitive process of item-checklist construction that involves various forms of validation, such as evaluation of how the checklist corresponds to other established constructs, etc. Perhaps most importantly, the cross-cultural researcher need not have a fully developed understanding of the informant's emic experience prior to collecting data. In fact, TAT data may actually be among the richest sources for developing an approximation of emic understanding in field settings, particularly when it is combined with sociohistorical analysis, and other ethnographic work that helps the social scientist further contextualize the informant's emic narrative framework.[5]

Nevertheless, when it comes to the analysis of TAT responses, we do not find it advisable to abandon all forms of a priori structure. In keeping with many others who have used the TAT (e.g., McClelland, 1987) we suggest that one can use a standardized system for scoring spontaneous manifest content according to specified a priori criteria, which is quite distinct from creating specific a priori items for use by the informant. One must keep in mind, however, that when using a standardized scoring method to assess an individual's "personality," all we have

---

[5]An excellent example of this type of multi-disciplinary social-sciences approach can be found in the volume by Wagatsuma and De Vos (1984).

thereby obtained is a quantitative-categorical scoring of the spontaneous narration of the informant, and nothing more.

To apply this type of data towards an assessment of personality dynamics, the researcher or clinician often is compelled to infer underlying motivation in keeping with the researcher or clinician's preferred theoretically derived etic structural framework. For example, if an informant generates a story that contains repeated expressions that can be scored as concern over success or failure (in response to a standardized stimulus that often invokes stories about a task to accomplish, such as Card 1) such preoccupation may be taken as evidence of a theoretically posited inner motivation to accomplish a goal, or more negatively, to a fear of failure or a concern with meeting parental expectations, etc. In such a case, on the basis of psychological theory one might infer that unresolved needs or inner difficulties have motivated the individual to spontaneously voice a desire to achieve, or, perhaps instead voice negative concerns over achievement, or voice an ambivalent relationship with authority figures, etc.

The very premise of the TAT as a psychological assessment is the concept of projection, which is an imputed psychodynamic mechanism. Any descriptions of external causal agents or consequential causal sequences or imputed intentionality that are provided in the TAT-elicited narrative must be based on some inner psychological mechanisms. As will be clear throughout the volume, we certainly have our own ideas about what those mechanisms might be, and projection is certainly among them. Yet we feel that it is necessary to argue against superficial or overly ready interpretations. For example, if an informant makes the very commonly obtained reference to the death of the father and a conversation between mother and son on Card 6BM (the mother-son card), one might want to interpret that as evidence of some latent hostility toward the father. On the other hand, such expressions could also be seen as the narratively required stage setting for the story that actually focuses on the informants more salient concerns with problems (or successes) to be found in the communication between the older woman and the younger man in the story. And how should we interpret the response to the same card that lacks reference to death? Would it be interpreted as a denial of death? And would the denial be based on an effort to cope with real fear of death as a force that acts from outside, or is it the denial of a death-seeking impulse endogenous to the informant?

Such quandaries that result from etic interpretations of the presence of inner needs, drives, etc., are not within the scope of the scoring system we are presenting in this volume. By using the word "concern" rather than "need" in our description of the scoring system, we avoid any necessity to relate an expressed concern directly to the motivated behavior of the specific person expressing it. We also thereby reiterate our emphasis on consciously experienced concerns. We must also emphasize that themes expressed consciously are not necessarily produced only as a result of unconscious dynamics within the individual person. They may also (or instead) reflect the person's internalization of socially constructed themes at varying degrees of superficiality or profound identification (i.e., varied levels of personal relevance).[6]

Narratives, although they are produced by individuals, remain nevertheless cultural products. What is elicited in stories, or revealed in other written or spoken materials, may be relatively salient expressions of patterns of thought and concern found in the group or the social context of which the individual is a member. An individual may participate in received or group-derived concerns without being the individual who acts them out in personal behavior. Perhaps even more importantly, an individual may fully participate in and identify with received or group-derived concerns without having internally developed the concern out of personal psychodynamic processes. Thus it is not always safe to impute the presence of a deeper level of intrapsychic needs or motives as psychodynamically underlying an individual's manifest expression of culturally prevalent concerns.

Furthermore, themes expressed may not even be experienced by the informant as self-relevant. Their self-relevance may instead be only implicit, and perceived only in the eyes of an etic interpretive system. Being implicit, they may not necessarily be experienced as part of the objectified self of the informant as it is seen in his or her own eyes. Instead, they may be experienced as actually present in the world, external to the experienced self. Obviously one must remember that etic interpretation about the inner presence or inner locus of various putative inner motives has moved one step beyond a quantitative notational recording of the frequency of occurrence of various categories of responses. Such interpretation thereby moves beyond what we consider the requisite initial step of quantification for the purpose of comparative psycho-cultural analysis.

The initial step in the use of TAT material in comparative psycho-cultural work is the notation of a relative frequency of appearance of concerns. This can then be used in at least three ways. (1) One can compare specific individuals with others in their cultural group, and differences found thereby can be interpreted as indicative of recurrent internal preoccupations specific to the individual. (2) One can document the prevalence of concerns among members of a cultural group. The appearance of concerns in a large portion of individuals from a given cultural group can indicate a prevailing or at least widespread presence of recurrent concerns within the cultural group. (3) Furthermore, if the method of obtaining data is relatively well standardized, it can also be used as a method for comparing the relative presence or prevalence of the various types of concerns among different social or cultural groups, and for comparing changes over developmental or historical time. It is in these two latter usages that we have found the TAT, and our categorical scoring system, to be of substantial value for the field of cultural psychology. The former usage, in contrast, is of greatest value in clinical diagnostic settings, or for life span developmental research.

---

[6]See Spiro (1984) for valuable discussion of the degrees of internalization of cultural patterns.

One of the great values of the TAT is that is based on the presentation of standardized stimuli which produce normative responses in any given social group. For the purposes of comparative psycho-cultural analysis, we have been most interested in noting and comparing the normative frequencies of specific interpersonal and self-reflexive concerns as they appear in stories from various cultural groups. One finds very similar stories appearing in quite varied groups, but they may appear frequently in some groups and less frequently in others. For example, the achievement theme that is common in responses to Card 1 (boy with violin) appears only rarely among Amazonian indigenous people, but it does appear even there. The farm scene (Card 2) is another example. In stories produced by North Americans, one rarely hears of children going back to the farm to take care of parents. In Japanese and Korean stories, they do. But the frequencies also vary by subgroups. Among alienated Koreans living in conditions of racial and economic oppression in Japan, family concerns are rarely expressed, whereas among Korean immigrants in Los Angeles, one commonly finds family concerns expressed in response to Card 2.

Additionally, in all groups one occasionally finds stories that are unique to the group, although they may or may not reach normative proportions for that group. In our later chapter (chapter 7, volume II) comparing American and Japanese delinquent youth and normal controls, we find occasional stories given by Japanese youth in which a mother murders her delinquent son and then commits suicide. The senior author has never found such a story in any other population than the Japanese. It reflects thoughts that are uniquely Japanese in respect to the degree of responsibility of mothers for the proper behavior of their children. Samples obtained in Kenya by Emmit Evans (chapter 3, volume II) are almost unique in their production of stories where expressions of frustration over achievement issues can cause the protagonist to resort to the possibility of criminal behavior. This reflects the extent of social anomie in present day Kenya. One is reminded of Merton's (1968) contention that criminal behavior is seen as an alternative path for the expression of achievement concerns when some segments of a population find socially legitimate achievement goals are blocked or unavailable to them (see chapter 3, volume II).

One can also find longitudinal shifts over historical time in the frequencies to be found even within the same social group. Certainly the Kenyan example mentioned above reflects current social and economic conditions in Kenya as well as a cultural heritage that prepares individuals to face such circumstances with deviant responses. In Japan in the 1980s and 1990s, we found nonnormative responses to Card 7 BM (two men talking) that involved corrupt politics or corrupt business deals (see chapters 3 and 4, volume II). In contrast, in the samples obtained in the 1950s such concerns never appeared at all. Again, we see that stories told in response to TAT stimuli reflect emerging social concerns. In the Brazilian samples from the 1990s we see similar stories of corruption appearing with considerable frequency in all the sampled Brazilian social groups (see chapter 10, volume II).

The collection of stories from informants, as mythology or folklore, is a traditional anthropological technique. Yet the stories elicited by the TAT are somewhat different, in that they are spontaneously elicited by standardized stimuli rather than being generated as a retelling of a previously known and possibly rehearsed story. Clearly, culturally derived mythological themes will be incorporated into the perceptual experiences individuals bring to their narratives. But the stories are not folklore in the traditional sense of the term, and our interest in them is directed toward neither the individual-personality-oriented narrative analysis of the psychologist, nor the wandering idiomatic or isomorphic variants of stories often of concern to anthropologists. Our method is distinct from and somewhere in between folklore and personality or life-theme analysis.

As is the case in any field work that involves folklore, stories, and so forth, the processing of verbal narrative information may require translating from one language to another. When this is necessary, it produces potential semiotic problems that need special attention. The problem of translation has been central for the hermeneutical or interpretive task and for the "human sciences," and we do not offer any special solutions here. As Cramer (1996) has discussed, narrative theory emphasizes the importance of context for correct interpretation of meaning, and we also want to emphasize the importance of contextualization. However, we would also emphasize that the initial suggested step in analysis is the coding of manifest content, prior to the leap toward imputed latent content. Clearly, even with manifest content, the very meaning of individual words does require contextualization, as well as the application of an available heuristic system. Yet we feel that it is best if the heuristic system be kept as explicit as possible, rather than being shrouded in an unarticulated idiosyncratic process or "personal reading" by the researcher.

The use of any clearly articulated heuristic or learning system, such as that provided by our system, does favor consideration of particular potential meanings. In the case of our system, we emphasize particular affective or instrumental meanings of narratives that we have found to be of emic importance in varied cultural settings. Nevertheless, even the use of well-defined heuristic categories and subcategories does not eliminate some problems with shade or nuance, and there may sometimes remain some degree of doubt about the certainty of meaning in any semiotic interpretation. However, we believe that correct meaning can most legitimately be read into any given narrative (whether translated or not) if that reading does not depend solely on individual words, but depends instead on meaning that flows out of the whole continuity of the narrative as it is given by the informant. This reading is then further legitimized if it is contextualized by the researcher's broader experience with the cultural group being studied, and by the researcher's familiarity with patterns or "constellations" of salient concerns that make sense within the informant's cultural framework and social context.

Based on the presence of constellations of salient concerns within cultural groups, we have been interested in identifying "molecular" patterns of thought about social interaction that are held collectively within a given culture or within a selected social segment of a population. If these patterns are contextualized with ethnographic and sociological data, knowledge about childhood socialization, etc., they can also be informative about psychological-developmental issues that affect members of the group generally. For example, as we will illustrate in chapter 11, volume I, Japanese TAT responses that are scored as responsibility concerns can reasonably be interpreted as evidence of unconscious guilt. The transgenerational transmission of this psycho-cultural pattern can be traced to child socialization patterns, and can also be found manifest in Japanese patterns of adult social relating, corporate and other organizational structures, etc. Although this imputation of the presence of unconscious guilt does involve an etic analytical process, whereby we attempt to move beyond simple notation of frequencies to begin to identify patterns, this differs from the clinical applications most commonly used for the TAT. Unlike our clinical colleagues, for the most part, we have been only been peripherally interested in the integrated personality patterns of particular individuals. Instead, thematic concerns are seen as occurring in a highly contextualized manner, not only as the products of the endogenous psychological processes of the informant, but also as reflective of the larger social-cultural-historical circumstances, as well as culturally derived or culturally patterned intrapsychic adaptive strategies (De Vos, 1974, 1978; De Vos and Hippler, 1969).

Again, we emphasize that the key to this approach to psycho-cultural analysis is the contextualization of the narratives. From the psycho-cultural perspective, this requires that the researcher refrain from interpretation based solely on the manifest content of the TAT responses. As with all narrative analysis, the meaning must be contextualized, and in the case of psycho-cultural analysis, the scope of that contextualization must be broad. Social scientists and critical theorists, however, have the risky tendency to look mostly outwards to broaden the contextualization of their narrative interpretation. The contextualization must go both ways: (1) toward some psychological theory of the workings of mind, and attempts to etically systematize possible meanings relative to inferred mental processes for perception, categorization, experience, etc.; (2) toward the outer context, towards the shared beliefs, social role expectations, economic, historical and institutional contexts as well as the idiosyncratic personal life-history of the informant as determined by study of family and community contexts. The combination of both inward and outward contextualization is necessary to enable the social scientist to correctly understand the "psycho-cultural meaning" of TAT responses. What this means in practice is that the social scientist cannot be content with discipline-limited frameworks, whether they be the sociologist's class-based or social-constructionist explanations that exclude any sophistication in reference to psychological or biological mechanisms, or whether they be psychodynamic or child-developmental explanations that exclude the very real historical realities of gender, class and caste-based discrimination, and the social-historical context of family socialization patterns. The psycho-cultural use of the TAT requires a move beyond the narrative itself, to see the narrative as it is framed in the psycho-social-historical ontogenetic context.

Dilemmas of Empirical and Interpretive Reporting in Comparative Work

We know that quantification can disguise as well as enlighten. A presentation of numerical differences in respect to a set of categories that have been defined or invented by the investigator leaves a critical reader wondering about the arbitrariness of the categories. The process of using directed interviews or surveys that are constructed around a priori categories may force the data to fall into the pre-specified categories. One wonders whether other relevant data is sometimes not considered because there was no category available in which to place material for consideration or for tallying. As noted elsewhere in this chapter, the senior author has criticized McClelland's cross-cultural examination of need achievement (McClelland, 1961; Smith, 1992) for leaving no way to consider responses alternative to those scorable in his system (De Vos, 1973b).

Our present system allows one to investigate the relative saliency of other issues that appear in TAT material. Our system for scoring data in this respect is more comprehensive, and enables the scoring of complex patterns of response. As we have discussed in the first section of this chapter, one can use the categorical system to identify "molecular" patterns of salient concerns in given groups. The tables constructed in some of the chapters in Volume II, which use our system for scoring the manifest content of TAT cards, allow for this type of quantitative comparison of patterns of concerns between groups.

The use of a complex scoring system does not obviate some of the limitations associated with constraining a researcher's perceptual processes to working within an a priori categorical system. It does, however, eliminate the problem of requiring the informant's responses to be limited to a priori categories. Our system provides for the scoring of twelve major categories, various dimensions that cut across these categories (see chapter 2, volume I), and numerous empirically derived subcategories. It therefore allows a substantial degree of complexity in the scoring that can parallel the complexity of the material. This can obviate some of the difficulties of objectively scoring the substantially complex fantasy or narrative material that is obtained using the TAT.

As discussed earlier, there is another problem with the use of projective-thematic test material, which is also a problem for most of the social sciences, i.e., the tendency toward overly hasty interpretation. In clinical practice, where one has the opportunity of repeated interaction with a client, this may be addressable over a period of time. As evidence accumulates over time, each interpretation can serve further exploration of the new material that is regularly generated in the clinical setting. In field-based psycho-cultural research, however, one's data are often collected and presented with little opportunity for timely follow-up investigation. One always wonders how much primary data is actually necessary in any presentation before one can make a generalization in respect to any social group when only some of its members have served as informants or have been given psychological tests.

Projective tests, as well as other ethnographic materials have occasionally been used to reach sweeping conclusions about particular groups without any presentation of sufficient supporting behavioral data on which basis the inferences were made. In fact it is often easier to relate to or accept theoretical statements made as a matter of opinion than it is to deal directly with material that may at times be discomforting, in addition to taking time to peruse and consider. Thus when one wishes to use projective tests comparatively, one is continually faced with the problem that previous users of the tests may have produced inferential generalizations without a thorough presentation of direct evidence. This make comparative use, and an evaluation of the reliability of methods difficult.

Despite much prevailing professional psychological opinion that doubts the advisability of any use of projective tests cross-culturally, over the past forty years the senior author has insisted on such continued use of the Rorschach and TAT as projective tests that can be used with sufficient validity (e.g., De Vos, 1952, 1954, 1973b; Miner and De Vos, 1960; De Vos and Boyer, 1989; De Vos and Kim, 1993). Some forms of comparative quantification are indeed possible if one makes the methods of analysis, and the actual content of the categories considered directly available for scrutiny by skeptical readers. If one has the opportunity to see actual elicited material, as we will be presenting in the present volumes, it becomes very clear that the narratives elicited by the TAT are informative, and that they can provide the basis for rich and meaningful interpretation. Yet that interpretation must be preceded by some degree of discipline in noting the manifest content of the responses, as well as disciplined effort to contextualize the interpretation in social, cultural, historical, and ontogenetic terms. One must continually resist making analytical inferences in the absence of adequate contextualization. The worst forms of this, for example, the blatant ethnocentrism of many early ethnographies, can be easily identified. Yet the imposition of ethnocentric and inappropriate etic systems by social scientists continues.

Another problem with comparative psycho-cultural research is in the area of how comparative interpretations are made when one finds unique or varied patterns in distinct groups. One of the primary problems in this area comes from a tendency on the part of some to erroneously translate normative group differences into predictions about the behavior of individual members of a group. The use of our categorical scoring system does not preclude such erroneous interpretations. Properly trained social scientists know the psychological basis of these kinds of erroneous inferences, and know the statistical reasons for their falsehood. Basically, regardless of the validity of inferences drawn from categorical analysis of material provided by individual informants, no generalization can be expected to necessarily hold for all or even for most members of any group.

Nevertheless, what can be both theoretically and empirically identified as positively or negatively adaptive social behavior, or positively or negatively adjustive internal psychological functioning are not equally distributed throughout various populations. There *are* normative psychological and social differences that do differentiate among groups. And these differences can be legitimately seen to indicate differences in degrees of successful adaptation. This produces a problem of comparative interpretation, when one attempts comparative evaluation of group well-being.

Relative indices of psychological health have been constructed on the basis of etic psychological theories. These indices can be compared across groups, and the relative occurrence of adaptive or maladaptive patterns can be identified and compared. To do comparative psycho-cultural analysis one *must* recognize such relative distributions. Yet one must be careful about the types of conclusions that are drawn from such findings. Ideally, by thorough psycho-cultural investigation and contextualization, one can help explain the social, psychological, and cultural causality behind such differences as well as the more general social, economic, and political consequences that ensue from the real presence of variously adaptive psycho-cultural patterns in any complex society.

In some instances, unfortunately, normative results obtained from specific groups have been thought to reflect too negatively on the total group considered. Ironically, rather than reinforcing the importance of further scientific investigation and causal explanation, this has strengthened the opinion among some that tests that reveal group differences should not be utilized in cross-cultural comparisons. Some have even claimed that the presence of group differences should cause one to question a test's validity. Unfortunately, rather than challenging this point of view by addressing real scientific issues, rather than seeking to develop more stringent methods of analysis to enhance validity, granting committees have instead under-funded or abandoned psycho-cultural research as impolitic (i.e., not P.C.). In some cases, legislative bodies have prohibited the use of data obtained with reliable psychometric instruments. Rather than attempting to further explain findings of group differences of a seemingly negative nature, it is easier to level off-hand criticism against psychological assessment. Indeed the operational concept "personality" itself, has by some, been brought into question as an impossible non-scientific field of inquiry.[7]

From his own experience both in normative work, and in looking at features of psychopathology found cross culturally, the senior author has been impressed with the universality of positive and negative forms of psychological functioning to be found in all groups, albeit with radical differences in their incidence of appearance, or despite differences in the social sensitivity directed to various forms of deviant behavior. The ability to translate clinical judgment from one culture to another is doubted by many more relativistically inclined anthropologists. We are not of this school of thought, having seen mental mechanisms used universally, in

---

[7]Much of this criticism goes unpublished, but occurs behind the scenes at publishing houses and funding agencies.

some instances even to a degree that produces similar patterns of structural malfunctioning, regardless of widely variant cultural settings.

As the present volumes attest, results from comparative studies that we term "cultural psychology" (De Vos and Hippler, 1969), indicate clearly that individuals from some class and/or ethnic backgrounds fare substantially better in terms of their apparent psychological functioning as compared with individuals from other class and/or ethnic backgrounds. Yet when such disfavorable psychological comparative results are obtained, they may be accounted for by some who use ready and psychologically superficial sociological explanations of direct social pressures or social discrimination. Those with ideological commitments may favor one variety of explanation over another, ranging from imputations of relative biological aptitudes to concerns about examiner bias and implicit discriminatory attitudes on the part of investigators. As evidenced by the historical use of Piagetian tasks cross-culturally, there *are indeed* legitimate concerns about the cross-cultural validity of various forms of psychological testing. This becomes most problematic if test results obtained are then translated into evaluative judgements that result in a justification of social discrimination, if they are used in support of apparently racist attitudes, or if they are used to support sanctimonious self-congratulatory ethnocentrism.

Nevertheless, it is obvious to us that there *are* enduring psycho-cultural patterns that originate historically from a variety of forces, including forms of social discrimination, as well as religious or other value systems, cosmological beliefs, patterns of childrearing, patterns of economic exchange and institutions of commerce, and even from such seemingly socially benign and underrated forces as geography and climate. It does not seem such a mystery to us that one should find a wide variety of forms of human suffering, and that in the face of this variety, some patterns of human adaptation are more successful than others in establishing psychological and social well-being.

As social scientists, how are we to explore discomforting areas that arouse adversarial political or ideological responses? What is the responsibility of a psychologist, anthropologist, or sociologist, as a social scientist to report or further investigate uncomfortable data? Can social sciences remain free of political pressure? One clearly feels such pressures while working in the area of psychological adjustment and social adaptation in different ethnic groups.

In scientific inquiry should disturbing results not lead us to further dispassionate exploration to better ascertain causality in human experience and social behavior? Yet social sciences are increasingly moving towards politically and rhetorically motivated, ideologically based interpretive and critical analyses, often in the absence of sufficient empirical basis (D'Andrade, 2000). By failing to provide comparable data from a variety of cultural settings, and by relying instead on interpretive and rhetorical analysis, this contemporary approach has the effect (perhaps intended) of virtually disabling objective comparative analyses. What is needed in social sciences, although not to the exclusion of grounded interpretation, is a consistent intermediate step, that of noting and reporting the occurrence of identifiable types of events, whether they be behavioral observations, dimensional measurements obtained through the use of reliable instruments, or the unmediated thematic contents of narrative products. We see our use of the TAT, and our scoring method as but one effort to address the objective scientific-methodological requirements of such an essential task.

The Need for Valid Quantifiable Data for Cross-Cultural Comparison

The initial purpose in developing a scoring system useful in categorizing spontaneous thought was to compare specific social settings or individuals living in different cultural contexts in some systematic manner that would be communicable and replicable. Over the years, that initial purpose has evolved into the system we are presenting in the present volume. Our own use of the method is clearly related, in our minds, to an explicitly considered developmental psychodynamic theoretical paradigm for interpretive analysis that we also discuss in the present volumes. However, the method itself functions to structure the researcher's categorical perception, leading to an understanding that is based first on a level of necessary objective quantitative scoring to record manifest conscious content, before attempting any interpretive generalizations. Moreover, legitimate comparative analysis must start with some normative consideration of what is relatively salient in the conscious content of a group. Further interpretation can occur only subsequent to such recording and systematic organization of materials. Therefore, in this volume we illustrate a methodological approach which lends itself to the useful quantification of experiential, emic data.

We recognized the need for a systematic scoring system early on. Beginning in 1948, William Caudill and George De Vos were using projective tests as part of a more general attempt to investigate the post-war adaptation of Japanese Americans in the Chicago area after their release from wartime internment camps. Caudill had examined TAT-elicited stories obtained from Japanese Americans in Chicago empirically, using no a priori scoring system to order his data (Caudill and De Vos, 1956). After seeing this process, De Vos concluded that some more systematic quantification would be necessary to handle the very large amount of data to be assembled at Nagoya in the 1953–1954 project. The first categories to be considered where those used originally by Henry Murray and others at Harvard (1938). While potentially useful, the approach was too trait-like in character, comprising a list of "needs" and "presses" that one might expect to find present in some balance in a given individual. Murray's system had no unifying underlying framework directed toward the psycho-cultural themes in which we had specific interest at that time. Furthermore, the need-press dichotomy did not seem to be a helpful distinction, since specific "needs" were also used by Murray to indicate achievement stories that were continually dramatized in the context of repayment for nurture and other family role situations that were manifest in the Japanese data.

In considering their approach we found that McClelland's conception of a need for achievement tended to confound concerns with standards for excellence with concerns with competence or mastery and interpersonal competitiveness. Their criteria for scoring was not useful in respect to the patterns elicited from the Japanese in which concerns with competence or mastery had to be distinguished from the sense of long-range purpose manifest in either American or Japanese achievement motivation. McClelland and his associates, in their quantitative comparisons of individuals on specific traits, did not tabulate several specific conflictual themes involving achievement so that they could be compared for possible cultural differences. For example, the Japanese were continually concerned with problems of possible inadequacy interfering with achievement goals. In contrast, American control samples were concerned with questions of whether one wanted to apply oneself to a task or not, or how one should deal with the force of parental pressure inducing the assumption of future goals (De Vos, 1973b). We felt, therefore, compelled to develop categories for scoring that would allow for more exhaustive quantification that dealt more systematically and exhaustively with alternative concerns and their interactive blending.

The McClelland approach remains concerned with individual personality patterns in which a specific trait is relatively present or absent within the individual or groups of individuals. Even where they are interested in comparisons of the relative frequency of evidence for specified motives between cultural groups, they have not emphasized the delineation of what we call "molecular" patterns of relative saliency of a variety of concerns that *are* present even where the researcher's particular sought-after trait might be absent. They are not interested in the complex overall patterns and relative saliencies of a variety of instrumental or expressive concerns within individuals from among a given social or cultural group. In contrast, from the perspective we describe in the present volume, the interesting peculiarities of a culture are to be found in the manner in which various concerns are interrelated and how they pattern out in a variety of social contexts.

We feel very strongly that an overall conceptual scheme for scoring TAT responses must be able to code for the wide variety of possible material elicited. It cannot be limited by the specific immediate interests of particular researchers. For example, we consider it to be a reflection of specific American ethnocentrism that none of the researchers within the McClelland, Atkinson tradition (Smith, 1992) attend to spontaneous content related to expressive interpersonal concerns with social support or family cohesion; nurture, protection, or dependency; social harmony or conciliation; or concerns with social acceptability in the form of esteem, shame, debasement, etc. Affiliation is considered by them only as individually defined companionate closeness.

The emphasis throughout their works is with individualistic concerns with achievement, defined more in economic terms than in terms of social dedication; they are concerned with individualistic perceptions of personal power rather than avoidance of some of his designated social or psychological presses (e.g. "Blamavoidance").

From a developmental psychodynamic theoretical framework, wherein social expectations that are experienced interpersonally become internalized, Murray's etic distinction between what is an inner need as opposed to an outer-derived expectation seemed somewhat artificial, and perhaps less theoretically relevant than other distinctions that could be made. A more emic-experiential interpersonal approach avoided any reference to a differentiation between bodily derived needs or drives and socially induced concerns. It seemed more feasible to pay attention to the informants expressed interpersonal concerns without having to designate what was an internal need or motivation versus an external press. We, therefore, have chosen to use the term "concerns" rather than "needs" in our presentation of the method. In this regard, it was interesting to note that protagonists in a story would sometimes be described as taking active, or passive or defensive stances. And informants would often provide indication of judgmental or evaluative positions regarding the events in the story. Additionally, informants would commonly make reference to questions of social status and expected role behavior. These various dimensions of activity, evaluation, and social position were of greater obvious importance to a multidisciplinary social scientist who was interested in the sociocultural framework of experience, and a comparative psycho-cultural analysis.

In the early 1950s, McClelland (1961) with other colleagues (i.e., Atkinson, 1958; McClelland, Atkinson and Lowelle, 1953; Shipley and Veroff, 1952; Veroff, 1958; Smith, 1992) were developing rather extensive, systematic work with what Murray had termed "need achievement" (n achievement). McClelland considered n achievement to be a motivation socialized differently in different social contexts. With their collaborators, McClelland, Atkinson, and Veroff developed a very precise, well elaborated series of criteria for scoring n achievement. They used similar methods to create precise scales for measuring needs for "affiliation" and "power." They began applying these measures to the analysis of the fantasy of children and adults in various contexts including that of economic development (McClelland, 1961).[8]

The very evident need to achieve, and the culturally induced motivational pattern underlying this need had become a concern that Caudill and De Vos found central to understanding the collectively apparent patterns of adaptation taking place among the Japanese Americans in Chicago. However, McClelland and his associates, in seeking for a quantitative focus, limited themselves for the most part to three basic concerns, and were ignoring some other salient themes that kept recurring in the sequential logic found embedded in the Japanese TAT stories. For example, the McClelland approach did not allow for any complex examination of

---

[8]More recently others have offered several other indices of "needs" or "orientations" such as complexity, uncertainty, and responsibility. See Smith (1992) *Motivation and Personality: Handbook of Thematic Content Analysis*.

social authority; both achievement and power are contextualized as competitive entrepreneurial advancement.[9] While competitiveness is emphasized, the word, cooperation, does not appear in Smith's index, nor do any of the words related to social harmony, care and nurture, or social acceptability or esteem as a social concern.[10] We have found many social concerns not scored or indeed scorable, within the measures developed within their tradition.

Such a system pays no heed to continual human concerns with group belonging or behavior consciously perceived in the context of being a group member. It pays no direct heed to *social status*, or to ethnic or class concerns or one's *social role* as part of instrumental or expressive social considerations. In our work, from its inception, we have become more focused on an overall conceptual organization of interpersonal patterns in which achievement or affiliation plays but a relative part in the context of other possible *social* as well as *individual* preoccupations.

The initial work by De Vos in Japan broadened out into an attempt to grasp the Japanese culture as a social system. His psycho-cultural approach was to understand how much the system, as observed from the outside, also operated within the conscious perceptions of its members. He was attempting an approximation of their emic experience, that is, he sought to get inside the perceptions of the Japanese as they functioned, first within the family, then within peer group and community, in educational institutions, in religious beliefs and practices, and then within more broadly approached political, commercial-business, and various professional pursuits (see Wagatsuma and De Vos, 1984). In this effort, he paid special attention to patterns of deviancy and crime as well as socially conforming behavior.

Cultural Continuity, Internalization, and Achievement Motivation

In the late 1940s, in Chicago, Japanese were moving into the high delinquency areas of the city whose inhabitants were being thoroughly studied by sociologists at the University of Chicago and by both sociologists and psychologists at the Institute of Juvenile Research. Sociologists at the Institute had intensively

---

[9]The word "competition" is even used by McClelland in his basic definition of Achievement as, "Competition with a standard of excellence" (see Smith, 1992, 155 ff.)

[10]For example, the word "dependent" is mentioned only once in Smith's volume (1992, 208) in respect to being a possibly "deficit-motivated aspect of affiliative needs." Dependency is not indexed as a need nor mentioned in the entire volume. Any sense of social or economic deprivation, poverty, social harmony or nurture or dependency are never mentioned. However, they have been salient social concerns found in many individuals among the samples we have investigated.

documented the patterns of juvenile crime in the inner city of Chicago with its special "zone of transition." On the basis of their previous studies of the negative effects of ghetto living among other groups, psychologists were predicting patterns of personal and family breakdown and various other forms of social alienation for the Japanese being released from the internment camps where they had been moved by the American government during World War II. However, when several of us began to study the incoming Japanese-Americans we found that they were not performing as negatively as would be expected of members of a minority facing strong, continuous discrimination. Here was a group of people who had been subject, not only to the usual forms of racially directed prejudice, but who been wrenched from their homes on the American west coast by their government and put into special camps for several years. Yet, they were not behaving according to negative predictions. How were we to explain why Japanese children and youth, unlike the other minorities residing in Chicago's zone of transition, were doing so well in school, and those old enough, were finding jobs and advancing in their occupations? Despite massive discrimination, their political allegiances remained quite conservative and were characterized by loyalty to the American society.

As a result of our collaborative work with Japanese in Chicago, William Caudill (who used the TAT) and George De Vos set forth some psycho-cultural contentions about internalized achievement motivation as related to a continuing cultural pattern based on primary family socialization (Caudill and De Vos, 1956). Our findings contradicted a straight sociological approach to discrimination. We advanced what was then still a novel idea that cultural patterning was more determinative of minority adaptive behavior than were immediate sociopolitical conditions of severe discrimination.

This theme was pursued in subsequent work with normative samples of Japanese in Japan starting in 1953 (De Vos, 1973b; De Vos and Boyer, 1989). This contention has been reinforced more recently with findings in the United States about the positive adaptive occupational and educational patterns and psychological adjustive patterns of more recently immigrating Koreans, whose family and community interaction patterns bear striking resemblance to Japanese immigrants of two generations ago (Lee and De Vos, 1981; De Vos, 1983; De Vos and Kim, 1993). Examination of patterns of minority adaptation both in the United States and Japan has led us to decry sociological theories that consider delinquency or deviancy solely in terms of the immediate situational social factors such as those operative in American city ghettos. Such theories do not explain why different minority groups viewed longitudinally over several generations develop different patterns of adaptation in response to similar exposures to discrimination and economic hardship.

In looking at the relative adaptation of minority children of different minorities in both the United States and Japan it should be very evident that cultural, psychological, and sociological factors *all* play a role in the behavior of minorities. Unfortunately such even-handedness is not found in the writings of many social scientists, who are prone to give most weight to one or another favorite pattern of causality. For example, anthropologists attempting to examine persistent culture patterns are too prone to dismiss psychological universals and advocate a nonjudgmental cultural relativism that ignores the fact that some forms of culturally persistent socialization are more problematical than others, either from the standpoint of mental health or from the standpoint of socially or politically adaptive functioning in situations of change.

Both the unexpectedly better adaptation in the face of discrimination of the Japanese and Koreans as minorities in the United States, and the continuing problems manifest in some other minorities (both in the United States and Japan) bear continual examination and explanation in a comparative context on all levels of analysis. Structural psychological problems can remain severe as they are passed on from one generation to the next by the inadequate or less adaptive parenting that is more common to some historically debased minorities. It follows therefore, that psychological problems of a maladjustive nature are not simply or solely to be ameliorated by a diminution of outer social discrimination. What has been remarkable about Japanese emigrants wherever they have settled, even in rather different social settings, is the similarity of the reported adaptive pattern. This holds true whether one looks at samples from the United States and Canada in North America, or from Brazil, Peru, or Argentina in South America. In volume II, we present data that enables us to attempt comparison of elicited fantasy among these groups.

In the results reported in some of the chapters of volume II, we also turn to an exploration of forms of cultural continuity such as those to be found in the expressed concerns of youth. For example, in Brazil (chapters 8, 9, 10, volume II), can we find continuities of social attitudes that stem from historical forms of political and social exploitation of large segments of the Brazilian population? Does this heritage from past Portuguese colonialism remain active in the expressed concerns of young Brazilians even today? Is such a heritage of exploitation still to be found both inside the family, and in outside status relationships? One instance of such a sociocultural-historical heritage can be seen in Brazilian attitudes about work. Is work an active or a passive verb? It appears that "work" for some does not mean a path to social advancement, but instead work is seen as "being put to work," to be exploited by others in dominant social positions, be they employers, government officials or one's own parents. As we will discuss in a subsequent chapter, our TAT method has enabled us to ask how the Japanese Brazilians as a subgroup reflect or fail to reflect this kind of social attitude that is readily found among other Brazilians.

For another example, in the United States we have noted (Caudill and De Vos, 1956) the differential responses among various minority groups to educational adaptation within American society. On the one hand, a number of the Asian groups are doing relatively well, have taken to the school system in a positive way and are over-represented numerically according to population at many of the American major undergraduate and graduate institutions of advanced learning. Other groups, such as Mexican Americans and African Americans, have done relatively poorly in the American setting. What is the situation elsewhere in respect to the adaptation of ethnic minorities with particular histories of discrimination within a majority dominated school system? The recent work of Marcelo Suárez-Orozco (1989) on Central American immigrants and with Carola Suárez-Orozco (1995) on a recent generation of Mexican Americans has been a continuity with this area of research.

Status Inequality as Reflected in the TAT

In ongoing psycho-cultural research, the senior author has continued to investigate the relative saliency of achievement motivation as but one instrumental concern among the variety of other possible instrumental or expressive social interests or preoccupations. It became obvious very early on that achievement concerns were closely interconnected with the broader pattern of interpersonal concerns, most importantly to family and social status concerns. Starting in 1948, De Vos and various colleagues have been using the TAT to study comparatively the social attitudes of Japanese and class differences among American youth. Subsequently, they have examined samples of minority Korean youth in Japan and in the United States, and have conducted studies in Europe and Latin America, as well as Japan and Korea. One continuing focus of this research, among the students and colleagues who have worked with G. De Vos in a variety of cultural settings, has been an examination of the attitudes of adolescent youth from various social strata, related to school performance and to future occupational interests. The most recent and still ongoing collaborative ventures have been involved with youth from ethnic and social strata found in Brazilian and Venezuelan societies in South America. From the study of youth we can gain some indirect reflections of cultural continuities in thought, as well as some changing attitudes related to shifting social circumstances. Throughout these various collaborations, we have been concerned with the effect of minority status on the social attitudes of specific minorities starting in early childhood, but most readily available during the period of high school and college attendance.

Empirical Derivation of the Present Scoring System

As mentioned above, William Caudill and George De Vos had used respectively the TAT and the Rorschach tests in their investigation of post-war adaptation of Japanese Americans in the Chicago area. A strong achievement drive was quite evident throughout the projective test materials as well as in the interviews conducted with the Issei (first generation) immigrants and their Nisei (second generation) children (Caudill and De Vos, 1956). This work on the personality and psychological development of Japanese Americans came to the attention of Professor Tsuneo Muramatsu of Nagoya National University in Japan. In 1952, the

Fulbright scholar exchange program was initiated for Japan. Muramatsu asked both Caudill and De Vos to come to Japan and participate in organizing and carrying out a program of research on Japanese personality and culture at Nagoya University. De Vos accepted and journeyed to Nagoya in 1953 to work on research in the department of Psychiatry in Japan for two years where a team of researchers would gather a normative sample of psychological and sociological materials from two cities and three rural settings (De Vos, 1973b).

Subsequently De Vos worked intermittently (for about ten years from 1959 to 1968) on studies of delinquency formation and crime in Japan (Wagatsuma and De Vos, 1984). During the 1960s, then again in the late 1970s, De Vos worked with present-day Japanese minorities; the *Burakumin*, the descendants of a former outcaste segment of premodern Japanese society similar in social function to the ex-untouchables of India (De Vos and Wagatsuma, 1966); and the Korean minority (Lee and De Vos, 1981), whose residence in Japan dated from the Japanese occupation of Korea from 1910 to 1945.

From the inception of joint work in Nagoya on the cultural psychology of the Japanese, De Vos was faced with the necessity of developing some systematic methods for analyzing the large amount of data that was to be gathered from a basic sample of approximately 2,400 rural and urban Japanese. To help analyze subjects given a Problem Situation Test as well as the TAT (De Vos, 1973b), he gradually developed a series of "interpersonal concerns" to help order the variety of psycho-cultural themes that can be spontaneously elicited in interviews or projective tests concerned with fantasy about social behavior.

The scoring system as presently published has been developed over a period of fifty years. Each of the major categories considered has been progressively further divided into numerous subcategories that were encountered in actual stories. In keeping with a generally recognized problem that comprehensive TAT scoring systems are difficult to learn (Cramer, 1996), the large number of subcategories in the present system does indeed take some time to learn. But, the key here is to understand that the specific subcategories are to be seen not as absolute, but as providing confirmatory heuristic clues to the scorer. They can be seen to be very helpful to the scorer in that they initially help to define the parameters of the twelve major categories. As the scorer gains increased experience with the system, and as the subcategories are used with increasing familiarity, the internal logic and inter-connectiveness of the system becomes increasingly apparent. There is no way to avoid this learning and familiarization process. However, once the system has been learned, a trained scorer may even find himself or herself parsing the larger world in terms of the system's scoring categories. The categories have a compelling heuristic value.

It must be noted that the possible thematic concerns evoked by any research procedure are selectively limited by the stimuli presented. For example, the Harvard-published set of TAT cards in most general use is highly limited in what they elicit. Depending on the pictures selected, different subcategories become emphasized. Each card utilized has a different cluster of possible stories, which, also differ with the social, or cultural background, age and gender of those tested. Most of the specific samples of individuals tested with the TAT do not produce examples of all, nor even many of the possible categories. Any particular group does not utilize more than a minor percentage of the possible subcategories listed.

It is also to be noted that, for the most part, the categories and subcategories included came into being as a result of TAT stories gathered in a number of different social groups over many years of usage. Many of the less frequently evoked subcategories we have included have appeared only in one or two cultural groups. However, these less frequently elicited subcategories are sometimes the most useful in demonstrating how cultural patterns influence groups differently. Some subcategories are very rare in occurrence in Japan, but more apparent in samples taken elsewhere such as those obtained from ethnic and class segments of Brazilian, Mexican, and Venezuelan society.

Moreover, not all the subcategories listed can be evoked by the cards we have most used. Not all, therefore, have initially actually appeared in TAT stories. Some subcategories of concern initially became apparent to us based on discussions with informants in other contexts. In Japan, for example, we have had numerous interviews in the context of ordinary family life in rural and urban areas, with small merchants and artisans, with minority individuals and their families, with educators in primary and secondary schools, with professional personnel in psychiatry and in the field of delinquency and crime.

Some subcategories related to religion and the supernatural were the result of attempting to score special concerns covered in discussions with Japanese religious personnel about religious beliefs. Some religious concerns were also found in writings of both Americans and Japanese about personal biographical and autobiographical experiences of a number of authors, varying from William James to some Japanese leaders of new religions. We found that Asian religions personify different interpersonal attributes in conceptualizing the supernatural. Emphases in relationship with the dead or with a supernatural deity vary greatly. Also what has been historically emphasized in a personification of the supernatural in western Christianity differs with the historical period considered.

Looking at how Japanese view deviant behavior in their society and what is considered immoral, criminal or irresponsible has also been particularly informative. Forms of sanctioning behavior and concepts of authority, responsibility, and legal punishment have considerable similarity to what is found in American society, but there are notable differences, as we shall presently discuss.

There has been more than one instance of occurrence of practically every one of the subcategories now listed. They are not a priori inventions, although they have been arranged in as logical a sequence as possible based on our developmental psychodynamic theoretical framework. We are fairly confident in the scope addressed by the twelve major categories of the present scoring system. Nevertheless, the usage of this system will be necessarily different in emphasis when it is applied to tests other than the TAT, or when it is used to score the content of interviews with informants in a variety of circumstances. Clearly there will always be room for addition and modification of the categorical and sub-categorical structure of a system such as this. There is always the possibility that new subcategories will occur empirically that require inclusion. What we set forward in the present volume is the synthesis of empirical experience gained over a period of fifty years. That is but a short period of time in the larger span of time. Although the present form taken by our system is derived from a substantial body of work, it will no doubt continue to require changes over time.

Collaborative and Supervisory Experiences: The Use of the TAT in Various Cultural Settings

During his activities as a clinical psychologist, and throughout his professional years, George De Vos has used the TAT as part of test batteries in the diagnosis of clinical cases. As a research specialist, however, he has been more interested in normative research with different cultural groups than in individual analysis. He has used the TAT extensively in twenty years of collaborative research work with the TAT in Japan. He has also worked collaboratively in a number of different settings, in Asia, Europe, as well as in North and South America. These numerous collaborative projects have involved the use of TAT materials obtained from a variety of other cultures. Some of these efforts have been published and some remain unpublished. In what follows, we briefly describe material obtained from some of these various collaborative or supervisory projects. Some of these efforts shall be illustrated in greater detail in volume II.

The initial research conducted in Japan involved collaboration with a psychiatrist, the late Dr. Fumio Marui of Nagoya National University, conducted in Nagoya from 1953 to 1955 (Muramatsu et al., 1962; De Vos, 1973b). For that work, we initially developed a Japanese set of TAT cards by altering the features or background of some of the published Harvard cards. To these cards we added a number of experimental cards to elicit themes of motherhood, aging, or poverty and other topics of specific interest to our research group at the time. In standardizing the Murray-like Japanese cards we were able to have them so matched as to obtain no statistical differences between the original and the Japanese version. Several of our minor projects were initially done with the Japanese version. Later, we felt, since results were so indistinguishable, there was actually no further salient value in using the altered cards in comparative studies. Japanese could use Caucasoid individuals in making up narratives with equal facility to those with Japanese features. In all subsequent work we went back to using the original Harvard set with the addition of three cards from our Japanese set that were not matched in the American series. In work in the 1960s with the late Eiji Murakami of Nagoya University Department of Education (De Vos and Murakami, 1974) we used both the Murray cards and some selected from our Japanese experimental series (see chapter 5, volume II).

Work with the Japanese materials obtained in the 1950s and 1960s was in the main done over several years, first at the University of Michigan, then at the University of California, with the late Hiroshi Wagatsuma (De Vos and Wagatsuma, 1959, 1961; Wagatsuma and De Vos, 1962, 1984) (see chapter 4, volume II). Additional material from other Japanese samples was collected in the 1980s. In addition to working with Nisei and Sansei Japanese-Americans in the Sacramento area of California, anthropologist John Connor, on a Fulbright grant to Japan, collected a more recent sample of TATs from Japanese college youth. From that data, Connor and De Vos were able to compare more recent records with previous records in regards to examining patterns of achievement motivation that were evident in the records (Connor and De Vos, 1989) (see chapter 6, volume II).

Collaborations have extended beyond the Japanese samples. In the late 1950s, the anthropologist June Helm, with George De Vos, examined Canadian Indian TATs obtained from Slavey and Dogrib Indian communities located in the MacKenzie river basin of the Northwest Territories (see excerpts from Helm, De Vos, and Carterette, 1960 in chapter 13, volume I). De Vos also worked with the anthropologist Melford Spiro and psychologist Leslie Rabkin on their twenty-year longitudinal follow up of Israeli Kibbutzim, which had utilized both Rorschach and TAT records (see chapter 1, volume II). He also worked with some of the materials Spiro brought back from Burma and from the Ifaluk Atoll in the Western Pacific. He has also examined some of the Navaho American Indian materials of the late Dorothea Leighton.

Korean TAT materials were obtained in Japan, Korea, and Los Angeles by anthropologist Kwang-Kyu Lee, and political scientist Chansoo Lee (De Vos and Kim, 1993) (see chapter 7, volume II).

In Europe, at the University of Paris (V) George De Vos assisted psychologist Jean Galap with TAT materials taken from Martiniquans who had migrated to the Paris area. In Belgium, at the Catholic University of Leuven in the late 1980s he worked with anthropologists Philip Hermans (see Hermans, 1999) and Antoine Galley on materials obtained from Turkish and Moroccan immigrants to Brussels.

Most recently De Vos has been occupied with collaborative work with psychologists from Latin America. While on a Fulbright grant, Professor Cicero Vaz of the Catholic University in Porto Alegré, Brazil, visited Berkeley for a year in 1989–1990 to work with him. Professor Vaz subsequently obtained TAT materials from a number of Brazilian ethnic groups both from the Amazon (chapter 12, volume II) and from the southern state of Rio Grande do Sul (chapters 8, 9, 10, volume II) with which we have been working since a subsequent visit to Brazil sponsored by the Fulbright program in 1991. While doing graduate dissertation work in Brazil, Dr. Takeyuki Tsuda of the University of California at San Diego also obtained a special sample of Japanese-Brazilians from both the cities of São Paulo and Porto Alegré (chapters 8, 9, 10, volume II). Professor David Ephraim of the National University in Caracas also came to work with George De Vos at Berkeley, on a Fulbright grant during 1993–1994. He had obtained a number of TAT samples from the ethnically diverse population of Venezuela, and provided some additional materials from a Protestant-Canadian population of Vancouver (chapter 11, volume II).

George De Vos has also supervised a number of dissertations which included TAT materials from Ireland (Scheper-Hughes, 1979, see chapter 1, volume II), Kenya (Evans, 1974, 1975, see chapter 3, volume II), the Philippines (Manlove, 1990, see chapter 13, volume II), Japan (Vaughn, 1988, 1996, see chapter 6, volume II), Central American immigrants in the United States (Suárez-Orozco, 1989, see chapter 15, volume II), Mexico (Suárez-Orozco and Suárez-Orozco, 1995, see chapter 15, volume II), Dorsch De Voe (see chapter 14, volume II), and from students in training for the ministry (Kirsten, 1991, 1993). He worked with students on TAT and Problem Situation tests supplied by the late Sinologist, Wolfram Eberhard, and late social worker, Kenneth Abbott, working with materials obtained from Chinese in Taiwan and San Francisco, and from Japanese war brides and their husbands in San Francisco (Abbott, 1970, 1976; De Vos, 1973a; De Vos, Hauswald, and Borders, 1979).

Eric De Vos has used the ICSS to analyze non-TAT materials, including material from African American women in Michigan. Using a combination of interviews, card sorts, and paper and pencil questionnaires that pertain to interpersonal concerns, he has examined social-status concerns and interpersonal attitudes at the time of pregnancy (E. De Vos, 2000a). He has also collected TAT responses as part of research on Tibetan refugees living in the United States (E. De Vos, 2000b). He is presently working with stories collected from athletes on a college football team, members of an NFL football team, and undergraduate college tutors. He and a student have also modified several of the TAT cards, changing the visual stimuli into verbal depictions for use in a study of blind teenagers.

As we shall illustrate in the chapters in volume II, the TAT materials, and other interview material collected in these various projects, were all amenable to organization in terms of the scoring categories demonstrated in this volume. These studies have offered abiding evidence of the validity of using the TAT cross-culturally as a means of eliciting conscious attitudes about society and self. They give witness to the universal appearance of basic dimensions and "elemental": components of the human experience of interpersonal relationships, regardless of the society considered. When adequate cooperation is obtained in the testing situation, TAT stories richly reflect different conscious preoccupations of individuals from different societies and from different social settings within a society.

Notes

Abbott, Kenneth. 1970. Harmony and Individualism. *Asian Folklore and Social Life Monographs, Vol XII*. Taipei: Orient Cultural Service.

———. 1976. Culture Change and the Persistence of the Chinese Personality. In George De Vos (Ed.), *Responses to Change: Society, Culture and Personality*. New York: D. Van Nostrand.

Archer, Robert P., Mark Maruish, E.A. Imhof, and Caroline Piotrowski. 1991. Psychological Test Usage with Adolescent Clients: 1990 Survey Findings. *Professional Psychology Research and Practice*, **22**: 247–252.

Atkinson, John William. 1958. *Motives in Fantasy, Action, and Society: A Method of Assessment and Study*. Princeton, N.J.: Van Nostrand.

Bellak, Leopold. 1954. *The Thematic Apperception Test and the Children's Apperception Test in Clinical Use*. New York: Grune and Stratton.

Blum, Gerald S. 1950. *The Blacky Pictures: Manual of Instructions*. New York: Psychological Corporation.

Caudill, William and George A. De Vos. 1956. Achievement, Culture and Personality: The Case of the Japanese Americans. *American Anthropologist*, **58**: 1102–1126.

Connor, John W. and George A. De Vos. 1989. Cultural Influences on Achievement Motivation and Orientation Toward Work in Japanese and American Youth. In David Stern and Dorothy Eichorn (Eds.), *Adolescence and Work: Influence of Social Structure, Labor Markets, and Culture* (pp. 291–326). Hillsdale, N.J.: Lawrence Erlbaum Associates.

Cramer, Phebe. 1996. *Storytelling, Narrative, and the Thematic Apperception Test*. New York: The Guilford Press.

D'Andrade, Roy G. 2000. The Sad Story of Anthropology 1950–1999. *Cross-Cultural Research*, **34**(3): 219–232.

De Vos, Eric S. 2000a. Social Support, Interpersonal Styles, and Reactions to the Pregnancy among African American Expectant Mothers. Paper presented at the 29th Annual Meeting of the Society for Cross-Cultural Research, New Orleans, La., February 23–27, 2000.

———. 2000b. Family Responsibility, Conflict Resolution and Achievement Motivation among Tibetan Refugees. Paper presented at the 29th Annual Meeting of the Society for Cross-Cultural Research, New Orleans, La., February 23–27, 2000.

De Vos, George A. 1952. A Quantitative Approach to Affective Symbolism in Rorschach Responses. *Journal of Projective Techniques*, **16**(2): 133–150.

———. 1954. A Comparison of the Personality Differences in two Generations of Japanese Americans by Means of the Rorschach Test. *Nagoya Journal of Medical Science*, **17**(3): 153–265 (reprinted: no. 34, 1966).

———. 1973a. *American Japanese Intercultural Marriages*. Taipei: The Chinese Association for Folklore.

———. 1973b. *Socialization for Achievement: Essays on the Cultural Psychology of The Japanese*. Berkeley: University of California Press.

———. 1974. Cross-Cultural Studies of Mental Disorder: An Anthropological Perspective. In Gerald Caplan (Ed.), *American Handbook of Psychiatry*, Vol. 3. New York: Basic Books.

———. 1978. Adaptation and Adjustment: Cross-Cultural Perspective on Mental Health. *Colloquia in Anthropology*, Vol. 2 (pp. 21–45). Fort Burgwin Research Center, S.M.U., Taos, New Mexico.

———. 1983. Achievement Motivation and Intra-Family Attitudes in Immigrant Koreans. *The Journal of Psychoanalytic Anthropology*, **6**(2): 125–162.

De Vos, George A. and L. Bryce Boyer. 1989. *Symbolic Analysis Cross-Culturally: The Rorschach Test.* Ruth M. Boyer and Horace Miner, Contributors. Berkeley: University of California Press.

De Vos, George, Lisabeth Hauswald, and Orin Borders. 1979. Cultural Differences in Family Socialization: A Psycho-Cultural Comparison of Chinese and Japanese. In Albert M. Craig (Ed.), *Japan: A Comparative View* (pp. 214–269). Princeton, N.J.: Princeton University Press.

De Vos, George and Arthur E. Hippler. 1969. Cultural Psychology: Comparative Studies of Human Behavior. In Gardner Lindzey and Elliot Aronson (Eds.), *The Handbook of Social Psychology,* Vol. 4 (pp. 323–417). Reading, Mass.: Addison-Wesley Publishing. (revised).

De Vos, George and Eun-Young Kim. 1993. Koreans in Japan: Problems with Achievement, Alienation Authority. In Ivan Light and Parminder Bhachu (Eds.), *California Immigrants in World Perspective.* New Brunswick, N.J.: Transaction Books.

De Vos, George and Eiji Murakami. 1974. Violence and Aggression in Fantasy: A Comparison of American and Japanese Lower-Class Youth. In William P. Lebra (Ed.), *Youth, Socialization and Mental Health* (pp. 153–177). Honolulu: University Press of Hawaii.

De Vos, George and Hiroshi Wagatsuma. 1959. Psycho-Cultural Significance of Concern over Death and Illness Among Rural Japanese. *International Journal of Social Psychiatry,* **5**(1): 6–19.

———. 1961. Value Attitudes Toward Role Behavior of Women in Two Japanese Villages. *American Anthropologist*, **63**(6): 1204–1230.

———. 1966. *Japan's Invisible Race: Caste in Culture and Personality.* Berkeley: University of California Press.

Evans, Emmit B. 1974. Kenyan Secondary School Students: A View Toward the Future. Ph.D. Dissertation. Berkeley: Department of Political Science, University of California.

———. 1975. Secondary School Education, Unemployment, and Crime in Kenya. *Journal of Modern African Studies*, **13** (March): 55–66.

Freeman, Mark P. 1993. *Rewriting the Self: History, Memory and Narrative*. New York: Routledge.

Helm, June, George A. De Vos, and Teresa Carterette. 1960. Variations in Personality and Ego Identification Within a Slave Indian Kin-Community. National Museum of Canada Bulletin, No. 190, *Contributions to Anthropology*, Part II.

Henry, William E. 1956. *The Analysis of Fantasy*. New York: John Wiley and Sons.

Hermans, Philip. 1999. The Expression of Guilt by Moroccan Adolescents: Ethnocentric Interpretations by Western Teachers and Social Workers. *International Journal of Educational Research*, **31**: 303–316.

Josselson, Ruthellen. 1996. Revising Herself: Women's Identity from College to Midlife. New York: Oxford University Press.

Kirsten, Ronald D. 1991 (unpublished). *An Investigation of the Religious Experience of Anglo, Black, Chinese, and Hispanic American Baptists*. Graduate Theological Union.

———. 1993. *Heinz Kohut's Nuclear Person: A Self Psychology/Religious Model of Maturity*. Ph.D. Dissertation. Berkeley: Graduate Theological Union.

Lee, Changsoo and George De Vos. 1981. *Koreans in Japan: Ethnic Conflict and Accommodation.* Berkeley: University of California Press.

Manlove, Robert F. 1990 (unpublished). *Ozamiz: A Case Study in Urban Anthropology*. Ph.D. Dissertation. Berkeley: University of California.

McAdams, Dan P. 1993. *The Stories We Live By: Personal Myths and the Making of the Self.* New York: Guilford.

McClelland, David C. 1961. *The Achieving Society.* Princeton, N.J.: D. Van Nostrand.

———. 1987. *Human Motivation.* New York: Cambridge University Press.

McClelland, David C., J.C. Atkinson, and E.L. Lowelle. 1953. *The Achievement Motive.* New York: Appleton-Century-Crofts.

Merton, Robert K. 1968. *Social Theory and Social Structure.* Glencoe, Ill.: The Free Press.

Miner, Horace and George De Vos. 1960. *Oasis and Casbah: Algerian Culture and Personality in Change.* Ann Arbor: University of Michigan Museum of Anthropology. *Anthropological Papers*, no. 15.

Morgan, Christina and Henry A. Murray. 1935. A Method for Investigating Fantasies: The Thematic Apperception Test. *Archives of Neurology and Psychiatry*, **34**: 289–306.

Morgan, W.G. 1995. Origin and History of the Thematic Apperception Test Images. *Journal of Personality Assessment*, **63**: 237–254.

Muramatsu, Tsuneo, et al. (Eds.). 1962. *Nihonjin Bunka to Pasonarititi no Jishõ-teki Kenkyu* (The Japanese: An Empirical Study in Culture and Personality). Tokyo and Nagoya: Reimei Shobõ.

Murray, Henry Alexander. 1937. Techniques for a Systematic Investigation of Fantasy. *Journal of Psychology*, **3**: 115–143.

———. 1938. *Explorations in Personality.* New York: Oxford.

———. 1943. *Thematic Apperception Test Manual.* Cambridge, Mass.: Harvard University Press.

Rabinow, Paul and William M. Sullivan. 1979. *Interpretive Social Science: A Reader.* Berkeley: University of California Press.

Scheper-Hughes, Nancy. 1979. *Saints, Scholars, and Schizophrenics; Mental Illness in Rural Ireland.* Berkeley: University of California Press.

Shipley, T. and J. Veroff. 1952. A Projective Measure of Need for Affiliation. *Journal of Experimental Psychology*, **43**: 349–356.

Smith, Charles P. 1992. *Motivation and Personality: Handbook of Thematic Content Analysis.* Cambridge and New York: Cambridge University Press.

Spiro, Melford. 1984. Some Reflections on Cultural Determinism and Relativism with Special Reference to Emotion and Reason. In Richard A.Shweder and Robert A. LeVine (Eds.), *Culture Theory: Essays on Mind, Self, and Emotion* (pp. 323–346). Cambridge: Cambridge University Press.

Suárez-Orozco, Carola and Marcelo Suárez-Orozco. 1995. *Transformations: Migration, Family Life, and Achievement Motivation Among Latino Adolescents.* Palo Alto: Stanford University Press.

Suárez-Orozco, Marcelo. 1989. *Central American Refugees and United States High Schools.* Palo Alto: Stanford University Press.

Vaughn, Curtis. 1988. *Cognitive Independence, Social Independence, and Achievement Orientation: A Comparison of Japanese and U.S. Students.* Dissertation. Berkeley: University of California.

———. 1996. Socialization and School Adaptation. In D. Shwalb and B. Shwalb (Eds.), *Japanese Child Rearing.* New York: Guilford.

Veroff, J. 1958. A Scoring Manual for the Power Motive. In J. W. Atkinson (Ed.), *Motives in Fantasy, Action, and Society* (pp. 219–233). Princeton, N.J.: D. VanNostrand.

Wagatsuma, Hiroshi and George De Vos. 1962. Attitudes Toward Arranged Marriage in Rural Japan. *Human Organization*, **21**(3): 187–200.

——. 1984. *Heritage of Endurance: Family Patterns and Delinquency Formation in Urban Japan.* Berkeley: University of California Press.

Worchel, F.T., L.L. Aaron, and D.F. Yates. 1990. Gender Bias on the Thematic Apperception Test. *Journal of Personality Assessment*, **55**(3–4), 593–602.

Chapter 1

The Self in Society: Theoretical Perspectives on Social Construction and Conscious Experience

Social or interpersonal perceptions turned inward, self-reflexively, are integral to what is often termed the "self." Following the social philosophies of Dewey (1890), Cooley (1909, 1912), and George Herbert Mead (1934), American social scientists have commonly seen the self as an "internalization of social feedback and societal values" (Hoyle, Kernis, Leary, and Baldwin, 1999, 6). In this tradition, the symbolic interactionists have developed usable concepts of a self-reflexive and interactive self that functions in the context of social roles and expectations. Over the course of this century this tradition has generated a substantial body of empirical research. Unfortunately, as noted by D'Andrade and Strauss (1992), this was largely focused on situational determinants of behavior, with less emphasis on psychological structural determinants. In recent years, however, psychologists have begun to explore empirically how mental representations of the self function as one component of the motivational and self-regulatory systems of the individual (Hoyle, Kernis, Leary, and Baldwin, 1999). Nevertheless, in its effort toward mechanistic explanation, this tradition does not yet sufficiently address the experiential, emotional, and conative components of selfhood as a socially and culturally mediated experience.

We suggest that social science, when it examines self-reflexive human thought, should systematically explore how humans both objectively perceive, and subjectively experience themselves interactively, in their social roles. We suggest that this be done via a psycho-cultural form of analysis that looks comparatively at social groups, and at differences in the patterns of conscious concerns expressed by individual members of those groups. In this framework, we consider the self as an operational concept, useful for understanding and comparing consistently held patterns of human conscious concerns and motives in their sociocultural contexts.

Whatever the group or social segment of a population we seek to understand, in any sociocultural context there are shared or collectively held human conscious concerns and motives. Durkheim (1898), in his effort to develop a sociological method, initially called our attention to this idea that a society shared "collective" representations. Following Vygotsky, many developmental psychologists have also come to recognize that an individual growing up in a community learns to think and to define feelings and interpersonal relationships within a shared language and by way of shared experiences.

Looking at self in this sociocultural developmental context, we can see that the forms or patterns taken by the developing self awareness differ along with other collectively shared dimensions of culture. Culturally structured experiences, from childhood on, guide the person's *perception of internal experience related to the externally perceived social world.* Socially constructed normative perceptions and normative expectations for the self become part of personality patterns that are more or less prevalent among members of any given social group.

The expressed concerns found manifest in narratives produced by members of any group can be informative about the sociocultural mediation of behavior and underlying systems of thought. In our two volumes, we shall demonstrate the presence of cultural *differences in thought about social relationships* as we find them in verbal responses to standardized stimuli. We shall also demonstrate that one can structure a comparative psycho-cultural analysis by using a systematic categorical scheme as the basis for scoring and analyzing narrative content.

Thus a central intent of the present volume is to present a notational recording/scoring system of interrelated categories, and to demonstrate that this content-focused system can help to organize a comparative examination of conscious human experience. We can record what individuals verbalize as they express the content of their consciousness while they respond to given stimuli, whether they be interview questions, specialized tests, or a series of pictures such as those used in the Thematic Apperception Test (TAT). The scoring system we present in this volume can clarify the relative saliency of themes that appear in human thought, thus enabling the comparison of diverse groups or diverse segments of complex societies. What can be revealed by this type of narrative analysis are not only idiosyncratic differences among individuals but also cultural influences on a culturally prevalent sense of "self" and/or basic social attitudes found operative within a social group.

Our presentation of the scoring system (Interpersonal Concerns Scoring System, or ICSS) focuses on the use of the Thematic Apperception Test, but is applicable to other forms of expression whether elicited in interviews or by other systematically presented stimuli. The ICSS can be used to code a variety of narrative productions, as they are found represented in simple or complex forms in interview materials, folklore, and literary productions, as well as on specially devised projective tests directed toward eliciting social attitudes or personality configurations.

As we have described in the Introduction, the need for this cross-culturally applicable categorical system grew out of efforts toward a psycho-cultural comparison of Japanese Americans and other Americans in Chicago after World War II. The production of narrative responses to the TAT was one method for eliciting manifest expressions from members of these social groups that could then be compared across the groups. These initial data and data subsequently obtained in Japan made it clear that some method for objectively coding or categorizing responses was needed before any comparative analysis could be performed. As we collected material from a wider range of cultures, we ultimately identified a universally applicable set of basic dimensions and "elemental" components of human experience. The categorical system described in this volume is based on those dimensions and components of experience (see chapter 2, volume I).

As we discussed in the Introduction, there are dangers to the use of the TAT, or any method that involves analysis of narrative content. Foremost among them is the fact that social scientists often wish to make interpretations as to the underlying personality implications of the materials elicited through such methods. Or, they may want to make inferences as to the social institutional processes that produce them. We have also been concerned with an exploration of the extra-conscious "structural" mechanisms governing consistencies in observable behavior.[1] For example, as we discuss in several of the illustrative chapters of volume II, when we examine certain sequences in stories given in response to the TAT, some culturally normative behavior patterns can be usefully related to underlying personality issues such as unconscious patterns of guilt[2] that are only very indirectly revealed in

---

[1]See our more detailed discussion of levels of analysis in social theory in De Vos and Suárez-Orozco (1990), chapter 1: Self in Society: A Multilevel, Psycho-Cultural Analysis. See also De Vos (1984).

[2]For example, where we discuss the scoring of responses in the "Responsibility" (R) category, we note that unconscious patterns of guilt are only very indirectly revealed in conscious thought in the Japanese. The context in which an experience of guilt arises can differ widely in societies within the Western tradition and in Japanese, but it has been our contention that guilt appears in some form in every society, as it is a universal human experience.

conscious thought.[3] However, such theoretically guided interpretive moves are not the initial step in comparative psycho-cultural analysis.

Although an interpretative approach has been an important purpose of our research and has been involved in the development of the scoring system, the major purpose of this volume is not to teach interpretation. Instead, we intend to present as objective a method as we have found possible, a system for scoring the *manifest* content of verbal products that can be applied across different cultural groups. This is for the purpose of clarifying the nature of the "self" and its intra- and inter-personal aspects as they are found to be both similar and different in emphasis or in structure in a variety of cultural contexts.

Experiential Versus Structural Analytic Perspectives

There are many approaches to the understanding of human thought and behavior. We believe that it is essential to distinguish between what are termed, in recent academic parlance, "emic" and "etic" approaches.[4] In an extension of the use of such terminology in linguistics, this is a distinction now made in anthropology. As we read this distinction, what is important is that an emic approach involves a description and analysis of cultural behavior based, as best possible, on the informants' conscious thought patterns, including the informants own interpretations of behavior and social patterns. This contrasts with an etic approach of an outside observer that is guided by a theoretical system with categories and patterns of causality possibly unknown to the group whose behavior is being interpreted. For example, sociologists who use an etic approach are concerned with behavior that

---

[3]Aspects of a person's evaluative being can be so transparent experientially that they are not self-consciously apparent to the individual (Hutchins, 1980, as cited by D'Andrade and Strauss, 1992). One of the advantages of using a method like the TAT is precisely its ability to elicit revelations about these kinds of evaluative concerns. This kind of cognitively transparent unavailability is quite distinct from the psychoanalytic concept of a "repressed unconscious." A mode of perceptual or evaluative experiential being can be so pervasively present that it is irrelevant for reflection. Where such transparent aspects of being are operative, the full implications of a person's conscious expressions are not necessarily available to the individual. Sometimes, only a movement beyond normal cultural participation leads toward conscious self reflection about ones own transparent experiential biases. This is one of the advantages of etic structural analyses, and is one of the most important benefits of comparative psycho-cultural research.

[4]These terms are derivative from linguistic analyses of human speech related to sounds and nuances of sound that are in the awareness of a speaker ("phonemic" distinctions), as distinct from actual differences in sound that one does not actually distinguish while speaking but are in the awareness of an outside analyst ("phonetic" distinctions). For example, the Japanese do not make a phonemic distinction between "l" and "r" sounds, which can be recognized phonetically.

is predictable by an examination of the social system, that is, the various "institutions" that give structure to the behavior of members of a society, without necessarily referring to individual conscious experience or even individual behavior. Psychologists' etic explanations for behavior also apply theoretically structured inferences about the presence of intrapsychic mechanisms or processes or "constructs" that may also be unavailable to conscious emic experience.

From an etically applied system of analysis, one comes to recognize in various cultural contexts a predictability of behavior as it is patterned by economic or political systems. There are patterns of social status or hierarchy found in a class structure or a caste system. There are predictable patterns of collective thought and behavior organizing kinship, family roles, etc. Many social scientists may prefer to concentrate solely on how institutions (social, political, economic, etc.) are structured into continuing predictable patterns. From this approach we also learn how human thought and behavior is structured into continuing patterns of interactive social roles that are related to social categories such as age and gender, and into social hierarchies that define the status positions into which individuals are socialized. It was from this vantage point that Emile Durkheim (1898) formulated his contentions that one could examine and analyze prevailing patterns of thought in any particular society in structural terms as collective representations including a "collective conscience" or a collectively held thought pattern that includes moral structure.

In the biological sciences there is also an etic or structural level of analysis that is relevant to understanding human behavior. Behavioral biologists (ethologists) have been concerned with how behavior reflects underlying psychophysiological and neurological patterns, and this is often seen in developmental biological terms (see, for example, Schore, 1994). On this level of etic analysis, behavior can be considered a product of developing psychophysiological mechanisms that are influenced by differential socialization experiences as they occur within different cultures.

Above this psychophysiological or biological level is yet another structural level on which behavior is examined independently of biological mechanisms. At a psychological level, the search for behavioral predictability leads to the construction of psychological concepts such as "internal representations" or "internalization," "cognitive schemes," "decision making," "motivation," "goal-directed behavioral programs," etc. On a more global and often psychodynamic level, psychologists have posited a whole host of etic theories that describe what is most often termed "personality." In this effort they posit the existence of structural elements of personality, such as the ego, or other self-regulatory or motivational elements. Some psychologists with less dynamic theoretical emphasis focus on statistics-based measurement of etic constructs such as "traits." These are all efforts to establish a scientific account of predictability in human behavior based on etic descriptions of structures that organize behavior around consistent forms of psychological coping that remain relatively though not entirely invariant across situations.

Varied terminology is applied to such structures, depending on a continuing diversity in theoretical orientation. In psychoanalytic theory, for example, there are concerns with "ego," "superego," and the unconscious defined as structures that organize and guide interactive behavior in predictable patterns. Such motivational or structuring forces are conceived of as existing (to some degree) outside of the ordinary conscious awareness of the members of a social group, although they may also be experienced (to some degree) subjectively as they are part of a subjective social awareness.

One can distinguish between "self" as behavior experienced consciously-subjectively, and "ego," which is intentional or coping behavior considered etically by an outside observer or analyst. Etically describable ego coping mechanisms are governed by internal structures of which the individual has only partial or periodic awareness, and of which the social scientist has only imperfect theoretical description.[5] On the other hand, the emically experienced self (either as a direct experience of "being" or as a reflectively perceived object) may be quite distinct from an etically defined "ego" system. We turn now to a discussion of the self in terms of "emic" experience.

Self as an Emic Concept

The direct, determinative effects of continuities in human consciousness or "experienced being" itself cannot be ignored by simple reduction into behavioral explanations that refer to preexistent structural systems, at whatever level of mechanistic analysis. The transformative force of "emic" conscious experience must also be considered. A major concern of social sciences must be to explain consciousness itself as an actuality in a lawful universe. Despite materialistic reductionist attempts to explain away consciousness or a belief in consciousness and intentionality, as was done by the Behaviorists in psychology or some Marxists in sociology, there is the uncomfortable ability for humans to become aware of a universe in which life forms are not only self "conscious," but are capable, in collective endeavor, of affecting their own destiny through intentional action as represented in the varied achievements of human technology and industry, achievements of interpersonal cooperation, and in intrapersonal mental or behavioral development.

---

[5]In several chapters of Status Inequality, De Vos and Suárez-Orozco (1990) discuss three basic mechanisms of coping, and their development, derived from Freud's etic description of ego functioning. The mechanisms include: (1) intake, i.e, the interoceptive mechanism related to the development of empathy and resonant interaction in human psychology; (2) boundary protective or exclusory functions, starting with denial, developing into repression and concentration in human thought; and (3) contrastiveness and the experience of power or control, which develop from early forms of projection into analytic human thought.

What is often overlooked in philosophical discussions of the supposed mind-body dichotomy is the fact that the consciousness found in particular individuals is always only a partial reflection of a greater reality. It is never complete. It is only part of a more general complex discourse inherited, negotiated, and modified transgenerationally by participants who coexist in a living culture comprised of many members (Schwartz, 1978). Graphic and written records are also part of this shared consciousness conceptualized as "collective representations" by Durkheim (1898), or the "super-organic" by Kroeber (1927). An individual consciousness is always incomplete. It is always a developing component of a shared or trans-personal cultural process.

Culturally structured and bio-psychologically structured patterns can produce generational-historical behavioral continuities, and these are an important element of what we know as "culture" (E. De Vos, 2000). Research in the social sciences may focus on mechanisms or processes at either biological, psychological, or sociological structural levels for identifying determinative patterns and their effects. Singly considered social-structural or bio-psychological explorations of the determinants of human thought or behavior can never be complete. To be complete, these explorations must be directed toward a multidisciplinary multilevel understanding of the multiple and interconnected causes that determine human development (E. De Vos, 2000) yet in which human conscious experience is of central import. What is ultimately determined by such development is the person's experience of selfhood, i.e., an experience of being that is situated in a socio-culturally constituted world, in "discriminatively constructed" or "relative" reality (Thurman, 1984, 360), and that is causally related to that world through emotional, attitudinal, and pragmatic conscious human intentionality.

However, despite the obvious developmental and causal interconnectedness of human existence, it is common for human beings to define themselves in terms of separateness and individuality. A conscious sense of individual incompleteness itself is found in many religious representations, and the experience of this incompleteness is sometimes expressed in terms of agony. Past human attempts to conceptualize the total universe, including the intentionality exhibited by life forms, have usually been embedded in religious belief systems that included "supernatural" forms of intentionality as part of the explanatory system that helps us to overcome some of the terror of an isolated human existence (see chapter 14, volume I).

In the effort to free the sciences from any form of religious belief, scientists since the nineteenth century have often preferred to utilize forms of mechanical reductionism in their explanations rather than turn to the daunting task of explaining a universe affected by living intentionality and conscious manipulation. This unfortunate dehumanizing and erroneously lopsided derivation of Descartes' dualistic framework has left us with a science that is more comfortable with a mechanical universe in which no consciousness exists. Scientists seek to reduce thought to mechanism, rather than examining conscious thought as an elemental component of a complex social life form.

Even where thought has been of interest in the western tradition, philosophers have generally sought to explain consciousness by examining individual thought. Yet, perhaps that endeavor is too narrow. Just as the reproductive functioning of a coral reef cannot be explained by examining individual coral, humans as social animals and reproductive units cannot be explained without reference to the transpersonal social processes and communication patterns that govern their adaptation. Perhaps thought patterns are collectively produced and collectively resident entities that exist on a higher organizational level than the single individual. If that is so, the living entity to be examined is a society and its collective forms. That is the essential sociological insight. Yet if there is no room for intentional consciousness in sociological explanation, then this essential sociological insight has failed us.

As envisioned by the theologian Pierre Teilhard de Chardin in his concept of the "noosphere" (Teilhard de Chardin, 1959), we see today a complex global society that is becoming increasingly centered around the exchange of information over the Internet. As we further develop the global communication system, we may also be creating a new social entity, in which each of us as an individual is now but one component, much as a single cell is but one component of a body. An understanding of how the new global information society functions adaptively will be an essential task for social scientists in coming decades. We will need to understand the higher-order processes that are required to maintain the integrity of the global system. We will be seeing the development of various forms of self-reflexive, self-regulating, self-protective, higher-order processes as the global information society grows its own regulatory and protective mechanisms. These may come to constitute a global version of what at the individual level we know as a self, with both self-awareness and (hopefully) a conscience.

To return to a less super-organic level, it is our contention, nevertheless, that the experiential world of the individual person cannot be simply reduced in its totality to extra-conscious governing mechanisms of either a "social system" or to the biological and psychological dynamics of a personality structure. Nor can it be reduced to the totality of these systems, etically conceived. Inner conscious experience has its own idiosyncratic determinative impact on continuity or change in social and personal behavior. The explanation for relative cultural stability or change is not completely reducible to structural analysis. The stability or change in human consciousness itself is an equal participant in what happens. For example, increasing conscious awareness of how economic or social forces operate may have a revolutionary social effect. Likewise, increasing awareness of underlying personality problems may have an effect on the individual's control over personal behavior. Increasing awareness of a biological basis for some behavioral patterns (e.g., mental health or illness, sexual orientation) can lead to a reconstitution of personal and social attitudes and changes in normative expectations.

Although behavior must always be contextualized within overarching determinative structural systems, changes in conscious perception of social or interpersonal relationships, or changes in personally understood goals and values, can have a certain degree of functional autonomy (Allport, 1968) and comprise a definite force in social change.

The study of human social behavior must not overlook the conscious and intentional dimensions of the human being, yet this is commonly the case in social sciences. Benjamin (1988, 1995) contends that this oversight is not accidental, but reflects a pervasive and historically gender-related incapacity to relate well as "intersubjective" beings who are capable of mutual "recognition" (see chapter 10, volume I). According to Benjamin, developmental psychodynamic forces move us away from a feared dependency toward a defensive infantile omnipotence that leads to various forms of domination and submission. This movement produces subjective modes of thought that lead to the analytic objectification of human beings and the natural world, which become objects of study and ultimately objects of control and subjugation. Benjamin points out that even where intersubjectivity is addressed by philosophers, such as Habermas (1970) or other culture-theorists who use symbolic discourse-analytic methods, the analytic method itself retains this objectification, and does not recognize the full scope of intersubjectivity. Intersubjectivity is not only a linguistic process, not only a "seeing-of" the other, it is an emotional or empathic interrelatedness, or a "being-with" the other. True "recognition" requires this latter form of empathic interrelatedness.

Rather than countering the analytical objectification of human beings with a movement away from objectivity, Benjamin suggests instead that we redirect our efforts toward understanding intersubjectivity more directly. Our method for narrative analysis centers on exactly that: the direct recognition of intersubjective processes. For, as we have said, we have great respect for the importance of consciousness in effecting social change. Yet without objective recognition of the subjective experiences of human beings, efforts to change social processes based on ideology alone have serious limitations. The ideologue remains idealistic in intent and entirely *inner*-subjective in practice, rather than scientific in intent and *inter*-subjective in practice.

The principal limitation in the implementation of all ideologically derived solutions is that it is difficult to arrive at the point of intervention, idealistically conceived. In all human affairs, particularly any efforts toward the implementation of social change, one can never begin with a clean slate. Every generation transmits to the next some continuity of the patterns of differential socialization that produced it. Only through a gradual process of bringing these mechanisms into consciousness in the overall population does social change proceed intelligently. That is, in fact, an important purpose of this present volume, as we attempt to convey a method for recognizing the emic experiences of the "other's" subjectivity, and thereby explore at the psycho-cultural level the patterns and processes of differential socialization that must be the nexus for any effective social change aimed at optimizing the human experience and minimizing suffering. Rather than abandoning objectivity, instead, through the direct recognition of the other and the categorical documentation of experiential patterns found in the subjectivity of the other, we attempt to apply objectivity to the comprehension of intersubjectivity. This is a move that can ultimately enable human liberation from existing systems of which the participants themselves may not be aware.

Inner-directed awareness that is aimed at an exploration of conscious experience itself can liberate the individual from habitual perceptual and behavioral patterns. To the extent that awareness is directed toward conscious observation of social role-governed behavior, or toward an understanding of the sociocultural or developmental bases of inner experiential states, and even toward appreciation of the role of consciousness itself as a directive force, a person may begin to transcend the control of unconscious directive forces that constitute the psycho-cultural framework of his or her existence. This has been the basis of many transcendence-oriented religious, spiritual-practical, as well as psychotherapeutic transformative traditions. This recognition of the importance of consciousness is also the basis for efforts directed toward a larger scope of transcendent liberation, as reflected, for example, in our optimism about the importance of an educated citizenry in a democratic society.

The self's own conscious experience of itself is not entirely an individually constructed experience. As much as it relies on the individual's inner-directed attentional mechanisms, it also is firmly embedded in social experience as well as ecological context (Neisser, 1993). Our own perspective is somewhat contrary to (perhaps broader than) the individualistic definition of self-consciousness common in both eastern and western psychology, wherein self-exploration is seen as turning *inward* (even if toward a transpersonal *atman* or collective soul as in Hindu thought). In contrast, we consider the self, especially when examined cross-culturally, to be experienced in *interactional* and *interpersonal* terms (Hsu, 1985) as well as in *introspective* revelations. As we develop analytical systems for identifying constituents of the self, it is useful to make the distinction between inner-directed and outer-directed constituents of self experiences (regardless of whether or not the distinction is emically experienced).

The distinction made by Markus and Kitayama (1991) between individualistic and collectivistic selves illustrates the point that we cannot rely on emic experience as the sole basis for scientific understanding of the self. For example, despite what many western individuals think subjectively about themselves as being individuals, we see the western self as far more collective in its development within the individual than the individualistic-collectivistic distinction would have us believe it to be. This observation may not have been lost on Markus and Kitayama (1998), but it may have been lost on many western students of personality who accept their distinction with perhaps less subtle understanding. If we attend to the issue of inner-directed versus outer-directed self concerns, we find that the western self is nevertheless largely a socially constructed being, regardless of its individualistic pretensions. We identify at least three major ways in which this is the case.

First, even within the western tradition, a commonly held conception of the origin of the "self" is that we experience the other "seeing" us, and we know ourselves in the attributed eyes of the other (Mead, 1934). Considered in this manner, the emic experiential "self," is subjectively experienced as a reflectively perceived objectification (E. De Vos, 2000). This type of thinking about the origin of a person's self as being based on a social-interactive dialog with others is at least as important in the contemporary western tradition as is an interest in the self's inner, or more privately motivated individualistic concerns.

A second way in which the western self is seen to be socially constructed (which differs from the idea of dialogic social construction) involves the existence of a prevalent or accepted cultural model of personality or selfhood to which the individual is explicitly exposed and which structures the individual's self perceptions and conceptualizations (as has been noted by Markus and Kitayama, 1998).

We see these ideas of a socially constructed, objectified, self-reflective, or "dialogic" self that is framed in terms provided by culturally prevalent models as addressing only two facets of the socially derived self. A third way of seeing the western self as essentially social comes from studying interactions between maturational forces and social-environmental forces in bio-psychological development. We are learning that there is very little that is nonsocial about the developing human bio-psychological system. There is now plenty of convincing evidence that early interpersonal experiences become embodied as patterns of neurological and physiological organization, and that these patterns serve as an enduring basis for later emotional regulation and interpersonal interactions (Schore, 1994). Personal characteristics that are developed in this manner are not merely socially constructed conceptual frameworks in a cognitive system, nor merely socially reinforced behavior patterns. They are not simply a cognitively experienced reflection of the self's attitudes as they are attributed to the other in a self-objectification. They represent a direct and enduring social regulation of biological systems at the level of neurological and physiological organizations that persist through life (E. De Vos, 2000).

These early experiences produce not only hardware, but also states of experienced "being." Experiences that are first obtained as relational experiences become integrated into a continuing identity that has inner experiences of its body, its emotions, its feelings (Chodorow, 1978). These experiences are directly experienced as states of being, or "flavors" of subjectivity, and they are often states of being-in-relationship-with (with a generalized other, with specific others, with objects or places, and with our cosmos). These become integrated into an experiential repertoire with which future subjective experiences are also flavored, and around which we establish a sense of continuing identity or selfhood that is experienced in its relationships with the larger world (E. De Vos, 2000).

By influencing patterns of early experience, socioculturally constructed family systems and care giving patterns determine the child's capacity to later engage in socially acceptable behavior, or to participate (or fail to participate) consensually in the larger set of agreements that constitute society. It is only upon ontogenetically organized biological structures and processes, and the experiential possibilities or states of being they enable, that the social construction of the self is built. There is always an actual living being who engages in the dialog.

We also acknowledge that some form of etically structured descriptive terminology about an objectified self exists as part of all culturally defined perceptual systems. This is indicated by the presence of person-descriptive adjectives in all languages. Furthermore, it is characteristic of the human experience to develop explanations about why people behave the way they do. Where specialized members of a culture have developed systematized etic constructs around these types of explanations, such constructs may become more generally used, and may thereby influence emic experiences of members of the cultural group.

Such etic constructs, such as "the unconscious," for example, can become part of the everyday landscape. To the extent that an individual has developed his or her own "naive" explanatory theory of personality, such a theory that initially may be applied etically toward others may also be applied reflexively toward the self. This can then become a basis for further emic experiences. Additionally, culturally derived descriptive or adjectival terms may become emic as the terms are applied during self reflection or self description. For example, some people are seen as "wily" or "humorous," etc., and may come to see themselves in those terms. Who we think we are, and the terms with which we describe ourselves, will be borrowed from our culture's language and models and applied towards ourselves in an awareness of the self as an objectifiable thing that can be described and explained. Yet this self-descriptive construction functions only as it interacts with the more primary experiential being.

Methods that rely on adjective-based description have dominated western personality research for several decades. From our perspective, such dimensional efforts are not interesting unless they reflect actual experiences of human selfhood, in its full complexity. The field in general has moved far from Raymond Cattell's (1950) early efforts to develop dimensional analysis as an objective and reliable adjunct in support of a complex and interesting understanding of human beings.[6]

What is relevant from the adjective-based perspective as applied to our perspective, is that some subjective experiences of selfhood do indeed rely, in part, on linguistically determined self-description. What begin as socially available descriptive categories may become the basis for emic experience of self. Additionally, self-descriptions are involved in some aspects of self-regulation, and exert directive force over behavior if the person seeks to adhere to either socially normative or personally desired standards. The person may even be rigid in his or her own self-characterizations, in ways that serve to direct behavior very strongly and narrowly. Yet the person may or may not be consciously aware that such self-

[6]The presently popular effort to reduce human personality to a few dimensions based on the use of adjective checklists and factor analysis, for all its statistical sophistication and even its cross-cultural replicability (McCrae, Costa, del Pilar, Rolland, and Parker, 1998), remains to our view a glorification of the nominalist fallacy, and a substantially insufficient approach, whether one is interested in understanding human experience or explaining human behavior.

regulations are occurring. Similarly, in the realm of social structural analysis, individuals who function in various social role settings may be either more or less conscious of the cultural or class patterns that govern their behavior as they either successfully or unsuccessfully enact or interact with perceived or experienced social roles.

Yet, as we have said above, the social scientist need not rely on emic experience as the sole basis for scientific understanding of the self. We must base our efforts at psycho-cultural analysis on the emic experiences of our informants, but we cannot limit it to them.[7] We can also benefit from developing our own system for categorizing and interpreting the emic experiences of others. Whatever the balance of descriptive or explanatory understanding that is achieved, whether emically or etically by the informant or by the social scientist, each person can have only an imperfect understanding of the psychological regularities and irregularities that govern the behavior of self and others. Each of us can, at best, develop a version of this awareness that is based on our own culture's ethno-psychological insights as well as its blindness.

What we seek, through comparative psycho-cultural exploration, is some capacity to move beyond the unavoidable ethno-psychological and idiosyncratic limitations of individual human experiences. We attempt to accomplish this through the analysis of consciously produced thematic content found in narratives. Our effort emphasizes the intermediate "emic" level of human social perception. Each specific expression of a human concern is produced as a specific culturally embedded instantiation of conscious experience. By conducting field research in a variety of sociocultural settings, we have obtained a wide range of narratives that illustrate the presence of diverse emically experienced self-relevant human concerns. Each of these concerns can be seen to comprise the set of "elements" or specific concerns that can then be configured into "molecular" patterns of concerns that distinguish individuals and cultures from one another. When taken as a whole, the extent of concerns, and their molecular configurations that we have found expressed in a wide range of cultures help us to move beyond an ethno-psychologically narrow understanding of what it is to be human.

The present volume derives from our effort to address the methodological need for a system of scoring that converts the manifest content of emic thought patterns into cross-culturally comparable etic elemental categories that quantitatively illuminate the presence of cultural differences in the emic perception of social relationships.

In the Introduction, we presented how we came to focus on the Thematic Apperception Test as a method through which to study human consciousness. We

---

[7]In contrast to the work with the TAT presented here, our work with symbolic analysis using the Rorschach Test (De Vos and Boyer, 1989) is on a structural psychological level dependent on an etic, psychoanalytic approach to the unconscious as it is revealed in responses to the Rorschach considered cross-culturally.

also discussed a variety of methodological issues that we have come to recognize as we have used the method over a period of fifty years. In chapter 2, volume I, we shall delineate the conceptual scheme around which our scoring system is organized. In the next twelve chapters we will describe, in detail, the various conceptual dimensions that form the basis of the categories used in our scoring system. Volume II presents a set of studies by a variety of authors who were influenced by our conceptual system and who used the scoring system as an integral component of their research activities.

Study of the Self: Patterns of Integration and Cohesion in Society

We would like to illustrate how an integrated social science can help us understand an issue such as social cohesion, which has been of special interest to us in understanding the development of the self (De Vos, 1992). It was our study of the self as it exists in the context of dynamic family patterns in Japan that initially alerted us to the unavoidable requirement that social sciences consider the force of consciousness and emic experience among the determiners of social structures and processes.

In the various social sciences, studies of social organization very often center around the regulatory or political forces that hold society together. From a motivational psycho-cultural standpoint, however, what actually is involved in the maintenance of relative social cohesion, or in the appearance of internal conflict within a society, is a far more complex interplay of expressive needs as well as individual or collective instrumental pursuits. These are framed within individuals as ways of being and mentally represented patterns for behavior, including regulated social interaction. Social cohesion depends on the subjective experience of some form of sanctioning. If there were no continuing social sanctions, internally as well as externally applied, society would fall apart. Thus the patterns of external power and intrapersonal self-restraint are central to understanding a society.

Humans are guided by a plurality of social passions (including a need for power) that create the possibility of conflict. Hobbes (1928) saw the exercise of control and coercion as the binding force holding together human societies. This entails a relative exercise of power. The largest element of power is the ability to command the recognition and the services of others. Hobbes calls into play the idea of society developing a "social contract" as a means of avoiding continual conflict.

In successful societies, social tensions and tendencies toward dissolution are alleviated by recognition of a sense of justice and legitimacy as opposed to any active sense of potential exploitation. Locke (1924) saw that through a recognition of an identity of instrumental interests, society sets up regulatory systems of government which reduce continual tendencies toward friction. There is a presumed mutual recognition of a need for regulation, standards of justice, and legitimate authority.

What is lacking in a number of social philosophers, such as Hobbes, Locke, or Marx, is some psychological consideration in human consciousness of the human capacity for internalization. The development of self-constraint and a sense of social responsibility that leads to autonomous behavior cannot be seen as strictly dependent upon Hobbesian external sanctioning or coercion or a Lockean instrumental recognition of mutual gain as the only regulatory considerations.

Marx, in his vision of the history of western culture found in nineteenth-century societies, social systems that had been governed by a corrupt and decaying feudal nobility. These stratified face-to-face societies were being supplanted by a more impersonal exploitation of industrial workers by the bourgeoisie, a class that avoided direct interpersonal relationships with their "inferiors." In his view, the separate national states would be overthrown by the antagonistic forces being engendered in them, principally by the general social alienation separating social classes one from another, and by the increasing alienation of the worker from any personal identification with his occupation. Marx's vision is a European historical vision that remains disturbingly realistic to a modern western observer (see De Vos, 1984).

Important in this vision, and central to it, is the moral dilemma of individualism as related to maximizing instrumental personal gain, and the consequent impersonal instrumental exploitative use of humans in a social structure determined by impersonal economic forces. In Marxist terms, humans are conceived of as rational animals. A person who lives in a class society may find it profitable, hence satisfying economically, to exploit those with less power and status, or to seek the status necessary to do so. Yet the satisfaction that is derived from exploitation of others may not be entirely economic, and the desire to be free from exploitation by others is also not entirely rational, nor necessarily conscious. What is overlooked in the Marxist idealization of a classless society is that its human ideal is itself basically *expressive* in nature. At the base of Marx's conception is a culturally specific, implicit expressive moral supposition that humanity *must* undergo a transformation from selfish instrumental motives toward those embracing a less selfish, expressive togetherness in society.

Expressively engendered feelings of moral outrage are aroused in a universalistic conscience that seeks for an idealized democracy. Outrage may hinder true social-scientific objectivity about the complexity of human psychology.[8] Adherence to underlying unexamined expressive goals hinders a more objective understanding of the complexity of *both* instrumental and expressive, rational *and* irrational sources of collective behavior in society, whether East or West. In brief, the Marxist materialist instrumental interpretation of human psychology remains both

[8]Although we may agree with this outrage, we must emphasize the importance of scientific objectivity if we are to successfully overcome tyranny and bondage of any sort.

ethnocentric and too simplistically rational and instrumental. In our view this is the principal failure whereby Marxist "materialism" never escaped its roots in German idealism and British instrumental social theory.

A Marxist materialist interpretation of history fails to sufficiently acknowledge that irrational, non-economic moral motivations have been playing as great a role in western history as those materialistic forces that direct society toward economic maximization and the concentration of capital. Such moral motives also are clearly represented in western Christianity (Durant, 1957). In contrast, Emile Durkheim (1898) in his sociological theory saw the development of inner constraints and a sense of belonging as basic to socialization within any group. Expressive needs as well as instrumental interests bind humans together, however simple or complex the society. Indeed, some human expressive needs, whatever the society, *are* constructively directed toward a mature form of social interaction in which expressive human needs are given some priority.

Previous work by De Vos and Suárez-Orozco has been concerned with status inequality in a number of different social contexts, ethnicity, class, caste, and gender relationships (De Vos, 1966, 1967; De Vos and Suárez-Orozco, 1990). Considered only from the perspective of power, or other instrumental considerations, decision making related to purposeful behavior is unequally distributed along status dimensions, and the pattern of distribution will vary in the different forms of status inequality that are found in distinct social systems. But the social perceptions of these relationships, in Japan or elsewhere, are interwoven with expressive needs. Thus patterns of social accommodation that minimize possible conflict cannot be understood without some examination of the interplay of various forms of anticipation. These anticipations include the thought that the individual's emotional and expressive needs will be met by respectful subordination within the system (De Vos and Suárez-Orozco, 1990).

In discussing patterns of social cohesion that characterized traditional Japanese social structure, De Vos has argued (De Vos, 1992) that the western concept of social class cannot be directly applied without serious distortion of the social dynamics to be observed in Japanese patterns of status inequality. Indeed, Japanese are very hierarchical in their social awareness. However, the Japanese have a sense of self as part of a *cohesive social hierarchy*, existing both inside the family and in the outside community. It is not enough to simply label such acquiescence in a subservient social role with the ideologically derived concept of "false consciousness." This kind of social participation must be understood in its own cultural-historical and developmental-psychological context, and not in terms that are limited to those that emphasize the impersonal and exploitative class stratification that occurred in Western Europe historically.

Social concerns and their attendant attitudes are a reflection both of *culturally patterned motivation* within the self and the *culturally patterned perception* of how interpersonal roles are enacted in particular social settings by others. Viewed psycho-culturally, modern organizational structures cannot continue to operate effectively without some mutually reinforcing resonance that originates in the personality structure or the social perceptions of the participants (Spiro, 1961). Socialization practices experienced in childhood prepare individuals to live in an adult society that reflects an ethos, an emotional climate, ways of being, and social definitions of status that seem "natural" to its members. Thus the forms of status inequality or equality found in any society may be at least partially in tune with expectations engendered from childhood on. Again, it is not enough to label this as "false consciousness." It is necessary to understand the nature of these expectations, and the developmental psychological processes that produce them. We feel that the nature of these expectations can best be discerned through an empirical rather than ideological exploration of the spontaneously expressed concerns of individual members of a social group.

The present volume is offered toward facilitating the scientific exploration of human concerns through which one can identify relevant preoccupations about power, control, etc. that may be operative in the society (i.e., influencing social forms related to status, power, etc.). Such an emic exploration can substantially improve our understanding of social structures and processes as they are experienced by participants. This may be particularly important where we are attempting to understand these social forms as they are found in cultural contexts that differ from our own, and where we may lack immediate insight into the operative preoccupations of members of the group under study.

Whether one studies one's own society or another society, it is never safe to assume any uniformity in conscious concerns. In any given society, one can find diverse patterns of emic experience in diverse cultural sub-groups. The very fact that such diversity exists in a large society may substantially complicate the situation such that sociological explanations for observed events will be found wanting if they fail to consider the effects of the diversity of culture-based human conscious experience. Therefore, we suggest a scientific and comparative psychocultural approach rather than an ideological approach to understanding social status and social cohesion.

Notes

Allport, Gordon. 1968. *The Person in Psychology: Selected Essays*. Boston: Beacon Press.

Benjamin, Jessica. 1988. *The Bands of Love: Psychoanalysis, Feminism, and the Problem of Domination*. New York: Pantheon.

———. 1995. *Like Subjects, Love Objects: Essays on Recognition and Sexual Difference*. New Haven, Conn.: Yale University Press.

Cattell, Raymond B. 1950. *Personality: A Systematic, Theoretical, and Factual Study*. New York: McGraw-Hill.

Chodorow, Nancy. 1978. *The Reproduction of Mothering: Psychoanalysis and the Sociology of Gender*. Berkeley, Calif.: University of California Press.

Cooley, Charles H. 1909. *Social Organization: A Study of the Larger Mind*. New York: Scribner's.

———. 1912. *Human Nature and the Social Order*. New York: Scribner's.

D'Andrade, Roy G. and Claudia Strauss. (Eds.). 1992. *Human Motives and Cultural Models*. New York: Cambridge University Press.

De Vos, Eric S. 2000. Biocultural and Experiential Bases of Cultural Continuity and Change. In A.L. Communian and U.P. Gielen (Eds.), *International Perspectives on Human Development*. Lengerich: Pabst Science Publishers.

De Vos, George A. 1966. Conflict, Dominance and Exploitation in Human Systems of Social Segregation: Some Theoretical Perspectives from the Study of Personality in Culture. In A.V.S. de Reuck and Julie Knight (Eds.), *Ciba Foundation Symposium on Conflict in Society* (pp. 60–81). London: J. and A. Churchill.

———. 1967. Psychology of Purity and Pollution as Related to Social Self-Identity and Caste. In A.V.S. de Reuck and Julie Knight (Eds.), *Caste and Race: Comparative Approaches* (pp. 92–315). London: J. & A. Churchill.

———. 1984. *The Incredibility of Western Prophets*. Amsterdam: University of Amsterdam Press.

———. 1992. *Social Cohesion and Alienation: The United States and Japan*. Boulder, Colo.: Westwood Press.

De Vos, George A. and L. Bryce Boyer. 1989. *Symbolic Analysis Cross-Culturally: The Rorschach Test*. Berkeley: University of California Press.

De Vos, George A. and Marcelo Suárez-Orozco. 1990. *Status Inequality: The Self in Culture*. Newberry Park, Calif.: Sage.

Dewey, J. 1890. On Some Current Conceptions of the Term "Self." *Mind*, **1**: 58–74.

Durant, Will. 1957. *The Story of Civilization: Part VI*. New York: Simon & Schuster.

Durkheim, Emile. 1898. Représentations Individuele et représentations collective. *Revue de Metaphysique et de Morale*, **6**: 273–302.

Habermas, Jürgen. 1970. A Theory of Communicative Competence. In H.P. Dreitzel (Ed.), *Recent Sociology* (no. 2). New York: Macmillan.

Hobbes, Thomas. 1928. *Leviathan*. London: J. Dent & Sons.

Hoyle, Rick H., Michael H. Kernis, Mark R. Leary, and M.W. Baldwin. 1999. *Selfhood: Identity, Esteem, Regulation*. Boulder, Colo.: Westview Press.

Hsu, Francis L.K. 1985. The Self in Cross Cultural Perspective. In A. Marsella, George De Vos, and Francis Hsu (Eds.), *Culture and Self: Asian and Western Perspectives*. New York and London: Tavistock Publications.

Hutchins, Edwin. 1980. *Culture and Inference: A Trobriand Case Study*. Cambridge, Mass.: Harvard University Press.

Kroeber, Alfred L. 1927. *The Superorganic*. New York: The Sociological Press.

Locke, John. 1924. *On Government: Two Treatises*. London: J. Dent & Sons.

Markus, H.R. and Seiichi Kitayama. 1991. Culture and Self. *Psychological Review*, **98**: 224–253.

———. 1998. The Cultural Psychology of Personality. *Journal of Cross Cultural Psychology*, **29**: 63–87.

McCrae, Robert R., P.T. Costa, G.H. del Pilar, J.P. Rolland, and W.D. Parker. 1998. Cross-Cultural Assessment of the Five-Factor Model: The Revised NEO Personality Inventory. *Journal of Cross Cultural Psychology*, **29**: 171–188.

Mead, George Herbert. 1934. The I and The Me. In Charles Morris (Ed.), *Mind, Self and Society* (pp. 152–164). Chicago: University of Chicago Press.

Neisser, Ulric. 1993. The Self Perceived. In U. Neisser (Ed.), *The Perceived Self: Ecological and Interpersonal Sources of Self-Knowledge*. Emory Symposia in Cognition, 5 (pp. 3–21). New York: Cambridge University Press.

Schore, Allan N. 1994. *Affect Regulation and the Origin of the Self: The Neurobiology of Emotional Development*. Hillsdale, N.J.: Erlbaum.

Schwartz, Theodore. 1978. Where Is the Culture? Personality as the Distributive Locus of Culture. In George D. Spindler (Ed.), *The Making of Psychological Anthropology* (pp. 417–441). Berkeley, Calif.: University of California Press.

Spiro, Melford. 1961. Social Systems, Personality, and Functional Analysis. In Bert Kaplan (Ed.), *Studying Personality Cross Culturally* (pp. 93–127). Evanston, Ill.: Row, Peterson.

Teilhard de Chardin, Pierre. 1959. *The Phenomenon of Man*. New York: Harper & Row, Publishers.

Thurman, Robert A.F. 1984. *The Central Philosophy of Tibet. A Study and Translation of Jey Tsong Khapa's "Essence of True Eloquence*." Princeton, N.J.: Princeton University Press.

Chapter 2

Basic Dimensions in Conscious Thought: Categories Studied in the Present Volume

We see the need to consider a broad set of categories of conscious human concerns if we are to understand social structures and processes. The present volume derives from our effort to address this methodological need. In the Introduction we presented how we came to focus on the Thematic Apperception Test (TAT) as a method through which to study human consciousness. Here in Part II we shall use a series of chapters to fully delineate the conceptual scheme around which our scoring system is organized. In volume II we then present a number of ethnographic studies, by a variety of authors whose work was influenced by our conceptual system for organizing their data and who used the TAT as a major component of their research activities.

An Etic Classification of Human Thought

For purposes of systematic etic objective analysis, we have found that the emic content of human consciousness can conveniently be classified in the Interpersonal Concerns Scoring System (ICSS) within ten basic interpersonal categories and two additional impersonal ones (see Table 2.1 and Appendix A). Each of these etic categories in turn can be further elaborated into a number of subcategories as will be discussed in the following chapters. Cutting through or intersecting the various major categories are eight dimensions or parameters that characterize some human universals of either an implicit or explicit nature. Bear in mind that this is an etic system, organized outside of the collective representations of any society (Durkheim, 1898; Farr, 1998), but it permits us to order various implicit emic categories that we have found to already exist in conscious verbalizations elicited from individuals in a wide variety of social and cultural settings.

In addition to the twelve categories, we have found it helpful to think in terms of eight dimensions that cut through the categories. Our presentation of the twelve categories will make reference to these eight dimensions, so we shall begin with a discussion of the eight dimensions (see Table 2.1).

Eight Intersecting Dimensions in Analyzing Human Categorization

Dimension 1: The Personal—Impersonal World

There is conscious recognition in every society that there are some distinctions between animate and inanimate objects. There is also a distinction between events that are described in terms of impersonal causation in contrast to those that are due to human or supernatural intentions. In our scoring categories we have noted this division between the *Personal* and the *Impersonal* as a major dimension separating the categories.

The major focus of our study of human motives and attitudes is on human interaction—on an interpersonal social world, and on the inner, self-oriented world. Most of our scoring categories reflect concerns about this personal, intentional world. However, as human beings we do not live entirely in a personal world. We also have a continual consciousness of how we are involved with an inanimate, natural world governed by impersonal forces and filled with material, inert objects. We have varying attitudes toward this involvement that can include a mix of positive or negative attitudes toward the forces of nature, the environment, and the various objects we find in it. The study of consciously motivated behavior would be incomplete without some method for categorizing this involvement with the impersonal as well as the personalized world.

We therefore score two impersonal thematic categories of human concerns that are distinct from, but often complementary to, or integral with, the *social-intentional* personal environment. We use the categories of Objects (O) and Fate or Kismet (K) to score for conscious attention to inert objects or fateful, dynamic events impinging upon the individual (see Table 2.1).

Dimension 2: An Instrumental—Expressive Dichotomy

Most of the content of narratives we have seen is not about objects or impersonal events, but rather emphasizes events that occur in the personal and interpersonal realms of human experience. We have found it most facilitative to divide these human—personal concerns into two major categories. Following the work of Parsons and Bales (1955), we have found that motivated behavior related to interpersonal concerns can be usefully classified as having either *instrumental-regulatory* or *expressive-affective* emphases. We see this as a consciously experienced distinction between the *purposefulness* of intentionality on the one hand and the *experience of aroused emotional or affective states* that may lead to action on the other hand. Additionally, some affect-driven behavior may be purely expressive, i.e., it seeks or expresses affective states without further intended purpose. Although this distinction between purposefulness and affective experience may not always be directly conscious to many informants, we find it advantageous to use this etically derived distinction as a basic dimension of our system. This distinction is managed in our category system by separately categorizing narrative content that emphasizes expressive *feeling,* and content that emphasizes instrumental *consequence or regulatory concerns.*

Humans are commonly aware of inner affective states that arise in social situations. Such awareness, and behavior prompted by it, has been termed "expressive" in nature. In contrast, "instrumental" concerns refer to behavior that takes place in the context of purpose and regulation. In a social context, instrumental behavior is constrained by rules, moral directives, and standards that measure relative accomplishment and social conformity. As we discuss elsewhere, there are underlying psychological-developmental structures involved in the complex interrelationships among these distinct yet interacting sets of human concerns.[1]

Expressive behavior or expressive elements of narratives can be distinguished where the aroused *feeling* is more salient than the desired or feared *consequence* of the behavior. Although positive or negative consequences relative to purpose or intentionality are seldom lacking in narratives, what we would consider to be expressive are concerns that emphasize the inherent sense of gratification or pain in either the behavior itself, or in the situation or relationship in which the behavior is expressed.

Feelings of pleasure or pain often move beyond an immediate somatic experience, and become integrated into experiences of an interpersonal nature, so a wide variety of interpersonal concerns are infused with expressive or emotional characteristics. Thus for our category system, in addition to the primarily internally-oriented (*self or intrapersonal*) category of Pleasure (P), we also use four *interpersonal* categories: Nurturance (N); Affiliation (F); Esteem (E); and Harmony (H) to organize our scoring of expressive concerns (see Dimension 3, below).

---

[1]In De Vos and Suárez-Orozco (1990) we make our own attempt to delineate some personality-structural mental mechanisms underlying the concerns reflected in various categories of narrative content. We do not consider our psychodynamically and developmentally oriented effort to constitute an overall theory of personality. For comparative approaches to personality theories we must refer to other publications, such as those of Salvatore Maddi (1996) and Hall, Lindzey, and Campbell (1998). For our present purposes of developing a system for scoring the manifest content of expressive concerns found in conscious experiences as they are communicated, we classify content within the logic of our own categorization system, rather than attempting thorough reconciliation with any extant theory of personality structure or personality dynamics.

Table 2.1

Interpersonal Concerns Scoring System—ICSS

Expressive Categories

Thematic Concerns *Positive* *Socially Sanctioned* *Active*	*Indeterminate* *or* *Unresolved*	*Negative* *Socially Unsanctioned* *Active*	*Negative* *Socially Unsanctioned* *Passive*
Self-Oriented (S)			
P Pleasure, Play, Suffering, Sadness (within oneself) (self-expression)			
Satisfaction Curiosity Creativity Enjoyment	Indifference Boredom Discomfort	Masochistic behavior Asceticism	Suffering Depressed Mad
Vertical, Donor-Recipient, Status Positions (V)			
N Nurture, Succor, Protection			
Donor (on behalf of someone)			
Nurture Care, Help, Comfort	Pity Wish to give or help	Withholding Unapproachable Selfish	Unable to give
Recipient (receive from someone)			
Dependent Grateful Edified Trusting	Distrustful Insecure Fear of want	Rivalrous Envious	Bereft Abandoned Deprived

Horizontal Reciprocal Relationships (H)

F Affiliation, Isolation, Closeness, Communication

(contact with someone)

Love Intimacy Reunion Communicative	Loneliness Fear of commitment Seduction	Rejection Betrayal Neglect Isolation	Loss Separation Deserted

Vertical, Horizontal, and Self-oriented (V, H, S)

E Esteem, Evaluation, Depreciation, Shame

(directed toward or accorded to others)

Respect Awe Recognition of status	Worry about not being appreciated	Disdain Depreciation Disparagement	Incapable of according recognition

(directed to self)

Self-respect Popularity	Doubt about worth Sense of shame	Self-abasement Disgraceful behavior	Inner defilement Worthlessness

Vertical and Horizontal (V, H)

H Harmony, Concordance, Discord, Hostility

(with others)

Harmony Peaceful relations	Concern about cohesion or discord Fear of threat	Violence Quarrel or injury Revenge	Hurt Injured Bewitched

IMPERSONAL CONCERNS WITH OBJECTS OR POSSESSIONS

Attention to Objects Possession, the Environment, or the Body

O Objects

Possession	Desire to own	Bad appearance	Loss

Table 2.1 (cont.)

INTERPERSONAL CONCERNS SCORING SYSTEM—ICSS
Instrumental Categories

Thematic Concerns *Positive Socially Sanctioned Active*	*Indeterminate or Unresolved*	*Negative Socially Unsanctioned Active*	*Negative Socially Unsanctioned Passive*
Self-Oriented (S) A **Achievement, Alienation, Withdrawal** (will do) (internalize goals, goal oriented)			
Ambition Purpose Persistence Commitment	Uncertain Commitment Daydreaming	Criminal activity Asocial ambition	Withdrawal Alienation No motivation
Self-Oriented Internalized Judgment of Performance (S) C **Competence, Mastery, Failure, Incapacity** (can do) (concerns with doing well)			
Avowal of capacity Excellence	Doubt or worry about capacity	Failure due to incapacities Bungled	Incapacity Inadequacy Chagrin
Vertical, Superordinate-Subordinate Status Positions (V) D **Control, Dominance, Autonomy, Compliance, Submission** Superordinate (must do)			
Proper authority Influence Censure	Uncertain exercise Ambivalent leadership	Exploitative Corrupt use Unfair Manipulative	Feckless Inept assertion of power
Subordinate (reactions to authority)			
Liberation Autonomy Compliance	Ambivalence Uncertain about obedience	Rebellion Trickery Rebellion	Submission Submissive fawning

Self-Oriented Internalized Social Status and Self-Judgment (S)			
R Responsibility, Guilt, Dereliction (ought to do) (internalized moral standards)			
Duty Assumption of obligations and controls	Regrets over commission or omission	Indulgence Wrongful behavior	Escape, avoidance, or denial of obligations
Horizontal reciprocal or peer relationships (H)			
M Mutual: Competition or Cooperation			
Competitive (competitive goals)			
Regulated games Contests	Envy	Unethical competitive behavior	Capitulation Withdraw from competition
Cooperative (mutually realized goals)			
Concerted behavior Mutual trust	Distrust Disagreement	Plotting Deception	Betrayed Exploited

IMPERSONAL CONCERNS WITH FATE

K Fate, Kismet			
Fate, Impersonal Forces of Nature or Society, Uncontrollable Events			
Good fortune Wealth	Anxiety about events Fear of illness	Accidental hurt Evil eye	Death Mishap

The positive and negative dimensions of expressive behavior are partially defined by states of excitement or arousal and/or by the presence of obvious emotional experiences such as surprise, fear, anger, sadness, joy, love, or comfort, as well numerous complex combinations of emotional experience (Plutchik, 1994). These experiences are mediated in humans by the interaction of cognitive interpretations of personal and situational factors, combined with patterns of neuroendocrine functioning (Lazarus and Lazarus, 1994). As we discuss in the chapter on Pleasure-Pain, there are diverse patterns of cognitive-neuroendocrine function associated with diverse emotional experiences such as active or aggressive expressions, or passive or anxious-avoidance experiences.[2]

There also are diverse patterns of neuroendocrine arousal to be found in response to essentially instrumental activities. This endocrine arousal can comprise one component of the experience of difficulty or challenge that is often associated with demanding situations. Thus the experience of purposeful force or causality in humans is seldom completely freed from an affectively driven excitement. For example, when a group of athletes move from lip-biting concentration to leaping from the bench upon winning a championship game, they are providing clear evidence of the continuing expressive dimension of experience that is wedded to virtually all instrumental activity. Even where it is largely instrumental it often retains expressive associations, and virtually everything we do as human beings involves some pattern of neuroendocrine-cognitive affective functioning. In every culture one finds designations of the direct or sublimated emotional states accompanying instrumental or regulated purposeful behavior. Despite the ubiquity of this affective component of experience, we nevertheless believe it is essential to distinguish between various elements of narratives that differ in their emphasis on expressive or instrumental content.

To be categorized as "instrumental," or purposeful, regardless of any attendant affectivity, the behavior or fantasy depicted in the narrative must be described as primarily motivated toward achieving a goal or meeting a standard by which behavior is judged. Reference must be made to some type of instrumental purpose or consequence. Often this type of action is perceived in the context of rules and regulations. A time dimension also often emerges in narrative descriptions of this type of action, and the behavior is seen as a purposeful means toward an end rather than as a means to immediately experience the emotion or aroused state inherent in the action itself.

---

[2]The delineation of various categories of emotional experience are a subject of unending discussion in Psychology. For example, see Ekman and Davidson (1994), Lazarus (1991), Lazarus and Lazarus (1994), or Plutchik (1994). It is beyond the scope of this volume to enter critically into the various theoretical discussions in respect to human emotions or forms of excitation.

As we shall presently discuss in detail, there are basic instrumental categories of persistent motive or Achievement (A), and concern with ability or Competence (C). Our category of Control (D) includes all concerns related to interpersonal authority or control as well as autonomy or freedom from dominance. It subsumes narrative concerns in which an individual is seen either as exercising control or is in a situation of being controlled or seeking freedom from control by others. Additional instrumental categories include Responsibility (R), and Mutual Purpose (M). Some of these are more *inter*-personal, and others more *intra*-personal (see Dimension 3, below).

Although expressive and instrumental components can be found in most behavior, one or the other consideration usually predominates in narratives. Where they are both present they are both scored. The prevalence of one or the other will often emerge from both quantitative and qualitative analyses of the patterns of response. Where it can be determined, the predominant subcategory is noted (in examples in this volume, we indicate this by underlining the predominant category code).

Dimension 3: Intrapersonal—Interpersonal Concerns

Narrative elements can also be differentiated according to whether they refer to concerns that are directed or focused *within* the conscious self or whether they refer to events that are interpersonal, i.e., occurring *between or among* individuals. Our category system therefore distinguishes between concerns that are more *interpersonal*, and those that are more self-oriented or *intrapersonal.*

Interpersonal concerns grow out of the basic interaction patterns of human beings that are inherited as part of our legacy as social primates and mammals (Henry and Stephens, 1977). They are built upon neuroendocrine and physiological systems that mediate sexual behavior, dominance behavior, parental behavior and other forms of affiliative and combative behavior that occur within primate social groups. They are elemental to our own species and appear in every human social group. They are inherent in childhood, and become socialized or "bioculturally constructed" in the context of culturally constituted attitudes and behavioral-interactional patterns (E. De Vos, 2000). Cultures differ as to how the various interpersonal concerns are relatively emphasized, interrelated or blended with one another in "molecular" compound patterns that may be quite culture-specific. For example, Achievement in Japanese is often narrated as occurring as part of family nurture or responsibility, whereas Americans more often describe Achievement themes in an individualistic context (De Vos, 1973).

Individuals also are concerned with their inner experiences, independent of any concern with others. We commonly see reference to experiences that pertain to personal statements of purpose, gratification in achievement, experiences of pleasure or enjoyment, as well as personal evaluations, such as self-esteem. These can be seen to be self-oriented or *intra*-personal. The categories of Pleasure (P), Competence (C), Achievement (A), and Responsibility (R) are substantially *intra*-personal, although culturally-constituted value systems will nevertheless be implicitly if not explicitly operative in any intrapersonal concerns. To accommodate the distinction between self-evaluated esteem and an *inter*-personal evaluation of social-acceptability, the Esteem category (E) includes two sets of subcategories. One of them considers acceptability or evaluation by others, the second focuses upon self-esteem or internal feelings of worthiness, which themselves depend on internalized social attitudes.

Dimension 4: Horizontal or Vertical Interpersonal Concerns Versus Self Concerns

An essential characteristic of human beings (as well as other animals) is that they see themselves as located in some dimensional space, which is often defined by relative social position or social status (Henry and Stephens, 1977). Status concerns appear as some forms of consciously considered instrumental or expressive behavior in all human societies (De Vos and Suárez-Orozco, 1990). These status concerns can be seen as being either *horizontal* or *vertical* in their orientation.

Status concerns about the roles taken within peer group, family, gender, or age-different situations (whether implicit or explicit) are either "horizontal" or "vertical." Within interpersonal concerns one can find conscious status considerations of *equivalence*, reciprocity, or mutuality, which can be termed "horizontal" concerns, where there is no attention drawn to higher or lower status.

Relationships that are described as involving reciprocal interactions, group cooperation, competition among rival peers (Mutual Purpose, M), mutual Affiliation (F), group Harmony (H), etc. can be seen as horizontal. Horizontal relationships may often involve some element of status differential, but this may not be the most salient aspect of the expressed concern. For example, harmonious relationships commonly involve individuals with different status positions. But in these situations, concerns with status differentials may remain secondary to the internally experienced affective states that are expressed as socially disarming behavior and integrative congeniality. Additionally, evaluations of acceptability among peers (Esteem, E) may also be expressions of horizontal interaction. Expressively salient horizontal concerns can be seen as parallel to instrumentally salient horizontal concerns, such as those involving mutually beneficial goal directed cooperation or socially regulated competition (M).

In contrast to these horizontal concerns, "vertical" concerns pertain to *non-equivalence in status,* power, dominance, being a giver or a receiver, etc. In any expression of concern with nonreciprocal relationships between individuals of unequal status, one can see evidence of a vertical status dimension, whether the concerns are instrumental, emphasizing awareness of relative dominance (D), or expressive, involving a donor and a recipient of nurturance, comfort, or protection (N). This verticality is addressed in our categories as a set of subcategories that mark consciousness of either donor-recipient or superordinate-subordinate positions taken in interpersonal relationships.

Evaluations of personal acceptability (E) can also occur in the context of status concerns that reflect vertical relationships.[3] Many expressively salient concerns with hostility or social esteem are vertical in the sense that individuals feel consciously subject to the internally unpleasant feelings of shame and the possibly overwhelming fear of malice and destructiveness of a dominant malign power. The instrumental, possibly punitive power of recognized authority (D), however, must be distinguished from affectively driven concern with disparagement (E) or hostile intentionality (H) wherein no regulatory considerations are apparent.

Dimension 5: Group Versus Dyadic Involvements

In some subcategories of *inter*-personal relationships there are *individual-group* relationships. In others the preoccupation is specifically *dyadic-triadic*, i.e., inter-individual occurrences that happen between two or perhaps three individuals.

It is sometimes important to distinguish between concerns that reflect dyadic involvement with others from those that involve group activities. The Harmony (H) and Mutual Purpose (M) categories include many subcategories that are related to group activities or group concerns. One example of this is the category of Mutual Purpose (M) where competitive or cooperative concerns can reflect the actions of individuals, or collective action, as in the distinction between a duel over a matter of honor versus a war. Other examples include categories concerned with group cohesion, group ritual participation, etc., from the Harmony (H) category. In the Esteem (E) category there are subcategories pertaining to family or group shame, or group-based respect or appreciation of others. One also finds issues related to group sanctioning in the Control (C) category. Here and there in the other categories, one can find examples of group rather than individual or dyadic concerns.

Dimension 6: Behavior Evaluated as Positive, Indeterminate, or Negative

Most human experiences are judged to be either positive or negative. They involve some attention to the *relative desirability* or *social approbation* of what is being perceived. There are implicit, if not explicit, socially or personally acquired judgments or evaluations about most social behavior or situations. For most of us, there is no complete detachment or neutrality in the observation of experiences either within the self, or regarding what occurs between or among individuals.

This dimension refers to the distinction between positive and negative outcomes of situations in terms of the consequences relevant to self-oriented or interpersonal-social concerns. The Positive-Negative evaluation of a situation is most easily scored if the informant has directly provided an explicit evaluation, or an indication that the event is evaluated relative to some normative standard. Thus positive and negative evaluations can be seen as a distinction between behavior that

---

[3]There are also internally oriented or internalized concerns about self-esteem that are categorized in the Esteem (E) category.

is normatively socially sanctioned positively versus behavior that is socially sanctioned negatively.

We recognize that this aspect of our category system imposes an inferential etic structure, based on our evaluation that certain behavior is usually socially positive versus socially negative in the eyes of the narrator. In the category system, a division between positive and negative holds even if there is no explicit reference made to evaluation. For example, in the category for Harmony (H), concerns that refer to harmonious outcomes, peace or reunion among family members, etc., are grouped together in a section of subcategories that are related to positive cohesion, reconciliation, group maintenance or protection. In contrast, unresolved attitudes such as anger, desire for revenge, etc., are considered indeterminate. They could lead to negative outcomes, but they have not yet become manifest in outward behavior or consequence, and could ultimately resolve positively, thus are indeterminate.

Hostile, cruel, selfish active behavior that disrupts harmony, or the passive experience of being victimized in some way, are among the negative subcategories. Thus negative subcategories may be either active or passive. As Table 2.1 indicates, in every major category we have made a distinction between subcategories that reflect Positive, Indeterminate, Negative-Active and Negative-Passive outcomes.

Dimensions 7 and 8: Active-Passive, Resolved-Unresolved Distinctions

Within each of the categories, there are distinctions made between subcategories that pertain to *active* and *passive* positions taken by the protagonist, and the *resolved* or *unresolved* characteristics of the situation. Depending on the explicitly expressed, or evident implicit attitude of the informant, there is a further division of narrative material of each of the major categories into four columns in Table 2.1:

(Dimension 7) Active-Passive positions in respect to action. The subjective experience in respect to action is that one is either an *initiator* or an active *respondent* to an action versus being a passive *recipient* of incurred activity. Note, for example, individuals in a vertical or subordinate status position may nevertheless be active or initiate action. For example, someone may actively seek God's help.

(Dimension 8) Resolved-Unresolved situations. A sense of action is either expressed as completed or left in some form of an unresolved state. This is conceptually distinct from the issue of indeterminacy relative to the positive or negative outcome as discussed in Dimension 6. However, our category system does not maintain this distinction with separate categories. Unresolved and indeterminate refer to different characteristics, but are subsumed under the same subcategories in the scoring system.

These latter three considerations (Dimensions 6, 7, 8) are distinguished by use of the subcategories (A, B, C, D) within each of the major categories noted on Table 2.1 and in Appendix A.

The "A" subcategories include positive active concerns. The protagonist does something. There are both socially and inwardly considered *positive* activities and attitudes. An example is hard work toward achievement.

The "B" subcategories comprise unresolved or indeterminate situations or attitudes. Some situations are narrated without revolution. The concerns are not expressed as actualized outcomes, but are expressed as potential outcomes that have not yet occurred and therefore remain inactive or unresolved. Expressed intentions have not yet been acted upon. Thought about something does not lead to action. For example, in the Achievement (A) category "thinking about" successful accomplishment is scored under some subcategory of "B." In the Harmony (H) category, there are various types of fears about things that might happen to produce discord. Or there are concerns of envy, jealousy, anger, etc., which might produce discord if they were to be acted on. On the other hand, concerns for group or family cohesion could be considered positive, in that if they were to be resolved, the outcome would be positive. In the Responsibility (R) category, one can have unresolved negative concerns about regret for having done or not done something. However, one can also have unresolved concerns about how to exercise responsibility, which could be seen as having a potentially positive result if future action were to ensue. Thus, although the unresolved situations might lead to either positive or negative outcomes, so long as they are expressed as being unresolved they are scored under the B category.

The "C" subcategories are negatively perceived active situations. The protagonist does something "bad" or negative in the view of the narrator. For, example, criminal behavior can be seen as a means to accomplishment.

The "D" subcategories comprise descriptions of negatively incurred passive states. The narrator sees an individual being inflicted upon by someone or some event. Or, for a different example, passive withdrawal from a purposeful task is scored under "D" as a negative-passive Achievement concern.

Other Dimensions

Other possible dimensions of interaction in stories are periodically evident, but for our purposes, we have found them to be too prone to subjectivity or insufficiently salient to have them require systematic scoring as part of our analysis of manifest content. Note, for example, how our scoring system makes no attempt to score the *intensity* of any conscious concern in what is verbalized. Judging intensity can be very problematic, as it may exist more in the judgment of the scorer than in the thought of the informant. Without explicit statements of intensity it is impossible to judge.

In understanding this explication of dimensions or categories, it will be helpful to refer to the accompanying chart and to Appendix A. What is necessarily abstract in initial presentation should become clearer with the presentation of more detailed, illustrative material throughout the following chapters.

In summary, Table 2.1 gives an overview of how the basic scoring categories are divided along the basic divisions of *instrumental* and *expressive* personal concerns, as well as concerns with inert *objects* and *impersonal* events. Then, further, basic internally oriented *self* concerns (S) are separated from *vertical* (V) and *horizontal* (H) status considerations. Depending on the explicitly expressed, or evident implicit attitude of the informant, there is a further division of narrative material of each of the major categories into four columns. They are: (1) socially and inwardly considered *positive activities* and attitudes; (2) *indeterminate-unresolved* situations or attitudes; (3) *negative-active* behaviors; and (4) *negative-passive* incurred situations. In the chapters of Part II, where the specific subcategories are described, you will find that these elements of the category system are represented by the code letters A, B, C and D, respectively.

The Twelve Major Categories

In the twelve chapters comprising Part II we shall examine, in turn, each of the major categories of the ICSS coding system. To give illustrative content to what would otherwise be an unduly abstract presentation, in each chapter we describe the category from both the psychological and social perspectives that comprise our psycho-cultural approach.

First, the category is discussed in the context of what a psychological perspective can contribute regarding physiological and psychological development as the bases for universal characteristics of human thought and emotion relevant to the specific category of human concerns.

Additionally, from a sociological perspective we consider relevant cultural factors, and give a specific social and cultural contextual basis for the thoughts or emotions that we use as illustrative examples of the category. For this purpose we frequently draw on the Japanese cultural tradition which does, in some instances, contrast very significantly in the shaping of thought and emotion from the formative experiences encountered within any western cultural setting. We may note, en passant, many of the premises of psychology as a scientific discipline have been shaped by a western tradition, sometimes without sufficient critical examination from a cross-cultural perspective.

The Five Expressive Concerns

We categorize expressive human narrative communication in a fivefold division. Each of these categories reflect negative as well as positively considered consciously experienced affective arousal (see Table 2.1). Chapters 3 through 7, volume I, consider each expressive category, in turn.

(a) *Chapter 3, volume I,* considers narrative material that makes reference to internally experienced Pleasure and suffering (P). There are a variety of pleasurable or painful sensations. Some are located directly in body sensations, others arise from aroused curiosity or excitement, from feelings of elation or depression, serenity or anxiety, from experiences of being frustrated or being satisfied. Developmentally, immediate physical sensations are progressively socialized into "meaningful" perceptions of inner arousal. Pleasurable sensations are inherently reinforcing and sought after in sensual activity and by self-inducing altered mental states.

Activities in which these states are sought are conditioned by social-contextual experiences. Yet when individuals are expressing intrapersonal emotional states, there are a limited number of basic classifiable universal emotional states, or considerations of affective excitement to which they refer. Basic experiences of affective arousal to discomforting or pleasurable stimuli become linked culturally to particular social contexts and particular role relationships. They become incorporated into a particular culturally constructed language system, which may be interesting in its own right to the ethnographer. Nevertheless, for our purpose of cross-cultural comparison, although a speaker of the Japanese language can communicate more variant gradations of the pleasurable experience of touch or texture, these variations can be subsumed under more broadly derived etic categories of affective experience.

In inner perception, experiences that are not immediately sensorially pleasurable can come to be experienced as pleasure when socially contextualized. For example, inherited mammalian playfulness and basic cognitive curiosity about new experiences, in humans can become transcended socially into aesthetic pleasure in an appreciation of human creativity. "Ecstatic" experiences or unusual states of excitement may become sought after or avoided, depending on a socially defined context. Similarly, negatively perceived pain and suffering can come to be experienced contextually in response to socially constructed mental as well as physical forms of perceived injury (e.g., ethnic slurs), or transmuted into a positive sense of endurance, socially defined.

It is even possible, as for the Japanese, to reinterpret suffering by considering it as good for character formation and eventual self-realization. By so doing the person may express suffering in a more complex context. This requires that we see the element of suffering as part of a more complex "molecular" experience that combines emotion and purpose, having both expressive and instrumental goals. We shall discuss throughout this volume how few human narratives are limited within only one scoring category. Using our system, the contextualized experience of suffering can be multiply scored. Yet, whatever the nuance molecular cultural pattern in which it occurs, suffering can still be scored as suffering, and pleasure can still be scored as pleasure, in addition to whatever form it takes.

In chapter 3, volume I, we use material extracted from three previous studies to demonstrate how stories are scored under the pleasure category. We illustrate how nuance differences between groups were apparent in the manner in which some of the pleasure responses were evoked as part of a more complex interpersonal context.

One set of examples are from a group of Korean immigrants to the United States, whom we compared with minority Koreans residing in Japan (see chapter 7, volume II). Overall our scoring system delineated how the Koreans coming to the United States were much more positive in all their inner emotional experiences contrasted with the considerable personal alienation and flatness of affect evident in the narratives of minority Koreans living in Japan.

Another set of examples come from a study comparing ethnic samples in Brazil (see chapter 8, volume II). One notes how Japanese Brazilians, compared with Italian, Portuguese, or Afro-Brazilians are more prone to directly express curiosity or creativity among their direct expressions of positive pleasurable activities.

Further examples come from a comparison of Venezuelan and Canadian youth (see chapter 11, volume II). Again some nuance differences became readily apparent.

(b) In *chapter 4, volume I*, we describe how we categorize vertically defined social experiences related to Nurture, help, and protection (N). One can recognize the complementary roles or positions motives of both donors and recipients in this category. For example, the needful state of being dependent upon a donor to supply nurture, help and protection (such as that experienced by the infant) is a dependent position that can readily be distinguished from the position of the parent, which is defined in terms of giving care and protection. Both poles of these types of asymmetrical vertical relationships are reflected in our category of Nurture.

The child recipient experiences a "dependent" relationship from a position of relative helplessness. Various aspects of an emotional need for security and comfort or a more practical need to receive succor or nurture from specific others continue into adult life as a set of important interpersonal themes for many people. Social roles are commonly structured around donor-recipient positions. Where we see an expressed concern with a donor-recipient relationship, we categorize the narrative theme using the Nurture (N) category.

The donor or dominant role positions can be experienced positively or negatively. The parental role or the role of the provider or protector is generally seen positively. Although generosity is usually seen to be an expression of benevolence or constructive intent, it may not always be so. Giving can involve an exploitation of the recipient, as the donor develops a sense of superiority relative to the recipient. Additionally, there are emotional experiences of withholding or deprivation, an incapacity or unwillingness to give.

The recipient position can also be seen positively or negatively. Subordinate social status can be experienced by the individual as a positive source of protection and nurturance. Yet participation in these role relationships from a subordinate status can also be reflected in expressed concerns about autonomy and independence. There can be envy experienced by those in need. There can be a cynical manipulation of the donor by the recipient, as is sometimes seen in the modern "welfare" society, or in some family relationships. There can also be an unwillingness to receive, as in the unwillingness of a child to receive the advice of an authority.

Societies rely on the continuance of both succoring and recipient behavior among their members, and numerous patterns of social interaction reflect these themes. To the extent that they involve donor-recipient roles, these interactions retain their vertical character. Interdependence is not non-dependence. It is not a horizontal equality, it is a reciprocal dependency that is nevertheless vertical at the moment of giving and receiving. There are social forms that involve horizontally reciprocal or mutual relationships of other kinds, and they are considered in the categories such as Affiliation, Harmony, Mutual Purpose.

Religious practices and beliefs also are relevant here. What may be, in its most primitive basis, a physical sense of hunger can also be experienced as a mental hunger, to be assuaged by a relationship with a benevolent outer presence. Experiences of inner insecurity can be assuaged by assurances of succoring protection by a caring, enveloping force. The complex patterns by which dependency and interdependency are intertwined in human experience can be seen represented in religious ritual, where vertical reciprocity is commonly established through an act of propitiation. In such an act, one simultaneously offers a gift or "service," and maintains a reverential or deferential status relationship with the more powerful external power, yet at the same time manipulatively expects the powerful other to act favorably towards ones own instrumental or emotional purposes.[4]

To illustrate how we score these kinds of themes, we turn to narrative material collected in Japan, and elsewhere (see chapter 4, volume I). For example, in chapter 10, volume II we discuss nurturance in the context of mentorship. The donor-recipient relationships experienced in Japan differ radically from those emphasized in the North American culture.

(c) *Chapter 5, volume I*, considers how we categorize horizontal reciprocal experiences of Affiliation, closeness, and communication (F).

The earliest experiences of the mutual warmth of mammalian physical closeness and resonant interaction continue to be a relevant form of experience throughout life. They are transmuted into socially constructed patterns of communication, contact, intimacy, empathy and sympathy. As children mature, and the character of the child-parent relationship changes, there is a progressive change in the relative strength of nurturant versus companionate concerns. With development, family-based intimacy progressively turn outward toward reciprocal peer contacts, eventually becoming adult concerns with friendship, marital intimacy, and relationships with a next generation. Positive developments lead towards more mutual and reciprocal affiliative experiences. Negative experiences include states

[4]There may be other religious experiences that are not vertical in this way, but they would then be considered under other categories, such as Harmony or Pleasure (see chapter 14, volume I).

of loss, isolation, loneliness, and experiences of faulty understanding or poor communication. These kinds of concerns are coded in the category Affiliation (F).

Robert Blood (1967) found, in comparing marital couples in Japan and the United States, while in many respects expressions of love or satisfaction in marital relationships were similar, there was a most notable difference in the expectation and realization experienced in respect to companionship. The two societies differed in respect to expectations of horizontally defined intimate companionship (F) or vertically defined care and nurture (N). As might be anticipated, marital satisfaction in Japan could be attained without the same degree of companionate intimacy that was expected in American marital relationships. The donor-recipient vertical relationships (N) discussed in chapter 4, volume I, were more evident in Japanese marriages, consistent with the expectations found in Japanese society generally. The American expectation of a more reciprocal form of marital intimacy (F) was consistent with other features of contemporary American culture discussed in chapter 5, volume I.

(d) *Chapter 6, volume I*, considers the concern with social acceptability and sensitivity to evaluations of Esteem, appreciation or social acceptability (E).

Affective arousal related to esteem is basic to a human capacity to experience a sense of shame. In addition to direct sanctioning involving a potential for direct punishment, the social world in any culture also induces conformity by more subtle, expressive means governing social acceptability. Humans become governed to varying degrees by a potential to experience what is termed *shame* in English. Shame depends on a continuing awareness of others potentially making an evaluation of one's behavior, appearance, or degree of appropriate physical, moral, or spiritual acceptability. Therefore, various forms of accorded social esteem are implicit forms of sanctioning related to a human need for appreciation and response.

In humans, there gradually evolves interpersonal sensitivity to group forms of approval or disapproval growing out of early dyadic parental regard or disapproval. There is a need for inner enhancement that depends upon receiving positive social regard from important others. Thus esteem concerns can retain personal perceptions of *status* differentials and distinctions marking horizontal and/or vertical social relationships of unequal acceptability as well as power. In addition to such evaluative considerations, these can also have socially regulative functions that can be more or less internalized as part of the self, or remain perceived as external social pressures being exerted by others. Social pressure toward acceptable behavior or appearance can also be seen as directed toward others, witnessed as the selective withholding of appreciation, or active public degradation of others.

Evaluative attitudes that are expressive in nature must be distinguished from instrumental-regulatory judgments. A judgment emphasizes instrumentally oriented discrimination that may be supported by effective regulatory control over behavior and social purpose. Judgmental attitudes may lead to social sanctioning to induce proper behavior or to punish transgressions of social or family order. Judgments of self and others may be made relative to what can be termed internalized standards or the precepts and directives that govern behavior.

Judgments are to be differentiated from *evaluations* that are focused on the emotions aroused by the acceptability or rejection of self or others. As we later develop the terms, *evaluative* considerations relate to feelings that increase or decrease social distance that determine the *acceptability* of the person considered. As such, they are affectively laden expressive considerations. These patterns can include beliefs about the supernatural that involve a sense of personal purity, worthiness, or unworthiness (see chapter 14, volume I).

Evaluations and judgments may be somewhat difficult to distinguish, as both can be related to social sanctioning. However, we attempt to distinguish between the affect aroused in a situation and the instrumental intent to directly control or regulate behavior. In both cases there is an internalization of social standards that occurs in the process of human socialization. Yet shame is directed more expressively toward social appearance. Guilt is directed more instrumentally toward behavioral conformity induced by intimidation or physical forms of punishment as well as *intra-punitive* attitudes.

In the context of the evaluative category in chapter 6, volume I, we consider, for example, the special case of the Koreans in Japan, where there are several unresolved issues arising out of past and present social disparagement. In recent years the Japanese government has attempted to rectify the social depreciation of the Korean minority by better acknowledgment of the separate social and cultural history of Korea. However, the present legally anomalous status of Koreans in Japan makes any assuagement of social disparagement a difficult task. Prevalent pejorative attitudes about a minority ethnic position within the Japanese state make it psychologically incumbent upon many Koreans to resist assimilation. Only when their past cultural background is accorded respect and they are given the right to be overtly of Korean background as a Japanese citizen can *Korean Japanese* inwardly accept the historical fact that they are destined to function as resident citizens of Japan in future generations. This experiential dilemma is well represented in the TAT evidence we obtained in Japan (De Vos, 1992).

(e) In *chapter 7, volume I*, the final expressive category is delineated. In this chapter we consider human concerns about interpersonal Harmony or discord (H).

The natural aggressive drives of all mammals are potentially adaptive and can aid self-preservation. The sympathetic nervous system and other neuroendocrine mechanisms prepare the body for emergencies which may result in protective antagonistic acts. In humans, anger is a basic, subjectively experienced emotion related to such chemical processes. In antagonistic interaction with others, affective arousal has socially destructive as well as personally defensive potentials. Given such aggressive potentials, it is inevitable, from infancy on, that experience with the frustrating intentionality of others arouses states of interpersonal confrontation that may become socially disruptive (McKee and Leader, 1955).

The converse human expressive need for congeniality is sometimes neglected in psychological studies. There are also pleasurable feelings entailed in the assumption of conciliatory attitudes. Humans are affectively influenced by a developing diffuse sense of belonging to a group, or a sense of *sharing* in something larger than the individual self. Developmental psychology has begun to seriously address the importance of transpersonal or relational processes in the development of the individual infant's mechanisms for emotional regulation, language skills, and even morality (Damon, 1988; Fox, 1994; Schore, 1994). Readiness to participate in harmonious and reciprocally regulated activity appears to be an essential component of human experience from the very earliest moments of extra-uterine life.

Beneath conscious expressions and concerns about harmony or discord one may find mammalian social-behavioral patterns that are quick to deflect antagonism away from any dyadic or in-group disruption. Whether it is automatic and biologically based or socially conditioned, integrative conciliatory behavior harnesses or prevents arousal of animosity between individuals. These behavioral mechanisms operate more or less effectively to *repress* or suppress behavior and thought that would be socially disruptive. An internal *consciously experienced* need for harmony also appears vital towards overcoming possible discordant interactions or confrontations which could irreparably disrupt one's group as well as one's individual relationships.

Cross culturally there are radical differences in conscious social values related to the maintenance of group harmony, or the situations that arise in society that cause serious discord and abiding hostility. Confucian social endeavor in China and Japan was frequently expressed in terms of salient social values related to the achievement of harmony in society (De Vos and Murakami, 1974). From that perspective, an ideal societal harmony can only be maintained when each individual inhabits his or her assigned social role properly. There was aesthetic as well as moral pleasure possible through adhering to the Confucian religion of the family as it was evident in Japanese and Koreans (Slote and De Vos, 1998).

One learns to be harmonious with others by practicing self-discipline. The very concept of "self" for many Chinese, Koreans, and Japanese is a relational self in which what one is (or what one is to become) is defined by one's social relationships. Sensuality that can be immediately gratified has much less value. Refined pleasures are transmuted into aesthetic forms. Where the Italians have learned to appreciate the taste of bitterness in the liquor called Campari, past generations of Japanese have taken the bitterness of life and distilled of it a moral virtue in pursuit of social harmony. A concept central to the traditional sense of social role in Japan was a sense of dedication and the long-range satisfactions to be gained from realizing one's social destiny in idealized harmony.

The Five Instrumental, Regulatory or Goal Oriented Concerns

Instrumental or goal oriented concerns have certain parallels to the five expressive categories just considered. Chapters 8 through 12, volume I, deal with each in turn. Self-oriented concerns with instrumental Competence (C) and Achievement (A) run parallel to the Pleasure-pain expressive category (P). There are parallels between concerns with guilt that center on the regulatory concerns of the Responsibility category (R) and the evaluative interest about shame that are found in concerns with social Esteem (E). There are parallels between Nurture (N) and Control (D). There are parallels between the instrumental category of Mutual Purpose (M) and the expressive categories of Harmony (H) and Affiliation (F). There are many ways in which these categories are interrelated, and these issues are discussed in further detail throughout this volume.

(f) *Chapter 8, volume I*, discusses a need for Achievement (A) as a harnessing of human drive potential into socially defined purposeful behavior. Achievement is marked by determination, persistence, a *will* to succeed, or motivation to accomplish or complete tasks once initiated. Definitions of successful achievement are to be found in some form in every culture. In its positive direction achievement is guided by positive social purpose. As an aspect of internalization during childhood, each individual is socialized to strive toward the realization of socially defined short and long-range future goals. Goals are essential to adult gender roles, family roles, as well as extra-familial role expectations about occupational accomplishment, etc. In complex societies there may be a wide range of role expectations that are selectively internalized. Class and caste considerations delimit what becomes the socially acceptable achievement motivation of particular individuals. Gender and age specific definitions in most societies contain rules to set boundaries on what are considered to be proper goals and the proper means to be taken in the realization of goals.

In an internalized instrumental concern the emphasis is either on "will do" or "can do." Achievement self consciously involves a sense of purpose activated by a *will* to accomplish what become a desired goal. A sense of achievement is self-oriented—whereas a sense of "control" is interpersonal. As indicated in the chapter on Control (D), a conceptualization of a "power" drive, as interpersonal is related to, but is to be distinguished from a purposeful, instrumentally directed sense of volition. Such volition per se is related to the internalized standards manifest in Achievement (A).

Considerable research has concentrated on instrumental concerns related to an imputed basic underlying motive termed a need for achievement (n Achievement). In contrast to the use of the term need Achievement in the research of McClelland and others (McClelland, 1987; Smith, 1992), we limit our category of Achievement (A) to focused determination and a persistent will to accomplish. In our system, concerns with competence (can do, C), rivalry or cooperation (with or against, M) are distinguished from achievement as separate instrumental concerns.

Achievement concerns, per se, are a question of a "motive" or "will" or purpose to succeed in taking on some self-defined or socially approved future goals. As indicated in chapter 9, volume I, the negative of Achievement (A) is not failure, but alienation. Failure, when due to the individual, not to circumstance, is an inner assessment related to a concern with competence or mastery; failure is the negative of Competence (C).

The negative of achievement is anomie or alienation. It is a loss of purpose or the willingness to arrive at goals by breaking social rules or by resorting to criminal behavior (De Vos, 1980). Thus the (A) category encompasses active "anomic" goal-directed behavior that is considered "criminal" or illicit in nature, as discussed by Merton (1949). An individual who goes outside the proper means to achieve political, economic, or social success risks being seen as deviant, even *criminal*, practicing "anomic" behavior, i.e., behavior that is unregulated—without rules. Such behavior is generally subject to punitive sanctioning by society at large.

Negative Achievement also includes forms of social alienation and passive withdrawal wherein there appear a loss of involvement in goals, no sense of purpose, or on an existential level, no satisfactory meaning to existence. Chapter 3 by Evans in volume II of this series illustrates Kenyan narratives about criminality resulting from a sense of frustration about legitimate achievement. Chapter 14, volume I, discusses the sense of alienation found in suicidal individuals in Japan and elsewhere.

In chapter 8, volume I, we examine some of the sense of frustration and alienation related to the minority status of Koreans in Japan. See also the TAT evidence we present in chapter 7, volume II.

(g) *Chapter 9, volume I*, examines how narratives of self-directed instrumental, purposeful behavior involve judgments of ability and personal mastery or Competence (C). These include self-judgments which can be related either to a sense of confidence or inferiority (in the sense of self-efficacy, as distinct from self-esteem, Bandura, 1986). Intentionality in humans appears early as an innate need for instrumental mastery (White, 1959, 1961). It is involved in acquiring confident control over one's own body, its motoric functions, and the purposeful manipulation of objects. This innate "self" oriented need has a biological basis. It is embedded in a requirement of the nervous system for stimulation and information and is a basic development out of our mammalian heritage. Out of an inner sense of causal empowerment grows an increasingly conscious attempt to gain competence in one's functioning.

The earliest form of mastery is that related to a sense of intentionality and the locus of potential power or agency.[5] It evolves as one's self-conscious intentions are internally experienced as successful or not when directed toward attaining future results (Competence C). A concern for mastery or competence (C) in intentional activity is integral to the psychological origins of the exercise of control over others. However, the sense of mastery in the experience of exercising control over the external environment is to be distinguished from that involved in controlling

---

[5]See the cogent discussion of White (1959, 1961) on the development of a need for competence as an essential of human development.

interpersonal interactions in situations of dominance and subordination discussed in the context of Control (D). As we shall try to develop in the several subsequent chapters on instrumental concerns, there are experiential, self-reflective differences that must be noted in distinguishing mastery or Competence (C) internally considered, from a need to Control (D) others in interpersonal situations.

The concern with Competence is a *self-oriented* instrumental category in our scoring system and includes a general, diffuse or specifically focused sense of relative "confidence" in dealing with one's ability in the manipulation of inanimate objects, or more generally in cognitive-intellectual problem solving.

The converse of a sense of empowerment through mastery is a sense of failure or ineptness. In different societies, explanations for failure vary. Situations of failure must be scored or double scored in respect to the explanations given by the informant. Some failure is attributed to one's own incapacity. Other explanations can refer to impersonal causality, such as happenstance, bad luck or a lack of proper opportunity or supporting context. There are fateful events beyond human control (see chapter 13, volume I, on Fate K). They may also refer to the impersonal working of an inexorable social system which defeats individual effort, no matter how promising.

One's own failures may be due to the interference of others. One's talent may not be rewarded by social success. Our Competence category allows us distinguish an inner experience of failure to perform well from experiences defined by social recognition (considered under the E category of Esteem), intentional interference (considered under the D category of Control), or fate (K). Instrumental explanations for failure can involve unfair authorities (Control D), being cheated by rivals or unfair forms of competition (Mutual Purpose M), irresponsible or profligate behavior distracting the individual from one's task (Responsibility R); or not infrequently, there is a lack or loss of internal motivation (Achievement A).

In some groups causal explanation for failure rely, if not on fateful external forces, on malevolent hostile intentions of a supernatural source (see chapter 7, volume I, on Harmony H). Supernatural malevolence may be believed the cause rather than the impersonal forces of nature. For example, in some groups reported in the anthropological literature, a crop failure is not due to the impersonal vagaries of climate, but due to the magical practices of an enemy, or the anger of a displeased deity. Thus explanations for failure can be expressive as well as instrumental.

Among expressive explanations for failure are not only the negative effects of intentional malice (Harmony H), but also lack of socially nurturant support (Nurturance N), or sufficient appreciation of one's efforts (Esteem E). One may apply social standards internally, and judge oneself as a failure (C) if one does not receive sustaining social approval or support. Nevertheless, one may also apply internal standards independent of social appreciation. Mozart or Rembrandt may have felt internally capable (C) regardless of the vagaries of social appreciation given their work. An inner directed individual will have both a sense of competence relative to personal standards (C) and an internal drive that leads to persistence in creative achievement efforts (A), despite the absence of reinforcing monetary or adulatory recognition.

In several chapters in volume II that describe illustrative research, we shall note, in some detail, differences between Americans and Japanese in their explanations given for failure. In many Japanese narratives, failure is due to personal incapacity, very often due to a physical or bodily deficiency (C). Japanese are highly internalized and self-reflective rather than externalized in respect to explaining why there is worry about, or actual failure in performance. Some possible personal inadequacy of a physical or mental nature can become an abiding concern. They seldom allow themselves to consider consciously any lack of motivation (A) or their own personal resistance to accepting an imposed task (D). They are much more ready to attribute failure in an intended task to their own personal insufficiencies, which are subject to improvement. Americans, in contrast, in their narratives much more readily attribute noncompletion of a task as due to loss of interest or lack of motivation in applying oneself to what is expected of them (A). Failure is often seen as a form of resistance to authority (D) and/or a problem of internal motivation. This is why failure is seen so readily by Americans as the logical opposite of successful achievement. For Americans, and the American psychologists who study this topic, causal attributions about achievement refer to innate ability as a stable characteristic of the person, and to motivated effort as an unstable characteristic (Weiner, 1992). This is in contrast to the Japanese emphasis on developing personal capacity through hard work that leads to self-improvement.

(h) *Chapter 10, volume I*, describes categories related to issues of legitimate or illegitimate Control, dominance, or influence (D). There is use of instrumental sanctions by those in superordinate positions of power to govern, regulate, advise, or direct the behavior of those in status subordinate positions. Some narratives refer to issues of the legitimacy of authority or the autonomous or resistive reactions of those in subordinate positions. The desire to exercise "power" as dominance in a social context is considered a pan-human concern as are concerns with autonomous control over one's purposeful instrumental activities and relationships. Any social group socially defines the exercise of authority over another, in both positive and negative terms. Concerns over the limits of legitimate exercise of authority are found in every society. Limits of autonomy or "self regulation" are also of universal concern.

Superordinate or authority power involves the potential use of punitive sanctions assuring enforcement. Society exercises some delegation of police power assuring socially desired conformity. Some form of legitimate "heteronomy" being subject to the law or authority of another is found in all societies. Compliance by a subordinate, whether adult or juvenile, is expected in response to the proper exercise of authority. However, any improper dominance or excessive use of authority is negatively defined in different societies in different ways, as is any improper form of rebellious resistance. Any concerns about social dominance are scored under the Control (D) category.

One can see these issues from a developmental perspective. Through infancy there arises a more differentiated, realistic self-awareness of one's limitations and the presence of external intentionality which cannot be made subject to the self. Throughout its progressive development, a contrastive mechanism (De Vos and Suárez-Orozco, 1990) becomes intimately related to the dynamic human experience of "voluntarily" exercised intentional power and intellectual control interpersonally. The need to control may be directed to person or objects. In some instances, the infant or child may continue to use defensively some sense of omnipotence or grandiosity to protect the self against an alternative experience of utter helplessness (Adler, 1956).

From early on, by keeping cognitive control, some form of intentional power is experienced *within*. One "wills" things to happen. One can find means of inducing desired behavior in others. For example we may consider that among one's first "commands" are acts of crying to gain desired attention. There later develops control over musculature and motility in moving. This experience of inner initiative in the exercise of power is maintained by a contrastive defensive differentiation of inner volition separate from outside force.

In its later transmutations a contrastive ego mechanism can finally lead to the attainment of objective, analytic, logical thought as a basic mode of coping with, and controlling the environment, or individuals in the social environment. The primary adjustive progression is a growing capacity to use thinking (i.e., intentional problem solving) as a means of internal control as well as extending control outwardly over both the natural and social environment.

Discussion of power or social control also includes concern with the adult establishment of some forms of autonomy and self-control as legitimate in given social situations. There are in every society, regulations for legitimate changes in status over the life course (De Vos, 1975), from a previous subordinate position to one of further compliance or of self-actualization in independent social purpose (De Vos, 1972). This is particularly apparent in definitions of adulthood and its influence on internal family dynamics. Historically, in many societies, social definitions concerning the position of women within the family or society have been shifting in respect to the legitimate autonomy of women at some time in the life trajectory.

Seen from a social perspective, there remain radical differences in how authority is perceived in a society organized around an age-graded social hierarchy and one that idealizes individual endeavor (De Vos, 1975). In chapter 6, volume II, we consider some of these differences that are evident in Japanese narratives as compared with those produced by Americans. In Japan, social optimism is engendered about changes of status that go with aging in a cohesive age-graded social system. In this context, mentorship is portrayed as a constructive aspect of authority. In direct contrast to American society, in modern Indian, Chinese, Korean, or Japanese families there remains much emphasis on deference behavior extending past adulthood related to age-graded offices which helps reinforce social interdependence and cohesion in family and community. Such enforced deference behavior causes less conscious social resentment than that required by socially alienating class or ethnic differences. It is difficult for a contemporary American, when looking at social hierarchy in a Confucian society, to understand the conscious emotions attached to age grading and its complex relationship to both instrumental mastery on the one hand or expressive dependency on the other. A dependent relationship in Japan may be perceived positively as instrumental as well as satisfying an expressive need for dependency (De Vos, 1975).

(i) *Chapter 11, volume I,* considers issues that arise consciously in respect to self-control, or Responsibility (R). Instrumentally oriented judgment of one's behavior come to be located to some degree internally. Authority becomes internalized in humans as part of social development. Judgment of one's behavior occurs both in terms of externally perceived social rules and in respect to regulations that are self-imposed.

Seen developmentally, the Responsibility (R) category is related to the appearance in childhood of what has been defined in religious or moral terms as a "conscience." Internalized awareness of potential punishment, as well as an increasing awareness of one's own capacity to do harm to others causes avoidance of personally unacceptable behavior. Such avoidance is aided by the easily aroused memory of previous experiences of *guilt* that resulted from past transgression. This human capacity transcends simpler mammalian forms of intra-group constraint. Interpersonal as well as internally perceived problems arise over the proper internalization of *duties and social regulations*.

The negative concerns with Responsibility are very often experienced as a tension between pleasure or self-indulgence versus duty and obligation. Human passions are seen to interfere with proper dutiful performance of one's social responsibilities in marriage or in occupational endeavor, for example. Human weakness is seen as a lack of self-control and a loss or avoidance of proper purpose in improper selfish pursuits often defined in religious terms as "sin."

There are basic cultural differences in how responsibility or guilt is defined. There are also notable differences in a sense of responsibility as related to one's status or class position within a society. For example, in Japan, during modernization, the universal education given to both boys and girls was directly based on samurai neo-Confucianist concepts of loyalty and responsibility. It further espoused an age-graded sense of purposeful endurance toward the realization of instrumental goals of achievement with a continuing emphasis on hierarchy within the family roles, as is discussed in chapter 11, volume I.

(j) *Chapter 12, volume I,* on Mutual Purpose, considers mutual instrumental, purposeful interactions with others (M). Interactive instrumental activity is either of a competitive or cooperative nature. Usually seen horizontally, or in group contexts, mutually reciprocal relationships can be perceived either as *competition* between or among peers or associates in some socially defined context, or can be about *cooperation* in mutually beneficial, goal-directed, interactive behavior.

The narratives subsumed under this category are to be distinguished from expressive, affiliative concerns (Affiliation F). The narrative concerns grouped under (M) are about realizing instrumental *goals*, rather than focusing on the expressive *feelings* of togetherness or separation that may accompany interactive activities. The instrumental aspects of cooperation are also to be distinguished from concerns located within the category of Harmony (H). These latter depict the *feelings* about concerted action rather than the *goals* involved. They depict the hate or hostility in a rivalrous situation rather than any instrumental goals. Both instrumental and expressive concerns can frequently be consciously described as intertwined. If so verbalized, one needs to double score such descriptions as *both* instrumental and expressive.

Some psychological studies find the appearance of cooperation or competition in very early childhood. Early aggressive interactions initially appear to be instrumental, directed toward competition over toys, etc. Only later does aggressive behavior appear hostile, or directed with injurious intent (see the discussion and references noted in chapter 12, volume I). What begin as frustrated instrumental concerns with possession, whether or not they involve recourse to projected feelings of hostility, can become linked with internal experiences of destructiveness that become experientially linked with a perception of possible negative consequences to others. This sense becomes a basis for future guilt formation and early moral awareness as discussed in chapter 11, volume I.

While frustrated instrumental intentions can be directed expressively into hostile feeling, they can also seek expression in further instrumental socially approved competitive behaviors. Sometimes they are redefined into cooperative endeavors. Either of these instrumental activities avoids arousal of potential guilt feelings.

Socially considered, patterns of competition and cooperation can be related to social status and social mobility. One can also see social-historical changes in patterns of cooperative or competitive group behavior. Patterns differ based on whether those involved in the group behavior are of elite versus subordinate or minority background within the majority society. To cite such an instance, we can refer to our interviews with Koreans or Japanese in Japan conducted during several research projects (Lee and De Vos, 1981). Our studies especially illuminate the type of dilemmas experientially faced by members of some minority groups in which individual advancement is opposed by considerations of group loyalty (see chapter 12, volume I).

The Impersonal World: Inert Objects and Fateful Events

In *chapter 13, volume I*, we consider how to score two *impersonal* thematic categories of human concerns: Objects (O) and Fate-Kismet (K). These categories cover basic scoring of *impersonal* concerns.

(k) People express numerous attitudes or concerns about inanimate objects. There can be preoccupation with objects that can be manipulated, or with persons treated as manipulable inert objects, without consideration for their own intentionality. These concerns are scored in the (O) category.

Preoccupations with one's body or one's personal possessions are also scored within the (O) category. There could be a large number of topics considered as possibly salient in this regard. We have limited our scoring to explicit and directly expressed attitudes toward inert objects (O), the depersonalization of living 'things,' and any impersonal relationship with objects that comprise the natural world.

Robert Manlove in chapter 13, volume II, reports on his extensive use of the TAT as part of his research activities in the Philippines. In this context he illustrates how status differences related to respect are readily evoked by a special card on which two young men are wearing clothes that define their social class. Attention to their clothes in their narratives bring to mind values related to what is locally termed *amor propio* or (self-esteem).

Concerns with bodily integrity appear in various forms in different cultural groups. In chapter 13, volume I, we cite as an example our work with a Canadian Indian community. In the late 1950s, G. De Vos worked with anthropologists June Helm and Teresa Carterette on Rorschach and TAT test materials obtained from a Slavey Indian community living on the upper Mackenzie River in Canada's Northwest Territories (Helm, De Vos, and Carterette, 1960). They demonstrated some of the interpretive possibilities related to pervasively occurring TAT narratives that expressed a manifestly unreasonable fear that objects would be stolen from them.

(l) There are also expressions of concern about fateful, impersonal events. Destiny or "fate" is often experienced as a nonpersonal or "natural" force and as not controllable. There are fatalistic, passive, resigned, or unresolved, non-accepting attitudes expressed about these kinds of events that originate from outside the person. Our category for Fate or Kismet (K) allows us to consider these external, dynamic occurrences of either a positive or negative nature. Specifically we are referring to concerns about nonintentional forces and occurrences that impinge upon and shape human events, including social forces, dynamic systems and fateful events such as accidents, injuries and death.

The categorization as to what is an animate or inanimate force can differ drastically from culture to culture, and from person to person. Additionally, confusion between intentional causality and mechanistic causality are seldom totally resolved in religious or magical thought current in every society (see chapter 14, volume I). What might be assumed to be impersonal by a researcher might be experienced consciously, emically, as intentional or personal by an informant. It is important to limit scoring in the impersonal subcategories subsumed under (K) to those concerns that are emically experienced as nonintentional by the narrator. Events that are experienced emically as supernatural intentionality must be scored in other categories (see chapter 14, volume I). This is one area where ethnographically contextualized understanding is essential.

A cross-cultural topic worthy of much greater consideration than can be given here is normative cultural attitudes about impersonal events, chance or fate, accidents, good fortune or misfortune. There are impersonal, natural, or social forces; destinies of inherited wealth or poverty; war, or natural catastrophes; the unexpected appearance of illness; or the sudden accidents that impinge upon every individual. What is the relative saliency of fate in the thought of particular individuals? Depending on how impersonal forces are understood or conceptualized, fate, variously conceived and variously termed, intervenes in characteristic ways in different cultures.

Conclusion

Thus we have presented our initial delineation of major dimensions and categories of human concerns. We will now turn to the task of a more detailed description of our system for scoring the manifest content of verbal communication that is organized around what is actually said by individuals, as they describe their emic perceptions of human concerns in different social settings.

In the chapters of Part II we explore the various human concerns regarding social belonging and social interaction, and self-oriented concerns as they are expressed by individuals from a wide variety of cultural contexts. In those chapters we will focus our presentation on the scoring system itself (the ICSS), and how it is divided into categories and subcategories that have helped us encompass what individuals communicate to one another in conversation, or in fantasy material elicited by a specific test such as the TAT. Such expressions may reflect general underlying coping mechanisms at work beneath human consciousness to which we shall only indirectly refer as we focus on the categories of interpersonal concerns that appear on the conscious level in various forms of human expression.

In volume II of this two-volume series, in a series of chapters that describe empirical studies, we shall present more detailed examples of how the scoring system can be effectively used in cross-cultural research, as the basis for normative descriptions of salient concerns found within specific cultural groups that permit valid psycho-cultural comparisons.

Notes

Adler, Alfred. 1956. *The Individual Psychology of Alfred Adler*. New York: Basic Books.

Bandura, Albert. 1986. *Social Foundations of Thought and Action: A Social Cognitive Theory*. Englewood Cliffs, N.J.: Prentice-Hall.

Blood, Robert O., Jr. 1967. *Love Match and Arranged Marriage: A Tokyo-Detroit Comparison*. New York: Free Press.

Damon, William. 1988. *The Moral Child.* New York: Cambridge University Press.

De Vos, Eric S. 2000. Biocultural and Experiential Bases of Cultural Continuity and Change. In A.L. Communian and U.P. Gielen (Eds.), *International Perspectives on Human Development*. Lengerich: Pabst Science Publishers.

De Vos, George A. 1972. Social Stratification and Ethnic Pluralism: An Overview from the Perspective of Psychological Anthropology. *Race*, April.

———. 1973. *Socialization for Achievement: Essays on the Cultural Psychology of the Japanese.* Berkeley: University of California Press.

———. 1975. Apprenticeship and Paternalism: Psycho-Cultural Continuities Underlying Japanese Social Organization. In Ezra Vogel (Ed.), *Modern Japanese Organization and Decision Making*. Berkeley: University of California Press.

———. 1980. Delinquency and Minority Status: A Psycho-Cultural Perspective (chapter 6). In Graeme Newman (Ed.), *Crime and Deviancy: A Comparative Perspective* (pp. 130–180). Beverly Hills: Sage Publications.

———. 1992. *Social Cohesion and Alienation: Minorities in the United States and Japan.* Boulder, Colo.: Westview Press.

De Vos, George A. and Eiji Murakami. 1974. Violence and Aggression in Fantasy: A Comparison of American and Japanese Lower-Class Youth. In William P. Lebra (Ed.), *Youth, Socialization and Mental Health* (pp. 153–177). Honolulu: University Press of Hawaii.

De Vos, George A. and Marcelo Suárez-Orozco. 1990. *Status Inequality: The Self in Culture*. Newbury Park, Calif.: Sage Publications.

Durkheim, Emile. 1898. Représentations Individuele et représentations collective. *Revue de Metaphysique et de Morale*, **6**: 273–302.

Ekman, Paul and Richard J. Davidson. 1994. *The Nature of Emotion: Fundamental Questions*. New York: Oxford University Press.

Farr, Robert M. 1998. From Collective to Social Representations: Aller et retour. *Culture and Psychology*, **4**(3): 275–296.

Fox, Nathan A. 1994. The Development of Emotion Regulation: Biological and Behavioral Considerations. *Monographs of the Society for Research in Child Development*, **59**(240): 2–3.

Hall, Calvin S., Gardner Lindzey, and John B. Campbell. 1998. *Theories of Personality* (4th edition). New York: John Wiley & Sons.

Helm, June, George A. De Vos, and Teresa Carterette. 1960. Variations in Personality and Ego Identification Within a Slave Indian Kin-Community. National Museum of Canada Bulletin, No. 190, *Contributions to Anthropology*, Part II.

Henry, James P. and P.M. Stephens. 1977. *Stress, Health and the Social Environment: A Sociobiological Approach to Medicine.* New York: Springer-Verlag.

Lazarus, Richard S. 1991. *Emotion and Adaptation*. New York: Oxford University Press.

Lazarus, Richard S. and Bernice N. Lazarus. 1994. *Passion and Reason: Making Sense of Our Emotions.* New York: Oxford University Press.

Lee, Changsoo and George A. De Vos. 1981. *Koreans in Japan: Ethnic Conflict and Accommodation.* Berkeley: University of California Press.

Maddi, Salvatore R. 1996. *Personality Theories: A Comparative Analysis* (6th edition). Pacific Grove, Calif.: Brooks/Cole.

Manlove, Robert F. 1990. *Ozamiz: A Case Study in Urban Anthropology.* Unpublished Ph.D. dissertation. Department of Anthropology, Berkeley: University of California.

McClelland, David. 1987. *Human Motivation*. New York: Cambridge University Press.

McKee, J. and Florence B. Leader. 1955. The Relationship of Socio-Economic Status and Aggression in the Competitive Behavior of Preschool Children. *Child Development*, **26**: 135–142.

Merton, Robert. 1949. *Social Theory and Social Structure.* Glencoe, Ill.: The Free Press.

Parsons, Talcott and Robert Bales. 1955. *Family Socialization and Interaction Process.* Glencoe, Ill.: The Free Press.

Plutchik, Robert. 1994. *The Psychology and Biology of Emotion.* New York: Harper Collins.

Schore, Allan N. 1994. *Affect Regulation and the Origin of the Self: The Neurobiology of Emotional Development.* Hillsdale, N.J.: Erlbaum.

Slote, Walter and George De Vos (Eds.). 1998. *Confucianism and the Family in an Interdisciplinary, Comparative Context.* Albany: State University of New York Press.

Smith, Charles P. 1992. *Motivation and Personality: Handbook of Thematic Content Analysis.* Cambridge and New York: Cambridge U. Press.

Weiner, Bernard. 1992. *Human Motivation: Metaphors, Theories and Research.* Thousand Oaks, Calif.: Sage Publications.

White, R.W. 1959. Motivation Reconsidered: The Concept of Competence. *Psychological Review*, **66**: 297–333.

———. 1961. Competence and the Psychosexual Stages of Development. In Donald W. Fiske and Salvatore R. Maddi (Eds.), *Functions of Varied Experience.* Homewood, Ill.: Dorsey Press.

Chapter 3

The Many Faces of Pain and Pleasure: The Emotive Self

Over the course of human life, what begin as inner experiences of sensory stimulation, motoric activity, and various patterns of physiological arousal or quiescence are gradually integrated with experiences of meaningful perception and self-conscious purposeful intentionality. Internally directed perceptual processes often bring these patterns of stimulation, activity, and arousal into conscious awareness. They, thereby, contribute a hedonic dimension to the various states of experiential being that constitute our "emic" experience of "self," even as these states of inner experience become linked with externally focused and socially derived meaning and purpose. Ultimately, emotional experiences are recruited into socially interactive patterns. They are differentiated in terms that are derived from representations common to the person's face-to-face social group. Nevertheless, they retain their character as *internally* located elements of experience that must be categorically distinguished from other more externally located elements of experience.

Prior to the experience of meaning and purpose (developmentally speaking), the person has sensory (including interoceptive) experiences that can produce a wide variety of states of comfort or discomfort (Blass and Ciaramitaro, 1994). Emotion researchers have identified numerous stimuli that elicit emotion-like patterns of behavioral and physiological response. Some sensory experiences may elicit expressive responses indicative of anger, fear, or social interest. Others may initiate orienting responses or information-seeking behavior.[1] Responses indicative of experiences of comfort, discomfort, and curiosity, as well as a variety of other responses that appear to be expressive of affective states can be seen occurring from early infancy on (Fox, 1994). Experiences of being calmed or disturbed in the presence of people or other external objects become associated with patterns of sensation and behavior, such that the person's interaction with the social world from early on is imbued with an affective flavor.

Some primary emotions, visible even in social patterns, appear to be relatively innate and unlearned. Some perhaps begin asocially but are shaped through social interaction. Some secondary emotions are clearly social in nature, and are inseparable from social stimuli and social consequences. Whether of social or intrapersonal origin, emotional experiences are present in almost all human interactions, and are communicated by facial, bodily, vocal, or verbal gestures to others who reciprocally share the communicative pattern. In infancy, these interactive and communicative experiences may form the core of much of our early conscious experience, and become the core of the experience of inner regulation, intentionality, and continuity that we commonly know as the "self" (Schore, 1994).

As we develop more complex webs of meaning, intentionality, and social relationship, the affective flavors of our experiences do not disappear. They instead come to make sense as causally related with meaningful events, with personal goals, and with meaningful dimensions of social interaction (social status, respectability, etc.). Humans often come to consciously define these inner experiences within a cultural framework, and on the basis of shared social or cultural representations. Basic experiences of affective arousal to discomforting or pleasurable stimuli become linked to particular social contexts and role relationships. They come to be experienced and communicated not only through unmediated expressive behavior, but also through common linguistic forms and through socially structured interactions. The specific behavior used to either directly express or verbally refer to emotional states are highly varied and depend heavily on the specific expressive and linguistic vocabularies available to the individual informant. Not only are there considerable within-group differences in this regard, the matter becomes even more complex when we investigate cross-culturally. Depending on language usage there are considerable semantic differences in how inner experiences are labeled or represented. We would nevertheless contend that however great these variations and the differentiation to which one attends individually or as part of a cultural norm, there are basic commonalities in human inner experience toward which we can reduce the widely varied or nuanced expressions of emotional experience.

While linguistic and cognitive-representational considerations have served as a foundation for much of the psychological study of emotions (Mandler, 1984), they are not the only basis on which to proceed in developing a categorical structure for

---

[1]For discussions of theories of emotion and emotional development, see Isen (1984), Lazarus (1991), Plutchik (1994), Sroufe (1984), and Stein, Leventhal, and Trabasso (1990).

scoring inner affective experiences. One might also want to proceed from neuropsychological or physiological perspectives. Among those who have studied the neuropsychological basis of emotional experience (e.g., Buck, 1999; Berlyne, 1971), it has become clear that there are distinct yet interrelated neurological systems whose activity is associated with distinguishable types of emotional experiences. For example, two important dimensions that have been identified by Tucker and Williamson (1984) are the "depression-elation" dimension and the "anxiety-relaxation" dimension. It is clear that distinct patterns of brain activity and patterns of physiological activity are associated with various types of emotional experience (Davidson, 1993; Mason, 1986a, 1986b). Given that the same types of biological structures are going be present (albeit in developmentally modifiable forms) in all cultural environments, we should expect to see universal dimensions of emotional experience expressed across cultures. Although emotion theorists have not agreed completely on any single set of "basic emotions" to be found universally, there is indeed evidence of substantial commonality across cultures and even across species in the use of facial features and vocalizations to express basic human and mammalian affective experiences (e.g., Ekman, 1970, 1973; Ekman, Friesen, and Ellsworth, 1972). These almost certainly are largely based in commonality of inherited neurological and physiological systems. Yet there are limits to the specificity with which biological bases can presently be related to the nuances of our culturally embedded, linguistically, and socially mediated experience.

Regardless of language, or nuanced refinements of definition, we widely share a variety of emotional states as humans. On the positive pole, there are expressions of an inner experience of happiness or joy. There is sensuality. There is excitement. There are ecstatic experiences, however varied their description and social relevance may be cross-culturally. There are playfulness and humor. There are curiosity and satisfaction. There is a sense of relief after tribulation. In humans one finds a wide variety of "esthetic" pleasures, however they may be expressed.

On the negative pole, there are universal experiences of physical discomfort. There are states of sadness, anxiety, boredom, disgust, despair, or depression. There are recognized crazed conditions of acute or chronic malaise. There are a number of negative or unresolved experiences of emotion that involve either active or passive attitudes.

In developing a system for categorizing this complexity, we have proceeded from emic concerns that have appeared spontaneously in responses to projective test materials or in other narrative materials expressing human experiences. Because we are most concerned here with emic experience and less concerned with testing theories about an underlying emotion system, our scoring system does not attempt to enable any final classification of responses into basic emotion categories. Nor are we interested in abstracting the underlying emotion from the culturally constituted context in which it is emically experienced.[2] Nevertheless, we have been informed by theory and research on emotion as we have developed our category system.

Categorization of Internally Focused Expressive Concerns

Whether the meaning or purpose of a person's experiences are ultimately framed as expressive "concerns" (as we term them), or as instrumental and purposive "concerns," and whether they are associated within intrapersonal or social realms, most experiences are imbued with some affective flavor. The enjoyment of various kinds of pleasure (as well as varieties of curiosity) and the avoidance of various kinds of discomfort remain basic to most human experience. Therefore, the first basic category of inner-oriented concerns in the scoring system is the Pleasure-Pain category (P).

Because pleasure and discomfort are basic to so many other human interests, they are often described in the context of situations where other concerns are also present, perhaps represented psychologically as components of a cognitive-behavioral, goal-corrected, purposive system (Mandler, 1984). By inference, one might expect the presence of specific emotional experiences in the context of specified goal-outcome or behavior-outcome settings (based on various cognitive-behavioral theories of emotion). Yet even where one might expect to find them, concerns with pleasure and discomfort are not always revealed directly in conscious thought, nor in narrative responses to the Thematic Apperception Test (TAT).

In our scoring system, subcategories of pleasure or pain, Pleasure (P), *are scored only when specific attention is consciously directed to them and referred to as internal experiences.* We do not infer their presence based on external circumstances. Because they are often directly expressed in a story context or in a recounting of thought or behavior, responses that fit this category are also frequently double scored with other categories. Most frequently, even when attention is directly called to inner intrapersonal states, a double scoring is necessary, since impersonal or accompanying interpersonal considerations are also at least partially conveyed in some form.

When someone consciously describes an inner condition of being "happy" it is usually about something or some personal relationship. Seldom does the inner experience fail to involve others, or something external that is of value to the narrator. Nevertheless, these expressed concerns may or may not directly involve feelings toward others, or feelings attributed to others in the social environment. Sometimes there are responses in which the individual, without giving any further

---

[2]We do not structure our system to match any of the numerous extant systematized abstractions such as the "circumplex" model proposed by Plutchik (1994). Instead, we retain our framework of Positive-Active, Inactive or Unresolved, Negative-Active, and Negative-Passive, as described in chapter 2, volume I.

concrete context for the feeling, refers to an affective state such as "happiness" or "sadness," or some expressions that suggest moods of elation, excitation, anxiety, or depression. When possible, it is helpful to inquire further in regard to such responses by asking the follow-up question: "What about?" Most often, but not always, people will have some idea as to the interpersonal social concern or impersonal external thing to which the experience of pleasure or pain is related.

There are certain forms of pleasurable or painful experiences for which the person cannot consciously articulate externally related concerns. Regardless of an absence of any such articulated relatedness, the concern is, nevertheless, emically real, and must be scored, albeit separately. When the Pleasure (P) category is scored separately it is because the affective experience is considered deeply, internally, *self-oriented* and is the sole focus of the expressed narrative. In such a situation, interaction with the "other" or another person is conveyed as a peripheral consideration or not conveyed at all.

Intrapersonal States

The expressions of inner states included in the pleasure-pain category (P) are essentially "intrapersonal" as distinguished from the "interpersonal" concerns noted in the following four chapters, wherein we discuss Nurture (N), Affiliation (F), Harmony (H), and Esteem (E). These categories, as well as the presently considered Pleasure (P) category are all "expressive" rather than "instrumental" in content.

Intra-personal concerns also often refer to purposeful behavior. There are numerous inner-oriented thoughts that refer to purposeful, or goal-oriented, considerations related to issues of mastery or Competence (C), Achievement (A), or Responsibility (R). These three inner-oriented instrumental categories are considered in subsequent chapters, where we examine our various categories of concerns with purposefully directed behavior or thought.

The Positive-Negative Dimension

Category (P) concerns refer to some *affective* state of either a positive (PA), negative active (PC), negative passive (PD), or unresolved nature (PB). As described in chapter 2, volume I, these letter designations are carried throughout all categories in the scoring system, according to the following general distinction: the letter "A" designates *positive active* situations. The letter "B" marks current inactivity or lack of resolution. The letter "C" marks *negative active* situations, and the letter "D" designates *negative passive* situations.

The subcategories utilize words in lower-case letters that are relatively easy to use to typify the material subsumed under each subcategory. For example, *PA-joy* designates various expressions of emotional pleasure, states of happiness, feelings of joy. *PB-bored* designates various expressions of ennui, boredom, or an expressed sense of indifference.

Further Distinctions

In our experience in scoring specific responses in the pleasure-pain category and its subcategories, we find six subdivisions to be useful.

Bodily Sensation. The first set of subcategories pertain to *Physical Pleasure-Pain; bodily sensations of pleasure or physical suffering.* These responses are narrative expressions of physical states in which the narrator pays direct attention to the body and its sensations.

Curiosity-Excitement. The second set of subcategories are states of *Curiosity-Disinterest; exploratory excitement, boredom.* These more cognitively oriented subcategories include mental excitement, exploratory curiosity, anticipation of surprise and new experience, or the negative converse of boredom or disinterest.

Elation-Depression. The third set of subcategories covers *Elation-Depression; happiness, joy, ecstasy, hyper-sensorial experiences.* These responses are expressions of happiness or the converse of despair.

Serenity-Anxiety. The fourth set of subcategories are considerations of *Serenity-Anxiety.* Tucker and Williamson (1984) describe this in terms of an "anxiety-relaxation" dimension. The negative states of anxiety are well reported and studied. What is less often considered is how the opposite pole of such states is an inner experience of quietude and calm, such as may be obtained in meditative states or by active relaxation.

Satisfaction-Frustration. The fifth set of subcategories are those of *Satisfaction-Frustration; contentment; dissatisfaction.* There are narratives that are characterized by expressions of frustration as well as statements of deep satisfaction within one's inner consciousness.

Complex States. In the sixth set we have some subcategories that seem more complex. They may overlap the above five distinctions; these kinds of states may include aesthetic pleasures, pleasure in nature, and various statements related to an intrapsychic component of religious experiences.

The Categories, in Full Detail

We proceed now to a detailed presentation of the category system.

A. *Subjective Inner States* ***PA***

Physical Pleasure	
PA-body	Physical or sensual—food, drink, bodily functions
PA-sensual	Sensuality in sexual or other bodily functions
Curiosity; Surprise, Exploratory Excitement, Ecstasy	
PA-curious	Curiosity and discovery
PA-surprise	Positive unanticipated event or discovery; new experiences, sudden waking from a dream
PA-joke	Joking or the unexpected in humor
PA-excite	A positive sense of excitement
PA-ecstasy	Ecstasy, religious state, or altered consciousness
Elation; Happiness, Joy, Play	
PA-joy	Emotional pleasure, happiness, joy, mirth
PA-play	Play, recreation or relaxation
PA-memory	Happy memories
Serenity; Quietude	
PA-relief	Relief, relaxation, or restorative feeling after an ordeal or difficulty
PA-meditate	Meditation—peace, quietude
Satisfaction; Contentment	
PA-satisfy	Pleasure in productivity accomplishment, in music or work, etc.
PA-order	Sense of order, composition, or harmony
PA-vicar	Vicarious pleasure in the happiness of others
PA-purge	Activity to relieve strong feelings; catharsis
PA-endure	Satisfaction while enduring through ordeal
Mixed	
PA-esthetic	Aesthetic pleasure: a) aesthetic, b) graphic, c) plastic, d) music, etc.
PA-nature	Pleasure in nature, in nature or in the environment
PA-god	Happiness in god or religion
PA-hope	Feeling of hope and optimism

Physical Pleasure. These subcategories cover various forms of *physical* pleasure related to food or drink (PA-body) and *sensual*, tactile, or sexual pleasure (PA-sensual). As we shall indicate, sexual desire never remains simply pleasure. It becomes deeply interpersonal and sex is better subsumed positively or negatively under other, more contextually specific categories such as *Affiliation*, *Dominance*, *Appreciation*, *Competence*, etc. (see the relevant chapters below).

Curiosity; Exploratory Excitement. Curiosity (PA-curious) is addressed here as a form of affective excitement in something new, and perhaps, a sense of surprise in discovery (PA-surprise). A sense of novelty in experience can be perceived as a pleasure, or in some circumstances, potentially a threat (PB-surprise). The sociologist W.I. Thomas (see Thomas and Znanicki, 1927) considered the excitement of "new experience" one of four basic human "wishes." When curiosity results in successful understanding or is seen in the context of purposeful behavior and information seeking related to problem solving, it becomes most often integral to concerns with Mastery or Competence (C), and as such, is discussed in chapter 9, volume I.

Excitement in aroused behavior is to be distinguished from the emergency aggressive responses of individuals involved in the active manipulation of the environment. In the Hindu pantheon, Brahma the creator, the personification of creativity is to be distinguished from Shiva, the god who causes change through destruction (see chapter 7, volume I, on Harmony and Discord).

Certain forms of excitement (PA-excite) are stimulating and sought after positively as peak experiences. White (1959) and Fiske and Maddi (1961) in their understandings of human development consider that there is a continual seeking for excitement on a neurological basis. Human activities are not all directed toward tension reduction, rather, a certain state of elevated tension can become a desired inner state. White posits an expressive "effectance motivation" which is partially transmuted into a "competence motivation" in instrumental concerns with mastery (see chapter 9, volume I). States of excitement can become addictive—as in the excitement of gambling.

There is a further level of excitement to be found in what can be termed *ecstatic pleasure* (PA-ecstasy). These states may occur or be induced individually or in group social contexts; in secular or in sacred religious contexts. They may be brought about by chemical ingestion. In many cultures these sought-for states are defined in a religious context where there is a sense of diffusion or a loss of boundaries of the self and a sense of oneness with the universe, as was described by mystics such as St. Teresa. Schwartz (1976) describes the "metastable" state induced by participating in a cargo cult in New Guinea natives. He discusses how a state of intense excitement in cult activities, once experienced, is sought after again and again. This sought-for repetition of excitement is the heart of addiction, a psychological or physiological dependency, inducing sought-after repetitions of intense, sometimes blissful excitement. When the excitement expressed is consciously goal directed and the conscious context is related contextually to problem solving, the expressed activity may be better categorized in the *Competence* or *Achievement* categories (see chapters 9 and 12, volume I).

Elation; Play. Most frequent is some expression of elation such as an inner feeling of joy or happiness (PA-joy). In extreme form it can be described as "bliss."

Humans have a developmental capacity toward mental pleasure in the act of learning. Excitement and attentiveness at first allows for learning without a need to maintain a purposeful goal direction. Playfulness (PA-play; PA-joke) and curiosity are pan-mammalian pleasurable activities further developed within conceptual symbolic systems of human thought guided by pleasure as well as purpose. Learning later becomes progressively instrumental and focused as cultural content is inculcated into instrumentalized goal anticipatory patterns by the society through the mediation of family and community. Internally stimulated innovative behavior may be rewarded as creative or discouraged as deviant. These may be expressed as an inner state of happiness brought on by recall of past memories of a positive nature (PA-memory). There is sometimes mentioned some nonspecified positive feeling about one's memory of experiences viewed at a distance.

Serenity; Quietude. There are periodic expressions of a sense of relaxation or relief after ordeal (PA-relief). There are pleasurable expressions of meditative states that produce a desired inner state of peace and quietude (PA-meditate).

Satisfaction; Contentment. Pleasure can be perceived as an auxiliary satisfaction experienced in work (PA-satisfy). For example, the satisfactory "pleasure" of playing music is distinct from a goal-oriented drive to learn music in accordance with standards, but the inherent pleasures of music help induce one into the "work" of disciplined application toward the standards that define music for a group. From the beginning, instrumental and expressive components in the exercise of a talent must be independently evaluated, even though they are usually blended or combined in various degrees of relative saliency in all human achievement–oriented activity. A sense of intellectual mastery may be instrumentally directed, but never loses an underlying sense of pleasure. (A double scoring may be indicated with either instrumental *Achievement* or *Competence*, depending on how the expressive satisfaction is focused upon in a narrative.)

One can find direct pleasure in a sense of order, harmony in one's environment (PA-order).

There is a human capacity to experience pleasure in the pleasure and happiness of others. There is the inner experience of vicarious pleasure through the witnessing of the pleasure or success of another (PA-vicar). Japanese women can take pleasure in the activities of their children, deriving from them a strong source of internal satisfaction and pleasure.

There are pleasurable experiences related to activities relieving one of strong affect in a sense of catharsis (PA-purge). We have received expressions of a positive affective state related to a sensed capacity to endure through tribulation; an inner state of self-maintenance through ordeal (PA-endure).

Some More Complex States of Inner Pleasure. In humans, tactile, olfactory, gustatory, auditory, visual, and kinesthetic sensibilities are given cultural coloring and can be transmuted into positive or negative "aesthetic" experiences (PA-esthetic). In some individuals there is consciousness of a direct pleasure in acts of creativity or in innovative behavior. Very often this is scored as a positive sense of competence. The excitement and pleasure of creativity is to be distinguished from purposeful, problem-solving behavior in which there is concern over one's capacity (*Competence*), responsibility (*Responsibility*), or success (*Achievement*) in the instrumental mastery of a problem. A human drive toward mastery does usually involve some state of heightened excitement as a driving force seeking affective as well as instrumental resolution. When such affective experience is mentioned narratively it should be double scored (PA-esthetic). An inventor is someone with an achievement orientation directed toward social purpose. In some expressed attitudes invention is more dedicated to solving a social need. Inventiveness, however, can also be a form of play when pleasure outweighs purpose. One must record both the expressive and instrumental components when they are both verbalized in the consciousness of the action or thought of the individual.

One may express a possible inner state aroused by the experience of the natural environment (PA-nature). In some few expressions we have scored comments of individuals who express a happiness they have experienced in the thought of god or religion (PA-god). Some individuals express directly an inner sense of hope or optimism (PA-hope).

B. Unresolved Concerns with Pleasure and Pain ***PB***

Unresolved Physical Discomfort	
PB-tired	Tired or sleeping
PB-body	Physical discomfort
PB-hunger	Hungry or thirsty
PB-rage	Inner impulse of anger not specified
Disinterest; Boredom	
PB-surprise	Surprised
PB-bored	Boredom, indifference, ennui
PB-sated	To be sated or jaded
Unresolved Emotional States	
PB-denial	A directly expressed denial of emotional expression
Anxious Condition	
PB-trouble	Troubled or disturbed
PB-anxiety	Unspecified general anxiety
PB-exist	Existential anxiety about human mortality
Frustration; Discontent, Dissatisfaction	
PB-satisfy	Lack of resolved pleasure or satisfaction
PB-dislike	Expression of dislike or discontent; dislike of situation or circumstance
PB-sulk	Sulking; in a pout
PB-work	Displeasure in relation with the work situation or occupation
PB-defer	Deferred pleasure

Mixed

PB-torn	Ambivalent or uncertain emotional state
PB-stress	Internally stressed condition

There are a number of undefined, unresolved, or undefined affective states that need to be categorized.

Unresolved Discomfort. A sense of being tired or without energy is a frequently expressed condition (PB-tired). There can be expressions of chronic physical discomfort (PB-body). An individual may suffer an unsatisfied physical need such as hunger or thirst (PB-hunger). Anger is another basic emotion sometimes experienced without interpersonal content. There are some who depict individuals feeling a diffuse anger or an inner sensation of rage with no target or sense of how to resolve the feeling (PB-rage).

Disinterest; Boredom. A state of surprise remains unresolved when not further delineated (PB-surprise). A vague sense of threat may be suggested. Individuals may become concerned with a loss of interest, a sense of undefined ennui (PB-bored). We may infer that such a state arises with no accompanying conscious awareness of how positive anticipation of social interaction may be blocked by internally unresolved problems about personal investment in others. Instead the individual is focused on the lack of satisfaction to be anticipated in any self-focused activities. Such a sense of boredom or ennui is an acute or a chronic unresolved condition. Conversely, an individual can experience an unresolved sense of being jaded or over-sated with physical or mental experience (PB-sated).

Unresolved Emotional States. There is sometimes some immediate expressed denial of any experience of emotions (PB-denial).

Anxiety Condition. We score among our "unresolved" subcategories various forms of anxiety or malaise (e.g., discussion in Spielberger, Gorsuch, and Lushene, 1970). There can be a mention of a vaguely defined unresolved emotional state. There can be vague mentions of being troubled that are not further specified (PB-trouble). Individuals may experience directly an unresolved inner state of anxiety which is diffuse and without focus (PB-anxiety). There may be a basic existential anxiety about one's continuity or existence through time—a sense of human mortality (PB-exist).

Frustration; Discontent, Dissatisfaction. One may express directly an inability to feel pleasure or satisfaction (PB-satisfy). (Insatiability in the specifically expressed forms of greed or envy are to be scored below under PC.) Dislike of ill-defined circumstances may be mentioned (PB-dislike). Seeing someone sulking or in some undefined snit can be expressed occasionally (PB-sulk). An unresolved tension may be concerning displeasure in regard to work (PB-work). There may be a sense of unresolved tension related to some deferred inner pleasure (PB-defer).

Mixed or Unspecified Resolution. These may be infrequently evident as a concern; some basic ambivalence about a situation that should be pleasurable but is internally conflictual (PB-torn). There is also experienced a sense of internal stress or tensions which may be more or less specified as to cause (PB-stress).

C. *Negative Categories Related to Arousal* ***PC***

Undue Active Physical State	
PC-sensual	Nonspecified undue sensuality; overindulgence of the senses
PC-lust	Out of control, nonfocused sexual experiences, a negative perception of one's lustful nature
Crazed State	
PC-crazed	Crazed state caused by unusual mental reactions to external events
Negatively Judged Elation	
PC-cruel	Pleasure in cruelty; sadism
PC-evil	"Sinful" or evil pleasure (to be double scored when context makes it necessary)
Agitation	
PC-unrest	Continually agitated, unable to attain serenity
Frustration; Dissatisfaction	
PC-anger	Diffuse unfocused experiences of anger
PC-unsated	Insatiability or overindulgence, i.e., gluttony, avarice
Mixed	
PC-pain	Self-inflicted punishment or suffering
PC-suicide	Injurious or suicidal acts or thoughts

Undue Active Physical States. Undue sensuality without any interpersonal context may be experienced negatively (PC-sensual). Lust is very often singled out as an out-of-control, not properly directed, sexual body experience. There can be a negative perception of an individual's driven, lustful nature (PC-lust).

Crazed State. One can dramatize a crazed state caused by unusual mental reactions to external events (PC-crazed).

Negatively Judged Excitement. A consciousness of sadistic pleasure (PC-cruel) can be additionally scored in concert with another scoring designating the specific context (pleasure in the injury of others, etc.). The are expressions of "sinful" or evil pleasure (PC-evil) (to be double scored when the context makes it necessary). Sins of "profligate" pleasure are usually scored in the context of guilt and negative responsibility (see chapter 9, volume I).

Agitation. There may be expressed an experienced continual agitated state, an inability to attain serenity (PC-unrest).

Frustration; Dissatisfaction. One sometimes finds expressed without other content an unfocused sense of anger or inner rage (PC-anger). Such responses are very rare since there is usually some interpersonal scene depicted that allows for scoring under the Harmony (H) category. There are internal states of insatiability in respect to food or internally perceived addictive forms of acquisition (PC-unsated). There are figures depicted as representing insatiability in a search for wealth or individuals given to insatiable overindulgence, i.e., the deadly sins of Gluttony, Avarice.

Mixed. Self-inflicted pain can be a subject of concern in expressions of masochism (PC-pain) or double scored as an act of aestheticism (PC-pain; DSB-obey). A nonspecified suicidal act may be scored by a special subcategory (PC-suicide). Sometimes suicide is seen as a means of avoiding some form of unbearable suffering. Sometimes there seems to be some social context (Jacobs, 1971).

In every culture, one can find some forms of active physical or mental pleasure that are socially condemned as personally or socially injurious, and are negatively perceived. Pleasures in forbidden acts are condemned within the religious systems of many cultures. In the earlier western Christian tradition, for example, there were the seven deadly sins: sloth, anger, lust, pride, envy, gluttony, and avarice. These were acts or attitudes considered to be especially abhorrent to the Christian deity. Contextually these "sinful" experiences are usually considered both in interpersonal or intrapersonal contexts. Sloth was often related to a failure of an internal sense of Responsibility (see chapter 11, volume I). The deadly sins are most often interpersonal failings. Lust can be seen as an improper form of Affiliation (chapter 5, volume I). Pride is a problem of Esteem (see the negative active category of EDC-disdain, chapter 6, volume I); anger is a failing of interpersonal Harmony (discord or violence in interaction with another, chapter 7, volume I). Envy is more varied, but most often appears in the context of Nurture (chapter 4, volume I) or competitiveness (chapter 12, volume I). Gluttony and Avarice may be overtly related to an undo relationship with objects (chapter 13, volume I). Sins of "profligate" pleasure are also commonly scored in the context of guilt and negative responsibility (see chapter 11, volume I).

Nevertheless, transgressions of a moral code are often described in the narratives as being states of insatiability or lack of control and should be scored within the present category, either as a body sensation or a form of uncontrollable dissatisfaction. For example, destructive behavior can be seen as a direct concern with evil in pleasures of one sort or other (PC-evil), but may also be double scored in its specific context (e.g., vandalism is also scored with OC-vandal). A consciousness of sadistic pleasure (PC-cruel) might be additionally scored in concert with another score that designates the specific context (e.g., the exploitation of others, DDC-exploit see chapter 10, volume I).

D. Passive States of Malaise ***PD***

Pain; Bodily Sensations, Physical Suffering	
PD-sex	Sexual activity viewed as unpleasant
PD-suffer	Suffering
Passive State of Negative Excitement	
PD-shock	Reaction of shock to events
PD-sloth	Sense of an incapacity to mobilize effort or interest
Depression	
PD-denial	Denial of emotions, incapacity to feel (acute or chronic)
PD-sad	Sad over specified situation
PD-submit	Masochistic pleasure in submission
PD-sorrow	General or unspecified grief or sorrow (crying, etc.)
PD-depress	Depression, despair
PD-suicide	Suicidal despair
PD-witness	Witnessed or imagine present or past unpleasantness
Pervasive Anxiety	
PD-anxiety	Diffuse sense of anxiety
Frustration; Dissatisfaction	
PD-thwart	Unspecified frustration or discontent
Mixed	
PD-mad	Madness caused by possible internal personality factors
PD-disorder	A sense of disorder or disarray
PD-disgust	Disgust in contact with unaesthetic people, objects, or behavior
PD-lost	Wistful over lost innocence

Pain; bodily sensations, physical suffering. Specific attention can be drawn to the unpleasantness of sex (PD-sex). There are relatively frequent expressions of suffering (PD-suffer) related to various circumstances.

Passive State of Negative Excitement. There are narrative descriptions of a person in deep shock (PD-shock). There can be a paralyzing sense of shock as a reaction to some events. One can express a sense of an incapacity to mobilize effort or interest (PD-sloth). One can also express an inner sense of indulgence coupled with an incapacity to mobilize effort.

Depression. There are narratives describing someone in a state of incapacity to feel (PD-denial). The most frequent forms of self-concerned displeasure have to do with sadness over some specified situation (PD-sad). Such stories should usually be double scored. We distinguish such responses from those in which nothing is specified as causing sorrow or sadness (PD-sorrow). These may be expressed as some Masochistic state of submissiveness. There are relatively frequent narratives depicting despair or depression (PD-depress). The nature of depression is a widely discussed topic. Often it appears without expressed interpersonal contact (e.g., Beck, 1967). These depressed states may be more specially noted as an individual contemplating suicide (PD-suicide).

We also consider under these subcategories modes of narrative experience in which the protagonist is 'distanced' from a situation or event by putting it in the past. It may be a pleasant memory (see above, PA-memory). It may, however, be an unpleasant memory, dream, or witnessed event (PD-witness). In such stories, an individual can be depicted as remembering, imagining, or dreaming of a scene before his or her eyes, or simply as witnessing a scene without being directly involved. Such stories may indicate a form of distancing that removes one from a less controlled direct affective involvement. This mode or narration can be seen inferentially as a defensive one. We double score such distancing as PD-witness, while also scoring the actual interpersonal behavior being depicted. In chapter 5, volume II (Table 5.4) we document that some stories of violence are depicted in such a way that the immediacy of violence is avoided by having the protagonist or "hero" of the story be a dreamer of a violent act, or a mere passive witness to violence.

Anxiety. There is occasionally depicted an uncontrollable sense of diffuse anxiety (PD-anxiety).

Frustration; Dissatisfaction. There is also a sense of deep, terminal frustration that preoccupies the individual (PD-thwart), but in most instances it is contextualized and can be scored under another category as part of an unresolved interaction.

Mixed. Some forms of crazed behavior are expressed as resulting from an internal state or personality condition. When they are uncontrolled and undesired, and experienced negatively, sometimes due to a physiological aberrance, they can be defined by members of a society as some form of psychopathology and classified in our subcategories under mixed (PD-mad). One may experience a profound sense of disorder or disarray (PD-disorder). One may experience disgust in contact with unaesthetic people, objects, or behavior or the sense of disgust aroused by a person or a situation (PD-disgust). Disgust is an emotionalized state different from a sense of anxiety and has to do specifically with some horror of contact with contaminated objects or people (Ekman, 1973). One may describe a wistful resignation to the loss of innocence (PD-lost). Mixed category expressions may need to be double scored. For example, in its extreme form, disgust might be found coupled with racist evaluative concerns about socially degraded individuals,[3] and would then need to be scored with an Esteem subcategory as well.

---

[3]See a full discussion of interpersonal attitudes related to contempt and disgust in chapter 6, volume I. For a recent full treatis on disgust as a basic emotion see Miller, *The Anatomy of Disgust* (1997).

People may attribute broader intentional or expressive meaning to various kinds of passively incurred *suffering* and ordeal. When negative affective states are in the context of interpersonal relationships they can be scored under other expressive categories which follow. For example, ordeals of suffering are sometimes contextualized as part of a social identity. An expressive sense of suffering can become an aspect of a particular ethnic or gender role identity, and can become means of manipulating of others (for example, see the categories of Esteem, Responsibility, Control, etc.).

Illustrative Complex Scoring of Responses from the TAT Including Expressions of Positive or Negative Pleasure

In what follows we will use material extracted from three previous studies (described further in chapters 7, 8, and 11, volume II) to illustrate how stories are scored under the pleasure category.

The first sample was of a group of fifty Korean immigrants to the United States compared with fifty minority Koreans residing in Japan (see chapter 7, volume II). These were compared on Cards 1, 2, and 17. The Koreans coming to the United States were much more positive in all their responses compared with the considerable personal alienation evident in minority Koreans living in Japan.

The second study compared ethnic samples in Brazil (see chapter 8, volume II). One notes how Japanese-Brazilians, compared with Italian, Portuguese, or Afro-Brazilians, on Cards 1, 2, 3BM, and 16, are more prone to directly express curiosity or creativity among their direct expressions of positive pleasurable activities.

The third study compared Venezuelan and Canadian youth specifically on Card 6BM (see chapter 11, volume II). Again some differences became apparent. For example, the Canadians on several cards depicted the necessity for practicing endurance as a positive attitude to be used in facing life alone. Emphasis is sometimes on a capacity to endure, even without satisfaction in the process. Some other stories depict the negative feelings of an isolated older person.

Because affect is so often embedded in larger contexts, as one generally might expect there are almost no stories of a simple, internally directed expression of affect in these samples. Nevertheless, we can illustrate how nuanced differences between groups were apparent in the manner in which some of the pleasure responses were evoked as part of a more complex interpersonal context, even where the other categories scored were of paramount concern.

Korean Records: Positive States (PA)

From a sample of responses to Card 17 (a man on a rope) by Korean immigrants to the United States:

(KLA [Los Angeles] f) (Card 17) He climbs the rope. He must be climbing up a mountain. Maybe he will go to the top of the mountain easily. He is a person who *enjoys* mountaineering. He *enjoys* rock climbing.

[CA-test AA-self PA-joy]

(KLA m) (Card 17) The man is an *inquisitive* person and he likes to see games. He is climbing on a rope to see a game free. He will enjoy seeing the game and will *satisfy* his risky attempt.

[PA-curious PA-satisfy AC-illicit]

(KLA f) (Card 17) This picture is a circus performance. The man is climbing on the rope. He is prideful before an audience. He is *satisfied* with his occupation in the circus. He will continue in this job.

[CA-present ESA-status PA-satisfy]

By a minority Korean residing in Japan:

(KJ [Japan] m) (Card 17) Should I look at picture lengthwise or crosswise? He is playing a fool. His face suggests he is playing a fool. He is *playing* as for a show, for a show booth. He is masculine. This is more cheerful one than the other pictures. I don't mind if he is naked or not. This is the most masculine and cheerful picture.

[ESC-detract-s SEA-approve OB-body PA-play]

As we discuss in chapter 7, volume II, throughout their materials there were more positive stories in all the categories given by the Korean immigrants to the United States as compared with minority Koreans residing in Japan (see also De Vos and Kim, 1993). On Card 17 (the man on a rope), the story listed above was the single story provided in the Koreans in Japan sample that could be scored as depicting a positive pleasure response, but note that it has a deprecatory tone aimed at the protagonist who is seen as playing a fool.

Inactive or Unresolved Issues (PB)

We find more stories of an unresolved nature among Korean residents of Japan as compared with the United States immigrant Koreans.

(KLA m) (Card 17) He is an acrobat. He climbs up the rope. He seems to be an old man but he is healthy. He is a veteran acrobat. He is full of confidence in climbing on the rope. He is looking at somebody. He has a slight feeling of *repugnance for his job* but he will climb to the end of the rope.

[OB-body CA-able CA-test PB-dislike]

(KJ m) (Card 1) Well, he is practicing the violin, and it seems that he is *tired of playing* the violin. And now he sighs, looking at the violin. He is completely *fed up with it*. And after all, when he is asked if he wants to quit the violin, he cannot decide. I don't know.

[PB-tired PB-bored AB-waver]

(KJ f) (Card 1) He was scolded by his mother once because he quit playing it. He feels *gloomy because he has to go practice* again. He will *not* be a violinist.

[NDA-scold PB-work DSC-family]

(KJ f) (Card 17) I wonder if he is going upwards or downwards. Maybe he is going upwards. He is searching for something desperately. This does not let me feel anything but *fear*. I don't know.

[PB-anxiety]

Negative-Active Pleasure (PC)

As a category (PC) is rarely scored in any of the present illustrative stories. There is the only one from the Japanese-Korean sample:

(JK m) (Card 1) He was receiving the lesson of the violin from a tutor. As he could not make a good sound however, he was *annoyed*, and then— . . . that is all.

[NSA-edify CC-Failure PC-anger]

Negative-Passive Affective States (PD)

Expressions of a negative-passive affective states (PD) were found among Koreans in Japan, as expression of sadness, sorrow (unspecified sadness), or a denial of affectivity. Sadness is scored as 'PD-sad' when the context of the sadness is defined. It is scored as 'PD-sorrow' when it refers to an affective state with no specification of the cause of the sadness.

(JK m) (Card 2) A fantastic picture. It is a scene that appears in someone's dream. This one (left) seems *too sad*. He (center) is cultivating a field. What is this woman? [on the right] She seems *worried* about something. This picture is fantastic as well as realistic.

[PD-sorrow PB-anxiety CB-worry KD-misc]

(JK m) (Card 2) I've seen this picture before . . . the past. . . . May I say it in a word? There is no past, present, or future. It exists *without time or feeling*.

[PD-denial]

Brazilian Records: Positive States (PA)

In another study comparing ethnic samples in Brazil from Japanese-Brazilians (De Vos, 1997): one notes how Japanese-Brazilians, compared with Italian, Portuguese, or Afro-Brazilians, are more prone to directly express curiosity among their direct expressions of positive pleasurable activities:

> (J m) (Card 1) Thinking about playing, whether he could hear how it sounds, *curious to know* who invented it, and how one gets sound out of the instrument. He wants to play and to know how the violin functions. Intends to learn his music.
>
> [AB-think PA-curious CA-future]

> (J f) (Card 1) He wants to learn how to play the violin . . . [shows] *curiosity and interest* in playing the instrument. He will probably be able to play some day.
>
> [AB-think PA-curious CA-future]

> (J m) (Card 1) Trying to fix . . . is this a violin? *Trying to understand*, or trying to produce a sound. Or *admiring* the instrument. Paper, on a table . . . trying to be able. . . . About how to play . . . will be able to play in future. At his age, will be able to do it.
>
> [PA-curious PA-esthetic OA-please AA-persist CA-future]

A blank card evokes symbolically concepts of order, creativity, purity, and endurance, which are all Japanese cultural concerns. In some instances, these are expressed with an explicit pleasure component, and in others, these are expressions that more correctly coded in the Competence (C) category.

> (J f) (Card 16) (blank) Street vendor *tired* asleep and started dreaming . . . a different world . . . animated/upbeat . . . pursue life. *Happy*. One *plays*, and knows lots of people. Suddenly, wakes up and sees that being together is not reality.
>
> [NSD-means PA-play PA-happy PB-tired FA-sympathy]

> (J m) (Card 16) (blank) White is purity—it means that there are *no differences*, no racism, that *all is equal, and in order.*
>
> [PA-order HA-symbol]

> (J f) (Card 16) (blank) *Happy* family *in the field*, with children—*among trees, grass.*
>
> [HA-family PA-nature]

> (J m) (Card 16) (blank) Should not forget the past. Make a white sheet first, then, decide what is important one by one. This is hard when you are confused. But one must forget things to a certain extent and then *start ordering them anew* from what is most important.
>
> [AA-purpose CA-create PA-order]

Portuguese-Brazilians gave different expressions to the same Cards 1 and 16. For example, a need to be aided is found in several stories:

(P m) (Card 1) The lonely boy. Once to *relieve* himself, the boy named Rafael decided to make a story which talked about our world. He locked himself in the bedroom and began his story. His mother said that it is nonsense, since he is yet too young to make stories. But the boy insisted on his story and went to his bedroom and there he shut himself. He spent hours and hours upon his text until, at a time, he finished the text. Soon after that he went downstairs, to the living room, and called his mother: "Mom come to see the story I made." Then mother read son's story and found it great, for she had never thought that the boy had evolved that much. Rafael became so *cheerful* that he went again to the room to write new stories. The days passed and the boy grew. At the school the boy was already a great student. At 15 years old he started to make his own book and so he wrote more books and became famous.

[FB-alone <u>AA-counter</u> PA-relief EDA-praise PA-joy ESA-fame]

(P m) (Card 1) A boy is deciding what he is going to do in order to study, but he was turned out of the school. He thinks of how he is going to get a job. Then I think, will I have to work as a garbage collector? Working as a garbage collector is too much running! But one day I went to a school and they accepted me, but the headmistress said that if I made one single disorder or difficulty I would be turned out again. Then I studied as hard as I could and passed from year to year. I reached college and wanted to be a lawyer, and thought: "Lawyer is a very good function and I'll have a family to celebrate this *joy*."

[KD-thwart AB-decide CA-present <u>AA-counter</u> ESA-approved PA-joy]

(P m) (Card 1) Once upon a time there was a boy who *liked very much playing* violin, *beautiful*, but he didn't know how to do it. As his grandfather was already too old he could not teach him to play violin. Then the boy grew and learned to play, and became a great violin player.

[PA-esthetic CB-able NDD-unable <u>AA-persist</u>]

(P f) (Card 1) It was in a little house where lived Elisabete, a very poor girl. She would like to go to school but her father couldn't afford the enrollment. A lady decided to pay the enrollment, for she was very sorry for the girl. When she arrived at home her father asked why she was so *cheerful*. She answered that a very rich lady had decided to pay her enrollment. In turn, she should visit her every morning.

[D-goods NDD-unable <u>NDA-active</u> NDB-pity PA-joy RA-duty-o]

(P m) (Card 16) Once upon a time there was a boy who *liked very much* riding a bike. But one day a tragedy happened: he was riding his bike, when a car bumped him. His mother was desperate, for the doctor had said he would never be able to ride a bike again. But with some time he got better, and again he was riding a bike.

[PA-play KD-accident <u>CA-defect</u> NDB-body]

On Card 1, the Afro-Brazilian sample only showed few stories of creative interest. In contrast to the use of Card 2 by others (see chapter 8, volume II) idyllic nature responses were especially apparent in response to Card 2 in this sample.

(AB m) (Card 1) He is *thinking of what he is doing* in making a little house. He is deciding whether he shall make a house, a building, or a church.

[CA-create PA-curious AB-waver]

(AB m) (Card 1) Once upon a time there was a boy who liked to play violin . . . always *enchanted about playing* violin . . . always dreamt of success, of being the best v. player. [no ending]

[PA-curious AB-dream MVA-work]

(AB m) (Card 1) Some time ago there was a boy who *liked very much playing* violin but he had no violin. He thought that the violin was cheap and started saving money. And when he discovered that the violin was very expensive—knew that he couldn't buy it—he became very *sad.* Till one day a rich old man decided to give him a violin . . . *became very happy* and went playing violin down the street.

[PA-play NSD-means PD-sad NDA-reward PA-satisfy]

(AB m) (Card 2) (farm scene) These are many people, *having fun* at the place where they are, *close to nature, field or forest.* Those people worry about the environment very much, and they are so strongly linked to nature that they *suffer deeply* when they see what is happening to the planet.

[PA-play PA-nature KB-crisis PD-suffer]

(AB m) (Card 2) This is the farmer's teacher. Some time ago there was a teacher on a farm which had no classroom. Then they had a meeting and decided that they had to make a classroom for the teacher to give classes. Everybody began to help building the classroom. The teacher became *very happy* and on the first day of classes they made a party. Everybody ate and drank, and the students became *very happy*, for they had got a classroom to study in. And so the teacher could give her pupils classes.

[MTA-task NDA-social HA-rite PA-joy PA-satisfy NDA-advice]

(AB f) (Card 3BM) Janaina, along with her *deep sorrow*, sat on the floor with her head leaning against the sofa. She was crying because her parents quarreled too much, because they were poor and couldn't afford her studies. Janaina stood up, wiped her tears and asked her parents to stop quarreling. They sat together in the living room in order to hear what Janaina had decided: "Dad, Mom, I have thought a lot and made a decision. I am 14 and in spite of everything I can read and write. So I decided to work." Her parents became happy for her having made this decision. Finally all of them *became happy.*

[PD-sad HC-discord HA-pacify KD-means NDD-unable RA-duty-o PA-joy]

(AB m) (Card 16) It is a person. Today she is planting a tree. This tree has grown and she is *happily picking the fruits* today.

[AA-self PA-satisfy PA-nature]

(AB f) (Card 16) On a certain day, a very beautiful and healthy girl was born. While growing up, she was a very *cheerful and happy* child. When she was 16, she heard her father and her mother saying that she had only two more years of life. She became very *sad* and stopped being that cheerful, happy girl. Her life, for her, had finished at that very moment. She didn't want to talk to anyone, and she also didn't want to go out to the street. She only wanted to weep and to become angry with everybody. After one year, she decided to go to a doctor in order to make a check-up. She found out that she wouldn't die anymore, and with that news she became cheerful again.

[PA-joy KD-ill PD-sad FC-flee PC-anger KA-recover]

Italian-Brazilians have a variety of positive pleasurable themes. Many are around work and family roles:

(I f) (Card 2) There is a person working, plowing the soil; the horse is pulling the plow. There is another person who is thinking, looking out somewhere. There is a girl who is going to school, or who is going to study at a friend's. This person who is plowing thinks this will be a nice kitchen garden to cultivate. The woman is thinking that someday she will go to that place. The girl is studying and, to be somebody, goes to take liturgy at the Church. They will try to get what they want. She will graduate. She will go to that place. He will be lucky. The man who cultivates the kitchen garden is central. The three people are making what they want to do. They *take pleasure in good order.*

[HA-family RA-work KA-luck PA-order AA-self]

(I f) (Card 16) There was in the sky a *beautiful white bird*. It was flying *happily*. But it was suddenly shot by a hunter, and it fell and fell until it came to the ground. It was very hurt. The hunter didn't find it. There was a happy boy who was walking until he found the pigeon. As he felt sorry for her, he decided to take her home and bandage her. Many days passed, and the pigeon began to fly again.

[PA-esthetic PA-joy HC-cruel HD-hurt NDB-pity NDA-charity]

Inactive or Unresolved Issues (PB)

In our sample of Brazilian-Japanese there are several expressions on Card 1 of being tired or feeling dislike about playing the violin related to being obliged to practice by parental pressure. In the other groups enforced obligation to study is inferentially due to school authority, not parents.

(J f) (Card 1) Wants to study the violin by himself and is writing a song, but done it so many times, getting tired.

[AA-self PA create PB-tired]

(J m) (Card 1) Child is practicing the violin and is learning how to play, but is *bored*. Can't play well although he has practiced, therefore bored. Attitude is expressed in the position of his hands.

[AA-persist PB-bored CB-difficult]

(J f) (Card 1) He *does not like* the violin, but will play it. By his manner, children act like this, they do not have lots of persistence. He has difficulties now, but will eventually be able to play. His parents will force him to do so.

[PB-dislike AD-endure RA-duty-o DSA-family CA-future]

(J f) (Card 1) He is thinking whether he should study or not, but is with doubt. He *doesn't like* anything like this, but he is obliged to do this, to wait, because of his parents. He will quit the violin in the future.

[AB-waver PB-dislike RA-duty-o DSA-family AD-withdraw]

(J f) (Card 1) Thinking and troubled . . . can't think of a solution. So he decided to play the violin for relief.

[PB-trouble CD-finish PA-relief]

(J f) (Card 1) Someone has just come in. I wonder who it is.

[PB-surprised]

In the Portuguese stories no direct parental pressure was mentioned, simply a dislike of studying or dislike of the violin:

(BP m) (Card 1) *Ambivalent about having fun* or being studious. He dutifully studies and finishes school.

[AB-waver PB-torn RA-duty-s AA-persist]

(BP m) (Card 1) *Tired*. Doesn't manage to do his homework. Has to work, forgets homework, loses grade.

[PB-tired RD-work RA-work DDA-punish]

(BP m) (Card 1) Given a violin for birthday. He *didn't like it much*. Then he decided to take violin classes and now is a violinist.

[NDA-reward PB-dislike AA-persist]

By two Italian-Brazilians questionable motives, or a feeling of discontent or ennui:

(I f) (Card 1) The boy is studying because he needs to get a good grade, but he does not feel like studying, he is *sleepy*. He did not study and he won't do well at the test. He thinks that it is a notebook or a violin. He feels bad about it because he wanted to do well, but he was sleepy because he had to help his father and didn't sleep at night.

[ESA-approve AD-motive PB-tired RD-work RB-regret RA-duty-o]

(I m) (Card 6BM) A 52-year-old lady found out that *her son used drugs. She told him to get out of her house.* He said he wouldn't do it anymore. He finally went to a clinic specialized in drug addicts. He used drugs because he was *discontented with the world.*

[RC-abuse FC-reject RA-reform PB-dislike]

By Afro-Brazilians:

(AB f) (Card 1) Once upon a time there was a boy called Rafael who had violin classes on Mondays, Wednesdays, and Fridays, but he didn't like the classes very much, for they were too *boring*.

[PB-bored AD-motive]

(AB f) (Card 6BM) He is sad about wife's death. Neither he nor his mother knew how to tell his children the truth. Very *nervous*, he asked mother for advice. Mother, also nervous, was standing near window asked him to calm down and to keep cool: "When your children arrive we will tell them."

[KD-death FD-fate PB-trouble NSA advice NDA-teach]

Negative-Active Pleasure (PC)

Few such stories appeared in any of the Brazilian groups. There are three stories of acting on or thinking about suicide on Card 3 given by Japanese-Brazilians. They do not appear in other Brazilians:

(J f) (Card 3BM) In a room, a girl was crying. No one knows why. There is one side of her that is trying to *commit suicide* but she could not completely succumb to this side of herself, but there was always this threat. She used to *try to cut her wrists.*

[PD-sorrow PC-suicide CB-decide]

(J m) (Card 3BM) The girl is like a person carrying a rock. She feels that she is like a rock—hard. She feels she *can end her life* here—that life will end like a rock. But she feels that things can't be this way. Therefore, she is *crying*.

[PC-suicide PD-suffer CB-decide]

(J f) (Card 3BM) A woman is in desperation because she drank too much. She is maladjusted and very *depressed* after fighting with her parents. She has started drinking and has arrived in this state and is currently *thinking about suicide*.

[RC-abuse HC-discord PD-depress PC-suicide]

There is only one story of cruelty given by a Portuguese youth. Note that it is scored as an HC story, not PC, because there is no expression of taking pleasure in the cruelty. Such an expression would have been needed to code this within the PC-cruel category. Instead this is a story of personal sacrifice by the maid to maintain harmony.

> (P m) (Card 3BM) A boss, a very bad man, had a very good maid. Once asked to bring coffee, but coffee warmed over . . . boss threw it on her face. She was so kind remained still. He swore badly at her and sent her away. The maid no place to go, no clothes. The boss then felt sorry for her, called her to the living room and said: "Never more over-warmed coffee, for I only drink fresh-made coffee." The maid was very *happy* and everything remained at peace.
>
> [DDC-exploit HC-injury HC-cruel HA-sacrifice NSB-means NDB-pity PA-happy HC-pacify]

An internal state of anger is expressed by an Italian youth:

> (BI f) (Card 1) It must be a boy studying; his face looks somewhat *angry*; he must be thinking. He is alone. The boy is *mad* because he can't learn. Before he was playing. He must be about 12 years old. He is studying for the test. He takes the test on the following day and does it badly.
>
> [CD-chagrin PC-anger CD-failure]

Negative-Passive Affective States (PD)

Note that the contexts for sadness differ. In the Japanese there is sadness due to discord or failure. In others it varies from failure, to imminent parting, or sadness about death. But sadness is also caused by a sense of deprivation in several of the favela stories. (There are also themes of some kind loss or breakage of an object. The latter is especially apparent in Afro-Brazilians, who are most concerned with economic deprivation throughout their TAT responses.)

> (J m) (Card 6BM) He appears *sad* at this moment. He is apparently with his mother. They are sad about something that occurred in the family. He is sadder than she. The problem is with him. He lost his job or has trouble with some woman. The problem is some factor with him, not only about family problems.
>
> [PD-sad CC-failure]

> (J m) (Card 6BM) The son did something wrong. There is a difference between them and the mother has become *sad and upset*.
>
> [RC-wrong HC-discord PD-sad]

(J f) (Card 6BM) This is the *obasan* (lady/aunt) and a grandson. There is a fight going on. The youth said something to the obasan and she is with a *sad* face or there is something sad going on. Someone has died.

[HC-discord PD-sad KD-death]

Potential failure appears as a theme given by a few Portuguese-Brazilians:

(P f) (Card 1) . . . Fair, small, thin boy, *sad* expression, wanted to learn to play instrument at home, but couldn't afford a single lesson. Decided to work and got a job. What he earned wasn't enough. Finally dutifully worked for teacher in exchange for lessons. Succeeds.

[OB-body PD-sad KD-means AA-counter RA-work]

(P m) (Card 1) *Sad* because he couldn't play well . . . difficult. Wants to quit; it is now packed for selling . . . boy looks for another instrument, easier to play. If one day he wants to learn violin he will make it.

[PD-sad CB-difficult AB-torn AB-waver]

(P f) (Card 1) . . . given violin. As present. But doesn't know how. Will have to take lessons. But remains *sad* because he can't learn.

[NSA-reward CC-failure PD-sad]

(P m) (Card 1) The sad boy is reading; *depressed.*

[PD-depress]

Sadness can be about family dissension or illness, a theme appearing on several of the cards among Favela youth:

(P f) (Card 1) Parents are separating; *miserable*, isn't able to concentrate.

[FC-gone PD-suffer CD-begin]

By an Italian-Brazilian sadness is in the context of failure:

(I f) (Card 1) It is a boy, *sad* for not knowing to do something; he keeps thinking of what to do. He was trying to make a task. He isn't able to do it.

[PD-sad CD-failure]

By a German-Brazilian, family discord is the direct issue:

(G m) (Card 6BM) A son telling his mother a sad story, and she became *sad* too. The mother is looking out of the window, and he looks to the ground as he tells story. The son tells the story that he wants to leave. He can't stay home any longer. And he leaves. Indeed, he is so determined. He leaves because of family quarrels.

[PD-sad FD-split HC-discord]

Note the numerous expressions of deprivation and incapacity related to sadness among the Afro-Brazilians in response to Card 1 (see chapter 8, volume II):

> (AB f) (Card 1) *Sad.* Liked playing. Violin got broken. Parents no money. Spent hours fondling it. Father felt sorry. Took extra work for repair wanted to see son smiling and playing again. Father had it repaired. Boy improved. Becoming great violinist.
>
> [PD-sad OD-broke NDD-means NDA-devote CA-improve AA-persist]

> (AB f) (Card 1) *Sad*, looking at his violin. He can't play. I think he wants to, but he can't.
>
> [PD-sad CD-begin]

> (AB m) (Card 1) Some time ago there was a boy who liked very much playing violin but he had no violin. He thought that the violin was cheap and started saving money. And when he discovered that the violin was very expensive—knew that he couldn't buy it—he became very *sad.* Till one day a rich old man decided to give him a violin. Became very happy and went playing violin down the street.
>
> [PA-esthetic NSD-means PD-sad NDA-reward PA-comfort]

> (AB m) (Card 1) There is a boy seated. He was thinking of a violin that he would get. Then, he would not be given the violin anymore; he became very sad and in the end he wasn't given the violin.
>
> [PD-sad OB-want NSD-means]

> (AB m) (Card 1) The boy is thinking and staring, staring, staring in order to understand what was inside his imagination and that is now appearing before him. He looked in order to understand what it was, the strange object which he wasn't able to decipher. He thought, thought, and understood that this strange object was his *depression* materializing itself.
>
> [CB-difficult PD-depress]

> (AB f) (Card 1) Marcelo was a *very sad* boy; he had neither friends to play with, nor brothers or sisters. He was alone. But one day Marcelo intended to study and made his mother put him in the school. Marcelo began to study. He learned new things so that he can teach them to other people. Now Marcelo wants to leave school, for he thinks he already knows everything, but deep inside he knows nothing. This is Marcelo's story.
>
> [PD-sad FB-alone AA-nurture CB-able AD-withdraw]

> (AB m) (Card 1) He quarreled with his parents, then he became *sad* and went to his room in order to think. Then he thought and decided to talk to his parents.
>
> [HC-discord PD-sad FA-mend]

Canadian and Venezuelan Comparisons: Positive States (PA)

Venezuelan youth and Canadian college students were compared in another study, specifically comparing responses to Card 6BM, depicting an older woman and younger man (see chapter 11, volume II). Only two responses directly attending to themes explicitly describing positive pleasure were elicited from the Venezuelan youth, none from Canadians. In one, autonomy in marriage leads to happiness, but the bride dies. Another stresses both sadness and happy memories.

> (V f) (Card 6BM) This is a fellow that was studying in the military academy. He graduates with honors and comes back home. Tells his mother how happy he is, and mother was also happy until he tells her that he is going to marry. His mother asks if she has a social position, if she has money. He says that no but that it doesn't matter to him. She gets angry and says that she is not going to let that wedding happen, that they have a social position to respect. He says no. At the end mother accepts and he marries and well . . . *they live happy* until the muchacha dies.
>
> [AA-self CA-present EDC-status HC-discord <u>DSA-free</u> PA-joy KD-death]

> (V m) (Card 6BM) I see sadness in both personages. Maybe it is the death of a relative. The women is asking God peace for her relative who died. He looks at the body of a man, maybe his father, and *remembers happy memories*. He knows that he has to be resigned. She also remembers how both saw their children growing up, and that he is now better that he is with God. They both go ahead with a positive mind.
>
> [PD-sad KD death NSA-pray PA-memory <u>KA-accept</u> PA-relief <u>NSA-god</u> KB-hope]

The Canadians on several cards depicted the necessity for practicing endurance as a coping attitude to be used in facing life alone. Emphasis is sometimes on a capacity to endure, even without depicting any satisfaction in the process. Some other stories depict the negative feelings of the isolated older person:

> (C f) (Card 6BM) It is not a sure relationship between two. Bad news. It is an aunt, not a mother and a son because they don't look close enough. She is trying to deal with the situation by staring out, getting peace from scenery. He doesn't know what to do . . . yet he is still being respectful. He is also *deeply hurt* by news of the death. She leans on a chair and stares out. He will go for long walk. He has aggression *and energy inside that has to get out.* [seeking catharsis]
>
> [KD-death <u>FB-distant</u> PA-meditate PB-stress]

> (C m) (Card 6BM) He would like to comfort. There is a strong emotional attachment. He is simply unable to express himself. There is an emotional gap. Uncle passes away. The nephew still cannot reach aunt and he leaves. She *will deal with grief* on her own.
>
> [KD-death NDD-comfort FA-love <u>FB-distant</u> PA-relief]

Inactive or Unresolved Issues (PB)

The Venezuelan and Canadian youth give relatively few stories manifesting unresolved affect in their responses to Card 6BM:

> (V m) (Card 6BM) There was a discussion or *surprise* for he did something unexpected. The present is uncertain. There is *confusion and even pain* by the impression the man gives, by his hand, holding the hat. There may be also anger, and there could be an uncertain future between them, it is for the women to clarify and normalize the situation.
>
> [PB-surprise PB-trouble HC-discord HB-role]

> (V m) (Card 6BM) The mother was *surprised.* She didn't expect it. She cannot believe it. He is telling her he is leaving home because he is going to study somewhere else.
>
> [AA-self PB-surprise FB-split]

> (C m) (Card 6BM) A mother and son. Somebody has died. A son-in-law comes to console. She is looking out, remembering her husband. He doesn't know really what to say. They might talk about the person over a cup of tea. He's *sad* and she's still *in shock.* She carries on the best she can. It is a sort of *denial.*
>
> [KD-death NDA-comfort FB-distant PD-sad PD-shock PB-denial]

Negative-Passive Affective States (PD)

Card 6BM evoked a number of negative-passive stories (PD) from both Venezuelan and Canadian youth.

> (V f) (Card 6BM) He has to leave and both are *sad.* She is consoling him. The son has to go because the decision has already been made, but doesn't want to. At the end, I think they are going to embrace each other and they will understand that the trip is necessary.
>
> [FB-parting PD-sad NDA-comfort FA-love KA-accept]

> (V f) (Card 6BM) News is given to a mother of death by accident. He is concerned for her. It is difficult to face the situation and give hope to this mother. She feels *depressed*, tears, that pain that is carried inside when someone loved dies.
>
> [KD death NDB-pity NDB-unable FD-fate PD-depress]

> (V f) (Card 6BM) Something has happened before. A grandmother. He came to tell her his work problems; he is finished with his sweetheart or crashed the car or someone died in the family. She has a face of susto, in *shock.* He feels sorry to have to tell her. She needs time to recover. He will do anything to help. Someone very close died.
>
> [FA-inform FD-split KD-death PD-shock NDA-active]

(V f) (Card 6BM) Two people preoccupied about someone they have in common, a woman I suppose, that is sick. It is grave. And the women is thinking that it is not possible, that something like that happened to her. And he also preoccupied on how it is going to finish. That she would die soon. They both think on the way to help her so that she doesn't suffer and she is *suffering*. Could be his sweetheart and her daughter.

[KD ill-die MTA-task NDA-comfort PD-suffer]

(V f) (Card 6BM) Something happened before. Bad news. *Cannot believe what happened.* They will embrace after that. They learned something; they lost money in the bank or a relative died.

[KD-misc PD-shock FA-share KD-death OD-loss]

Resignation to fate, or Competence (C) in coping by being capable of enduring is stressed in several Canadian stories (see chapter 11, volume II):

(C m) (Card 6BM) He's come to tell her news. They are not related. He *feels pain* and confused. She's been expecting him. Just a matter of time. He told her that her husband passed away. She was prepared for it. She is *sad* but she will carry on with everything. She's keeping her *grief* inside. She's a tough lady. She knew she was going to lose him and has already accepted it. She'll never get over loss, but it will get easier. And she will keep herself busy.

[PD-sad FD-thought FD-fate KA-accept PA-relief]

(C f) (Card 6BM) He is mourning the loss of his father. The wife is in *denial*, the son is more angry. A rocky relationship in the past but, a turning point. For a short term conclusion, there is no change. If I were to be positive: in the long run they will become closer, not farther apart.

[KD-death PD-sad PB-denial PB-anger HB-split FA-mend]

(C f) (Card 6BM) A mother concerned with her son. He seems to be confessing her something, and mother is *astonished.* She cannot even speak. She is very tense. He is a little far out, far from reality, only remembering his past. I believe his mother will embrace him and forgive him. (He felt the need to tell something to his mother. He is afraid to face her.)

[RA-apology PD-shock PB-trouble NDA-pardon]

(C m) (Card 6BM) A mother and son. Both are *sad.* He did something done wrong. She is rejecting him, turned away ashamed. He broke the law. Trying to please and help. Forged a check to give her money. She will eventually forgive him. He feels very hurt and wants her to accept him again. He will be relieved if she does that. She will but in her deathbed.

[PD-sad RC-illicit FC-reject ESB-shame NDB-means NSA-forgive PA-relief]

Death or suffering is final in several stories:

(C m) (Card 6BM) Her son is working at this place to raise money to go to school or move out of town. He has not told his mom this. . . . Eventually, she finds out, the son was hinting to her. She is disappointed because she thought he would stay and help her out. She was dependent on him, but felt he needed his independence and to go on his own. She knew he wanted to move out and experience life. She becomes jealous of his new decision. She feels she will be isolated and won't cope with life anymore. So she tries to prove that his job now is good and that he knows this town and is familiar with this town. He says: But it's too familiar and he needs more friends and experiences. . . . She still can't believe in his decisions. Thinks he should at last stay for his mom, because he owes it to her for all she's done . . . he doesn't agree with his mom and goes off. The mom is *depressed*, feel there is no hope and no one to lean on, and she ignores attempts by other people to support her. So eventually she lives in isolation and dies of old age and malnourishment.

[AA-persist FB-parting NSB-help FA-sympathy FB-jealous <u>FB-alone</u> NDA-advice PA-curious RB-duty NSD-no-help PD-depress NSC-refuse KD-death]

(C m) (Card 6BM) Mother is elderly and has a terminal illness like cancer. Obviously he is upset and *grief* and that sort of thing. He has never been an emotional kind of guy; maybe is but doesn't show. . . . He didn't show many emotions. He worries about what people will think when she dies. That he might not care. This is a major problem for his whole life. His father was the same and he will pass it on to his kids. Maybe when on his deathbed he will at least understand why his children will not seem too upset.

[KD-ill-die PD-sad <u>FB-shy</u> <u>NDD-comfort</u> ESB-appear KD-defect]

(C m) (Card 6BM) Looks like someone died. The dad died. The mother and son are *mourning*. The funeral just ended. They aren't very close and not talking about it. They both want to get on, do their own thing. They both feel alone. That's about it. Not much exciting happening in this picture.

[KD-death PD-sad FB-distant <u>FB-alone</u>]

(C m) (Card 6BM) A man and his mother. They have visions in completely different directions about their lives. She's *despairing*, and he doesn't know why. There is much space between them. They are not connecting. The scene ends without any emotional interaction that has substance. They'll shake hands when he leaves and then continue on in the same mind-set as before. Both are unwilling to give a little bit to break the detachment.

[PD-depress FB-empathy <u>FB-distant</u> <u>FC-flee</u>]

(C f) (Card 6BM) Both are in shock. Bad news. Mother and son. She told him the bad news. The father has died. They are in *shock*, staring into space. They can't believe it. They are not comforting each other. Each is in own world. He is thinking how to reach out. Should I touch her or hug her? She's spaced out. He turns away and leaves.

[KD-death PD-shock <u>FB-distant</u> FB-aware NDD-comfort]

Illustrative Samples of Scoring in Volume II

Volume II includes chapters that illustrate the use of this scoring system. Throughout chapters in that volume I can find additional examples of material scored with the [P] category.

Notes

Beck, Aaron T. 1967. *Depression: Clinical, Experimental and Theoretical Aspects*. New York: Hoeber.

Berlyne, D.E. 1971. *Aesthetics and Psychobiology*. New York: Appleton-Century-Crofts.

Blass, E.M. and V. Ciaramitaro. 1994. A New Look at Some Old Mechanisms in Human Newborns: Taste and Tactile Determinants of State, Affect, and Action. *Monographs of the Society for Research in Child Development*. Serial No. 239, Vol. 59, No. 1.

Buck, Ross. 1999. The Biological Affects: A Typology. *Psychological Review*, **106**(2): 301–336.

Davidson, Richard J. 1993. Parsing Affective Space: Perspectives from, Neuropsychology and Psychophysiology. *Neuropsychology*, **7**: 464–475.

De Vos, George A. 1997. Heritage of Exploitation: A Brief TAT Report on South Brazilian Youth. In Stanley Renshon and John Duckitt (Eds.), Culture and Cross Cultural Dimensions of Political Psychology. *Political Psychology*, **18**(2): 437–474.

De Vos, George A. and Eun-Young Kim. 1993. Koreans in Japan: Problems with Achievement, Alienation Authority. In Ivan Light and Parminder Bhachu (Eds.), *California Immigrants in World Perspective*. New Brunswick, N.J.: Transaction Books.

Ekman, Paul. 1970. Universal Facial Expressions of Emotion. *California Mental Health Research Digest*, **8**: 151–158.

———. (Ed.). 1973. *Darwin and Facial Expression: A Century of Research in Review*. New York: Academic Press.

Ekman, Paul, Wallace V. Friesen, and Phoebe Ellsworth. 1972. *Emotions in the Human Face*. New York: Pergamon Press.

Fiske, Donald W. and Salvatore R. Maddi (Eds.). 1961. *Functions of Varied Experience*. Homewood, Ill.: Dorsey Press.

Fox, Nathan A. 1994. The Development of Emotion Regulation: Biological and Behavioral Considerations. *Monographs of the Society for Research in Child Development*, **59**(240): 2–3.

Isen, Alice. 1984. Toward Understanding the Role of Affect in Cognition. In Robert S. Wyer Jr. and Thomas K. Srull (Eds.), *Handbook of Social Cognition* (Vol. 3). Hillsdale, N.J.: Lawrence Erbaum Associates.

Jacobs, Jerry. 1971. *Adolescent Suicide*. New York: Wiley.

Lazarus, Richard S. 1991. *Emotion and Adaptation*. New York: Oxford University Press.

Mandler, George. 1984. *Mind and Body: Psychology of Emotion and Stress*. New York: W.W. Norton.

Mason, J.W. 1986a. A Review of Psychoendocrine Research on the Pituitary-Adrenal Cortical System. *Psychosomatic Medicine*, **30**: 576–607.

———. 1986b. A Review of Psychoendocrine Research on the Sympathetic-Adrenal Medullary System. *Psychosomatic Medicine*, **30**: 631–653.

Miller, William I. 1997. *The Anatomy of Disgust*. Cambridge: Harvard University Press.

Plutchik, Robert. 1994. *The Psychology and Biology of Emotion*. New York: HarperCollins.

Schore, Allan N. 1994. *Affect Regulation and the Origin of the Self: The Neurobiology of Emotional Development*. Hillsdale, N.J.: Erlbaum.

Schwartz, Theodore. 1976. The Cargo Cult: A Melanesian Type-Response to Change. In George De Vos (Ed.), *Responses to Change: Society, Culture and Personality*. New York: D. Van Nostrand Company.

Spielberger, Charles David, Richard L. Gorsuch, and R.E. Lushene. 1970. *Manual for the State-Trait Anxiety Inventory*. Palo Alto, Calif.: Consulting Psychologists Press.

Sroufe, L. Alan. 1984. The Organization of Emotional Development. In Klaus R. Scherer and Paul Ekman (Eds.), *Approaches to Emotion* (pp. 109–128). Hillsdale, N.J.: Erlbaum.

Stein, Nancy L., Bennett Leventhal, and Tom Trabasso (Eds.). 1990. *Psychological and Biological Approaches to Emotion*. Hillsdale, N.J.: Erlbaum.

Thomas, William I. and Florian Znaniecki. 1927. *The Polish Peasant in Europe and America*. Edited by Eli Zaretsky, 1984. Urbana, Ill.: University of Illinois Press.

Tucker, Don M. and Peter A. Williamson. 1984. Asymmetric Neural Control Systems in Human Self-Regulation. *Psychological Review*, **91**: 185–215.

White, R.W. 1959. Motivation Reconsidered: The Concept of Competence. *Psychological Review*, **66**: 297–333.

Chapter 4

Motives to Give, Succor, and Protect: The Fulfillment of Insufficiency and Dependency

Vertical Attachments: The Child as Recipient— The Adult as Giver

The first substantial human relationships (developmentally speaking) involve dyadic interactions between the infant and its mother and/or one or more primary caregivers. Later in life, forms of dyadic closeness can include various forms of intimacy and interrelatedness between any two people. Intense positive feelings associated with this type of intimacy form the basis of feelings that we often characterize as "love," "affection," "fondness," etc. These terms refer to aspects of the continuing attachment that commonly develop between human beings who share intimate time (Hazan and Shaver, 1987). Some aspects of these intimate relationships are primarily "affiliative" and emphasize a feeling of communicative closeness. These aspects of relationship involve mutuality and reciprocity, and can be seen as being horizontal in respect to social status. In contrast, there are aspects of relationship that emphasize the provision or receipt of nurturance, succor, and/or security and protection. These aspects of relationship can be characterized as non-reciprocal and vertical, wherein individuals are either donors or recipients and in differential status positions relative to each other. In regards to these aspects of a relationship, each individual may be either fulfilling or frustrating the donor or recipient efforts of the other.

It is helpful to distinguish these components of interpersonal attachment, and we consider them separately with our category system. In the following chapter on

Affiliation (A), we discuss aspects of relationship that grow out of early experiences of mammalian closeness and communication and the mutual sharing of warmth and interpersonal contact. These aspects of relationship are later expressed as concerns with friendship, peer, or group affiliation; the intimacies of adult sexual and reproductive behavior; and, various forms of contact and communication in social institutional relationships, including family and community. In contrast, the present chapter covers those aspects of relationship that are asymmetrical, and involve non-reciprocal giving and receiving. As we shall presently discuss, there is a variety of concerns related to efforts to give and receive that we score within the Nurturance (N) category.

The human infant initially exists in a condition of complete dependency and must rely on the succoring and protective components of parenting behavior for its survival. Although the phenomenology of the infantile experience of dependency may or may not be readily accessible to us as memories or inferential reconstructions later in life, it is very likely that among the first conscious experiences of selfhood are those of dependent needs, and either the frustration of fulfillment of those needs. Whatever the subjective experience might initially be, the developing self of the helpless infant must integrate the internal experiences of insufficiency or satisfaction that come to be more or less resolved in a dependent relationship with an external other.

Through experiences of receiving succor or nurture from outside beings, there develops in human consciousness an inner sense of fulfillment and security. Primary forms of attachment and relative security are well discussed in the writings and research findings of Bowlby, Ainsworth, and colleagues (e.g., Ainsworth, Blehar, Waters, and Wall, 1978; Bowlby, 1969; Anisfeld, Casper, Nozyce, and Cunningham, 1990). A sense of basic trust in an outside other is built up out of such early experiences. An experience of having one's needs satisfied leads to an optimism about potential future gratification, and a capacity to sustain oneself with future hope and trust that one will be eventually satisfied (Erikson, 1963).

What is less often discussed is the fact that to give to others is also a basic human pattern. There are biopsychological or neuroendocrine bases for the patterns of behavior that ensure some continuity of the species through an internal evocation of what is recognized as parental behavior (including both maternal and paternal behavior) such as nurturing, succoring, instructing, and various forms of protective behavior.[1] From the parent's side, to provide nurturance and protection to a dependent child may be as much an imperative as is the need to receive, from the side of the child. However much these patterns are inherent in our mammalian nature, among humans such behavior depends heavily on learning and on the transgenerational transmission of patterns of neuro-behavioral organization. These

[1]See the volume on mammalian parenting by Krasnegor and Bridges (1990). Hormonal mechanisms have also been found to be involved in dominance behavior, as we shall discuss later, in the context of instrumental or purposeful behavior.

begin in utero, as the mother's psychophysiological systems transplacentally mediate the neurological organization of the fetal brain. The process continues postnatally, as the infant participates in the give and take of affect-regulatory communication with caregivers. It continues through childhood and perhaps throughout life, as parenting is increasingly directed toward equipping the child to function adequately in the outside world, through advice and educational facilitation.

Eventually, and to varying degrees of success in different individuals, the child begins to more or less autonomously regulate its physiological and behavioral systems, such that it can directly fulfill its own needs, and secure its own safety to a substantial degree.

Giving and Receiving

Giving becomes as much a human need as does a continuing sense of dependency on others. Through social experiences, the complementary roles of giving and receiving are both incorporated into internal representations of role relationships. Through some combination of the activation of built-in, species-wide behavioral programs, and the internalization of cultural scripts that frame interpersonal behavior, the child who has received becomes the adult who is capable of giving. The relatively satisfied recipient of parental nurturance also increasingly develops a capacity for bestowal upon another. This process is practiced in various ways.

The developing need to give or care for others can be sometimes witnessed in the relatively early play of children (Murphy, 1937). They can, and do express active nurture of others. For example, culturally derived scripts can be seen as they are acted out in fantasy play and in pragmatic uses of language. The child who instrumentally directs scripted instructions or commands toward an action figure is practicing an externalization of the inner-directed speech by which it is learning to regulate its own behavior. The child playing with a doll may expressively experience the joy of vicariously receiving what the child itself is bestowing on the toy as a self-surrogate. Caring for pets may also serve as opportunities to practice these skills. Through this kind of solitary play, and also in scripted play with other children, the child practices both giving and receiving, a simultaneous ownership of both aspects of relationship.

What was initially internalized in the context of a dependent role becomes externalized, such that the giving and receiving roles are reversed. Ultimately, the human being becomes capable of taking either side of the complementary roles. These skills become essential if the former child is to become the successful parent. Gender roles pertaining to nurturance are also developed through this type of process. Although an active capacity to care for or succor others is developed in both males and females, the role behavior through which it is to be satisfied may become defined differently via socially-constructed, gender-specific role expectations.[2]

Impulses that lead us to nurture or protect our offspring may also be recruited into broader social contexts. Economic or material support of the needy or any general "humanitarian" protection of the weak or the handicapped, or the protection of animals, is an extension of this succoring need beyond the immediate family or social group. Those who have, in the past, received nurture can readily experience compassionate identity with others who are dependent. This may also be indicated by experiences of compassionate sensitivity to the needs of those over whom one maintains some power or responsibility. Indeed one often finds that the impulse to bestow upon or succor others is only one component of interactions that involve disparate positions of relative adequacy and power. If they are positively structured, active donor participants in such interactions may feel "good" about their concern for others. The converse, passive or receptive positions in such vertical relationships, may also be experienced positively, as a sense of gratification felt while receiving care.

The early experience of a recipient position is one origin of vertical interpersonal status differentiation that is experienced in many ways throughout social life. Subordinate social status can be experienced by the individual as a positive source of being protected and nurtured, provided that the individual remains deferential and fulfills the expectations or directives of the superior. The previous rewarding of "proper," expected behavior in a recipient role becomes a powerful source of social regulation. A legacy of social belief or a personal fantasy of a caring superior remains, whatever the reality may be.[3] As noted by de Grazia, in *The Political Community* (1948), the Roman coinage bearing the face of Augustus bore also the slogan of his "plenty" and his assuring promise of continuous abundance.

Seen from this perspective, the acceptance of forms of social exploitation by subordinates can be readily understood as the persistence of a positively experienced anticipation of satisfaction in a dependent social role.[4] In an adult, a need to

---

[2]The extent to which hormonally regulated and developmentally organized neurobehavioral patterns interact with social experiences to produce differences between "maternal" and "paternal" behavior in males and females is not clear in humans. What cannot be disputed is that there are clear sex differences in parenting behavior in many species (Krasnegor and Bridges, 1990), even those that lack culture and lack the human history of sexist socialization patterns. Explanations for gender differences in human parenting behavior must consider the contributory if not entirely deterministic contribution of neurobehavioral differences between male and female humans.

[3]See especially further discussion of dependency in the Japanese context in De Vos (1984) and Caudill and Weinstein (1969).

[4]Such expectations might seem incomprehensible or be seen as evidence of "false consciousness" from a "rational" instrumental Marxist or other western sociological perspective.

feel gratitude for being taken care of becomes a continuance of the expressive experiences of childhood.

Often such positive images of subservient roles appear in the collective representations of a culture, and may comprise a substantial component of a religious system as it defines the relationship of the individual with a superior supernatural force (Firth, 1940). Depending on the religious tradition of one's society, gratitude can be perceived as involved in a personal relation with a deity who is pictured as all-giving, caring, and protective. A physical sense of hunger that has become increasingly mental as well as physical in nature, may be assuaged by such a benevolent outer presence.[5] Clearly some religious experiences can be discussed in this light, and we note in more detail in chapter 14, volume I, how inner insecurity can be assuaged by assurances of succoring protection by a caring, enveloping, supernatural force.

Gratitude can also be engendered as a component of other types of religious experience, perhaps less superstitious in nature. For example, incipient feelings of gratitude for having been given to can be aroused and themselves requited by loving others. In the Tibetan Buddhist system of mind training there is evocation of a sense of profound gratitude toward all sentient beings (each of whom are seen as having been one's own mother, at one time or another over the course of beginningless time). This evocation is one step toward the development of Bodhicitta, or a profound and compelling compassion for all sentient beings. It enables compassion to be strengthened on the basis of reciprocity for past recipient experiences.[6]

The Tibetans also have a practice known as "exchanging self for others," in which the practitioner substitutes himself or herself into the situation of others, taking on the suffering of others, and giving his or her own happiness to others as an exchange. While, for the Buddhist practitioner, this may usually be primarily a mental exercise, it may also function to prepare the individual with habit patterns that reduce self-cherishing behavior and facilitate compassion in real-life situations. For the westerner, perhaps the most famous example of this practice is Christ's sacrifice of his own body, his willingness to give his own life as a substitute for the

---

[5]This idea that the satisfaction of basic needs serves as a basis for the satisfaction of transcendent or "meta" needs is addressed by Maslow (1955, 1962). Maslow postulated two basic motivations: a growth motivation (and associated B-cognition) that pertain to the satisfaction of higher or transcendent needs, and a deficit motivation (and associated D-cognition) that pertain to deficiencies including dependency needs. We differ somewhat from Maslow in that we see at least some of the transcendent needs to reflect continuities of basic needs, albeit in sublimated forms, perhaps serving loftier, or, one might even say more affluent goals that are economically enabled by the satisfaction of more fundamental needs. At least some of the "meta" needs may reflect continuities of more basic needs. We also differ from Maslow in how we stress the distinction between instrumental and expressive needs.

[6]See Geshe Kelsang Gyatso's commentary on Shantideva's Bodhisattvacharyavatara (Gyatso, 1994), specifically pages 256–264, which describe prescribed meditations on the equality of self and others, and pages 264–273, on the exchange of self for others.

sins of others. There are analogous stories of self-sacrifice to be found in the Jataka stories of the previous lives of the Buddha (Cowell, 1990).

For the sincere Christian practitioner, meditations on Christ as the sacrificial lamb can engender a sense of profound gratitude that becomes an obligation to follow in Christ's footsteps. A newly awakened capacity to experience gratitude for receiving Christ's love, as symbolized by his sacrifice, is often basic to a religious conversion experience in some forms of Christianity. The need to care for others can become self-sacrificial in some circumstances, and a self-sacrificing saintly role can be found occasionally among some religiously inclined individuals, but very rarely elsewhere. We respect a Mother Teresa, but do not anticipate such behavior as part of an ordinary family role or business relationship. Her reason for her own dedicated behavior was the religious image of a self-sacrificing Christ. Whether in the course of repaying such a debt the Christian follows Christ's example as a symbolic act of generosity, or as a symbolic act of self-destructive martyrdom, may depend on various other aspects of the individual's social, cultural, psychological, and spiritual development.

Insufficient Nurture: Its Consequence

Developmentally, healthy individuals reach a sufficient level of social maturity to become donors. However, insufficient early dependent gratification, and unresolved dependent needs, may produce chronic or acute "personality problems" that may interfere with such a progression. If one does not have sufficient experience of receiving it is most difficult to become a giver to others. More subtly, socialization patterns that produce such insufficiencies may also contribute to the prevalence of particular personality configurations one finds more or less prevalent in given societies. Work with juvenile delinquents has revealed that a sense of material want or resentment about supposed or actual economic deprivation is not related simply to actual poverty, but also to an emotionally deprived childhood. In some, as a consequence of neglect and deprivation, there is no guilt or compunction about "taking" from others. A sense of inner deprivation is sometimes externalized as part of a general sense of injustice experienced as living in an ungiving, unheeding world.

In a dyadic relationship, the dependent and helpless child must seek gratification through the expected responses of a significant other on whom the child is dependent. Yet this "other" is a separate person with his/her own motivation, and thus may thwart wishes, or in some instances, deliberately withhold gratification from a child. This pattern of dependent need and withholding may continue as an element of adult relationships as well.

In both children and adults, an ungovernable inner sense of rage can become the active reaction to an acute sense of personal helplessness that is felt when dependent needs are not met. This may remain as an underlying unconscious frustration, which may become expressed as an aggressive or destructive act directed toward the person or group on whom one is dependent. By a "show" of rage or making a histrionic display in response to an impasse or frustration, one might hope to induce acquiescence, or somehow positively activate the person who is the source of frustration.

In both adults and children, there are instances wherein one may be incapable of expressing rage outwardly, or one may not dare attack directly the object of a felt frustration since one remains heavily dependent on that particular person or social group as a source of potential gratification. The ego defends against the possibility of harming the source of dependent gratification by redirecting or deflecting anger (Horney, 1937). In children, a destructive "tantrum" can be deflected back onto the child's own body, as the child throws the body against the floor, walls, or furniture, even to the extent of inducing pain and injury. Adults may engage in similar self-destructive behavior, including dangerous driving, substance abuse, etc.

In studying suicide in Japan we found several examples of acutely experienced outbreaks of self-directed anger. Such anger can result when there is an acute social rupture experienced by one who is totally invested in, and thereby dependent upon, a given professional or social role (De Vos, 1968, see also chapter 14, volume I). In general, for Japanese, there may be recourse to surrogate objects in an attempt to assuage one's sense of continuing dependent needs,[7] or if rage is aroused,[8] there can be recourse either to an available, vulnerable outside scapegoat, or one's physical, bodily self as an object.

The ego's effort to contain or redirect anger is not always successful. Rage may sometimes be directed toward the source of gratification, which may be followed by experiences of deep remorse and anxiety over the potential termination of nurturance. In children, this can involve physically striking the parent, or in extreme cases can involve the killing of a parent. Similarly, in situations of spousal abuse, the perpetrator may be acting on an experience of extreme dependency and helplessness. In such situations, the abuser may nevertheless engage in behavior that harms or even kills the loved one.

The redirection of helpless anger may not result directly in violence. For example, there are passive forms of isolation and withdrawal resulting from a sense of frustrated dependent need found in some Irish adults. Nancy Scheper-Hughes (1979) in her volume, and in chapter 1,volume II, discusses such resultant behavior in considering a form of emotional withholding experienced by some Irish youth that relates to a relatively high incidence of mental illness in rural Ireland. In the next section of this chapter, we will discuss how a pattern of neglect contributes to the idealization of independence that characterizes the American cultural landscape.

---

[7]See Harlow (1973) and Kramer (1992) on dependency surrogates.

[8]Bowlby (1973) discusses early childhood rage at separation, and problems with reunification.

Idealizations of Independence

Humans as social animals cannot forego some continuing forms of group or individual dependency. Children often remain dependently linked with their adult guardians (or, in the case of street-orphans, with a provisory adult society) in vertical, dependent relationships through childhood and into adult life. The life-course patterns exhibited by this continuation of dependent expectancies into adulthood differs markedly from one society to the next, and one family to the next. Nevertheless, dependency remains universal as a common and often powerful human concern. Such concerns persist, either overtly or covertly, into adulthood in all cultures. Dependency and autonomy are never completely absent from the conscious concerns of many people.

Dependency or nurture is often a generational issue. In many societies the experience of being grateful or expectations of receiving the gratitude of others are age graded. Gratitude for past favors received can either be redirected toward one's own children or returned toward the more aged by succoring and caring for elders such as parents or mentors, whether or not they are in actual need. In some situations, these age-graded expectations may lead to gratitude that is institutionally exhibited even where not genuinely experienced internally.

Societies differ as to how dependent interaction may be consciously viewed positively, negatively, or with ambivalence. Some cultures, more than others, emphasize increasing independence, autonomy, or even detachment as more appropriate to status as an adult. In some contexts, the movement toward autonomy can be reflected in acts of resistance or rebellion that can even be seen positively. Or, they can be found as functional independence that nevertheless remains compliant with adult advice. Varying combinations of these can be found, depending on the overall functioning of the family system, as well as social norms incorporated into the family system from the expanding social world of the child.

For example, there are considerable differences among Japanese, Korean, and American cultures in how dependency issues are expressed or communicated in the context of unequal status relationships (e.g., see Lee and De Vos, 1981). A belief in a caring God is a continuance of a dependent personal relationship in many seemingly socially and personally "independent" European entrepreneurs. A dependent belief in God is not usually examined as part of their "Protestant ethic" in an American Psychology, any more than is a deep belief in an interdependent family examined as it influences Asian businessmen.

American Psychology, with its individualistic instrumental emphasis, has contributed relatively few studies of any adult human need to give, to protect, to provide *security for other adults*. Nor are continuing adult concerns with gratitude or repayment for receiving succor or nurture given much systematic study. There is an uneasiness about considering "altruism" as a human trait. The emphasis in social psychology, for example, has been on group processes in an *instrumental* framework concerned with decision making, attitude change, or organizational behavior, etc. With this instrumental focus the emphasis has been on numerous studies of instrumental power or relative influence, and the various forms of vertical needs related to dominance, control, etc. Expressive experiences about emotions governing nurture among adults has received less direct attention.

In the motivational studies of McClelland and his associates, no attention has been paid to the entire category of vertical nurturant behavior or feelings of gratitude (McClelland, 1987; McClelland, Atkinson, Clark, and Lowelle, 1953). "Expressive" behavior has only been studied by them in an overall *horizontal* context of "affiliative" needs. Vertical relationships were only studied in terms of instrumental concern with the relative instrumental exercise of "power." Their instrumental concept of "need-achievement" was related to a perceived positive transcendence of childhood dependent needs, fostered by parents as part of "independence training."

In American developmental psychology, generally, there is an explicit value put on independence as a stage superseding childhood dependency. Even an early provision of emotional security, without any direct intention to produce independence, is seen as eventuating into forms of secular self reliance that are evaluated as superior to any form of continuing vertical interdependence among adults (Bowlby, 1940, 1952). Only where relationships are defined in a form of horizontal reciprocity are any interdependent needs depicted positively. For example, the positive resolution of Erikson's stage of intimacy versus isolation (1963) requires the attainment of an equal mutuality among peers (see our next chapter on affiliation (F)).

In Japanese culture by contrast, there are not such "problems" over continuing dependency in adults. Concern about nurturing continues to be consciously expressed positively in lifelong extensions of vertically conceived family-like relationships, very often as an aspect of age-graded roles extending even to the workplace. Certain forms of continuing social dependency may be viewed very positively in such a hierarchical culture (Doi, 1973; De Vos, 1975, 1993; Vogel and Vogel, 1961).

Yet we should note that the independence of the American ideal is not so well realized, in actuality. In complex modern societies, even the fully mature secular adult remains relatively helpless and mystified in the face of technology that is beyond the skills of the lay person. Most of us do not independently obtain cooking and heating fuel; build, repair, or manufacture spare parts for the technological/material objects we use on a day-to-day basis. Even the internal combustion engine, a technology that has been with us for several generations, is beyond the comprehension and mechanical skills of most Americans. In this way, the modern world is very different from our ancestral past. Aware of this limitation to autonomy, some individuals may attempt to "live off the land," or at least periodically attempt some form of wilderness experience, or "extreme" experiences, where one's life is entirely in one's own hands. The benefits of this type of experience for adolescents is recognized by programs such as "Outward Bound," which helps young people make the transition into the self-reliance-based, self-confidence that is expected of the idealized adult.[9] These kinds of efforts may be seen as attempts to establish or recover an idealized sense of instrumental competence in what has become an increasingly interdependent and perhaps, for some, an unacceptably dependent modern American adult lifestyle.

The reality of this dependency is perhaps best illustrated by the fear with which some Americans anticipated the millennium and the potential danger that the "Y2K" bug might produce a collapse of the technological infrastructure. Such concern over the potential failure of the infrastructure and the security it provides, if even it were to last for only a few hours or days, was a clear expression of our virtually complete technological dependency.

Perhaps at the core of this is a conflation of autonomy and independence, and a conflation of dependency and affiliation. Actual dependency needs for succor and protection may be a small portion of the social interactions that we commonly call dependency. Essential mammalian emotional needs for comfort, tenderness, intimacy, and closeness (and the converse needs to comfort others, etc.) are essentially affiliative needs. Yet they are often closely linked to dependency needs for succor and protection such that they become symbolically and behaviorally associated. Additionally, limited personal competencies make us instrumentally reliant on others, even where we may be functionally autonomous in the sense of having the internal means for self-regulation. For some people, an experience of needing others (whether for comfort or for instrumental assistance) and the feeling that others need them, is experienced as a threat to a sense of autonomy. Through seeking to maintain or strengthen autonomy, they may do themselves a disservice by denying the satisfaction of legitimate human needs for affiliative closeness and dependent security or the gratification that comes from an expressive act of giving to others.

Because dependency developmentally begins as a state of helplessness, any form of human need for others that are symbolically associated with dependency feelings may reactivate unconscious experiences of diffuse helplessness. A fear of this helplessness may underlie the idealization of autonomy and the denial of neediness and even become the disdain of dependency one sees in American culture. This remains a major difference between Americans and Japanese. For the Americans, competency and ability are often conflated in our ideology of the self, such that a behavioral failure is experienced as lack of ability and an admission of incompetence is tantamount to an admission of unredeemable and permanent incapacity which is experienced as a childish dependency. For the Japanese, in contrast, a failure is perceived as something that can (and should) be overcome not only by self-improvement, but also by dependent, grateful reliance on a giving mentor.

---

[9]A traditional version of this among some North American native groups, known as the "vision quest," may have served similar purposes for the young person at the threshold of adulthood, although also having explicit spiritual implications.

It is interesting to note that the pattern of child rearing McClelland and associates called "independence training" is a conflation of these dimensions. Independence training is in fact simultaneously a form of "non-affiliation training" in the sense that the child is socially isolated and left alone. It is a form of "autonomy training" in the sense that the child becomes responsible for autonomous behavioral self-regulation. By requiring the child to self-comfort, self-regulate, and fend for itself, the "independence training" pattern neglects basic human needs related to all three dimensions: affiliation and nurturance, as well as control. The early helplessness of the American child who experiences independence training thus is a simultaneous helplessness with regard to affiliation, self-control (autonomy), and nurturance. It is not surprising that continuing fears in adults around experiences that symbolize or are associated with loneliness, loss of freedom, and scarcity or lack of nurture are so easily cross-activated. It is also no mystery that there are overgeneralizations and conflations of these dimensions in American Psychology.

Horizontal Affiliation Versus Vertical Nurturant Relationships

Nurture-oriented caring relationships (i.e., those that begin as primarily vertical) do not usually transform into relationships of reciprocal intimacy (see the following chapter on affiliation). Givers and receivers are usually intertwined in lasting *non-equivalent* vertical social relationships that psychologically cannot be readily transformed into forms of reciprocal interaction. Where dependency needs are not in balance, as is the case in many marriages, there are risks that it will be difficult to achieve true intimacy. In such instances, lasting relationships may involve deeply emotional experiences around physical, emotional, and/or material dependent needs, yet without the participants attaining any actual communicative closeness in thought or in mutual understanding. Prior status differences usually prevent a strongly vertical relationship from becoming prevailingly reciprocal in any affiliative sense of *mutual* intimacy, thus precluding whatever further affiliative satisfactions that might be gained in more mutually equivalent psychological closeness or intimacy. This may be a source of problems for the establishment of truly intimate relationships between men and women in settings where gender-linked behavior patterns and associated expectations of provisory and controlling verticality may conflict with efforts toward mutuality. Evidence of this can be found in the higher incidence of divorce among marriages where there is a reversal of normative income differentials such that she earns more than he. This situation may be experienced by some men as a personal failure to fulfill gender-role expectations pertaining to issues of provision and control (Riesmann, 1990).

Only rarely do relationships that are initially established on the basis of giving and taking later come to involve equal-status reciprocity. Implicitly it is extremely difficult to change a mentorship/apprenticeship into a collegial relationship. One especially witnesses this in the Japanese society, where the age-grade emphasis remains institutionalized (Wagatsuma and De Vos, 1984). Yet even within relationships that are primarily organized around a vertical nurturance component, there may nevertheless be other attendant aspects of the relationship that are reciprocal, such as mutual respect, turn-taking in communication, cooperative instrumental behavior, etc. Nevertheless, with respect to the provision and receipt of succor and protection, as well as advice, etc., such a relationship generally maintains its essential vertical character.

In the context of balanced dependencies that one finds in successful intimate partnerships, what may appear to be horizontal or mutual nurture may not in actuality be horizontal. It can involve a series of donor-recipient role reversals that maintain their verticality (whether the roles endure for a short term or a long term). For example, one partner in a marriage may be able to provide more effectively for the family at one time, whereas that may be reversed at other times due to economic factors such as unemployment, career changes, etc. One partner may experience a period of increased emotional need in response to external stressors, and the other partner may be able to respond to that immediate dependent need, only to find the roles reversed under other circumstances.

An individual's role adaptations in response to changing circumstances for the dyad may appear to produce transitional periods wherein the vertical emphasis of the nurturant relationship is diminished, and more horizontal or reciprocal nurturant relationships appear to temporarily prevail. Additionally, the division of labor (however that is customarily constructed) that occurs in cooperative families may delegate the individual's giving and taking into various specific role domains, such that both giving and taking roles are experienced concurrently by both members of a dyad. Although this may appear to be horizontal, the various nurturance components of relationships retain their vertical character. Individuals may take on "responsible" roles without any sharing of intimate thought in a successful interactive adaptation to changing needs.

Over the course of life, the dependency roles between parents and their children are often reversed. The parent who once provided for others may eventually require nurturant care (see stories given to Card 6BM in chapter 11, volume II). Where children become intentionally involved in caring for their elders, this becomes a role reversal, and the verticality of the nurturance is reversed, at least for some aspects of the relationship. Nevertheless, an adult child who cares for an aged parent may continue to feel grateful for parental advice, may receive financial assistance and other benefits of family participation, even while taking care of the elder's basic needs. This domain-specific pattern of role relationships can be seen as similar to the division of labor within other dyadic relationships.

Where the parent and adult child can establish a relationship that is primarily based on mutual purpose, affiliation, harmony, etc., the emphasis on nurturance in the relationship may be diminished and truly mutual interactions between parents and children may occur. But for most people, the initial and continuing intrapsychic as well as practical importance of dependency issues, for both the parent and the child, will interfere with the establishment of true instrumental mutuality among peers in parent-child relationships, even where some domain-specific reversal of dependency does occur. This comes out very clearly in responses to Card 6BM in chapter 11, volume II on mother-son relationships in Canada.

North Americans often avoid direct involvement in parental care (often by leaving it in the hands of overworked caregivers in understaffed care facilities). It may, on the one hand, be seen as evidence of the degree to which gratitude and reciprocal obligation has or has not become a compelling force in the child's mind. But on the other hand, it may reflect the persistence into senescence of the parent's own refusal to accept a dependent role in adulthood, as the parent refuses to acknowledge an increasing dependency, in a continuing denial of the intrapsychic conflict that arises from idealizing an autonomous self.

Quasi-Religious Functions Related to Nurture, Power, and Regulation: Actuality, Illusion, and the Consciousness of Exploitation in Japan

Gratitude and the Confucian Ideal

Confucian beliefs and practices in the family context were directed toward a form of self-actualization that fulfilled many of the basic functions one might otherwise expect of a religious system (De Vos and Sofué, 1986). In looking at basic elements of Confucianism, we see that the central concepts of reverence and gratitude are the essence of a religiously directed human, not supernatural interaction. As they are manifest in Japan, they are associated with *kokoro,* the Japanese concept of "heart," combining reason, will, and feeling in social action.

Without relying on ideas of supernatural intervention, Confucianists nevertheless insist on the maintenance of some superordinate ethical principles governing the behavior of man that could not be reduced to the material forms of causality found in western science. There are indeed "mystical" concepts of ultimate religious unity for many Confucianists who do not have any concept of a personal deity governing life. Wang Yang-Ming (Tu, 1986) considered innate knowledge of the good as forming "one body" with all things. Integrity is the principle of "heaven" applied to everyday things.

A Confucianist can express sentiments of reverence and gratitude in a family context that in the West are only found in a totally supernatural context. For the Japanese, the family system provided a sense of dependent security similar to that found by westerners who "place their trust in God's hands." For some, a sense of reverence related to incurred benevolence can also be related to an extraordinary being such as Amida Buddha, although, more characteristically for Japanese it remains localized within the normative human social realm. It could be directed toward the person of a particular superior, although it is initially developed in relation to the gratitude felt toward parents. In contrast, for many Americans, expressive concerns with gratitude are expressed most often in religious terminology in respect to relations with a deity. In the West, such concerns are less central to family and community relationships.

Among Japanese, gratitude is frequently expressed as a feeling of unrepayable "*on*" (Lebra, 1969). On, as benevolent giving from elders to be repaid, came to be heavily imbued with a reverential sense of something so precious, and indeed so sacred, that it can never be totally realized by an ordinary self. Such inner experiences of respect and gratitude are basic to Japanese Confucian-inspired thought. There is a continuing gratefulness for what is received and a need to return the gratitude by some individual acts, be they morally defined in terms of good and bad action, material bestowal upon others, or as an ascetic sacrifice of present pleasure to achieve a greater future purpose. Responsible behavior is deemed repayment for what has been received.

This core concept of grateful repayment is important in Japanese familial relationships. In Japan, the traditional role of nurturing mother [which persisted at least into the 1960s, as we can illustrate from research data, including the Thematic Apperception Test (TAT)] was defined consciously in a very self-sacrificing manner. In the Confucian model of parental care, this capacity for self sacrifice was idealized, and the expression of gratitude was directly related to an awareness of parental efforts.

This concept of gratitude has been centrally operative in what is termed *Naikan*, a quasi-religious form of therapy practiced with some delinquent youth, who through good offices come to experience new, previously unacknowledged reasons for gratitude. Newfound gratitude helps overcome various past experiences of deep resentment over neglect or deprivation felt toward parents that had been transmuted into negative behavior directed toward other social authorities and society more generally (De Vos, 1984).

Although a failure to receive adequate nurturance may predispose a youth toward delinquency directed at society more generally, the normative pattern is the receipt of adequate nurturance in the family context. This is then transmuted developmentally into an experience of continuing dependency and gratitude, directed outward toward society more generally. In the 1960s we became bemused by the relative absence of feelings of being exploited reported by those in poor economic circumstances in Japan (Wagatsuma and De Vos, 1984). Yet with an understanding of Japanese socialization processes, we can attribute such observations to indicate the presence of continuing dependency or interdependency feelings that are operative in occupational settings as well as in the primary family. Furthermore, we found that the dependent needs of a subordinate were frequently actually met by someone in responsible authority. Nurturing attitudes and guilt over failures to nurture were overtly expressed by some heads of small companies, and resembled what we usually found evident in a family setting.

The Role of the Sensei or Mentor

A permanent dependent relationship with a mentor can be seen in positive terms in a Confucianist framework, wherein the sentiments of reverence and gratitude that are expressed toward the previous generation can only be understood in terms of the sacred.[10] Being accepted into a dependent mentoring situation was considered very important for one's career by young Japanese men. But the actual benefits derived from mentorship do not fully account for its intense symbolic value.[11] One could almost consider that some adolescent Japanese at the turn of the century, like Lorenz's ducklings, went through a phase wherein they became "imprinted" by a teacher, or "*sensei*"—the person "born before." Some retained throughout their careers a grateful veneration for their master. There remains still for some a romanticized image of the sensei, somewhat akin to a youthful image of a first love. In contrast, for the Westerner to find oneself an object of veneration or gratitude can be discomforting. The Westerner does not know what to do with it. Such behavior is sometimes decried by secularized Japanese as well, who prefer "dry" to "wet" emotional attachments, as it has been phrased.

Today, the search for direct contact with a teacher cannot be realized in the large classes of a university. As we noted elsewhere (De Vos, 1973), many Japanese college students attending large classes feel intense alienation. Radical students quickly change their ideology once they are taken into an organization after graduation and put into the hands of some older member of the organization for in-house training. In Japanese culture, the mentor remains a transcendence of the parental relationship in providing vocational guidance.[12] It was even customary for merchants during the Tokugawa period to send their sons out to be apprenticed to another shop, rather than receiving all their training at home.

Mentorship is a two-way relationship. In its Confucian context, it is as important to the sense of self-dignity and accomplishment of the master as it is to the pupil. This makes sense also from a Western perspective. Erik Erikson (1963), in describing various stages of the life cycle, sees a successful aging process as

---

[10]As defined by Durkheim (1947). See the more detailed discussion of the sacred in chapter 14, volume I, below.

[11]The woman's pattern of dependency is quite different and cannot be discussed in detail here. It is complicated by leaving one's family as a bride. The informal continuity of relationships between mother and daughter, though they remained strong in Japan, are given scant or no comment in the Confucian writings. Women in the workplace are for the most part considered as "temporary." Their major social role is still conceived of as wife and mother, thus dependency issues of adult women are handled quite differently from those of adult men.

[12]This idea has also been discussed by Robert Bly, who has advocated the importance of mentoring for young men. As Bly (1992) has described it, the mentor serves as a "male mother" (p. 36) for the young man, so that the young man can retain benevolent guidance as he steps out from under the wing of the mother.

involving a sense of generativity turned toward social continuity into the next generation. Many aging Japanese are as concerned with such a successful bestowal as they were with receiving nurture when young. This generational continuity is found in the occupational world in Japan.

The emotional tone between older and younger is what makes a sense of hierarchy bearable, even desirable for those raised within Confucian family ideals. In this cultural atmosphere, equalizing relationships is not a goal. One equalizes basically only with friends of the same age. There has remained to some degree a present-day mythology in Japan about the ideal company president. He is a folk hero who exemplifies the ideal exercise of power and control for the benefit of his workers, as well as producing a product that will benefit the populace at large. The purpose of gaining power as head of a company is to become a benevolent figure. Power is not for its own sake but to help others. Realizing ambition is not an individualistic achievement, it is to be able to bestow favors on others. One becomes a boss or "*kacho*" in order to be a sage advising the younger people coming up through the firm (De Vos, 1973). Older men are not only teaching younger men, but "taking care" of them.

There are indeed those who seek to actualize this culturally shared fantasy. There is gratification to be derived from playing such a role. It is a repetition of an idealized family setting in which parents take care, provide for their children, even to the point of self sacrifice. Ideally, the deepest gratification to be attained is to make enough money to be a philanthropist in the original meaning of the word. There are periodically such figures to be found in Japanese industry. Beliefs in this pattern of social success are thereby reinforced. Contrary to the emphasis that is put by some observers on the situational ethic of Japanese, actual ethnological observation of an urban community convinced Wagatsuma and De Vos (1984) how much "public service" is present in some urban Japanese communities.

The Role of Successful Elders in Voluntary Organizations

Although giving and taking relationships are defined in familial terms, many older Japanese do get beyond immediate concern with their own family. They get involved with social causes as individuals donating to others, time, energy, as well as financial support. When we examined community activities related to delinquency in Arakawa ward, a district of petty artisans and merchants in northwest Tokyo (Wagatsuma and De Vos, 1984) we found a plethora of voluntary organizations actively engaging both the men and women of the ward.

One such activity will serve as illustration. A number of men over fifty-five became *hōgōshi,* voluntary probation officers, supervising from two to four delinquent youth remanded to their charge by a probation official. This was not simple surveillance; a mentoring-like relationship was attempted. The recidivism rate of youth working with a hōgōshi was relatively low. Because these hōgōshi came from the same ward as their charges, they knew their life pattern and could establish close communication. Big Brother was indeed watching, but with a benevolent, insightful form of control.

For many older Japanese men in Arakawa ward, leisure time was utilized for such social causes as neighborhood betterment. The prevailing social atmosphere constrains one to join a number of organizations. But among many middle-class office worker families in neighboring wards it was mainly the housewives who were so occupied, since their men were away at work. It was artisans, merchants, or shopkeepers, men working at home, who were drawn into such activities.

It was obvious in some instances, that it was the social network that forced them to enter a number of local "voluntary" groups. The Japanese, too, have Rotary clubs and their "Rions" (Lions) who roar together with their fellow boosters, joining in benevolent community projects as found in the smaller cities of the United States. Kiwanis clubs in both the United States and Japan, for example, co-sponsor exchange programs for youth. Collectively, Japanese volunteers consider themselves bestowing some good on the community. This development in Japan may not be directly Confucian in origin, but it is important to consider the type of traditional social self-actualization related to responsible status that is engendered by such activities. In contrast with the dissolution of family and community in the United States, Japanese family and local community organizations are maintaining coordination, despite the individualizing and socially isolating pressures of modern mass society everywhere.

Deprivation Related to Minority Status

Experiences of deprivation do not necessarily originate only in childhood, they can occur during adulthood related to poor economic circumstances and various forms of social discrimination. Varieties of this can be found among ethnic minorities that have been victims of economic and social exploitation. Ethnic minority status in a particular society can be related to certain unresolved issues not only around material-economic forms of deprivation, but also in a negative inter-twining of economic and emotional issues. If economic and social hardships persist over generations, they can come to affect whole communities and become trans-generationally transmitted cultural patterns of reaction to discrimination and deprivation. In members of a minority group who have experienced a long tradition of discrimination, it is common to see a combination of defensive hostility toward the dominant group with attitudes of economic dependency on social aid programs. The expressive, helpless, and dependent feelings that are cultivated in aid recipients further risk injury to self-respect. Under these circumstances, deviousness and an expediential attitude can become a balm to the ego. As a way to salvage some sense of initiative, power, and self-respect, the individual may see himself or herself as expediential rather than abjectly dependent. One finds instrumental means of being devious in how one "takes" from the donor system.

Minority groups who have experienced several generations of social deprivation may seek to exploit whatever welfare agencies are set up. We can turn again to Japan to illustrate this (De Vos and Wagatsuma, 1966). One can find this expediential attitude among the Japanese ex-pariahs, or "Burakumin." The Japanese government has been pressured successfully by the formerly outcaste Burakumin to ameliorate housing and school deficiencies. Burakumin have developed certain expectations that they are "due" economic assistance from the majority society. They see it as a right that goes with their minority status. We cited graphic evidence of the prevalence of such dependent, demanding attitudes among Burakumin, as compared to their relative absence among ordinary Japanese (De Vos and Wagatsuma, 1966; Wagatsuma and De Vos, 1984).

Individuals in the majority culture sometimes are angered when they discover some form of "relief cheating." It confirms their prejudice concerning the worthless nature of the individuals who are being helped through the efforts of the more humane elements within their community. American society today expresses considerable division of opinion concerning the effects of its welfare policy in this regard. What is not faced sometimes is that the donor is also gaining personal gratification for being a "giving" person, not heeding that this gratification is at the expense of the self-respect of the recipient.

A sense of responsibility for nurturance expressed among Japanese does not readily extend beyond the majority community. For example, the Japanese sense of paternalism and mentorship is not as readily extended to younger Korean workers in Japan. Japanese labor unions, as well as management, ignore the special plight of Koreans. The Japanese admit that the Koreans have "human rights," but their dubious legal status makes it uncertain whether these rights include general welfare or simply emergency aid in times of dire need. While the more militant, politically oriented labor unions are more likely to take up the cause of minorities than are the prevailing company unions, Koreans are generally seen by the union membership as competitors rather than as peers in need of assistance.

Labor unions serve both instrumental and expressive functions within Japanese society. In some cases, they may be simply interest groups. In other cases, they may impart to those who belong a sense of interdependency and brotherhood, a sense of affiliation and mutual care. Neither the instrumental nor the expressive functions of Japanese labor unions, however, are very effective for Koreans, given their lack of legal status. In fact, many of the legal problems concerning the Korean minority in Japan are related to the underlying fact that many Japanese do not feel a social compunction to provide care for "foreign," "inferior" Koreans.

In general, private welfare agencies are fairly rare in Japan and religious organizations play only a minor role. The family remains paramount. In the United States, in contrast, some ethnic and religious minorities have pioneered such agencies. Under conditions of ethnic or religious discrimination, an incentive to maintain one's group identity can come from the expressive gratification that comes from giving to and receiving from peers within the ethnic or religious community. One benefits from knowing that one can turn somewhere for help and comfort in times of stress or tribulation. Conversely, for some individuals, a sense of social belonging implies a responsibility or a need to nurture those of one's own group who are less fortunate or who are still young and inexperienced.

American Jews, for example, from a very early period have set up professional agencies to care for their distressed members. These agencies very often have extended public service to others outside the Jewish group and the same has been true for many Catholic charities. Programs that are politically oriented may also use welfare as a means of gaining loyalty. In Japan, the Ch'ongnyon and the Mindan, as voluntary organizations, are supposedly set up to provide nurturing functions within the Korean community. However, we found that their political objectives and interests usually took priority, and their funds were only in small part directed to help people in need within the Korean community.

Consciousness of Exploitation and the Gratification of Dependency

A psycho-cultural analysis of hierarchical aspects of society can benefit from a thorough consideration of the subjective experience of being cared for or being exploited, whether from an expressive or an instrumental standpoint. One can find in any society some exploitative activities that are part of an instrumental exercise of power or control over others, even where the prevailing ideology does not frame it this way. Despite the Confucian ideal described above, one can observe that the attitudes expressed by superiors were not always in accord with actual behavior. Nevertheless, an abiding illusion that one will be cared for was evident among many workers.

In Japan, any alienated class-consciousness of a Western type has been offset considerably by a history of economic and social paternalism. By the 1960s, this social form was still being experienced as relatively satisfying by both those in the subordinate as well as those in superordinate positions among the small entrepreneurs we examined. Expressions of concerned paternalism seemed to offset the alienating processes involved in more directly impersonal instrumental situations of potential class exploitation (Wagatsuma and De Vos, 1984). From our more psychological-motivational point of view, paralleling Nakane's (1970) more strictly sociological structural analysis, paternalism in Japan worked because there was some interdependent, personal, psychological identification between subordinate and superordinate individuals. Status differentials in Japan did not completely depersonalize, alienate, or cause a lack of emotional concern between those found on different levels of a Japanese status hierarchy. Therefore, there was possible an emotional interchange of a type that has been very rarely experienced between present-day superiors and subordinates in Western economic or commercial settings.

One wonders whether the Western manager or owner has learned to think so completely impersonally about a workforce as a consequence of personal developmental-psychological experiences, or as a consequence of a trained capacity to think in abstract, impersonal, ideological terms. Western economic theory is, by and large, impersonal. Its determinative operative forces are economic. Marketplace decisions are "rational." The laws of supply and demand are impersonal, mechanical forces; human decision-making starts with the assumption that any person given the opportunity will maximize one's own material benefits rather than impose irrationally based constraints on oneself for the good of one's group or one's subordinates. From this rational perspective, a Western observer might even concede that an apprenticeship situation could be tolerable if one could anticipate future privileges to be reached by seniority. Such a possible long-term benefit is probably more quickly understandable than is the idea of being satisfied in a lifelong dependency.

Personal, emotional concerns and what are defined in Western economics as "irrational" considerations are handled with difficulty in Western economic formulae. The presence or absence of familial attitudes, therefore, has only a secondary role, if any, in modern economic theory. Paternalism is seen as a negative term in western business. In contrast, impersonal abstract thinking of this nature was notably lacking in the Japanese tradition. In Japan, paternalism remained real and positive in the shared collective representations of many. What we observed,[13] in the underlying social attitudes embedded in the roles of apprentice and patron in Arakawa ward in Tokyo in the 1960s or in the urban and rural samples we investigated in the 1950s, to some degree, is still operative among some small-scale entrepreneurs. Their attitudes have remained as an undercurrent in the economic and cultural historical processes at work in the course of Japanese industrialization generally.

Those in the *oyabun* (parent-role) positions did indeed relate very often to their subordinates as if they were their charges. In a number of organizations they were not simply dealing with impersonally conceived contract labor from whom

---

[13]As stated in the introduction of this book, the greater part of firsthand empirical evidence and experience that deepened our understanding of social cohesion, nurturance, as well as status inequality in Japan was obtained, first by two years of research at Nagoya University from 1953 to 1955 which included interviews in both rural and urban settings, and second by Keiichi Mizushima, Hiroshi Wagatsuma, and George De Vos in the course of several years research in the 1960s among the Burakumin of the Kansai area, and among the merchants and artisans of Arakawa Ward in Tokyo (De Vos and Mizushima, 1967). However, subsequent repeated visits and the extensive reports and writings of others as well as the plots of films and literary works strengthens the contentions made in this chapter (see also Abegglen, 1958; Cole, 1971; Dore, 1958; Nakane, 1970; Vogel, 1963). During our work in Arakawa ward during the 1960s (Wagatsuma and De Vos, 1984) a great deal of discussion with the small entrepreneurs involved exploring how patterns of apprenticeship functioned in respect to both the instrumental and expressive aspects of this dying tradition.

one seeks to obtain maximum productive output. The subordinate, even when worked too hard, was not totally depersonalized or treated as a machine.

An examination of Japanese pre-war legal structure demonstrates that the subordinate has been legally at the mercy of the superior. Yet, what is imperfectly understood even by the Japanese themselves in examining their own social science theory is the degree to which there remained implicit constraints that limited the decision making of the superior. These constraints were not established in law, but were enforced simply by collectively held representations or "scripts," and associated affective feelings that governed behavior. In the small manufacturers with whom we had contact (De Vos, 1973), we found some inner conflict between the emotionally satisfying features of the idealized superordinate role of the Japanese employer-as-giver, and the instrumental advantages to be gained by economic exploitation of one's subordinates.

From the other side, culturally patterned dependent expectations on the part of subordinates did, in certain instances, distort their perception of the degree to which they were at times victims of exploitation on the part of their superiors. Yet the Japanese saw the apprenticeship situation as a reciprocal payment of present labor for future-oriented training in a skill. Although apprentices were paid poorly, if at all, the apprentice was learning a necessary trade through which he could later realize himself and earn his own living. Indeed, very frequently an apprentice inherited his master's job, sometimes even his family. This is not to deny that in many situations there was a lifelong perpetuation of *kobun* (child status), where the individuals remained sub-adult and maintained an emotional and financial dependency on an *oyakata* (parent figure) who periodically rewarded his followers by symbols of appreciation or nurture. Such ties remained highly emotional, internally reinforced by potential guilt should the subordinate not repay his benefactor. What is often missed by the Westerner, and even by more modern Japanese, is the fact that guilt also arose on the part of some benefactors should they fail to give proper care to subordinates.

The master who took on an apprentice might be seen etically from outside the system as one who economically exploited the labor of the young by paying them pitiful salaries under the pretext that they need years of training in order to learn a skill well enough to function independently. The same behavior perceived emically, internally and subjectively may be phrased quite differently by the participants; this internal cultural perception at times demanded the capacity for considerable denial or distortion of the raw objective fact of exploitation when it occurred.

One cannot prophesize how long these attitudes will be maintained in the face of stronger countervening social forces. Suffice it to indicate that they have continued to exist post-war for some time as influences that helped set the tone of contemporary Japanese organizational behavior as well as family life.

One could contend that instrumental or economic exploitation does not exist emically as a social problem until it is consciously perceived collectively and overtly defined as such by groups subjected to it. Yet, even individuals who feel exploited cannot often translate their individual realization into collective revolutionary effort. Others may not perceive the exploitation. The lack of readiness for the Japanese worker generally to perceive himself or herself as exploited was a point of considerable frustration for leftists in Japan. One may generalize that a majority of Japanese workers, in their collectivities at least, chose to continue to think in positive personal terms about their superiors rather than to perceive themselves as exploited impersonally by them simply as a means toward economic gain. Those who thought differently could not gain a critical mass to express discontent.

Any objective appraisal of Western cultural history since industrialization makes it clear that the class system in many Western nations has been alienating, not just in Marx's sense of the economic alienation of the working class from the fruits of its labor. The alienation runs much deeper, manifesting as weakening emotional ties and increasing mutual antagonism between different occupational strata of the society, even where the working class has not been self-aware of this class division in political or economic terms. The social cleavages resulting from differential status in modern American and European societies are not bridged by the type of familial morality that has continued to some degree even within the modern Japanese social system. One can generally say that Western postfeudal bourgeois societies have not been knit together in the way one continues to find in Japan. The continuity of the premodern feudal Japanese mythology of quasi-parentage or extended quasi-familial vertical networks of obligations may have served as a constraint on raw exploitation during the process of modernization.

The failure of the dialectical-materialist leftist organizer in the face of this paternalistic aspect of Japanese society perfectly illustrates the fact that social scientists can benefit from an adequate cultural psychology. The instrumentally oriented Westerner, and even in some cases the modern Japanese, fail to adequately comprehend and certainly fail to value the psychological gratification that comes from expressive components of participation in hierarchical social forms.

Western and leftist theorists do not like the fact that traditional Japanese "paternalism" also gratified a continuing expressive need for dependency on the part of many in the subordinate role. Such gratification in the context of economic exploitation is prevailingly generally considered irrational in both personal and economic terms. Yet among Western capitalists there is a growing instrumental realization (informed by the Japanese model) that one must oil the morale of one's workers at least as well as one's machines to maintain productivity without too much disruption or need for costly replacement. Some would see this attention to the psychological well-being of workers as simply feeding the false consciousness of the working class. Those who espouse the ethnocentric modern and postmodern Western values that all members of a society should strive for a sense of independent and equal adulthood, are disturbed by any acceptance of permanently dependent or subordinate roles as positive features of a society.

If one is to successfully apply Marx's insights about false consciousness, class-consciousness, the origins of consciousness from material conditions, and the central role of consciousness as a determiner of history, one must recognize that conscious experience does not arise immediately from material conditions. It is always mediated. It is always framed in terms provided by the culture, such that material conditions only become a determining force by way of culturally mediated emic experience. These experiences are constructed developmentally into mental representations that guide both personal and collective perception and behavior. But the complexity of this cultural mediation of consciousness is not adequately addressed in the Marxist framework. Although the individual's social class certainly does frame many aspects of perception and consciousness, there is far more complexity to a cultural framework.

The human experience of social participation in stratified societies cannot be seen in terms of exploitation alone.[14] From the comparative developmental psycho-cultural perspective described in the present volume, one sees both expressive and instrumental dimensions as they are reflected in social forms. One can see that these social forms may serve to address emotional well-being, as well as economic well-being, in the context of enduring patterns of child rearing, socialization, and social cohesion. To label the richness of such cultural mediation of human experience as nothing more than "false consciousness" might itself be nothing more than a psychologically naive ethnocentric denigration (now in the guise of postmodernism, deconstructionism, and critical theory) of the internal structure of an enduring, successful, and relatively gratifying culture.[15]

Regardless of the ideological spin one might ultimately give to the presence of social patterns such as we have described in Japan, the social scientist cannot overlook the abiding force of history as it is reflected in thematic cultural representations. These received representations frame and distort perception in such a way that a continuity of functional social cohesion might be maintained despite massive changes in political and economic systems. For comparative psycho-cultural purposes it is best to note and record the fact that these thematic representations are present in the emic experience of the informant, without peremptory ideological interpretations that preclude data-based cross-cultural comparisons.

Scoring Expressions of Nurturance/Succorance/Protection or Withholding/Deprivation/Helplessness

Nurturance (N), and its instrumentally oriented counterpart, Control (D), cover the two basic expressive and instrumental "vertical" categories operative in unequal status-defined human social relationships. These categories must be kept distinct from those instrumental or expressive concerns embedded in "horizontal" or

---

[14]For a cogent discussion of the expressive components of power relationships, see Benjamin (1988).

[15]This is not to say that Japanese psychological experience is nonproblematic.

mutually reciprocal expressive status relationships categorized under Affiliation (F), and forms of instrumental cooperation-competition, Mutual Purpose (M).

Vertical relationships related to giving or receiving involve both a donor (D) and a recipient position (S). Let us first consider the scoring categories related to a donor's acts of giving, help or protection.

Protagonist as Donor

The A categories are positive. Unequal relationships can be generally perceived and defined in donor-recipient terms as nurturing, helpful, or protective "love."

A. Positive Nurture, Succor, Protection ***NDA***

NDA-nurture	Love, nurture; physical care
NDA-reward	Rewards, gifts, etc.
NDA-means	Material, educational, or economic assistance
NDA-comfort	Emotional comforting
NDA-nurse	Nurturant feeding or restorative care
NDA-secure	Giving or attempting protection and security
NDA-advice	Advice, instruction, guidance
NDA-active	Helpful activities on behalf of someone or group
NDA-family	General familial (acts done for the family); adoption
NDA-social	Acts done for community, society
NDA-rescue	Rescue or saving someone
NDA-devote	To be devoted to acts of sacrifice as an act of nurturance
NDA-charity	Benevolent act (often in religious context)
NDA-god	Rewarding deity; God's help, magical protection
NDA-prayer	Prayer for another
NDA-ritual	Protective or beneficial rituals
NDA-magic	Benevolent use of magic
NDA-help-s	Self remedial or self helping behavior
NDA-memory	Nostalgic nurture or care for others
NDA-disown	Denial of support from undeserving recipient

An activity to *nurture* or *protect*, i.e., to *bestow upon* or *succor* others is part of human maturation that progressively appears in our active interaction with others from positions of relative adequacy and power. Positively structured, active participants feel "good" in the act of caring for others (NDA-nurture).

The giving of gifts or the bestowal or rewards is a gratifying activity (NDA-means; NDA-rewards). Donor activities include assisting in the material or economic well-being of others (NDA-means). There is giving of emotional comfort (NDA-comfort). Various forms of care, feeding, or restorative nursing are essential to succoring (NDA-nurse). Security and protection are two of the main forms of nurturant care (NDA-secure). Part of the nurture of parents or other, later mentors, is directed toward equipping the immature child or needful adult to function adequately in the outside world through succoring advice and educational facilitation (NDA-advice). There are, additionally, numerous helpful activities that see to the well-being of others we can score under the subcategory of active assistance (NDA-active). There is, in parents, general or specific expressions of a desire to nurture, succor, and protect members of one's family by activities on their behalf (NDA-family).

There is interest in general "humanitarian" protection of the weak or the handicapped, and the protection of animals (NDA-social). Active rescue or saving someone from a difficult situation can occur (NDA-rescue). The desire to care can become self-sacrificial in some circumstances (NDA-devote).

Charity is an extension of this succoring need beyond the immediate family or social group. The act may be done in a religious context (NDA-charity). One may pray for the benefit or well-being of someone (NDA-prayer). God's help is depicted as playing an active role. God is seen as an active protagonist in an event (NDA-god). There is expressed concern in some religious contexts for forms of beneficial ritual that may be of assistance to others (NDA-ritual). There are narratives describing a benevolent use of magic (NDA-magic), such as in the tale of Cinderella and her fairy godmother.

There can be an expression of self-remedial or self-help behavior. One expresses a capacity to take care of oneself. Some individuals express their capacity or need for some form of self help as a resolution of their difficulties (NDA-help-s). One may narrate a nostalgic memory of previous acts or a previous capacity to help or supply nurture (NDA-memory). There are perceptions that it is necessary to deny support to an undeserving potential recipient, such as a wayward child (NDA-disown).

B. *Concerns or Worry Over Giving or Helping* ***NDB***

NDB-pity	Sense of pity, compassion for another's need or travail
NDB-welfare	Concern with another's well-being
NDB-body	Concern with bodily problems of another
NDB-means	Concern with material problems of others
NDB-lack	Lack of another to nurture (childless)
NDB-unable	Wanting to help unresolved (presently lacking resources or knowledge to be helpful)

NDB-thwart	Frustrated or rebuffed desire to help
NDB-reject	Fear of having one's nurturant acts rejected

The NDB categories include unresolved concerns about giving, seen from the position of a would-be donor. There may be a sense of concern about the social or emotional needs of another (NDB-pity). One may have an unresolved concern about the welfare or well-being of another (NDB-welfare). There may be concern about the physical or mental problems of another (NDB-body). One may have concern about someone's material or economic problems (NDB-means).

One can sense a deep need to give, but be without an available recipient (NDB-lack). This is most frequently experienced when in a state of being childless. One may lack the necessary resources or the required knowledge to be of assistance and have a consequent sense of helplessness in wishing to help another (NDB-unable). One may experience a direct sense of frustration over one's inability to act (NDB-thwart). There may be a fear of having one's assistance rejected (NDB-reject).

C. Withholding, Abandonment ***NDC***

NDC-hard	Hard and ungiving, stern, unapproachable
NDC-selfish	Selfish lack of concern for others' needs
NDC-deprive	To withhold materially or educationally
NDC-comfort	To withhold or deprive emotionally
NDC-succor	Refusal of help or succor
NDC-desert	Abandonment of a needy one
NDC-protect	Refusal to protect
NDC-legal	Withholding of assistance due to a legal technicality
NDC-repay	Provide something to force repayment later
NDC-indulge	Overprotection, indulge, inducing dependency

Some potential or expected donors are depicted as hard and ungiving, stern, unapproachable (NDC-hard). There may be a description of a selfish lack of concern about the well-being of another. Heedless egocentric behavior can cause loss or deprivation (NDC-selfish). There are negative-active expressive acts of deliberate material withholding (NDC-deprive). There are negative-active expressive acts of deliberate emotional withholding (NDC-comfort). There are negative openly expressed refusals to help (NDC-succor). One may narrate about an active abandoning of another in need (NDC-desert).

There are refusals to protect (NDC-protect). There can be a form of withholding of help or causing deprivation through resort to legal technicalities (NDC-legal).

There may be depicted an act of giving as a means of forcing an individual into a forced reciprocity of an unfair nature to force repayment later. Inducing excessive dependency can be viewed as not good for someone who is in a recipient position, or someone who should become more independent for one's own good. In Japan there are instances of consciously giving to a particular child for the purpose of future repayment of dependency. Such an attitude can be frowned upon by some informants (NDC-repay).

There can be a conscious perception that excessive indulgence of another or overprotection is actually a form of negative behavior (NDC-indulge).

A negative emotional state can stimulate active withholding as a malicious, aggressive act. If destructive in intent, such activity must be double scored (HC-hostile) for its destructive or hostile intent.

D. Omission, Inability, Ineptitude ***NDD***

NDD-neglect	Deprivation through neglect or omission
NDD-unable	Inept and unable to help or take care of someone
NDD-comfort	Unable to provide emotional support
NDD-means	Unable to support financially

There are chronic insoluble negative-passive states experienced by a potential donor. There is a chronic, passive state of neglecting a potential deserving recipient (NDD-neglect).

One may experience a sense of inner incapacity to give or to help one in need (NDD-unable). One may feel internally incapable of giving emotional support when needed (NDD-comfort). One may not have the means to support someone financial or materially (NDD-means).

Protagonist as Recipient or in the Dependent Position

The recipient position is also represented in A, B, C, D, subcategories:

A. Receiving Nurture, Succor, Protection ***NSA***

NSA-trust	Trust in receiving care or protection
NSA-assist	Actively seeks assistance or help
NSA-reward	Given rewards, gifts, etc.
NSA-means	Given material, educational or economic aid
NSA-comfort	Given emotional aid
NSA-nurse	Given bodily succor
NSA-secure	Given security, protection, or blessing

NSA-edified	Given advice, intellectual or educational aid
NSA-grateful	Grateful behavior or feeling
NSA-forgive	Seeks forgiveness for past action or omission
NSA-god	Being taken care of by God
NSA-prayer	Seeking for protection or care of a deity, magic
NSA-malice	Counter-protection from malevolence
NSA-s-help	Becomes independent, needs no help
NSA-memory	Memory of being taken care of

In the recipient position, one is aware of a sense of trustful dependency on outside donors (NSA-trust) and one may seek assistance or advice (NSA-assist).

Many of the subcategories scored from the experience of being a recipient are the obverse of those already considered from the position of a donor. One can be rewarded or given gifts (NSA-reward). One can be a recipient of material support (NSA-means), receive emotional comforting (NSA-comfort), experience bodily care (NSA-nurse), be afforded protection (NSA-secure), receive advice, intellectual help, educational aid (NSA-edified).

Feelings of gratitude are aroused to be requited by some form of loving response (NSA-grateful). It is considered a positive feeling for many to seek forgiveness from another for past actions in a relationship (NSA-forgive). This sought-for forgiveness can be viewed as something that another can bestow as a loving act. This seeking can be thought of as part of a religious relationship with a deity.

One's sense of inner insufficiencies can cause a continuing need to receive which, depending on the culture, may be conceptualized as coming from human or supernatural sources (NSA-god). In the West, many seemingly "independent" individuals remain in a dependent relationship to a deity perceived as both powerful and giving, with a compassionate "love for mankind."

The act of prayer itself is a positive experience for many. Technically defined, prayer is a form of supplication with positive anticipation of benevolent bestowal. But prayers may be performed without thinking too explicitly about what it is that one is to receive. Some prayers are performed as an expression of gratitude for what has already been received (NSA-prayer). There is also the specific experience of receiving, having received some religious counterprotection against malice or malevolence (NSA-malice).

Some cultures, more than others, emphasize increasing independence and detachment as more appropriate to the adult status, wherein one should be able to find inner resources in time of felt need. Self help can, therefore, be seen positively (NSA-s-help).

One may depict a past memory of receiving care or nurture (NSA-memory).

B. *Insecurity, Unresolved Worry over Sustenance* ***NSB***

NSB-help	Needs help, succor, or support
NSB-depend	Uncertain about emotional dependency
NSB-insecure	Fear of withdrawal or absence of care or protection
NSB-means	Fear of economic want
NSB-social	General uncertainty about security
NSB-other	Wants other than what given
NSB-deprive	Fear of deprivation by another
NSB-loss	Fear of losing something, or being stolen from
NSB-distrust	Distrust about receiving
NSB-envy	Unresolved envy over what another receives
NSB-jealous	Jealous and uncertain about one's dependency, related to rivalry about receiving nurture
NSB-god	Questions or distrust of God's goodness
NSB-bless	Uncertain about receiving blessing as support

For those experiencing or describing a recipient position, there are a number of unresolved experiences of needing help or protection (NSB-help). One may be uncertain about emotional dependency or the availability of comfort (NSB-depend). There may be fear of possible withdrawal of care or protection (NSB-insecure). There may be insecurities related to economic assistance (NSB-means). Various anxieties stem from uncertainty of social support (NSB-social). There may be depicted a situation that one is dissatisfied with what is proffered or given (NSB-other).

Some insecurity may be felt over the possible withdrawal of support and the deprivation that may ensue. There may be a chronic fear of possible withdrawal of protection (NSB-deprive).

There may be concern about potential loss (NSB-loss). Among Canadian Indians, Athabaskan Slavey and Dogrib of the Northwest Territories, June Helm elicited frequent stories of anxiety about being stolen from or losing some possession (Helm, De Vos, and Carterette, 1960, see also chapter 13 of this volume). This was despite the fact that cases of actual stealing were extremely rare in their small communities. Such anxieties were very often expressed by those with younger siblings who had lost the attention and affection of the mother when it was redirected solely toward a newborn.

There may occur a sense of underlying distrust about being able to rely on another, or others, to meet one's expectations (NSB-distrust), or a state of unresolved envy over what another receives (NSB-envy). There may arise jealousy about a possible shift toward another by a giver or protector (NSB-jealous).

In a religious context there may be questions arising about God's goodness (NSB-god), or fear of a withdrawal of divine blessing (NSB-bless).

C. Undue Demands, Covetousness ***NSC***

NSC-rivalry	Rivalrous over getting nurturance
NSC-envy	Active envy, coveting another's nurture
NSC-demand	Improperly dependent, demanding, wanting
NSC-refuse	Refusal to receive nurture, gift, etc.
NSC-injury	Injurious act to self or others sense of deprivation
NSC-suicide	Injurious act (self or other) to force nurture

Those in a recipient position may be depicted as actively, even destructively rivalrous over getting care or nurture (NSC-rivalry). There may be active envy of a more favored individual (NSC-envy). These may sometimes be double scored with hostile acts (HC-hostile). Someone may be seen as excessively demanding of others (NSC-demand). They may refuse what is offered in an unreasonable way (NSC-refuse).

There may be injurious or negative acts done out of a sense of deprivation (NSC-injury). There can be self injurious or suicidal acts related to a sense of extreme deprivation. Some suicides can be symbolic forms of forcing attention or nurture (NSC-suicide).

D. Passive Sense of Deprivation, Abandonment ***NSD***

NSD-lack	Insufficient help
NSD-comfort	Being emotionally deprived
NSD-means	Being economically or materially deprived
NSD-parent	No parents; homeless
NSD-deserted	Being or having been abandoned
NSD-no-help	No help possible
NSD-sustain	Incapacity to sustain oneself; helplessness
NSD-suicide	Despair; lack of economic and/or emotional support
NSD-intake	Inability to accept assistance or help

Some experience a chronic insufficiency as to what is available there is some giving or care, but it is not enough to satisfy need (NSD-lack). One can sense being emotionally deprived (NSD-comfort), or one may express a sense of chronic economic or material deprivation (NSD-means). One may express a sense of chronic deprivation by some individual, most often a family member.

Some individuals suffer from a state of homelessness, of being orphaned with no sustaining individuals from whom to receive nurture (NSD-parent). Others suffer from a sense of being abandoned and helpless (NSD-deserted).

One may suffer a sense of chronic depressive deprivation, realizing no help is possible (NSD-no-help). There are some expressions of desperation about the inability to sustain oneself (NSD-sustain). There can be despair over lack of economic or emotional assistance to the point of suicide (NSD-suicide). There are sometimes expressed feelings of an inability to accept help, even when it is needed (NSD-intake).

Some Illustrative Examples of Scoring in the Nurture Category

In the previous chapter we illustrated the complex scoring of categories by drawing from previous studies. Let us here illustrate some scorings within the Nurture category. In this instance we shall again consider some responses of the Brazilian samples given to Card 7BM, a scene depicting a younger and older man in a close conversation (see chapter 10, volume II).

Among the Japanese Brazilians a number of stories are about long-range advice:

> (J f) (Card 7BM) A young man here appears to be angry or jealous. The older man is sheltering him and trying to teach what is right. But the youth has lots of remorse.
>
> [HB-resent FB-jealous NDA-advice RB-regret]

> (J m) (Card 7BM) A professor or a father and son. He is talking and *explaining to the son.* About life in general . . . the son will obey. . . . It is difficult for a son of this age to listen to a mother's counsel.
>
> [NDA-advice NDA-advice DSA-comply NSD-intake]

> (J m) (Card 7BM) They are discussing and examining their own experience. The older man is talking about the characteristics of life and is *giving advice, like a parent.*
>
> [FA-sympathy NDA-advice]

> (J m) (Card 7BM) A father and son again. The father is trying to explain the situation to the son, about life. He is counseling him about how to live, to study, to work, and to better the family. The son listens to the father and learns from him. The opinions of older people are always valid.
>
> [NDA-advice NSA-advice NDA-family CA-expert]

> (J m) (Card 7BM) This is a senior of greater age and a youth. The elder is comforting. As his son lost his wife and he is discouraged/exhausted. The other is comforting him. He will overcome this state. He is journeying through a transitional, temporary stage. All people go through this phase.
>
> [NDA-comfort KD-death PD-depress PA-endure]

> (J f) (Card 7BM) Not the father, but an uncle or another relative. He is a good friend of the younger man and is speaking with him about his girlfriend because he

has a relationship problem. The elder has lots of life experiences and knows a lot and so he is helping the youth. They are good friends.

[FA-friend FB-problem CA-expert NDA-advice]

(BJ fy) (Card 7BM) Louis was thinking in a room. He is in the room doing business. No, I will change the story. Gumersindo is sad with his son, Manuel, because he is suffering about a patient who brought a lawsuit against him. This is about treatment, about what a dentist should do. They are dentists. This should not have happened because Manuel has a diploma. For Manuel, to be a dentist was always his life. Due to having committed dental errors, everything has ended for him.

[NDA-comfort HB-f-anger CC-failure]

(J f) (7BM) Uncle or another relative. Good friend speaking with him about his girlfriend because relationship problem. Lots of life experiences, knows a lot so he is helping youth. They are good friends.

[FA-friend CA-past FB problem NDA-comfort]

The older man can be seen as nurturant among the Italian-Brazilians as well:

(I m) (Card 7BM) A trial. Lawyer is giving him an orientation so that his accuser doesn't speak any nonsense. He is instructing the young man to defend himself from the other accuser's lawyers.

[MVA-smart NDA-advice]

(I m) (Card 7BM) A drunkard [younger figure] used to go home drunk. One day his wife separated. Both wanted a son. They fought in court. He drinks in order to relieve the expectation. The judge's decision came and he lost. He kidnaped his son. He told his father what he had done, who convinced him to bring son back. The wife lodged a complaint in the police. He went to his wife and confessed that he had done it and apologized. She forgave him. They kept separated. His father took him to the hospital to treatment in order to stop drinking. Later he was cured and went to visit his son with love and care. He had been a drunk since he got married.

[RC-abuse HC-discord RC-illegal NSB-help NDA-advice RA-apology NDA-active NDA-love]

(I m) (Card 7BM) Father and son were talking about a play they had seen. The father asked the son how he liked it. His son said that he had found it very beautiful. And his father told him that he would take him again to see plays, and to other places too. Then in order to reward his father, the son himself decided to stage a play, to show to his father and family.

[FA-friend PA-esthete NDA-edify NDA-reward]

(I m) (7BM) Drunkard has wife and children. Wife separated. Kidnaped his son. Told his father went to his wife and confessed father took him to the hospital cured and went to visit his son with love and care.

[RC-abuse RC-illegal FC-reject NDA-active RA-reform]

Some Brazilian Portuguese stories in summary:

(P m) (7BM) Father gives son advice. Study to become great engineer.

[NDA-advice AA-inspire]

(P m) (7BM) Advice of older friend.

[NDA-advice]

(P f) (7BM) Man sad, other man is comforting him. He will be very happy.

[PA-sorrow NDA-comfort PA-joy]

(P f) (7BM) Father wants son to succeed. To have a good job give his own children good studies, and good family life.

[NDA-advice NDA-family]

(P m) (7BM) Father a judge. Son soccer player. Both rich. Both give half their wealth to poor.

[KA-social KA-wealth NDA-charity]

Some Afro-Brazilians:

(AB f) (7BM) Peevish man turned out of his house. Neighbor takes him in. He's grateful.

[FC-reject NSD-means NDA-rescue NSA-grateful]

(AB m) (7BM) Son gives much desired picture to his father.

[PA-esthete OB-want KC-poor NDA-reward]

(AB m) (7BM) Rich colleague gives means to poor friend to succeed with violin. Reaches friends social class.

[KA-wealth NSD-goods AA-self NDA-means MTA-task EDA-status]

(AB f) (7BM) Peevish man turned out of his house. Neighbor takes him in. He's grateful.

[FC-reject NSD-means NDA-rescue NSA-grateful]

Illustrative Samples of Scoring in Volume II

Other illustrative examples of the scoring of [N] category responses are found throughout the verbatim responses found in chapters 9, 10, 11, and 12 in volume II.

Notes

Abegglen, James. 1958. *The Japanese Factory: Aspects of Its Social Organization*. Glencoe, Ill.: Free Press.

Ainsworth, Mary, Mary Blehar, E. Waters, and S. Wall. 1978. *Patterns of Attachment: A Psychological Study of the Strange Situation.* Hillsdale, N.J.: L. Erlbaum Associates.

Anisfeld, E., V. Casper, M. Nozyce, and N. Cunningham. 1990. Does Infant Carrying Promote Attachment? *Child Development*, **61**: 1617–1627.

Benjamin, Jessica. 1988. *The Bonds of Love: Psychoanalysis, Feminism, and the Problem of Domination*. New York: Pantheon Books.

Bly, Robert. 1992. *Iron John: A Book About Men.* New York: Vintage Books.

Bowlby, John. 1940. Influence of Early Environment in Development of Neurosis and Neurotic Character. *Int. J. Psycho-Analysis*, **21**: 154–178.

———. 1952. *Maternal Care and Mental Health.* Geneva: World Health Organization.

———. 1969. *Attachment and Loss, Vol. I, Attachment.* New York: Basic Books.

———. 1973. *Attachment and Loss, Vol. II, Separation: Anxiety and Anger.* New York: Basic Books.

Caudill, William and Helen Weinstein. 1969. Maternal Care and Infant Behavior in Japan and America. *Psychiatry*, **XXXII**: 12–43.

Cole, Robert E. 1971. *Japanese Blue Collar: The Changing Tradition.* Berkeley and Los Angeles: University of California Press.

Cowell, E.B. (Ed.). 1990. *The Jataka, or Stories of the Buddha's Former Births*. Oxford: The Pali Text Society. (First published by the Cambridge University Press, 1895).

de Grazia, Sebastian. 1948. *The Political Community: A Study of Anomie*. Chicago: University of Chicago Press.

De Vos, George A. 1968. Suicide in Cross Cultural Perspective. In H.L.P. Resnick (Ed.), *Suicidal Behaviors: Diagnosis and Management* (pp. 105–134). Boston: Little, Brown, & Co.

———. 1973. *Socialization for Achievement: Essays on the Cultural Psychology of the Japanese.* Berkeley: University of California Press.

———. 1975. Apprenticeship and Paternalism: Psycho-Cultural Continuities Underlying Japanese Social Organization. In Ezra Vogel (Ed.), *Modern Japanese Organization and Decision Making*. Berkeley: University of California Press.

———. 1984. Religion and Family: Structural and Motivational Relationships. In George A. De Vos and Takao Sofué (Eds.), *Religion and Family in East Asia*. Senri Ethnological Studies No. 9. Osaka: National Museum of Ethnology.

———. 1993. A Cross-Cultural Perspective: The Japanese Family as a Unit in Moral Socialization. In P. Cowan, J. Field, D. Hansen, M. Scolnick, and G. Swanson (Eds.),

Family, Self, and Society: Toward a New Agenda for Family Research (pp. 115–142). Hillsdale, N.J.: Erlbaum Associates.

De Vos, George A. and Keiichi Mizushima. 1967. Organization and Social Function of Japanese Gangs. In Ronald Philip Dore (Ed.), *Aspects of Social Change in Modern Japan* (pp. 289–325). Princeton University Press.

De Vos, George A. and Takao Sofué (Eds.). 1986. *Religion and the Family in East Asia.* Berkeley, Calif.: University of California Press. (Revised).

De Vos, George A. and Hiroshi Wagatsuma. 1966. *Japan's Invisible Race: Caste in Culture and Personality.* Berkeley: University of California Press.

Doi, Takeo. 1973. *The Anatomy of Dependency.* Tokyo: Kodansha.

Dore, Ronald Philip. 1958. *City Life in Japan: A Study of a Tokyo Ward.* London: Routledge & Paul.

———. 1965. *Education in Tokugawa Japan.* Berkeley: University of California Press.

Durkheim, Emile. 1947. *The Elementary Forms of the Religious Life.* Trans. J.W. Swain. Glencoe, Ill.: The Free Press.

Erikson, Erik H. 1963. *Childhood and Society* (2nd edition). New York: Norton.

Firth, Raymond. 1940. The Analysis of Mana: An Empirical Approach. *Journal of the Polynesian Society*, **49**: 483–510.

Gyatso, Geshe Kelsang. 1994. *Meaningful to Behold: The Bodhisattva's Way of Life* (4th edition). London: Tharpa Publications.

Harlow, Harry F. 1973. *Learning to Love.* New York: Ballantine.

Hazan, C. and P. Shaver. 1987. Romantic Love Conceptualized as an Attachment Process. *Journal of Personality and Social Psychology*, **52**: 511–524.

Helm, June, George A. De Vos, and Teresa Carterette. 1960. Variations in Personality and Ego Identification Within a Slave Indian Kin-Community. National Museum of Canada Bulletin, No. 190, *Contributions to Anthropology*, Part II.

Horney, Karen. 1937. *Neurotic Personality of Our Times.* New York: W.W. Norton.

Kramer, G.W. 1992. A Psychobiological Theory of Attachment. *Behavioral and Brain Sciences*, **15**: 493–541.

Krasnegor, Norman A. and Robert S. Bridges (Eds.). 1990. *Mammalian Parenting: Biochemical, Neurobiological, and Behavioral Determinants.* Proceedings of the National Institute of Child Health and Human Development Conference on "Biological and Behavioral Determinants of Parental Behavior in Mammals," held in Leesburg, Va., Sept. 8–11, 1987. New York: Oxford University Press.

Lebra, T. 1969. Reciprocity and the Asymmetric Principle: An Analytical Reappraisal of the Japanese Concept of *On*. *Psychologia*, **10**: 129–138.

Lee, Changsoo and George A. De Vos. 1981. *Koreans in Japan: Ethnic Conflict and Accommodation.* Berkeley: University of California Press.

Maslow, Abraham Harold. 1955. Deficiency Motivation and Growth Motivation. In M.R. Jones (Ed.), *Nebraska Symposium on Motivation.* Lincoln: University of Nebraska Press.

———. 1962. Some Basic Propositions of a Growth and Self Actualization Psychology. In *Perceiving, Behaving, Becoming: A New Focus for Education.* Washington, D.C. Yearbook of the Association for Supervision and Curriculum Development.

McClelland, David. 1987. *Human Motivation.* New York: Cambridge University Press.

McClelland, David, with J.W. Atkinson, R.H. Clark, and E.L. Lowelle. 1953. *The Achievement Motive.* New York: Appleton-Century-Crofts.

Murphy, Lois B. 1937. *Social Behavior and Child Personality*. New York: Columbia University Press.

Nakane, Chie. 1970. *Japanese Society*. Berkeley: University of California Press.

Riesmann, Catherine H. 1990. *Divorce Talk: Women and Men Make Sense of Personal Relationships*. New Brunswick: Rutgers University Press.

Scheper-Hughes, Nancy. 1979. *Saints, Scholars, and Schizophrenics*. Berkeley: University of California Press.

Tu, Wei Ming. 1986. On Neo-Confucianism and Human Relatedness. In George A. De Vos and Takao Sofué (Eds.), *Religion and the Family in East Asia.* Berkeley, Calif.: University of California Press. (Revised).

Vogel, Ezra. 1963. *Japan's New Middle Class*. Berkeley: University of California Press.

Vogel, Ezra and F. Vogel. 1961. Family Security, Personal Immaturity, and Emotional Health in a Japanese Sample. *Marriage and Family Living*, **23**: 161-166.

Wagatsuma, Hiroshi and George A. De Vos. 1984. *Heritage of Endurance: Family Patterns and Delinquency Formation in Urban Japan*. Berkeley: University of California Press.

Chapter 5

Resonance, Closeness, and Communication: Affiliative Concerns in Human Relationships

Affiliation (F) is a basic expressive category marking horizontal relationships of physical, emotional, and intellectual closeness, or its converse, a sense of distance from others, loss of relationship, and isolation. It is built upon the capacities for experiencing mammalian resonance, whether physical, emotional, or intellectual. It is experienced as participation in a variety of communicative forms that entail physical proximity and mutual physical movement and/or emotional and mental understanding. Its absence is experienced as an awareness of being disconnected, rejected, or misunderstood. These concerns are frequently expressed in terms of the various exigencies of establishing or maintaining intimate friendship and loving relationship.

The Genesis and Contexts of Affiliation

Horizontal human relationships of the affiliative mode start from the experience of pleasurable mammalian contact in exchanging bodily warmth. The horizontal mammalian experiences of bodily warmth begin in concert with the more vertically ordered nurturing or succoring needs. The experience of closeness and warmth in early infancy occurs in the context of close physical contact between infants and caregivers. The experience of being understood comes from the interpersonal communication and mutual ontological validation that is constituted by the reciprocal attunement of infants and caregivers.[1] These early forms of closeness and communication are basic to the continuing human concerns about *psychological* and *physical* intimacy, that are expressed in various ways developmentally as efforts towards maintaining reciprocal contact and expressive understanding.

As we have noted in the previous chapter, concerns about the maintenance of a sense of closeness and mutual understanding are to be distinguished from the more vertical donor-recipient nurturance considerations. Both of these categories are commonly conflated in descriptions and experiences of the emotions and behavior that humans term "affection" or "love." We think it is advantageous to keep them separate, analytically.

Both horizontal (affiliative) and vertical (nurturant) needs pervade the earlier developmental periods. As the vertical and dependent nurturance requirements of immaturity become gradually transcended, individuals may nevertheless remain linked by forms of social bonding that continue the earlier affiliative relationship (Hazan and Shaver, 1987). There is a progressive shift with age toward some degree of individuation or independence, and toward an increased emphasis on horizontal-reciprocal concerns, even within child-parent relationships. Additionally, the arena for the expression of these concerns changes. As human psycho-sexual maturation proceeds, affiliative needs that are initially expressed within the family eventually come to be expressed in the context of broader reciprocal peer contacts. Such concerns eventually become central elements of adult intimacy and friendship, discourse, and sexual intercourse.

Where such affiliative concerns appear to be related to the *expressive* component of feelings engendered in horizontal relationships, these are addressed with the ICSS as the Affiliation (F) category. This is to be distinguished from concerns that emphasize mutual activity that serves instrumental purpose (which we will discuss later), as we find in either cooperative or competitive horizontal relationships. In our system, mutual instrumental activities are categorized as Mutual Purpose (M), not as Affiliation (F).

There are substantial individual differences in the degree to which affiliative bonds remain part of the independent adult lifestyle. There are also clearly cross-species differences in patterns of adult affiliation. Animals of some species remain closely bonded in interactive groups, whereas others become isolated after the period of immature dependency has ended. Within humans, individual differences may reflect variability in inherited tendencies as well as variability in personal developmental experiences. Differences across human social groups may also reflect culturally mediated patterns or styles of normative social interaction, including social-role constraints related to factors such as family roles, social status or gender.

---

[1]For an interesting discussion of some parallels between object relations theory and Sartre's existentialist position on ontological validity, see chapter 6 of Seinfeld (1993).

Family relationship patterns are often characterized by dependent interactions. However, the growing child begins to seek out and express friendship with those who share similar interests yet who are situated outside the immediate family. Psychologists have for decades observed the early development of peer group activities in nursery settings (e.g., Bronson, 1981; Maudry and Nekula, 1939). By the middle of the second year, children have begun to move towards interactive play with other children. Early imitative and object-focused interactive is gradually replaced by sociodramatic pretend play or fantasy play. Such sociodramatic play can be seen as a practice ground for the child's mental representation of social reality, and centers around social role enactments that are culturally appropriate (Farver and Shin, 1997). By three years of age, children are clearly aware of complementary social roles (Howes, Unger, and Seidner, 1989), and these can include vertical social roles, such as parent and child or doctor and patient, as well as more reciprocal peer roles.

Social participation increases in complexity between the second and fifth years, and once the period of isolated play has been passed, the affiliative and cooperative character of childhood play is readily apparent. Yet not only is there evidence of social togetherness and mutual purpose, one sees conflict as well. In childhood one sees evidence of the beginnings of competitive behavior, which is apparent in aggressive acts, both instrumental and hostile (Coie and Dodge, 1998; Hartup and Laursen, 1993).

In observing individual differences it is apparent that the infant's first social relations particularly with the mother, as well as parenting styles, more generally influence to some extent the attitude and behavior of a child with peers (Buhler, 1931;[2] Sroufe, Egeland, and Kreutzer, 1990; Sroufe, Egeland, and Carlson, 1999). The more "independent" the child and securely attached the child, the earlier and more successful are the child's ventures into peer relationships that involve horizontal or reciprocal interaction (Bowlby, 1988).

Any general statement about a progression away from vertical dependency toward horizontal and interactive relationships between autonomously functioning individuals must be qualified, however, with the recognition that the emphasis on what is desired or expected differs from society to society. Societies differ in their emphasis on hierarchical dependency or on equality and reciprocity in adult relationships. A sense of age-graded mentorship discussed in the previous chapter, for example, may be more pronounced in some societies compared with others.

---

[2]Buhler (1931) in her pioneer work, found three patterns of early interaction: (a) the "socially blind" children who ignore the presence of others; (b) the socially dependent who monitors his or her behavior according to another child's reaction; (c) the socially independent child who is self involved, but friendly and can be consoling or helpful of another. These approaches are influenced by relative age. A younger child assumes a more dependent attitudes with older peers.

In hierarchically age-graded societies, relationships may remain more pervasively defined in vertical terms. As noted above, in traditional Japan, some spousal marital relationships, for example, emphasize nurturant concerns and de-emphasize companionate needs (see, for example, Blood, 1967). Hierarchical cultures are sometimes more comfortable in having all positive relationships defined vertically rather than horizontally. The need for friendship and mutual intimacy remain secondary. In more egalitarian settings there are shifts in status toward more horizontal forms of interaction. Age and gender differences may be less defined in hierarchical terms.

In some settings, inter-generational relationships may cause discomfort when roles are not clearly defined as horizontal or vertical. There can be mutual alienation related to incompatible attitudes or expectations and a lack of mutual understanding of age-specific points of view. Sometimes generational relationships are complicated by attitudes of underlying dominance expressed as inappropriate attempts at unwelcome succor or by younger adults harboring unresolved feeling of continuing dependency resulting in unresolved internal conflict. Such conflict may become complex in nature. For example, unresolved needs can be deflected into either excessive demands or avoidance of social affiliation.

The Complexity of Interpersonal Concerns in the Sexual Arena

Sexual interest and interaction starts early and matures toward dyadic relationships subsequent to puberty. The age of expected sexual interest and the appropriate or tolerated forms of contact differ widely with culturally defined expectations. We cannot go into this complex topic in any detail, but we must note that it is essential to distinguish the pleasurable physical sensations of sexual excitation from the complex social context of sexual behavior as a psychosocial process. Sexuality is not normally experienced non-interactively as simple sensual pleasure (P). Sexual arousal is generally blended with mental states that are marked by a variety of both instrumental and expressive concerns.

It is safe to say that all sexual interest, whatever the sexual orientation, can *potentially* involve affiliative needs for contact to some degree. Sexuality is often experienced as part of a conscious desire for affiliation and is often expressed as efforts to maintain continuous or enduring affectionate closeness. Yet sexual behavior, per se, cannot be assumed to be always affiliative in intent or in satisfaction (Cook and Wilson, 1979). Furthermore, even where there is an affiliative component to sexuality, sexual needs as experienced are often not simply affiliative or "loving." They can often be enmeshed in very complex modes of human interaction (Benjamin, 1995).

While part of sexual satisfaction is found in the responsive warmth of close body contact with others, for some, sexual pleasure may not be experienced as simply affiliative, but may become more fused with other positive expressive vertical nurturant-succoring needs. It can involve acts of withholding, or be blended into acts of giving. Sexual encounters can also be blended negatively with a sense of inner insufficiency, insecurity, or insatiability. For some people, sexual activity is a reciprocal exchange between individuals of equal status. For others, it is never so considered.

Expressively considered, sexuality can be symbolic of deep harmony, or an aggressive, injurious act (H). It can even become blended with active or passive sado-masochistic desires for injury or destruction. Sex can be part of an evaluative dimension (E) whereby another or the self is judged. Positively considered, it can be an appreciative act with a socially desirable "other." Negatively considered, the performer can be exhibitionistic or perform sex as an act aimed at the debasement of the partner. It can also be experienced as an act of self debasement or self destruction.

Instrumentally, vertically considered, sexuality can be contextualized in a desire for control (D). In a horizontal dimension, it may be experienced competitively as an arena for outperforming others (M) or for cooperative conquest (M and D). For some, sex is instrumentally *self* oriented. Some experiences of sexual behavior are in a context of manifesting personal competence (C) or the partner is considered as a successful achievement of a targeted social status goal (A). For others, sexual intercourse can become a duty, or even a social role responsibility (R).

Sexuality can also be experienced impersonally. In some cases, either the self or the other can be seen to be a "sex object" or an "object of desire," and we often see possessive terms (e.g., "my lover") used in discourse regarding sex. Sexual depersonalization can manifest as forms of sexual slavery or ownership. Instances where the depersonalized sex object is seen as a possession (O) can be distinguished from instances in which the object is seen as a person subject to control (D), although both categories may co-occur.

Sex can also be experienced as determined by fate (K). Acts of sexual submission (or even sexual proceptivity) may be experienced fatalistically, as one gives up one's own free will to the flow of the moment. Such fatalistic experiences can be distinguished from acts of submission or proceptivity experienced as duty (R).

Therefore, while, very often, expressions of interest in or recounting of sexual behavior involves some affiliative concern of a positive or negative nature, verbal references to sexual interest or sexual behavior have to be scored or categorized according to the emic expression in which it is contextualized by the individual informant. These experiences are not necessarily affiliative in their intention or expression.

Chronic Incompleteness: Unresolved Affiliative Needs

As social animals, it is a characteristic of self-conscious human beings to experience a sense of incompleteness. Our sense of personal incompleteness is usually assuaged consciously, however, through attempts at establishing further *affiliation* through closer intimacy with others in dyadic ties. For some, the sense of separateness can only be overcome by some form of fusion of the self with a larger purpose. Often, as described in the above chapter on Nurture, when an individual experiences an abject feeling of needful *dependency* (N), a giving presence such as a provident God is sought out. Additionally, a sense of closeness to a supernatural being may be experienced in some forms of religious conversion (James, 1935). In religious reverie or meditation, an individual may experience a transformation of ordinary perception into an extraordinary transcendence of the separated self. In the English language a Christian "espousal" is not only a wedding to a religious belief but also necessitates active advocacy which produces a sense of belonging. Political allegiances may also act as such an assuagement.

Problems over the unsuccessful development of a satisfactory social identity that helps overcome social distance and isolation occur frequently in modern, complex, changing societies (see Riesman, Denney, and Glazer, 1950; Gordon, 1976). On an existential level some individuals may develop a profound sense of loneliness, a sense of distance that cannot be bridged (e.g., see Weiss, 1973; Peplau and Perlman, 1979; Wenz, 1977). The complex interrelationship between a lack of meaningful instrumental purpose and a sense of social isolation is dramatized in modern existential literature and discussed in existential philosophy.

In *Being and Nothingness*, Sartre (1943) concluded pessimistically regarding the possibility that one might attain ontological validity through relations with others. Instead, according to the existentialist metaphysics, it is only through the exercise of free will (as demonstrated through intentional action) that one's existence can be established (de Beauvior, 1975). Thus, Sartre ultimately suggests action, often consisting of political praxis, i.e., participation in some form of political movement, as a means of attaining ontological validity. Although the existentialist analysis denies a validating role for relationship and emphasizes individual free will as the sole basis for ontological validity, the existentialist's practical advice nevertheless returns us to social relationship, in the form of social praxis, as a means for overcoming existential "nausea" (see Sartre, 1962).

But, since we may never overcome an abiding sense of our inner insufficiency and incompleteness, we may also continually seek out satisfaction of our dependent needs by remaining subject to the expectations of others in face-to-face social encounters. As we consider in the following chapter, our behavior is often constrained so as to gain, or maintain, satisfactory social acceptability and the *Esteem* (E) of others.

Many religious thinkers and writers have attempted to communicate the experience of a quest for ultimate meaning in those who have lost a sense of primary attachment (see chapter 14, this volume). Either a religious conversion experience can occur, or one achieves a sudden dedication to social meaning of a political or ideological nature.

In some acute psychotic experiences, a mystical oneness may become cosmic in nature. A mystical experience can also be defined in positive terms in some religious contexts. Some mystical or meditative practices encourage a loss of boundaries between the experience of self and the cosmos, perhaps thereby reducing a sense of separateness or individuality. In contrast, some religious traditions, such as mainstream Christianity and Islam and some sects of Buddhism promise a continuity of an individualized "soul" or mind stream throughout eternity that finds spiritual unity with God or continued rebirth in other lives. This apparent paradox may be resolved in some Buddhist traditions, wherein the experience of one's being as a separate self that has inherent existence is acknowledged to be an illusory fabrication, whereas the continuity of one's personal karma through future lives is certain. The individual is thus encouraged to develop the conviction (based on meditative experience) that one's true essence partakes of the essential continuity and inclusiveness of all life linked inseparably in a completely causal universe that is nevertheless affected by the individual consciousness as a seat of moral responsibility. For some, the gnawing pain of personal isolation and hopeless separation that is expressed in the Existentialist's nausea may be symbolically healed or assuaged by entertaining such beliefs.

Egoistic Suicide

A failure to overcome profound existential "nausea" can lead to what Durkheim called "egoistic suicide" (see chapters 17 and 18 in De Vos, 1973b; see also chapter 14, this volume). In this sense of what can be termed "social meaning," we can grasp Durkheim's basic perception of society as a "reality existing prior to the individual." Should the individual become personally alienated from any response to social expectations, and further suffer the consequences of anomic loss of self regulation, he or she can become bereft of meaning and suffer further extreme forms of intolerable malaise (see Horowitz and French, 1979).

A prevalent form of suicide among some elderly is more directly consciously *affiliative* in some cases and experienced as an intolerable loss. Among some aged individuals are those who have suffered the loss of a mate of long standing. Others, however, may be coping with the increasing infirmity or the pain of failing health. For such individuals there seems in documented instances to be insufficient external emotional investment remaining to sustain interest in life.

The loss of a vital interest can lead to death without recourse to actual suicide. We do not yet well understand the role of our will to live in recovery from illness or in other related phenomena. In the aged, the loss of a marital companion or the final completion of some task is sometimes closely followed by a form of devitalization that results in death. This withdrawal of positive cathexis from body functions to the point of producing death is not viewed as deliberate and is usually not seen as related to suicide. Nevertheless, such a loss of a will to live, whatever its origin, is an essential element in egoistic suicide.

Loneliness Scales Compared with Scoring of Loneliness in Spontaneous Narrative

Standardized yet ambiguous stimuli [such as the Thematic Apperception Test (TAT)] provide opportunities for respondents to spontaneously voice their concerns. A person's descriptions of his or her apperception can be interpreted as evidence of internal preoccupation. For example, those who have unresolved or negative issues regarding affiliation with others may express those concerns, whereas other individuals responding to the same stimuli might instead refer to positive affiliations. The relative *spontaneous* appearance of some concerns in specific individuals can thereby be compared with others who are responding to the same stimuli. Additionally, the overall context in which affiliation concerns are framed, such as issues of social acceptability, nurture, etc., enriches the potential for meaningful theoretically guided interpretation. Affiliative concerns about acceptance or fears of rejection may co-occur with concerns about loss of security, incurred anger, irresponsibility or failure to live up to expectations, incompetence judged harshly, failures of mutual purpose or individual achievement, etc. The application of a scoring system such as the ICSS can provide a complex picture of the distinct configuration of a person's affiliative concerns, and how they fit into a larger experiential framework.

Many efforts in psychology, however, are aimed at more limited or focused measurement of specific psychological "constructs." What is most common is the use of checklists comprised of items that are provided to the respondent in an a priori manner. These checklists often reflect a researcher's desire to measure imputed psychological "constructs" that arise from theoretical speculation. Such checklists are usually constructed initially based on the face validity of the items. Their validity is then assessed using various statistical methods for empirical validation, such as factor analysis. The danger of the use of a priori item checklists, however, is that they may suggest issues that are not inherently salient to a given informant, thereby biasing his or her responses, and consequently failing to accurately assess the idiosyncratic and contextual concerns of the individual. The potential problems that may follow from this as checklists are applied in cross-cultural work should be obvious.

The validation process can include efforts to empirically correlate data obtained using the instrument that is being validated with data collected using other (sometimes more established) measures for assessing the same construct (or measures that assess other theoretically related constructs). Our method for collecting spontaneous narratives that describe apperceptive experiences contrasts with the checklist approach. Nevertheless, it can be useful to compare some of the dimensions obtained through theory-derived construct-oriented psychometric methods with those obtained using our more empirical narrative-analytical method. For example; in the context of systematically assessing loneliness with the UCLA Loneliness Scale, Russell, Peplau and Cutrona (1980) identified four useful factors that they found to be meaningfully correlated with other relevant measures.[3] The factors they identified in their work allow us to comment upon how such a loneliness scale corresponds to our expressive categories of Affiliation (F) and Esteem (E). In the items they used these investigators in our opinion seem to indicate an interrelatedness of some concerns about loneliness with special concerns over social acceptability.

What they labeled "Affiliative Motivation" was the most highly loaded with the items from their "Loneliness" list. These items suggest that a need for closeness is, indeed, central to affiliative concerns. Such issues are salient to many of the concerns we score below under Affiliation (F).

A second factor they labeled "Social Risk Taking" also contained positive measures of assertiveness, extroversion, self-esteem, and negatively, introversion and sensitivity to potential rejection. What this factor seems to measure as part of affiliative concerns is a confident readiness to anticipate positive interaction with others, versus some underlying anticipation of rejection felt by some. Our scoring system of (F) categories includes expression of both positive and negative anticipation of belonging or rejection, or uncertainty. Loneliness can be an abiding or unresolved concern of some individuals who can be considered "introversive" psychologically. They are, therefore, more prone to variety of spontaneous expressions in this regard. Also, concern with rejection, either already experienced, or anticipated, is relatively strong in some individuals compared with others.

Their factor analysis revealed a set of items that loaded on a factor they labeled "Social Desirability." This factor was found to be unrelated to other measures of loneliness. One can see why. What loaded on this factor are essentially concerns we have subsumed under our category (E), that covers concerns with social acceptability or appraisal, which we shall discuss presently in detail in the next chapter.

A remaining factor they termed "Negative Affect." The items that loaded on this factor were strongly related to the dimensions assessed by anxiety and depression scales. In examining their items, one can see how negative affect is linked with problematic relationships. In our scoring system, where expressions of either depression or anxiety occur in the context of a problematical relationship they are usually scored appropriately in our affiliative (F) category. But, where there is no interpersonal context described, expressions of depression or anxiety are subsumed under our Pleasure category (P), discussed in a previous chapter.

---

[3]See also Nerviano and Gross (1976), Peplau and Perlman (1979), and Peplau, Russell, and Heim, (1979).

Group Closeness in Social Perception and the Maintenance of Group Cohesion

Being alone—isolated or alienated—is intolerable for most human beings. A felt necessity for a sense of belonging or affiliation can be expressed frequently through one's close identity with a group. A sense of group belonging also affords a means of finding one's harmonious place in an entity larger than oneself (see chapter 7, volume I, on Harmony). Total social isolation without face-to-face contacts and communication afforded by some form of group membership or intimate personal contact is difficult to maintain.

The basic human need is for some form of intimacy, companionship, and affiliation and this can be best found among those with common emotional experiences. An outsider cannot readily provide the same kind of understanding. Members of an ethnic group, for example, can provide a mutual sense of intimacy and communication for those sharing past common experiences. In this regard, a generalized ethnic identity may sometimes supplant more directly personal and intimate one-to-one relationships. Group belonging can compensate for individual difficulties in achieving intimacy.

The threat of separation from the group is one of the most stringent of human sanctions. Ostracism for behavior against the group is a far more potent social sanction than the more personal punishment or legal restrictions imposed on an individual from the outside. In order to maintain a sense of belonging with a group, the individual will strictly monitor personal behavior. As we shall presently discuss, such mechanisms are very visible in Japanese American groups, especially among peers, and as such have kept the delinquency rate very low. Curiously, in some groups, peer group sanctions may make it difficult for a school system to discipline an individual. Conformity to the demands of the school against the resistance of the peer group may result in severe sanctions of the member (De Vos, 1992, chapter 4). One is not to undertake individual development at the expense of group belonging. Individual action can be an implicit threat to the group's cohesiveness and resistance to the hated majority outside.

A generation gap or antagonisms between the generations is potentially present in group behavior. An individual may more readily find satisfying and intimate companionship with peers of similar ethnic origin than with primary family members of a different generation.[4] This aspect of group affiliation overlaps with a consciousness about social acceptability as discussed further in the following chapter on Esteem.

---

[4]This process was especially noted among Mexican American youth in some interviews of a young prison population where the ethnic peer group had quickly replaced the primary family as a point of social reference (see also, De Vos, 1992, chapter 7).

The Function of the Peer Group as an Agent of Social Communication

An important consideration cross-culturally is how identity formation is related to the self through the influence of peer group participation (Sherif and Sherif, 1964; Sherif, 1967). In multiethnic contemporary societies, the functioning of the peer group in social self-identity formation and social communication patterns differs greatly depending on the continuing interaction of a complex number of cultural, social, and psychological determinants. Such concerns are often neglected in both psychological and social structural analyses.

First, viewed in a cultural-historical perspective, there are major differences in respect to the types and degree of cohesion of family patterns arising from past traditions (Riesman, Denney, and Glazer, 1950; Miller and Swanson, 1958). These family traditions influence community cohesion, which in turn influences the peer group formation and social communication occurring within the minority communities. The relative adaptability or non-adaptability of the peer groups in which ethnic children function in a pluralistic society is determined by the effectiveness of the social sanctioning of youth by their community or family. Some ethnic minorities maintain stronger sanctioning practices than do others, where control is weaker. Past cultural traditions of the primary family influence how a child interacts in the new social atmosphere of peer groups and other social contacts related to minority status.

Viewed *socially,* in situations of change, tensions within particular families or weakness of effective sanctioning within a reconstituted ethnic community can occur. A child operates in a new social setting. New patterns of peer group relationships will appear. Age-specific memberships are selectively chosen during childhood and adolescence by individuals, depending on the closeness or distance of rapport within the primary family. The peer groups available, as well as the primary family, help determine not only how a changing ethnic identity will be developed, but how social role expectations will change and how certain collective representations will be more salient than other alternative ways of viewing society (see De Vos and Suárez-Orozco, 1990, chapter 1).

Cognitive or Perceptual Patterns of Social Communication and Group Rapport

At the level of social role interactions, past cultural traditions can be seen to help determine the nature of continuing family cohesion, the traditional roles played within the family and the way the family transmits concerns about social status. This traditional pattern will already include some expected definition of how peer groups are to function.

Examined on a psychological level, *cognitive and perceptual structures* that underlie communicative patterns are formed first in the context of family. But interaction with a peer group can either reinforce or go counter to what was previously developed. As suggested by the research of Witkin and his associates (e.g., Witkin and Berry, 1975; see also, Vaughn, 1988), there are differences in prior cognitive structures related to how peer groups come to interact. Family patterns differ not only in respect to the degree of interactive cohesion maintained, but in the forms of discipline practiced toward children and the nature of communication that may facilitate or impede certain forms of cognitive maturation or "cognitive style." Different cognitive styles are later reinforced in peer group interaction.

Ethnic groups differ in emphasizing the selective utilization of given mental mechanisms involved in learning social adaptation. Therefore, one will find psychocultural differences in cognitive style in parent-child communication and later forms of interaction both within the family and outside. Groups will differ in the typical pattern of discipline utilized in affecting behavior. Families will differ in the degree of consistent, hierarchical, or nonhierarchical differences within family roles. These emphases, in turn, will be influential in how peer groups operate.

How families are accepted or rejected by children in a multiethnic social structure becomes reflected in peer group patterns. A major influence on how peer groups function is the structuring of present social animosities derived from traditions of past social stratification or degradation that influence peer group activities. Some peer groups become defensive, enclaved, and antagonistic toward outsiders. Other peer groups become accommodative and influence the individual toward more accommodative relationships with members of other groups. The present sociological environment will provide some degree of acceptability or inclusion for each minority group due to specific historic circumstances, the forms taken by discrimination, and the place of a minority group in some preconceived past historical pattern of ethnic class, caste, and sex role status expectations.

In sum, patterns of peer group socialization and group identity formation fostered in early and subsequently continuous peer relationships will be as salient as parental relationships, depending upon the complex interaction of sociological and psychological variables examined on more than one level of analysis.

Family Cohesion Versus Peer Group Orientation: Some Ethnographic Comments

Our cross-cultural work with crime and delinquency as well as minority status has led us to consider the interaction of peer group allegiance and family cohesion of central concern in understanding the development of horizontal affiliative relationships.

Reference Group Theory Reconsidered

Whereas Muzafer and Carolyn Sherif (1964, 1967) have used reference group theory as a powerful instrument for understanding social processes in communities, the emphasis too often in the use of these concepts has been on the conscious face-to-face affiliation of individuals. Relatively less attention is paid to the dynamic, sometimes conflicting interrelationship between the internalized conscience, more or less acquired in the family, and the immediate peer reference group influence. Apparent in those individuals who have strongly internalized a family identity is the maturation of a social identity somehow more tuned to prior family directives and therefore relatively less susceptible to immediate group influences. Such "inner directed" individuals, to use Riesman's term (Riesman et al., 1950) in some sense have more autonomy (inner regulation) and are less subject to the vagaries of immediate social pressures to conform to group influences.

In minority groups where family interaction is generally less cohesive, or in individuals residing within a particular family where regulatory conflicts are greater, there is more dependence on the reference group as a secondary medium of socialization. This *priority of peer group over family* is quite apparent in many acculturative situations. Especially where the families are less cohesive, the parents may become viewed as "foreigners" or as out of date. Children are alienated from the past adult community and seek social identification as defined among their peers. This has been a notable process in the more assimilative "Americanization" of previous generations of ethnic minorities coming from Europe. But for European immigrants, the reference group itself was defined as "American" by the growing youth. More recently, however, for youthful Mexican Americans, African Americans, Puerto Ricans, and Chinese Americans in San Francisco, the peer reference group itself may become "acculturated," but serves to maintain a separateness in social orientation that prevents ready identification with the majority white population.

This peer group alienation has traditionally operated in a similar fashion among Native Americans. Their social group has been historically overrun by an expanding European population; but they have resisted any incorporative definitions by the white culture. Note well, however, how this type of separateness is maintained in peer group orientation and is somehow directly related to a sense of adult status degradation directed toward their parents coming from the outside. It is in such situations of relative adult status degradation that the family moral authority of socially alienated parents has itself been replaced by a defensive peer group orientation. This occurs over several generations in some traditionally degraded groups.[5]

---

[5]This topic warrants far more explication than can be pursued here.

Peer Group Sanctioning

In self-preservative reactions, the peer group, throughout the life span, continually tends to sanction against individuals trying to leave a group. The mechanisms employed can be subtle or directly coercive. An account told to us by another anthropologist is a paradigm of such peer group pressure. A Native American Apache high school graduate, upon being awarded a college scholarship, came home afterward only to receive a severe beating and to find his dog killed by his peers. Change of reference orientation in a member of the group can be experienced as a threat to the collectivity.

This threat is not simply to the cohesion of the group, but to the implicit defensive posture of the group against the intrusion of alien expectations of accomplishment that would entail an examination of personal inadequacies. Contrastively, youthful minority peer groups more often are used to ward off the expectations of adulthood defined in majority terms. In a plural society, minority peer groups not only resist the demands of the dominant society, they sometimes prepare their members for a sense of coming failure. Collectively maintained defensive attitudes both prevent attempts to succeed, and prevent any critical self-examination for unsatisfactory life circumstances. The group collectively helps place blame for any personal failure on majority prejudice. To attempt to succeed individually, and then fail is to acknowledge the possibility that failure is in the self, or in the inferiority of the group to which one belongs.

Hence, there is a negative circle in which one cannot try to succeed in generally accepted social terms without becoming personally alienated from one's group. The negative stance of the minority group ironically perpetuates the very need to defend against implications of inferiority, by denying the competitive goals thrust upon the group by a disparaging host society that already judges a group incapable of picking up the challenge. Those with partial African ancestry particularly are caught by this dilemma between the necessity for personal endeavor, and their readiness to put blame on severe past caste discrimination for any frustrations when they arise. African American conservative authors (e.g., McWhorter, 2000) who seek to assess motivational problems in youth are immediately subject to severe professional and personal attack. Even in the academic community, it is difficult to address issues other than discrimination in examining poor performance in minorities. Yet, those with a broader view can acknowledge the similarity of circumstances faced by all minorities dealing with the more subtle forms of present-day discrimination in multiethnic America. The presence of discrimination does not explain differences in reaction to discrimination.

Family Expectations Versus Peer Group Acculturation

The more horizontal peer groups in minorities provide an affiliative bond for those losing affective attachments marked by vertical generational age grading in traditional societies. An important issue in discussing subcultural modes of adaptation related to any minority situation is the conditions under which youth become antagonistic not only to the majority society but to their own parental generation. Another issue is how they develop shared collective representations specific to their face-to-face social group.

Contrasted with the frequent conflict between the peer group, the parents, and the school found among African American and Mexican American children, what one sees in contemporary Japan as well as in many Japanese American children in the United States is a peer-group affiliative orientation which mutually reinforces an intense emotional commitment to the formal learning processes of the school (Lewis, 1995; Schwalb and Schwalb, 1996; Werner, 1979).

However, the fact that harmony of peer group and family directives did not hold up in all circumstances in Japanese Americans is well illustrated when comparing the striking record of the American-born Nisei within the regular American school system with the very poor results obtained in teaching Japanese in the Japanese-language schools established in the 1920s and 1930s by Japanese parents. Parents wanted their children to preserve the language and culture of their homeland. However, the special Japanese language schools to which children were sent after regular school hours did not "take." There was great implicit as well as explicit resistance to learning the Japanese language among Nisei. In this instance, the peer group reinforced the more general social attitudes found among the children of other immigrant groups who resisted learning the parental language. Such resistance has been a characteristic of the social self-identity of American immigrants rather generally and was also adopted by the first sizable generation of American-born Japanese (De Vos, 1966).

In regular schools, however, the social attitudes shared by the Japanese community and by Japanese families were reinforced by the collective activity of the Nisei peer group. In this respect, behavior of Japanese in the ordinary public schools resembled that of middle-class American children rather than lower-class children. The automatic American social self-identity taken on by the Nisei child resembled, therefore, the assimilative patterns taken on by waves of European immigrants in the American cities. That is to say, the language of the Japanese child, as happened with European children in Chicago and New York schools at the turn of the century, became the lingua franca—English. Any attempt to maintain at least a bilingual heritage, as in most immigrant ethnic minorities, was defeated by peer group resistance. Spontaneously, English became the "natural language" of most American-born children of immigrants.

Such an acculturative peer group pattern contrasts very directly with alternative patterns more frequently found among some groups: African Americans and Mexican Americans as well as Hawaiians. Symbolically, separate modes of speech—"Black English" (now sometimes termed "Ebonics") "Latina," "Pidgin"—are reinforced in dissident peer groups as part of the continuity of a different identity. One must note that in these extreme cases, the peer group also goes counter to any socially assimilative type of school interaction. It is noticeable now that Mexican American and Black peers tend to create a separating interaction with the other groups of a school population. They are equally alienated from their own parental generation who, in good part, hope that their children will do well in school to guarantee them an adequate future.[6]

Whereas in some of the earlier European immigrant situations separate gangs of youth would form, the general language of the peer group usually became English regardless of other ethnic differences in response to the schools. Depending on cultural and class background, the American school was variously used as an adaptive instrument by the children of immigrants for social and educational advancement. It was not accidental that immigrant eastern European Jews with a tradition of scholarship did relatively well in the schools and children of immigrant Poles of peasant background did relatively poorly.

Again, to reiterate, one has to look back to specific cultural traditions in the use of cognitive styles within the family, including verbal communication between parents and children from early childhood. Moreover, it is very important to consider differences in the methods of childhood discipline used to foster internalization of modes of cognitive functioning. The matter is further complicated by the fact that characteristic patterns of parental discipline contribute to subcultural patterns of peer group interaction that aid or hinder learning in the schools. There are also subcultural variations in the type of interaction established between the family and the peer group as primary reference groups. These interactive processes continually contribute not only to the development of social self-identity in the children of migrants or minorities, but these processes effect the patterns of learning used by the child in the school.

Examined on a cognitive psychological level, of crucial issue is how parental discipline, whether deliberately or inadvertently, causes forms of internalization that emphasize particular cognitive coping mechanisms and that are receptive to the collective representations of a specific social segment of the total society. The development of thought is not only related to *how* a child internalizes the standards and values of the adult society, but it also in turn affects the availability of adaptive

---

[6]Again, one must note the difference generally cited in the sociological literature between *cultural* or *behavioral* assimilation, and *structural* or *social* assimilation. Some groups can assimilate the dominant culture, but be excluded from the dominant group, or *choose to* remain socially separate. There was a division among Japanese American Nisei in the 1930s between those who readily interacted with majority peers and those who kept to themselves, but maintained the same social patterns as the majority in the high schools they were attending. They remained socially separate by deliberate choice.

patterns allowing for the utilization of abstract thought and modes of intimate communication.

One must then ask, how do characteristic forms of internalization previously fostered in the family relate to the complementary use of the peer group as a further formative influence in the final development of an identity that defines satisfactory adult economic and social roles and specific forms of thought? These important questions deserve systematic research inquiry.

Avoidance of Personal Isolation Related to a Minority Identity: Minorities in Japan

Problems of ethnic identity can arise if self-affirmation signals that one is leaving the group. This decision leads to rejection or enforced isolation in the larger society and as such, involves severe psychological strain. For example, former outcastes (De Vos and Wagatsuma, 1966) who having tried to "pass" (as regular Japanese) for some time find the isolation intolerable, tend to finally return to their own group, giving up promising professional careers bought at the cost of complete social estrangement and personal isolation. The whole topic of individualism and alienation is related to problems of group maintenance. For some, a sense of group belonging is the ultimate meaning of life. An attempt to pass may completely strip away this meaning and cause total alienation.

As noted (De Vos, 1973b), the vertically oriented family in Japanese culture may provide a deep sense of psychological security *without* supplying intimate communicative companionship to any of its members. Regardless of the priority given to direct companionate types of intimacy and contact, the Japanese family affords other forms of warmth and a sense of belonging for the individual. A need for affiliation is usually directed more toward the satisfaction to be gained from intimacy and close contact between specific individuals outside the family, either in bonds of peer group friendship or in some heterosexual attachments.

With Korean Japanese, our psychological materials (Lee and De Vos, 1981) emphasized a very strong sense of personal alienation in contrast with the cohesive family concerns found in majority Japanese records. One may infer that the Korean family in Japan often provides less expressive gratification, not only in intimacy (F) but in harmony (H), self-respect (E), and nurture (N) for those related to a disparaged minority status in Japan. Marginality and being apart are sources of inner agony and tension.

In our study of minority Koreans in Japan, we noted, for example, that an extreme complexity of peer group involvement in identity can occur. A conflicting identity of being a despised Korean is difficult to avoid in a culture in which the individual's parents do not speak Korean but Japanese; where their legal status remains that of foreigners; where the father is often unemployed or works ambiguously at a dubious occupation; where the mother is very often constrained to work as a bar hostess; where the children are not supervised with the constancy that they need, especially in early childhood; where the Korean child is often ridiculed as dirty and uncouth, or feared as tough and belligerent by his Japanese mates. Under such complex, socially unrewarding circumstances, the Korean youth finds it most difficult to resolve with any finality his chronic problems of belonging, even with the help of peer group socialization.

Individual instances reveal how complex this problem can become. In some of the individual cases we have studied, a Japanese peer reference group at times accepts the individual Korean child without any negative reference to his background. At other times, however, the individual must make selective identification with either a Korean group against Japanese or join a Japanese group in which there is animosity expressed toward Koreans. Yet, in other instances, some individuals who are accepted by a Japanese group will, in peer group conflicts in school, be forced to make a loyalty choice which at times can pit him against other Korean youth. The situation can become very complex for the individual.

Looking at the problem longitudinally, both in childhood and in adolescence, the same individual may at one time make an identification with Japanese peers, and at other times become affiliative with other Koreans of his own age. In this movement back and forth, the individual is often struggling with internal conflicts of a self-deprecatory nature (E). If a person should too readily identify with the degraded Korean community, he or she may experience a sense of worthlessness. Yet at any given rebuff or setback in relation to majority Japanese, whether based on prejudice or not, what comes into focus very often is a basic lack of self-confidence (C) derived from the inescapable knowledge that one is of Korean origin. In some cases, however, a secure family identity leads to a persistence and a sense of dedication to personal achievement (A) and overcoming barriers to accomplishment.

In general, ethnic group membership, even in disparaged minorities, may supply the forms of contact and affiliation necessary for day-to-day living. But some individuals may give up social group needs because they feel a prior positive strong *instrumental* need for personal *autonomy* (D; see chapter 10, volume I) and independence or individual instrumental advantage through personal *achievement* (A; see chapter 8, volume I). Negatively, they may have a stronger need to escape personal disparagement or social embarrassment to maintain self *esteem* (E; see chapter 6, volume I). As they search out their own goals, they may be willing to become distant and uncommitted to previous attachments. For many, however, the continuing need for affiliation is too strong to cut ties. Few can accomplish the coldness necessary for distancing oneself from others without some internal discomfort.

For Koreans as well as the former outcastes in Japan, the relative strength of their need for affiliation is interrelated to whether or not an individual chooses to pass by cutting overt ties, leaving his own family and childhood friendships behind in seeking an individual route of social mobility. Whatever their inner willingness to pass, at least on the surface, individuals who seek to leave their group are also subject to various forms of interpersonal sanctioning. The principal threat, of course, is that of ostracism and rejection by the group. A group that in turn feels rejected by a former member can become even physically destructive toward a perceived deserter or traitor. In some cases the sanction employed is exposure, being "outed" a sanction more readily being considered in recent trends among minority group individuals such as homosexuals. For many, the threat of isolation or of aggressive rejection can be a very heavy sanction that keeps them within the group.

Korean youth and children of Burakumin in Japan seem to do relatively poorly in school for similar reasons found to operate in some American minorities, such as among African Americans or Mexican Americans (De Vos, 1980). Individuals do not identify or internalize standards and expectations set for them by members of the external majority (see chapter 11, volume I). Instead, the peer group becomes the principal source of affiliative gratification, discouraging acquiescence and conformity to the school as an institution. The peer group also becomes the arena for demonstration of prowess and competence (C; see chapter 9, volume I), the source of esteem (E; see chapter 6, volume I) related to an appreciative judgment received from other youth.

The absence of affiliative stories can be informative. In our TAT research with minority Koreans, for example, we see that fewer positive expressions of affiliative concerns are to be found among alienated minority youth whose fantasies are often expressive of distance or non-relatedness in the figures perceived in the TAT cards (see chapter 7, volume II). Such a lack of affiliative stories where they can be expected can be interpreted as indicating some form of alienation. We must also note impressionistically that Korean Japanese youth in many instances are stronger in their disregard of family or adult authority simply because there is less gratification to be gained from interdependent family relationships.

Affiliation is sought in peer group relationships that are frequently delinquency oriented and antagonistic toward social authorities, including teachers and others functioning in Japanese administrative agencies. These attitudes of protective association (N; see chapter 4, volume I) and antagonism (H; see chapter 7, volume I) toward the outside are sometimes perpetuated into adulthood by both Koreans and Burakumin (De Vos and Wagatsuma, 1966; Lee and De Vos, 1981).

Korean Japanese seem to seek out individual affiliations in marriage. Although their Confucian tradition emphasizes vertical family role patterns rather than intimate companionship, today, they seem less prone to concern themselves with family considerations. One notes that among younger Koreans, just as among younger majority Japanese, there is a greater desire for finding closeness and intimacy in the marital bond. Indeed, romantic love today in some few instances transcends the social barriers set up between Koreans and lower status Japanese. Such marriages can compound problems of identity on the part of the Korean partner. He or she is faced with the necessity to affirm or deny Korean affiliations outside of marriage and at the same time to maintain solidarity with his or her mate. There are numerous instances of difficulties arising in mixed marriages owing to external pressures of family or internal problems of divided loyalty (De Vos, 1973a). In turn, mixed marriages produce children who have their own identity problems, who must decide on their principal allegiances and the principal groups from which they will seek out companions.

The Scoring Categories Related to Affiliative Concerns

*A. Positive Contact, Communication, or Reunion **FA***

Closeness

FA-empathy	Resonance, sympathy, empathy, understanding
FA-inform	Seeking closeness through communication
FA-friend	Friendship
FA-love	Love and warmth in a relationship: physical closeness
FA-sex	Sexual relationships viewed positively
FA-trust	Emphasis on trust in an affiliative relationship
FA-similar	Affiliation through a sense of similarity (kinship, ethnicity, gender, class, physical appearance)
FA-share	Affiliation through a sense of shared experiences or similarity in past experiences
FA-ties	Affiliation valued more than concern with objects or other activities
FA-injury	Injurious act to self or others as an act of love (includes euthanasia)

Positive Coping with Separation or Reunion

FA-distant	Contact despite distance
FA-solitude	Hermetic solitude viewed positively
FA-travel	Travel for a friendly visit
FA-console	Self consoling; coping with separation
FA-happen	Reestablishment of contact broken due to external circumstances
FA-mend	Reestablishment of relationship broken due to discord, etc.
FA-rite	Ritual of amity or restoration of relationship
FA-death	Dyadic reunion in death
FA-mystic	Closeness to the ineffable or merger with the sacred
FA-casual	Casual relationship, nontraumatic

Continuities in Companionship and Sexual Attraction. Among adults, affiliation marks a need for continuing reciprocal contact and closeness. Capacities for understanding can be noted in expressions of sympathy or empathy with the needs of another for closeness. There may be expressed a direct sense of closeness in the form of sympathetic understanding, or empathic awareness (FA-empathy). There may be a seeking for a closer understanding through imparting information, establishing communication (FA-inform). Concerns with friendship relations are among the most frequent expressions of affiliation (FA-friend). What is termed friendship, however, can differ in different social contexts. Peer group ties start in childhood: their form may change but they are found throughout the life trajectory. In some societies peer relationships remain gender specific or age-graded, in others, peer reciprocity can transcend age and sex differences.

This need for closeness may be combined with various forms of what are termed love relationships, very often as a form of either nonmarital or marital companionship (FA-love). Love can be explicitly depicted as a sexual bonding (FA-sex). The basic trust that is first fostered in early maternal relationships (Erikson, 1963; Ainsworth et al., 1978) later come to characterize both horizontal companionate (FA-trust) and vertical nurturing relationships (NSA-trust).

There are various other expressions of affiliation and a sense of similarity related to group belonging (FA-similar). These similarities may be on the basis of kinship, ethnicity, gender, class, or physical appearance. Affiliation may be due to some specified sense of shared experiences or past ordeal (FA-share). For some, closeness may sometimes be possible only within one's own ethnic group with the mutual sharing of familiar experiences. Personal ties can be directly compared as more valued than other activities or interests or concern with objects (FA-ties). One may express a positive feeling about a casual relationship with no ties or future commitment (FA-casual). One even finds expressions of an injury to self or others as an act of love or closeness (FA-injury). Euthanasia may be double scored under this category (FA-injury NDA-active) with a form of succor.

Positive Coping with Separateness or Reunion. Affiliation can be kept despite being separated to some circumstance a sense of emotional closeness can overcome geographic distance (FA-distant). A positive sense of affiliation receives some very complex expressions, such as positively experienced solitude and detachment from others (FA-solitude). One can be consciously self consoling and cope positively with separation (FA-console).

Among major positive affiliative concerns are reestablishment of relationships that have been broken or interrupted due to circumstances. There may, for example, be a reunion of family after the death of a member, or one may travel to renew an affiliative relationship (FA-happen). There can be the reestablishment of relationships broken due to discord (FA-mend). There can be concern with rituals symbolizing amity or restoration of relationship (FA-rite). There are fantasies of some reunion after death (FA-death), or a mystical closeness or mergers of a religious nature (FA-mystic). One may also view a casual, transient relationship in positive terms (FA-casual).

B. *Unresolved Problems Related to Affiliation* ***FB***

Felt Need; Wanting Better Contact or Expressions of Warmth	
FB-aware	Awareness of the sorrow or discomfort of another
FB-shy	Shyness
FB-isolate	Frustrated affiliation; inability to communicate
FB-alone	A deep sense of unresolved isolation or aloneness
FB-longing	Loneliness or longing for someone, homesick
FB-apart	Concern with possible or actual separation, temporary or not (due to circumstances)
FB-wait	Waiting for someone
FB-reach	Worry about getting close or communicating
Problematic Relationship	
FB-problem	Undefined problem in relationship
FB-thwart	Thwarted in establishing a desired relation
FB-unruly	Passionately involved, helplessly in love
FB-accord	Lack of mutual understanding; unfamiliarity
FB-cry	Crying after a falling out
FB-distant	Unresolved feeling of emotional or attitudinal distance
FB-separate	Separation required by other purpose
FB-neglect	Sense of being neglected in a relationship
FB-jealousy	Fear of being replaced; rivalry about attention or regard
FB-envy	Envy of the closeness of others
FB-distrust	Distrust, anxieties about sincerity
FB-unmet	Discontent, dissatisfaction in a relation
FB-unsuited	Incompatibility in a relationship
FB-commit	Unresolved commitment
FB-split	Unresolved after attempt at split
FB-result	Negative influence of lover or peers
FB-observe	Observing without contact
FB-alien	No relationship depicted among the characters in a story
FB-identity	Problem about social identity

Felt Need; Wanting Better Contact or Expressions of Warmth. Someone may be aware of the sorrow and discomfort of another without the ability to come close enough to assuage or to comfort (FB-aware). In attempting to establish a relationship there are concerns with shyness (FB-shy). There may be a deep sense of unresolved isolation (FB-isolate). In a transitional state one may sense unresolved isolation or aloneness (FB-alone). One may experience loneliness in longing for a specified other, one may feel homesick when away (FB-longing). There may be worries about an impending or possible separation (FB-apart). One may be in an anticipatory state, waiting for someone with some anxiety (FB-wait). There may be worry about how to get close or communicate with another (FB-reach).

Problematic Relationships. One may express a sense of problem about a relationship without specifying its nature (FB-problem). One may experience an unresolved frustration in attempting to establish a desired love relationship, due to a number of possible reasons, from lack of opportunity to lack of response from the desired other (FB-thwart). One may become passionately involved or fall hopelessly in love (FB-unruly).

There may be an expressed sense of lack of mutual understanding which frustrates a relationship (FB-accord). Some figures in stories are depicted as crying due to some form of falling out (FB-cry).

What may be experienced with discomfort is some inability to communicate (FB-inform) which frustrates a sense of desired closeness. What may be felt in various situations are a sense of emotional distance, and inability of one's partner, or oneself to have, or develop, any sense of satisfactory closeness (FB-distant). One may be separated due to pursuing another purpose or activity (FB-separate).

There may arise a sense of being neglected (FB-neglect), or jealousy about losing the affections of one's lover (FB-jealousy). There can be envy of the perceived affiliative closeness of others compared with oneself (FB-envy). As in the case of early experiences of constancy in nurture, constancy in affectionate interchange from an early period leads to a later readiness to be trustful in, or optimistic about, reciprocal relationships. Events may stimulate a direct conscious concern, distrust, or worry about lack of sincerity (FB-distrust) is a problem. It may be more often experienced in love relationships or friendships formed outside the basic family unit. There may develop discontent with a partner or dissatisfaction with a relationship (FB-unmet). What may be unresolved is some particular dislike which must be scored under disharmony (HB dislike), whereas a sense of basic incompatibility (FB-unsuited) is scored as unresolved affiliation. In contemporary love relationships there is a great deal of worry about the depth or intensity of commitment (FB-commit).

There are unresolved feelings about reestablishing a relationship after an actual break is attempted. One can be uncertain whether or not the split is permanent (FB-split).

One can be concerned with the negative influence of a peer or a love relationship, either on the part of another, or on oneself (FB-result). One might become an observer rather than a true participant in a relationship (FB-observe).

There are a number of stories given by informants that are marked by a lack of relationship among individuals. We use a subcategory here to tabulate and score such stories (FB-alien). Finally there are unresolved concerns with a closeness or belonging to a group (FB-identity).

C. *Negative Acts in an Affiliative Context* ***FC***

FC-split	Separation (sometimes not explained); flight from contact; withdrawal
FC-drift	Loss of feelings or closeness of another with time
FC-reveal	Reveal an uncomfortable secret
FC-neglect	Neglect of another
FC-deceit	Deception of a spouse or family member
FC-desert	Abandon friend or lover
FC-reject	Rejection and divorce
FC-triangle	Triangular relationship
FC-sex-rej	Sexual rejection of a partner
FC-betray	Deception or betrayal of a friend, lover
FC-seduce	Seduction of a sexual or nonsexual nature, also impersonal lust
FC-impose	An imposed continuance of a relationship
FC-selfish	Disregard of another; incapacity to be sensitive to another
FC-demand	Excessive demand or excessive focus (emotional or physical)
FC-affect	Inability to accept affection
FC-union	Suicide with another to create union (double score with HC-injury)
FC-injure-s	Injury to self and other due to loss of a relationship (double score with HC-injury)
FC-suicide	Injurious act to self after the hurt of a love object (double score with HC-injury or HC-murder)
FC-pact	An affiliative pact leading to injury of both for selfish motives

The most general negative affiliative act is simply leaving or separating with no explanation given (FC-split). There are a variety of reasons for breaking or harming an affiliative relationship with an individual or group. There are various possible conflicts between instrumental needs to accomplish or answering the call of responsibility and a possible consequent separation from a loved one or a social group (FC-selfish FC-split). In some instances there is an awareness of one's active lack of affection resulting from preoccupation with achievement at the expense of interpersonal closeness. Such expression can be double scored (AA-self FC-split). For some, successful social mobility may seem to dictate cutting ties with family or social group. Conversely, members of a group may experience the relative instrumental success of one of its members as an act of betrayal (AA-self MTC-betray; see the chapter on Mutuality). Groups sanction their members not to become too different in status or personal accomplishments. Interethnically, differences arouse distrust. Questions of interpersonal trust can arise in both instrumental acts of cooperation as well as in expressive affiliative relationships.

What may be expressed is a sense of drifting apart and losing affection for another which is a slow form of desertion (FC-drift). There may be a sense of disregarding another's feeling, or being neglectful (FC-neglect). One may deceive one's family, friends, or lover (FC-deceit). There may also be an abandonment of a friend or lover. Desertion or rejection of someone occurs in a number of contexts (FC-desert). More active negative resolutions are found in active rejection or formal divorce (FC-reject). There are forms of rejection of others as ugly (FC-reject EDC-disgust) or uninteresting (FC-reject EDC-other) to be double scored with depreciation (see below).

Complex situations develop in triangular love relationships (FC-triangle). There may be a sexual rejection of a partner (FC-sex-rej). There may be acts of betrayal (FC-betray), or seduction (FC-seduce), or the use of a partner impersonally solely for sexual purposes.

One may seek to impose a relationship on another (FC-impose). One may become demanding, or put an excessive focus on a relationship (FC-demand). From the perspective of active, negative relationships, one may view a person as actively warding off the positive feelings forwarded by another due to being unable to experience the closeness on another (FC-affect).

Affiliative relationships can be injurious or damaging. There are self-injurious acts committed in seeking for another (FC-injure-s), including suicide (FC-suicide), because a relationship is broken. In Japan, there were even suicidal pacts (FC-pact) marking very complex affiliative relationships. There were several instances in our Japanese materials of an injurious act to self and another to create union after death (FC-union). Some of these negative affiliative concerns or expressions should be double scored with HC-injure as described in a following chapter. For example, injurious acts to self and other because of the loss of a relationship (FC-injure-s) can also be double scored with HC-injure. There can result an injurious act to self after the hurt of a love object. These materials can be double scored with HC-injure or HC-murder.

D. *Incurred Loss, Separation, or Isolation* ***FD***

FD-fate	Loss of love or friend due to circumstances, including death or a need to choose between loved ones
FD-death	Death following a loss of affiliation
FD-social	Loss of love due to social obedience
FD-split	Final separation (double score when necessary as due to discord, punishment)
FD-cold	Indifferent coldness or neglect of other person

FD-affect	Inability to feel affection or other feeling
FD-rejected	Loss due to rejection or divorce
FD-autonomy	Loss of love object or friendship due to another's assumption of an independent life or autonomy
FD-isolate	Experience an isolate, lonely existence
FD-no-one	No-one; homeless, bereft of companionship
FD-seduced	Seduced into a negative relationship
FD-thought	Inability to share thoughts or comprehend another
FD-shunned	A person may be shunned by ones' social group
FD-retreat	Retreat from others due to feeling hurt

As we noted above, fear of separation can be a most abiding concern governing behavior. The anguish of actual loss can be more profound and abiding. There are several nonpersonal circumstances leading to such an experience of affiliative loss (FD-fate). One may lose another through death (FD-fate KD-death), which is the final separation from a loved one (see chapter 13, volume I, for a discussion of fate). There may be death depicted as a result of personal loss of a relationship (FD-death). One may passively experience the loss of a loved one due to the social demands that cause an irreversible separation (FD-social).

One may suffer an enduring loss through the necessity for a child or someone to assume a separate independent life or achievement (FD-split DSA-free or FD-split AA-self). Affiliative needs in American society are often contrary to achievement activities. In the research of McClelland on American achievement motivation he found an inverse relationship between expressive, affiliative concerns and instrumental achievement needs. In contrast to his results, no such incompatibilities were found to be as characteristic for the Japanese (see below).

One may incur separation or become isolated (FD-split), due to a number of interpersonal difficulties. Some of these can, for example, be double scored in our system to specify whether separation is due to discord (FD-split HC-discord), or incurred as a form of social punishment inflicted by society on a loved one (FD-split NDA-police). One may experience some form of active rejection from another. One may experience loss due to betrayal. One such circumstance is suffering a divorce (FD-rejected).

One may suffer the chronic indifference or coldness or neglect of another person (FD-cold). There may be a resultant neglect of another in situations wherein the loved or needed individual is more occupied with other activities. Neglect by another on whom one depends is sometimes sensed more basically as deprivation. In children it is sometimes difficult to differentiate whether lack of nurture or lack of contact is uppermost in the experience of an unsatisfactory relationship with a parent. The feeling of having been neglected, for example, is very common in Japanese delinquent youth (Wagatsuma and De Vos, 1984, chapter 9). A child may be neglected out of the mother's distracting sexual desires. This is a cautionary fear often expressed in Japanese fantasy materials.

Conversely, one may be subject to an inner incapacity to love or accept affection (FD-affect). One may experience final rejection by another person (FD-rejected), or may lose the relationship due to the other's assumption of an independent lifestyle (FD-autonomy).

A person may experience a life of chronic isolation (FD-isolate). A deep abiding sense of loneliness or isolation marks the continuing inner experience of some individuals. "Separation anxiety" is an early experience transmuted into various fears of social isolation chronically experienced by humans (de Grazia, 1948). One may feel homeless, bereft of any other relationship, bereft of companionship (FD-no-one). A person may feel seduced into a negative relationship (FD-seduced). There may be an inability to share thoughts or to comprehend another person or a different life orientation (FD-thought).

There are circumstances under which someone may be subjected to shunning behavior. Such a social sanction may isolate someone as a result of the person's unacceptable behavior (FD-shunned). One may retreat from contact with others due to feeling hurt, or due to a fear of being hurt again (FD-retreat).

Some Complexities in Scoring Interpersonal Affective States

It is commonly the case that affiliative concerns co-occur with other concerns, such that one must double score the responses.

Trust and Distrust. Affiliative concerns may also reflect issues of trust. The state of distrust is subsidiary to, but more specific than, the generic category of anxiety, and it is characterized by doubt, suspicion, loss of confidence or faith, or reliance upon another. As a more specific form of anxiety, it is expressed most often as an unresolved emotional state. It usually involves a relationship with another person that has become problematical.

Trust issues can be double scored, for example, where there are affiliative or nurturant questions concerning the reliability of another. These can be concern in competitive or cooperative situations. They can also be a concern in dominant-subordinate instrumental relationships. This appears as a sense of not being able to rely on an established relationship as it is currently constituted. Distrust may be aroused by any behavior of another that becomes suspicious.

Trust is an anticipatory attitude that involves optimism, a sense of confidence, and faith. Trust and distrust are most often preconscious and not conscious except when directly expressed as part of situations of cooperation or in an affiliative relationship.

Vertically, trust appears in the assumption of protection or of being taken care of by a superordinate figure (N). In the instrumental direction it appears in compliance with authority (D), in the assumption of the legitimacy of authority and trust that authority will not be misused. In religion, trust and distrust are expressed as having faith versus living in an ungiving, unjust world. Distrust appears directly expressed in the nurturant category related to potential deprivation or potential withholding. In the instrumental category it remains latent in assumptions of authoritarian dominance and exploitation.

On the horizontal level, trust appears in the assumption of fidelity and steadfastness in affiliative relationships (F). In the negative sense it appears as worry about possible rejection or loss of interest in another to oneself; or as in active concerns with betrayal in a love relationship. On the instrumental side, trust sometimes is directly expressed in cooperative ventures (M), and in related reciprocity among peers. In a negative sense, it appears as a worry or concern about betrayal.

In the self, there is a positive self-regard; in the negative sense, there is a distrust in one's own character in one's own abilities to maintain acceptability and accord from others: some people have no confidence that they will be acceptable. Trust also appears as self-confidence and an anticipatory sense of having the capacity to succeed in tasks (Competence, C). In the negative form it appears as an anticipated sense of failure and lack of ability to perform properly.

Jealousy. Jealousy is an expressively constituted feeling of vulnerability related to distrust concerning the possibility that someone may replace oneself or take from oneself a possession, or an object of affection, or one's envied status, and it's attendant social regard. It appears in various contexts.

One can become jealous of one's status of being the one most favored in a dependency relationship, when the one on whom one is dependent is perceived to be envied by others. There can be a jealous fear of being replaced (NSB-jealous).

In affiliative relationships there can be a jealous fear of being replaced as an object of affection (FB-jealousy). Being jealous of one's mate is particularly emphasized in some societies. Elaborate precautions may be taken to protect oneself from the incursions of others on ones beloved, or conversely, in distrustful love situations, from the possible wayward affections of a loved one (FB-distrust FB-jealousy).

There may be jealous fear of losing something precious (objects or possessions) to another (OB-jealous; see chapter 13, volume I). Some people express jealous fear of the increasing competence of another; a fear of competitive encroachment (MVB-jealousy; see chapter 12, volume I). There can be disruption of group harmony or cohesion due to within-group jealousy or envy (HB-jealous; see chapter 7, volume I). One can be jealous of one's authority. Jehovah was perceived as a jealous god (DDB-jealousy; see chapter 10, volume I).

Envy. Envy is the converse of jealousy. Envy can lead to actively attacking another while jealousy is usually an inactive, distrustful state or can lead to behavior which is perceived as defensive self-protection. In affiliative situations that evoke envy, someone else already has the desired object whereas in jealousy the subject is in possession of the desired object. Envy is usually a currently unresolved state pushing for resolution. Instrumentally it can be part of a complex emotional state related to a desire to possess or to be capable of something manifested by another. It can be directed toward the good fortune, reputation, or social prowess that one does not have oneself, and so one is desirous of acquiring it or destroying its possession by another.

Envy appears in several of the scoring categories. It can appear as a discordant emotion usually implying interpersonal malice (HB-envy). A frequent form of envy within a family is coveting the nurturance received by another (NSB-envy). Some can express envy of the affiliative closeness of others (FB-envy). There can be envy of the regard or status afforded another (EDB-envy). Some express envy of a competitor's ability (MVB-envy). There can be envy of the influence or authority exercised by another (DSB-envy). There is envy of possessions of others (OB-envy).

Complexities in Scoring Sexual Attitudes or Expression

As mentioned above, sexual behavior itself is very seldom reduced to a physiological act. Its social import and accompanying affectivity is varied and complex. There is no prime category locating where to score sexual behavior. Most often, however, in narratives sexual behavior becomes interactive with questions of affiliative commitment. Marriage, in contrast, can refer to social situations including expected commitment and responsibility. Extramarital sex includes various forms of behavior that can be negatively sanctioned by social authority.

Contextually, concern with sex can be located in any expressive category. The emphasis can be on the act as pleasurable, as self-enhancing, as nurturant, or affiliative. It can be positively described in the context of harmony or negatively with discord or injury.

Simple sexual pleasure itself is seldom mentioned explicitly (PA-sensual). Most often it appears as sexual attraction for another and expressed as involving the attractions of love (FA-love). If so, when necessary it should be doubled scored within the context of the interpersonal relationship directly expressed in the story. For example, there may be problems of unresolved commitment (FA-love FB-commit). Where sex remains casual or unresolved, there may be concern on the part of one or another of those involved with potential separation (FA-love FB-apart), and can be so double scored.

Sexual attraction can also be depicted in the context of instrumental concerns. For example, sexual behavior can be coupled with concern over responsibility (R; see chapter 11, volume I). A sex liaison can be a matter of responsibility or duty; it can arouse a sense of guilt when it is seen as irresponsible or profligate in nature. It can be double scored either with guilt (FA-love RB-guilt), or under negative active responsibility as extramarital adultery (FA-love RC-ex-sex), as premarital outside of a sanctioned relationship (RC-pre-sex), as involving unacceptable forms of activity (RC-perverse). The story may be presented as a case of the avoidance of responsibility or avoidance of commitment (RD-personal).

Instrumentally, a sexual liaison can be contextualized by some as an instrumental achievement or a concern with competence. However, such concerns are rarely expressed overtly as such. Attainment of a sexual liaison may be a form of social achievement for family as well as for the individual.

Expressive or instrumental purposes may be intertwined in sexual relationships. They may involve family harmony or family success or family obligation (HA-family MTA-family RA-duty-o), and may be in conflict with unresolved or frustrated expressive feelings of personal affiliation (FB-thwart). The resolution of such conflict may be seen either negatively as separation (FC-split) or positively (FA-love). It can possibly be double scored with autonomous freedom from family domination (FA-love DSA-free).

As in the latter resolution, sex and marriage can be seen as related to resolving problems of dominance and subordination within families or social groups or submitting to them (DSD-family).

Sexual relationships may evoke problems of capacity or adequacy (CB-worry), although again these are seldom brought up in spontaneous stories in the TAT. These concerns, however, appear frequently in fiction.

Where an objectification of the self or the other describes a person as a sex object or a possession, an object category may be appropriate whether the objectification is positive (e.g., OA-own, OA-please), unresolved (e.g., OB-want, OB-worth), negative active (e.g., OC-display), or negative passive (e.g., OD-used). Where the sexuality is fatalistic, it may also appear as positive, unresolved, or negative (e.g., KA-accept, KB-mishap-s, KC-hurt-s, KD-hopeless).

Triangular Relationships. Sexual liaisons can be competitive in nature, sometimes involving triangular situations. Triangular relations occur in various social contexts where discord is involved. The basic nature of triangular relationship is that two individuals are in an equivalent relationship in respect to a third and where there is tension between them. Some of these relationships involve themes of jealousy or envy (see above).

Most of these relationships are heavily concerned with expressive issues, although instrumental concerns may be interwoven. For example, in a mother-daughter-in-law relationship a question of control may involve the priority of loyalty or affection of the son. In a sibling relationship there may be a question of priority of affection of a parent for a child. Very often there are family situations which may involve instrumental questions of control and they can involve issues of competition, capacity, or success.

Frequently, triangular relationships involve the affiliative category, where there is competition or jealousy in love relationships. Triangular relationships may involve unfaithfulness on the part of the spouse or a conspiracy (MTC-plot) to remove an unwanted other member of the relationship. Conspiracies involve negative active cooperation and are usually seen as instrumental collusion. In triangular discord (HC-triangle) narratives are often doubled scored with betrayal

(FC-betray) or jealousy (FB-jealousy). In a case of covert conspiracy toward betrayal, it is scored as deception or betrayal coupled with cooperative conspiracy (FC-betray with MTC-plot).

Illustrative Samples of Scoring in the Following Chapters

In several of the chapters of volume II we have included actual illustrations of scoring of several of the subcategories included under the [F] category. Especially notable are the verbatim responses found in chapters 9, 11, and 12, volume II.

Notes

Ainsworth, Mary, Mary Blehar, E. Waters, and S. Wall. 1978. *Patterns of Attachment: A Psychological Study of the Strange Situation.* Hillsdale, N.J.: L. Erlbaum Associates.

Benjamin, Jessica. 1995. *Like Subjects, Love Objects: Essays on Recognition and Sexual Difference*. New Haven: Yale University Press.

Blood, Robert O., Jr. 1967. *Love Match and Arranged Marriage: A Tokyo-Detroit Comparison*. New York: Free Press.

Bowlby, John. 1988. *A Secure Base* (2nd edition). New York: Basic Books.

Bronson, Wanda C. 1981. *Toddler's Behavior with Agemates: Issues of Interaction, Cognition, and Affect.* Norwood, N.J.: Ablex Pub. Corp.

Buhler, Charlotte. 1931. The Social Behavior of Children. In Carl Murchison (Ed.), *Handbook of Child Psychology* (2nd edition) (pp. 374–416). New York: Russell & Russell.

Coie, J. and K. Dodge. 1998. Aggression and Antisocial Behavior. In William Damon (Series Ed.) and N. Eisenberg (Vol. Ed.), *Handbook of Child Psychology: Vol. 3. Social, Emotional, and Personality Development* (5th edition) (pp. 779–862). New York: Wiley.

Cook, Mark and Glenn Wilson (Eds.). 1979. *Love and Attraction*. Oxford: Pergamon.

de Beauvior, Simone. 1975. *The Ethics of Ambiguity.* Secaucus, N.J.: The Citadel Press.

de Grazia, Sebastian. 1948. *The Political Community: A Study of Anomie*. Chicago: University of Chicago Press.

De Vos, George A. 1966. *A Comparison of the Personality Differences in Two Generations of Japanese Americans by Means of the Rorschach Test.* University of Hawaii Social Science Research Institute, Reprint No. 14.

———. 1973a. *American Japanese Intercultural Marriages*. Taipei: The Chinese Association for Folklore.

———. 1973b. *Socialization for Achievement: Essays on the Cultural Psychology of the Japanese.* Berkeley: University of California Press.

———. 1980. Identity Problems of Immigrant Minorities: A Psycho-Cultural Comparative Approach Applied to Korean Japanese (chapter 31). In Roy Simon Bryce-Laporte (Ed.), *Source Book in the New Immigration: Implications for the United States and the International Community* (pp. 321–328). New Brunswick, N.J.: Transaction Books.

———. 1992. *Social Cohesion and Alienation: Minorities in the United States and Japan.* Boulder, Colo.: Westview Press.

De Vos, George A. and Marcelo Suárez-Orozco. 1990. *Status Inequality: The Self in Culture.* Newbury Park, Calif.: Sage Publications.

De Vos, George A. and Hiroshi Wagatsuma. 1966. *Japan's Invisible Race: Caste in Culture and Personality.* Berkeley: University of California Press.

Erikson, Erik H. 1963. *Childhood and Society* (2nd edition). New York: Norton.

Farver, J.A.M. and Y.L. Shin. 1997. Social Pretend Play in Korean and Anglo-American Preschoolers. Child Development, **68**: 544–556.

Gordon, Suzanne. 1976. *Lonely in America.* New York: Simon & Schuster.

Hartup, W. and B. Laursen. 1993. Conflict and Context in Peer Relations. In C. Hart (Ed.), *Children on Playgrounds: Research Perspectives and Applications* (pp. 44–84). Albany: State University of New York Press.

Hazan, C. and P. Shaver. 1987. Romantic Love Conceptualized as an Attachment Process. *Journal of Personality and Social Psychology*, **52**: 511–524.

Horowitz, L.M. and R. French. 1979. Interpersonal Problems of People Who Describe Themselves as Lonely. *Journal of Consulting and Clinical Psychology*, **47**: 762–764.

Howes, C., O. Unger, and L.B. Seidner. 1989. Social Pretend Play in Toddlers: Parallels with Social Play and with Solitary Play. *Child Development*, **60**: 77–84.

James, William. 1935. *The Varieties of Religious Experience.* (1902). New York: Random House

Lee, Changsoo and George A. De Vos. 1981. *Koreans in Japan: Ethnic Conflict and Accommodation.* Berkeley: University of California Press.

Lewis, Catherine. 1995. *Educating Hearts and Minds: Reflections on Japanese Preschool and Early Elementary Education.* New York: Cambridge University Press.

Maudry, Maria and Maria Nekula. 1939. Social Relations among Children of the Same Age During the First Two Years of Life. *Journal of Genetic Psychology*, **54**: 193–215.

McWhorter, John. 2000. *Losing the Race: Self Sabotage in Black America.* Glencoe, Ill: The Free Press.

Miller, Daniel and Guy Swanson. 1958. *The Changing American Parent.* New York: Wiley.

Nerviano, V.J. and W.F. Gross. 1976. Loneliness and Locus of Control for Alcoholic Males: Validity Against Murray Need and Cattell Trait Dimensions. *Journal of Clinical Psychology*, **32**: 479–484.

Peplau, L.A. and D. Perlman. 1979. Blueprint for a Social Psychological Theory of Loneliness. In Mark Cook and Glenn Wilson (Eds.), *Love and Attraction.* Oxford: Pergamon.

Peplau, L.A., D. Russell, and M. Heim. 1979. Loneliness: A Bibliography of Research and Theory. JSAS. *Catalog of Selected Documents in Psychology*, **8**: 38.

Riesman, David, Reuel Denney, and Nathan Glazer. 1950. *The Lonely Crowd: A Study in the Changing American Character.* New Haven, Conn.: Yale University Press.

Russell, Daniel, Letitia Peplau, and C. Cutrona. 1980. The Revised UCLA Loneliness Scale: Concurrent and Discriminant Validity Evidence. *Journal of Personality and Social Psychology*, **39**(3): 472–480.

Sartre, J.P. 1943. *Being and Nothingness.* New York: Washington Square Press.

———. 1962. *La Nausee.* Paris: Gallimard.

Schwalb, David and Barbara Schwalb. 1996. *Japanese Childrearing: Two Generations of Scholarship.* New York: Guilford.

Seinfeld, Jeffrey. 1993. *Interpreting and Holding. The Paternal and Maternal Functions of the Psychotherapist.* Northvale, N.J.: Aronson.

Sherif, Muzafer. 1967. *Social Interaction: Process and Products.* Chicago: Aldine.

Sherif, Muzafer and Carolyn W. Sherif. 1964. *Reference Groups: Exploration into Conformity and Deviation of Adolescents*. New York: Harper & Row.

Sroufe, L.A., B. Egeland, and E.A. Carlson. 1999. One Social World: The Integrated Development of Parent-Child and Peer Relationships. In W.A. Collins and B. Larsen (Eds.), *Minnesota Symposium on Child Psychology: Vol. 30. Relationships as Developmental Contexts: Festschrift in Honor of Willard W. Hartup* (pp. 241–261). Mahwah, N.J.: Erlbaum.

Sroufe, L.A., B. Egeland, and T. Kreutzer. 1990. The Fate of Early Experience Following Developmental Change: Longitudinal Approaches to Individual Adaptation in Childhood. *Child Development*, **61**: 1363–1373.

Vaughn, Curtis. 1988. *Cognitive Independence, Social Independence, and Achievement Orientation: A Comparison of Japanese and U. S. Students*. Dissertation, University of California, Berkeley.

Wagatsuma, Hiroshi and George A. De Vos. 1984. *Heritage of Endurance: Family Patterns and Delinquency Formation in Urban Japan*. Berkeley: University of California Press.

Weiss, Robert S. 1973. *Loneliness: The Experience of Emotional and Social Isolation*. Cambridge, Mass: M. I. T. press.

Wenz, F. V. 1977. Seasonal Suicide Attempts and Forms of Loneliness. *Psychological Reports*, **40**: 807–810.

Werner, Emmy E. 1979. *Cross-Cultural Child Development: A View from the Planet Earth.* Monterey, Calif.: Brooks Cole.

Witkin, H. A. and J. W. Berry. 1975. Psychological Differentiation in Cross-Cultural Perspective. *Journal of Cross Cultural Psychology*, **6**: 4–67.

Chapter 6

Esteem: Evaluative Concerns with Social Acceptability

A Need for Recognition and Social Acceptability

Humans are clearly sensitive to approval or disapproval, and a person's inner sense of worthiness often depends on having received approval from others (Crowne and Marlowe, 1964; Maslow, 1970). One of the abiding "four wishes" advanced by sociologist W.I. Thomas was the wish for "recognition" (Thomas and Znaniecki, 1927). The idea that recognition from another is a basis for the person's capacity for self-regard throughout life is also central to contemporary object-relations perspectives in the psychoanalytic tradition (Benjamin, 1988). It would appear that a need for positive social recognition is basic to human beings, in some form, in every culture. We categorize such concerns with the category of Esteem (E).

Our basic expressive attitudes toward the self can be enhanced or deflated depending on approval and disapproval, beginning with that which was initially given to the child by primary caregivers. This is continued throughout life in social relations with a peer group, or with others. The individual continues to savor the positive regard that is received for appropriate appearance or behavior, and seeks to avoid negative social evaluation. To varying degrees in different individuals, "self-respect" continues to be based on "proper" dressing, speaking, or bodily comportment that produce positive social regard.

The abiding need for recognition and social acceptability is used in various ways by human cultures as a means to regulate human behavior. Contemporary views on childhood socialization acknowledge the importance of this need for recognition, with the concept of "socialization from the inside" (Ainsworth, Bell, and Stayton, 1974; DeHart, Sroufe, and Cooper, 2000). The according (or withholding) of social appreciation, respect or Esteem (E) is an implicit form of social sanctioning. Where the individual is deemed unworthy of positive social recognition, instead of having a sense of self-respect or self-esteem, the person experiences some form of humiliation or a sense of unworthiness. Approbation can also lead to greater affiliative (F) closeness. Where it is denied, as in forms of ostracism, it can eventuate in retreat and isolation (see chapter 5, volume I). Humans are governable to varying degrees by their aversion to such negative *expressive* experiences.

Expressively operative concern with appreciation must be distinguished from concern with *instrumental* judgment and punishment. Instrumental sanctioning involves direct control or coercion related to punishment meted out by those with social authority or power. Such instrumental forms of sanctioning by authority are considered under the category of Control (D). Where instrumental transgressions occur, purposeful restitution or rectification is called for. In contrast, where one has experienced social disapproval or humiliation, efforts to repair one's self-esteem or social "face" are called for.

Both forms of sanctioning, the instrumental and the expressive, can become internalized, and can serve self-regulatory functions. Instrumental social authority can be internalized and directed toward the self, by way of the human potential to experience *guilt*. Guilt may even be experienced where there is no immediate threat of punishment from outside (see our discussion of Responsibility in chapter 11, volume I). Just as guilt is a form of internalized control that compels desired behavior, there is also to some degree in most individuals an internalized sense of relative worthiness or worthlessness, known as pride and *shame*.

Much has been written in the psychodynamic literature about shame as it is related to guilt.[1] The two may be distinguished with respect to their intrapsychic origins. Freud considered shame to result from the development of an "ego ideal," i.e., the component of the superego that develops out of experiences of social approval or disapproval. In contrast, guilt is seen as the result of unconscious destructiveness that was initially directed outward, but that is turned back on the self as punitive "judgment" and the anticipation of injurious retribution, if not annihilation (Fenichel, 1945). Thus intrapunitiveness draws its energy from unconscious hostile-destructive intentionality as it is redirected against the self.

As social approbation is internalized, self-referential expressive feelings of approval or disapproval may occur even where there is no immediate direct external audience or "other." Thus evaluations can become divorced from immediate social opinion, and instead reflect the individual's internal evaluative system. Whether such evaluations remain socially derived or become increasingly idiosyncratic, a capacity for internal self-evaluation can serve as a basis for autonomous regulation

---

[1]See chapter 11, volume I, in this volume. See Piers and Singer (1953). See also Tangney and Fischer (1995) for contemporary coverage of the "self-conscious" emotions, including shame and guilt.

of behavior. The self acts in ways that do not produce negative self-evaluations. Ultimately, the cognitive mechanisms that support such evaluations may be developed into a more widely applied evaluative capacity. Any percept can potentially be appraised relative to standards of acceptability, whether the standards are aesthetic or pragmatic.

As we have constituted it, the category of Esteem (E) includes concerns with both *self*-oriented or internally derived personal assessments of acceptability as well as social-evaluative interactions with others.

Some Interweaving of Expressive and Instrumental Concerns

Esteem as Related to Harmonious Interaction

Because mutual positive regard is often a component of harmonious interactions, this evaluative dimension of Esteem (E) is related to, but must be distinguished from, the category of Harmony and Discord (H) discussed in the next chapter. While a positive evaluation may facilitate harmony because the individual is considered to be more acceptable as part of the group, the category of Harmony (H) reflects the peacefulness or discord in social involvement rather than any evaluation of behavior or appearance. However, a negative antagonistic attitude aimed at hostile or destructive action (discord) can utilize expressions of negative evaluation and derogation. A sense of unworthiness, whether directed toward another, or toward oneself can have both conscious and unconscious destructive purpose. We score the destructive purpose only when it is directly expressed as such.

In the effort to avoid conflict and maintain or restore social harmony, individuals may passively inhibit or actively alter their comportment to avoid criticism or self-criticism. The frequency with which humans attend to issues of social conformity indicates that many people do not become completely independent of their group's evaluative framework. Although some degree of social conformity reflects adaptive psychological functioning, some individuals experience a distressing or continually unresolved sense of potential unworthiness. This can cause them to fear contact in social interaction and can produce forms of social avoidance (e.g., shyness). For other individuals, the avoidance of social appraisal may derive from real knowledge based on previous social experience. Where social contact cannot be avoided, self-deprecatory or deferential acts may occur, to blunt the impact of anticipated disapproval, or to minimize the occurrence of disruptive feelings of anger that might lead to overt conflict. Where such prophylactic action is depicted as a means for the avoidance of conflict, or for the maintenance of harmony, it may need to be double scored with Harmony (H) and Esteem (E).

Esteem as Related to Instrumental Concerns

Evaluative considerations are also linked to a sense of instrumental mastery or Competence (C). As we shall discuss in chapter 9, volume I, a sense of confidence, or its converse (i.e., worry about inadequacy or failure), can be a salient instrumental concern. A person may be concerned about possessing the internal means necessary to accomplish a goal. Developmentally,[2] a sense of mastery or competence may be closely associated with early evaluative interactions with parents or peers. The exhibition of competent behavior may directly produce positive social regard, and such social regard may in turn energize the seeking of competence. Thus issues of instrumental competence and social esteem may be closely intermingled in phenomenological experience.

In order to assess one's own competence as being either satisfactory or unsatisfactory, one must have some implicit or explicit evaluative standards in mind. The same or similar cognitive capacities may be involved in self-evaluation, whether the evaluation is directed toward expressive concerns with social acceptability or towards instrumental concerns with competence. However, goal-oriented concerns about competent action must be distinguished from concerns with the receipt of approval or recognition (from either self or others) that might also result from competent performance.

Whereas there certainly are evaluative aspects to any concern with adequacy or competence, we score narrative depictions of such concerns in an instrumental category. Such evaluations of instrumental competence may or may not have any relation to the sense of relative social acceptability that is central to the considerations within the Esteem (E) category. Where there is a depiction of a concern about adequacy in the context of an *audience*, or any depiction that reflects issues of *approbation*, one can see evidence of expressive concerns intertwined with instrumental goals. In such instances one must double score.

Situations of competition and rivalry may also involve evaluative concerns. Experiences of relative worthiness or unacceptability may be produced in the context of competitive interactions. Victory or loss in an instrumental arena may be experienced in expressive terms as conferring superiority or inferiority vis-à-vis others. Thus a self-evaluative component can often be seen in situations of Mutual Purpose (M) (see chapter 12, volume I). Additionally, depictions of exhibitionist performance in competitive situations may reflect a concern with self-enhancement through the achievement of social recognition and power or social dominance. The competitive arena (M) can be a venue wherein Competence (C) becomes a vehicle for establishing Control (D) and earning the Esteem (E) of others. Winning a contest can also be depicted as a goal-oriented form of Achievement (A).

---

[2]See White (1961).

Individuals may be preoccupied with the way in which personal Achievement (A) can be related to social approval. As we shall discuss in chapter 8, volume I, achievement concerns in many cases are internalized and self-oriented. Nevertheless, for some individuals (actors, dancers, singers, musicians), acts of achievement may be viewed as social performances that take place before an evaluative audience. The instrumental goals in such instances cannot be separated out as independent of expressive interpersonal considerations of group or peer approval, and double scoring as Esteem (E) and Achievement (A) may be necessary.

When competition, competent performance, or achievement is clearly depicted as a positive seeking of recognition or a negative seeking of the humiliation of others, then the expressive aspects of the activity must be scored.

Concerns with social evaluation can sometimes also be related to instrumental concerns with personal Responsibility (R) (see chapter 11, volume I). For example, the mechanisms at work in Japanese guilt over failure to meet socially defined standards have been previously described (De Vos, 1973, chapter 5). In Japanese, guilt can be experienced as related to the transgression of social standards and social expectations. Such failure can be seen as injurious to the family in general, and often the mother in particular. Considered on their most superficial level, some Japanese themes that depict a failure of personal responsibility seem to be more consciously related to concerns with social assessment and possible social disapproval. Not readily expressed by the Japanese is an awareness of the hurt done to those of one's family as a result of social transgression. Nevertheless, in the traditional Japanese mentality, neither purposeful acts of achievement nor transgressions were seen as being simply of individualistic import. The inner experience of the Japanese does, however, include an experience of having hurt others by inviting disapproval of a self that is experienced as integral with a group. Acts of failed responsibility, therefore, are not just individual failures, but also are destructive of family or society. Although superficially appearing as expressed concerns with shame, the underlying psychodynamic process and inner experience may be more complex. Experiences of guilt over social transgression that occur in some situations may also reflect elements of unconsciously intended destructiveness (see representative stories in chapter 11, volume I). In such situations, a potential for guilt may be projected outward as a hypersensitivity to social appearances, while in actuality it is a hypersensitivity to one's own capacity to hurt. In the case of delinquents (Bennett, 1960) negative behavior relates to a sense of resentment over deprivation or neglect. Being resentful, they do not feel guilty because their destructiveness is weighed in the balance of not having received. Such mechanisms may defend the person against the conscious experience of guilt over profligate or otherwise irresponsible or injurious behavior.

Where instrumental concerns are expressed in conjunction with depictions of relative status or esteem, the full complexity of possible concerns must be considered when scoring. A judgment must sometimes be made as to which is more salient, or whether there is indeed sufficient manifest content to serve as a basis for double scoring.

Esteem and Instrumental Concerns Related to Social Status

The assignment or attainment of social status involves an evaluation of the individual in relative terms (i.e., relative to some social reference group within which differential status can be accorded). Anthropologists (e.g., Warner et al., 1963) recognize a difference between *achieved* and *acquired* social status. Status may be afforded an individual on the basis of group membership as well as on the basis of individual evaluation. In either case, differential social status reflects evaluations of the degree to which individuals or groups are or are not seen as socially acceptable, on some dimension of social evaluation.

Prestige systems of social inequality in society, whereby a group member is afforded status by virtue of membership, are related to *group-acquired* status. This can be seen in economic, political, or kinship terms. In most social systems, whether simple or complex, higher status can usually be acquired and maintained economically, by the control of material resources or wealth. It can also be acquired and then maintained politically, through a developed capacity to dominate or influence by the manipulation of personal or group power. Status may also be maintained through the possession of "awesome" or "aweful" power (such as that possessed by a supernatural being or priesthood) that elicits deferential responses from others. These issues shall be discussed further in the context of concerns about Control and social dominance (D) (see chapter 10, volume I, also chapter 14, volume I) as well as below, in this chapter.

In a traditional, kinship-oriented society it is not so easy to change accorded status, even with the acquisition of wealth, or even with political power. In a changing society, however, *individually achieved* status may become more salient than the status acquired without personal effort through an inheritance of group-based status. Achievement motivation, as ordinarily defined in modern societies (in contrast to tradition-oriented societies) is not static but is a dynamic force for changing social status. Personal achievement is seen as taking place within some system of social stratification in which individuals do not attempt solely to repeat the past role of a parent. Instead, successful achievement is gauged by evidence of a capacity to take risks in the exploration of opportunity, to excel competitively, or to innovate. Such activities are sometimes described in terms of their relationship to social status or social approval. When social status concerns are alluded to in narratives about Achievement (A), the narrative must also be double scored with reference to the Esteem (E) concern.

Culturally conditioned social evaluations can become internalized, as the individual recognizes and/or adopts the evaluative attitudes of the social group. Thus a sense of one's relative status can become a part of one's own identity as a social self. Positive evaluations of the self are generally maintained when one's own behavior, or one's accorded status, continues to be evaluated as worthy. This can manifest as a continuing preoccupation with how to properly stimulate attitudes in others that enhance one's own status, partly as a means to attain or retain actual social status, but also as a means for attaining a desired level of self-esteem, internally. Even the mature individual who feels relatively comfortable with his or her social identity will make continued use of internalized social attitudes as part of the self.

The Audience and a Concern with Observed Performance

Individual Versus Group Evaluation

In human societies, one is evaluated by one's group membership as well as on an individual basis. Thus there are complex interactions between *personal* and *group* identity, particularly as this is related to forms of social appreciation and disparagement. In some individuals, a personal sense of pride or shame is closely linked to in-group approbation or disapprobation. For others, there is a greater concern with how one is seen by those outside the immediate group. An individual's behavior or appearance can be seen as inviting positive or negative attitudes directed toward the group. Some forms of social sanctioning are therefore specifically directed toward maintaining the group's social image by controlling the individual's behavior.

There are specific group differences, as well as cultural differences in the degree to which members are consciously alert to possible observation and evaluation by others. This was brought to our attention especially by examining the Thematic Apperception Test (TAT) records of Israeli youth from a Kibbutz compared with other Israeli youth.[3] In their TAT fantasies as well as in actual work, the Kibbutzim frequently performed achievement-oriented activities *in the presence of others*. The records left a strong impression that mentioning an audience of peers in Kibbutzim stories was more frequent than what was found in other samples of records both in Israel and elsewhere (see also chapter 2, volume II).

Concern with an audience can occur in either an instrumental or an expressive context, or in a blending of both. It can be related to worries about social acceptability in the eyes of authorities or peers as they evaluate one's adequacy in accomplishing required tasks. It can be related to more internalized concerns with mastery in the classroom or workplace. An audience that is in an authority position, or that might possibly exercise punitive or controlling authority, is somewhat different from an audience where one has an emotional need to gain approbation or warm appreciation. For semantic purposes we have chosen to distinguish audiences that exercise instrumental *judgment* and associated sanctions from audiences that

---

[3]These records were shown to me in personal communication by the late Martin Wolins, Professor of Social Welfare at Berkeley, who had gathered TAT material as part of his comparative research on children in institutions (Wolins, personal communication, 1959).

provide expressive *appreciation*. As we use the terms, the act of "judgment" is instrumental and regulatory; "appreciation" involves primarily an emotional exchange. In scoring narrative depictions, one must distinguish, first, the relative *presence or absence* of an outside audience, and whether it consists of one, or many others. Second, one notes whether there are any possible consequences of the audience's presence relative to Esteem or Control, etc.

The Artist and the Audience

To the extent that any creative act or artistic performance is social activity, it has a more or less specified audience or reference group. The interactive communication that is exchanged between artist and audience may be complex, and may be based on both instrumental and expressive dimensions of the artist's and audience's intent. Though intertwined in all art forms, these two dimensions nevertheless can be distinguished in respect to relative saliency in specific contexts.

An artistic performer, whether writer, painter, filmmaker, musician, etc., may experience an instrumental intent to influence an audience through some communicative act. The artistic act, therefore, may reflect concerns related to power or control. The individual may even seek to forward certain ideas as a political or social goal. In the sense of being self-consciously "an artist," some individuals are continually self-judgmental, seeing themselves as meeting or not meeting internally defined criteria of instrumental success or failure in respect to the standards of their medium, or in respect to the goal of influencing others. These types of goal-oriented self-evaluations of relative artistic mastery or social impact reflect instrumental concerns related to the categories of Control (D), Competence (C), and Achievement (A).

Most artists also experience some need for an emotionally receptive audience and may suffer when appreciative response (E) is not forthcoming. For some, self-esteem is continually influenced positively or negatively by audience reactions. However, some individuals need an audience more than others do, and this can take various forms. Some "performers," such as actors, musicians, or singers, draw immediate emotional sustenance or sense power through direct contact with the audience [scored with the Pleasure (P) category]. They thrive on audience reaction, and for some this can become almost an addictive form of sought-after ecstatic excitement. The "entertainer," by contrast with the "artist," may be most concerned with audience approval rather than with the standards of performance or any inner excitement derived from the performance. Other artists may be most concerned with what the critics have to say later about the performance. Some artists can be content with knowing that they have expressed what they hope to express, even though they know that very few people may ever fully appreciate them or understand their communicative intent.

Some may find audience appreciation irrelevant, or even offensive, if it is seen as adulation rather than understanding. Some artists experience a form of disdain for their audience and may even become overtly hostile. One may infer that this arises from a conflict between an internally harsh judgment of competence and what may seem to the artist to be undeserved adulation received from an uncomprehending or naive audience. Such was the case with Dylan Thomas on his American tour before his death. At some times in the course of their careers Bob Dylan and Miles Davis have also appeared to become disdainful of their audiences. Artists, as opposed to entertainers (whose primary motive is to please), may have an internal vision of a very selective audience they are seeking to reach in expressive communication; it is this audience which is their idealized reference group, or their ultimate source of appreciation. Such an audience is seldom found in actual public performance.

Negative Social Evaluation of Others

Status differences can be used with antagonism in the hostile degradation of others. Questions of depreciation, denigration, or contempt are among the most socially sensitive issues governing ethnic or minority relations (see De Vos, 1972, 1975, 1978, 1984). They are also deeply embedded in social class relationships (see Sennett and Cobb, 1972). Whether the exploitation of others is manifest as a class or a caste system, it will often involve some form of expressive exploitation through the use of evaluation to establish a subjectively experienced superiority of the exploiting group, and a subjectively experienced inferiority of the unworthy group. Individual, family, or group pride and an experience of self-worth is thus obtained contrastively at the expense of those who are subject to denigration. Psychological mechanisms of projection and displacement are deeply involved in the disparagement of others (De Vos, 1967).

The Operation of Projection and Displacement in Disparagement

Opposite to the intake mechanism, which allows for the integration of new experiences within the self, is the mechanism of expulsion which rids the self of what is unacceptable, and allows for the "not-me" to be experienced as externally located (see De Vos and Suárez-Orozco, 1990, chapter 1). An understanding of the ways in which this "projective" mechanism is used in a social context is central to any understanding of the disparagement of others on either an individual or group basis.

There can be a collective expulsion of undesirable thoughts or behavior. What is disgusting or not acceptable is more easily attributable to others outside the group, than to those considered within. A collective use of projection can result in the particular scapegoating of specific outsiders or low status group members (see De Vos and Suárez-Orozco, 1990, chapter 1). Collective projection is much less readily identified than is individual paranoia.

Projection is readily recognized as "paranoia" when an individual idiosyncratically maintains delusions of persecution in a fearful defense against some outside threat impinging upon the suffering individual. Projection is not as easily clinically defined in situations where the mechanism is used in displaced disparagement of others as a means of maintaining an enhanced sense of self. This mechanism is not usually only individual in context, but more frequently can become central to the maintenance of a defensive group identity. In-group enhancement is very often based, partially at least, on an ability to perceive outsiders in a contrasting pejorative sense. For example, among many American Indians, other groups were termed "non-people." In all groups, outsiders can be negatively evaluated in reference to traits that may be equally present, but not recognizable, as characteristic of one's own group.[4]

The mechanism of "projection," collectively as well as individually, remains widespread in human society in a more or less primitive form. In its progressive transmutations, it is also variously involved in forms of magical thought. More progressively it is found in forms of analytic, discriminating intellectual analysis. It is necessary to the achievement of scientific objectivity. Projection, then, is the earliest appearing manifestation of the operation of a basic, continually operative coping mechanism.

In its social manifestations, displacement appears as *pejorative displacement*, often appearing as part of attitudes defining ethnic status inequality. Status inequality encourages extensive use of the mechanism of displacement turned toward those more vulnerable and less powerful. Affective reactions, such as anger aroused by a superior, can be displaced downward by expressing them toward a vulnerable member of a lower status class, caste, or ethnic group. Both projection and displacement are involved in the various manifestations of ethnic-racial scapegoating and other related social phenomena (see De Vos, chapters 4 and 5, 1992; Suárez-Orozco, chapter 4, 1989). For example, in the past, some lower status white southerners, rather than feeling victimized by those above, felt safe to periodically displace violence, venting their feeling of low status onto Blacks as "beneath" them, more ignorant, more dirty and inferior, even using religiously inspired concepts such as seeing them branded by the "mark of Cain."

As pointed out cogently by Stein (1980a, 1980b), group formation, as well as intragroup processes, creates the defensive need for inside/outside complementarity. Projection and displacement permit intragroup solidarity and prevent fission at the expense of negative relationships with those outside. Analysis of the expulsive mechanism in interaction with patterns of intake affords us some further insight into

---

[4]German Nazis saw Jews as obscenely concerned with money, although that may have reflected their own concerns with a national economic crisis.

the use of projection as it involves both a collective as well as a personal need to represent power and control as internal experiences. (This is discussed further in chapter 9, volume I, on Competence.)

It has often been pointed out how a society can externalize its internal tension by going to war to "defend itself" from its neighbor. The use of groups of individuals outside the society is a fairly well-recognized form of a *pejorative displacement* of internal tensions. As such, war can be as much or more an expressive act as it is a means of instrumental gain at the expense of others.

So, too, the peopling of the external world with supernatural, malevolent forces, demons, witches, and warlocks permits a displacement of tensions from within the person or social group onto outside sources of malevolence or pollution (Kluckhohn, 1962). Such behavior obviously can be far more expressive in nature than instrumental in intent.

Similar forms of expressive exploitation are found in the scapegoating of vulnerable social segments within the society itself. There is scapegoating or projective function of an out-caste group. In many societies where women are held in lower status, such scapegoating may be more subtle and less direct.

The recognition of this expressive dimension is complicated by the fact that the disparaged group does have instrumental utility and the dominant group has a continuing feeling of dependency toward this group and toward the functions that it performs. These functions can be both those of a menial, instrumental nature and those of an expressive, psychological nature. The dominant members, therefore, want the outcaste or subordinate group to continue the exercise of its functions and cannot eliminate them or practice irretrievable violence, lest it is no longer capable of performing its services. Additionally, the outcaste or disparaged group is necessary for the maintenance of a secure definition of superior social status on the part of the dominant groups. It fits on the bottom of a hierarchy of virtue by exemplifying inferiority in its varying forms.

It is interesting to note that a mythology of contentment with one's status is attributed to a continuously disparaged group. It is claimed of such groups that they "like to be where they are" or that they realize themselves by the proper exercise of their functions. When conflict appears, it is often attributable to outside sources of agitation. For example, some conservatives or racists have in the past considered that unrest among American Blacks in the South had been caused by "Communists" or Northern radicals. According to such reasoning, if left alone, Blacks would have remained content with their inferior lot. The same erroneous opinions are found in India. Gerald Berreman (1960) demonstrates very cogently that the alleged contentment of the Indian untouchables and lower castes is similarly a myth when one actually examines the true conscious feelings of members of these submerged groups.

For those individuals who have some source of continuing insecurity relative to their status either as men vis-à-vis women, or as members of a dominant social group, a sense of threat is countered by some symbolic affirmation of their status demanded of those in the legally and socially subordinate group. Any diminution in deference behavior can result in immediate sensitivity, and in the use of coercion or even violence to reaffirm dominance.[5] Periodically, when there are sources of increased tension or insecurity, the individual, in concert with others of his group undergoing a similar sense of tension, may seek alleviation by recourse to culturally or institutionally available acts of scapegoating involving particular members of a subordinate group. As a collective act, such as an act of lynching or gang rape, the scapegoating can also serve to reaffirm dominance and to intimidate the subordinated group to prevent further overt challenge or manifest conflict.

The psychic energy necessary to maintain a projective system remains continual in those individuals bedeviled by processes with which they cannot cope internally. The need for some form of external projection remains unceasing. Bettelheim and Janowitz (1964), in a classic systematic psychological and sociological study of both anti-Semitism and anti-Black attitudes in the United States, found that prejudice in individuals is inversely related to the strength of integration of the ego. Individuals who manifest relatively weak integration of the ego do not seem to be able to manage inner conflicts without resorting to some form of projection or displacement. Individuals who cannot manage sources of intrapsychic tension are especially prone, therefore, to continual recourse to institutional scapegoating.

Collectively held and socially reinforced representations help to sustain individual psychic structures. By resorting to historically available sustaining group beliefs, whether they be of a positive or a negative nature, the individual can gain some relief from internal tension, since the energy demanded to believe in a collectively held social myth is much less than that necessary to create and maintain an individual projective system. A true believer in some form of socially accepted prejudice is less threatened. Where a cultural pattern provides an acceptable delusion as part of a belief system, one can more easily maintain a level of acceptable social adjustment and solidarity with others. Whereas the weight of maintaining individual projections might be unbearable, and lead to a form of behavior defined as psychopathological, social projections shared collectively within a group permit some form of psychic balance to be maintained without any overt emically perceived social malfunctioning.[6] Under ordinary conditions overt conflict does not appear. However, when stress becomes unmanageable, some overt form of violence may erupt.

To the degree to which the system of dominance in society, be it hierarchical in castes or stratified into class segments, is internalized, and to the degree that systems of social self identity are mutually accommodating, conflict remains

---

[5]Witness the racially motivated killing of a Black youth by working class Whites in New York City (August 1989) where the Black youth was supposed to be dating a White woman.

[6]In preindependent Algeria, elaborate projective systems involved Jews and French in schemes to rob Algerians of their potency. Women, as hopeless inferiors, could not be trusted outside the house (see Miner and De Vos, 1960).

minimal. Given situations of social change and the possibilities of taking on new definitions of social self identity, either from cultural incursions from outside the traditional society or on the basis of internal social changes, situations of conflict become more evident. In the modern age with its rapid social change one may predict an increasing tempo of internal social conflicts becoming visible in segmented social orders. The resurgence of ethnic conflict that has followed the fragmentation of the former Soviet Union and its satellite nations may reflect this kind of process.

The Socialization of Disgust

Ekman (1992) has given us graphic representation of the universality of facial expressions related to what we can define as disgust. Disgust is a basic physical reaction related to a sense of rejection of touch and contact involving not only the injection of noisome material in the mouth but contaminatory touch of any part of the body or, by extension, of objects belonging to oneself or others. Visual objects can be disgusting to sight. There is some indication that the closer to possible contact the greater the reaction. We see in the reactions of contempt and disgust related to individuals discussed above in the instance of caste that these feelings can be socialized from early childhood on so as to be aroused by some form of symbolic association. Disgust in every culture is as much subject to socialization as are any *interpersonal* expressions of hate, fear, love, or sexual desire. Disgust differs in degree from other emotions by having a unique sense of the danger of what it feels like to be too close, to have to smell it, see it, or touch it. Disgust uses images of sensation or suggests the sensory experience merely by describing the disgusting thing or person (Miller, 1997).

The Reverential, the Heroic, and the "Aweful"

Conscious evaluations extend beyond the ordinary in both directions. Human evaluative expectations extend into the world of the supernatural and the uncanny. In the negative direction are severe evaluations of contaminatory untouchability. The demonic can, in various ways, epitomize disgust. Attitudes of purity, respect, and reverence extend toward concepts of deity, but they also include a sense of the charismatic and the heroic embodied in some special humans that inspire a sense of awe and evoke a desire in one to approach and partake of a special emanation of prowess or beauty. To approach such a being raises a need for special preparation to be worthy of proximity or touch, not to be disgusting to the awesome figure or deity. Such narrative material in both directions is scorable under (E).

Some Religious Representations of Purity and Awe

The extremes of any social evaluations of social acceptability or pejorative displacements are found cross culturally in religious representations of purity and awe. This category includes religious concerns with acceptability related to one's deity. In positive or negative religious terms there are forms of personal and group depreciation related to ideas of purity and pollution.

In the history of anthropology, one of the pioneering major insights of W. Robertson-Smith (1894) was that in many early religious collective representations one often cannot distinguish between the holy and the satanic, the awesome and the awful. The good and the bad were not separated in the realm of the supernatural. This idea was later taken up by Emile Durkheim (1947) and extended further in his discussion of the nature of the sacred. Smith saw that *respect* for an elevated god is an advanced development in religious conceptualization from a more generalized feeling of fear-induced awe held toward the supernatural. Gradually awe becomes less a question of fear, and more one of respect. Deference can be accorded completely out of respect rather than out of a feeling of being under the subordination of power.

Such stages in development can be seen ontogenetically in the development of childhood religious conceptions. From its early inception the concept of the supernatural has both instrumental and expressive facets. Power evokes both submission and reverence. Power is also bestowal of benevolence. Historically, the idea of a god that is all good is a stage of moral development which succeeds more inchoate concepts of power and magic, both malevolent and benevolent. Such feelings become related to adhering to regulations seen as coming from powerful beings. They also become related to being pleasing or relatively attractive to the deity. They may lead to some sense of power or mastery in oneself as one of the elected of God.

> To know that one has the mysterious powers of nature on one's side, so long as one acts in conformity with certain rules, gives a man strength and courage to pursue the task of the subjugation of nature to his service. To restrain one's individual license, not out of slavish fear, but from respect for a higher and beneficent power, is a more developed moral discipline of which the value does not altogether depend on the reasonableness of the sacred restrictions. (Robertson-Smith, 1894)

This description of Smith's is an almost direct representation of the concept that Freud later proposed as identification, in which the child learns to suppress and repress the disavowed as a means of enjoying the love and approval of his parents and of some representation of God. Through a denial or a projection of the disavowed, the child brings within a feeling of closeness if not identification with the powers that regulate the moral order, be it the parents or later, when one assumes the religious beliefs of one's group, either of a beneficent, guiding deity

(N) or a jealous and terrible god (D), ready to visit disease, starvation, or natural catastrophe as punishment upon his possibly wayward subjects.

As to social acceptability as related to purity, nowhere is the unconscious psychological symbolic nature of ritual behavior more clearly apparent than in the ritual acts of purification that follow what is considered contamination. Most religions have incorporated some form of cleansing ritual. These are often used around the act of birth to bring the woman back into contact with her social group. In Japan, Shinto ritual used symbolic forms of ablution and cleansing related to the purity of white as a color and the cleansing property of water; similarly in Christianity, baptismal water symbolically cleanses the individual from the impure state of original sin. This baptismal cleansing is not the removal of individual guilt, but of a past collective guilt of humanity. The individual starts anew in a relationship in which there is hopefully an internalization of a sense of potential guilt which governs future behavior.[7]

One must distinguish between different uses of the concept of purification. In some contexts it can be related to potentials for guilt and to consciously considered socially responsible behavior. For example, in the Vajrayana Buddhism of Tibet "purification" appears in a context of the *rectification* of behavior, and an acknowledgment of the consequences of one's own acts. In some meditative visualizations, light and liquid emanate from enlightened beings and serve the purpose of purification. Yet there are also requirements to generate regret, restitution, and an intention to refrain from future negative actions.[8] Seeking purification of this sort requires adherence to behavioral proscriptions and prescriptions in a future temporal orientation that regulates future behavior and alters the conditions that affect the ripening of negative karma.

In this sense there is seeking absolution from self-inflicted punishment. Note that this religiously guided thought about "purification" is much more relevant to our discussion of the instrumental categories, considered below. We further discuss there distinctions between fear of punishment considered in chapter 10, volume I, under Control (D) and an inner recognition of the consequences of one's behavior considered under categories of Responsibility (R) (chapter 11, volume I). Semantically, in either instance, the terminology used can also include the word "purification." But what is actually represented can be less a problem of concern with social acceptability, and more a problem of an internalized intrapsychically considered sense of responsibility or fear of wrathful judgment (see chapters 10 and 11, volume I). Often the two are mixed, yet must be distinguished analytically.

---

[7]Technically, individual guilt only starts with the internalization of responsibility (see chapter 11, volume I).

[8]There are numerous descriptions published on the "Four Opponent Powers." For example, see Dhargyey (1974) or Pabongka (1991).

The Social Evaluation of Women and Female Functions: Gender Displacement and Social Regard

We should note that some current work in feminist psychology and anthropology approaches the question of women and gender status inequality from different perspectives. Some feminist theorists tend to equate and reduce the exploitation and depreciation of women to instrumental "class" factors (Collier, 1988; Nash and Safa, 1986). They overlook the dynamic expressive elements of social derogation that mark caste and gender relationships. Other theorists distance themselves from a simple sociological Marxist paradigm and delve instead into what they consider to be the differential dynamics of gender development as culturally mediated variants of psychological development that produce what are termed "feminine" psychosocial traits (Chodorow, 1978; Dinnerstin, 1976; Gilligan, 1982; Strathern, 1988).[9] In our judgment it is the *projective negative evaluation* of traits of the opposite sex that remains the source of difficulty in gender relationships.

One form of evaluative social differentiation based on concepts of purity and pollution is the periodic sequestering of women as "impure," most often directly related to taboos concerning menstruation and childbirth (De Vos and Suárez-Orozco, 1990, chapter 5). Menstrual functions in a number of societies are intertwined with concepts of gender inferiority, even acts of degradation including absolute prohibitions on women serving in a priesthood that requires an elevated state of relative holiness and purity (Buckley and Gottlieb, 1988).

The "Aweful"

The religious conceptions of pollution found in the defined ritual impurity of women goes beyond any concept of ordinary dirt or contamination. It is not the simple avoidance of what is unpleasant or disgusting. As is all ritual pollution, it remains unconsciously, if not directly consciously, interpenetrated by feelings of respect and deep fear characterizing what is "aweful." This inner confusion of supernatural power with the fear of pollution contributes to the sense of the demonic and has its pan-human origins in the early primitive confusion found in symbolic representations characteristic of infantile associative mental processes (Bettelheim, 1962).

Religious representations of the mysteries of menstrual bleeding are ambivalent in nature. This fear of the uncontrollable appearance of blood in menstruation and childbirth is related unconsciously to feelings of destruction and mutilation, and to the excretory loss of dead materials from the body. It is, therefore,

---

[9]For overviews of concerns in the anthropology of women, see Martin (1987), Reiter (1975), Rosaldo and Lamphere (1974), and Strathern (1988).

not difficult to see how concepts of contamination also become related to the appearance of menstrual bleeding. However, this female function usually brings on even more deeply emotional attitudes. Any deep fear of contamination is more than simple disgust, there are intermingled mixtures of awe and of mysterious power as well.

Feelings of awe, as is true for reverential fear, are universally apparent in representations of the mysteries of sex, birth, death, and fertility as power (Graves, 1948). Fear can represent an acknowledgment of power. Where power attributed to individuals is too awesome to be easily acceptable, the fear can be transmuted into some form of disparagement. Menstrual taboos, world wide, suggest not only disgust but fearful power (Bettelheim, 1962; De Vos, 1963; De Vos and Suárez-Orozco, 1990; Buckley and Gottlieb, 1988).

The bloody business of birth has about it something of the supernatural in the mysteries of generativity and suggests, in many cultures, the linkage of women's genital functions to the "awful" or the demonic. Some of the most basic feelings of awe are related to concepts concerning fertility and the power of creation. In the history of religions, there are numerous occasions where these feelings are combined symbolically in representation of a female deity. In Anatolia from the early Hittite period and before, as well as in the early Greek (Graves, 1948) and in many Melanesian cultures (Bettelheim, 1962; Herdt, 1981, 1982), an awesome, birthing female power is revealed in religious symbolism. In some symbolic rituals such as those of New Guinea (De Vos and Suárez-Orozco, 1990, chapter 5), men appropriate to themselves such generative power along with their elevation to the male status of adulthood at the expense of women who remain socially disparaged.

The appearance of female witches in the West, which persisted even into the last century, provided some outlet for representations of the negatively evaluated demonic that was imputed to female nature. In some instances there was a demonization of the power of postmenopausal women symbolized as fearful hags. At certain periods in European history, unconscious projections concerning witchcraft, mostly on the part of older women, rivaled concerns with the despised "dirty" Jew, who was also seen as representative of the demonic and a source of fear and hatred. In short, feelings of contamination related to women's sexual functioning must be seen as psychologically similar to those feelings which reinforce exclusory caste, ethnic, and racial attitudes (De Vos and Wagatsuma, 1966).

There is no way, of course, of segregating women permanently in all areas of life. Nevertheless, in many societies in which a male priesthood is established, women are not allowed to partake of the most elevated of sacred functions. Celibacy is espoused as a means of maintaining purity. Belief in women's impurity is sufficient to justify the prevention of their participation in many forms of ritual life. In societies that have severe menstrual proscriptions and in those having severe caste proscriptions, it is the higher caste or the dominant males that enforce the social sanctions. In these contexts, deference behavior may be expected from the subordinate. The superior is sensitive to any lack of deference that may be a signal of possible retributory attitudes on the part of the subordinate, and this may contribute to a superior's "status anxiety."[10] We may assume, therefore, that not only can social sanctions be related to questions of ritual impurity and sexual integrity, but they also can reflect underlying tensions related to status anxiety.

In other words, political dominance when related to a social hierarchy in which there is considerable expressive exploitation of another social group, begets fear on the part of the superordinate. The fear itself begets more stringent political sanctions related to unequal status. In turn, the sanctions themselves repeat the convoluted vicious circle of psychological concern with an asymmetrical social relationship.

Our concept of status anxiety (De Vos and Wagatsuma, 1966) is as pertinent to the discussion of the social segregation of women in male-dominated societies as it is to the segregated unequal status occurring within caste, or multiethnic societies with specially despised social minorities. This concept can be related to affiliative and companionate problems in Arab cultures (Miner and De Vos, 1960), or other patriarchal societies where there are minimal caste feelings, but more stringent, unresolved feelings about the basic inequality of women related to their supposed impurity as well as inferiority attributed to their supposed lack of capacity for self-control.[11]

Caste becomes related to irrational, fearful emotions related to questions of relative social acceptability, whatever the exploitative economic or political aspects of relative social status. Marxist theory, which is instrumentally oriented in understanding human behavior cannot deal with the irrational forces governing sexism and caste-based disparagement. These can not be explained solely by reference to rationally derived class advantages.

Social Pride: Appreciation or Depreciation in Interethnic Relations

There are many complex issues raised by multiethnic relationships within a single society or political state. Ethnicity has a historical dimension which becomes involved in the group assessment of the majority or a minority. Defensively, an ethnic identity requires some way of taking pride in one's heritage. Affirmation of ethnic pride is used to counter the potential derogation or humiliation of others.

---

[10] See the discussion of status anxiety in De Vos and Watagsuma (1966).

[11] The supposed lack of self-control can be found even in the psychoanalytic tradition. In Freud's description of superego development, it is suggested that the male's response to castration anxiety involves a more powerful investment of defensive "identification with the aggressor," which leads to a more effective internalization of the parental voice as superego than is accomplished by the female's response to penis envy. See Chodorow (1978) for a discussion on this.

Ethnic situations become more complex when more than one heritage is involved. Mixed marriages occur in any multiethnic state, raising questions of status identity for the children of parents of different ethnic backgrounds. In situations imputing nothing pejorative to either ancestry, a child will happily identify with a more complex heritage. The child can acknowledge both ancestral backgrounds without conflict over the expediency or the integrity of being identified one or other way.

Social identity may be far more complicated when there are severe differences in social acceptability whether one is of single or mixed ancestry. "Passing" discussed elsewhere (chapter 8, volume I) may be practiced. One seeks to hide one's ancestry, disavowing a disparaged heritage.

In a racist society, wherein certain ethnic groups are considered inferior to others, intermarriages between the dominant and the inferior groups can be deemed contaminatory, and the children of such liaisons forced to identify with their less acceptable minority heritage. In some situations of conflict, however, children faced with the need to choose between parental heritage will sometimes voluntarily opt for the minority identity, seeking to protect the heritage of the more demeaned parent out of a sense of honor and personal integrity.

Let us again turn to Japan to illustrate some problems of social acceptability.

Koreans in Japan: Some Unresolved Issues of Past and Present Social Disparagement

Whatever the present society there is no society without minority citizens. The history of any society needs to be retaught in more complex ways. The Japanese, as a modern society, cannot sustain the illusion of separate origin. Their cultural heritage is interwoven with that of Korea, past and present. No cohesive multi-ethnic state can afford to emphasize one cultural heritage as "innate" or as superior to another. In recent years, the Japanese government has attempted to rectify the social disparagement of their Korean minority by better acknowledgment of the separate social and cultural history of Korea.

However, the present legally anomalous status of Koreans in Japan makes any assuagement of social disparagement a difficult task. Prevalent pejorative attitudes about a minority ethnic position within the Japanese state make it psychologically incumbent upon many Koreans to resist assimilation. Only when their past cultural background is accorded respect and they are given the right to be of Korean background as a Japanese citizen can hyphenated *Korean-Japanese* accept the historical fact that they are destined to function as resident citizens of Japan in future generations.

Glazer and Moynihan (1975) cite the conclusions of Dahrendorf (1969) that an internal dynamic evident in many heterogeneous populations is the increasing awareness on the part of minorities as well as the majority, of manifest incongruities in the social values of modern states. Dahrendorf considers that an unresolvable conflict has arisen everywhere between modern egalitarianism and the differential patterns of social achievement realized by different class or ethnic segments of a population. In this context, the Korean case is an interesting one both historically and in the contemporary international industrial scene. Certainly, the Japanese also now espouse "human rights," yet they remain socially discriminatory and deprecatory toward Koreans in such a way that the Koreans in Japan do not achieve up to expected educational and occupational levels in their society.

According to sociologist Dahrendorf (1969), "selection of norms always involves discrimination, not only against persons holding sociologically random moral convictions but also against social positions that may debar their incumbents from conformity with established values." In other words, his thesis is that every society emphasizes norms and established values selected from a diverse set of possibilities. Once the selection is made historically of what is "good" and what is "bad," individuals and ethnic groups are defined by different levels of success in attaining these desired status conditions. These norms may define physical traits, character traits, or particular talents that are differentially socialized within different groups. Therefore, a conflict occurs between the idea that all people should have equal instrumental opportunity and the differential possibility of achieving the *social acceptability norms* of a given society.

This form of analysis, at first glance, certainly pertains to the relationship found between Koreans in Japan and the Japanese majority. But there is more to it. Viewing the psychologically expressive features of their social situation, one sees that Koreans also become disadvantaged by their particular socialization experiences within a "racially" oriented society that subjects Koreans to forms of early experienced disparagement that impair the functioning of Korean youth in their educational and vocational adaptation.

The intensity of negative feelings on the part of Japanese must be considered a part of clashing personality variables between the majority Japanese and their debased ex-colonial minority. In considering why Japanese depreciate Koreans personally, one must also consider the force of negative projections on the part of Japanese who are subject to internal pressures about accomplishing stringently defined social goals (De Vos, 1973). Koreans are considered by Japanese to exhibit various socially disavowed traits concerning overtly expressed aggressive behavior, and seem to hold different expressive values dangerous to those of the majority who must constrict themselves to attain vocational ends. In short, Koreans are easily used as scapegoats by Japanese who have applied to them stringent expectations concerning self-controlled, goal-directed behavior.

As noted by Dahrendorf, countering the forces leading to inequality of status are those forces in most contemporary societies related both to humanitarian ideals of acceptance (E) and the bestowal of welfare benefits on the needy and the disadvantaged (N). We have mentioned how such processes are at work in Japan (Lee and De Vos, 1981), although programs broadening welfare in Japan remain ambivalent about their "foreign" ethnic minority. Here the question of citizenship related to Japanese racist attitudes becomes a critical issue. Moreover, because Japanese consider them "racially" different, Koreans by and large have either refused or have been unable to become Japanese citizens.

The situation of Koreans in Japan has come to resemble the problems faced by *non-citizen* non-European migrant laborers in Europe. Koreans continue to be treated in racist terms parallel to what we find among certain segments of European migrant labor. In Europe, North Africans and Turks were brought in as unskilled labor to solve immediate industrial needs without considering the consequences of what proves to be continuous residence of a population not considered "assimilative." The social effects of possible permanent residence on the part of new minority families was not considered at the time foreign labor was introduced by industrial concerns interested only in economic profit. In France, for example, Arab and Senegalese workers are now the focus of attitudes more racially discriminatory than those expressed toward Spanish and Portuguese workers. In Belgium, it is the Moroccans and Turks who are seen as visible problems (De Vos and Suárez-Orozco, 1990, chapter 8). There were consequent expressive "racial" attitudes lying latent in majority populations that became manifest when the children of migrants entered the public schools and responded differently from majority children. These new social problems are a complex social by-product of a simple attempt at gaining immediate instrumental economic benefits, not consciously considered exploitative in nature.

While in general agreement with much of the theoretical focus in contemporary sociology, we nevertheless find many sociological approaches insufficient because they do not sufficiently emphasize salient differences between *caste* and *class* in European or Japanese social attitudes. In addition, there is simply insufficient attention paid to the differences in *psychological vulnerability* of some groups compared with others as they face attendant attitudes of degradation related to unacceptability. These vulnerabilities are interrelated with attitudes of possible inferiority vis-à-vis the dominant denigrating group. The Koreans in Japan illustrate patterns to be found both in contemporary Europe and in the United States.

Part of the problem is not that Japanese and Korean cultural values are different, but ironically that they are so similar in their Confucian traditions. In contrast to themselves, Koreans see Japanese as better practitioners of the Confucian virtues. They find themselves in broken marital situations, living in degraded residence conditions within Japanese society. They are socially disparaged as inferior in their vocational pursuits. In such conditions, they are self-consciously failing to properly exercise their deeply felt traditional values and they do no credit to their family lineage. They are therefore doubly vulnerable to negative evaluations coming from seemingly more virtuous Japanese. To generalize: *similarity of values* with the majority can lead to as great a psychological vulnerability on the part of a degraded minority as may result from any differences in traditional values.[12] In caste-like situations especially, other psychological processes besides simple instrumental exploitation are at work. These expressive features create a true difference in the historical aftermath. Stratification in a caste society endures even after the economic advantages of exploiting a particular group have come to be outweighed by the manifest disadvantages, economic and social, of maintaining a segregated society.

It is therefore important to understand that the present social degradation of Koreans is not simply a result of "class exploitation," despite all the features of economic exploitation we have documented in our study (Lee and De Vos, 1981). It is equally important, in this instance, to consider the plight of Koreans in Japan historically as the result of expressively driven thinking of a type peculiar to the Japanese as they interrelate with individuals socialized in a "Korean" psycho-cultural milieu.

Koreans in Japan have responded to their present conditions by an ethnic consolidation not dissimilar in some modes of social adaptation to those that have been occurring in the African American population. In each instance, group members have come to recognize that their submerged, exploited condition occurs within a "racist" society. In our judgment, "caste" and so-called racial attitudes are psychologically identical.

Many Koreans are ambivalent about espousing a simple Marxist explanation for their own plight, although Marxist militancy has indeed been a most active unifying force through which a good number of both Koreans and Burakumin have sought redress. It is not that a Marxist explanation lacks certain cogency; it is that it does not explain fully the Japanese inability to socially accept either the Korean people or their own ex-untouchable Burakumin as we discussed elsewhere (De Vos and Wagatsuma, 1966). Despite the historically different circumstances in the two cases, both bear expressively prompted similarities. They are both marked by a Japanese form of racism. Moreover, Marxist "working class solidarity" between Burakumin and Koreans does not readily cross their ethnic differences as well as the "racial" or "caste" barriers they both experience in relation with majority Japanese. Their specific forms of ethnic identity are driven by emotional forces that becloud possible mutual instrumental purpose. One can question the overall saliency of worker solidarity concepts as applied to hierarchically organized contemporary Japan.

The racism that has affected northwestern European states has much in common with the situation in Japan, despite independent cultural-historical origins. However, true class attitudes in Europe and Japan, as examined above, are different in intensity and structure. There is worker solidarity in Europe to a degree not found

---

[12]Such negative self-evaluations are also apparent in African Americans who are, despite assertions to the contrary, an integral part of an American society that disparages them. Overall, they do not comprise a separate culture, but share common values and aspirations.

in Japan. The Japanese have not been alienated by class differences in a manner true for Europeans (De Vos, 1975).

Appreciation Versus Disparagement

Ultimately, perhaps, the issue of social acceptance and dignity is the principal concern of any ethnic minority. The Japanese themselves, sensitive to appreciation or deprecation from outsiders, generally have been deprecatory and derogatory toward Koreans. They cannot accept different Korean customs; they cannot even accept Korean eating habits. The poverty to which Koreans have been historically subjected is used to classify them as *inherently* uncouth and uncivilized. In this respect, direct parallels to race relations in the United States are very apparent. The Japanese cannot accept some aspects of the freer interpersonal expressions, both positive and aggressive, that Koreans manifest. These go against the greater degree of self-constraint exercised by the Japanese. This self-constraint has been particularly apparent in Japanese society from the time of the annexation of Korea through the pre-war militaristic period, and it has been maintained by many into the post-war era.

It is difficult for any majority group to accord equal value to the alien and sometimes tempting behavioral patterns of others which may stimulate tension in themselves. Only a very open, self-possessed individual who arrives at his own behavior out of choice rather than out of severely internalized constraints can accord acceptance to others behaving differently from himself. The Japanese have great difficulty in feeling comfortable in cultural settings other than their own. This discomfort is not limited to their contacts with Koreans but includes contacts with other peoples throughout eastern and southeastern Asia.[13] The Japanese have been quick to disparage and derogate what is different from their own expectations. Their sense of uniqueness, their susceptibility to criticism, and their need for approval are the opposite sides of a readiness to disparage and disapprove of others. For Japanese, Europe and the United States are an "audience" that may possibly withhold the equal acceptability of Japanese and Japanese in the family of "superior nations."

In short, Koreans have been vulnerable to scapegoating because their behavior is thought to be not thoroughly "Japanese." Their anomalous status within Japanese society continues. The deviant behavior of some is used by many Japanese as supportive evidence for maintaining a massive deprecatory attitude toward all Koreans. One need not belabor the point that Koreans are deprecated not because they eat garlic or have a higher delinquency and crime rate, but because they have

---

[13]Their relations with Europeans and Americans are more complex. They more overtly envy some of the desirable features of Western societies, while also seeing them as less refined in many respects. The Japanese cannot give up their sense of uniqueness.

been, since the turn of the century, used psychologically by majority Japanese as vulnerable objects of projection of what is disavowed internally. They are ready targets for the displacement of frustration and anger.

This brings up the crucial problem that some members of a disparaged ethnic minority themselves become subject to self-hatred and self-disparagement. We have written at length on this topic in a discussion of self-hatred among the Japanese Burakumin (see De Vos and Wagatsuma, 1966, passim). The presence of self-depreciation among some alienated Koreans was equally apparent. No theoretical statements can better express these processes at work than the actual writings and comments we gathered from those who must deal with their own damaged self-esteem.[14]

The use of educational practices to resolve the complex issues of minority identity involves irreconcilable instrumental and expressive difficulties. For example, there is at present no consensus among Korean parents in Japan whether a child should use its Korean name in school or in public. Emphasis on immediate, practical, instrumental adaptation by appearing to be Japanese may sacrifice pride, the validity of being "Korean," and one's sense of self-worth. Conversely, a too rigid insistence that being Korean resides in objective criteria, such as language proficiency or dress, may be impractical for Koreans who plan to continue to live in Japan. Furthermore, being aggressively Korean represents an identical adversarial view shared with those Japanese who claim that Japanese ethnicity is essential for "true" Japanese citizenship.

This majority Japanese position does not permit Koreans in Japan to maintain ethnic self-esteem by being both a Japanese citizen and of Korean ethnic origin. In a modern, industrial state—whether it be France, the United States, Israel, Germany, or Japan—this equation of citizenship with a particular ethnic ancestry is no longer legally or socially tenable. In the mobile societies of today, where birth and continual residence in a new setting is increasing, no modern state can judge allegiance or responsible membership by maintaining a narrow, defensive ethnicity as criteria for citizenship. This contrastive separation diminishes or incapacitates individuals from any group. No state, or so-called nation can adapt to the future by systematic denial of entry to those of external cultural origin. Minority groups cannot escape considerable damage from the prevention of social as well as cultural assimilation. Affirmation of origin is different from a defensive maintenance of difference. A defensive minority identity, by its very nature, is maladaptive in a complex modern society. If Korean identity in Japan can be maintained only through attending a Korean language school, which handicaps the individual in the formal Japanese school system, then the individual becomes subject to continuous conflict, both external and internal.

Conversely, if the Japanese school system implicitly derogates the legitimate right to citizenship as well as the dignity of Korean ancestry in discouraging the use

[14]Some of these comments are presented in Lee and De Vos (1981) chapters 13 and 14.

of a Korean name at school, then the child perhaps has no alternative but to resist Japanese education at a cost to his sense of personal worth. The fact is that most children of Korean ancestry growing up in Japan will not speak Korean as their native tongue. They are culturally assimilated. They will speak Japanese. Nonetheless, there should be no need for them to become socially assimilated only by derogating their previous cultural tradition, a tradition in which, as citizens of Japan, they may no longer directly participate in during daily life. They may, nevertheless, wish to continue a symbolic sense of ancestry.

Categories of Esteem and Social Acceptability

The category of esteem is complex in so far as one must distinguish whether it is the protagonist who is appreciating or depreciating another person, or whether an evaluation is perceived from the standpoint of the recipient. This latter situation includes various forms of self evaluation as enhancing or derogating.

Protagonist as Donor

*A. Positive Evaluative Attitudes **EDA***

EDA-respect	According respect
EDA-awe	According awe and reverence
EDA-holy	Appreciation of another's holiness or purity (related to religion)
EDA-status	Positively perceived status
EDA-family	Appreciation of another's family or lineage
EDA-ethnic	Appreciation of another ethnic group
EDA-praise	Appreciation or praise of another
EDA-fame	Famous or recognized person
EDA-appear	Physical appreciation of another (beauty, strength, etc.)
EDA-reclean	Reestablishment of another's status after degradation or pollution

Respect as an expressive experience (EDA-respect) is to be distinguished from obedience as an instrumental submission to authority. A feeling of awe may be directed toward figures with special talents in holiness, in wisdom, in artistic performance, or in military prowess. Arising out of the infantile state of relative helplessness there is a human tendency to sense awe and respect to be accorded those who manifest power or special talent. There develops a human deference to what has been termed "charisma." These early experiences of infancy can continue to be directed to elders in an age graded social system or focused on supernatural beings in religious beliefs and practices (EDA-awe). There can be verbalized a sense of the special holiness or purity accorded an individual or group (EDA-holy).

From the standpoint of the donors of appreciation, deference may be accorded to members of special groups on the basis of family lineage or other markers of social status (EDA-status). One may have a special comparative appreciation of someone's family (EDA-family). There are special evaluations of individuals or groups that are considered ethnically separate. Some outside minority groups are held in high esteem (EDA-ethnic).

There is a general social recognition of special talent. One willingly recognizes special positive attributes in another person (EDA-praise). One form of social appreciation is what is termed "fame" (EDA-fame).

One may have a sense of appreciation for the beauty or physical appearance of another (EDA-appear). In some societies there are rituals of cleansing or reestablishing the good name or social acceptability of those previously depreciated (EDA-reclean).

B. Unresolved Evaluative Attitudes ***EDB***

EDB-lessen	Disappointment in another
EDB-appear	Concern with the appearance of another
EDB-evaluate	Uncertain or undisclosed evaluation
EDB-torn	Unresolved respect toward another
EDB-envy	Envy of the regard or status afforded another
EDB-status	Concern with social status of another

Some behavior or impropriety can cause one to feel a disappointment in another, or a lessening of previous esteem (EDB-lessen). The concern may be directed toward the dubious appearance of another (EDB-appear). One can note uncertain or ambiguous attitudes expressed in regard to others (EDB-evaluate). One may develop uncertainty or ambivalence about the respect due another (EDB-torn). There may be awareness of envy of the regard or status received by another (EDB-envy). More often one expresses unresolved concerns with social status and social acceptability of another (EDB-status).

C. Negative Evaluation of Others ***EDC***

EDC-disdain	Pride, arrogance, disdain, humiliation, degradation of another
EDC-group	Depreciation or degradation of a group
EDC-contempt	Expressing contempt despising another
EDC-sarcasm	Sarcasm, teasing; verbal dueling

EDC-insolent	Rude or insolent behavior toward a superior
EDC-brash	Brash, no respect for others feelings or opinions
EDC-status	Defensive use of status against other/others, chauvinism, sexism, etc.
EDC-moral	Moral self righteous toward another
EDC-expect	Devaluating expectations of another
EDC-disgust	Finding another repulsive, ugly, or disgusting
EDC-slander	Slander, calumny
EDC-lessen	General disparaging of society, disillusionment

In this category are included forms of negative expressive actions or attitudes expressing either excessive self-enhancement by disdaining others or direct humiliation or depreciation of others.

Excessive pride or arrogance about oneself or one's group may become expressed in an active need to humiliate or humble the pride of others (EDC-disdain). However, expressions of depreciation (EDC-group) may not be necessarily accompanied by self or group enhancement. There are forms of derogation in which the other is seen with contempt and is actively despised (EDC-contempt).

There are milder forms of depreciation to be noted in teasing behavior or heavier forms of verbal sarcasm (EDC-sarcasm). Among the negative forms of excessive self-enhancement at the expense of others are brash behavior, arrogance, and various forms of humiliation and degradation of individuals or groups. There may be insolent, rude behavior expressed either to superior or to peers (EDC-insolent). Brash behavior (EDC-brash) manifests an inordinate lack of concern with the possible opinions of others.

There are various forms of using one's status against others. One may be chauvinistic about one's country at the expense of others. For example, there are various forms of sexism used to put another person down (EDC-status). Often depreciation has a moral or moralistic flavor and appears as some form of self-righteous behavior in which others are derogated (EDC-moral). One may deflate, disparage, and so disappoint the expectation of appreciation of another (EDC-expect).

A person may be put down as ugly, disgusting, or repulsive (EDC-disgust). There may be the practice of vilification, slander, or calumny (EDC-slander). Finally there may be derogation of society based on a general sense of disillusionment (EDC-lessen).

D. Ineffectual or Unseemly Evaluation ***EDD***

EDD-withhold	Withholding of recognition
EDD-unable	Incapable of giving recognition
EDD-awe	Excessive regard for another
EDD-praise	Excessive praise, flattery, or adulation

There can be a passive withholding of expected recognition or response (EDD-withhold). An individual may be incapable of expressing appreciation or giving recognition (EDC-unable). There are excessively deferential attitudes according another undeserved obsequiousness (EDD-awe), or awarding undeserved praise of others (EDD-praise), that we have allocated to this category.

Protagonist as Recipient

A. Positive Evaluative Attitudes ***ESA***

ESA-status	Positively perceived social-professional status
ESA-family	Pride in one's family or lineage
ESA-ethnic	Ethnic pride as self-appreciation
ESA-worth	Self-respect, sense of worth or acceptability
ESA-praised	Appreciated
ESA-loved	Loved, popular
ESA-approved	Approval of an audience, authority
ESA-appear	Approved appearance: physical characteristic
ESA-pride	Others are proud of self
ESA-demure	Self-effacing, modest, "shy" as a virtue opposite of self-forwarding
ESA-fame	Recognition of achieved status (fame)
ESA-heroic	Recognized as heroic in deeds
ESA-awe	Receiving awe or deference
ESA-restore	Restoration of honor by sacrificial act
ESA-pure	Pure or purified, in religious terms

Individuals may be recipients of some form of positive evaluation from others, or from oneself, as members of groups or families, whether or not they are respected or appreciated by others individually (ESA-status). There may be a sense of having one's family appreciated by others and having a sense of positive pride about family lineage (ESA-family). They also may have a sense of pride about social group, or ethnicity (ESA-ethnic).

Individuals are concerned positively about having self-respect (ESA-worth). There are a number of situations in which one receives some form of appreciation or regard or receives praise from someone (ESA-praised). One may become popular and be loved by others (ESA-loved). One may receive the approbation or appreciation of an audience for one's performance (EDA-approved). Often this category is double scored with one of positive competence when there is also an expressed awareness of positive ability (EDA-approved CA-present). One may be appreciated for appearance or physical characteristics (ESA-appear). One can receive indications that one's family or friends have become proud of an individual (ESA-pride). One may be appraised positively as self-effacing, modest, shy, as virtuously opposite of self-forwarding (ESA-demure).

The level of appreciation may be considerable so that an individual becomes renowned or famous (ESA-fame). Individuals may be made to feel that they are considered heroic by others (ESA-heroic) or have become aware that they are objects of awe or deference (ESA-awe). One may restore personal or family honor by a sacrificial act (ESA-restore). Japanese suicide in *seppuku* is an example of maintaining family honor. One may experience oneself as being pure or having become purified, seen in religious terms (ESA-pure).

B. Unresolved Evaluative Attitudes ***ESB***

ESB-esteem	Insecure self-respect or self-esteem
ESB-praised	Worry about being appreciated
ESB-shamed	Worry about negative evaluation of others: embarrassment
ESB-appear	Worry about appearance
ESB-accepted	Worry about being accepted
ESB-regard	Unresolved regard or recognition of peers
ESB-ignored	Worry about being ignored
ESB-teased	Concerned with being teased
ESB-unworthy	Concern about unworthiness
ESB-status	Doubt about social acceptance or status
ESB-expose	Worry about compromising exposure

There are ambivalent unresolved or insecure forms of self-evaluation or self-esteem (ESB-esteem) and general worries about being appreciated (ESB-praised). There may be worries about the possible negative evaluations of others leading to a sense of shame (ESB-shamed). There may be special worries about personal appearance (ESB-appear). There are special concerns about being accepted by a social group (ESB-accepted), gaining regard or recognition (ESB-regard), or worry about being ignored (ESB-ignored) or teased (ESB-teased).

There may be worries about being morally worthless or unworthy (ESB-unworthy). There may be doubt about having acceptable social status (ESB-status). There may be special concerns about having some compromising personal or family secrets become public (ESB-expose).

C. Negative Active Evaluation Related to Self ***ESC***

ESC-conceit	Narcissistic preoccupation or pride
ESC-exhibit	"Showing off" unduly exhibitionistic
ESC-lessen	Disappoint someone, lose other's esteem
ESC-detract-s	Self-depreciation (general)
ESC-group	Self-depreciation related to one's group
ESC-appear-s	Active self-depreciative sense of ugliness
ESC-hate-s	Sense of active self-hatred
ESC-abase-s	Self-abasement before others
ESC-disgrace	Behavior brings disgrace on family or group
ESC-injury	Hurt to self or others due to loss of status
ESC-suicide	Suicide due to loss of social regard
ESC-honor	Vengeance related to personal or family honor (double score with HD-revenge)

Self-oriented evaluations of one's behavior can either be excessively positive or negative. Excessive forms of self-preoccupation or undue self-evaluation are defined as "narcissistic" in nature (ESC-conceit). The motive for some activities can be more to gain the attention of others (ESC-exhibit) than because one enjoys the acts performed, or because one has developed a well-defined inner need for accomplishment. Childish self-exhibition can become later cloaked, or transmuted, into more acceptable adult displays of talent or beauty.

One's behavior or revelation can cause one to lose the esteem of others (EDC-lessen). Humans generally exhibit a basic reactive vulnerability to social as well as personal depreciation, belittlement, debasement, degradation, denigration, defamation, or defilement, and such excessively negative evaluative attitudes can be actively directed toward the self (ESC-detract-s), or be directed toward oneself as a member of a social group (ESC-group). There are special concerns over social acceptability related to disapproved group behavior, or what in some societies are considered hereditary taints or ethnic inferiority.

"Ugly" appearance and behavior is stigmatized socially.[15] Some individuals can become excessively self-critical and openly self-disparaging about their

[15]See Goffman (1963), for an extended discussion of the agonies of self-presentation and the manipulation of behavior to avoid stigma.

personal appearance (ESC-appear-s). In our study of the Burakumin pariahs of Japan, a group that was treated socially much as the untouchables of India even after their official emancipation in 1872, we found not infrequently some display of self hate (ESC-hate-s). Some individuals seem to develop various forms of self-abasement in particular social circumstances (ESC-abase-s).

One may bring active disgrace on one's family by a variety of activities (ESC-disgrace). A loss of status, actual or imagined, can result in self-destructive behavior, or in the injury of others (ESC-injury). One form of suicide found in Japan, for example, was the taking of one's life after making a socially compromising mistake, or an imagined loss of status due to the mistakes of others for whom one was technically responsible (ESC-suicide).

Concern with "honor" is a salient feature of a number of societies. Family and individual honor was a mark of the samurai. Sicilians have been notably sensitive about the sexual honor of their women. Concerns with honor often involve physical retaliation for social slight (ESC-honor, double score with HC-revenge).

D. Negatively Incurred Evaluations ***ESD***

ESD-unfair	Unfairly unappreciated
ESD-shamed	Feeling of being shamed, humiliated, mortified
ESD-shunned	Being shunned for one's behavior
ESD-disgraced	Family or group shamed by another member
ESD-exposed	Exposed or revealed for bad behavior
ESD-infamy	Considered notorious or infamous
ESD-base	Sense of worthlessness
ESD-impure	Sense of impurity or defilement
ESD-illusory	Disillusionment with the self

There are a number of negatively incurred evaluations experienced by individuals and groups. One may feel very unfairly treated chronically due to withheld appreciation (ESD-unfair). One can be caused to sense mortification or the humbling of pride. Individuals can be made to feel shamed, humiliated, or degraded (ESD-shamed). One can experience being shunned by one's society on the basis of real or fancied wrongdoing (ESD-shunned).

Family members can feel they have been disgraced by one of the members of their family (ESD-disgraced). Individuals can feel exposed (ESD-exposed) when a socially disapproved act they sought to hide becomes revealed. Some become infamous or notorious (ESD-infamy) as deserved or undeserved victims of social disapproval. Individuals may suffer from a deep sense of personal worthlessness (ESD-base) and lack of self-acceptance. Such attitudes become internalized in women in some societies related to generally abhorrent attitudes about menstruation. Women or outcastes can come to consider themselves as hopelessly impure.

Some can feel sullied or made impure by unwitting participation or being forced into forms of defiling social behavior, others feel basically impure (ESD-impure). Social attitudes toward prostitution, for example, can be severely sanctioning even when there are no actual punitive laws.

There can occur a sense of disillusionment about oneself. Finding one's past self-regard has been based on illusory self-concepts (EDS-illusory). There are also rare conditions in which the individual cannot accept social approval or praise, but shuns the approbation of others (ESD-praise).

Illustrative Samples of Scoring in the Following Chapters

In several of the chapters of volume II we have included actual illustrations of scoring of several of the subcategories included under the [E] category. Especially notable are the verbatim responses found in chapters 7, 10, and 13, volume II.

Notes

Ainsworth, Mary, S. Bell, and D. Stayton. 1974. Infant-Mother Attachment and Social Development: Socialization as the Product of Reciprocal Responsiveness to Signals. In M. Richards (Ed.), *The Integration of the Child into the Social World* (pp. 99–135). Cambridge: Cambridge University Press.

Benjamin, Jessica. 1988. *The Bonds of Love: Psychoanalysis, Feminism, and the Problem of Domination*. New York: Pantheon Books.

Bennett, Ivy Lee. 1960. *Delinquent and Neurotic Children, A Comparative Study*. New York: Basic Books.

Berreman, Gerald. 1960. Caste in India and the United States. *American Journal of Sociology*, **66**(2): 120–127.

Bettelheim, Bruno. 1962. *Symbolic Wounds; Puberty Rites and the Envious Male*. New York: Collier Books.

Bettelheim, Bruno and Morris Janowitz. 1964. *Social Change and Prejudice, Including Dynamics of Prejudice*. Glencoe, Ill.: Free Press.

Buckley, Thomas and Alma Gottlieb (Eds.). 1988. *Blood Magic: The Antropology of Menstruation*. Berkeley: University of California Press.

Chodorow, Nancy. 1978. *The Reproduction of Mothering: Psychoanalysis and the Sociology of Gender*. Berkeley, Calf.: University of California Press.

Collier, J. 1988. *Marriage and Motherhood in a Classless Society*. Stanford: Stanford University Press.

Crowne, Douglas P. and David Marlowe. 1964. *The Approval Motive: Studies in Evaluative Dependence*. New York: Wiley.

Dahrendorf, Ralf. 1969. On the Origin of Inequality among Men. In Andre Beteille (Ed.), *Social Inequality*. Baltimore: Penguin Books.

DeHart, G.B., L.A. Sroufe, and R.G. Cooper. 2000. *Child Development: Its Nature and Course* (4th edition). Boston: McGraw-Hill.

De Vos, George A. 1963. Menstrual Taboos and Chi Square. Review of William N. Stephen's "Oedipus Complex: Cross-Cultural Evidence" in *Contemporary Psychology*, **8**(11), 434–438.

———. 1967. Psychology of Purity and Pollution as Related to Social Self-Identity and Caste. In A.V.S. de Reuck and Julie Knight (Eds.), *Caste and Race: Comparative Approaches* (pp. 92–315). London: J & A. Churchill.

———. 1972. Social Stratification and Ethnic Pluralism: An Overview from the Perspective of Psychological Anthropology. *Race*, April.

———. 1973. *Socialization for Achievement: Essays on the Cultural Psychology of the Japanese.* Berkeley: University of California Press.

———. 1975. Dangers of Pure Theory in Social Anthropology. *Ethos*, **3**(1), 77–91.

———. 1978. Selective Permeability and Reference Group Sanctioning: Psycho-Cultural Continuities in Role Degradation. In Milton Yinger and Stephen Cutler (Eds.), *Major Social Issues—A Multidisciplinary View* (pp. 9–24). New York: Free Press.

———. 1984. Ethnic Identity and Minority Status: Some Psycho-Cultural Considerations. In Anita Jacobson-Widding (Ed.), *Identity: Personal and Socio-Cultural.* Stockholm, Sweden: Almquist and Wiksell International.

———. 1992. *Social Cohesion and Alienation: Minorities in The United States and Japan.* Boulder, Colo.: Westview Press.

De Vos, George A. and Marcelo Suárez-Orozco. 1990. *Status Inequality: The Self in Culture.* Newbury Park, Calif.: Sage Publications.

De Vos, George A. and Hiroshi Wagatsuma. 1966. *Japan's Invisible Race: Caste in Culture and Personality.* Berkeley: University of California Press.

Dhargyey, Geshey Ngawang. 1974. *Tibetan Tradition of Mental Development.* Dharamsala, India: Library of Tibetan Works and Archives.

Dinnerstin, D. 1976. *The Mermaid and the Minator.* New York: Harper & Row.

Durkheim, Emile. 1947. *The Elementary Forms of the Religious Life.* Trans. J.W. Swain. Glencoe, Ill.: The Free Press.

Ekman, Paul. 1992. An Argument for Basic Emotions. *Cognition and Emotion*, **6**: 169–200.

Fenichel, Otto. 1945. *The Psychoanalytic Theory of the Neurosis.* New York: W. W. Norton.

Gilligan, C. 1982. *In a Different Voice: Psychological Theory and Women's Development.* Cambridge, Mass.: Harvard University Press.

Glazer, Nathan and Patrick Moynihan. 1975. *Ethnicity: Theory and Experience.* Cambridge: Harvard University Press.

Goffman, E. 1963. *Stigma.* Englewood Cliffs, N.J.: Prentice-Hall.

Graves, Robert. 1948. *The White Goddess; A Historical Grammar of Poetic Myth.* New York: Creative Age Press.

Herdt, Gilbert H. 1981. *The Guardians of the Flutes: Idioms of Masculinity.* New York: McGraw-Hill.

———. 1982. *Rituals of Manhood.* Berkeley: University of California Press.

Kluckhohn, Clyde. 1962. *Navaho Witchcraft.* Boston: Beacon Press.

Lee, Changsoo and George A. De Vos. 1981. *Koreans in Japan: Ethnic Conflict and Accommodation.* Berkeley: University of California Press.

Martin, Emily. 1987. *The Woman in the Body: A Cultural Analysis of Reproduction.* Boston: Beacon Press.

Maslow, Abraham H. 1970. *Motivation and Personality* (2nd edition). New York: Harper & Row.

Miller, William I. 1997. *The Anatomy of Disgust.* Cambridge: Harvard University Press.

Miner, Horace and George De Vos. 1960. *Oasis and Casbah: Algerian Culture and Personality in Change*. Anthropology Papers. University of Michigan Museum of Anthropology No. 15.

Nash, J. and P. Safa. 1986. *Women and Change in South America*. Boston, Mass.: Bergin and Harvey.

Pabongka, Rispoche. 1991. *Liberation in the Palm of Your Hand: A Concise Disrouce on the Path to Enlightenment*. Boston: Wisdom Publications.

Piers, G. and M.B. Singer. 1953. *Shame and Guilt: A Psychoanalytic and Cultural Study*. Springfield, Ill.: Thomas Publishing Co.

Reiter, Reyna (Ed.). 1975. *Toward an Anthropology of Women*. New York: Monthly Review Press.

Robertson-Smith, William. 1894. *Lectures on the Religion of the Semites*. London: Black.

Rosaldo, Michelle Z. and Louise Lamphere (Eds.). 1974. *Woman, Culture and Society*. Stanford: Stanford University Press.

Sennett, Richard and Jonathan Cobb. 1972. *The Hidden Injuries of Class*. New York: Random House.

Stein, Howard. 1980a. Bowen 'Family Systems Theory': The Problem of Cultural Persistence and the Differentiation of Self in One's Culture. *The Family*, **8**(1): 3–12.

———. 1980b. Culture and Ethnicity as Group-Fantasies: A Psychohistoric Paradigm of Group Identity. *Journal of Psychohistory*, **8**(1): 21–51.

Strathern, M. 1988. *Gender of the Gift*. Berkeley: University of California Press.

Suárez-Orozco, Marcelo. 1989. *Central American Refugees and U.S. High Schools: A Psychosocial Study of Motivation and Achievement*. Stanford, Calif.: Stanford University Press.

Tangney, J.P. and K.W. Fischer (Eds.). 1995. *Self Conscious Emotions: The Psychology of Shame, Guilt, Embarrassment, and Pride*. New York: Guilford.

Thomas, William I. and Florian Znaniecki. 1927. *The Polish Peasant in Europe and America*. Edited by Eli Zaretsky, 1984. Urbana, Ill.: University of Illinois Press.

Warner, W. Lloyd, et al. 1963. *Yankee City*. New Haven, Conn.: Yale University Press.

White, R.W. 1961. Competence and the Psychosexual Stages of Development. In Donald W. Fiske and Salvatore R. Maddi (Eds.), *Functions of Varied Experience*. Homewood, Ill.: Dorsey Press.

Wolins, Martin. 1959. Personal communication.

Chapter 7

Harmony Versus Discord: Humans as Socially Accommodative Animals

The natural aggressive behavioral tendencies of all mammals are potentially adaptive and may function to aid self-preservation and increase reproductive fitness. The sympathetic nervous system and related hormonal suffusions prepare the body for emergencies and support various forms of self-protective behavior (whether combat or escape) (Cannon, 1929). Humans are biologically predisposed to patterns of behavior such as posturing, facial expression, and vocalization that communicate antagonism or a readiness to meet a threat (Birdwhistell, 1970; Ekman, 1970, 1973; Ekman, Wallace, Friesen, and Ellsworth, 1972). In humans, the basic subjectively experienced emotions related to such chemical processes are anger and fear, or in their extreme forms, rage and terror. The ability to face potential antagonism is sometimes termed "courage."

In antagonistic interactions with others, affective arousal and its subjective and behavioral correlates can have results that are not only self-defensive, they can be socially destructive. The human is physically capable of terrible, destructive activity when sufficiently aroused. Where antagonistic impulses are directed within one's group, harmony breaks down into discord, which can threaten further group cohesion or even group viability. Antagonistic impulses are generally allowed to remain directly destructive only when directed outside the group (e.g., there are group defense activities aimed at within-group survival), or when directed at individuals within the group who are perceived as a threat to social stability.

Socially disruptive arousal and its behavioral consequences are readily activated in humans, from infancy on. Where anger arises in the context of human interactions it is commonly related to the frustration of one's own need-related intentionality, or frustration that stems from the intentionality of others whose interests or actions may be in conflict with one's own. Antagonism may or may not be related to forms of social inequality, but is often so, for mammals commonly live in groups that are marked by dominant and subordinate status and role differentiation. While certain forms and degrees of antagonism are tolerated, the potential for more dangerous or destructively disruptive interactions remains, and status differentials are periodically reinforced by physical sanctions, thus maintaining some degree of harmony within the group for periods of time.

As with other mammals, human social processes are structured so that the harm that ultimately derives from disruptive antagonistic tendencies is reduced. Harmony is maintained not only by external sanctions, but also by internal mechanisms that inhibit untoward behavior that would otherwise interfere with the individual's adherence to specialized or differential roles. Conciliatory postures and other communicative signals are available that mollify rather than antagonize relationships within the group, thus reducing interactive discord, possible injury, or other disruptive effects of aggressive-hostile arousal. One sees accommodative body signaling between group members (De Vos 1993b, 1998).

Antagonistic potential may or may not be readily apparent, it may be relatively unconscious, it may be consciously suppressed, or it may even be intentionally masked through dissemblance in expressive communication. For example, smiling is socialized to disarm as well as to express inner satisfaction; congeniality may be used to be socially disarming whether or not it reflects inner consensus. Beneath what may or may not be conscious uses of emotional communication for social harmony, one also finds accommodative ego mechanisms that operate more or less effectively to repress or suppress socially disruptive behavior and thought. Potentially destructive impulses are also sublimated to some degree within most human societies, and can be expressed as instrumental behavior such as that found in socially approved competition. On the other hand, in some instances, the ego mechanisms can malfunction and become counterproductive to harmony in the social group.

What is scored as Harmony or Hostility (H) in our system can also be seen in positive terms to be an active seeking after nondiscordant feelings. On the positive side, we find a human autonomic nervous system that predisposes us to feelings of comfort and "relaxation" in the presence of others. The human is capable of affective sharing and instrumental cooperation, expressed archetypically in the social procurement and consumption of food or in shared olfactory and tactile experiences of collective shelter. Thus harmony may be seen not only as a reduction of aggressive impulses through postural and kinesthetic inhibition, etc., but also in positive terms, as the attainment of a desirable state of relational being and both social and aesthetic comfort. Harmony is also realized positively by body and mind through ritual practice, both in the presence of others and alone in ritual context. Developmentally and psychodynamically speaking, one might say that harmonious group interactions are a continuation of a primary infantile resonant state that precedes the objectification of the self in self-consciousness (E. De Vos, 2000). Group harmony may involve an expansion of the affiliative/resonant communicative experiences of infancy beyond the caregiver-infant dyad, to the level of a larger group.

Humans are emotionally influenced by a sense of belonging to a group or a sense of sharing in something larger than the individual self. There is an aesthetic pleasure to be derived from harmonious interaction, wherein the individual accepts and participates in appropriate role behavior such that group harmony is achieved. Perhaps an appropriate comparison would be with the satisfaction one attains as a member of a choir or musical group or from participation in religious ritual, wherein one's individual and narrowly constrained contribution forms but one piece of a larger whole.

For such harmony to be achieved, individuals must be capable of playing respective yet integrated roles. Integrative continuities in human social life necessitate more than sanctioning by evaluations of social acceptability, by instrumental coercion, or by the operation of an internalized conscience. Human beings also internally experience needs for harmony, for concord, and for behavioral regularity or stability. In a social context, the satisfaction of these pro-social needs is provided by the presence of complementary social roles (whether vertical or horizontal). Appropriate role enactment can therefore be experienced positively. Thus one can say that continuities of social integration are facilitated when individuals find that role-structured social interactions satisfy basic human prosocial needs.

One might say that the human sense of social and personal integration and continuity are directly countered by the possibility of divisiveness, decay, dissolution, and death. At the cultural level, these issues can be represented in philosophical or religious terms and images or prophetic visions. In the Indian pantheon the god Shiva represents change through the destruction of what is. The god Vishnu represents the forces of integrative continuity. The destructive forces of nature are also used as representations of the dangers lurking within human society or within the human psyche. The person may use external representations of the self or society as symbols of an inner sense of being dissolute or suffering an inner decay. Social disintegration from within is always a real possibility for any society, and may be as dangerous for the group as would be any destructive interactions between groups. Yet humans also spontaneously reconstitute new group structures and processes following periods of disruption. Expressions of concern with social decay or with its converse, social cohesion, may reflect inner concerns over the dangers of dissolute behavior and self-destructiveness, on the one hand, or with converse intrapsychic efforts at integration and growth, cohesive, interpersonally oriented social ritual, on the other.

Concern with the alternatives of peacefulness or hostility are basic expressive considerations in any cultural context and cannot be subsumed under other categories. Our H scoring category (harmony/conciliation—discord/hostility) covers, on the positive side, various expressions of specific needs, such as the need for concord, and the avoidance of eruptions of mutual antagonism or injury within human groups. The category also includes courageous or combative activity performed in an aroused emotional state that produces action for the benefit of individual or group harmony. Such a state of active arousal is the opposite of responses depicting aroused passive anxiety caused by facing an external threat.

On the negative side this category includes various forms of hostile aggressiveness appearing in discordant, violent, and destructive behavior, and in aroused fear thereof. In brief, it reflects a variety of expressive concerns with accommodative social integration or the opposite, destructiveness, or dissolution.

Conciliation and Harmony as a Social Need

One learns to guide interpersonal behavior to maximize a positive interactive sense of the self participating in harmonious group activities. This basic positive social need for harmony is often neglected in conscious western thought. Scoring categories set up to consider social concerns generally neglect the issue of harmony as a positive need. Instead of being granted its status as a basic and central concern, the need for accommodative social harmony and stability is often treated simply as an absence of discord, while one pursues other interests, rather than a sought-for inner state of positive activities in the presence of others. Or, it may be reduced to reflecting another form of affiliative concern.[16]

A useful metaphor to consider is the orchestra. The accommodative pleasures of playing in an orchestra are not derived from an "affiliative" character of social aggregation. Instead, orchestral performances that succeed in producing harmony, despite the contributions of multiple instruments, require complementary role performances of the various musicians. Harmony as an affectively experienced expressive pleasure is enhanced by complementary role performances regardless of the relative status position of the performers or the state of intimacy between them in other contexts. They may or may not have relationships outside their roles as orchestral musicians, yet they agree consensually to perform a socially defined range of behavior to produce a mutually positive affective experience.

Harmonious social processes may be relatively intolerant of individual innovation. The orchestral musician is not to indulge in innovative behavior at the expense of the expectations of others. Refinement or the perfection of socially defined or allotted accommodative behavior, not creative change, is the goal of self-development when social harmony is expressly desired.

Even in American Jazz, where individual improvisation is encouraged, there are accepted ranges of behavior and the emphasis is on the establishment of a

[16]See the sense of togetherness used by Thomas and Znaniecki (1927), in the discussion of the "Four Wishes."

"groove" through consensual interpretation and reinterpretation (albeit somewhat spontaneous) of a group theme. This can sometimes be experienced intensely as a transcendence of self. Musicians report "magical moments" where the groove is experienced as a clarity of communication among the musicians present. Even a momentary sense of pride or self-conscious concern about acceptability can get in the way to the extent that the magic is broken. Through participation in group activity, where behavior is constrained yet free for the expression of competent virtuosity, an experience of shared selflessness becomes possible. Any "ego trip" becomes an obvious disruption unless it is accompanied by a sense of humor. Music is basically an expressive rather than an instrumental activity for its participants, and moments of musical magic are experienced when group harmony is realized and there is a shared experience of transparency. Participation in a musical consort can be seen as a metaphor for the assumption of social roles.

Concordant behavior relies on the human capacity to find mutual agreement or processes whereby disagreement takes place without threat to a larger social concordance. Societies find ways to accommodatively structure disagreements so that they remain nonthreatening, or become incorporated into the process of mutual co-regulation. Consider the difference between a formal debate and a heated argument. Some societies are more tolerant of confrontation than others. For example, in Japan, more extreme measures are taken to assure consensus or to avoid evidence of any open confrontation than is true for similar settings in American society (De Vos, 1972).

Conciliatory behavior can be immediately brought into play when smooth interplay is threatened. In a society consciously based on interpersonal group harmony, from childhood on there can be developed a heightened sensitivity to what might cause adverse affective arousal in another. Expressive comfort is experienced when confrontation is avoided, sometimes at the expense of one's wayward personal feelings or possibly divisive personal opinions.

Confucian societies emphasize a self-consciousness that is interactional, a self that spontaneously seeks expressive realization in harmonious and integrative relationships derivative of the expectations defining one's social role in concordant terms (Tu, 1986). Harmony and social stability are directly considered and sought after as a pleasurable state in the thought of eastern Confucian–influenced societies (De Vos, 1992, 1993b, 1998). They emphasize the pleasures to be found in propriety and in proper role performance. The development of the self, and the enhancement of self-regard is realized in the context of a mutual performance of social roles. In Confucian China, stability was sought after; change was suspect. Sometimes change is to be avoided as bringing about social discord, disruption, even dissolution of the social group.

One cannot work with material from Asian cultures without being impressed with the continual consciously expressed concern with harmonious relationships, defined often in terms of family role behavior (De Vos, 1992, 1993a; De Vos and Sofué, 1986). This expressive consideration is not equally in evidence in the consciousness of individuals from more individually oriented western societies. In our judgment, as we have previously written, the study of instrumental achievement motives from a western perspective neglects the contextualization of the achievement motive within an emotional matrix of expressive feelings about the family.

One must note that positive concerns with harmony are in some respects "vertical" in nature. They are sometimes blended with positive attitudes about formal authority in the realization of collective goals (see chapter on Control, D). The collectivity is often experienced as the controlling force rather than having individuals considered dominant personalities or single authorities. Verticality can therefore be found in the individual's expressively toned compliance with expectations of a collectivity. This culturally accentuated experience is to be distinguished from a more instrumental concern with dyadic personal dominance exercised by single individuals.

In the Japanese context, as compared to an American setting, the role aspects of the self are more directly posited in all expressive concerns, but especially in a concern with harmony. This direct conscious emic concern with harmony in relationships is an emphasis derived from their Confucian family heritage. In making cross-cultural comparisons, it is interesting to note how relatively seldom themes of concern with peaceful interaction or concern with establishment of a "harmonious" relationship are evoked in American interviews. Neither discord nor harmony is usually conceptualized in social role terms by Americans.

Antagonism and Its Discontents

Our inborn affectively driven capacities for aggression and the arousal of antagonistic responses go counter to our needs for social harmony. However, as we indicated above, innate aggressive predispositions can become positively transmuted and harnessed to social purposes by deflection or some form of social sublimation such as condoned competitive or group protective behavior. Aggression can be instrumentally socialized toward the removal of obstacles or impediments to actualizing goals as well as the defensive protection of oneself from externally inflicted injury. Negatively expressed, with aroused affectivity, it can become what is termed "hostile" or "dissolute" behavior. We prefer to avoid using the term "aggression" only in its negative sense. Therefore we have chosen a consistent use of hostile, or hostility, to refer more explicitly to behavior driven by strong affectivity in a negative direction.

Hostile expressive behavior related to specifically contextualized concerns with *discord* or *injury* starts very early. One's sensing of internal or external intentional destructive wishes is basic early experiences occurring before there are definite boundaries separating inside and outside. Sometimes these internal states can be projected out or become part of the early "splitting" process being studied in contemporary psychoanalytic theory (Kernberg, 1975; Seinfeld, 1996).

There are equally early, bodily states of aroused fear. These become gradually less diffusely experienced and are progressively localized in perceptions of animate and inanimate noxious or destructive threats coming from the outside. Conscious fear experienced from a passive position, seen psychodynamically, can be generated by one's own destructive impulses projected outward as well as by the real potential of being attacked by outside malevolence. Human consciousness has to deal early on with internal maneuvers against a sense of potential annihilation.

When aroused in a social context, anger, or even rage, is a possible response to various forms of petty frustrations occurring within the family: in sibling rivalries; in negative feelings toward parents over being disciplined; in rivalries for affection; and in reactions to a sense of deprivation or neglect. Because rage generally arises when there is conflict between individuals, it is quite rare for an individual to experience a suffusion of rage without having it directed or displaced toward some definable individual or social situation. Rage can also be directed inwardly in an act or impulse toward acute self-destruction or can be more or less buried in dissolute social behavior.

Directly discordant interpersonal concerns can range from mild forms of disagreement to direct acts of violence. A readiness to anger can give rise to a chronically discordant, antagonistic view of basic relationships or can be re-channeled into negative feeling directed toward more distant others. Just as sexuality is not limited to an appearance in affiliative situations, aroused hostility or antagonism is not limited to any single contextual category. However, the direct expressive experiences of anger and a need to injure, or a fear of violence must be distinguished from acts so instrumentalized that the potentially negative components of an aggressive drive instigating them are no longer socially or even consciously visible.

Limitations of Consciousness in Pursuit of Harmony

Human aggressive tendencies are transmuted and socialized in a variety of forms. All instrumental, goal-oriented behavior can well utilize some forms of aggressive energy.[17] Achievement, acts of mastery and competence, any form of socialized competition harness aggressive energy. Superego formation or an internalized sense of responsibility necessitates some adequate internalization of more hostile or punitively directed aggression that may be experienced internally as a potential for guilt. What we categorize as Control (D) and all forms of authority are judged socially in accord with the improper or proper assertion of aggressive, even destructive potentials in punitive sanctioning behavior. However, to be socially

---

[17]See further discussion in the following chapters on instrumental control or competitive behavior.

acceptable in a modern society, legitimate punishment must subordinate, disguise, or repress the hostile-aggressive aspects of the action in the name of legitimate instrumental purpose.

In considering formation of the social self, one must examine the defensive selectivity of perception and experience that influence the interpretation of social reality so that negative perceptions of one's social group are screened out. Usually, in a relatively well-functioning culturally conditioned ego, those ideas that are dangerous or contradictory to one's primary group membership will not be allowed to come into consciousness. They may either be totally "denied" or unconsciously "repressed." This patterning of consciousness we have termed "selective permeability" (De Vos and Wagatsuma, 1966). It is related to how some degree of self-consistency is maintained within a socially defined self. Dangerously inconsistent or discordant elements that are potentially disruptive are protectively kept out so they do not upset the viable homeostasis necessary for the continuity of harmonious social interaction.

What we term the mechanism of "exclusion" (De Vos, 1990; De Vos and Suárez-Orozco, 1990) as it interacts continually with mechanisms of intake and expulsion (described elsewhere) has been explored extensively in the clinical psychoanalytic literature most primitively as "denial," then in neurotic symptoms as "repression."

Negative thoughts are not only screened out or repressed. Sometimes "suppression" is operative, that is, the negative thoughts rise to consciousness, but are not revealed to others so as to maintain group harmony. We have remarked how the Japanese concept of "sincerity" is semantically different from its usual translation into English. When a Japanese is being "sincere" he or she is behaving in accord with or conforming to accommodative role expectations, whatever the inner thoughts or feelings to the contrary. Outer, visible behavior is consciously controlled so as to not be disruptive to one's group. An American who is sincere is expected to express what he or she feels, even if such expression is possibly confrontational. In many social circumstances, Japanese conform, not because they necessarily internally repress negative or contrary thoughts. Suppression rather than repression is evident. Conversely, in respect to attitudes held toward parents, Japanese are apt to be more repressed about negative feelings than are Americans. Psychoanalysis is more deeply challenging to many Japanese who find it *unconscionable* to hold conscious feelings of resentment or hostility, especially toward a mother (De Vos, 1984). Repression when used too generally can inhibit thought in some circumstances, as we shall discuss below in respect to the instrumental development of mastery in school achievement in some ethnic or social minorities. We shall describe, for example, how selective permeability functions in the defensive maintenance of a conforming social identity among peers (see chapter 9, volume I, on Competence, C).

In discussing differences between classes or ethnic groups there is a prevalent misconception, which is that the cultural modes of living or language patterns in themselves are so different that they are the cause of lack of understanding and the source of antagonism between individuals from different groups. To the contrary, for purposes of argument one could say that it is not the differences in behavior themselves that cause misunderstanding, but a self-protective need to preserve distinguishing barriers between individuals and groups. Distancing operations which cause individuals to experience events differently are particularly noticeable where caste or even gender distinctions are being used by one segment of the population against the other (see discussion in chapter 6, volume I, on Esteem, E). Differences are maintained as a barrier to any possible assimilation process, or they are used selectively in a defensive way by those subordinated to enable the individual to maintain his or her integrity when meeting with lack of acceptance in situations of possible social assimilation.

As we shall further discuss in chapter 10, volume I,[18] "exclusion" and its manifestation as the Freudian mechanism of repression is basically different from "expulsion" as manifest in negative projections that help contrast groups from one another. The energy used in exclusion is automatically invested in a barrier that unconsciously keeps out disruptive experiences. In effective repression there is no awareness of dynamic defensive forces within or without, although considerable energy may be expended to keep unacceptable feelings unconscious. In contrast, in expulsion, energy is invested in a conscious, contrastive sense of possible confrontation, or in perceptions related to a potentially threatening or negatively perceived "outside." When one uses expulsion, one must continue to contend with what has been defensively projected, because it remains as part of an external world that is perceived to be threatening.

In our scoring system, however, one scores *consciously* expressed attitudes, not unconsciously operative drives. Hence, direct conscious hostility and violence in human behavior or fantasy, as well as minor confrontations or disagreements, in so far as they remain primarily *consciously* expressive concerns, are scored under the presently considered category (H). What we may want to infer to be the presence of underlying but unconscious aggressive behavior is not scored. For example, competitive, instrumentally focused behavior that might be construed to be unconsciously destructive, yet which is only consciously verbalized as directly goal oriented, is scored under the Mutual Purpose (M) category (see chapter 12, volume I). In achieving one's positively considered ends one may have to destroy what impedes its realization without attending consciously to any experience of an expressive need to destroy, or any conscious sense of being gratified by destructive action.

Sometimes, however, descriptions of destructive behavior used for instrumental purposes include reference to a negative hostile intent on the part of the protagonist. In such instances, we must double score in the (H) category and the (M) category. Whatever emphasis there might be on instrumental purpose, these

---

[18]See also chapters 1 and 4 in De Vos and Suárez-Orozco (1990) on psychodynamic mental mechanisms.

kind of responses still require a double scoring with the Harmony (H) expressive category. This must be done whenever there is some conscious indication of awareness of an expressive hostile component. For example, any affect-driven forms of violence exercised from a dominant controlling status position, when accompanied by expressions of cruelty, etc., must be scored under Harmony (H) as well as Control (D).

The Need for Harmony in the Confucian Self

Subjectively, any uncontrolled potential for hostile destructiveness can arouse anxiety. To avoid such attendant anxiety, one learns to search for atmospheric in-group harmony and concordance and the espousal of normative regulations as assuring future peace. The achievement of harmony in society is a basic tenet of Confucian ideology and Confucian social endeavor. This can only be accomplished when each individual inhabits his or her role properly. Behavior that is in accordance with role expectations assures relative harmony within a group.

One learns to harmonize by practicing self-discipline. The very concept of self is a relational self in which what one is (or what one is to be) is defined by relationships. A person gains both purpose and pleasure out of any placement in an orchestra regardless of the status of the instrument played. There is a future time orientation in the realization of pleasure in learning music because much practice is necessary before skillful harmony results. Pleasure occurs with the aesthetic refinement of a skill, individually or collectively realized. It is not crude and direct. Sensuality that can be immediately gratified has much less value. Refined pleasures are transmuted into aesthetic forms. Central to the traditional social role in Japan was a sense of dedication and the long range satisfactions to be gained from realizing one's designated social destiny.

Let us now explore briefly the aesthetic as well as moral pleasure possible through the Confucian religion of the family as it was found still evident in Japanese and Koreans in our past research activities (Slote and De Vos, 1998).

A Basic Need for Belonging as Expressed in Altruism and Dedication

Immediate concerns about harmony appear readily in human consciousness, as do the basic underlying needs to "belong" that we discuss elsewhere in relation to existential anxiety. What also periodically appear on a conscious level are various forms of personal *dedication* of a social or religious nature that mark one's expressive need for social life. Such feelings about social purpose must be considered in respect to their expressive functions as well as in their instrumental functions related to particular goal-driven activities. Purpose can be put in terms (either or both) of general nurturant and harmonious social dedication as well as in terms of individualized goals. For some individuals, a social self consists of being part of something larger than the individual. But, in other instances, the psychological necessity to lose oneself in a cause or a religious commitment may be necessary in order to survive a diffuse feeling of inner insufficiency.[19] Social purpose is so intimately related to social idealism and to highly esteemed social values that it is difficult to examine this subject dispassionately. Such social dedication is "sacred" to members of most cohesive cultures or groups. In some societies, however, excessive social dedication strikes no responsive chord and seems to be a form of madness. For example, in the 1957 film directed by David Lean, *The Bridge on the River Kwai*, the American outsider perceives both British and Japanese role dedication as excessive to the point of both sides being mad in how they conceptualize the social honor of their military.

Problems of Internal Social Discord in Japan and Korea[20]

Factionalism Among Koreans in Japan

It is true for Koreans as well as for other groups that sometimes the ideals espoused are little exercised in actuality. The history of the Koreans in Japan shows much within-group political discord, as well as many examples of mutual antagonism, hostility, and resentment expressed by family members toward one another. The many voluntary organizations available to Koreans have been a source of emotional satisfaction and of a sense of harmony, but they have also been a means of expressing dissension and antagonism toward the outside. The instrumental goals of group cooperation to which they are supposedly dedicated sometimes become secondary to discordant expressive needs that break out in factional strife.

Individuals can find considerable emotional support as well as mobilization of energy by joining a professional or worker's group. Church membership has been useful as a means of expressing cohesion and a sense of belonging. But the division of the homeland and the consequent divisive political climate has caused Korean groups to dissipate much of their potential energy on internal discord rather than on the development of plans that could become instrumentally productive. Suspicion and wariness characterize internal group processes; there is constant concern over the presence of spies. Some leaders, acutely aware of this divisiveness, take great pains to avoid internal criticism of fellow members, but the leadership role remains a difficult one.

In brief, Koreans in Japan, in the past as well as witnessed in our interviews during the late 1970s, generally found their need for harmony dissipated by deep and abiding discords, and traditions of past divisiveness. Political groups still manifest longstanding splits between North and South, between progovernment and

---

[19]See discussion of suicide in chapter 14, volume I (see also De Vos, 1968).

[20]See Lee and De Vos (1981).

antigovernment groupings, between Christian and non-Christian. Whereas many Korean Japanese with considerable justification blamed these cleavages on the fact that they were pawns in a power game in which the chief players were the Soviet Union and China, the United States and Japan, they attempted to face the fact that discordant factionalism is also caused by the seeking of personal gain on the part of particular Koreans.

Social movements rising from within a minority group, such as the Koreans, often attempt to unite the group to achieve a new sense of harmony within. The most expedient mechanism for achieving internal harmony is to find some means of deflecting socially disruptive behavior onto outside individuals or groups. For example, the North Korean–oriented groups and their schools have sought to further their internal group solidarity by expressing discord toward those "less virtuous" in the Korean community. This is a well-researched mechanism in social psychology. Displacement of internal tensions onto an outside enemy is basic to ethnocentrism wherever it operates. But it is indeed an unfortunate destiny of many minority groups to embody in their subordinate social traditions forms of discord that are more internally expressed than externally displaced.

A dominant majority benefits more from displacement of discord by scapegoating, since it can do so without fear of retribution from the scapegoated minority. We have documented how at the time of the earthquake in 1923, Koreans became victimized as scapegoats in Japan. The ease with which Koreans were seen as a criminal disruptive element within Japanese society was obvious in journals and newspapers of the 1920s as well as in word-of-mouth accounts of the disorders that followed. The Japanese could think better of themselves if a crime could be attributed to Koreans. It gave them a sense of compensatory superiority to have within their society a disparaged minority to whom criminality and political radicalism could be attributed.

It is ironic that in the world arena, the Japanese in turn at this time were experiencing the implicit disparagement (E) underlying the United States policy barring the in-migration of Orientals despite the so-called Gentleman's Agreement of 1924. Only since World War II have racist attitudes toward the Japanese become absent from official American foreign policy and its immigration laws.

In order to attain internal harmony, Koreans today, both at home and in Japan, often have recourse to labeling the Japanese collectively as the enemy. It is easier to deflect hatred onto all Japanese rather than to distinguish those who are indeed prejudiced from those who are accepting and potentially helpful. Hence, Koreans sometimes behave with anger and hostility toward all Japanese, irrespective of their personal guilt or innocence. This reciprocal stereotypic attitude of hatred contributes to acts of animosity on both sides.

Most Korean groups exercise particularly heavy sanctions against group members who take Japanese citizenship. Since the Japanese also reject them, naturalized citizens of Korean origin have set up their own group, the Seiwa Club, in several Japanese cities. This name can be roughly translated as "the realization of harmony." Naturalization is a form of avoiding passing by openly acknowledging one's Korean background and at the same time asserting one's Japanese citizenship. Finding themselves in a fairly precarious position and generally isolated, naturalized Korean Japanese hope to make their position more acceptable or tolerated by others.

Perhaps the greatest problem that we have noted is how disruptive the circumstances of discrimination have been to the harmonious functioning of the Korean family. The destruction of the male's occupational prowess, and the wounding of his sense of dignity results in spasmodic acts of compensatory discordant masculinity at home. It also results in disparagement (E) of the husband by his wife within the home setting. Confucianist values, in which the wife ideally plays a subordinate role to the head of the house and sees to it that the children are obedient to those in authority (D), are not well exercised in many Korean homes. This leads to a sense of worthlessness about their family on the part of growing children. The family relationships themselves become bonds of aggressive displacement, of mute frustration, and of inescapable ignominy. The family is not a haven but a place of alienation. As noted below in respect to achievement motivation (see chapter 8, volume I), many youths express their feelings in some form of delinquent behavior that eventuates in a criminal career (A).

In-Group Solidarity and Out-Group Hostility Among the Japanese Burakumin

In-Group Solidarity

In order to live in the face of strong social discrimination and prejudice, the ordinary Japanese outcaste minority Burakumin has to rely heavily upon his or her own group (see De Vos and Wagatsuma, 1966; also, Wagatsuma and De Vos, 1984). In the late 1960s when we were studying employment patterns, we found that with the exception of government service, one could not easily take a job in the majority society unless one had the capacity to successfully "pass," and few succeeded in getting into the big firms. Most of the Buraku individuals have had to stay within the community and make their living there. A considerable number of individuals living in Buraku communities remained on some form of public relief, having little opportunity for self-support.

Those who worked within the community depended upon their employer. Usually the relationship with the employer has been a very paternalistic one, the traditional pattern of mutual obligation involving financial protection and income security. Occupations within the communities studied in Kobe and Kyoto were mainly in the leather industry, shoe-making, animal slaughtering, metal or rag picking, and the handling of corpses and burial of the dead. Each of these occupations is controlled by a few bosses. The working conditions and income may not be very acceptable for the individual employee, but when dissatisfied he had almost no alternative choice. Jobs outside were hard to come by, and if he was "disloyal" to one employer, he risked the possibility that his attitude would be conveyed to other bosses so that he will have a hard time getting into another occupation. Therefore, obedience and passivity toward bosses were strongly sanctioned. As long as an employee remained passively loyal and hardworking, he could enjoy a modicum of emotional and financial security. If, for instance, he or his family members got ill, the boss would protect him and help defray medical expenses. As far as the poor were concerned, individualism was discouraged.

Social solidarity was reinforced within the community by a feature which in itself creates caste status, namely, enforced endogamy. Insofar as we have been able to determine, in-group marriage is still the rule. Only occasionally will an individual make a "love" marriage with a person of non-outcaste background in the face of the difficulties engendered. As in the case of relations between Blacks and Whites in the United States, differences in caste position do not prevent sexual relationships between men and women, even though unhappiness rather than marriage often results.

As in all endogamous groups, the number of individuals of proper age is limited by the size of the community as well as by relative status within it. This allows relatively little room for individual choice, particularly in wealthier families. In most Buraku there were certain individuals, usually middle-aged or older women, who took on the role of matchmaker. Such a person needed to be one that people could especially trust.

A sense of family solidarity or family relatedness within the Buraku is thus created because in actuality, most of the individuals are related in one way or another due to the high rate of endogamy. According to one of our informants, expressions such as "we are like one family" were much used. Everyone knows everyone else. Children are accepted in every house. When a child is afraid of an angry father, he will simply flee into a neighbor's house and will at times sleep there or eat there on a very casual basis. Parents do not worry, even when the child does not show up at home for two or three days, as long as they are sure the child is within their community.

Ritually, the social solidarity of the Buraku has been also partly reinforced by participation in services and worship at a segregated Buddhist temple. In the middle of many Buraku communities, one will characteristically find a very well-built, large Buddhist temple, which often makes an impressive contrast to the shabby-looking houses in the vicinity. There is some indication that the Burakumin tend to maintain adherence to their Buddhist religion with a greater tenacity than that now noted generally in Japan. Most Buraku temples belong to the Shinshu sect, which may be partially due to the fact that Shinran, the founder of the sect, taught that, with Buddha's intercession, outcastes would receive full-fledged social status, if not in this life, then in a later incarnation. Few, perhaps, hold this traditional belief today.

A number of the individuals are seemingly very pious and devoted and donate a considerable amount of money to their temple so that it can be kept in good repair. There is also evidence that in the Tokugawa period the government at one time decided to have all whom they termed *Eta* belong to the Shinshu sect so that there may have been people at this time converted by force from their own sects to Shinshu.

Ambivalence toward the meaning of achievement outside of the community plus a concern with the psychological and marital security of their children can lead parents to enforce children's continued participation in Buraku life. The primary family in this way can maintain continuity and social solidarity and sanction the necessity for endogamy within the group.

Out-Group Enmity

People too readily assume that the problems caused by social discrimination can be soon resolved if the majority society changes its attitudes and becomes more accepting of the discriminated individual. This overlooks the fact that there are often strong inducements in the socialization pattern of discriminated individuals which will make the maintenance of their minority status important to them in their psychological integration regardless of amelioration in outside attitudes toward them. Some of the reputation of the Burakumin for being aggressive seems to have some basis in fact. The relations between aggressive behavior, out-group enmity, and patterns of socialization in the Buraku were evident to us. Hatred of the outer society and hostility toward the majority society become a part of the individual's total personality structure; they are not simply immediate angry reactions to prejudice and discrimination.

Interviews, both within and outside the communities, revealed that Burakumin are considered to be somewhat more impulsive and volatile than other Japanese and, as a related trait, hostile and aggressive to individuals from the outside society. There is also some evidence that in socialization practices, the Burakumin tend to be less restrained in the expression of aggression toward their children. According to some informants, parents, especially fathers, do not hesitate to resort to physical punishment in handling children. Not only shouting loudly or wildly but also slapping and hitting on the head or cheeks are common expressions of disfavor when provoked. Counteraggression on the part of the child toward either parent, especially the father, is not permitted. Children within the Buraku community also often fight one another. When such fighting becomes too serious, however, it tends to be discouraged.

These patterns may be related to the perception of the outside community by the Burakumin child, as well as the adult. Any hostility and hate stimulated within the family or peer group by these aggressive control methods are readily displaced toward people of the outside community, who are judged to merit it considering their prejudice and discrimination. At the same time, it is not implausible to explain the father's physical aggression toward his own children as a partial displacement of hostility induced in him by his relations to the outside community. One must quickly qualify, and say that while there is no valid quantification of the alleged greater aggressiveness of the Burakumin child, the informal evidence does point in this direction.

The time when we were studying them, the Buraku child was probably also more sexually aware than was generally true for the total Japanese society. There was less hiding of sexual relationships, and the children seemed to develop less of a "latency" period than was true in the more restrained Japanese household. In general, there seemed to be less stringent impulse control demanded of either sexuality or aggression of the Buraku child. The adult relationships witnessed in childhood also illustrate the fact that role modeling adults do act impulsively and can give vent to their feelings when they are under the influence of strong emotions.

The Scoring Categories Related to Harmony or Discord

A. Positive Harmony, Cohesion, Reconciliation; Group Maintenance or Protection ***HA***

Internal Harmony

HA-depict	Descriptive appropriate role behavior
HA-family	Expressions of harmonious family relationships
HA-group	Harmonious interaction or group concordance
HA-conform	Conformity to preserve group harmony
HA-agree	Agreeable, congenial, good-natured disarming role behavior
HA-pacify	Attempted mollification, mediation, or conciliation of discord
HA-forgive	Forgiveness to reestablish group or mutual togetherness
HA-mend	Reestablishment of harmony
HA-reunite	Group reunion occasioned by death, usually a family member
HA-symbol	Symbolic peace
HA-rite	Group ceremony or ritual; religious activity, attendance
HA-god	Belief in the harmony of God's world or in a divinely or perfectly ordered cosmos

Positive Defensive Postures

HA-courage	Courage enabling one to face personal adversaries or opponents
HA-secure	A sense of harmonious within-group security
HA-combat	Righteous combativeness or defensive aggression, or protest to preserve group

HA-engulf	Dedication; loss of self in political or religious group; engulfed in a movement as an expression of role dedication toward group maintenance, including self-sacrifice

Internal Harmony. In this scoring category, we note simple descriptions of expected role behavior in daily activities as the simplest form of social harmony (HA-depict). We distinguish expressions of harmony among family members (HA-family) from those marking social or peer groups more generally (HA-group). One can note special acts of conformity, in which there is giving up personal predilections to preserve group or family harmony (HA-conform). Attention is paid to manifest "agreeable," "congenial," "good-natured" behavior that is socially "disarming" (HA-agree). Some behavior is mollifying or conciliatory (HA-pacify). There can be acts of forgiveness that reestablish harmony in a personal relationship (HA-forgive). Mediation, negotiation, or other means can be depicted as ways to re-establish harmony within a group (HA-mend).

There are situations wherein harmony is reestablished, sometimes occasioned by an external event such as the death of someone, very often a family member (HA-reunite). One may note some symbol of peace (HA-symbol). Attention can be drawn to an expression of togetherness or group harmony by some ritual behavior (HA-rite). Occasionally attention is drawn to the overall role of the deity or a divine power in creating or maintaining an internally regulated, or perfectly harmonious cosmos (HA-god).

Positive Defensive Postures. There is direct conscious awareness of courage as a desirable affective integration. Courage enables one to overcome debilitating anxiety. It allows one to face off personal adversaries or opponents and face off possible external threats (HA-courage).

Security is established within a given social perimeter and a distinction can be made between a secure and rewarding concordant in-group and potentially harmful out-groups. Experiencing expected and anticipated normative within-group behavior creates possibility for relaxation, or a inner sense of peacefulness and harmony (HA-secure).

There are positive expressions of combative protection of the group by means of some aggressive, even violent behavior (HA-combat). One finds expressions of personal dedication to a group cause. One can become so engulfed in a political or religious movement that little remains of a sense of self apart from one's group (HA-engulf). There are manifest forms of self-sacrificial behavior toward group maintenance that may even involve self-injury or self-annihilation.

B. *Unresolved or Potential Discord; Fear of Malice* ***HB***

Unresolved Anger	
HB-dislike	Unresolved dislike
HB-anger	Anger (sometimes nonspecified)
HB-inhibit	Represses, inhibited physical violence
HB-revenge	Desire for vengeance
HB-envy	Envy
HB-jealous	Jealous of one's love
HB-hurt	Hurt feelings
HB-resent	Unresolved resentment regarding real or imagined deception or injury
HB-family	Concern about family cohesion
HB-group	Concern about group cohesion
HB-unrest	Condition of social unrest
HB-split	Concern about potential removal from family
HB-control	Unresolved anger, irritation over being pressured or controlled
HB-torn	Ambivalence about expected social role participation
HB-break	"Fed up" with a social or personal situation; desire to break ties
HB-role	Possible conflict between role expectations
HB-deceit	Deceit to avoid anger or preserve harmony
Impending Fears	
HB-fright	Frightened, not specified as to source
HB-f-attack	Feared attack (animal or human)
HB-f-anger	Feared anger of another
HB-f-fury	Fear of potential violence
HB-f-repay	Fear of possible vengeance
HB-f-envy	Fear of envious behavior
HB-f-super	Fear of malevolent supernatural
HB-f-magic	Fear of magic
HB-god	Questions about religious harmony

Unresolved Anger. There are a number of unresolved states of anger or interpersonal discord (HB-dislike). One may harbor unresolved inner agitated states of anger or hostility toward others (HB-anger). There may be an inner experience of an impulse to violence which is not acted out (HB-inhibit). There may be unresolved feelings that involve a desire for vengeance (HB-revenge).

There may be unresolved envy (HB-envy) or a hostile sense of jealousy aroused about another's intrusion on one's possessions or relations (HB-jealous). There are various forms of hurt feelings (HB-hurt). Among specified negative states of anger or fear are states of hostility or resentment over past injury that cannot be expressed. In some instances, these states, defined as resentful, may be related to an imagined injury (HB-resent).

Paralleling affirmative feelings about family and group cohesion are feelings of insecurity in respect to family (HB-family) and/or group (HB-group) harmony.

There may be broader fears about social unrest in a more general context (HB-unrest). There may be specific worry about a possible split or internal factional discord (HB-split). There may arise unresolved anger about being pressured, or controlled by others (HB-control). An individual may become ambivalent about continuing participation in a family or group (HB-torn). There may develop a pent-up desire to break away from expected role participation (HB-break).

There are major forms of anxiety or ambivalence related to inner conflict between role expectations and group cohesion (HB-role). The worry or internal tension may be in respect to an unresolvable conflict appearing between conflicting loyalties. There may be the practice of deceit to avoid anger or seen as a means of preserving harmony (HB-deceit).

Impending Fears. From a passive position of feeling threatened there are a number of possible unresolved fears. There can be expressed an unspecified sense of fear or threat (HB-fright). More specifically considered is some direct fear of attack (animal or human) (HB-f-attack). One may fear the potential anger of another or feel personal vulnerability to another's anger (HB-f-anger). One may express some sense of being a victim of potential violence (HB-f-fury). The expressed fear may be of some possible act of vengeance (HB-f-repay). The fear may be that of envious behavior (HB-f-envy). There may be a fear of the malevolence of a supernatural force (HB-f-super). There may be fear of the use of witchcraft or sorcery (HB-f-magic). One may have questions about religious harmony (HB-god).

C. Negative Active Discord, Destruction, Violence ***HC***

HC-discord	Anger, quarrel, or discord
HC-hostile	Some form of specified or nonspecified hostility toward others to make them suffer
HC-verbal	Abusive verbal attack; excessive nagging
HC-beat	Physical expression of violent; beating
HC-injure	Physical injury of another
HC-cruel	Cruelty, sadism, inflicting psychological trauma
HC-rape	Rape; force used in sexual situation
HC-murder	Homicide
HC-elder	Generational animosity

HC-triangle	Discord in triangular relationship
HC-faction	Factional behavior; also excluding a group member
HC-selfish	Inconsiderate behavior causes hurt
HC-revenge	Revenge (when with physical violence double score)
HC-control	Dominance as a gratification of power at the expense of another (double score with DDC)
HC-contempt	Expression of repugnance or contempt causing hurt (double score with EDC-contempt)
HC-vandal	Vandalism, arson, wanton destruction
HC-rake	Dissolute or self-destructive behavior
HC-suicide	Suicide anger directed toward self
HC-magic	Malevolent magic

Antagonism and its consequent injurious behavior when aroused varies in intensity from subtle covert forms, through verbal attacks, toward forms of physical attack of a violent nature.

Some form of interpersonal quarrels are the most frequently expressed simply as some form of mutual discord (HC-discord). There are a variety of nonspecific hostile acts to cause others to suffer (HC-hostile). There are abusive forms of verbal attack (HC-verbal). Women are more apt than men to use verbal means of attack. Verbal assault can become almost violent in nature. Physical forms of assault are more characteristic for men (HC-beat). Violence can be inflicted to the point of physical injury (HC-injure). There are pleasurable acts of physical and psychological cruelty of a sadistic nature (Garma, 1944) that range from the subtle to the obvious in causing suffering in others (HC-cruel). The most extreme forms of violence are rape (HC-rape) and murder (HC-murder).

There are specific forms of hostility related directly to generational differences between elders and the next generation (HC-elder). Discord often specifically involves a triangular sexual relationship (HC-triangle). There are various forms of factional behavior that becomes internally disruptive to a group (HC-faction).

There are inconsiderate or selfish, malicious acts that are hurtful to others (HC-selfish). For example, there can be an injurious exclusion of a group member or members to cause suffering. Revenge can be either a nonphysical or physical nature (HC-revenge). When there is physical injury it should be double scored (HC-revenge HC-injure).

Dominance can be a hostile gratification of power at the expense of another (HC-control) (double-score with DDC-despot). Contempt or repugnance can be expressed in an assaultive injurious manner. As such, it is to be double scored with negative esteem (HC-contempt EDC-contempt). There are wanton acts of destruction, that may not be directed toward single individuals, but express some form of excitement or satisfaction found in the act of destruction itself (HC-vandal).

Dissolute behavior is disintegrative. It leads to self-destruction, but also may have a disintegrative effect on others in one's social group (HC-rake). Suicide is an extreme form of self-destructive behavior (HC-suicide).

In the realm of the supernatural there is belief in the efficacy of practicing malevolent magic, sorcery, or witchcraft that can be used in causing ill to another (HC-magic).

D. *Passively Incurred Discord or Dissolution* ***HD***

HD-hurt	To feel hurt by another or others
HD-injured	To be physically injured by others, to be made ill
HD-crime	Victim of an assaultive crime
HD-death	To incur the violent death of someone
HD-withheld	To feel hurt by destructively intended withdrawal or withholding (double score)
HD-maligned	Victim of malice, or being maligned
HD-vilified	To be hurt by derogation or disparagement, or social injury (double score)
HD-decay	Dissolution, decay, or decomposition of an individual, group, family, or society
HD-paranoia	Delusions of persecution
HD-deviled	Taken or captured by supernatural being
HD-bewitched	Bewitched, or injured supernaturally

Viewed from the perspective of the victim of assaultive or violent acts, the most frequent expression is one of being reduced to tears by being hurt by another. There are situations of retreat from others due to feeling hurt (HD-hurt). One can experience being a victim of deliberate withholding. Such responses are double-scored with withholding (HD-hurt NDC-withhold). There a numerous forms of incurred injury or a sense of being made ill by another (HD-injured). One can be a victim of an assaultive crime (HD-crime). One can be the victim of the assaultive death of someone close (HD-death). One can feel hurt by destructively intended withdrawal or withholding (HD-withheld) (double score with NDC-deprive).

Sometimes there is an experience of being a victim of general social malice or being maligned for a variety of reasons (HD-maligned), or being hurt by derogation or disparagement or derogation (HD-vilified) (double score with esteem).

There can be a sense of dissolution and decay that effects group morale. One may experience a sense of general social decomposition (HD-decay). There are also to be noted delusions of persecution (HD-paranoia). There may be narrated experiences of being taken over, captured, or possessed by some demonic force or being (HD-deviled). An individual can sense being bewitched or somehow injured by supernatural means (HD-bewitched).

Interrelationships of Expressive and Instrumental Categories and Complexities of Scoring

Distinguishing Aggression from Other Concerns

The category of Harmony-Discord (H) is representative of how our scoring categories overlap into blends that are themselves significantly present or absent in particular groups. For example, we have found among Japanese, more than among Americans, that conscious emic concerns with harmony are usually defined as most salient in terms of social roles that characterize family relationships or occupational functions.

A positive sense of harmony can be expressed either apart from or blended with hedonic, affiliative, nurturant or evaluative considerations that we have considered in previous chapters. Scoring within the (H) category may appear to overlap with other expressive instrumental categories of Affiliation (A), Nurturance (N), Esteem (E), and Pleasure-Suffering (P). Yet where the narrative emphasis is on the *harmony* or concordance of relationships (H) this is to be distinguished from the *hedonic* (P), *nurturant* (N), *affiliative* (F), or *evaluative* (E) features we have discussed in previous chapters. For example, as discussed in chapter 6, volume I, in the context of Esteem (E) and social acceptability, negative evaluations of others may also contain some consciously destructive components. A sense of antagonism may also be consciously present in negatively perceived Affiliation (F, chapter 5, volume I) or in acts of withholding in nurturing situations Nurture (N, chapter 4, volume I).

Guilt and Responsibility. Concern about family Harmony (H) is sometimes double scored with an abiding sense of social Responsibility (R). We have described the mechanisms at work in Japanese guilt over failure resulting in an expressive sense of worthlessness. Failure for a Japanese is *injurious* to the family in general, and often the mother in particular.[21] We have argued that all experiences of guilt have elements of such unconsciously intended destructiveness. The forms of guilt consciously related to the transgression of standards and social expectations we consider negatively under the category of responsibility to be described below. In our system one does not, however, score for unconscious intent.

Psychoanalytic theory attempts to describe the manner in which an underlying primitive destructive intentionality, or fears of externally antagonistically perceived destructiveness becomes part of a socialized, internalized "superego" and a pattern of self "control" or responsibility (Fenichel, 1945). A sense of extended possible

---

[21]See chapter 5 in De Vos (1973), and see chapter 11, volume I, this text.

sequences through time, or a differentiated awareness of consequences, become the core of a sense of social Responsibility (R). As we shall discuss in chapter 11, volume I, integral to this awareness is a capacity to experience a potential for intrapunitively directed guilt for possible transgressions or omissions of expected social behavior.

Some experienced concerns with *guilt* or *remorse* are related directly or indirectly to a consciousness of having brought *injury* to another. Among Christians unworthiness may imply injuries to a loving Jesus who is repaid poorly (inferentially injured) by sinful behavior. Insofar as this is more or less consciously considered, we can see the direct connection between a resultant sense of guilt and an unconscious intention to inflict injury. In all these situations one must remember to score the conscious verbalization, not interpretive suppositions about unconscious motives.

Punishment. As we shall discuss further under chapter 10, volume I, punishment is seen in all societies as a legitimate exercise of Control (D) by those in the superordinate status of authority. Conversely, from a subordinate perspective, aggression, in the sublimated form of self-assertion, is socially sanctioned as legitimate autonomy. In socially disapproved status violations, however, it is perceived as rebelliousness or as sub-adult delinquent acts against legitimate authority (De Vos and Murakami, 1974). Regardless of underlying affectivity, it is the essence of instrumental-regulatory behavior to focus on the *legitimate* or *illegitimate* use of punishment to control social behavior and the need for the harnessing of aggressive antagonistic propensities to socially sanctioned purpose. Punishment usually connotes the instrumental means used to bring about submission to regulation. "Retribution," in contrast, more often directly indicates a hostile intent which can be scored under negative Harmony (H). Vengeance can be seen as a positive or negative act. It should be double scored with what instigates it, be it physical or mental injury, dishonor, unfair competition, etc. Fear of violence from others is subsumed under discord as a passive unresolved category.

Anger. When anger is mentioned but is further left unspecified as an unresolved state, it can be located simply within HB-anger. More typically, however, anger mentioned in narratives depicts responses to something negative that has happened in a specified relationship. For example, it is frequently expressed as discord (HC-discord) in an affiliative situation, and should be double scored with an Affiliation (F) category. There can be a response to a betrayal by others, anger with oneself for letting someone down, etc. These would be double scored, depending on the resolution or lack of resolution of the specific situation.

When directly expressed in a specified context, anger should be double scored depending on the resolution or lack of resolution of the specific situation. For example, direct expression of the experience of anger felt by one in a control position toward a subordinate can be double scored with some Control (D) subcategory. Anger can be seen as a legitimate part of an authority situation, as in a parent rebuking a child, and hence indicates authoritative disapproval as a mode of control. When authoritative action is taken subsequent to the depiction of such a feeling, it becomes resolved as a positive active form of dominance (HB-anger DDA-scold) and is double-scored as such.

Complexities in Regard to Killing or Injury. Expressive malicious acts involving the killing of another (HC-murder) can be complex in nature. Murder can be seen also as protective of loved ones, in self-defense, etc. When it is deliberate and with malice, it is single scored (HC-murder).

When the act of killing is purely instrumental, it is not scored under the Harmony (H) category, but is scored elsewhere. For example, manslaughter does not need to have any intentionality. Inadvertent injury is a fate category (KD-mishap). However, an injurious act may lead to concerns with guilt over unintentional injury (KD-mishap RB-guilt). Killing or injury may be seen as an instrumental act of unfair competition (MVC-remove AC-crime) having nothing to do with an expressive need for injuring another. Depictions of injury or killing another may be seen as acts of assuming necessary control in legitimate professional activity (DDA-police); or they may be seen as excessive (DDC-punish).

Expressions of Chagrin. Being angry with yourself can be experienced as "chagrin." If someone is internally vexed about failure, such expression has to be scored under the competence category (CD-chagrin). When such a concern or worry has to do with the sense of failure uppermost it is scored under negative competence. If, however, it appears within some expressive context as a form of mortification it may be related to wounded pride. It should be scored under the expressive evaluation category (ESD-shamed).

One's failure may be perceived as potentially adversely evaluated by others. Mortification is a compelling sense of damaged status. When the self-evaluative aspects of disappointment with behavior is in relation to others it is evident that we score it under negative evaluation. If both qualities of disappointment with ones competence and its evaluation by others are present we can double score (CD-chagrin ESD-shamed).

The Aggressive Element in Other Activity

Some amount of unresolved tension is part of all future-oriented goal-directed behavior. "Aggression" or active responses that bring on sensations that are relieved by a destruction or removal of obstacles can become socially "sublimated" into consciously directed instrumental or goal-oriented activity and disappear from the level of consciousness. In effect, on a conscious level they become part of some instrumental, purposely directed behavior rather than being simply displays of an emotional state. "Aggression" is not limited to socially negative situations. It may even be present in some sublimated form in all instrumental behavior. It is especially visible in such activities as sports competition or in the rivalrous play of games such as chess.

When harnessed socially, there is an inner approval of this experience of tension, with the expectation that it is to be resolved by behavior directed toward removing the discomforting stimuli and the positive accomplishment of a personal or social goal or some approved form of competitive triumph. In our scoring system we do not score directly the *aggression* that has been transmuted into patterns of concern with legitimate competition unless there is direct attention paid to the antagonistic feelings experienced with the behavior. We are scoring only manifest content. We do not score a possible underlying presence of aggression or underlying hostile or destructive motive unless it is explicitly expressed by an informant. In any instrumental context such as a competitive business situation or the punishment of a deviant individual, when a destructive affect is *overtly* expressed it must be double scored with its instrumental justification. Hostile behavior directly expressed in instrumental situations is usually viewed as less socially regulated.

Underlying aggression can fuel a continuing concern with a basic sense of mastery or competence. As behavior becomes instrumentally organized in goal directed patterns acting toward resolution, it can be more consciously defined as problem-solving behavior related to a sense of social purpose. As such, sublimated aggression also appears periodically as part of achievement concerns. However, as noted later in our discussion of the Competence (C) category in chapter 9, volume I, there is theoretical argument against the too ready supposition that all instrumental behavior stems from aggressive drives per se. Robert White argues cogently that an "effectance motivation" is innate in humans (White, 1959, 1961). It is an intentional motive which is related to a motoric and cognitive pleasure in the inner power that causes things to happen; it is an innately pleasurable form of excitement. Instrumentally directed, such motivation can become consciously "willful." An inner instrumental concern with volition become what we categorize as Achievement (A). Basic to a developing concern with achievement may be a concomitant attention paid to satisfactory levels of competence in one's operative functioning. As we shall further discuss, in chapters 8 and 9, volume I, while this concern with competence is related to achievement, it can be considered distinct from achievement motivation per se, and both should be distinguished from aggression (H).

Illustrative Samples of Scoring in the Following Chapters

In several of the chapters of volume II we have included actual illustrations of scoring of several of the subcategories included under the [H] category. Rather than repeat them here, we refer the reader to the verbatim responses found in chapters 4, 7, 9, 11, 12, and 13, volume II.

Notes

Birdwhistell, Ray L. 1970. *Kinesics and Context; Essays on Bodily Motion Communication.* Philadelphia: University of Pennsylvania Press.

Cannon, Walter B. 1929. *Bodily Changes in Pain, Hunger, Fear and Rage* (2nd edition). New York: Appleton-Century-Crofts.

De Vos, Eric S. 2000. Biocultural and Experiential Bases of Cultural Continuity and Change. In A.L. Communian & U.P. Gielen (Eds.), *International Perspectives on Human Development.* Lengerich: Pabst Science Publishers.

De Vos, George A. 1968. Suicide in Cross Cultural Perspective. In H.L.P. Resnick (Ed.), *Suicidal Behaviors: Diagnosis and Management* (pp. 105–134). Boston: Little, Brown, & Co.

———. 1972. Social Stratification and Ethnic Pluralism: An Overview from the Perspective of Psychological Anthropology. *Race*, April.

———. 1973. *Socialization for Achievement: Essays on the Cultural Psychology of the Japanese.* Berkeley: University of California Press.

———. 1984. *The Incredibility of Western Prophets.* Amsterdam: University of Amsterdam Press.

———. 1990. Empathy to Alienation: Problems in Human Belonging. In David Jordan and Marc Swartz (Eds.), *Personality and the Cultural Construction of Society: Papers in Honor of Melford E. Spiro* (pp. 222–242). Tuscaloosa, Ala.: University of Alabama Press.

———. 1992. *Social Cohesion and Alienation: Minorities in the United States and Japan.* Boulder, Colo.: Westview Press.

———. 1993a. A Cross Cultural Perspective: The Japanese Family as a Unit in Moral Socialization. In P. Cowan, J. Filed, D. Hansen, M. Scolnick, and G. Swanson (Eds.), *Family, Self, and Society: Towards a New Agenda for Family Research.* Hillsdale, N.J.: Erlbaum Assoc.

———. 1993b. The Rites of Pleasure: The Religion, Morality and Aesthetics of Bodily Propriety. In I. Dosamantes (Ed.), *Bodily Image in Cultural Context: Interdisciplinary Essays* (pp. 35–63). Los Angeles: DMT Publications.

———. 1998. Confucian Family Socialization: The Religion, Morality and Aesthetics of Propriety. In Walter Slote and George De Vos (Eds.), *Confucianism and the Family in an Interdisciplinary, Comparative Context* (pp. 329–380). Albany: State University of New York Press.

De Vos, George A. and Eiji Murakami. 1974. Violence and Aggression in Fantasy: A Comparison of American and Japanese Lower-Class Youth. In William P. Lebra (Ed.), *Youth, Socialization and Mental Health* (pp. 153–177). Honolulu: University Press of Hawaii.

De Vos, George A. and Takao Sofué (Eds.). 1986. *Religion and the Family in East Asia.* Berkeley, Calif.: University of California Press. (Revised).

De Vos, George A. and Marcelo Suárez-Orozco. 1990. *Status Inequality: The Self in Culture.* Newbury Park, Calif.: Sage Publications.

De Vos, George A. and Hiroshi Wagatsuma. 1966. *Japan's Invisible Race: Caste in Culture and Personality.* Berkeley: University of California Press.

Ekman, Paul. 1970. Universal Facial Expressions of Emotion. *California Mental Health Research Digest*, **8**: 151–158.

———. (Ed.). 1973. *Darwin and Facial Expression: A Century of Research in Review*. New York: Academic Press.

Ekman, Paul, Wallace V. Friesen, and Phoebe Ellsworth. 1972. *Emotions in the Human Face.* New York: Pergamon Press.

Fenichel, Otto. 1945. *The Psychoanalytic Theory of the Neurosis*. New York: W. W. Norton.

Garma, A. 1944. Sadism and Masochism in Human Conduct. *Journal of Clinical Psychopathology and Psychotherapy*, **VI**: 355–390.

Kernberg, Otto. 1975. *Borderline Conditions and Pathological Narcissism.* New York: Jason Aronson.

Lee, Changsoo and George A. De Vos. 1981. *Koreans in Japan: Ethnic Conflict and Accommodation.* Berkeley: University of California Press.

Seinfeld, Jeffrey. 1996. *Containing Rage, Terror and Despair: An Object Relations Approach to Psychotherapy.* Northvale, N.J.: Jason Aronson Inc.

Slote, Walter and George De Vos (Eds.). 1998. *Confucianism and the Family in an Interdisciplinary, Comparative Context.* Albany: State University of New York Press.

Thomas, William I. and Florian Znaniecki. 1927. *The Polish Peasant in Europe and America.* Edited by Eli Zaretsky, 1984. Urbana, Ill.: University of Illinois Press.

Tu, Wei Ming. 1986. On Neo-Confucianism and Human Relatedness. In George A. De Vos and Takao Sofué (Eds.), *Religion and the Family in East Asia.* Berkeley, Calif.: University of California Press. (Revised).

Wagatsuma, Hiroshi and George A. De Vos. 1984. *Heritage of Endurance: Family Patterns and Delinquency Formation in Urban Japan*. Berkeley: University of California Press.

White, R.W. 1959. Motivation Reconsidered: The Concept of Competence. *Psychological Review*, **66**: 297–333.

———. 1961. Competence and the Psychosexual Stages of Development. In Donald W. Fiske and Salvatore R. Maddi (Eds.), *Functions of Varied Experience*. Homewood, Ill.: Dorsey Press.

Chapter 8

Achievement as a Will to Accomplish: A Sense of Purpose in Human Life

Unique among our mammalian peers, humans have a self-awareness that often asks the question: "Why are we here?" We humans are seekers after meaning, we seek some purpose for our existence. As we turn that self-conscious awareness that seeks meaning not only inward but outward, and as we apply our recently developed scientific vision into the vast reaches of space, we find ourselves within an expanding mechanical universe. From this modern scientific perspective, we see a universe governed by natural law, in which a sense of purpose can be seen as a human fabrication. Yet this scientific vision is relatively new, and has not supplanted the human search for a purposeful existence. Whether we live with others in the simple habitations of hunter-gatherers, or on the plantations of agriculturists, or in cities with their vast diversity of specialized social roles, we humans have creatively imagined ways to explain our place in the universe and in society, and from that derive our sense of personal purpose.

The question of purpose has been partially or fully answered for many people by systems of belief or objective knowledge that order our existence. The quest for purpose has led us to develop various forms of religious belief that encompass the known world of space and time, looking back for explanations of origin and forward into some destined, yet to be defined future. Although not universal, in most cultures and for most of our historically recorded existence, humans have attributed (with various degrees of rationality) our arrival on Earth to some purposeful being who had a master plan, a being superior to ourselves to whom we somehow owe an existence. From this perspective it has followed that our meaning might be derived by bringing ourselves into line with this being's yet-to-be-fully-fathomed purposes and by abiding the superior being's regulations. The mechanistic perspective of the modern scientist has not entirely replaced these beliefs with psychologically satisfying explanations. The quest for meaning in the face of our capacity for objectivity has left us with forms of anxiety unique to humans. We may doubt our purpose, find ourselves abandoned or punished by supposedly uncaring or vengeful Gods, or find ourselves bereft of meaning in a heartless, atomistic, mechanical universe.

From a more existential perspective, however, in which the individual becomes responsible for the creation of meaning, we have come to realize that a sense of purpose is only to be found within ourselves, and the validity or actuality of our existence is only established as we act creatively and authentically in the world (de Beauvoir, 1975; Varela, Thompson, and Rosch, 1991). Thus, for many people, a capacity for meaning is enabled by an awareness of our own intentionality, as well as by the self-evaluations that refer to perceived and internalized expectations or values.

As we exercise our intentionality and develop goals or plan for the future, we appear to be driven simultaneously by an inner determination to actualize intentions, as well as being guided by society's standards for meaningful or "successful" endeavor. Self-oriented rather than interpersonally involved "conative" drives, or the human "will" can lead to a desire for superiority and perfection in achieving internal standards (Adler, 1956), although these standards may originally have been internalized based on social experiences and the transmission of cultural values. Experienced inwardly as an aspect of self-will or intentionality, a need for achievement can variously imply urges toward complexity and growth, efforts for aesthetic satisfaction, or as energy directed toward the realization of individual or social purpose. It can motivate unrelenting motoric as well as mental activity that is directed toward future actualization in the accomplishment of goals. In the negative direction, the lack of will can be experienced as forms of volitional inertia, as a disorienting, vertiginous loss of purpose, as the malaise associated with a profound loss of inner meaning, or as painful social alienation.

Internalized Will to Accomplish

Experimental psychologists have had a difficult time addressing issues of intentionality, and have preferred to focus on mechanistic explanations for the initiation of behavior. Human beings nevertheless experience the world in terms of their own capacity to make things happen, i.e., as a center of intentionality. Our experience of our own intentionality is so ubiquitous that explanations of events in the natural world commonly make teleological reference to intended or desired outcomes, even where the causation is in fact entirely mechanistic.

An understanding of causation is an essential component of this, and the capacity for recognizing causal patterns in perceptual experience appears to develop early in infancy (Leslie, 1984). Piaget's insight into the role that our own sense of purpose plays in a causal world was that the earliest experiences of dynamic effort are inextricable from the phenomenal experiences of the physical changes produced by the effort, such that there is no distinction made psychologically between dynamic effort and physical consequences. To quote:

> In conclusion, the point of departure of causality should, it seems to us, be sought in a diffuse feeling of efficacy which would accompany the activity itself but would be localized by the child, not in a self, but in the point of culmination of the action. This efficacy would therefor fill the little child's whole universe or rather would be localized in each familiar center of perception, whether it is concerned with objects perceived in the environment or the subject's own body. (Piaget, 1954, p. 228)

Thus the psychological causal universe is initially comprised of efficacy and its inseparable consequences. Only through experience, and the development of the capacity to mentally represent the variety of specific actions that generate specific anticipated outcomes, or the capacity for mental schemes that distinguish means from ends, does the child develop a capacity to distinguish the physical and intentional realms (Piaget, 1954).

As goals come to be represented independent of the actions that produce them, the energy of effort is harnessed, transmuted, and directed with intentionality toward future-oriented personal goals and a determined will to accomplish desired outcomes. Purposeful or "willful" behavior overcomes obstacles through persistence and personal endurance. To some extent the selection of desired outcomes reflects endogenous priorities related to internal need states of the organism: curiosity, etc. However, there are also goals based on *internalized* standards of excellence and moral values that are both implicitly and explicitly conveyed through socialization in all human societies. The will to succeed in the attainment of goals is internally experienced as a *self-oriented* motivational force, and is categorized in the ICSS in the category Achievement (A).

Considerable research has concentrated on instrumental concerns related to an imputed innate, basic underlying motive termed a "need for achievement" (*n* Achievement).[1] Definitions of successful achievement are to be found in some form in every culture. As an aspect of internalization during childhood, each individual is socialized to strive toward the realization of socially defined short- and long-range future goals. Achievement or accomplishment of a socially desired outcome can be a form of personal validation, wherein one has succeeded in meeting the standards of one's value system. In many modern societies, innovative behavior is valued. Achievement motivation in a changing society can therefore be

---

[1]The most notable efforts are found in the work of Murray initially (1938) and then McClelland and his many associates (1961, 1987). See also extended discussion on this research in the introduction.

instigated toward innovation and invention as personal goals. As we shall presently discuss at some length, there are also negative achievement concerns that include what the Durkheimian sociological tradition refers to as "anomic" or alienated social experiences, wherein the person experiences a lack of social purpose.

In contrast to the concept of a need for achievement in the extended research of McClelland and others (see introduction) (Smith, 1992), we limit our category of Achievement (A) more specifically to code for narrative expressions that refer to a focused and persistent will or determination to accomplish, or its converse, an alienated loss of purpose. As it is experienced consciously, what we score as Achievement involves a sense of purpose activated by a *will* to accomplish a desired goal, or the absence thereof. Concerns with Competence (C) or rivalrous endeavor (M) are distinguished in the ICSS as separable instrumental concerns. For purposes of contextual conciseness, concerns with ability are differentiated from Achievement concerns and are scored in the category for Competence (C). Among the *internal self-oriented* instrumental concerns, the emphasis is either on "will do" (A) or "can do" (C). Achievement can also be inner directed in relation to a sense of Responsibility (R) in respect to meeting internally experienced standards of excellence.

In addition to one's internalized sense of purpose, one may also experience *interpersonal* situations, where there is emphasis on either competitiveness and rivalry or purposeful cooperation. These are separately considered in the category of Mutual Purpose (M), as discussed below. One may also be conscious of the presence of an evaluative audience or "reference group" that is witness to acts of successful endeavor. Thus the social acceptability of our goal-directed actions may be called into question, as we have described in our discussion of the Esteem category (E). We may also be aware that personal endeavor can be directed toward the acquisition of wealth or possessions (as scored with the Objects [O] category), or toward the manipulation of others through the exercise of power. As discussed below in the chapter on Control (D), concerns with "power" exercised *interpersonally* are related to, but are to be distinguished from concerns with the purposeful, instrumentally directed, *self-reflective* sense of volition related to socialized standards that we score as Achievement (A).

Depending on the nature of the narrative, these concerns may be blended together, as they commonly are in conscious experience. If so, they must receive multiple scoring. In some cultures such as Japan, concerns about accomplishment (A) are seldom experienced without an accompanying concern over personal incapacity (C). In many stories of concern with personal competence the achievement need may be secondary or can be so completely lacking in the story as to not be scored. There may be a sense of rivalry with another as part of one's need to accomplish which must be double scored, both under the (A) and the (M) categories. There is also frequent Pleasure or Pain (P) associated with the realization of, or the failure to realize a positive accomplishment.

Achievement concerns are a question of a "motive" or "will" or an inner-driven purpose to succeed in taking on some self-defined or socially approved future goals. As indicated further in chapter 9, volume I, the negative of Achievement (A) is not failure. Failure, when due to the individual, not to circumstance, is an inner assessment related to a concern with competence or mastery; it is the negative of Competence (C). The experience of failure does not necessarily end a need to achieve. One may be spurred on to greater efforts to succeed despite concerns with personal incapacity.

One of the most central features of an urge to achieve is a sense of internal tension that leads to persistence in pursuing a task once initiated. Atkinson (1953) found that individuals with a high *n* Achievement recalled more uncompleted than completed tasks. They exhibited more persistence toward completing a task and doing it well. As Raynor and Entin have documented (1982), there is among achievers a strong future time orientation and a sustaining sense of purpose that fuels persistence in goal-directed behavior.

Alienation and Anomic Criminality: The Negative Sides of Achievement Motivation

There are a variety of negative forms that contrast with the purposeful, means-ends behavior involved in achievement. These can involve the active use of deviant behavior in the means taken toward attainment of goals, "anomic" lawlessness in behavior, the loss of a socially desirable positive goal orientation, or even more passive forms of withdrawn "alienation."

The otherwise apparently powerful need to seek socially acceptable future accomplishments can be lost, or can be transformed into the socially unacceptable anomic deviant patterns that sacrifice socially acceptable means in focusing on the desired ends. The desire to achieve "success" whether it is defined as wealth or some other socially approved status may not be given up in the face of social barriers or particular inner defects in character or ability. In anomic behavior, the compensatory means taken may instead violate social norms or regulations. Attempts at achievement outside the limits of proper behavior include criminal career patterns.

The sociologist Robert Merton[2] in his analysis of Durkheim's conception of anomie discusses anomic behavior in the success patterns of American industrial tycoons. The entrepreneurial urge can lead to legally dubious means taken to achieve success. There was in American society reluctant admiration about such financial success and a dubiousness about the role models presented for emulation. Today, in the American inner cities some with a strong need to achieve might become participants in the illegal distribution of drugs. The district attorney charged with the prosecution of the El Rukin gang, that was involved in drugs,

[2]Merton (1949), see especially pp. 125ff.

gambling and prostitution in Chicago in the 1980s, once commented that the individuals whom he was prosecuting would have achieved high levels of success if they had directed their entrepreneurial skills into legitimate economic pursuits.

Conversely, alienated withdrawal can occur when there is the loss of a sustaining purpose or goal direction. A sense of inner problems over purpose in life can lead to some form of existential crisis that ends in a passive withdrawal from motivated efforts. As we also discuss further, the inner stress of alienation is a central consideration in understanding the motives that lead to suicide.[3]

Alienation as an alternative to positive achievement striving is particularly visible in some ethnic minorities, as in the case of the Koreans in Japan.[4] Koreans were placed in a situation of denigration and contempt over several generations in Japan. Alcoholic withdrawal and criminal behavior are among the deviant, alternative passive or active negative reactions found in a considerable number of minority Koreans. A similar fate attends a high proportion of the ex-pariahs of pre-modern Japan, the Burakumin outcastes (De Vos and Wagatsuma, 1966).

Achievement Motivation as Related to Expected Social Roles and to Social Status Considerations

In complex societies there may be a wide range of role expectations that are selectively internalized. Class and caste considerations delimit what become the socially acceptable achievement-directed motives of particular individuals. Gender- and age-specific definitions in most societies continue to set boundaries on what are considered to be proper goals and the proper means to be taken in the realization of goals. Adult gender roles commonly establish defined expectations either about appropriate occupational accomplishment and/or optimal realization of domestic parental roles, etc.

An individual who goes outside the proper means to achieve political, economic, or social success risks being seen as deviant, or even as a *criminal* practicing "anomic" behavior, that is, behavior that is unregulated or without proper rules.[5] Such behavior is generally subject to punitive sanctioning by society. In contrast, successful achievement of role-appropriate desired outcomes can be met with positive regard from others. As we have discussed in the context of expressive needs related to social evaluation, individual effort toward the realization of what is valued in personal talent as well as physical attractiveness is recognized and rewarded by social Esteem (E) or conversely with denigration and disrespect. The category we use to define achievement themes does *not* refer to conscious concerns with esteem per se, but more directly to a *self-oriented* awareness of a purpose that

[3]De Vos (1992, chapter 2). See also chapter 14, volume I, below.

[4]See chapters 13, 14, in Lee and De Vos (1981).

[5]From the Greek *nomia*-regulation, law or custom: *a*-without.

must be realized through acts of will directing behavior in a time sequence toward a goal. If awareness of social evaluation is also expressed it must be double scored. As discussed in chapter 6, volume I, on Esteem, when status concerns are directly alluded to in any Achievement (A) narrative, one must double-score with (E).

Achievement motivation, as ordinarily defined in modern societies in contrast to tradition-oriented ones, is not static but is a dynamic force for social change: it is seen as taking place within some system of social stratification in which individuals do not attempt solely to repeat the past role of a parent but work to win higher status through a capacity to take risks, to excel competitively, or to innovate.

Goal-orienting values are not static, even in simple societies. No society is without historically embedded exemplars of the ideal, as personified in the social roles of individuals such as the political leader, the scientist, the artist, the teacher, or the spiritual mentor. In some societies, the maternal role can also be idealized for women as a standard of personal accomplishment; in other societies successful fathering, or parenting (more generically considered) may serve similarly as exemplars of achievement.

In narrative elements that are coded as Achievement (A), one commonly finds mention of a particular activity or social role position that an individual would like to attain. There is also some mention of the effort necessary to become such a person. Behavior that is guided toward the realization of a goal of higher achieved social status is, by definition, highly instrumental in nature, yet is also experienced as a reflection on the self, as it is seen embedded in status relationships.

In every culture, higher status can also be realized, in ways more subtle than direct economic or political means, by those individuals who exemplify or express the "sacred" (Durkheim, 1947), or represent the basic unquestioned values of the society. Such an individual is accorded some form of relative social status reflecting his or her position in a hierarchy of the sacred or in an ordained status. Such status positions exist in even the most instrumentally oriented societies. Such hierarchy is especially apparent in caste societies. Achievement can be sought in the hierarchy of socially acceptable holiness as we discussed in the context of Esteem. Even in a caste system such as the traditional Hindu society, where achievement patterns are severely limited by birth status, there are concepts of gaining holiness in a future existence through efforts exerted in the present lifetime toward spiritual evolution.

Distinctions Between a Career and a Job

One must distinguish different ways of seeing a "job" or career. On the one hand, a job can be seen as a vehicle for self-actualization in a sought-after career. On the other hand, a job can be a means of financial security or wealth. We shall further discuss the use of a "job" as a means of financial security in chapter 13, volume I, where we discuss the impersonal categories centering on objects or possessions, including the acquisition of money and the vagaries of fate. When one looks at work as a means of sustenance or the acquisition of wealth for its own purpose, there is an impersonal relationship with the job, even though it may also be pleasurable.

In contrast, a fulfilling career implies self-enhancement and the realization of excellence. When Marx discussed the alienating effects of exploitative capitalism he was discussing the fact that exploited workers take a job because they must survive. They do what they do, as did Charlie Chaplin in his 1936 film *Modern Times,* in an environment of machines. In such a context, one produces goods for the marketplace and surplus value for the capitalist who owns the means of production. One obtains no personal identification with or ownership of the product of one's labor. An individual who sees work from that perspective is not working as a venue for achievement, but is merely surviving. Therefore, for example, when scoring the stories of Kenyan youth, Evans (see chapter 3, volume II) distinguished stories wherein a protagonist is seeking work or is unable to find a "job," from stories that express more internally motivated achievement themes, such as seeking success or being frustrated in such attempts and turning to anomic criminal "careers" instead. Many who find themselves in economically deprived circumstances are concerned with working toward survival rather than self-enhancement or achievement through attempts to pursue a career with longer range purpose in mind.

Concerns with Social Purpose: Comparisons of Americans with Japanese

There are very significant differences in Thematic Apperception Test (TAT) narratives about achievement elicited from the various groups represented in volume II. Japanese, for example, are more apt to show internalized self-oriented considerations about achievement interwoven with concerns with Competence (C) or a sense of family Responsibility (R). In contrast, Americans more characteristically express ambivalent motivation and concerns with parental Control (D), which indicates that the American achievement motivation is not as internalized as is that found among Japanese.[6]

In traditional Japanese society, an intense socialization toward the internalization of high standards entails a readiness to assume a subordinate apprentice role in an age-graded social hierarchy. As discussed in chapter 9, volume I, this leads to more conscious emphasis on going through formative stages of acknowledged incompetence. In the *Kabuki* tradition of assessing one's accomplishment in a craft, one measures oneself against ideal standards of performance rather than the competitive progress of one's peers, as is more often the case in American competitive settings discussed in chapter 12, volume I. Americans are less likely to

[6]See De Vos (1973, chapters 1 and 5) and Vaughn (1988).

describe the need for achievement as involving any willingness to undertake an age-graded task in which the young must first subordinate themselves to necessary discipline to achieve a long-term goal.

The Japanese did not concern themselves with negative tensions over any willingness to self-discipline, or to accept subordination or control as do Americans. Rather, they focused on inner concerns with inadequacy or incompetence as a necessary precondition in seeking greater mastery.[7] In an American youth, worry over incompetence is more apt to be judged as an admission of competitive inferiority, unworthiness or low self-regard, and therefore shameful. Prognostically, in assessing individual personality in an American TAT record, an expressed concern with incompetence would be interpreted as contextually different from the same concern expressed by a Japanese youth.

The Japanese do express considerable fear of failure in a variety of contexts. In some considerations of the Freudian concept of the *ego ideal* this could be possibly regarded as directly related to shame as the primary sanctioning motive. We have argued elsewhere that this supposition about the role of shame in Japanese culture is incorrect.[8] Suffice it to say here, instances of failure expressed by the Japanese in either spontaneous interview material or in projective protocols are more readily connected to guilt over its negative, destructive effects on the status of the family than to the individual's personal "face" or appearance in the public eye.

As will be mentioned in the discussion on Responsibility (R), the negative effects of failure for the Japanese are considered on a deeper level to be *destructive* acts doing greater injury to long-range family as well as personal objectives. This is distinct from the momentary injury suffered through temporary embarrassment. The unconscious destructive intentionality toward others that is connected to failure makes such failure a ready stimulus to guilt even though the individual has not been irresponsible in his conscious behavior. For Japanese, failure may be seen as an unconscious act of resistance (D) in situations whereas Americans more consciously express an alienated lack of purposive involvement (A) or even a direct unwillingness to undertake a task (A).

Achievement Motivation Is not Necessarily in Conflict with Social Cohesiveness or Social Sensitivity

From a comparative anthropological perspective, some of the presently available comparative studies of achievement motivation emphasize, implicitly if not

[7]See the various discussions of recent comparative research on the attitudes of Japanese school children compared with American counterparts in Stevenson, Azuma, and Hakuta (1988). They reinforce the contentions made by De Vos (1992).

[8]See discussion under Responsibility in chapter 11, volume I, below, and De Vos (1960).

explicitly, the somewhat ethnocentric preoccupation in middle-class American culture with analytic thought and what can be seen as socially disruptive individualistic and competitive (M) methods for achieving success. This is the pattern advocated by McClelland and others as a necessary universal for personal and societal economic advancement (e.g., McClelland et al., 1952, 1958, 1961; Child, Storm and Veroff, 1958). They see socially cohesive, expressive, affiliative needs (F) as counterpoised to the individual pursuit of instrumentally oriented *n* achievement. Whereas McClelland's generalization accounts well for behavior and expressed attitudes in many societies, we shall report in subsequent chapters, that it does not work well to explain the Japanese form of achievement motivation, nor even the behavior in Japanese Brazilians (see chapters 8 and 10, volume II).

From the vantage point of the Japanese and Japanese-American cultures which we have studied,[9] we find it questionable whether a theory of achievement motivation that emphasizes individualistic achievement can be applied cross-culturally without substantial modification. An opposition of "expressive" need affiliation and "instrumental" individualistic achievement, as is suggested by McClelland, does not hold up universally, for example, when one examines the internalized interpersonal attitudes operative within an economically successful yet cohesive Japanese society. The Japanese, as well as Japanese emigrants in both North and South America, remain much more concerned with internalized directives to achieve in a social context for family purposes rather than individualized goals. Similarly, Suárez-Orozco (1989) has found themes of family-oriented achievement expressed in Central-American immigrants living in North America.

Some Alternative or Deviant Expressions of Achievement or Alienation: Koreans in Japan and America

Individual Passing[10]

Instrumentally based definitions of social, occupational, economic, and political success or achievement are found in every society. In any pluralistic society that emphasizes the ascendancy of one group, the achievement of social success may well require one to disguise one's minority status origins. In effect, for some, achievement motivation becomes equivalent to "passing" into the dominant society. "Passing" can be distinguished from "acculturation." The individual who is passing experiences mainstream social membership as a pretense, to be accomplished through the assumption of social roles and attempts to affect normative behavior.

---

[9]See especially De Vos (1973, pp. 170–200), Caudill (1952), Caudill and De Vos (1956), Connor and De Vos (1989).
[10]This section adapted from Lee and De Vos (1981).

This also involves efforts to gain acceptance by masking one's past. In contrast, acculturation involves a less self-conscious identification with the mainstream society, without a sense of pretense. The term "passing," first used by light-skinned African Americans, is a universal phenomenon found in any hierarchical setting in which a person's background might be a disadvantage for the individual. Passing is practiced in any social setting in which some form of escape from community surveillance is possible. The complex urban environment makes some forms of passing more readily possible in modern societies. The problem, however, is more difficult in caste settings (which include racist societies) in which intermarriage is vigilantly interdicted.

In a more rigidly controlled class society, there are severe difficulties in passing, and the individual is also subject to exposure. Sometimes a class-specific linguistic usage or an inadvertent form of behavior betrays one's past affiliations. In the yet rigidly maintained class segments of British or French societies, for example, certain individuals delight in exposing or "outing" upwardly mobile pretenders. George Bernard Shaw's play *Pygmalion* is a humorous satire on this very topic.

In our volume on *Koreans in Japan* (Lee and De Vos, 1981, chapter 12), we note examples of why and how some Koreans have changed behavior and disguised their background to obtain success, especially in the less carefully monitored world of entertainment. In Japan, to be known as Korean today or to have any Korean background is still to court failure through ostracism. Intermarriage with Japanese is extremely rare, with the exception of marriage with those of Burakumin status. Even an entertainer of Korean background remains an anomaly. Some Koreans find it expedient to attempt to maintain a disguised background; but here expressive needs become counterpoised. They cannot maintain affectionate ties with family or friends located in the Korean community without exposing themselves in a socially vigilant society. The cost of passing is loneliness and isolation. Among those Koreans who choose not to pass there is continual ambivalence toward others who attempt it. There is sometimes some insistence that a passing individual maintain covert contacts or give some signs of allegiance to the minority group.

We have already noted how Koreans in Japan have been under constraint to use Japanese names and to deny their origins to obtain even marginal acceptability as "Japanese" citizens. In effect, many Japanese would not mind that Koreans try to "pass" and assimilate by becoming totally invisible; but this form of assimilation is impossible. It overlooks the continuing pull exerted by an inner sense of Korean integrity and ethnic solidarity as well as by Korean counter-reactions to discriminatory attitudes. The same persistence of a sense of overt pride in a minority social identity is now found among many of the former outcaste Burakumin who also insist on not "passing" and disappearing as disguised ordinary Japanese.

If the route of individualistically seeking to achieve by passing is given up, a Japanese Korean can respond to the resulting frustration of a need for achievement in five other predictable ways, some active, some passive in nature.

Five Forms of Response to Frustrated Achievement

(1) Protest. A frustration of ordinary achievement can turn into concern with being powerless. Some turn from consideration of goal-oriented achievement to concerns with power. There can be political dissidence, or social protest. Some forms taken are mature when measured in terms of a defined political goal. Some forms of protest are more expressive of pent-up frustration. Koreans in Japan have been motivated to take a wide variety of means to redress their social plight. Lee and De Vos (1981) have discussed the history of this social protest, including violent political radicalism, past and present. Alternatively, power can be sought symbolically in religious terms. It must be noted that a number of religious sects still vie with political groups for ideological commitment. For some, being anti-Japanese has resulted in conversion to Christianity.

From the Japanese perspective, Koreans have been and continue to be feared as a source of political and social violence. Looked at psychologically as well as socially, the social protest of Koreans in Japan displays a broad spectrum of adjustment patterns ranging from infantile destructiveness rationalized as social purpose, to mature espousal of a political cause deriving from a sense of common humanity and compassion. There is considerable factional strife related to the legitimacy of authority, especially among Korean youth in Japan, but also in Korea itself.[11]

(2) Innovation. There are various forms of innovative social behavior, some of it leading to individualistically achieved professional and business success, even within the heavily group-oriented Japanese society. Such innovative activities do not depend on sponsorship or inclusion in some form or ordinary Japanese organization. For many Koreans, some innovative pursuit in the Japanese entertainment industry, i.e., in restaurants or sports facilities, is a path to success. While some individuals achieve by passing, others do so despite maintaining their Korean identity openly.

(3) Professional Criminal Activity. Many socially alienated Koreans become involved in goal-oriented criminal activity. The Japanese criminal underworld contains many relatively successful Koreans, but even here, a great deal of disguise and passing is practiced. In our informal interviews with the police and with Burakumin and Koreans, we found that an uncomfortable topic was the high percentage of individuals with either Korean and Burakumin background who comprise underworld gangs. At the same time, these *Yakuza*, as they are known, like to consider themselves patriotic or true Japanese with romanticized virtues derivative from the premodern society. They support, and are sometimes supported

[11]See our discussion of the Korean contemporary ambivalence about authority in Korea (De Vos and Lee, 1981; De Vos, 1993).

by rightist politicians.[12] The functional similarity to the Mafia in the United States is striking.

(4) Delinquency and Assaultive Behavior. Alienation from positive social goals can become manifest in more expressive, less consciously goal-focused forms of deviant behavior (De Vos and Wagatsuma, 1969; De Vos, 1980, 1982; Wagatsuma and De Vos, 1984; De Vos and Suárez-Orozco, 1990). Expressively prompted acts of delinquency or crime are in contrast to more instrumentally organized forms of civil protest or criminal syndication. Unfortunately, Koreans are greatly overrepresented in various forms of nonachievement behavior, including delinquency. In the 1960s, we found that the rate of delinquency among Korean youth was seven times that found among ordinary Japanese. This pattern continues. When examined closely, much of youthful delinquent behavior, both in assaultive forms as well as in thievery, is expressive either of a deep sense of emotional and material deprivation or of an angry antagonism toward any form of official authority. This kind of delinquent behavior is not simply instrumental. Stealing is not simply an act of gain, but is an expression of a lack of capacity for experiencing emotional satisfaction.[13]

(5) Alienated Withdrawal. Especially among youth, there are evident unresolved difficulties in applying themselves to any future plans. One notes many cases of social and psychologically alienated *withdrawal* including suicide.[14] The rate of alcoholism among Korean men is extremely high. General disparagement of men leads to damaged parental authority due to alcoholism. There is also much evidence of personal self-disparagement and lack of confidence in one's abilities. A sense of emotional as well as economic deprivation also exists. What is evident is that the Korean family in Japan has been *vulnerable* to several generations of social disparagement.

In our empirical work in the field of delinquency in Japan (De Vos, 1990, 1992), not only did we document the uncommonly high rate of delinquency among Korean youth, but also the atmosphere of social *withdrawal* among Koreans living in marginal slums in discontented and broken families resulting from an atmosphere of social degradation. TAT narratives that show lack of future orientation, as well as forms of impersonality and disparagement, are reported below in chapter 7, volume II, and provide striking evidence of this type of response to chronic frustration.

Social disparagement has both indirect and direct consequences for family life. Koreans in Japan find it difficult to use their group identity as a means of

---

[12]See our discussion of gang attitudes and their history in De Vos and Mizushima (1967).

[13]Expressive attitudes toward authority are well evident in predelinquents as well as delinquents. See chapter 7, volume II, below. See also De Vos and Mizushima (1962, pp. 626–638); De Vos and Murakami (1974, pp. 153–177); Wagatsuma and De Vos (1984, passim).

[14]See also discussion of suicide in chapter 14, volume I; also, De Vos (1968).

countering moments of individual doubt about ability. Frequently, the minority individual cannot depend on a sense of confidence drawn from past group experience. He comes instead to share the prejudice directed at his group in a form of self-hatred.

These modes of reaction for Koreans in Japan are not dissimilar to those practiced by some African or Mexican Americans in the United States whose communities have experienced a similar history of racist and economic degradation and consequent frustrated achievement over periods of generations.

Achievement Among Koreans in the United States

The situation for immigrant Koreans is different in the United States. On psychological tests, this present generation of entering Koreans resemble, in both attitude and behavior, achievement-motivated Japanese immigrants of two generations past (De Vos, 1983). Ironically, the Confucian heritage shared by Japanese and Koreans with its emphasis on achievement activities in the context of social cohesiveness, as well as hierarchy within the family, can be better practiced in the United States by Koreans than in a disparaging and socially debilitating Japanese context. Those Koreans coming to the United States as immigrants do so voluntarily, seeking the promises of personal and family advancement. For the most part, the families remain intact. Coming voluntarily to the United States, they find here no history of specific degradation and unemployment. Ogbu (1978) discusses at length the difference between what he terms voluntary and involuntary minorities. He has found that minorities formed historically by willing migrants maintain more positive attitudes than minorities created by socially disruptive forms of colonization, enslavement, or other forms of involuntary group subordination. Our experience with Korean Americans corresponds with Ogbu's thesis.

One must note that social class issues are also involved. Among recent Korean immigrants, for example, the middle class is overrepresented. Members of immigrant families have, in many instances, already achieved some form of professional occupation prior to emigration. Although many must initially work at occupations beneath their specific training, they remain optimistic. They hold on to the conviction that their children at least, will succeed by climbing the American educational ladder, which they are indeed doing. Koreans are overrepresented in all the major top grade American universities.

In chapter 7, volume II, we report in detail the results we obtained from samples of TATs collected from Koreans in Japan as compared with those of Korean immigrants to Los Angeles. What is particularly clear in our TAT material, comparing Japanese Koreans with American and Korean American samples is the difference in future time orientation. The Japanese sample of Korean youth tested show almost no positive future time orientation. They avoid projecting into the future. In contrast, the new Korean Americans see the future in vital, positive terms (see chapter 7, volume II).

Affiliative Concerns Versus More Individualist or Competitive Learning in Hawaii

As discussed in chapter 12, volume I, where we describe research with Mexican Americans, it is crucial when examining classroom learning behavior to investigate how specific ethnic peer groups may be characterized by culturally prevalent patterns of cognitive organization as well as forms of interpersonal behavior. One finds this issue directly addressed in the studies of classroom competition and cooperation made by Ron Gallimore and Allen Howard (Gallimore, Boggs, and Jordan, 1974; Howard et al., 1971, 1974), who examined the learning difficulties of "culturally Hawaiian" children in American schools.

Hawaiian society no longer exists in isolation. The great irony is that Hawaiians have become a minority group in their own islands. Although the category "Hawaiian" includes all individuals with some trace of native Hawaiian ancestry, those who are considered culturally Hawaiian are not actually racially different from those who have become more assimilated to the dominant American cultural traditions. It is the children who remain "culturally" Hawaiian who show the greatest difficulty in formal school settings.

Howard and colleagues found that with such children, language and other institutional aspects of Hawaiian culture had largely disappeared, but the children had been socialized in ways that deemphasized individual competitive behavior and stressed the positive social virtues of peer group expressive affiliation. This affiliative pattern of interrelationship among Hawaiians was pervasive.

Howard and colleagues discuss how early parental interaction, especially between mother and child, is relatively nonverbal compared with middle-class American patterns. Both adults and children are more peer group oriented. Commitments to work-mate or childhood peers often supersede commitments to one's spouse or one's children. Howard points out cogently how investment of material or emotional resources has been directed toward a loose social network, rather than toward members of one's primary family. In a sense, one accumulates the goodwill of one's peers rather than material objects or intellectual problem solving behavior. Relationships today generally tend to be non-hierarchical. This finding about non-hierarchy in the Hawaiian and Samoan family and community conflicts with some other reported generalizations (Werner, 1979). (One must note, however, hierarchical differences between *Alii* or nobles and the commoners in the old Hawaiian traditions.)

Howard and colleagues applied these cognitive and social ethnographic patterns to the understanding of the lack of learning taking place in the formal school environment. Culturally, from the standpoint of the dominant American society, Hawaiian children have been described as intellectually unmotivated and present-oriented. Yet by interrelating ethnographic and formal psychological research methods, the researchers were able to make a rather cogent explanation of why teacher-pupil relationships did not produce positive learning behavior in schools. In effect, the Hawaiian culture-oriented children bring to the school a relatively nonverbal pattern of communication as well as an implicit orientation toward expressive affiliation with peers rather than an internalized instrumental need-achievement in which the child gains his primary satisfaction through his own goal-oriented activities. The Hawaiian affiliative pattern is not a problem until it interferes with performance in the school context that has been created by the dominant society, wherein Hawaiian children are expected to learn individually and to take on an individualistic and even competitive learning style.

Generational Changes in Adaptation: Alienation in Hawaiian Youth

In looking at minority adaptation, one must attend to changes from one generation to the next. Again, this generational continuity is where the peer group plays a special role in modern American minorities. While the writings of Howard (1971, 1974) and associates are useful to warn about the implicitly pejorative attitudes taken toward traditional cooperative peer-oriented minorities, they fail to relate their studies to changes in the experiences of debased minority status and its direct relation to patterns of contemporary social deviancy.

There have been, for example, longitudinal shifts in adaptation in respect to what has happened with Hawaiian youth over the past several decades. By the 1970s, youth in Hawaii were manifesting more self-consciously hostile and antagonistic behavior toward outsiders than did past generations. In effect, we may have seen, in some enclaves of Hawaiians, the development of those characteristics of a "subculture of poverty" (see Oscar Lewis, 1959, 1961, 1966) that are due to changes in self-concept vis-à-vis the majority society. The relationship of individuals to their peer group may differ with such changing relationships with mainstream society.

As Howard and colleagues (1971, 1974) point out, it was traditional in Hawaii to be oriented to the peer group as the primary reference group. However, the relationship of the peer group to the outside culture changes with changing social attitudes. Whereas in the past, the youthful peer group was not antagonistic to the adult society or to outsiders, one may have witnessed in the 1970s the growth of a youthful peer reference group that developed an antagonism toward the older generation as well as toward what they perceived as an encroaching White society that afforded them neither understanding nor respect, and patronizes them as entertainers for gaping waves of tourists interested in "native" behavior. A sense of loss of purpose as to social accomplishment was evident. They had lost status markers of traditional social accomplishment and not replaced them with the individualistic forms of achievement expected in the majority American culture.

Hawaiian youth became overrepresented in every category of "social problem" (Liliuokalani Trust, 1978), with a progressive increase in delinquent behavior. Their behavior has been described by some observers in recent decades as a reaction to new definitions of success in which the easier lifestyle of the Hawaiians had become contrastively perceived as "unsuccessful." When we look at what has happened with the Hawaiians in Hawaii, we find that there has been increasing concern in the majority society that some Hawaiians remain embedded within their traditional culture and are therefore not "integrated" with the middle-class achievement oriented goals of the dominant society. Hawaiians who were formerly content with a simple nonmaterial lifestyle are now perceived, even by themselves, as living in some relative degree of poverty.

There is some continuing argument over whether these observed patterns are part of the traditional Hawaiian culture or whether what is perceived as socially maladaptive behavior is due to the inundation of the old culture by present-day American industrial society. Adaptation is judged "emically" from within the minority itself, not just "etically" from the outside in terms of objective behavioral indices observable by the social scientist.[15] There may arise a general emic concern that a group "should" integrate, as in the case of the Hawaiians. This general social concern may help cause problems by changing the self-perception of the group itself from one that is "different" to one that is "inadequate."

As in the case of Hawaiians, the "adaptation" of any minority group must be examined longitudinally through time. The actual adaptation of native Hawaiians to the dominant American culture and its concern with individual achievement has been changing with social circumstances. One notes that some Hawaiian youth manifest both an increased sense of personal alienation as well as hostility toward members of other groups.

Thus, there has been a greater amount of delinquent behavior, more recently turning into overt violence, than there was in previous generations. It is not simply that the ethnic interaction patterns have become more difficult with the greater overall population density and with the influx of mainland Americans. It is also, whatever the previous Hawaiian culture, that the youth now growing up feel a sense of anger and antagonism which the previous generation did not feel with the same intensity toward outsiders. This is now made manifest in destructive behavior. The economic well-being of the Hawaiian group has not changed as much as their sense of relative deprivation (see Aberle, 1966) vis-à-vis the majority American society. This sense of relative deprivation does not inspire them to internalize individualistically conceived forms of achievement.

---

[15]The social judgments by the dominant society at large are also "etic" and may differ from those of the social scientist.

The Hawaiian youth do not "buy" the individualistic goals of American urban society. The role of the peer reference group in the development of one's contemporary social self-identity and its relationship to the process of internalization of certain norms is very complex. Among Hawaiian youth the peer group has turned antagonistic to the goals of majority America which are taught them implicitly, if not explicitly by their school teachers. In American society, today, we know that some minority youth groups become extremely antagonistic to any perceived authority trying to instill in them middle class patterns of social striving. They are susceptible or vulnerable to sanctioning only from their immediate peers. The teacher in the school becomes perceived as an alien requiring of them deportment out of key with their previous experiences or social needs. They do not internalize individualized goals toward future accomplishment in ways that can be actualized outside a peer subculture.

ICSS Categories Related to Achievement or Alienation

A. Positive Active Achievement or Purpose ***AA***

AA-self	Self-initiated activities toward the attainment of a goal
AA-persist	Persistence toward a goal, hard work—endurance
AA-inspire	Inspired by person or idealized achievement (including religious thought)
AA-counter	Compensatory achievement. Overcoming the past or avoiding future negative circumstances
AA-else	Alternative goal
AA-status	Achievement for status
AA-duty	Achievement as responsibility or duty
AA-nurture	Achievement to nurture others
AA-repay	Achievement as repayment for past nurture, etc.
AA-parent	Parent or mentor initiated activities toward the attainment of a goal
AA-peer	Peer group initiated activities towards the attainment of a goal
AA-moral	Moralistic statement about achievement
AA-purpose	Existential meaning; self-defined positive purpose of life
AA-divine	A sense of divine purpose inspiriting or guiding behavior

There are a number of general or unspecified statements related to a need for achievement. In the present scoring system we can distinguish more specifically, self-initiated activities towards the attainment of a goal (AA-self). Some individuals attend especially to the persistence necessary to reach a goal. Success necessitates hard work and endurance (AA-persist). There is achievement motivation that has been inspired. Sources of inspiration may be found within one's family in a parental or grandparent figure or some ancestor, or even in a sense of lineage. There may be inspiration by a mentor or some heroic figure. There are even religious figures or religious thought that become inspirational in causing idealization and a strong need for personal achievement (AA-inspire). Some achievement is compensatory in nature. It can consciously be due to a past poor environment or a re-vindication of past sorrow or degradation (AA-counter). There may be a positive sense of an alternative activity to that considered by family or others (AA-else). Achievement may be seen directly as related to an enhancement of social status (AA-status) considered rather abstractly rather than related to any specific audience, but when appropriate, this type of response can be double scored with an evaluative category.

This category requires other forms of double scoring related to family considerations. Some achievement is considered a form of responsibility or duty (AA-duty). Achievement may be consciously voiced as an active repayment for past nurture (AA-nurture) or acts of giving on the part of another (AA-repay). Achievement may be both a duty and a desire to nurture (AA-duty NDA-family). There is in Japanese materials frequent specification of responsible, nurturant motives as a force in achievement motivation (AA-nurture NDA-family). Achievement can be verbalized as a repayment for past acts of nurture or care, etc. (AA-repay).

There are forms of achievement that are self consciously seen as instigated by a parent or mentor who helped initiate goal directed activities (AA-parent). Some individuals see their own achievement needs being kindled by peers in a social context (AA-peer). There can be moralistic statements about achievement and accomplishment that demonstrate strong social or religious values (AA-moral). For some, existential meaning is found in a self defined purpose of life (AA-purpose). There may even be expressed a sense of divine purpose inspiring or guiding one's will toward accomplishment (AA-divine).

*B. Passive Inactive or Unresolved Commitment **AB***

AB-inactive	Inactivity but interested in a task
AB-dream	Daydreaming about achievement (unrealistic ambition)
AB-think	Thinking about the future
AB-decide	Undecided future goal or contradiction or ambivalence about alternative goals
AB-torn	Alternative goal as possibility unresolved
AB-waver	Vacillation or inability to arrive at a commitment
AB-endure	Questions about endurance or frustration tolerance toward the realization of a goal

AB-purpose	Worry over possible loss of purpose or meaning of life

There are various expressions of interest in achievement in the context of inactivity. These situations can be seen as states yet to be resolved by action or definite commitment (AB-inactive). There are situations of daydreams about future possibilities (AB-dream). Some of these wishes are of an unrealistic nature. There may be more purposeful, yet uncommitted thinking about future possibilities (AB-think). The situation may directly depict a situation prior to decision (AB-decide). Some of these undecided situations involve ambivalence (AA-torn) or are further specified by vacillation and a present stated inability to make a final commitment (AB-waver). Questions can be raised about endurance or tolerating frustration toward the realization of a goal (AB-endure). There may be an explicit worry about a loss of purpose or meaning for one's existence (AB-purpose).

C. Anomic or Lawless Behavior ***AC***

AC-illicit	Achieving through questionable activities
AC-crime	Direct criminal oriented activity toward a goal
AC-chance	Looking for opportunity for negative behavior
AC-bribe	Bribery to achieve
AC-plot	Plotting to achieve goal
AC-theft	Thefts and crime against property
AC-gang	Organized illegal activities
AC-motive	Dysfunctional activity due to insufficient motivation
AC-hurry	Impatience leading to abandonment of a proper long range goal
AC-asocial	Success at the expense of relationships with others
AC-injury	Injurious action to self or others due to alienation

There are modes of expressing an achievement motivation through questionable activities (AC-illicit). There are directly explicit forms of criminal behavior (AC-crime). There are situations of seeking out negative opportunities for advancing one's ambitions (AC-chance). There is the use of bribery, psychological or physical prostitution to enhance one's opportunities (AC-bribe). There is plotting with others to achieve one's ambitions (AC-plot). These should be double scored in their specific contexts. There are thefts and the use of other's property in self advancement (AC-theft), which should be double scored with the Objects (O) category when appropriate. Organized criminal activities (AC-gang) with explicit achievement motive can be double scored with a cooperative category (M) when there is explicit mention of cooperation.

There are forms of active dysfunctional activity due to lack of positive forms of motivation (AC-motive). There are rash or hasty forms of action to impatience and an inability to sustain frustration (AC-hurry). There are modes of achieving success at the expense of positive relationships with others (AC-asocial). Depending on context these patterns can be double scored with some form of negative affiliation or negative competition (M). There are injurious actions hurting others not directly involved in any competition, but stand in the way of some successful accomplishment (AC-injury).

*D. Alienation, Social Withdrawal, or Lack of Purpose **AD***

AD-motive	Lack of motivation
AD-mediocre	Mediocre attainment due to lack of strong purpose
AD-lack	Give up ambition due to lack of funds, proper education, opportunity
AD-bias	Give up ambition due to discrimination, unfair treatment
AD-refuse	Refusal of proffered opportunity
AD-withdraw	An alienated withdrawal from a task or goal
AD-purpose	Expressed alienated sense of lack of social purpose
AD-endure	Incapacity to endure or tolerate frustration necessary toward attainment of a goal
AD-dream	Escapist daydreaming (so seen by the storyteller)
AD-irony	Ironic form of distancing from social goals
AD-meaning	Attenuation of social meaning
AD-regress	Psychological withdrawal can result in a regressive psychotic state

The chief form of alienation is a direct expression of a lack of motivation in a particular pursuit (AD-motive). There may be expressions of dissatisfaction with some mediocre level of accomplishment related to lack of strong purpose (AD-mediocre).

Some may express giving up ambition due to lack of funds, proper education, opportunity (AD-lack). Some see someone giving up ambition due to discrimination, unfair treatment (AD-bias). There may be direct refusal of opportunity due to lack of motivation (AD-refuse). There can be a simple alienated withdrawal from seeking a goal (AD-withdraw). There are also more general expressions of a lack of social purpose (AD-purpose). There may be an expressed incapacity to endure or tolerate frustration to the degree necessary toward attainment of a goal (AD-endure). There is an alienated form of escapist daydreaming (AD-dream). There are those who become ironic about social purpose in one's own behavior or in respect to the behavior of others. Irony can be an act of social distancing from belief in social purpose (AD-irony).

There are more profound forms of attenuation involving loss of all social meaning in life. In their extreme form these conditions can result in some act of what Durkheim (1951) called "egoistic suicide." There may be an attenuation of all social meaning. One sometimes finds such terminal forms of alienation in the aged or in those who have lost others that have given life meaning (AD-meaning). Some of these latter conditions must be double scored with an appropriate expressive Nurturant (N) or Affiliative (F) category. There are extreme forms of psychological withdrawal that can even result in a regressive psychotic state (AD-regress).

The experiences scored in this variety of AD categories can also be accompanied by a sense of suffering of a physical or psychological nature. If so, they should then be double scored with the Pleasure (P) category.

Illustrative Samples of Scoring in the Following Chapters

In several of the chapters of volume II we have included actual illustrations scoring of several of the subcategories included under the [A] category. Especially notable are the verbatim responses found in chapters 1, 2, 3, 6, 7, 8, 12, and 13, volume II.

Notes

Aberle, David. 1966. *The Peyote Religion Among the Navaho*. Chicago: Aldine.

Adler, Alfred. 1956. *The Individual Psychology of Alfred Adler*. New York: Basic Books.

Atkinson, J.W. 1953. The Achievement Motive and Recall of Interrupted and Completed Tasks. *Journal of Experimental Psychology*, **46**: 381–390.

Caudill, William. 1952. Japanese-American Personality and Acculturation. *Genetic Psychological Monograph*, **45**: 3–102.

Caudill, William and George De Vos. 1956. Achievement, Culture and Personality: The Use of Japanese-Americans. *American Anthropologist,* **58**: 102–126.

Child, I., T. Storm, and J. Veroff. 1958. Achievement Themes in Folktales Related to Socialization Practice. In J. Atkinson (Ed.), *Motives in Fantasy, Action and Society* (pp. 479–492). Princeton: Van Nostrand.

Connor, John W. and George A. De Vos. 1989. Cultural Influences on Achievement Motivation and Orientation Toward Work in Japanese and American Youth. In David Stern and Dorothy Eichorn (Eds.), *Adolescence and Work: Influence of Social Structure, Labor Markets, and Culture* (pp. 291–326). Hillsdale, N.J.: Lawrence Erlbaum Associates.

de Beauvoir, Simone. 1975. *The Ethics of Ambiguity.* Secaucus, N.J.: The Citadel Press.

De Vos, George A. 1960. The Relation of Guilt Toward Parents to Achievement and Arranged Marriage Among the Japanese. *Psychiatry*, **23**(3), 287–301. (reprinted: no. 22, 1963; no. 42, 1967; no. 85, 1974; no. 161, 1986.)

———. 1968. Suicide in Cross Cultural Perspective. In H.L.P. Resnick (Ed.), *Suicidal Behaviors: Diagnosis and Management* (pp. 105–134). Boston: Little, Brown, & Co.

———. 1973. *Socialization for Achievement: Essays on the Cultural Psychology of the Japanese.* Berkeley: University of California Press.

———. 1980. Delinquency and Minority Status: A Psycho-Cultural Perspective (chapter 6). In Graeme Newman (Ed.), *Crime and Deviancy: A Comparative Perspective* (pp. 130–180). Beverly Hills: Sage Publications.

———. 1982. Adaptive Strategies in American Minorities. In E.E. Jones and S. Korchin (Eds.), *Minority Mental Health* (pp. 74–117). New York: Praeger.

———. 1983. Achievement Motivation and Intra-Family Attitudes in Immigrant Koreans. *The Journal of Psychoanalytic Anthropology,* **6**(2): 125–162.

———. 1990. Empathy to Alienation: Problems in Human Belonging. In David Jordan and Marc Swartz (Eds.), *Personality and the Cultural Construction of Society: Papers in Honor of Melford E. Spiro* (pp. 222–242). Tuscaloosa, Ala.: University of Alabama Press.

———. 1992. *Social Cohesion and Alienation: Minorities in The United States and Japan.* Boulder, Colo.: Westview Press.

———. 1993. Problems with Achievement, Alienation, and Authority in Korean Minorities in the United States and Japan. In K.K. Lee (Ed.), *Studies of Koreans Abroad* (pp. 137–194). Seoul: Society for the Study of Overseas Koreans.

De Vos, George A. and Kwang-kyu Lee. 1981. Attitude Toward Authority: Dilemma of Ex-Colonial Society. In Changsoo Lee (Ed.), *Modernization of Korea and the Impact of the West* (pp. 150–162). Los Angeles: University of Southern California.

De Vos, George A. and Keiichi Mizushima. 1962. The School and Delinquency: Perspectives from Japan. *Teachers College Record,* **63**(8): 626–638.

———. 1967. Organization and Social Function of Japanese Gangs. In Ronald Philip Dore (Ed.), *Aspects of Social Change in Modern Japan* (pp. 289–325). Princeton University Press.

De Vos, George A. and Eiji Murakami. 1974. Violence and Aggression in Fantasy: A Comparison of American and Japanese Lower-Class Youth. In William P. Lebra (Ed.), *Youth, Socialization and Mental Health* (pp. 153–177). Honolulu: University Press of Hawaii.

De Vos, George A. and Marcelo Suárez-Orozco. 1990. *Status Inequality: The Self in Culture.* Newbury Park, Calif.: Sage Publications.

De Vos, George A. and Hiroshi Wagatsuma. 1966. *Japan's Invisible Race: Caste in Culture and Personality.* Berkeley: University of California Press.

———. 1969. Minority Status and Delinquency in Japan. In William Caudill and Tsung-yi-Lin (Eds.), *Mental Health Research in Asia and the Pacific* (pp. 342–357). Honolulu: East-West Center Press.

Durkheim, Emile. 1947. *The Elementary Forms of the Religious Life.* Trans. J.W. Swain. Glencoe, Ill.: The Free Press.

———. 1951. *Suicide: The Elementary Forms of the Religious Life.* Glencoe, Ill.: The Free Press.

Gallimore, R., J. Boggs, and C. Jordan. 1974. *Culture, Behavior and Education: A Study of Hawaiian-Americans.* Beverly Hills, Calif.: Sage.

Howard, A. 1974. *Ain't No Big Thing.* Honolulu: University of Hawaii Press.

Howard, A. (with associates). 1971. *Households, Families and Friends in a Hawaiian-American Community.* Working paper 19. Honolulu: East-West Population Institute.

Lee, Changsoo and George A. De Vos. 1981. *Koreans in Japan: Ethnic Conflict and Accommodation.* Berkeley: University of California Press.

Leslie, A.M. 1984. Spatiotemporal Continuity and the Perception of Causality in Infants. *Perception*, **13**: 287–305.
Lewis, Oscar. 1959. *Five Families*. New York: Basic Books.
———. 1961. *Children of Sanchez*. New York: Random House.
———. 1966. *La Vida*. New York: Random House.
Liliuokalani Trust. 1978. *A Survey of the Socio-Economic Status of the Hawaiian People Today*. Honolulu.
McClelland, David. 1961. *The Achieving Society*. Princeton, N.J.: Van Nostrand.
———. 1987. *Human Motivation*. New York: Cambridge University Press.
McClelland, David, with A.L. Baldwin, U. Brofenbrenner, and F.L. Strodtbeck. 1958. *Talent and Society: New Perspectives in the Identification of Talent*. Princeton, N.J.: Van Nostrand.
McClelland, David and G. Friedman. 1952. A Cross-Cultural Study of the Relationship Between Child-Training Practices and Achievement Motivation Appearing in Folktales. In G. Swanson, et al. (Eds.), *Readings in Social Psychology* (pp. 243–249). New York: Holt Rinehart and Winston.
Merton, Robert. 1949. *Social Theory and Social Structure*. Glencoe, Ill.: The Free Press.
Murray, Henry A. 1938. *Explorations in Personality*. New York: Oxford University Press.
Ogbu, John. 1978. *Minority Education and Caste: The American System in Cross-Cultural Perspective*. New York: Academic Press.
Piaget, Jean. 1954. *The Construction of Reality in the Child*. New York: Basic Books.
Raynor, J.O. and E.E. Entin. 1982. Future Orientation and Achievement Orientation. In J.O. Raynor and E.E. Entin (Eds.), *Motivation, Career Striving and Aging*. New York: Hemisphere.
Smith, Charles P. 1992. *Motivation and Personality: Handbook of Thematic Content Analysis*. Cambridge and New York: Cambridge U. Press.
Stevenson, Harold, Hiroshi Azuma, and Kenji Hakuta (Eds.). 1988. *Child Development and Education in Japan* (pp. 289–298). New York: Freeman.
Suárez-Orozco, Marcelo. 1989. *Central American Refugees and U.S. High Schools: A Psychosocial Study of Motivation and Achievement*. Stanford, Calif.: Stanford University Press.
Varela, Francisco J., Evan Thompson, and Eleanor Rosch. 1991. *The Embodied Mind: Cognitive Science and Human Experience*. Cambridge, Mass.: The MIT Press.
Vaughn, Curtis. 1988. *Cognitive Independence, Social Independence, and Achievement Orientation: A Comparison of Japanese and U. S. Students*. Dissertation, University of California, Berkeley.
Wagatsuma, Hiroshi and George A. De Vos. 1984. *Heritage of Endurance: Family Patterns and Delinquency Formation in Urban Japan*. Berkeley: University of California Press.
Werner, Emmy E. 1979. *Cross-Cultural Child Development: A View from the Planet Earth*. Monterey, Calif.: Brooks Cole.

Chapter 9

Competence and Mastery

We have found the need to distinguish a separate category of narrative themes that pertain to issues of competence and mastery. This category is used for scoring self-oriented themes that refer to one's capacity for competent understanding of the world, and one's capacity for skilled manipulation of the motoric functions of the body and the manipulation of objects. We see the capacity for the expert application of knowledge as a basic human characteristic that has developed out of mammalian curiosity and the inherited capacity for adaptive psychic functions that organize intelligent responses to external stimuli. Where this biologically derived capacity to know and master leads to successful understanding and successful manipulation of outcomes, it produces an inner sense of empowerment. Yet there are distinctions to be made with respect to the various ways in which causal empowerment is experienced.

As we discuss also in other chapters, one must note that the sense of causal empowerment can be focused on the manipulation of others, in its interpersonal context as Dominance (D). It can be experienced as related to the goal-directed sense of purpose that is reflected in the categories of Achievement (A) and Mutual Purpose (M). Where narratives emphasize the accomplishment of mastery itself, as distinct from (though potentially coincident with) the achievement of purposive goal seeking or interpersonal control or manipulation, we use the category of Competence (C) to score the thematic content.

Mastery: The Control of Causality

Hartmann (1958), White (1959, 1960, 1961, and 1963), and other ego psychologists found the traditional psychoanalytic account to be deficient in that it limited the consideration of drives to those related to sex and aggression. The ego psychologists recognized that there are reality-oriented mechanisms that produce adaptive interactions with the environment yet which do not develop from and are not in service of the other biological drives. Instead, they are seen themselves to be direct and distinct expressions of a biologically based requirement of the nervous system for novelty, for stimulation, and for the incorporation of new information that underlies much of our psychological development.

We are congenial with White's cogent attempt to establish the "effectance" motive as a way to handle problems in psychoanalytic theory as it pertains to understanding cognitive and behavioral development.[1] We suggest that the development of mastery grows out of the human capacity to develop a relatively nondistorted understanding of the world, and to accurately conceptualize and experience our causal relationship with the world. The movement toward mastery as an outcome of developmental processes in any domain of knowledge or action can be seen as consequent to the ubiquitous functional imperative of the biological structures that subserve the intelligent psyche, i.e., that they serve as mechanisms for behavioral adaptation. Furthermore, as Piaget has noted (1954), our epistemological development and behavioral adaptation is largely derived from our experiences with effective (or ineffective) actions that result from our attempts to assimilate the world with our prior epistemic schemes. Our understanding of reality is linked with causal outcomes, and therefore with our experience of power and force as it acts in the world (see also chapter 10, volume I).

In childhood development, an inner sense of ability progresses along with the capacity for nondistorted conceptualization of causal reality. Self-regulated instrumental functioning is not only a progressive autonomy from external regulation, but becomes an adapted autonomy that is free from more immature and distorted sensory-motor experience. In Piagetian terms, the manipulation of internal representational schemes and the voluntary control of purposeful action represents a growing *cognitive autonomy*. This autonomy can lead to a cognitive mastery that is increasingly effective through the more appropriate well-equilibrated manipulation of objects or concepts as well as people. Ultimately, relative degrees of success are experienced in problem solving directed toward the tasks that one has taken on. These serve as the basis for the development of an inner sense of competence and self-confidence.

The early sense of "causing" things to happen from within may begin with an infantile cry of hunger that results in feeding, although volitional control is gradually established over a whole range of behavior. In a movement toward autonomous self-regulation, volitional control is increasingly exercised over one's musculature and one's sensation seeking, and eventually over one's physiological arousal. However, this movement toward autonomy collides with the continued

---

[1]See Maddi's summary discussion of White's use of the concept of competence in relation to other psychodynamic theories of human development (Maddi, 1980, pp. 120–121, 354–359).

presence of external demands and the opposing power of external forces. The socializing agents of society demand acquiescence to external directives, as is discussed below in reference to the "D" category of *Dominance*, or *Control.* The child can maintain stubborn resistance to giving up a sense of inner control, and this comes in focus especially during the so-called anal period (otherwise commonly known by parents as "the terrible twos"). In our discussion of the Control (D) category (chapter 10, volume I), we trace the development of autonomy (self-regulation) from situations of hierarchical *inter*-personal control. Here in the discussion of Competence we trace the development of *intra*-personal knowledge about one's problem-solving ability and one's sense of mastery that moves from ignorance or lack of knowledge toward effective understanding. The sense of mastery (C) in the human experience of exercising *intrapersonally experienced* control over the environment is to be distinguished from that involved in *interpersonal* interactions in instrumental situations of dominance and subordination (D).[2]

Normally, we ultimately develop a realistic awareness of power and force, which is that they are situated both within and outside the experiential self. This distinction relies on the capacity for discrimination between inside and outside sources of causation, and the capacity to recognize the "other" as its own seat of subjectivity and intentionality (Benjamin, 1995). What is normally kept "within" developmentally is the sense of one's own intentional force or power.[3] What is normally recognized as coming from "outside" are the intentions of others, as well as the occurrence of "accidental" events that appear beyond volitional control (see chapter 13, volume I). The experience of power such as that derived from the early cry of hunger may also later be transmuted into the religious experience of the power of magical thought, vocal incantation, and invocation (De Vos and Suárez-Orozco, 1987). An inner intentionality may also be projected onto the world through the primitive defensive mechanism of projection, perhaps as an attempt to retain internal control. In the extremes of paranoid illness the defensive effort to retain internal control that is at the heart of projection may become obvious in grandiose fantasies of omnipotence.[4] At any level of severity, the projection of intentionality constitutes a defensive perceptual distortion that does not realistically

---

[2]One might consider here also the ideas of Alfred Adler (1956) regarding self-improvement or superiority seeking. However, in Adler's earlier formulation, self-evaluations regarding superiority were a reflection of underlying feelings of comparative competitive inferiority. Thus we consider them in the discussion of competition in chapter 12, volume I.

[3]See especially chapter 1 in De Vos and Suárez-Orozco (1990).

[4]In the psychoanalytic tradition, the ego mechanism of "projection" initially derives from conflict and anxiety around anal control, and has a twofold function. First, it can enable the expulsion of unacceptable or bad elements of the psyche from inside to an external locus. Secondly, it can produce an over extension of one's perceived realm of intentional control, such that it encompasses an unrealistically large universe.

acknowledge the presence of the autonomous volitional entities that are truly situated outside the self.

Where there is an outside "other," there is also the possibility of its internalization as a self-evaluative dimension of experience. Yet these self-evaluations can be of various kinds including both expressive and instrumental evaluations. The instrumental concerns we score with the Competence (C) category parallel the more expressive concerns we categorize with the Esteem (E) category. Although the same cognitive-evaluative processes for making judgments relative to a "standard-for-comparison" may be involved in both Esteem and Competence evaluations, the judgments refer to difference standards.

Esteem evaluations are made relative to standards that are based on social expectations and social regard. One's *self-esteem* is based on evaluative consideration of the worthiness of one's self and one's behavior whether in reference to one's actual *acceptability* either *interpersonally* in a social context or *intrapsychically* in relation to one's internalized standards of acceptability. These concerns with acceptability or feelings of self-respect and worthiness are *expressive* concerns. In contrast, Competence evaluations are made relative to standards of *effectiveness*, instrumentally considered. Evaluations are made as to whether one sufficiently "understands" a situation, or whether one has sufficient skill to address a challenge, or whether one's prior experiences lead to expectancies of future success in similar situations. These instrumental evaluations produce relative degrees of self-confidence or "*self-effacacy*," i.e., the expectation that one can act effectively to produce desired consequences in the future.[5]

We reiterate that there is an internal evaluative aspect to concerns with competence. One must have some implicit or explicit standards or expectations in mind in order to assess one's own competence as satisfactory, or conversely, what is negatively considered a failure in mastery. Despite the fact that social standards may also be used to evaluate one's competence, this remains a self-oriented judgment that is distinct from the social acceptability evaluation categorized in the Esteem category. Therefore, narrative content that refers to expectations of instrumental ability to *accomplish tasks* is scored in the Competence category, whereas references to expectations of the ability to *please others* are scored under the Esteem category. The Competence category is used to score themes that are *self*-oriented and instrumental, including general, diffuse, or even specifically focused experiences of relative "confidence" in dealing with the manipulation of inanimate objects, or in cognitive-intellectual problem solving.

---

[5]The work of Bandura and Walters (1963) and others illustrates the importance of efficacy evaluations as regulators of behavior within the framework of a self system.

Concerns with adequacy or competence must be distinguished from the Achievement (A) concerns discussed in the previous chapter.[6] A need for achievement per se emphasizes "willful" or volitional involvement with a task and goal-directed accomplishment. Some individuals remain more focused on adequacy, or the actual *ability* to perform rather than on the motivated *volition* directed to attain particular goals. Concern with adequacy is an attention to "can do" as distinguished from purposeful, volitional "will" or "want to do."[7] Research on achievement motivation espoused by McClelland and his associates recognizes the connection between "can do" and "will do," but does not adequately treat them as distinct dimensions of experience.[8]

The negative aspect of a concern with Competence or adequacy is *failure*, or an *inability* to accomplish one's purpose. Failure can be experienced as "I cannot do." This must be contrasted with concern with the failure to seek goals, or "I have no will to do" that is involved in problems with Achievement. These problems involve a sense of *alienation in motivation*, not a *failure in capacity*. Alienated behavior or attitudes appear either in active "anomic" criminal behavior performed in order to achieve one's instrumental ends (one "wills" to do even if illegal), or in a passive withdrawal due to an alienated loss of purpose (nothing is worth doing). Thus failures of achievement can be contrasted with failures of competence, because the former involve concerns with the absence of purpose itself, whereas with the latter it is the absence of capacity or ability. Additionally, there are differences between achievement and competence in the locus of the goal.

With competence, the goal seeking is internally directed toward the further development of the self and its capacity. With achievement, the goal seeking is externally directed toward the accomplishment of external purpose. This has implications for how competence and achievement concerns may be linked with other categories of concern. For example, one's failure to reach the goals of competence or mastery reflects on the self. Thus failure to reach the goal results in a failure of the self, seen directly. If this is turned in the affective direction, it may move in the direction of Esteem concerns, where failure due to inadequacy or

---

[6]As already mentioned, we find a conceptual difficulty in McClelland's concept of n-achievement in that he does not distinguish between uncertain motivations toward accomplishment and unresolved concerns with ability.

[7]All instrumental categories are about "doing." The Competence category (C) addresses the issue of "*can do*." The Achievement category (A) addresses the issue of "*will do*." The Control category (D) addresses concerns with "*must do*." The Responsibility category addresses concerns with "*should do*." The Mutual Purpose category addresses concerns with "*do with*" (in both senses, as "cooperating with" or "competing with.")

[8]See, for example, McClelland (1961); McClelland, Atkinson, Clark, and Lowelle (1953); McClelland, Baldwin, Brofenbrenner, and Strodtbeck (1958); McClelland and Friedman (1952).

inferiority can lead to a sense of worthlessness and shame, and success due to adequacy or superiority can become a source of pride and positive esteem.

Concerns with social evaluation may also be related to the presence or absence of motivation or the accomplishment of purposive activity (Achievement, A and Mutual Purpose, M). However, with achievement concerns the goal seeking is generally externally directed beyond the self. The negative achievement themes such as alienated withdrawal are not primarily concerned with another's opinion of oneself, they instead reflect the absence of legitimate goals. Failure to achieve or lack of involvement in a task (or the achievement of negatively defined goals such as anomic or criminal behavior) may involve transgressions that are more social-role related rather than directly personal reflections on the self. Thus success or failure to achieve relative to social expectations or social roles can be related to Responsibility (R) as we discuss in chapter 11, volume I.

There can be a connection of Achievement with a sense of guilt, whether for potential harm caused to others by a failure to fulfill obligations, or for perceived negative consequences of anomic action, or even for the accidental negative consequences produced by actions taken in good faith. In any case, where one has caused harm there is also a potential for concerns with punitive or retributive consequences. In this sense, we are congenial with Erikson's (1963) ideas that posit the development of initiative as being linked to the development of guilt. Certainly criminal achievement and a sense of culpability may evoke judgmental guilt as well as fear of punishment. In some social contexts, punitive consequences may involve the infliction of pain, but most often involve, and perhaps more effectively involve some withdrawal of social regard (E), shunning or isolation (F).

Obviously, this is not an exhaustive discussion of the complexity of how these various instrumental and expressive concerns are interrelated. For example, in criminal behavior shame may also be produced as a secondary vulnerability to negative evaluations of one's unsanctioned behavior when such behavior becomes publicly known to others (E). This is particularly true where the criminal behavior that has led to success has been motivated by status considerations of a compensatory nature. In such instances one may have initially been more motivated by social acceptability than by any inner sense of accomplishment, although this may be difficult to see in the manifest content of the narratives.

Although we distinguish analytically between narrative reference to the cognitive and behavioral processes related to mastery of task demands (C) and narrative reference to the conative processes related to purposive engagement with a task (A), in real-life experience these concerns are interrelated and there are instances when both are articulated together or with other categories. In such cases we must double score the narrative themes in both categories.

Presently we shall illustrate how concerns with competence can be developed into a special concern in a culture other than our own by considering self-development in Japan in respect to their continual concerns with competence.

Cultural Differences in Attributions Regarding Success or Failure

The negative pole of evaluative assessments of capacity, confidence, or competence is a sense of inability or personal incapacity. Failure in performance is the logical opposite of mastery. It requires a recognition that one has failed to solve a problem or fulfill an obligation due to personal limitations. However, cultures differ significantly in how their members explain personal failure. They vary widely in how they define concepts of relative inferiority or incapacity. Social values may emphasize or deemphasize individual differences in this regard. (We also touch upon individual differences in respect to concepts of competition considered in chapter 12, volume I.)

For a variety of reasons, it may become a serious social and political problem to consider differences in relative competence among the members of a group or between groups. It may also become psychologically unacceptable to assess one's talents or limitations with any objectivity. In an egalitarian society it may be disturbing to consider that some talents of an intellectual or physical nature are unequally distributed genetically among the members of a group. Therefore, explanations other than innate ability or innate incapacity are brought forward to rationalize, justify, or interpret failure. The initial success of John Watson's espousal of the behaviorist psychology may have its roots in these more pervasive American social values.

Explanations for success or failure generally involve attributions to four types of causes: effort, ability (both of which are internal causes), task difficulty, and luck (both external sources; see Weiner, 1992). How these types of attributions will be made in given situations will vary across cultures, and this is likely to also affect the researcher's own interpretation of causal process that are not made explicit in narratives.[9] With regards to the application of the ICSS scoring system, one must remember that narrative references to situations of success or failure must be scored or double scored in respect to the emic explanations given by the informant. These explanations can be impersonal as well as personal in nature. Some failures are attributed to happenstance, bad luck, lack of proper opportunity or supporting context, or other such fateful events beyond human control (see chapter 13, volume I, on Fate [K]). Personal failure also may be attributed to the impersonal or discriminatory working of an inexorable social system which defeats individual effort, no matter how promising the individual might be. One's talent may not be rewarded by social success. (Again, one must distinguish between an inner experience of failure to perform well, from the experiences defined by social recognition, which are considered under the category for Esteem). Mozart or

---

[9]Cross-cultural social psychology research on attribution has found differences in causal attribution (Brislin, 1993).

Rembrandt may have felt internally capable regardless of the social appreciation given their work. An inner-directed individual will have an internal sense of competence relative to personal standards that can lead to persistence in creative achievement efforts, despite the absence of reinforcing monetary or adulatory recognition.

In some groups, causal power is attributed to fateful external forces or even to the malevolent hostile intentions of a supernatural source (see chapter 7, volume I, on Harmony). Deliberate supernatural *malevolence* may be suggested rather than considering the *impersonal* forces of nature. For example, in some groups reported in the anthropological literature, a crop failure is not due to the impersonal vagaries of climate, but due to the magical practices of an enemy, or the anger of a displeased deity. Thus explanations for failure can be expressive as well as instrumental. Among expressive explanations are not only the negative effects of personal malice (Harmony [H]), but also lack of socially nurturant support (Nurturance [N]), or insufficient appreciation of one's efforts (Esteem [E]).

Instrumental explanations for failure can involve unfair treatment by authorities (Control [D]), being cheated by rivals through unfair forms of competition (Mutual Purpose [M]), irresponsible or profligate behavior that has distracted the individual from the task (Responsibility [R]). Not infrequently, there is reference to a lack or loss of internal motivation (Achievement [A]).

In the chapters in volume II, where we present illustrative research, we shall note in some detail, differences between Americans and Japanese in their attributions regarding failure. In many Japanese narratives, failure is due to personal incapacity, very often due to a physical or bodily deficiency (C). Japanese are highly internalized and self-reflective rather than externalized in respect to explaining why there is worry about, or actual failure in performance. Some possible personal inadequacy of a physical or mental nature can become an abiding concern. They seldom allow themselves to consider consciously any lack of motivation or their own personal resistance to accepting an imposed task. They are much more ready to attribute failure in an intended task to their own personal insufficiencies, although these insufficiencies are seen as surmountable through effort toward self-improvement.

In contrast, narratives produced by Americans reflect a readiness to attribute noncompletion of a task to a loss of interest or lack of motivation in applying oneself to what is expected of them (A). Failure is often seen as one optional form of resistance to authority (D) and/or a problem of internal motivation. This is why failure is seen so readily by Americans as the logical opposite of successful achievement, where in the ICSS, we see failure as the opposite of competence. For many Americans, achievement is a question of overcoming obstacles and difficulty through purpose and effort, rather than a question of developing personal *capacity* through the effort of hard work leading to self-improvement.

Studies of the causal attributions associated with the depressive cognitive style (Abramson, Alloy, and Metasky, 1990) confirm our findings from narratives provided by Americans. The normative American tendency to account for failure in terms of lack of effort or the excessive difficulty of an imposed task, but not to a lack of ability, is seen to be protective against depressive tendencies. An internal attribution of self-experienced deficiencies as the explanation for negative life experiences is one among several attributions that present risk for subsequent depression. Indeed, the Japanese sense of possible internal incapacity can lead to forms of depression which do manifest clinically in Japan. The Japanese emphasis on the long-range pursuit of self-improvement can be seen as a way to avoid immediate self-attributions of *hopeless* incapacity.

The difficulty in American culture with the explanation for failure manifests also on a sociopolitical level, as a split between the political right and left in explaining relative failure of ethnic, gender, or racial groups in situations that seem to indicate relative competence. Those more politically to the right are quick to attribute poor performance or relative failure to genetic or sexual differences or internal moral failure. Those more to the left are quick to attribute these to an unfair or discriminatory social system that either discourages or hampers motivation, or refuses to provide opportunities through employment and promotion of those against whom the discrimination is in effect.

Adherents of either position avoid the use of research instruments to gain better objectivity regarding the actual presence of actual discrimination or discriminatory attitudes. Some are also loath to accept appreciable differences in test results, where they are obtained, as *functionally* valid and objectively representative though they may be due not to biological differences but to a continuing legacy of past social discrimination that persists in its consequences. Some also neglect the practical importance of the fact that some of the effects of past discrimination are passed on generationally within family situations rather than simply reflecting a present outer social environment. Where there are generationally transmitted patterns, the effects of past discrimination may not be solely addressable through the removal of current discrimination. They must also be addressed more directly in the context of childhood socialization processes that occur in family settings where internalized evaluative and self-regulatory systems, as well as other self-development practices are engendered.

In the contemporary academic atmosphere, any psychological tests of relative performance ability are considered unfair or cross-culturally inapplicable by many American social scientists. There is also the further generalization that any form of testing devised in one culture cannot be used elsewhere. Such thinking may result from a legitimate desire to oppose prejudicial assumptions, yet at the same time, we must note that much present opposition to utilizing comparative research is itself based on a priori assumptions that are not empirically valid.

The present volume attests to the utility of cross-cultural methods that assume a common humanity whose psychological functioning transcends the different specific patterning of cultural experience. Comparison of narratives cross-culturally does not present us with direct measures of actual achievement or actual competence, but does provide us with evidence of subjective attitudes about confidence and the awareness of either ability or incapacity and a sense of failure. These subjective attitudes or awareness occur in every segment of every society and can be elicited for comparison. We note, for example, in comparing Brazilian youth in chapter 8, volume II, that Brazilian young women are far less positive about their abilities than are Brazilian young men. Conversely in chapter 1, volume II, Nancy Scheper-Hughes reports a greater sense of personal incapacity among Irish young men compared with Irish women.[10] How these attitudes are initially produced and how they actually translate into behavior and opportunities in a structured social context is another matter for empirical assessment, but that does not preclude the importance of documenting and comparatively analyzing subjective experiences as they are reflected in narratives.

Locus of Power Related to Self-Development in Confucian Thought

Approached psychologically, one of the important issues in respect to the effects of childhood training within a Confucian family is whether or not such training characteristically leads to passivity and resignation to circumstances, or conversely, to a growing sense of personal competence in achieving one's social expectations. Is one resigned through the inculcation of Confucian thought to be a passive respondent to uncontrollable circumstance, or is one prompted to seek out whatever instrumental means are available to bend circumstances to the advantage of one's primary social group? Is passivity and resignation, when it appears in some Japanese, due to the internalization of Confucian teaching per se, or to other social or personal factors occurring in given individuals? We strongly affirm that Confucian teaching leads both to positive concerns with competence and an active desire for accomplishment. We can examine how competence concerns underlie the use of magic or recourse to religious teachings.

How then are we to consider recourse to magic or prayer when it appears in Japan or in the West? Psychodynamically considered, magic usually entails an instrumental, or active practice to achieve some desire. Prayer, for some, is a form of meditation, but for many is a more helpless supplication for outside instrumental assistance due to a deep sense of inner insufficiency or *incapacity*. As we have discussed previously,[11] belief in magic can be related to forms of mechanical pre-causality found in children in which the locus of power is in some manipulative activity, either on the part of oneself or on the part of a knowledgeable technical specialist who can produce the desired change. Magical practices are a coping measure that, experienced inwardly, may entail a positive capacity to deal with a challenging situation. As Jordan has argued in examining the magical practices to

---

[10]See also Scheper-Hughes (1979).

[11]See especially chapter 3 in De Vos and Suárez-Orozco (1987, 1990).

which Chinese have recourse in geomancy,[12] or in divination, what may be cited as magical procedures used to improve one's fate can also be read as active instrumental behavior based on the shared folk beliefs that are used to ward off any easy acquiescence or resignation to fate. They are not experienced as indications of a passive resignation, but rather as competent mastery of environmental forces through knowledge and appropriate accommodative behavior.

A Religion of Self-Help

Among the Japanese, there are at times seeming acts of acquiescence to circumstances or acts of resignation in which the person uses the term "*akirameru*." One must note that this is a term, borrowed from Buddhism, that literally means "to become enlightened." In this usage, it does not actually refer to attaining enlightenment, and would be better translated as "seeing the light." The Japanese distinguish between forms of religion in which individuals appeal to outside power, "*tariki*," and religious activities employing "*jiriki*" or power from within. Appealing to the mercy of Amida Buddha is *tariki*. Zen Buddhist practices of meditation are *jiriki*. Confucian concepts of social role actualization are also *jiriki*. The resignation found in a Confucian adherence to one's role does not result in inactivity. Rather, it is a sought-for resolution between what is termed "selfishness" and the proper but more selfless active carrying out of one's expected role. Proper assumption of an expected role implies hard work and self-discipline, not resignation or withdrawal from challenge nor an appeal to external power to help one's fate. Socially realistic solutions to a problem are emphasized, rather than recourse to magic or the seeking of help through supplicating prayer. That would acknowledge a sense of passivity or inner helplessness and the need for the intercession of an outside intentional power to amend ones fate. Confucianist training, in contrast, emphasizes self-discipline.

The development of a sense of competence cannot be separated from any need to achieve, in the Confucianist tradition. One learns to put off present gratification, but with future social purpose and future social and occupational mastery in mind. A personal, inner sense of mastery in respect to the events occurring in the world about is the purpose of Confucian self-development as defined within one's prescribed social role. One senses internally one's active potential. One seeks to enhance an active locus of control *within* although it is framed in terms of social obligation.

Causality in this system is ultimately moral but morality is related to inner *will* and to emotional intensity in *ki* (spirit) or *kokoro* (heart), not to some submission

[12]Geomancy involves a concern with directions in locating housing or the use of land in placing a tomb, etc. See Jordan's paper on "Filial Piety in Taiwan: The Twenty-Four Filial Exemplars" in Slote and De Vos (Eds.) (1998).

to a potentially wrathful deity. This concept of "kokoro" for a Japanese, together implies active will, heart, and mind. Or, in Western psychological terminology it combines: conation (will, that is, the act or faculty of impelling or directing muscular or mental effort), affect (emotion), and cognition (thought). These are interfused with one another in social behavior resulting from our inner nature which is assumed to have an innate inner capacity for problem solving that can be developed with sufficient effort.

Age Grading and a Sense of Mastery in a Confucian Context

Rote Learning Before Verbal Explanation

There are social behavioral implications of a Japanese cultural emphasis placed on a present compliance as a means to future mastery. In Japanese socialization there is the direct training of the child's body into patterned expected behavior. Willful bodily movement is directed by outside intention as well as by inside volition (De Vos, 1993).

In more extreme cases, there are negative considerations. There can also be a molding of the child by a maternal emotional closeness that gratifies dependency as a means of control. One can note some lack of development of clear ego boundaries separating mother and child when such dependent bonds are maintained into adulthood (Doi, 1973). Considered from a clinical standpoint, one can see how the continuation of a dependent mother-child relationship into the adult period may cause a number of psychological disturbances. Suffice it to say that excessive attachment to a controlling mother can be a source of considerable personal malaise in a significant number of Japanese. However this underlying control is usually put to impelling the child toward the acquisition of instrumental competence.

Compliant motoric training of early behavior precedes critical comprehension; it prepares a child to be sensitive to the proximate physical cues that signal the intentionality of others in the actual social world. A motoric stage in both cognitive and moral perception is implicitly acknowledged and has long been utilized in Japanese concepts of training, whether in social comportment or in artistic skills. A child or an apprentice is expected to learn through pliant behavior before understanding *what* the action means or *why* it is being done. This is very apparent when one looks at traditional patterns of schooling and apprenticeship in Japan. Such motoric compliance is still expected in the learning of the martial arts.

From the very beginning, Japanese mothers, when compared with their American counterparts communicate through close body contact (Caudill and Weinstein, 1966). American mothers treat their infants as more separate, non-contiguous independent objects; verbal communication is emphasized from early on. Motoric learning though physical contact is more proximal than is learning through the distal sensory organs of hearing and sight, and is less directly subjected to the possible interference of critical cognitive mechanisms.

Rote repetition and memorization as well as behavioral participation in ritual has been used in a number of traditions to inculcate sacred scriptures. Note that such a pattern seems to be appropriate in the imparting of both a nonliterate as well as literate religious tradition. Children or adults are not usually expected to examine critically the beliefs derived from sacred sources. Direct memorization is the mode of incorporating the sacred. In contrast, secularized scientific investigation is based on the notion that all present knowledge is based on theory that must receive continuous critical examination. Ideally, there is also developed a willingness to doubt current orthodoxy. An enduring argument within pedagogy is about how much is to be first imparted by rote before encouraging a questioning attitude toward what is taught.

A successful example of such a motoric method of training is the Suzuki method of teaching children the violin. There are certain elementary pieces where everyone plays (that is, "moves") together, from the youngest child on up, imitating gestures and arm movements. The more adept are not excused from the elementary exercises; they play along with the little tots, as the younger ones are as best possible imitating their gestures. There is continuous participatory togetherness that creates willingness to practice in those less skilled. This method stimulates optimism about being able to reach the next difficult level of behavioral performance by playing next to those who are progressively more adept, but still part of a group. In the Suzuki method learning is social and behavioral, not individual and conceptual.

The Lineage Master as Model

In understanding the development of competence in traditional plastic and dramatic art forms in Japan as well as the martial arts, one must note how rote behavior continues on the long road toward an eventual mastery. There is no presumption that every practitioner will even eventually come to full comprehension. Francis Hsu (1975), has written with considerable insight into the continuity in art due to the tradition of the *iemoto*. An *iemoto* is the sole unchangeable master of a tradition. Upon death, this tradition is passed on to a successor. He is the only one who can modify or change anything. All others trained, or being trained, are subject to his final authority. Religious and philosophical traditions, as well as Noh drama, Kabuki, schools of flower arrangement, all have *iemoto*. In the Noh tradition, for example, only an experienced true master knows the meaning of the cryptic codes that describe the state of mind to attain both motorically and conceptually in attempting a particular role. The master doesn't attempt to impart such knowledge or secrets except to his immediate successor.

The emphasis on a direct lineage transmission that cannot be accomplished through written texts is found in many spiritual traditions. It is an essential component of the Tibetan Buddhist tradition. The first stanza in a well-known teaching text by the Tibetan master Je-Tsongkapa states: "Following a kind master, foundation of all perfections, is the very root and basis of the path. Empower me to see this clearly and make every effort to follow well."[13] As an undercurrent, sometimes explicitly recognized, there is a direct imparting of the master's capacities and power. In such lineage traditions, there is an explicitly acknowledged capacity carried by the master that cannot be transmitted in any manner other than direct, unmediated proximal communication. Written text or other forms of recorded transmission simply do not carry the weight of the direct transmission.

Over one's life span the master may disappear as a source of learning, but the process is internalized and continues within. A sense of inner competence in the Confucian tradition is not rapidly attained, but there is a continuous lifelong goal of seeking further inner development toward competence and mastery, with the actual master, or an idealization of mastery serving as the model. In scoring our Thematic Apperception Test (TAT) material we have found just such a pervasive concern with inner ability or competence in many Japanese records. It is coupled with a sense that hard work and endurance will ultimately achieve one's dedicated purpose. The Confucianist life trajectory is an optimistic one, wherein one looks forward to achieving eventual mastery.

Defensive Self-Identity and a Selective Permeability Limiting the Development of Competence

Here we consider how what we term "exclusion" continually interacts with mechanisms of intake and expulsion. Exclusion as a basic mechanism has been explored extensively in the clinical psychoanalytic literature, most primitively when it appears as a neurotic rigidification of coping that produces behavioral symptoms indicative of "repression."[14] One must also consider a more positive function for such mechanisms in the formation of the social self in nonclinical situations. Exclusory selectivity of experiences, or "selective attention," is a necessary component of healthy perception. Exclusory functions are found operative in all societies. Collective representations use perceptual exclusion to give consistency to social experience. What is excluded from conscious perception differs from one society to another and produces local interpretations of social reality that distinguish members of different social groups one from another. Such selectivity is part of a social identity formation process that functions to keep groups distinct.

We have used the concept of "*selective permeability*" to interrelate certain structural components of personality with how a reference group influences social behavior.[15] Structurally considered, repression works defensively in maintaining

---

[13]From *The Foundation of all Perfections*, as used by the Jewel Heart Dharma Center, Ann Arbor, Michigan.

[14]See especially chapter 1 in De Vos and Suárez-Orozco (1990).

[15]See especially De Vos (1978) and chapter 7 in De Vos (1992).

separation between proximate social groups. “Selective permeability,” as we use it, is an analogy, borrowed from biology, that compares the functioning of the ego with the functioning of a living cell. The continuity of the living cell as an organism depends on the adequate functioning of a permeable membrane that is selective in what it allows to come in. In an analogous sense the ego depends on a working membrane that selectively allows certain stimuli to penetrate as “experiences” that may or may not become an integral part of the functioning self.

This concept is helpful to us in considering how social distance is maintained individually as well as collectively between different cultural and subcultural groups. Selective permeability is involved defensively in what is or is not “internalized.” Specific experiences have varied degrees of saliency of influence in different reference groups. There are their different role expectations and special inducements or sanctions to take on a particular line of thought or behavior.

This consideration is related to reference group theory. The reference group provides structure of meaning to the experiences of its members. This framework of meaning becomes the selective membrane that renders particular experiences relatively salient. There is sometimes a conflict between reference groups in how they define the meaning of an event or an idea. The most important reference group for any individual will be that group identity that facilitates most readily a selective penetration of experience that is in line with a group defined “meaning.” There is a greater willingness, either consciously or unconsciously, to experience events in line with socially defined meaning as set forth by a primary reference group.

Usually in a relatively well-functioning culturally conditioned ego, those ideas that are dangerous or contradictory to one’s primary group membership will not be allowed to come into consciousness. They may either be totally “denied” or unconsciously “repressed.” This concept of selective permeability is related to the manner in which some degree of consistency is maintained within the social self. Dangerously inconsistent or potentially disruptive discordant elements are protectively kept out so that they do not upset the viable homeostasis necessary for the continuity of the living structure. What might sometimes serve positively for maintaining consistency can at the same time function negatively to inhibit a development of further competence. Growth of further adequacy demands some readiness, in a Piagetian sense, to “accommodate” experiences that disturb or cause acute discomfort. A future sense of relative adequacy or competence can be prevented by an inability to accommodate what are initially disturbing or threatening new experiences.

There is a prevalent misconception in discussions of group differences between classes or ethnic groups that any lack of understanding between individuals from different groups is caused by different cultural modes of living or language patterns. To the contrary, for purposes of argument one could say that it is not the differences in behavior themselves that cause misunderstanding, but a self-protective need to preserve distinguishing barriers between individuals and groups. Distancing operations which cause individuals to experience events differently are particularly noticeable where caste or class distinctions are being used by one segment of the population against the other. Differences are maintained as a barrier to any possible assimilation process, or they are used selectively in a defensive way by those subordinated to enable the individual to maintain his or her integrity when confronting lack of acceptance in situations of possible social assimilation. This defensive need may inhibit the acquisition of competence that threatens the stability of the social self, even where an actual opportunity for assimilation or upward mobility may exist for the individual. This can be seen in schools, where one can find a selective minority "non-learning" which persists in social segmentation.[16]

Note that "exclusion" and its manifestation in repression is basically different from both projection and displacement.[17] Projection is a mechanism that governs the expulsion from within of what is disruptive, and efforts to maintain control through externalization of intentionality. In projection a dynamic sense of intentional power from within actively opposes what has been disavowed and externalized. What is projected continues to be experienced, albeit externally, thus one must continue to contend with what is projected as part of the external world. In contrast, the energy used in exclusion is automatically invested in a barrier that unconsciously keeps out disruptive experiences. There is no necessary conscious, contrastive sense of confrontation with outside forces. In effective repression there is no dynamic defensive awareness of forces within or without, although considerable energy may be expended to maintain exclusion. The exclusory mechanism can lead to maladaptive non-learning.

The Lack of Competence or Confidence Among the Japanese Burakumin Minority

One striking parallel between the value systems of American and Japanese cultures is the emphasis on occupational and educational achievement in both societies. Members of both societies are well aware of the fact that they "should" apply themselves to personal training and education. Yet the minority individual, whether African American or Burakumin, also knows that he or she will face discrimination-based difficulties when applying for a job in the profession or skill for which the training has been sought (Ogbu, 1974, 1978). The individual must be willing and able to face a number of situations that can produce feelings of self-deflation and rejection. Although there may be some social inducement to make the effort to succeed, the potential for aversive outcomes may be more salient. An individual's confidence in attaining competence may be severely challenged when not supported from early childhood by consistent encouragement from significant others regarding one's true potential.

---

[16]Discussed in detail in chapter 7 in De Vos (1992).

[17]See the discussion of displacement and projection in chapter 6, volume I, on Esteem.

Based originally on psychological experiments with animals we have found that consistent exposure to aversive outcomes beyond the individual's control brings about an experimental neurosis known as "learned helplessness," in which the individual ceases all effort to avoid the negative outcomes (Seligman and Maier, 1967; Seligman, 1975). Parallels with this also appear to be related to some forms of depression in humans (Seligman, Abramson, Semmel, and von Baeyer, 1979). The result under such conditions is to not try, although humans have the additional cognitive capacity of discrediting the goal. A protective, defensive self-identity with a submerged group makes the need for trying unnecessary. Although a number of individuals from minority groups nonetheless have the strength of purpose and the ego capacities to survive despite discrimination, others react with general apathy and lack of involvement with the educational process (De Vos, 1982). Although such apathy may be expressed in terms of hostility and rejection of mainstream goals, it may actually spring from an inner lack of self confidence. Individuals who take this course do not allow themselves to be challenged since they are too uncertain about inner resources. They become defensively impermeable to the educational experience afforded them in public schools. This early deflation of self confidence is found in particular minorities both in Japan and the United States.[18]

This can manifest in testing situations as poor performance that does not reflect actual capacity. We can illustrate this by an example from research reported by De Vos and Wagatsuma (1966). In a comparative study of Binet IQ tests in a small city near Osaka, Japan, of the students tested in the majority Japanese group, 23 percent scored above 125, compared with 2.6 percent of the Buraku students. In the majority group, 32 percent scored between 109 and 124, compared with 19.5 percent of the Burakumin. In the majority, 23 percent scored between 93 and 108 compared with 22 percent of the Burakumin. Scores between 77 and 92 were reported for 12 percent of the majority compared with 18 percent of the minority. Whereas only 10 percent of the majority had IQ scores under 76, 37.6 percent, or *more than a third of the Buraku children scored under 76* in IQ. These intelligence test findings for the Burakumin of Japan can not possibly be indicative of differences in biological intelligence, for there is no racial difference between majority Japanese and the Burakumin. They are instead indicative of a massive resistance, both unconscious as well as conscious, to the educational efforts directed toward the Burakumin by the majority community. Whatever the attitudes of the teachers involved, the children are not responding positively to classroom situations. They are not as permeable to educational experiences as are the more receptive majority children (Ogbu, 1974). They are feeling defensively inferior to the majority Japanese.

---

[18]The comparative work of John Ogbu in a variety of cultural settings has reaffirmed these contentions (see especially 1974, 1978).

Categories of Competence, Mastery, Failure, or Incapacity

A. *Realization of Mastery and Adequacy in Problem-Solving Behavior* ***CA***

CA-present	Expression of present mastery, capacity, ability, or adequacy, including awareness of aging
CA-past	Expression of past mastery, capacity, ability, or adequacy
CA-future	Expression of future mastery, capacity, ability, or adequacy
CA-test	Demonstration of competence (passing a test or ordeal)
CA-endure	Capacity to endure or survive tribulations or difficulties in life
CA-body	Reference to one's capable body
CA-defect	Overcoming a handicap
CA-comic	Success despite inadequacy (the comic-comedy)
CA-repair	Capacity to repair
CA-improve	Self-improvement through persistence or hard work; mastery
CA-open	Open-minded and adaptive to circumstance
CA-expert	Capacity through experience
CA-able	Positive actualization of one's own occupation or destined role
CA-create	Positive sense of capacity to be creative
CA-model	Copy or use model to emulate, learn, or gain proficiency
CA-aware	Scientific causality and awareness to solve problems
CA-help-s	Self-help, self-improvement by internal reordering (meditation)
CA-relief	Internally achieved confidence as a relief from anxiety
CA-affirm	Affirmation of an achieved status
CA-know-s	Knowledge, perception (insight) into oneself
CA-know-o	Knowledge, perception (insight) into others
CA-magic	Supernatural or magical ability
CA-trance	Empowerment through a supernatural entity by entering a trance state

A narrative may explicitly refer to the adequacy involved in actualizing the protagonist's goals. Such responses should be double scored with an appropriate Achievement (A) category.

Positive concerns with competence include confident expressions of competence in respect to present, past, or future activities (CA-present, CA-past, CA-future). In specific terms there may be the successful passing of a test or having the ability to do so (CA-test). There is voiced capacity to endure or survive tribulations or difficulties in life (CA-endure).

There can be positive reference to one's body as capable (CA-body). There may be a sense of overcoming a personal handicap in realizing a successful level of personal adequacy (CA-defect). There may be a sense of confidence in instrumental realization despite some personal inadequacies. This is the sense of the comic in life. Inadequacy does not rule out a successful resolution of problems (CA-comic).

Confidence may be expressed about an ability to repair what is broken or defective (CA-repair). There is expression of modes of self-improvement to raise one's competence (CA-improve). One may value being "open minded," as a capacity to adapt (CA-open). One may become an expert and improve capacity through experience (CA-expert). There may be a positive actualization of one's own occupation or destined role (CA-able). One may have a positive sense of creativity, a capacity to be creative (CA-create). One may be able to use another as a role model to improve one's capacities by emulation (CA-model). There may be a positive assertion of scientific knowledge of causality, or an awareness of an ability to solve problems (CA-aware).

There may be referral to the means of self-help taken to improve one's general adequacy or self confidence including such methods as meditation (CA-help-s). The may a confident recovery from internal doubts or anxieties (CA-relief). Attention can be drawn to a capacity to affirm some kind of achieved status (CA-affirm).

There may be expressions of competence in achieving insight into oneself (CA-know-s), or adequate psychological perception of others (CA-know-o).

There may be fantasized positive recourse to supernatural or magical forms of competence (CA-magic). Empowerment may be achieved through a supernatural entity by entering a trance state (CB-trance).

B. Unresolved Issues of Personal Ability ***CB***

CB-help	Needs help to solve problem—outside assistance
CB-worry	General or unspecified worry, doubt, or anxiety
CB-arduous	Difficulty with a task, or emergency situation; need to solve a problem or enigma
CB-able	Worry, doubt about capacity, ability
CB-blind	Innocence or ignorance preventing adequate behavior

CB-age	Concern about diminishing ability with aging
CB-inferior	Worry, doubt about inferiority
CB-decide	Vacillation in a decision; making a decision with great difficulty
CB-chafing	Impatient, chafing, to complete task
CB-else	Secondary or compensatory goal of which one is capable rather than primary objective
CB-hope	Hope for the future capacity of another
CB-defect	Difficulty in repairing or overcoming a defect
CB-status	Worry about the capacity to realize a desired social status
CB-delay	Procrastination, put off starting
CB-weak	Concern about weakness in self-assertion
CB-prayer	Seeks supernatural assistance in a task

The individual may sense a personal incapacity in facing some situation and a need for help (CB-help). We also score here any general or unspecified expression of anxiety or worry (CB-worry). The rationale for this is that a sense of inability to cope underlies such expression.

There may be an unresolved sense of difficulty encountered in facing a task (CB-arduous). There are direct expression or worries or doubts about personal ability (CB-able). Being inept in coping may be due to being ignorant or innocent. One may be "blind" to what is called for in a situation (CB-blind). Age may cause worry about ability (CB-age). The worry voiced may be about a feared inferiority (CB-inferior). There may be an unresolved inability to make a coping decision (CB-decide). There may be a sense of impatience with oneself to be able to complete a task (CB-chafing).

There may be the consideration of a secondary or compensatory goal due to a lack of confidence in the attainability of one's primary objective (CB-else). One may hope (CB-hope) to attain the capacities that are possessed by another person (this may sometimes be double-scored with AA-inspire). The unresolved concern may be with something defective which one may not be capable of overcoming (CB-defect). There may be an experienced unresolved sense weakness in social status that is a form of handicap (CB-status).

There may be an expressed difficulty in starting a task and a problem with procrastination (CB-delay). One may express a sense of unresolved inner weakness in self-assertion toward one's task (CB-weak). One may seek supernatural assistance in working on a task (CB-prayer).

C. Ineptitude in Attempted Performance ***CC***

CC-inept	Ineptitude in proper performance of a task
CC-fake	Fraudulent or faked competence
CC-mental	Frustrated or bungled action due to internal factors of an intellectual order (lack of intelligence, of knowledge)
CC-body	Frustrated or bungled action due to internal factors of a physical order
CC-artist	Frustrated or bungled action due to lack of artistic capacity
CC-tragic	Failed action due to tragic flaw; tragedy
CC-loss	Injurious action to self or others due to failing professional, mental, physical, or sexual capacity
CC-break	Inept inadvertent breakage
CC-grand	Grandiosity

There can be failure to perform a task properly (CC-inept). There can be active fraud or a pretense of competence not actually possessed (CC-fake). There can be bungled action due to a lack of proper intelligence or sufficient knowledge to perform a task adequately (CC-mental). The incapacity to perform a desired action may be due to physical factors (CC-body). One may express a lack of artistic ability (CC-artist).

There may be tragedy consisting of failure due to some unexpected or minor defect or flaw in a noble protagonist (CC-tragic). There can be injurious action to self or others due to failing professional, mental, physical, or sexual capacities (CC-loss).

Inept handling can cause some breakage (CC-break). This generally must also be double scored with the Object category (O).

Individuals can suffer from a sense of grandiosity in respect to personal abilities. This may be to the extent of manifesting mental illness (CC-grand).

D. Withdrawal from Tasks Due to Ineptitude or Sense of Inner Incapacity ***CD***

CD-inept	Judged to be inept by others or by self
CD-mediocre	Mediocre attainment due to inability, not lack of purpose
CD-unable	Inability to initiate or do task
CD-finish	Inability to realize a task that has been started
CD-weak	Feelings of weakness, powerlessness, helplessness
CD-inferior	Sense of inferiority in relation to others

CD-sex	Sexual incapacity or ineptitude
CD-chagrin	Chagrin or a sense of mortification over one's incapacity or lack of mastery
CD-aide	A helpless incapacity to aid or ameliorate the conditions of others
CD-psycho	Psychotic withdrawal due to incapacity to solve problems
CD-belief	Inability to perform or protect due to countering beliefs or convictions
CD-age	Loss of ability due to age

One may be judged by others as being hopelessly inept (CD-inept). These responses are usually double scored with some subcategory under Esteem (E). There may be a feeling of hopeless mediocrity which causes withdrawal from a task (CD-mediocre). There may be an inability to initiate a task (CD-unable). The narrative may describe an incapacity to finish a task that has been initiated (CD-finish). There may be a feeling of weakness, powerlessness, helplessness (CD-weak). There may be an inhibiting sense of comparative inferiority in competitive situations causing withdrawal (CD-inferior). These responses are usually double scored with a Mutual Purpose (M) response. There may be specified forms of sexual incapacity or ineptitude (CD-sex). One's incapacity may be attributed to aging (CD-age).

There may be a sense of mortification or chagrin over a sense of personal incapacity (CD-chagrin). This should be double-scored with an Esteem (E) category. There can be a sensed inner incapacity to aid or ameliorate the conditions of others (CD-aide). Such concerns are most frequently double scored with some negative Nurturance (N) category. There are forms of psychotic withdrawal related to an inner sense of incapacity to solve problems (CD-psycho). There may be an inability to perform resulting from inhibiting belief or convictions (CD-belief).

Distinguishing Between Competence and Other Categories

In scoring manifest content in this category, one must attend to the context in which a concern over competence or failure is perceived. For example, for the Japanese, it is most often a self-oriented expression of dissatisfaction to be remedied by hard work toward successful accomplishment of goal. Such perceptions are double-scored with Achievement (A). If a sense of personal superiority or inferiority is expressed in a competitive peer context, it is double-scored, using one of the Mutual Purpose (M) categories for scoring competition. Success or failure can also be contextualized with expressive concerns over pride or shame related to possible appreciation or depreciation, scored as Esteem (E).

One notices a continuous inter-relatedness of Competence (C) and other scoring categories, but there are essential differences in focus that differ significantly between cultures. This chapter's earlier discussion in respect to the complex interweaving of Competence and other categories should make it apparent why it is helpful to distinguish explicitly between self-oriented concerns with *capacity, purpose*, and *worthiness*. If these are analytically distinguished in the process of scoring the narratives, one can then better see the culturally constituted molecular patterns by which they are interrelated.

Illustrative Samples of Scoring in the Following Chapters

In several of the chapters of volume II we have included actual illustrations of scoring of several of the subcategories included under the [C] category. Especially notable are the verbatim responses found in chapters 1, 2, 6, 7, 8, 11, and 12, volume II.

Notes

Abramson, L.Y., L.B. Alloy, and G.I. Metasky. 1990. The Hopelessness Theory of Depression: Current Status and Future Directions. In Nancy L. Stein, Bennett Leventhal, and Tom Trabasso (Eds.), *Psychological and Biological Approaches to Emotion.* Hillsdale, N.J.: L. Erlbaum Associates.

Adler, Alfred. 1956. *The Individual Psychology of Alfred Adler*. New York: Basic Books.

Bandura, Albert and Richard H. Walters. 1963. *Social Learning and Personality Development.* New York: Holt, Rinehart and Winston.

Benjamin, Jessica. 1995. *Like Subjects, Love Objects: Essays on Recognition and Sexual Difference*. New Haven: Yale University Press.

Brislin, Richard. 1993. *Understanding Culture's Influence on Behavior.* Fort Worth, Tex.: Harcourt Brace Jovanovich College Publishers.

Caudill, William and Helen Weinstein. 1966. Maternal Care and Infant Behavior in Japanese and American Middle-Class Families. In René Konig and Reubin Hill (Eds.), *Yearbook of International Sociological Association.* Switzerland: Broz.

De Vos, George A. 1978. Selective Permeability and Reference Group Sanctioning: Psychocultural Continuities in Role Degradation. In Milton Yinger and Stephen Cutler (Eds.), *Major Social Issues—A Multidisciplinary View* (pp. 9–24). New York: Free Press.

———. 1982. Adaptive Strategies in American Minorities. In E.E. Jones and S. Korchin (Eds.), *Minority Mental Health* (pp. 74–117). New York: Praeger.

———. 1992. *Social Cohesion and Alienation: Minorities in The United States and Japan.* Boulder, Colo.: Westview Press.

———. 1993. The Rites of Pleasure: The Religion, Morality and Aesthetics of Bodily Propriety. In Irma Dosamantes (Ed.), *Body Image in Cultural Context: Interdisciplinary Essays* (pp. 35–63). Los Angeles: DMT Publications.

De Vos, George A. and Marcelo Suárez-Orozco. 1987. Sacrifice and the Experience of the Sacred. *Journal of Psychoanalytic Anthropology*, **10**(1).

———. 1990. *Status Inequality: The Self in Culture*. Newbury Park, Calif.: Sage Publications.

De Vos, George A. and Hiroshi Wagatsuma. 1966. *Japan's Invisible Race: Caste in Culture and Personality*. Berkeley: University of California Press.

Doi, Takeo. 1973. *The Anatomy of Dependency*. Tokyo: Kodansha.

Erikson, Erik H. 1963. *Childhood and Society* (2nd edition). New York: Norton.

Hartmann, Heinz. 1958. *Ego Psychology and the Problem of Adaptation*. New York: International Universities Press.

Hsu, Francis. 1975. *Iemoto: The Heart of Japan*. New York: Halsted Press.

Jordan, David Folk. 1998. Chapter 15. Filial Piety in Taiwan: The Twenty-Four Filial Exemplars. In Walter Slote and George De Vos (Eds.), *Confucianism and the Family in an Interdisciplinary, Comparative Context*. Albany: State University of New York Press.

Maddi, Salvatore R. 1980. *Personality Theories: A Comparative Analysis* (4th edition). Homewood, Ill.: Dorsey Press.

McClelland, David. 1961. *The Achieving Society*. Princeton, N.J.: Van Nostrand.

McClelland, David, with J.W. Atkinson, R.H. Clark, and E.L. Lowelle. 1953. *The Achievement Motive*. New York: Appleton-Century-Crofts.

McClelland, David, with A.L. Baldwin, U. Brofenbrenner, and F.L. Strodtbeck. 1958. *Talent and Society: New Perspectives in the Identification of Talent*. Princeton, N.J.: Van Nostrand.

McClelland, David and G. Friedman. 1952. A Cross-Cultural Study of the Relationship Between Child-Training Practices and Achievement Motivation Appearing in Folktales. In G. Swanson, et al. (Eds.), *Readings in Social Psychology* (pp. 243–249). New York: Holt Rinehart and Winston.

Ogbu, John. 1974. *The Next Generation*. New York: Academic Press.

———. 1978. *Minority Education and Caste: The American System in Cross-Cultural Perspective*. New York: Academic Press.

Piaget, Jean. 1954. *The Construction of Reality in the Child*. New York: Basic Books.

Scheper-Hughes, Nancy. 1979. *Saints, Scholars, and Schizophrenics*. Berkeley: University of California Press.

Seligman, Martin E.P. 1975. *Helplessness: On Depression, Development and Death*. San Francisco, Calif.: Freeman.

Seligman, Martin E.P., L.Y. Abramson, A. Semmel, and C. von Baeyer. 1979. Depressive Attributional Style. *Journal of Abnormal Psychology*, **88**: 242–247.

Seligman, Martin E.P. and S.F. Maier. 1967. Failure to Escape Traumatic Shock. *Journal of Experimental Psychology*, **74**: 1–9.

Slote, Walter and George De Vos (Eds.). 1998. *Confucianism and the Family in an Interdisciplinary, Comparative Context*. Albany: State University of New York Press.

Weiner, Bernard. 1992. *Human Motivation: Metaphors, Theories and Research*. Thousand Oaks, Calif.: Sage Publications.

White, R.W. 1959. Motivation Reconsidered: The Concept of Competence. *Psychological Review*, **66**: 297–333.

———. 1960. Competence and the Psychosexual Stages of Development. In M.R. Jones (Ed.), *Nebraska Symposium on Motivation*. Lincoln, Nebr.: University of Nebraska Press.

———. 1961. Competence and the Psychosexual Stages of Development. In Donald W. Fiske and Salvatore R. Maddi (Eds.), *Functions of Varied Experience*. Homewood, Ill.: Dorsey Press.

———. 1963. Ego and Reality in Psychoanalytic Theory: A Proposal Regarding Independent Ego Energies. *Psychological Issues* Monograph 11. New York: International Universities Press.

Chapter 10

Status Inequality and Patterns of Social Control

The exercise of "power" or "influence" as dominance in a social context, and the subordinate's reaction to that exercise of power, are panhuman instrumental concerns (Dahrendorf, 1969; De Vos, 1966, 1971). To some extent they have their origins in our mammalian and primate ancestry, where dominance hierarchies can be found among both males and females of many species. Yet dominance concerns among humans also reflect psychological developmental processes and social institutional forces. Dominance is exercised over the behavior of others, very often over those in subordinate status positions or over those who for some reason are dependent or vulnerable to influence. The converse of interpersonal power and control, i.e., autonomy and inner "self regulation" are also of pervasive concern, and these can be seen in conscious concerns over the limits of legitimacy regarding the exercise of power. Issues of both control and autonomy have some impact on virtually all instrumental activities that occur in the context of human social relationships. Narrative elements that involve concerns with intentional regulatory control, power, or influence are scored as Control (D) with the Interpersonal Concerns Scoring System (ICSS).

Nietzsche (1923, 1924) in his concept of the superior being (*Ubermensh*) and his concept of a "will" to power, saw social dominance as a basic urge. Nietzsche also dramatized a human struggle to become free of internalized constraints. Similarly, in his "individual psychology," Adler (1956) also emphasized a will to power as a drive central to human development. Adler considered aggressive urges or drives as more important than sexual ones. A power drive can lead to pursuits that maximize self-interest and even to a Machiavellian manipulation of others. Seen in terms of social status, Adler saw this as an urge from "below" to "above."

As this drive is supposed to be manifest in vertical status situations directed toward others, it is a drive to overcome inferiority by gaining dominance or control of others. It also appears in a desire to prevail in situations of mutual competition.

From the developmental perspective, the exercise of control over others, or the submission to such control, can be seen as having a common psychological origin with concerns about mastery or competence. A conceptualization of a "power" drive as *interpersonal* control is also to be distinguished from the *intrapsychic* tensions inherent in a self-reflective sense of volition related to expected standards manifest in socialized achievement, as we have already discussed in chapter 8, volume I. Adler's two conceptions of superiority also recognized this distinction. One form of superiority-seeking is seen in terms of relative interpersonal status. The other form is seen as the seeking of an internally evaluated betterment of one's own self. Adler referred to personal "superiority" such as that achieved by an athlete bettering his own record. Experienced inwardly as an aspect of self will, superiority implies a continuing upward urge toward complexity, aesthetic efforts to be satisfied, and energy directed toward the realization of social or personally defined purpose. When self-directed rather than interpersonal in content, it can instigate unrelenting tensions that seek some actualization in accomplishment. In a negative direction are experiences of an inner sense of lack of will, loss of purpose, or social alienation. Thus superiority, in Adler's sense, also partakes of intrapsychic concerns with achievement (A) and/or relative competence (C). When self-oriented rather than interpersonally involved, the human "will" can lead to a desire for superiority and perfection in achieving *internalized* standards.

As mentioned in chapter 9, volume I, some self-reflexive inner judgments of ability related to Competence (C) or self-confidence, if experienced in a negative direction, can manifest as various concerns over incapacity and inferiority. The negative direction of competence concerns is a diffuse sense of intrapsychic inferiority. In interpersonally oriented theories such as Adler's (1956), a need to control others or to strive toward some self-relevant standard of perfection may be considered in many instances as *compensatory* for the underlying competitive feelings of relative inferiority children feel in comparison with adults. When there is a direct competitive comparison to others, *horizontal* vying replaces a *vertical* sense of relative powerlessness. There evolves the sense of Mutual Competition (M) discussed in detail in chapter 12, volume I.

As touched upon in the previous chapter on Competence (C) and continued in the following chapter on Responsibility (R), we consider how the individual develops both *intrapsychic* problem-solving concerns with what has been termed "mastery,"[19] and a self-reflective capacity for internalized regulatory moral directives in a "conscience" that has the capacity for moral judgment or responsibility. These *intrapsychic* developments are analytically distinguishable from the

---

[19]See especially White (1959, 1961).

forms of *interpersonal* control exercised in the influencing of others in instrumental situations and the forms of subordinate behavior reflected in either compliance with authority or autonomy from external directives.

As is evident from a consideration of this complexity, one cannot rely on the concept of the mammalian "dominance hierarchy" as a straightforward analogy for the Control (D) category of the ICSS. Dominance hierarchies are additionally related to issues of esteem or respectability as well as to issues of access to resources or resource utilization (Henry and Stephens, 1977). Thus the forms of vertical social interaction that occur in dominance hierarchies are more varied than those that are categorized as Control (D). Conscious concerns related to those additional dimensions of vertical social status or "dominance" may be categorized under the Esteem (E) and Nurturance (N) categories.

There are also forms of behavioral regulation related to Affiliative communication (F). This is particularly the case in early development, where the infant and caregiver are engaged in mutual communication that regulates both behavior and physiological arousal (Schore, 1994). Such co-regulation continues into more mature patterns of structured communication and affiliation. Additionally, interpersonal competitive or cooperative behavior categorized under Mutual Purpose (M) may involve some kinds of interpersonal behavioral regulation. However, cooperative or affiliative co-regulations are more "horizontal" and less "vertical" and are not categorized under the Control (D) category. The (D) category of Dominance or Control is limited to vertical considerations of imposed regulatory directives and the acceptance or rejection of those directives by would-be subordinates.

A sense of control is divided between control over material objects and a control over intentional beings. Instrumental concern with control or manipulation shades over into the treatment of living beings, human, flora, or fauna as possessions that give gratification, or as *objects* being moved or manipulated for the realization of one's individual purpose. The pieces on a game board such as chess are called "men," but they contribute no dynamic force of their own, they are moved as inert objects by the players of the game. Under the impersonal category of Objects (O) considered in chapter 13, volume I, we also see that humans can be depersonalized, treated as inert objects, with no consideration of possible intentional behavior on their part. Under the present category of Control (D) we include only forms of control exercised *interactively*. The relationship of control or influence is "interpersonal." For the D category to be relevant for scoring, an expectation of an interactive instrumentally oriented intentional response is required. What is present is either a desire to influence the intentionality of another or to be situated in a subordinate position subject to the external intentional influence of another.

Regardless of whatever possible psychodynamic or other theory-based interpretations one may wish to make, the first step in narrative analysis is to score the *manifest* content of any expressed concern. Thus, for example, we score expressed internal concerns with inferiority under the category of Competence, as discussed in chapter 9, volume I. Only expressed concerns with dominance or control either from a superior or inferior status position are scored under the presently considered Control (D) category. Expressions referring to horizontal instrumental competition are scored under the Mutual Purpose (M) category discussed in chapter 12, volume I, and so forth.

The Contrastive Mechanism and Intentional Control[20]

Developmental Issues

Prior to the elaboration of intentionality one experiences the world with the most primitive differentiations between pleasure and pain, satisfaction and distress, the attractive and the aversive. From early on, however, in the process of developing the capacity to manipulate the world through cognitive adaptations, some form of intentional power is experienced "within" (Piaget, 1927, 1930). One "wills" things to happen, and this can readily include the manipulation of other people as one finds means for inducing desired behavior in others. For example, we may consider that among one's first "commands" are acts of crying to gain desired attention and succor. Subsequently, greater control over skeletal musculature and voluntary locomotion develop.

Too much clinical focus on so-called anal control can deflect attention from the more general issues of muscular control that are involved in psychosexual development in different cultural settings. We discuss this more fully in the context of Japanese motoric socialization (De Vos, 1992, 1993) wherein "willfulness" in a child is perceived differently by Japanese mothers as compared with their American counterparts. The early forms of mental/conceptual control are related to the developing experience of causality externally and motoric control internally. In effect, the expulsive contrastive mechanism is central to the development of analytic cognitive differentiation while allowing a sense of intentional control, both conceptual and motoric, to be retained within the developing self. Projection, from the very beginning as it defensively expels that which threatens from within, at the same time helps the individual develop a separate sense of self in which the experiential locus of control is kept within and focused on a "will to do" motorically.

One experiences "voluntary" control over both one's thoughts and one's muscular or motoric activities. The experience of intentional power and the initial process of thinking itself are not separated. Indeed, much thought can remain inherently "magical." Mastery through thought that moves things externally,

[20]See additional discussion in "Sacrifice and the Experience of Power," chapter 3 of De Vos and Suárez-Orozco (1990).

whether through muscular control or through a magical sense of telekinesis, is an early part of an instrumental intentionality experienced within. Such early thought or other ego-centered activity is experienced as causing things to happen externally. This is well illustrated in Piaget's example (1927, 1930) where a child experiences his walking in the moonlight to influence the changing position of the moon. When the child steps forward the moon moves forward, when the child stops the moon stops.

In its most primitive form, intentionality may manifest as a sense of omnipotence, a sense of control from within, which occurs before self and non-self becomes well separated. Normally, once intentionality is experienced, a general contrastive discriminatory coping mechanism or "ego mechanism" appears, and the experience of inner initiative in the exercise of power is maintained by a contrastive defensive differentiation of inner volition or intention separate from outside force. Throughout its progressive development, this contrastive mechanism becomes intimately related to the dynamic human experience of "voluntary" intentional power exercised interpersonally.

In psychoanalytic terms "splitting" occurs (Summers, 1994; Kernberg, 1975; Volkan, 1981), which separates the self and outside objects contrastively. This splitting is linked to the beginning of contrastive evaluative judgments about a causal world.[21] As intentionality becomes linked with the prior differentiation between the pleasant and the unpleasant, the contrastive mechanism differentiates the experience of intentionality into a world of either satisfactory or unsatisfactory effort. The analytical contrastive mechanism is involved in affective as well as cognitive discrimination. In some instances, a sense of "affective dissonance" is prior to, and in the beginning more salient than, cognitive discrimination, although affect and cognition are inextricable one from the other from the very beginning (De Vos and Suárez-Orozco, 1990). From the beginning of self-awareness, experiences are constantly evaluated and judged as potentially self-enhancing or disparaging, Esteem (E), as well as potentially reinforcing or threatening.

As best possible, intentionality that induces "good-pleasure" is kept within as part of the self, and that which induces "bad-pain" is projected out, to become part of the not-self. Developmentally, there is a tendency for behaviors that "succeed" or produce positive external "controlling" outcomes to be retained as an accepted or acknowledged component of the self system. There are defensive maneuvers or mechanisms by which analytical, contrastive thought throws out the affectively less desirable of two dissonant perceptions and keeps what is more *control-maintaining* and *self-enhancing*. If possible, the person optimally avoids a sense of self that includes excessive identification of the self with negative characteristics such as worthlessness or helplessness, low self-esteem, and/or an ineffective inability to

[21]The discussion of "coping" or "defense" mechanisms is more fully developed in De Vos and Suárez-Orozco's volume on *Status Inequality: The Self in Culture* (1990).

"control" which can be later associated with other depressive symptoms (Seligman, 1975).

Intentional behavior and interpersonal relationships that produce undesirable outcomes may, with varying degrees of success, be excluded or unacknowledged, or ejected from oneself and experienced as intruding from the outside. In the seeking of closeness and distance with outside forces or persons, splitting is used to differentiate between the good or bad in outside forces or persons. One seeks to adhere or stay close to the good and avoid the bad, both within and outside. In normal development this produces a differentiated, realistic self-awareness of one's limitations and the presence of external intentionality that cannot be made subject to the self, yet with which one interacts interpersonally. In some instances, the infant, child, or adult may continue to use defensively some sense of omnipotence or grandiosity to protect the self against an alternative experience of utter helplessness (Adler, 1956; Benjamin, 1988). Alternatively, the primitive defense of projection is used to unrealistically exclude from oneself those aspects of one's own intentionality that have been experienced as excessively dangerous.

To the extent that distance is maintained by projective defenses, the farther out and distinct from self an intentional object is perceived to be, the more apt that object is to be invested with bad projections. Such contrastive and distancing evaluations are very alive within, but may be kept unrecognizable as part of the projecting self which does not see its own isolation as deriving from itself.[22]

The Contrastive Mechanism and Thought

The contrastive mechanism can ultimately lead to the attainment of objective, analytic, logical, sequentially organized thought as a basic (though not exclusive nor necessarily optimal) mode of coping with and controlling the environment. The maturation of the contrastive-expulsive mechanism produces a growing capacity to use thinking (i.e., intentional problem solving) as a means of maintaining internal control as well as assuring an internal locus of control over the external environment.[23] In this line of thought it is unnecessary to posit any new "internal" effectance capacities other than the functioning of basic ego mechanisms in response to the inner experience of power in causal sequences.

---

[22]One must note that not all awareness of good and bad involves splitting and projection. There are in the external social environment actual outside presences and events that are realistically classifiable in social and personal terms as "bad" or "good," and which through their own subjectivity and intentionality may themselves produce an interpersonal distance.

[23]We do not refer here to the specific usage of this term as specified by Rotter's "generalized expectancy for control" (Rotter, 1966), although that work addresses similar concerns with the attributed locus of causality from a social-learning perspective, with its emphasis on expectancies and environmental reinforcement.

As well as enabling appropriately differentiated motoric control, the contrastive mechanism expands control outwardly over both the natural and the social environment through symbolization and the consciously intentional "naming" of objects. In magical thought, to know the name is to control the object.[24] In medicine, "diagnosis" can be confused with explanation.[25] In personality psychology, adjective checklists and their analysis with forms of statistical wizardry (e.g., factor analysis) can take the place of an emic knowledge of human experience or an etiological understanding of the developmental organization of personality dynamics.

In extreme forms, contrastiveness can also become involved in defensive maneuvers termed "intellectualization" or "isolation."[26] In its more mature transformations, the distancing aspect of this mechanism can lead to the attainment of functional objectivity, as well as analytic and logical thought that is abstracted from the self. Where applied appropriately, and with sufficient non-projective sensitivity, this capacity can provide an effective mode of coping with, and ultimately controlling the environment through understanding of causal dynamics. Where applied inappropriately, and from an isolated or emotionally removed distance,[27] it can support forms of destructiveness and exploitation that are at the root of many social and environmental problems.

The mechanism of projection is widely evident cross-culturally; in certain institutionalized forms it comes to characterize culturally patterned belief systems.

---

[24]Robert Graves (1948) in the *White Goddess* writes at length of how the name of the Hebrew god had to be kept secret so that possible enemies could not seize control of "Him."

[25]If the physician can demonstrate nosological skill and identify the syndrome with a category term in Greek or Latin (diagnose) and then apply categorically appropriate treatment, there is a tendency to think its etiology is thereby explained, even where no actual causal understanding has been obtained. This commission of the nominalist fallacy may appease the insurance company and may give comfort to the patient, yet it cannot result in anything more than a magical cure based on empirical correlational experience, without an understanding of causal mechanism. Actually this is a form of what is termed "sympathetic magical control."

[26]The individual is self distanced from internally disruptive affectivity which is disparaged and rejected as causing loss of control. These defensive maneuvers have historically been especially present in middle-class western adolescents (A. Freud, 1937).

[27]Benjamin (1988) has noted that the analysis of language or discourse as the basis for studying intersubjective processes (Habermas, 1970) maintains an excessive degree of distance rather than fostering empathy. Benjamin sees such an analytical movement as an inadequate exploration of the full scope of intersubjectivity, and as a reflection of masculine-gendered tendencies toward analytical autonomy that ultimately support forms of domination, rather than the more feminine affiliative communion. We concur with Benjamin's description of such distancing as a notable deficiency in certain philosophical and scientific traditions, as well as its role in the instrumental exploitation of others that is a widespread feature of human societies. Our efforts to consider the full spectrum of human concerns in emic terms can be seen as an effort to avoid such distancing, yet without losing a desired degree of objectivity.

In some cultures, however, the disciplined use of logical classification into abstract categories is relatively lacking. Its eventual appearance depends on a transformation of earlier forms of contrastiveness into formal forms of analysis, made culturally available in collective representations. In some cultures, where the training of contrastiveness toward analytic forms of coping is relatively lacking, or is not generalized beyond limited domains of application, the disciplined use of logical classification or abstract formal analysis may only rarely be attained or be narrowly applied (Levy-Bruhl, 1923).

Psychodynamic bases for the persistence of earlier projective forms of thought may also be involved in some social settings. For example, in some societies, anxious suspiciousness and a sense of threat may continue to characterize social relations into adulthood. "Paranoid" projection can remain institutionalized in collective representations, and anxious suspiciousness may continue to characterize social relations. Less mature forms of contrastiveness are emphasized in the pre-logical processes which continue to operate within such a society. Schwartz (1975, 1976) described this as being prevalent among certain Melanesian societies of New Guinea.

Contrastiveness and Social Identity

Stein's discussion of how "splitting" is involved with social role formation and role maintenance (Stein, 1986) centers on the concept of "projective identification." As this term is presently used, a projected aspect of the self becomes a set of expectations about what one anticipates or even experiences as coming from a particular "other" (from what can also be termed a "transference object"). This can be seen as an effort to simultaneously disavow and transfer troublesome intra-psychic content while imposing the projection on the other as a form of control. This is a particular danger point recognized in the clinical setting if the therapist or clinician is not careful in handling a counter-transference and instead buys into the projective identification (see Fenichel, 1945; also, Gorkin, 1987).

Projection can produce an "identification" with others because one has attributed to them qualities actually occurring within the self but not experienced as being within. These projected qualities can then be taken back in to the self as if they originated from the outside yet with the added validation of group consensus, as occurs with some forms of group membership. To identify with these group values is also to adhere to the power of the collectivity as "we." This latter use of the introjective mechanism (i.e., to feel similarity with others in what can be seen as a "re-avowing" of the formerly disavowed) is in continual dynamic interaction with the contrastive mechanism that maintains distance from the disavowed (see chapter 2 in De Vos and Suárez-Orozco, 1987, 1990).[28]

There is a difference in cultural atmospheres between cultures that variously emphasize a readiness to the inclusiveness that is involved in the creation of an in-group ("we"). Such social identity processes were the case historically in Polynesia (Levy, 1973). Other societies emphasize the presence of a dangerous "they." Schwartz (1976), for example, describes the "paranoid ethos" of Melanesian societies. In such societies, the "me" is saliently experienced as "different from" others, whether or not the individual achieves a higher level of formal cognitive operations by maintaining a defensive perimeter.

A particular culture can emphasize a style of ego development that expects a member to seek individual mastery and to perceive self-control as an internal process defensively used against others. This brings about emphasis on the salient use of a projective mechanism of defense and its more mature transformations. In emphasizing personal control, a culture also emphasizes problem-solving behavior in which the individual is to become *self-reliant* rather than passively dependent on others or on any outside force to resolve one's problems. Collective security is abjured and individual prowess is emphasized. The individual takes the initiative in an instrumental manipulation of the social as well as material environment. This is the pattern found in "individualistic" social groups such as the Protestant mainstream in North America.

Some early forms of *differential socialization* and experience of unequal status relationships between the sexes within given social atmospheres may be conducive to later experience of conscious social distrust. There may be a close link between forms of gender-based exploitation and the use of contrastive mechanisms although these may not always develop into their more mature forms as abstracted instrumental objectivity. For example, we have described the relative presence of paranoid defenses manifest in a sample of Algerian Arabs (Miner and De Vos, 1960; De Vos and Boyer, 1989). One finds earlier forms of contrastiveness emphasized, even institutionalized, in the pre-logical processes that continue to operate within such a society. In this group there is relatively lesser movement toward the more mature rational objectivity.

Looked at in a modern social framework, highly internalized individuals are at times quite capable of individual rather than collectively adaptive social mobility, succeeding, for example, by abandoning past class or ethnic affiliative ties (De Vos and Suárez-Orozco, 1990, chapter 7). Such individuals do not use the social group attachments as a reference of self-evaluation and are freer to join other groupings in an instrumental or expediential fashion. They can act totally for self-interest

---

[28]Durkheim (1947) did not deal with this process on a psychological level and may have missed this from his sociological perspective.

instrumentally without taking the subjective feelings of self or others into account.[29] In *Social Cohesion and Alienation* (De Vos, 1992, chapter 7), we discuss in further detail how "Anglo" children when compared with Mexican American or Mexican children are less concerned with the feelings of others and more overtly competitive in their contrastive individuality (Madsen, 1967; Madsen and Shapira, 1970). A relative disregard of the consequences of their instrumental activities as they affect others may be observed.

It is in this respect, especially during the adulthood of the individualistic person, that some internal maladjustment may appear as difficulty in establishment of close affiliative relationships, even while the person is able to attain successful occupational adaptations. A competitive, results-oriented social system reinforces abstracted intellectual competence, economic achievement, and the controlling exploitation of the natural world. Yet it may at the same time variously devalue mutual affiliative and inter-subjective receptivity (Benjamin, 1988), the capacity for nurturance and interdependency, the maintenance of social harmony, as well as the more instrumental concerns of mutual purpose and responsibility that otherwise contribute positively to the quality of human relationships and society at large.

Autonomy or Social Compliance: The Subordinate Position

Legitimacy of Power

Discussion of power or social control also includes concern with the adult establishment of some forms of autonomy and self-control as the legitimate response to certain social situations. There are, in every society, regulations for legitimate changes in status from a previous subordinate position to one of further compliance, or to one of self-actualization in autonomous social purpose. This is particularly apparent in definitions of adulthood and the influence of role expectations on interpersonal domination in internal family dynamics and sexual politics, as well as in forms of class and caste-based exploitation. On a worldwide basis over recent decades, social definitions concerning the roles of women within the family or in society have been notably shifting in respect to the autonomy of women throughout the life trajectory. Similarly, the ideological justifications for caste and class discrimination have been weakening. Nevertheless, there remain pervasive forms of gender differentiation, as well as class and caste divisions that are produced by generational continuities in differential socialization and differential social opportunity.

---

[29]For a cogent discussion of the developmental and psychodynamic origins of a capacity for the self-interested exploitation of others, and for the failure to "recognize" the other's subjectivity, see Benjamin (1988).

Human liberation from domination is a perpetual process that involves overcoming structural mechanisms at the social level, psychological mechanisms at the psycho-cultural level, and physiological mechanisms at the biological level.[30] At the social level, societies have regulatory mechanisms that are based on what is held sacred in both religious and secular terms. The "sacred," whether religious or secular, may be defined as laws received from a divinity, or set down as regulations within a legal system. Societies also delegate power toward assuring the desired conformity. Individuals are placed in socially legitimized positions of superordinate authority, and are designated as having legitimate power to exercise towards the maintenance of order within both religious and secular regulatory systems. Some form of legitimate "heteronomy" (i.e., being subject to the law or authority of another), is found in all societies (see the DS categories discussed below in this chapter).

The exercise of authority over another is socially defined in both positive and negative terms. The exercise of such superordinate authority can involve the use of punitive sanctions to assure enforcement. Compliance by a subordinate, whether adult or juvenile, is expected in response to the *proper* exercise of authority. However, any improper dominance or excessive use of authority is negatively defined in different societies in different ways, as is any improper form of rebellious resistance.

At the psychological level, there is also a consideration of a potential for self-empowerment to overcome inappropriate domination. There are proper or improper assertions of "autonomy" or self-regulation. Socially or personally legitimated seeking of autonomy must be distinguished from what are viewed emically as inappropriate forms of disobedience or rebellion.

There are also circumstances in which individuals consciously seek out some external authority to regulate them, even where such regulation is not immediately

---

[30]As noted in the first paragraph of this chapter, structured systems of dominance and control are not solely produced by "human" patterns of exploitation. They are not structured by social and cultural processes alone. They exist not only among humans, but also on a widespread basis in other animal species, where their existence cannot be attributed to social or cultural "construction." Such widespread or pan-specific patterns can be most effectively explained by reference to developmental-biological, primarily neuro-endocrine or bio-behavioral processes (Henry and Stephens, 1977). It would be a major omission for the social sciences to not acknowledge such essential processes as they function to determine behavior in the human animal. The recognition that such biological determiners may be either incorporated into and even overwritten by sociocultural and psychological processes does not obviate the need to understand their functioning at the biological level. For, in the absence of substantial change at the genetic level, such biological determiners are perennial. They return anew with each generation, and must be addressed through socialization processes in each generation. An applied ideology that fails to fully comprehend and (in an informed manner) address underlying bio-behavioral processes cannot accomplish any lasting liberation from biologically structured forms of domination.

imposed from outside. Some individuals seeking to attain a sense of belonging may submit themselves temporarily or permanently to a leader or belief system that gives them regulation. Erich Fromm (1968), in his volume *Escape from Freedom*, discusses such a sequence of "anomy" or lack of inner regulation and identity diffusion experienced in Germans prior to the Nazi "ethnic affirmation" of Adolph Hitler. This sought-for submission to external authority is sometimes deemed necessary because a sense of inner regulation is found to be relatively missing in situations of general social anomy.

The Price of Gendered Autonomy and Isolation

What is sometimes characteristic of individualistic societies that emphasize personal autonomy at the expense of legitimate social regulation is that there is less emphasis on binding affinities (see the F category) or concern with the maintenance of social cohesion collectively (see the H category). That is to say, there is less positive maturation in the sense of being part of, as well as being different from others. Expressive needs for social harmony, togetherness, or interdependency are denied or diverted from consideration in an emphasis on self-oriented instrumental goals. However, one notes that in most societies a well-balanced socialized self is continually experiencing how it is related to the others in a social environment both vertically and horizontally, as well as experiencing a satisfactory sense of autonomy in social affairs.

As should be clear from many discussions in this present volume, we are congenial with the ideas expressed in Benjamin's feminist critique of the hegemony of instrumentally focused autonomy in modern society that exists at the expense of nurturant and affiliative modes of human interaction. We are also congenial with much of Benjamin's analysis of the psychodynamic origins of dominance and social inequality. Benjamin and other feminist theorists who have addressed the psychodynamic origins of dominance have traced it (in part) to the gender-differentiated socialization that occurs when male figures are not involved in nurturant care. As Benjamin sees it, the absence of male nurturance has forced males toward an excessive autonomy, as they seek to differentiate themselves psychically from the mother and identify with the father. As a potential method for addressing this problem, Chodorow (1978) and others have advocated an increased involvement of fathers in nurturant roles. For our part, we concur with the idea that a healthy human being is capable of both analytic autonomy from the regulatory pressures of the impinging stimulus field while also being capable of affiliative closeness that is not a submissive merging but a mutual recognition or interactive validation of the subjectivity and intentionality of the other.[31]

Bly (1990), Moore and Gillette (1990), and others (whom one might call "masculinist" theorists) have also recommended the adoption of more emotionally well-rounded (including nurturant), less emotionally immature, and less isolated roles for older males. Where masculinist theorists emphasize the importance of male nurturance and increased sensitivity to others, they may overlook the critical importance of infancy and early childhood as the optimal time for the intervention of paternal nurturance, opting instead to emphasize male mentoring of the young adult (as in apprenticeships). To some extent this is a legitimate reaction to the pervasiveness of institutionalized female mentoring from infancy through the elementary school years. The study of Japanese society, however, where nuturant male mentoring continues to play an important role, reveals that post-pubescent mentoring is not a cure-all that produces a non-exploitative and non-sexist society (see below, this chapter). Instead, it produces a society where the initial dependence of males on a dominant and possibly manipulative (though also nurturant) mother is translated for the adult male into a continued dependence on a dominant and possibly exploitative (though also nurturant) male mentor. This is then converted into an instrumental expectation of future dominance of the self over subsequent generations in a continuity of the vertical mentorship role. This is an example that illustrates that at least some kinds of male nurturance can coexist with continued vertical age-graded and sexist status differentials in a society.[32]

The Developmental Patterning of Authority and Autonomy

Active exercise of interpersonal dominance is transmuted from earlier passive experiences of being controlled within the family and appears as various forms of permanent status inequality. In humans, the relatively helpless infant or child continues to submit to dominance to maintain security and avoid fear of annihilation. Control or power is first experienced in a vertical interpersonal context as an

[31]In Benjamin's usage: "Recognition is that response from the other which makes meaningful the feelings, intentions, and actions of the self. It allows the self to realize its agency and authorship in a tangible way. But such recognition can only come from an other whom we, in turn, recognize as a person in his or her own right" (1988, p. 12).

[32]See also the discussion in chapter 2, volume I. An idealization of human development that would expect male nurturance alone to free us from the bonds of our primate ancestry and from the continuation of hierarchical systems of social organization would be naive. In the explanation of status relationships, one must also not neglect the legacy of our phylogeny that remains in the differential reproductive strategies of males and females and in sex-linked (though not necessarily gender-linked) differences in social-behavioral predispositions.

exercise of will from a dependent subordinate position (the DS categories below).[33] One's own intentionality or willful behavior comes in conflict with the intentionality of more powerful beings than oneself. One's behavior becomes adaptively "socialized," as it is progressively guided in accord with the expectations of parental or other disciplinary figures (including supernatural ones) who exercise continuous social or personal dominance.

A sense of inequality or inferiority as usually discussed in the context of psychological coping mechanisms, can appear very early in self-development. As the young infant first comes to experience instrumental intentionality or "power" in the increasing control exercised over the body and its motility, this is the beginning of a need for "autonomy" as well as personal mastery. With further maturation, concerns with mastery and individually selected purposeful behavior becomes more self-oriented eventuating into concerns that we have categorized as Competence (C). Concerns with authority, the exercise of power or dominance over another person, is to be distinguished from "mastery" as a self-oriented sense of power in excising successful resolution of a problem that we discussed in respect to our category of Competence. It is also to be distinguished from the "control over the world" that supports individual instrumental purposes such as those required for Achievement (A). These may involve a sense of "control" over a medium of expression or production rather than being directed into interpersonal domination.

In vertical relationships one must distinguish between a simple need for power and a desire to use influence to assist others. There may be a necessity to double score Control (D) and Nurturance (N).[34] There are Japanese stories, for example, in which the informant expresses, more or less openly, how nurture is used to influence the desired behavior of children, as well as conversely, how a position of authority allows one to take care of subordinates to their own benefit. Control is often experienced in the relatively benign affectively expressive vertical context of *nurture* and care and the awarding of security and contentment. One's own instrumental "willful" behavior is modified in accord with these expressive needs.

In some societies there can be a continuing interrelationship between the concerns we have categorized as expressive and instrumental. The nurturing person may have instrumentalized the giving of nurture or care as a means of maintaining control over a previously dependent child into adulthood as has been very evident in examining some Japanese mother–child relationships. What is also apparent in some Japanese social contexts in fantasy, if not always in reality, is that the

---

[33]See chapter 3 of De Vos and Suárez-Orozco (1990).

[34]McClelland and his associates (1987) do not distinguish in their scoring categories what we categorize under *Nurturance*, namely succorant needs of controlling figures (whether parents or civil authorities) to bestow care on others. They tend to subsume any stated desire to assist others or protect them as an expression of the power motive or a fear related to power. For example, see Veroff's discussion of the power motive (Smith, 1992, chapter 5, volume II). See also Benjamin (1988, 1995).

individual seeks to achieve instrumental dominance in order to exercise an expressive need for bestowing nurture on others in the form of benevolence. Conversely, as is indicated in the Japanese concept of "*amae*," an individual in a subordinate position can instrumentalize a subordinate role in such a way that he or she manipulates the expressive behavior of a superior so as to gain one's own purpose.

With psychosocial development there is increasing capacity for self-reliance in purposefully directed behavior. Constraints on behavior are decreasingly a question of immature capacities. Constraints on behavior and thought are due to forms of established social dominance that characterize different societies, as well as forms of internalized directives that occur in all human socialization [see the discussion of Responsibility (R) and self-control, below]. Complex societies are maintained in relative equilibrium with various forms of coercively reinforced status inequality as well as forms of internalized self-control governing behavior among adults related to economic-ecological and political situations.

Personal autonomy or self-regulation comes to be expected as attainable in given relationships. With changes of proper occupational or marital status come expected transcendence of some previous vertically defined relationships in family or community. In some societies, such as those of North America, to reach what is considered adulthood implies a basic equalization of former vertically defined sub-adult relationships. The gaining of a certain competence with adequate training can move one from a subordinate status as an "apprentice" to one of being a "master," on par with other masters, now superordinate to those still located in the position of apprentice. In strongly age-graded societies such as those of a Confucian tradition, there is continuing verticality related to age disparity throughout the life span, regardless of professional or occupational competence. Societies also differ widely in the degree or situations of relative gender parity defined in role expectations. Control is also defined in collective terms as exercised between socially defined subgroups in societies organized on the basis of class, caste, or gender. There are experiences of collective dominance or submission that are more or less acceptable to those participating.

Double scoring with an expressive category may be necessary. For example, one circumstance in which a change in relative status is sought is when there is experienced a need for greater empowerment of one's group (DSA-assert) to overcome present or past humiliation (ESC-group) (see the chapter on Esteem). Narratives in which dominance and humiliation are coupled have to be double scored. A concern with reputation can often be more related to social Esteem than to power.

There may be expressed an attempt to overcome (DSA-assert) a sense of collective vulnerability or weakness (CD-weak) in ethnic relationships with expressed hatred or resentment (HB-resent) over previous domination, which must be scored in its complexity.

We now will turn to consider some features of social control cross-culturally related to concepts of legitimate authority and control not usually considered in

American society. We will now discuss the vertical relationships of authority and deference that are operative in an essentially vertically organized society, in which age grading is a central feature defining unequal status. We draw on some of the author's previous writing about Japan for illustration (see especially De Vos, 1972, 1992; Lee and De Vos, 1981).

Age, Status, and Control in Confucian Societies

Age Grading and Future-Oriented Optimism

Social optimism about an upward change of status can be engendered in a cohesive age-graded social system. In considering authority and social status among adults, contemporary American society has not worked out a comfortable distinction between temporary vertical relationships that are found in age grading and status differences of a more permanent nature found in class or other social distinctions. Present-day Western societies in their efforts at democratization are progressively attempting to do away with concepts of seniority among adults, regardless of age. In the United States, this effort can be socially disruptive. It has sometimes been extended to a consideration of "children's rights" as something to enforce legally, especially should parents be considered too authoritarian.

In contrast, even in modern Indian, Chinese, Korean, or Japanese families there remains much emphasis on deference behavior related to age-graded offices which helps reinforce social interdependence and cohesion in family and community. Such deference behavior causes less conscious social resentment than that required by socially alienating class or ethnic differences. It is difficult for a contemporary American, looking at social hierarchy in a Confucian society, to understand the emotions attached to age grading and its complex relationship to both instrumental mastery on the one hand or expressive dependency on the other. For Americans, deference behavior readily demeans the individualistically oriented person. It is interpreted as submissiveness and possible weakness of character, or even a form of deviousness. It would seldom be considered, as with the Japanese, in a future time framework wherein non-demeaning patience is informed by an optimistic consideration of future possibilities of mastery by assuming the mentality of an apprentice.

A dependent relationship in Japan may be perceived positively as instrumental, as well as satisfying an expressive need for dependency. The age grading system moves one through an ideal life trajectory of a dependent childhood, a dependent period of learning as apprentice or bride, then assumption of positions of control in the middle years either within a family or an occupation, then a reversion to a more dependent old age, while inhabiting a position of high esteem and guaranteed status in old age. This ideal is not necessarily realized, and there are psychological prices paid in attempting its realization. For example, there may be personal problems well discussed by Doi (1973), that result from the over practice of *amae*, a manipulative form of dependency first directed toward parents by children, and later directed toward superiors by subordinates.[35]

Note that dependency for Japanese does not lead to any general social passivity, but may be related in some instances to vigorous social striving and occupational success (Vogel, 1963; De Vos, 1972). Nor are dependency and deference congruent concepts. Dependency refers to the continuing receptive need for gratification from someone in a position to bestow benefits; deference is an expression of respect, even reverence to someone superior in status. It may be totally instrumental or simply formal in other instances.

To properly understand age grading, one must examine more fully the concept of self-development in traditional Confucian education, whether it is that of an artisan apprentice, a would-be artist, or scholar. An anticipation of future power is the heart of the concept of apprenticeship in Japan as elsewhere (De Vos, 1975). Theodor Reik (1941), analyzing "moral masochism," provides an excellent description of the mentality of the apprentice, who by submission gains eventual mastery. One doesn't submit to comply, one submits to gain power. The sense of endurance itself may become pleasurable in enhancing an internal sense of "being able to take it," furthering the anticipation of one's future goals. "Patience" is not passive in nature; rather the individual is already actively engaged in a future purpose.

Patience in this context can be seen as an instrumental virtue, not experienced as demeaning to those who practice it. Instead it is recognized as a legitimate deferment of future goals. When one is conscious of inner capacities despite the tribulations of the moment, there is self-assurance that the proper energy will be there to realize one's goals at a future time. Things are going to change for the better if one can hold on and endure.

In the Japanese past, the apprentice worked very hard for little pay. In the past, a male apprentice worked up to fourteen hours without any right to complain. Maids were their female counterparts. Young girls were in this sense apprenticed to learn domestic duties in a higher status household. A complainer, male or female, would be sent home in disgrace, where the family would berate the "failure." An apprentice knew if he worked hard enough he could even have a "*Noren waké*," a symbolic splitting of the cloth designed with a house emblem that was strung across the doorway of a traditional establishment. The boss would "split" functions with him, making him a branch or a subsidiary master, or if he was quite successful, he might even marry the boss's daughter. The maid knew her subordinate learning from someone in higher status would enhance her own future marriage possibilities.

---

[35]We shall not enter into the more clinical topic of the problems that result from this continuing manipulative dependency among Japanese. There is a lack of development of a sense of a truly separate, unattached self that causes various forms of continuing malaise, and often interferes with rapport or companionship in marital relations.

In such a system of thought, one is tempering oneself to overcome future obstacles. The moral muscles are being exercised to strengthen oneself to triumph over future competition. Carrying daily burdens on one's back strengthens the spirit, even if the body is worn down sacrificially in service to a future cause. The traditional Japanese made a virtue of endurance (Wagatsuma and De Vos, 1984). Young men practiced endurance in their professions; young women inside the family. The young male office worker was in no better status than was the young bride. Even today, in entering a company at the bottom or in becoming an apprentice, one must submit to a system, and anticipate being rewarded only with time. Subsequent to World War II, there were developed wage scales and a work-week of about forty-five hours, officially. But often one was required to work overtime. The young man either as a worker or a member of management was still required to work very hard for relatively little pay. Wage labor has eroded this tradition in Japan, without completely doing away with the concept of age grading in modern industry.

Apprenticeship is almost totally a thing of the past in American society. There is an insistence on being paid equally for work, regardless of age. There tends to be an "all or none" in American systems of thought. All authority may be bad, especially any rule by an elderly gerontocracy. We should not have to wait to be gratified. Let us push aside those who are "Old and in the way." Everything must be leveled to bring about equality. Verticality in any form is bad. Everything has to be leveled and made more equal because equality is good.

Yet this ideological commitment to equality belies the actuality that American society is also strongly affected by class, caste (in this case racial), and gender-based exploitation and discrimination. The superficial ideology may constitute a massive denial of the reality of domination and the escape from domination that actually underlies the pathological anti-dependency and individualism of the American psyche. Benjamin has cogently discussed the origins of domination in an incapacity to tolerate the paradox that is required to achieve the mutual recognition of inter-subjectivity. To be able to afford recognition of the other's subjectivity one must relinquish one's own infantile omnipotence. But that runs up against the counter-vailing fear of dependency and the potential annihilation of the self in subjugation. In an escape from dependency, one moves back toward omnipotence, which becomes the autonomy and refusal of intersubjectivity that is so characteristic of American culture. Or one can resort to a self-subjugation in acquiescence, as an attempt to extract recognition from the other. At the social level, this unfortunately then manifests as a perpetuation of domination, on the part of both the dominant and the subordinate. In our society this is also gender-linked (Benjamin, 1988, 1995).

In contrast to the American pattern, in age-graded societies, hierarchy based on age can be reassuring, for one knows that with patience the automatic fact of aging will eventually accord respect and status. There is no such assurance accorded the aging individual in American society. On the contrary, one faces the problem of Willie Loman in Arthur Miller's American tragedy, *Death of a Salesman* (1949).

At some future time, one can expect to be dispensed with when no longer useful. This implicit message becomes explicit when one looks at sports as a profession. One is rewarded during the period of peak success, but is quickly discarded when injuries or infirmities make the individual no longer useful.

Age-Grading, Gender, and Role Complementarity[36]

There has been substantial concern with the need to address gender differences in the West. There is recognition about the past withholding of equal respect and opportunities for instrumental power in American society, when full adulthood was not granted women. For many in the West, the leveling of differences and the establishment of status equality between the sexes imply that one must establish a congruence of behavior, including a lack of continuing complementarity in family roles. In contrast, in Asian societies, although women now increasingly insist on greater economic parity as well as parity of respect, they are not as insistent on congruity in social roles within the family as are their American counterparts. They may still espouse some role complementarity. They do not tend to see a woman's role in the home as relatively powerless as do many American women.

To understand this difference, one must note how the age grading of women's roles is formally structured in patriarchal Asian societies. As discussed by Cho (1998), women could mitigate their feelings of powerlessness or a sense of inferior status while young. By exercising patience, a younger woman could later achieve the domestic power she saw exercised by older women. Women in Japan or in Korea sensed how with time one eventually moved into a higher status as a mother. Both husband and sons made her a provider for continuing dependency needs. A woman desiring control learned how to manipulate such dependency for her own purposes. In this Asian framework, role complementarity does not preclude the existence of an arena in which women could also exercise control and avoid an internal experience of subordination.

In sum, in considering hierarchy instrumentally in a Confucian social context, one must understand that ideally, at least, the system is not permanently demeaning to those in lower positions. The optimistic inner religious message of neo-Confucianism is one of age-graded instrumental self-development through the better exercise of one's social role. Expressively considered, rather than emphasizing success through changing status, the message points toward achieving personal purposeful satisfaction through self-improvement. Within the family, therefore, the mother does not try to compete with the role of father because it is seen as a higher role. The goal, instead is to become the mother of an instrumentally successful man

[36]See the discussion in "Caste, Race and Gender: A Psycho-Cultural Approach to Awe, Purity and Pollution," chapter 5 of De Vos and Suárez-Orozco (1990).

or men, which then becomes a basis for her own power, both vicariously and even directly as the success is reflected in family wealth and status.

Problematic Experiences of the Legitimacy of Authority in Minority Groups

Koreans in Japan: Disparagement Rather Than Acceptance Within a Confucian Hierarchy

To be a Korean in Japan is to come in conflict with the well-defined system of social hierarchy operative in Japanese society in which only majority Japanese are truly accepted, however lowly the position. Koreans remain placed "outside" and are subordinated and demeaned without any compensatory reward of anticipated upward change of status. Koreans are not brought in to "belong." They are not treated in a positive sense with the paternalistic care under which many Japanese are willing to be subordinated. They have no sustaining hope to be paid for their allegiance in the future. Since the emotional gratification that makes power or control relationships tolerable is not forthcoming, Koreans can only resent subordination. Exercise of dominance and submission between Japanese and Koreans remains strictly instrumental, with none of the emotional lubrication that reduces friction. It is harder for the Koreans to tolerate subordinate status and to view the Japanese as exercising legitimate authority with constraint and concern for the subordinate. They feel much more put-upon. Koreans tend to be very sensitive to the negative aspects of social control in their interpersonal relationships. They are not apt to create illusions of gratitude for benevolence received. Government or personal authority is perceived as exercised for the benefit of those in power rather than for benevolent purposes.

However, Koreans remain patriarchal Confucianists within their own families. It is their Confucian conscience that makes them *vulnerable* to degradation by Japanese! They see Japanese as exemplars of what they should be. Given their inability to actualize their responsible roles due to economic duress and despised status, some begin to consider themselves incapable and unworthy. Korean men expect to exercise Confucianist paternal authority. They avow male dominance in the family as part of the value of family life. Compared with Japanese, however, their authority is in doubt, and more apt to be reinforced by physical punishment.

Also, by and large, in regards to obligation and responsibility, Korean women allocated to lower social status are less concerned with maintaining family position through the seemingly submissive role behavior expected of middle-class Japanese women. We note that Korean women in Japan are less long-suffering and less constrained by submissive role behavior than are Japanese women. Although seen ideally as dutiful and responsible, they are also perceived as capable of aggressive even violent remonstration.

Expected role behavior differs with status among Japanese women; for example, as described in chapter 4, volume II, women from a fishing village were less constrained toward their husbands than were women from a farming village that prided itself on *samurai* ancestry (De Vos and Wagatsuma, 1961). In general, however, Japanese women traditionally practiced deferential behavior in fulfillment of the wifely social role.

Our case-history material would seem to suggest that the use of physical punishment for control of children by both parents is more accepted among Koreans in Japan than among Japanese. This impression gathered by hearsay has not been systematically documented. Although in our previous intensive family studies in Tokyo, we found instances among lower-class Japanese of the use of physical punishment, we could not characterize it as normative to employ physical punishment as discipline. As reported to us, lower status Koreans are more given to the exercise of physical force between husband and wife and between parent and child. In some respects, it seems to be a defensive act by one who is socially insecure.

Koreans in Japan are more prone to direct expressions of aggressive attitudes, and their actual comportment contributes to their being perceived by Japanese as more aggressive in their interpersonal relationships. In general, they are more accustomed socially to seeing expressions of aggression and are less upset by such behavior than are majority Japanese. They do not feel that the direct expression of aggression in language or comportment results in an irrevocable breach in a relationship, as do many Japanese.

For some Koreans, therefore, the exercise of power entails a capacity to enforce one's will by physical force if necessary. Korean children in school are also more likely to assert themselves against their Japanese peers. They can more readily intimidate. This difference in aggressive comportment may be historically related to differences in class origins. The Korean migration to Japan comprised mostly illiterate, impoverished rural groups who would have been less likely to practice forms of refinement in disputes. Koreans, finding themselves in a subordinate status, do not typically use long-range, devious, submissive tactics. They are more apt to lose patience, letting superiors know directly their true feelings or attitudes. This sometimes contributes to a confrontational atmosphere that disconcerts Japanese. To summarize, Koreans are more apt to see themselves as seeking autonomy than to express loyalty. They are more apt to be perceived by Japanese as aggressive, if not insubordinate.

Relative Indices of Delinquency and Crime Among Japans' Burakumin as a Reflection of Their Attitudes Toward Official Authority

Members of the Kobe family court, when interviewed in 1962, suggested that although the Burakumin outcaste group is a small minority of the population of Kobe city, they do indeed comprise a disproportionate number of cases of both family problems and delinquency coming before the court (De Vos and Wagatsuma, 1966). There is also court evidence from Kobe, as well as in Kyoto, that Burakumin inspire fear in the rest of the population. A number of Buraku children were brought before the court for intimidating peers; sometimes for demanding money or other property from children frequently a good deal older than themselves. Sometimes all a child has to do is to say that he comes from Bancho (a fairly large outcaste district) and the children threatened will turn out their pockets for him.

In some Buraku at least, community control seems to deflect delinquent activities outside the Buraku community. It was widely agreed by our informants that violence, acts of stealing, or other forms of antisocial behavior rarely take place within the outcaste community itself. Although children will be verbally aggressive toward one another, if physical aggression seems to be in the offing, an adult will quickly step in to make peace.

The Burakumin do not support outside authority should a child be accused of delinquent behavior. They stand behind and support the child against the authorities. What is important, seemingly, is that the children obey their parents rather than show any allegiance to the outside. When children are put on probation, they are usually put under the supervision of a voluntary "supervisor" within their own community. But since Buraku children do not indulge in delinquent activities within their own community, the *hōgōshi* (voluntary probation helper) actually does very little in the way of supervision and seems not to be active in preventing the individual adolescent from committing delinquent acts elsewhere. The recidivism rate is disproportionately high for Buraku children on probation.

The community is not at all supportive of court decisions to place a child in a correctional institution. When children have been committed to such an institution there have been hostile demonstrations at the court building and appeals to put the child on probation instead so that he does not have to leave the community.

A general attitude of hostility is directed toward the buildings that house the prefectural offices, police, and court. These institutions represent for the Burakumin the hated legal authority of the majority society, but also, in the case of the prefectural office, the place where the family registers are kept—the records which tie them to their Buraku social identity.

The police are the focus for considerable criticism. Policemen, it is implicitly understood, can only marry with the permission of a superior officer, which is given only after a careful scrutiny of the girl's family background. When the police were brought up in conversation, informants would often recall instances of policemen being refused permission to marry Buraku girls they were in love with because of the girl's "unfavorable" background.

A criminal career is one available for "passing." *Yakuza*, the generic name now used for the organized underworld, draw into their ranks youth who can contribute talent to their organizations.[37] If a Buraku youth is successful in becoming a member of a criminal gang or *yakuza* group, his outcaste background is discreetly forgotten. Therefore, the Buraku youth may feel more readily accepted in this career activity than in attempting to face the more overt discrimination that occurs in other occupational pursuits. In the same manner, Buraku women who become entertainers, bar girls, or prostitutes find it an easy way to pass and to remove themselves from the Buraku community.

Categories of Control

We turn now to a description of the categories of the ICSS that are used to score narrative concerns with issues of control. This category as we use it bears some resemblance to n-power used by McClelland and his associates (Veroff, 1958). However, our category is not concerned only with behavior as a "need" to dominate. Rather, it is focused on the relative salience of concerns about the exercise of authority as well as any desire to dominate or win over or influence others in less clearly defined status situations, as well as the converse concerns with submission, compliance, autonomy, rebelliousness, etc. Additionally, in this category we further distinguish between concerns that reflect the perspectives of superordinate and subordinate narrative protagonists.

From the Superordinate or Influential Position

A. *Positive Control, Compliance, or Autonomy* ***DDA***

DDA-control	Legitimate power, authority including family control
DDA-scold	Parental scolding, disapproval, censure
DDA-punish	Parental punishment
DDA-reject	Rejection of family membership as punishment
DDA-group	Group or peer pressure
DDA-lead	Lead or seek to influence peers (score with MVA)

[37]See our extensive discussion of the history of Japanese organized crime in De Vos and Mizushima (1967, pp. 289–325).

DDA-educate	Educational directives, or supervisory control
DDA-advice	Advice or persuasion (either peer or authority); mentorship
DDA-author	Exercise of proper civil authority or interdiction
DDA-police	Punitive community authority or surveillance
DDA-censure	Censure or disapproval from authorities
DDA-pardon	Pardon, absolution tolerance, or approval
DDA-mediate	Intervention or mediation in an authority context
DDA-trust	Put trust in or delegate to a subordinate
DDA-patient	Be patient or understanding with a subordinate
DDA-give	Instrumental giving used positively
DDA-free	Permission for another to assume autonomy
DDA-gambit	Instrumental sacrifice to induce behavior
DDA-curse	Supernatural punishment by legitimate authority
DDA-create	Creative act used to influence others
DDA-model	Influence others by serving as role model

Positive control or dominance includes all benign, legitimate exercise of authority, persuasion or guidance to achieve legitimate socially approved individual and collective purposes. Throughout, exercise of authority is defined as legitimate when it is for socially approved instrumental purposes and not for the expression of personal hostility or dislike.

Positively considered family control can include enforcement of proper behavior when necessary (DDA-control). Cautionary scolding can occur (DDA-scold). Punishment is not only condoned but expected as a responsibility of those who are considered maternal or paternal authorities (DDA-punish). Some punishment can even result in rejection of family or group membership inflicted on someone as deserved (DDA-reject). Such punishment can include expulsion from a home.

In some societies there are recognized forms of peer group control exercised over individual members including those participating in voluntary organizations or operating in business ventures (DDA-group).

The converse is also true; a peer may seek to influence, persuade, or convince a peer or colleagues on a course of action (DDA-lead). There is desire for a peer to become a leader or a person of influence over others. There are various forms of advice or persuasion exercised in social interaction that give successful direction to instrumental behavior. Such advice or persuasion reflecting a desire to control can be exercised from a peer. The emphasis could be either on a common goal, or simply the need for personal influence itself. There are stories involving leadership in collectively perceived goals that must be noted in considering possible double scoring with the Mutual Purpose (M) categories of cooperation. When a common goal is stressed persuasion has to be double scored as an act of mutual instrumental cooperation (see MTA-task below). There can be innovative or creative behavior that influences others (DDA-create). There may be behavior of an exemplary nature that is done so as to become a role model for others (DDA-model).

Educational directives or supervisory control are a proper vertical role. Societies have special educational institutions or delegated individuals that exercise authority over individuals in training. However, a mother or father can also assume an educational role (DDA-educate).

There are various forms of advice or persuasion exercised in social interaction that give successful direction to instrumental behavior. Advice from a position of authority is recognized and expected (DDA-advice). Such advice or persuasion reflecting a desire to control can be exercised from either peer or authority positions.

If there is a mutual argument in which the emphasis is not only on having influence for its own sake, but also on winning a competitively conceived argument, the response should be double scored. For example, there are various competitive situations in which one outwits an opponent or wins (MVA-smart), has a sense of inferiority, ineptitude, or being flawed (e.g., CD-inferior, CD-inept, CC-inept, CC-tragic, etc.) or is personally frustrated (MVB-anger). When actual personal animosity or discord arises one must double score (HC-discord) the discordant relationship.

Civil officials exercise various forms of positive authority directing behavior (DDA-author). There are various legal institutions, courts, or police who are involved in what are considered proper methods of punishment to be inflicted on errant individuals (DDA-police). There are various forms of disapproval or censorship considered socially proper (DDA-censure).

There are acts of pardon or absolution possible through which a proper authority, religious or secular, releases an individual from the consequences of past behavior (DDA-pardon). One can intervene or act as a mediator from a position of authority (DDA-mediate).

One can put trust in or delegate to a subordinate (DDA-trust). An authority can exercise patience when dealing with a subordinate (DDA-patient).

There are institutional forms of reward, or forms of giving used to induce proper behavior on the part of a group member (DDA-give). There are acts of an authority which sanction the autonomy sought by a subordinate (DDA-free).

There are even examples of sacrificial behavior on the part of an authority to induce proper behavior in subordinates. One dramatic example of this occurred at the end of World War II in which an envoy of the emperor committed suicide in front of rebellious troops to force them to obey the emperor's order to surrender. In a religious context, the sacrifice of Christ is considered to be a means of inducing good behavior in Christian believers (DDA-gambit). There is, in some religious contexts, belief in the proper punishing capacity of a supernatural force using a curse as ultimate authority (DDA-curse).

B. *Unresolved Legitimacy or Uncertainty About Authority* ***DDB***

DDB-result	Doubting consequences of authority to others
DDB-torn	Ambivalent about assuming authority
DDB-worry	Worry about how to exercise authority
DDB-rigid	Uncertain about rigidity in enforcing regulations
DDB-free	Uncertain or insecure over autonomy of another
DDB-licit	Ambiguity or the legitimacy of one's actions
DDB-order	Fear of chaos or disorder; a need for social control
DDB-jealousy	Jealous about one's authority
DDB-example	Fear of influence of one's past or present behavior as negative example
DDB-patient	Unresolved patience or understanding with subordinate

From the standpoint of a superordinate position one can express uncertainty about the consequences of one's acts in regard to others (DDB-result). One can express ambivalence over the necessity to exercise authority (DDB-torn). One can worry about how to exercise authority (DDB-worry). One can be uncertain about one's rigidity in enforcing regulations (DDB-rigid). One may be highly uncertain about allowing autonomous behavior on the part of a subordinate or former subordinate (DDB-free). From the standpoint of being in a superordinate position one can be uncertain about the legitimacy of one's position (DDB-licit). There may be fear of chaos or disorder or a need for social control (DDB-order). There are expressions of jealousy about one's authority (DDB-jealousy). One might become concerned that one's behavior may influence another by setting a bad example (DDB-example). One may be unresolved about exercising the proper patience or understanding with a subordinate (DDB-patient).

C. *Negative or Illicit Control or Resistance* ***DDC***

DDC-unfair	Unfairness or discriminatory authority
DDC-press	Undue pressure, or punishment
DDC-rigid	Undue inflexibility or rigidity in enforcing control
DDC-despot	Undue dominance or the exercise of power for its own sake (political or religious)
DDC-exploit	Exploitation of vulnerability
DDC-corrupt	Corrupt authorities
DDC-punish	Overexertion of punishment or destructiveness
DDC-result	Negative consequence to others (may be due to poor judgment)

DDC-capture	Capture of another person
DDC-manage	Manipulative control
DDC-give	Manipulative giving, or reward-inducing behavior
DDC-provoke	Provocative teasing
DDC-suicide	Threat or act of injury, suicide against subordinate
DDC-watch	Undue surveillance spying (police, etc.)
DDC-magic	Exercise magical control over another

Negatively perceived, superordinate behavior includes irrational or oppressive forms of dominance so as to instrumentally achieve one's own intentions at the expense of others. There may be unfair or discriminatory forms of authority (DDC-unfair). There are various forms of undue pressure to gain acquiescence (DDC-press). There may be perceived undue inflexibility or rigidity in enforcing control or unduly rigid or inflexible in responding to particular circumstances (DDC-rigid).

The most frequent form of negatively considered pressure is an exercise of an authoritarian dominance, which can include excessive forms of religious authority (DDC-despot). There are specific occasions in which an individual in a dominant position exploitatively takes undue advantage of another's vulnerability (DDC-exploit). There are depicted in some narratives, venal and corrupt forms of behavior by authorities (DDC-corrupt).

There can be overassertion through hostile, punitive measures, or destructive behavior including teasing or disdainful arrogance (DDC-punish). (Double score such material with an Esteem category, e.g., EDC-disdain or EDC-sarcasm.)

Some behavior by authorities is inadequate, and due to poor judgment can result in harm to subordinates or to others (DDC-result).

One can make instrumental or expressive use of another person by capturing, kidnaping, or other illegitimate forced captivity or another person (DDC-capture). There may be a variety of additional purposes for such an act of control, and these need to also be scored. For example, a kidnaping for ransom is an instrumental criminal act (DDC-capture AC-crime). An attempt to physically possess a captive may be for the expressive purpose of forcing one's affection upon another (DDC-capture FC-impose).

There can be evident a manipulative control of another (DDC-manage). Sometimes the manipulation is done through some form of inappropriate use of giving or rewarding to obtain desired behavior (DDC-give). In hierarchical societies, bestowing charity on others may be a means of control as well as potentially an act of debasement of others while enhancing one's own socially dominant position. Some rulers claim benevolent motives, but it remains obvious that their need for power most often remains paramount in motivating their seemingly giving behavior. These acts can be double scored with some *Nurturant* category (e.g., NDA-reward). One can use actual self injury, or the threat of self-injury, or suicide to force behavioral compliance (DDC-suicide).

There may be depicted undue surveillance or spying, police intrusions, etc. (DDC-watch). One can even be seen as exercising magical control over another (DDC-magic).

D. Excessive Passivity in Exercising Control ***DDD***

DDD-lax	Lax and too indulgent in training role; lack of proper supervision
DDD-neglect	Irresponsibility or neglect
DDD-inept	Inept or ineffective exercise of power
DDD-weak	Failure to punish others when expected
DDD-helpless	Failure to respond to rebellion, or a sense of helplessness about attack by subordinates
DDD-deluded	Paranoid delusions in respect to subordinates

There can be various forms of superordinate behavior that exhibit undue passivity. One can be too lax or too indulgent in exercising a training role, or lack proper supervision (DDD-lax). There are situations of irresponsibility or neglect (DDD-neglect). There are failures to assert proper authority, or a feckless inability to act when expected (DDD-inept). One views numerous such situations evident in American schools where authorities are unable to exercise proper discipline. There can be an inability to properly punish when expected (DDD-weak). There can also be a helpless passivity in the face of rebellion or some undue attack from subordinates (DDD-helpless). There are examples of highly anxious, paranoid delusional systems held against subordinates (DDD-deluded).

From the Superordinate or Autonomous Position

A. Positive Compliance or Exertion of Autonomy ***DSA***

DSA-permit	Asks permission of authority
DSA-assert	Autonomy or self-assertion from authority, family, peer pressure
DSA-mutiny	Overthrow of despotic authority
DSA-free	Escape from a status discrimination or from wrong scolding or punishment (family or authority)
DSA-free-s	Self-liberation; freeing self from excessive self-control or super-ego
DSA-comply	Proper compliance to family authority
DSA-author	Compliance conform with legitimate authority

DSA-trust	Trust in authority or superior
DSA-soothe	Supplication acts to please another
DSA-forgive	Supplicating forgiveness
DSA-appease	Instrumental donation or propitiation
DSA-persuade	Induced positive action by authority due to subordinate's persuasion or instigation
DSA-disobey	Disobedience as ultimate respect for authority
DSA-god	Belief in being subject to divine control
DSA-ritual	Ritual of supplication of the supernatural
DSA-prayer	Use of prayer

Seen from the perspective of a superordinate position, there are various forms of institutionally recognized control or dominance in society. From the standpoint of a subordinate position, control seen positively includes both respectful compliance as well as proper concerns with autonomy or resistance to tyranny.

Individuals may seek proper permission to follow their intentions (DSA-permit). There are various categories of behavior related to a proper realization of autonomy from improper or no longer appropriate forms of dominance whether by family or peers or civil authorities (DSA-assert). There can be legitimately perceived mutiny against unjust authority (DSA-mutiny). Positive self-assertion can be expressed as escape from status discrimination or wrongful subordination, scolding, punishment of one's family or outside authority (DSA-free). There are also forms of self-liberation that involve freeing oneself from excessive self-control or super-ego (DSA-free-s).

Viewed from the subordinate perspective, there are normative forms of compliance to family (DSA-comply) which in some cultural contexts can involve the subordination of mother to father. Individuals are subject to civil authority and comply to social authority (DSA-author). One can consciously put trust in authority (DSA-trust). There is the use of supplication or propitiation of a potentially punishing secular authority (DSA-soothe). There are situations where one seeks forgiveness for previous acts that displeased an authority (DSA-forgive). Appeasement may be practiced to undue previous activities or to instrumentally gain a more positive consideration of an authority (DSA-appease).

Subordinates can persuade those in dominant positions to do what they desire to happen (DSA-persuade). Japanese in subordinate positions, for example, have learned to behave in such a manner as to cause an authority to do what one wishes. This is called "*amaeru.*" We have termed such behavior "instrumental dependency" (De Vos, 1973, p. 49). If expressed positively, these are scored as DSA.

There are curious circumstances in which disobedience, technically perceived, is actually an act of ultimate obedience to the good maintenance of an authority or family head. Confucianism recognizes some such acts as expression of filial piety.

Some forms of civil disobedience can be viewed as acts that maintain proper civil government (DSA-disobey).

One may feel subject to divine control or religious force. In a religious context, suffice it to state here, few humans ever overcome some forms of inner constraint related to a more powerful supernatural (DSA-god). Religious practices are replete with forms of sacrifice and placation of supernatural power which can be perceived to be not only expressive of love or awe, but instrumental acts guaranteeing continuing well-being while avoiding the potential wrath of powerful beings. If there is an expressive sense of awe and admiration involved in compliance to a superior one must consider double scoring with another Control category [e.g., such as fear of punishment (DSB-punish) and the Esteem category (EDA-awe)]. Or, if there is a sense of gratitude for bestowal received, one can double score with Nurturance category (NSA-grateful).

Religious rituals of supplication to appease the supernatural may be described in narratives (DSA-ritual). Prayer is considered a form of supplication (DSA-prayer).

B. *Unresolved Legitimacy or Uncertainty About Authority* ***DSB***

DSB-punish	Fear of punishment by authority
DSB-torn	Ambivalent about legitimacy of authority
DSB-rebel	Concern with legitimacy of rebellion
DSB-obey	Reluctant obedience
DSB-ignore	Ignore or disregard authority
DSB-control	Uncertain of how to overcome dominance
DSB-advice	Uncertain about advice or guidance
DSB-pardon	Concerns with pardon or absolution
DSB-envy	Envy of the greater influence of another
DSB-approve	Need for approval
DSB-god	Awaiting God's judgment

From the perspective of a subordinate, there may be an abiding fear of punishment (DSB-punish). There may be uncertainty or ambivalence about the legitimacy of authority (DSB-torn). One may depict doubt about the legitimacy or appropriateness of an act or rebellion or disobedience (DSB-rebel).

There may be felt a chronic reluctance to obey (DSB-obey). There may be an unresolved ignoring or disregard of authority (DSB-ignore). One may express an uncertainty of how to overcome the dominance of another (DSB-control). There may be an uncertainty about the appropriateness or effectiveness of advice or guidance received (DSB-advice). There may be a chronic concern with receiving proper pardon or absolution for previous behavior (DSB-pardon). One may come to envy the greater influence or authority of another person and wish to ascend to his or her position. One may express an unresolved need for approval from an authority (DSB-approve). One may depict waiting for God's judgment (DSB-god).

C. Illicit Resistance or Manipulation ***DSC***

DSC-accuse	False accusations against a superior or authority
DSC-disobey	Defiant, self willed, lacking proper humility
DSC-family	Resistance or rebel against family authority
DSC-resist	Resist or rebel against tutoring or social authority
DSC-escape	Escape from family, jail; violation of interdiction
DSC-rude	Rude, disrespectful behavior
DSC-tantrum	Emotional blackmail (temper tantrums)
DSC-seduce	Seductive or "*amaeru*" behavior to influence others
DSC-manage	Manipulative to avoid any control
DSC-amaeru	Submissive to either gain instrumental goals or gain expressive gratification
DSC-give	Manipulative giving to please controller
DSC-injury	Injury to self to induce action of a superior

False accusations can be lodged against one's superior or some legitimate authority (DSC-accuse). Negatively viewed, subordinates may attempt both unwarranted hostile rebellion or contrariness or excessive compliance or submission. Many acts can be viewed as disobedience on the part of subadults (DSC-disobey). Acts of rebellion can be seen as specifically inappropriate in some instances when they are directed against the family (DSC-family). In other instances they are directed against what is perceived to be proper authority (DSC-resist). Breaking out of jail, resisting proper medical treatment, or evading any act of punishment is usually viewed negatively (DSC-escape).

One can evidence rude, disrespectful behavior (DSC-rude). There are forms of emotional blackmail ranging from temper tantrums to other forms of histrionic behavior (DSC-tantrum). There can be seductive behavior to influence decisions (DSC-seduce). There can be evident a manipulative control of another (DDC-manage). Amaeru is a form of dependent behavior to gain either instrumental goals or expressive gratification. There are any number of active manipulations of behavior on the part of subordinates. There can be submissiveness or acts of dependency to evoke attitudes of giving and protection in others. One can be submissive to gain either instrumental goals or expressive gratification. All of these can be categorized as (DSC-amaeru) if there is an expression indicating a non-legitimate manipulation.

These can involve instrumental generosity, giving, or doing unexpected positive acts from the subordinate position (DSC-give). There can be acts of actual or threatened injury to self or suicide (DSC-injury).

In any instance where an individual is seen as acting improperly in reaction to neglectful or otherwise inappropriate supervision on the part of an authority, such behavior can be double scored with reference also to the type of inappropriate action of the superordinate individual.

D. Excessive Passivity or Submissiveness ***DSD***

DSD-family	Excessive submission to family control
DSD-submit	Excessive submission to social authority
DSD-peer	Excessive submission to peer group
DSD-captive	Remain captive to a person or to a system of external or ideological control
DSD-fawning	Excessive fawning, obsequiousness, to gain instrumental ends

There are various forms of excessive obsequiousness or abject behavior in acts of submission. They may be abject behavior in respect to family control (DSD-family). There are various forms of excessive obsequiousness to civil authorities (DSD-submit). There are various forms of excessive obsequiousness to one's peer group (DSD-peer). Some individuals make themselves captive to the dominance of another, or remain dominated by a system of thought to which they do not rationally subscribe yet to which they behaviorally acquiesce (DSD-captive).

Excessive submission, fawning, or obsequious behavior can be for instrumental purposes, such as career advancement, eventual dominance, competitive gain, etc. (DSD-fawning). Acts of excessive submission may be specified as related to expressive needs for nurture, affiliation, sexual gratification, or some form of evaluative enhancement. When specified, these acts of submission can be double scored.

The Blending of Instrumental Controls with Expressive Motivations or Expressive Reactions

Punishment, as a sanction, has both instrumental and expressive aspects. Societies, social groups, and families differ in respect to favored means of punishment and in respect to those most feared by given individuals. Insofar as it is simply a function of legitimate authority, punishment is generally seen as a form of legitimate Control (D). As such, it may be seen as corrective and without negative emotional intent. When so considered the instrumental concerns may be paramount and it is classifiable simply under the category of Control (D). Among Japanese, however, physical punishment of children is more often conceived of as an outlet for unnecessary *violence* than it is in the United States. It is hard for them to conceive of punishment as being without some expressive component. Thus, as it is expressed in narratives, the need to establish or maintain control over others through punishment often goes beyond simple instrumental purpose, suggesting additional expressive motives that can be indicated by double scoring.

Punishment to insure desired behavior can take various forms related to the expressive state engendered in either the individual who is doing the punishing or the individual who is receiving the threat of punishment or its actual exercise. In the expressive behavior categories we note that there is destructive intent under some of the negative interpersonal concerns related to withholding (Nurture N), *rejection* (Affiliation F), and the *humiliation* (Esteem E) of others. Being punished by *isolation* (Affiliation F) or *deprivation* (Nurture N), also usually involves the arousal of negative discordant feelings. Various forms of passive *resentment* (Harmony H) can be scored under the (H) category whether or not there is mention of retributive intentions.

Punishment can be physical or mental, and can involve the intent to harm or injure in a variety of ways. In the expressive categories we note that destructive intent is scored under some of the expressive categories of negative interpersonal concerns. A threat of discord or injury in punitive acts is double scored with discord or violence (Harmony H). Where the emphasis is put on causing displeasure or suffering, it can be double scored as a negative Pleasure (P) category. Sanctioning by ostracism or isolation is another possible measure taken against children or adults. The individual incurs a form of negative Affiliation (F) or isolation which can be double scored. There may be a violence component as well and various forms of passive resentment that can be double scored with negative forms of Harmony (H). The destructive aim may be the debasement of specific individuals, where measures may even be deliberately taken to punish by some form of institutionalized or ceremonious ritual degradation. This can be double scored with some form of negative Esteem (E). Finally, there are various forms of deprivation and withholding which can be deliberately applied as a means of behavioral control (double score with Nurturance, N) (e.g., NDC-comfort). These potential expressive components of punishment are only scored, however, when they are visible in the manifest content of a response.

When such expressive responses are manifest, one might want to speculate further as to their possible meaning, but one must resist scoring beyond the manifest content. For example, the derogation of another may be compensatory in purpose, as an attempt to overcome a sense of one's own inferiority. It may be a response to a previously experienced degradation of a social, physical, or mental nature that has made one feel unacceptable to others. An irrational need for hostile, destructive dominance may stem from a past sense of material or emotional deprivation. Sadistic dominance and masochistic compliance may indicate elements of hostility, or they may indicate problems with ontological validation. Yet for the purpose of scoring and documenting the presence of narrative themes with the ICSS categories, one should record only what is expressed emically, not what is interpreted etically from the outside.

Illustrative Samples of Scoring in the Following Chapters

In several of the chapters of volume II we have included actual illustrations of scoring of several of the subcategories included under the (D) category. Especially notable are the verbatim responses found in chapters 2, 3, 5, 7, 11, and 12, volume II.

Notes

Adler, Alfred. 1956. *The Individual Psychology of Alfred Adler*. New York: Basic Books.

Benjamin, Jessica. 1988. *The Bonds of Love: Psychoanalysis, Feminism, and the Problem of Domination*. New York: Pantheon Books.

———. 1995. *Like Subjects, Love Objects: Essays on Recognition and Sexual Difference*. New Haven: Yale University Press.

Bly, Robert. 1990. *Iron John: A Book About Men*. Reading, Mass.: Addison-Wesley.

Cho, Haejoang. 1998. Male Dominance and Mother Power: The Two Sides of Confucian Patriarchy in Korea. In Walter Slote and George De Vos (Eds.), *Confucianism and the Family in an Interdisciplinary, Comparative Context*. Albany: State University of New York Press.

Chodorow, Nancy. 1978. *The Reproduction of Mothering: Psychoanalysis and the Sociology of Gender*. Berkeley, Calf.: University of California Press.

Dahrendorf, Ralf. 1969. On the Origin of Inequality Among Men. In Andre Beteille (Ed.), *Social Inequality*. Baltimore: Penguin Books.

De Vos, George A. 1966. Conflict, Dominance and Exploitation in Human Systems of Social Segregation: Some Theoretical Perspectives for Study of Personality and Culture. In A.V.S. de Reuck and Ruth Porter (Eds.), *Ciba Foundation Symposium on Transcultural Psychiatry*. London: Churchill.

———. 1971. Conflict, Dominance and Exploitation. In Nevitt Sanford and Craig Comstock (Eds.), *Sanctions for Evil*. San Francisco: Jossey-Bass.

———. 1972. Social Stratification and Ethnic Pluralism: An Overview from the Perspective of Psychological Anthropology. *Race*, April.

———. 1973. *Socialization for Achievement: Essays on the Cultural Psychology of the Japanese*. Berkeley: University of California Press.

———. 1975. Affective Dissonance in Primary Socialization: Implications for a Theory of Incest Avoidance. *Ethos* (Summer), **3**(2).

———. 1992. *Social Cohesion and Alienation: Minorities in the United States and Japan*. Boulder, Colo.: Westview Press.

———. 1993. The Rites of Pleasure: The Religion, Morality and Aesthetics of Bodily Propriety. In Irma Dosamantes (Ed.), *Body Image in Cultural Context: Interdisciplinary Essays* (pp. 35–63). Los Angeles: DMT Publications.

De Vos, George A. and L. Bryce Boyer. 1989. *Symbolic Analysis Cross-Culturally: The Rorschach Test.* Berkeley: University of California Press.

De Vos, George A. and Keiichi Mizushima. 1967. Organization and Social Function of Japanese Gangs. In Ronald Philip Dore (Ed.), *Aspects of Social Change in Modern Japan* (pp. 289–325). Princeton University Press.

De Vos, George A. and Marcelo Suárez-Orozco. 1987. Sacrifice and the Experience of the Sacred. *Journal of Psychoanalytic Anthropology*, **10**(1).

———. 1990. *Status Inequality: The Self in Culture*. Newbury Park, Calif.: Sage Publications.

De Vos, George A. and Hiroshi Wagatsuma. 1961. Value Attitudes Toward Role Behavior of Women in Two Japanese Villages. *American Anthropologist*, **63**(6): 1204–1230.

———. 1966. *Japan's Invisible Race: Caste in Culture and Personality.* Berkeley: University of California Press.

Doi, Takeo. 1973. *The Anatomy of Dependency*. Tokyo: Kodansha.

Durkheim, Emile. 1947. *The Elementary Forms of the Religious Life.* Trans. J.W. Swain. Glencoe, Ill.: The Free Press.

Fenichel, Otto. 1945. *The Psychoanalytic Theory of the Neurosis*. New York: W. W. Norton.

Freud, Anna. 1937. *The Ego and Mechanisms of Defense*. London: Hogarth Press.

Fromm, Eric. 1968. *Escape from Freedom*. New York: Avon Books.

Gorkin, Michael. 1987. *The Uses of Countertransference*. Northvale, N.J.: Jason Aronson.

Graves, Robert. 1948. *The White Goddess: A Historical Grammar of Poetic Myth*. New York: Creative Age Press.

Habermas, J. 1970. A Theory of Communicative Competence. In H.P. Dreitzel (Ed.), *Recent Sociology* (no. 2). New York: Macmillan.

Henry, James P. and P.M. Stephens. 1977. *Stress, Health and the Social Environment: A Sociobiological Approach to Medicine.* New York: Springer-Verlag.

Kernberg, Otto. 1975. *Borderline Conditions and Pathological Narcissism.* New York: Jason Aronson.

Lee, Changsoo and George A. De Vos. 1981. *Koreans in Japan: Ethnic Conflict and Accommodation.* Berkeley: University of California Press.

Levy, Robert I. 1973. *Tahitians: Mind and Experience in the Society Islands.* Chicago and London: University of Chicago Press.

Levy-Bruhl, Lucien. 1923. *Primitive Mentality.* Boston: Beacon Press.

Madsen, M.C. 1967. Cooperative and Competitive Motivation of Children in Three Mexican Subcultures. *Psychological Reports*, **20**: 1307–1320.

Madsen, M.C. and A. Shapira. 1970. Cooperative and Competitive Behavior of Urban Afro-American, Anglo Americans, Mexican Americans and Mexican Village Children. *Developmental Psychology*, **3**: 16–20.

McClelland, David. 1987. *Human Motivation*. New York: Cambridge University Press.

Miller, Arthur. 1949. *Death of a Salesman*. New York: Viking Press.

Miner, Horace and George De Vos. 1960. *Oasis and Casbah: Algerian Culture and Personality in Change*. Anthropology Papers. University of Michigan Museum of Anthropology No. 15.

Moore, Robert and Douglas Gillette. 1990. *King, Warrior, Magician Lover: Rediscovering the Archetypes of the Mature Masculine*. New York: HarperCollins.

Nietzsche, Fredrick. 1923. *Genealogy of Morals.* Trans. H.B. Samuel. London: Kegan Paul.

———. 1924. *The Will to Power to Power* (2 vol.). Trans. A.M. Ludovici. London: MacMillan, Ltd.

Piaget, Jean. 1927. *La Causalite physique chez l'enfant*. Paris: Alcan.

———. 1930. *The Child's Conception of Physical Causality*. London: Kegan Paul, Trench, Trubner & Co. Ltd.

Reik, Theodor. 1941. *Masochism in Modern Man*. New York: Farrar and Rinehart.

Rotter, J.B. 1966. Generalized Expectancies for Internal and External Control of Reinforcement. *Psychological Monographs: General and Applied*, **80** (1, Whole No. 609).

Schore, Allan N. 1994. *Affect Regulation and the Origin of the Self: The Neurobiology of Emotional Development*. Hillsdale, N.J.: Erlbaum.

Schwartz, Theodore. 1975. Cultural Totemism: Ethnic Identity Primitive and Modern. In George De Vos and Lola Romanucci-Ross (Eds.), *Ethnic Identity: Cultural Continuities and Change*. Palo Alto, Calif.: Mayfield Publishing Co.

———. 1976. The Cargo Cult: A Melanesian Type-Response to Change. In George De Vos (Ed.), *Responses to Change: Society, Culture and Personality*. New York: D. Van Nostrand Company.

Seligman, Martin E.P. 1975. *Helplessness: On Depression, Development and Death*. San Francisco, Calif.: Freeman.

Smith, Charles P. 1992. *Motivation and Personality: Handbook of Thematic Content Analysis*. Cambridge and New York: Cambridge University Press.

Stein, Howard. 1986. Social Role and Unconscious Complementarity. In George A. De Vos (Ed.), Insight and Symbol: Dimensions of Analysis in Psychoanalytic Anthropology. *Journal of Psychoanalytic Anthropology*, **9**(3).

Summers, Frank. 1994. *Object Relations Theories and Psychopathology: A Comprehensive Text*. Hillsdale, N.J.: The Analytic Press.

Veroff, J. 1958. A Scoring Manual for the Power Motive. In J.W. Atkinson (Ed.), *Motives in Fantasy, Action, and Society* (pp. 219–233). Princeton, N.J.: D.Van Nostrand.

Vogel, Ezra. 1963. *Japan's New Middle Class*. Berkeley: University of California Press.

Volkan, Vamik. 1981. Transference and Countertransference: An Examination from the Point of View of Internalized Object Relations. In S. Tuttman, C. Kaye, and M. Zimmerman (Eds), *Object and Self: A Developmental Approach* (pp. 429–451). New York: International Universities Press.

Wagatsuma, Hiroshi and George A. De Vos. 1984. *Heritage of Endurance: Family Patterns and Delinquency Formation in Urban Japan*. Berkeley: University of California Press.

White, R.W. 1959. Motivation Reconsidered: The Concept of Competence. *Psychological Review*, **66**: 297–333.

———. 1961. Competence and the Psychosexual Stages of Development. In Donald W. Fiske and Salvatore R. Maddi (Eds.), *Functions of Varied Experience*. Homewood, Ill.: Dorsey Press.

Chapter 11

Responsibility: Human Potentials for Guilt

The (R) category, Responsibility, seen developmentally, is related to the appearance in childhood of what has been defined in religious or moral terms as a "conscience." This human capacity transcends simpler mammalian forms of intragroup constraint. The internalization of standards as the basis of moral restraint and self-regulation in childhood has been studied extensively in Psychology (Power and Manire, 1992; Turiel, 1998). In psychoanalytic models of the human personality this is conceptualized as "superego" (Schafer, 1968).

Responsibility involves the internalization of control and the experience of the exercise of power discussed in the previous chapters. Subjectively experienced, tensions over possible punishment governing goal-directed behavior become a positive experience of meeting obligations, or a negative experience of transgressing what have become internalized moral standards. In Durkheimian terms, the individual experiences "internalized social constraint." In psychoanalytic terms, humans develop a "superego" that shifts feelings of being externally controlled by coercive reinforcement or punishment into self-regulatory control that is aided by feelings of guilt and the supervisory presence of a potentially self-punishing internal psychological agency. As the individual considers present transgression, this arouses memories of previous experiences of guilt related to previous transgressions. This serves internally as an aversive stimulus that leads one to avoid further consideration of personally unacceptable behavior, thereby producing a form of peremptory internal punishment.

This internally structured conscience or "superego" is part of the human capacity to anticipate the future consequences of behavior. Humans, in their well-developed forebrain, have gained a capacity to exist projectively both forward and backward in a temporal dimension. They can understand causality both temporally and spatially, not only in respect to interactive laws of nature but as participants in a social environment peopled by intentional beings who live in accordance to "natural" laws. The world itself can even be experienced as a "moral" world, wherein the "natural" laws that regulate the behavior of even putatively non-intentional entities such as the planets and stars are seen as somehow originating from a divine plan, with both benevolent and punitive purpose.

Hobbes (1924) was incorrect in generalizing that only the imposition of dominant force can keep human societies together. Systems based too directly or exclusively on force are inherently unstable. Societies built upon domination may persist for some time, but do so at a great economic and social expense, as well as by sacrificing the empowerment and psychological well-being of their people. In contrast, the achievement of relatively stable forms of social and cultural continuity is built on the establishment of moral authority and inner self-regulation. The presence of some degree of more or less satisfactory internalization among a significant number of people is also necessary for social stability, and this pattern does appear periodically in human history.

As noted in the previous chapter, internalized constraint by itself is usually insufficient for the maintenance of social order. External force or group sanctioning must also be continually available as an option to keep potentially destructive deviants better in line with social expectations. External forms of control are supported but not entirely supplanted by internalized knowledge of consequences, not only by memories of being punished but also by memories of having been capable of destructiveness aimed at others. In an interpersonal world, intentional, purposeful behavior has social consequences that are culturally defined in positive and negative terms, as either "good" or "bad." As noted throughout the present scoring system, interpersonal behavior usually is experientially classifiable as constructive, or positive; or, defined negatively, as socially or personally undesirable or destructive.

All normal human beings have the capacity to internalize an anticipatory evaluation of the consequences of intended behavior. Behavior can be judged as potentially leading to future negative sanctions applied by others, or as leading to the possible future experience of discomfort within. On this basis, intended behavior can be subject to anticipatory control before action takes place. The capacity to exercise punitive self-judgment, internally, is essential to the development of a "superego" or "conscience." The socialization of this anticipatory self-sanctioning mechanism utilizes a capacity to internalize knowledge of culturally patterned social responses to negative consequences. Behavior can also be judged ex post facto, when there is a later awareness of previously unanticipated consequences. When one does not comply with positive social directives, or when one performs delinquent or profligate social acts, "guilt" can then ensue. A sense of painful "remorse" can also follow.

As an internalized sense of responsibility develops, there is less conscious focus on one's simply being externally controlled by social directives. The tensions over fulfillment of social directives become increasingly independent of any immediately obvious outer pressures. The regulation of behavior becomes less consciously a question of compliance or resistance. Instead, a sense of positive and internal acceptance of responsibility guides one's own goal-oriented instrumental behavior, as it is directed in accord with the maintenance of approved social standards. If, on the other hand, one considers or initiates socially disapproved behavior, one's sense of internalized constraint is alerted by an awareness of "moral" consequences and potential guilt.

Socially and culturally supported categorizations as to what types of behavior constitute moral transgressions about which one should feel guilt differ substantially from society to society, and are commonly based in local religious as well as economic belief systems. Nevertheless, both forms of transgression, whether social or religious, are not necessarily scored as being primarily forms of negative responsibility. For, although the potential for experiencing guilt among its members is one of the mechanisms that fosters stability and continuity in human societies generally, moral belief systems serve a variety of other psychological functions. For purposes of scoring, negatively defined behavior (or "sins") may sometimes be better considered under a number of the other Interpersonal Concerns Scoring System (ICSS) categories, depending on the interpersonal considerations involved (see also chapter 14, volume I).

A neurotic or rigidified sense of guilt, such as an "overly punitive superego," as is examined in studies of psychopathology, is not the primary topic of discussion here. Instead, the focus in this category is on responsibility in the control of socially relevant causality or consequence, and not on any immediate affective state related to it. What we score with this category are narrative depictions of behavior that explicitly focus on an *awareness of responsibility* with respect to either social or personal consequences. The category of Responsibility (R) is used to score all narrative content wherein the focus is directly placed on an internalized sense of social obligations (i.e., duty or responsibility relative to behavior that *should* be done or *should* be avoided). The category is used to score all morality-focused considerations of "duty" or obligations in the performance of social roles as well as the negative states resulting from any active transgressions or any avoidance of expected duties.

Some form of guilt appears among socially responsible individuals in all cultures, although the contents of the experience and the contexts for its arousal vary widely. In considering moral behavior, duty, or obligation, one must consider it in its specific social context as it is produced through the emic experience of the informant. One must initially refrain from superimposing one's own moral standards as a basis for deciding whether any particular content reflects good or bad as is seen emically in the local sociocultural context of the informant. To illustrate the variability of socialcultural contexts of internalized responsibility, we will draw on our previous writings on Japanese culture (De Vos, 1960a, 1960b, 1970, 1973, 1986a, 1986b, 1992, 1993a, 1993b). As we shall presently illustrate, in the case of the Japanese, guilt can result from educational or occupational failure. Such failure is experienced more or less unconsciously, as a transgression that "hurts" the immediate social group, which has come to symbolically represent the nurturant and loving parent.

Duty and Responsibility: The Confucian Heritage in Japan

According to Dore (1965), between 40 percent and 50 percent of all Japanese boys and perhaps 15 percent of girls were already receiving formal education outside their homes by the time of the restoration of direct imperial rule in 1868. Not only was it the samurai who were educated, but those with sufficient means among the merchants or wealthy farmers would seek to provide education for their children, both girls and boys. It must be noted that what was available before 1868 was not any system of free or compulsory education. Voluntary education often involved some *nurturant* sacrifice on the part of the parents to provide a much-desired development of their children.

Boys were trained to develop self-motivated achievement toward excellence in a vocation. In addition to literacy, girls acquired the social graces that would make them more socially acceptable [see chapter 6, volume I, on Esteem (E)]. They were to be turned into socially desirable spouses with possibilities of marrying up in the status hierarchy. According to Dore (1965, 102), the notion of individual *self-improvement* was widely diffused. By the late Tokugawa period, in the 1800s, education was already established as a means to both social mobility through personal achievement as well as a means of realizing Confucianist moral concepts of self-development. Espoused by Meiji reformers after 1867, notions of already existent personal responsibility contributing to national self-improvement had prior common support when promulgated as part of essential school learning.

In the past, Confucian teachings afforded samurai their code for political leadership. Ideally it was not simply considered as a means of gratifying a need for power, but as a code defining how one fulfilled a social duty.

With the Meiji restoration of 1868 there was a diffusion of Confucianist thought into the total populace. There were explicit moral teachings in Confucianism that became part of the training of the children of merchants and farmers in primary schools. This was brought about by the establishment of universal education based upon Confucianist concepts newly interpreted in a familistic-nationalist framework. Education intensified the diffusion of the samurai ethic, not only through the merchants and townsmen, but also throughout the rural population.

In the Confucian tradition, politics was not to be the art of the possible, the choice of lesser evils, or the achievement of democratic compromise between conflicting interests. A good policy was one which could *benefit* everyone (see chapter 4, volume I, on Nurture and Care). Confucian government policy after 1868, as espoused by neo-Confucianist scholars, was not to be based on the political philosophy of a less complex hierarchical society in which political conflicts of interest existed between the producing ruled and consuming rulers. Enlightened government consisted in the kind of harmony brought about by nurturant benevolence that would enable the existing rulers to enhance the general contentment for the benefit of all (Dore, 1965, 118).

Loyalty toward superiors was to be cultivated. This loyalty was not simple obedience to a controlling *authority*, but an active moral anticipation of what would benefit one's superior. (There were many stories in the popular Confucian literature to exemplify heroic individuals dedicated to family or ruler.) A truly developed loyal person would seek out the ultimate benefit of the master rather than immediately gratifying any command. If need be, individuals might go against a superior's wishes, when, in their deep judgment, obeying immediate commands would be detrimental to any ultimate loyalty and ultimate well-being.

The downward diffusion of the Confucian ethic had a profound effect on Japanese family life that has lasted to the present day (De Vos, 1998). One cannot understand Japanese family dynamics without some reference to these educational influences. The rigid four-class structure was broken by the abolition of the samurai as a separate class. Yet, the universal education given to both boys and girls has remained directly based on samurai neo-Confucianist loyalty and responsibility, and has further espoused an age-graded sense of purposeful endurance toward the realization of instrumental goals of achievement with a continuing emphasis on hierarchy within the family roles.

As a cultural continuity, it had been the samurai, especially the samurai women, who had deeply internalized the Confucian ethic in respect to duty. The conception of woman's nature in the samurai class was one that stressed their capacity for self-control (R) and their capacity to maintain and enhance family honor and esteem (E). The entering bride was to be trained with necessary severity to this end through the authority (D) of her mother-in-law and other elder women. This attitude toward women, while it emphasizes the subordination to men, also sees women as truly capable of personal pride and self-control. It was not psychologically disempowering nor vilifying of women. This attitude is far different from the suspicious or distrustful attitude toward the moral integrity of women that marked some western Judeo-Christian and Islamic traditions, especially in the circum-Mediterranean area.

The Meiji Imperial Rescript on Education was an important document that explicitly made Confucian thought central to the moral education that was to guide the national polity. It was a sacred guide to be revered as laying down the religious tenets of social purpose for all Japanese.

The Japanese were very self-consciously aware of the inner tensions inherent in taking on Confucianism. It was viewed as supporting the intellectual-moral side of a continuing tension between instrumentally positive social obligation, or *giri* as opposed to more spontaneous, affiliative, or nurturant emotional social feelings, *ninjo*. To attend to giri was to comply ritually with the anticipated and expected behavior appropriate to one's social role. It was a more formal adherence to moral expectations as opposed to the spontaneity of love and other sometimes socially disruptive human emotions. All through the Tokugawa period, the townsmen and rural folk both were seen as more lively and less stuffy than those of the samurai class. However, with the universal educational system in Meiji, it was the samurai neo-Confucianist precepts that set up justification of moral order and proper behavior for all commoners as well as for the elite.

What is going on in Japan more recently has been an attempted shift to a search for more expressive, subjectively experienced happiness or "*shiawase*" as a desirable concept to guide educational policy. It is now a social goal to aim for a more spontaneous mode of existence. However, the Japanese are also very cognizant of the potential chaos of unregulated behavior resulting from too great a shift toward Western individualism. Conservative Japanese are very concerned that their society may become chaotic rather than liberalized. On the other hand, liberal Japanese are very aware that in the past individuals were coerced into conformity by exiguous group behavior. There is, among many Japanese intellectuals today, a strong wish to move toward a looser, less collective type of educational training, towards realizing a more individualized sense of self-regulation.

Japanese Confucian arguments (cf. Yamashita, 1984, 155 ff.), about moral cultivation (which ultimately were set forth in the Meiji Imperial Rescript on Education), are not too different from the early twentieth-century pedagogic arguments found in France and England as advanced by conservative collectivists (Fauconnet, 1920). In discussing educational policies, some interpreted Durkheim's concepts of how society is constituted "prior to the individual" as necessitating moral teachings in the schools. To ensure proper continuity, a society should inculcate moral teaching as central to school curriculum. Opposed to this line of thought were liberal individualists whose concept of human personality saw a natural maturation possible without such deliberate moral guidance. Those more individualistic in their orientation, as was Piaget (1932), would rely more on an educational system that fosters innate capacities in the developing child, that spontaneously unfold with maturation toward forms of moral reciprocity and objectivity in thought. Accordingly, children were to be given proper social encouragement rather than being rigidified behaviorally by indoctrination. Predominantly, cultivation of a religious social sense is to be kept separate from secular education in recent western educational philosophy.

Family and Group Responsibility in Japan

One can find, in Japanese history, various examples of what Westerners might consider extreme acts of responsibility related to family or occupation (De Vos, 1992, chapter 2). We have already discussed Japanese social sensitivity related to honor or esteem (see chapter 6, volume I). On a conscious level in Japan, the assumption of authority requires a strong sense of personal responsibility. If something goes wrong, including the improper behavior of a subordinate or family member, it is the one in authority who must assume responsibility.

In premodern Japan, there were variously defined expected practices of collective responsibility. For example, there were numerous instances in which several village heads were collectively punished for the behavior of an individual member of their village. In the local family context, the head of family would take responsibility for the errant behavior of any family member. Acts of public penance called *kinshin* were expected. Among the samurai, taking responsibility for failed behavior could involve, as a final act of responsibility, a ritual act of suicide called *seppuku* (which we know by the more informal term of *hara-kiri*) (De Vos, 1968).

The traditional cultural logic of seppuku as punishment for a warrior included the belief that an honorable suicide responsibly preserves the status of the *"ie"* or "house" of the offender. By the voluntary atonement behavior of one of its members, the remaining household was freed of any negative consequences. By submitting positively to the demands for ritual suicide, the offender affirms both the legitimate control, or authority, of his superiors and his own sense of responsibility to his family. He "cleanses" away any past deviation from the required code of honor and loyalty. If he did not do so, not only would he be put to death ignominiously, but his family, if not killed, would also be punished by loss of status and property.

So-called "double suicides" or "love suicides," *shinju* or "true heart" suicides, were a favorite theme of premodern tragic dramas. At the heart of such a tragic drama was the insoluble conflict between one's responsibility to one's family and one's love attachment to a socially unsuitable person.

In the frame of reference of the instrumental-expressive interpersonal concerns, various other forms of altruistic suicide in Japan could be seen culturally as both instrumental and expressive acts. There was both a sense of dedication to the well-being of the family we discussed in the context of Nurture (N) and Harmony (H), but also an explicit sense of duty and social responsibility. There were several forms of legendary sacrificial suicide, "*gisei jisatsu*," of heroic spouses or family members. These were explicitly related to their Confucian sense of family responsibility.

As we shall presently illustrate in this chapter, a favorite theme elicited in some Thematic Apperception Test (TAT) narratives we gathered in 1953–1954 and in 1960 (De Vos, 1973) was that of an ailing wife who, presuming herself to be a burden interfering with her husband's career purpose, out of an expressed sense of responsibility, removes herself by suicide so as to insure his continued dedication to occupational success. In a stringent definition of a woman's responsibility to the family into whom she has married, there was the ultimate thought to die to preserve and enhance the "*ie*," or house of her husband. Suicide in this context could be interpreted by Japanese as an edifying example of *responsible* dedication, as in the *junshi* ("following death") of General Nogi who followed his emperor in death in a suicidal act.

As we shall also discuss further below, a mother in Japan could, and does still, not infrequently threaten suicide as a deliberate means of controlling a rebellious or delinquent child (see Wagatsuma and De Vos, 1984). A mother's threat of suicide may be seen positively not only as an act of extreme responsibility for guiding her children to a proper future; it can also be viewed as a threatened "advice" suicide. It can be seen as an act of both *responsibility* and *control*, through a reproach to a rebellious underling or underlings. Such was the behavior represented in the suicide of the emperor's emissary in front of Manchurian army troops unwilling to surrender in 1945.

In a more negative sense, some suicides by mothers have been interpreted by some Japanese to signify atonement for a past irresponsibility and failure to maintain herself properly in her role as mother.

The Social Context of Deviant Behavior

Family Life and Delinquency

As discussed elsewhere (De Vos, 1960a, 1962; De Vos and Wagatsuma, 1969), the social behavior of minorities is related to acceptance or nonacceptance of official authority in a society.[1] This discussion anticipated the present examination of the internalization of social responsibility. Let us here note briefly this examination of the social internalization of authority in respect to patterns of delinquency in Japan.

In pursuing a number of issues raised concerning family interaction and the *selective appearance of delinquency* in particular children, we were particularly interested in how relative family cohesion was an important factor. We found to a highly significant degree that delinquent children lacked any sense of cohesive interaction between parents. As in the United States, a preponderant number of delinquents came from broken families. Delinquents generally lacked any signs of expressed affection, usually from both parents, and above all lacked responsible supervision and consistent forms of discipline. The delinquent child did not internalize much of a sense of responsibility. Rather, he often gave evidence of a deep sense of deprivation and neglect (Wagatsuma and De Vos, 1984).

In respect to whether the father's discipline was consistently severe or mild in nature, we found that 58 percent of the fathers in our nondelinquent sample showed adequate consistent discipline compared with *none* of the fathers of delinquents. Conversely, eighteen of the thirty-one fathers of delinquents evidenced withdrawal and or excessive laxity in their discipline. Only one father of a nondelinquent could be so categorized. In respect to mother's supervision, only two

---

[1]See an examination of this problem as revealed by the behavior and attitudes of Moroccan adolescents in Belgium in Philip Hermans (1999).

mothers of the delinquents obtained an optimal rating. In most instances, neglect was the most noticeable negative feature. Half of our sample showed definitely unsuitable maternal supervision. Of the mothers of our control sample of nondelinquents only one was rated less than good in this respect. On responses to a translation of the California Psychological Inventory, parents of delinquents showed relatively low socialization scores (indicative of delinquent attitudinal tendencies) in comparison with parents of nondelinquents (Gough, De Vos, and Mizushima, 1968; Mizushima and De Vos, 1967).

Our results led us to agree very strongly with the conclusions of Bennett (1960), who conducted an intensive comparison in England, of fifty delinquent and fifty neurotic children. She considered, in general, that personal instability in parents was related to the occurrence of broken homes, rather than broken homes per se having a direct causal relationship to delinquency. In her English samples, Bennett found a great deal of mutual incompatibility as well as immaturity and irresponsibility in one or both parents. In addition to the general findings of a positive relationship between unstable and discordant homes in English delinquents, she found antisocial tendencies latent if not manifest in parents of delinquents in sharp contrast with the social attitudes found among the parents of neurotic children.

When looking at the psychological dimension, we also agreed with her that the category "delinquent" is a heterogeneous one rather than one which points to any specific personality pattern. Again, Bennett's results stressed inconsistency or irresponsibility in discipline related to lack of internalization, which we found true for our Japanese delinquent sample. Despite totally different cultural traditions, our findings in Japan are consistent with intensive family studies in Britain such as that conducted by Bennett. We have also reported similar results from our somewhat less intensive study of Italian families (De Vos, 1980). Despite cultural variations, when one has intensive enough firsthand materials, one can readily assess the presence or absence of discord and affection as well as consistencies, inconsistencies, or inadequacies in responsible parental discipline and supervision.

In comparing a number of the variables that we could safely assess from our data, we found one other specific Japanese pattern worth noting in respect to role expectations and internalized responsibility. There was consistent evidence that the sibling position of parents is apparently related to the appearance of delinquency in a child. In Japan, it is the common observation that eldest sons are indulged more than other children in the family. It has been said often that in the pattern of urban in-migration in Japan, it is more often the second, and later sons and daughters of rural families who were constrained, by lack of future inheritance, to go to the city. Second sons were considered to be relatively neglected. Maternal and paternal interest was more directed toward the son who would become the family head. We were, therefore, interested in the relationship of sibling position to possible manifestations of delinquency, since one would presume the possibility of relative degrees of *neglect* or *rejection*[2] of younger siblings to occur within families. In contrast, first sons were indulged as a way of impelling them to assume more responsibility as future head of family. We found differences which reached significance, even given our small number of cases. In the sibling position of the delinquent sample, we found the position of middle or second son overrepresented. In contrast to the delinquent subjects, nondelinquent subjects tended to be either the oldest child or oldest or youngest sons.

Going back to the parents' generation to examine their sibling positions, we found that half of the fathers of our nondelinquent subjects were first sons, compared with one-quarter of the fathers of delinquents. Fifteen percent of the fathers of non-delinquents were second sons, compared with 60 percent of fathers of delinquents. These would appear to be indicative of the greater attention that has traditionally been paid to first-born sons and daughters than to those coming later in a sibling sequence.[3]

In examining the Japanese family tradition, one is made aware of how the father is very often respected for his social *role position* rather than for himself as an individual. In a Confucian culture, the father's position was considered unassailable within the family. This attitude of *deference* and *respect* (E), would prevail even should the father, considered from a personality standpoint, be insufficient in meeting the requirements of his role. Formal behavior in the family was defined by roles: the growing male child would witness what to expect in deference to a "father." Upon reaching maturity, he could expect to be afforded similar recognition no matter what he felt subjectively about his own inefficiencies. At the same time this role would demand of him the assumption of sometimes onerous responsibilities.

Delinquency and Minority Status

A careful breakdown of social grouping in Japan demonstrates very quickly that there are some socioeconomic and minority status variables within Japanese society that operate to some degree in a similar fashion to those reported in the United States.

Despite differences in overall numbers, variables reported in Japan for those becoming delinquent, such as broken homes and past records of truancy among what could be defined as lower-class Japanese, replicate very closely patterns reported in American studies. The two large minorities within Japanese society (the former outcastes or "Burakumin," and the Koreans) have comparatively high rates

---

[2]See the negative Nurture and Affiliation categories discussed in chapters 4 and 5, volume I.

[3]The second son was known as "the cold rice" son since he had to wait to be served sequentially to the point of relative neglect. It was the role of these individuals to leave the family and to seek their fortunes elsewhere, receiving no inheritance.

of delinquency among their youth (De Vos, 1980; De Vos and Mizushima, 1962; De Vos and Wagatsuma, 1966; see also chapter 10, volume I, of the present text). In the early 1960s, we were able to determine a delinquency rate among outcastes which was four and a half times that of the majority. Among Korean youth the rate was seven times that of majority youth! These figures confirmed the informal impressions of probation officers and other agencies working with juveniles in the area. Many of the minority youth in Japan do not appear to internalize the moral directives of the majority society (De Vos, 1993a). In a manner similar to what is found among some African American and Mexican American youths, the minority Japanese youth peer groups set up counter directives for their members. Let us illustrate this in somewhat more detail.

Problems of Assuming Responsibility Related to Minority Status: Koreans in Japan

Part of being socialized into a responsible membership in any society is the internalization of a moral code. In addition to proscriptions of negative behavior, a moral code emphasizes positive obligations for repayment to parents, responsibility to the group, and loyalty to the nation. The Korean minority is ambivalent about being governed in good conscience by standards and proscriptions to which they, as "innately inferior" to Japanese, are not assumed to be capable of adhering.

Animosity and resentment over discrimination, in one sense, frees the individual from assuming the internalized standards of the majority. A dilemma of identity for a Korean is whether he or she should attempt to meet the social obligations assumed by ordinary Japanese. In one of the chapters on Koreans in Japan (Lee and De Vos, 1981), we report the case history of a youthful Korean suicide. This individual was torn by internalized guilt and a sense of inner insufficiency in two respects: first, a guilt-ridden ambivalence about being or not being "Japanese" and its attendant expectations; second, guilt over not meeting maternal expectations combined with the knowledge of the total family degradation. He experienced at age eleven the death by freezing of his father who, one winter, had fallen into a gutter drunk on alcohol. He never witnessed his father receiving any respect from his mother. His own discreditable school behavior reflected on his mother's inadequacy as a parent and thereby hurt her. She reviled him for his inadequate behavior. Although such a youth feels guilty, he may also resent a parent who pushes him toward a course of behavior he is emotionally incapable of following.

For some Koreans, maintaining a Korean identity entails an antagonistic posture that condones illegal or deviant marginal activity. Alternatively, to become "Japanese" by passing is to accept as valid the deprecatory attitudes directed toward Koreans, including one's secret self. The individual is caught in a dilemma of integrity. One is caught by possible conscious or unconscious prejudices internalized as part of living in the larger society. Frequently the resolution of such a conflict is to resist passing, because to pass implies acceptance of Japanese judgments about one's own people and their past.

In a negative direction, there are advantages to avoiding responsibility. In an ethnically pluralistic society, an individual may retain his or her minority status to avoid certain obligations that are part of the role expectations of the majority. Conversely, one would expect some individuals from the majority to "drop out," identifying with a supposedly freer minority to indulge in behavioral patterns ordinarily forbidden. In the relationship of minority Koreans and Japanese, this latter move is not often made. A few Japanese, however, do identify themselves as Koreans. In Arakawa Ward, we found an example of a Japanese boy who put a Korean button on his cap to intimidate his peers. To be considered "tough," some Yakuza or gangster types use Korean speech mannerisms. Occasionally, some lower-class Japanese prefer to live in Korean or Burakumin ghettos because they favor such a lifestyle to living among their own group and its restrictive responsibilities. We found that such outsiders are tolerated in some instances, and rejected in others. Koreans are usually suspicious of any outsider who seeks to gain acceptance among them.

The maintenance of a Korean identity in Japan invariably implies some conflict over assumption or avoidance of responsibility and guilt. To the degree to which the individual has introjected a negative self-image, he or she may find a great deal of internal conflict about ordinary ethical standards. To assume the same moral, ethical, and social obligations as the majority Japanese may be distasteful or burdensome to many Koreans. Conversely, the avoidance of responsibility may at times be made easier through blaming the negative attitudes of the majority for one's avoidance of any form of responsible social commitment to society in general. Chapter 7, volume II, deals with the TAT evidence of personal alienation rather than achievement motivation found in the narratives of Koreans in Japan.

We now turn to a presentation of the categories and subcategories used for scoring these issues with the ICSS. We shall then further illustrate the scoring of Responsibility categories. As we do this, we will discuss how expressed concerns with responsibility can be found as elements in narrative sequences that also point to concerns with guilt, even where the guilt itself is not directly voiced in the narrative.

Categories of Responsibility

A. *Active, Responsible Behavior* ***RA***

RA-work	Work—daily tasks as a responsibility
RA-good	A "good" person; responsible products or activities or unspecified as to nature of "goodness"

RA-example	Behavior an example for guidance or training of others
RA-duty-s	Assumption of self-oriented or self-defined obligations or duties
RA-duty-o	Assumption of externally or socially defined obligations or duties
RA-order	Proper exercise of propriety, regularity, a positive sense of order
RA-control	Self control in order to accomplish goals or duties
RA-stoic	Stoic reactions to adversity
RA-sex	Responsible in sexual behavior
RA-reform	Taking responsibility for previous behavior by reform, or reparation, resolution of guilt
RA-apology	Taking responsibility by apology, confession
RA-expiate	To give oneself up for punishment as a means of expiation
RA-hurt-s	Self-punishment or injurious behavior as an act of taking responsibility for negative behavior
RA-buck-o	Taking responsibility for the behavior of another, e.g., family members, subordinates, etc.
RA-injure	Injurious behavior to self or others in taking responsibility for the negative behavior of others
RA-repay	Obligatory reciprocity; necessary gifts (Japanese "*giri*" relationships)
RA-ritual	Ritual or ceremonial obligations
RA-suicide	Suicide as an act of duty or responsibility

Individuals may talk about work as daily tasks (RA-work). Very often there is not direct attention drawn to the fact that daily activities are an automatic assumption of ones daily activities as part of one's expected social role.

An individual may be defined as a "good" person implying some form of moral righteousness (RA-good). Responsible behavior may be consciously considered as exemplary in nature (RA-example). That is, the individual is aware that one's own behavior is observed and emulated by others. Activities may be more directly described as a self-oriented or self-defined obligation or duty (RA-duty-s). A duty or obligation may be taken on without any evidence of external control; nevertheless it can be recognized as a socially defined obligation or duty (RA-duty-o). Individuals may be described as properly exercising propriety or having a sense of maintaining or perceiving a way to keep good order as part of one's activities or responsibilities (RA-order). One exercises self-control in order to accomplish goals or duties (RA-control).

One may express a stoic reaction to adversity due to a deeply internalized sense of one's duty (RA-stoic). Specific attention may be drawn to responsibility in sexual activities (RA-sex).

Various forms of responsible behavior may be expiatory in nature. One may consciously change, taking responsibility for previous behavior by reform, or reparation (RA-reform). One may take responsibility for previous acts by apology, private, or public confession (RA-apology). One may give oneself up for punishment as a means of expiation (RA-expiate).

Infrequently, one may even self-inflict punishment or injurious behavior as an act of assuming responsibility for negative behavior (RA-hurt-s).

One's concept of responsibility may include taking the consequences for the negative behavior of others under one's charge, including family members, subordinates, etc. (RA-buck-o). A sense of responsibility may extend to injurious behavior to self or others in taking responsibility for the negative behavior of others (RA-injure). We shall illustrate such conscious thought in Japan (see below, this chapter).

Responsibility may involve complex forms of reciprocal behavior. In some societies this may involve gift exchange or various forms of repayment for the previous behavior of others (RA-repay). Illustrative of such a sense of responsibility are found in what are termed "*giri*," obligatory relationships in Japan.

One's social role may oblige the person to conduct some form of expected ritual or sponsor and pay for a ceremony (RA-ritual). Marriage ceremonies in western cultures or a "potlatch" among northwest coast Native Americans are examples of such responsibilities. Where one feels it to be appropriate to the fulfillment of duty, one may even make the decision to use suicide as an act of responsibility (RA-suicide).

B. *Inner Concerns About Responsibility (Feelings Rather Than Actions)* ***RB***

RB-guilt	Guilt; unresolved repentance for present or past acts
RB-regret	Regret; ruefulness
RB-omit	To experience guilt or negative feelings for not having done something; guilt of omission
RB-duty	Unresolved duty or uncertain about how to be responsible
RB-resign	Unresolved resignation to the role behavior expected by others
RB-torn	Ambivalence about accepting responsibility
RB-role	Conflict between role responsibilities
RB-ideals	Internal conflict over social values or ideals
RB-legit	Ambivalent activities; questions of legitimacy

There are a number of inactive or unresolved states related to a sense of responsibility. Expressions of possible or actual guilt appear not infrequently (RB-guilt). One may suffer from a sense of regret over previous behavior (RB-regret). This sense of ruefulness may involve the conscious experience of a wish for repentance for acts done or expected acts not performed (RB-omit). There are both "sins" of transgression and omission or avoidance that equally result in some form of guilt. There may be some concern with an unresolved duty or uncertainty about how to be responsible (RB-duty). There may be some lack of resolution or resignation to the role responsibilities expected by others (RB-resign). This may be expressed as some form of ambivalence about designated duties (RB-torn).

There may be some internal conflict experienced as a result of incompatible expectations and duties between conflicting roles (RB-role). There may be internal conflicts related to conflicting social values or ideas of proper social ideals (RB-ideals).

C. *Excessive Irresponsible or Forbidden Behavior* ***RC***

RC-wrong	Wrongdoing unspecified; a "bad" person, unspecified
RC-group	Irresponsible group activities
RC-duty	To violate one's duty; corrupt authority
RC-rigid	Excessively rigid and inflexible
RC-control	Loss or lack of self-control
RC-indulge	General or unspecified acts of indulgence; sins of gluttony, laziness (sloth), lust with prostitutes, etc.
RC-messy	Messy or disorderly behavior; lack of inner or outer regularity, impropriety
RC-abuse	Self-indulgence, substance abuse (drink, narcotics, etc.)
RC-waste	Wasteful with money (gambling, etc.)
RC-rash	Rash, heedless, irresponsible acts
RC-illegal	Illicit or illegal acts
RC-ex-sex	Extramarital or prohibited sexual behavior (violating rights of legitimate partner)
RC-pre-sex	Premarital or nonmarital sexual behavior (with socially prohibited partner)
RC-perverse	Acts perceived as socially perverse; homosexuality, incest, fetishes, etc.
RC-mores	Violation of norms or customs, e.g., gossip, impoliteness and improprieties of behavior

RC-status	Status violation, such as wife or husband neglect duties; children behave badly against family expectations; rowdiness
RC-property	Irresponsible or invasive use of another's property or social space
RC-hurt-s	Excessive self-punishment due to guilt
RC-example	Setting a bad example for others
RC-evade	Use of role or authority for evasion of responsibility
RC-sacred	Religious sacrilege

There is consciousness of numerous irresponsible violations of social norms. We have listed a good number, but have not exhausted the possible specific categories that may be elicited, and there is always room for further specification of subcategories.

In many stories, the nature of the wrongdoing is not specified (RC-wrong). There is irresponsible group activity or activity influenced negatively by group adherence (RC-group). There are negative expressions of some direct violation of duty (RC-duty). An individual may be excessively rigid in a definition of duty, and by so being there may result harm to others (RC-rigid).

There are situations of loss of self-control (RC-control). There are acts of self-indulgence or laziness. Some are defined generally or unspecified as being a "ne'er do well" (RC-indulge). This subcategory includes the old "mortal" sin of sloth. A person's behavior may be seen as careless, slovenly, or messy. Such behavior is "disorderly" (RC-messy). There are also varieties of substance abuse: drinking, narcotics, etc. (RC-abuse). Some individuals are wasteful of resources or money, this includes irresponsible gambling (RC-waste). There are varieties of rash, heedless, reckless irresponsible acts (RC-rash). There are also a variety of irresponsible illegal acts (RC-illegal) that can be scored when the irresponsibility is emphasized rather the instrumental gain which is scored as anomic achievement (see AC-illicit, elsewhere). Some responses must be double scored.

Irresponsible behavior is very often sexual in nature. Extramarital behavior (RC-ex-sex) not only violates the norms but the rights of a legitimate sexual partner. There are premarital violation of norms (RC-pre-sex). Other forms of sexual behavior, regardless of the partner, can be seen as prohibited. Such behavior, including prostitution, may be socially considered as "perverse" or may be seen as unacceptable by the informant. This may include references to homosexuality, sodomy, incest, etc. (RC-perverse).

There are violations of norms or customs not legally defined [e.g., gossip, eavesdropping, impoliteness, and improprieties of behavior (RC-mores)]. There are what are termed "status violations." These can include mutual marital obligations, or vertical relations of subordinate to superior, children or sub-adults (RC-status). A woman can be seen as remiss in her domestic duties. Children may be seen as behaving badly against parental expectations or the expectation of teachers, indulging in rowdiness, for example. The category of Esteem (E) may be double scored, or scored alternatively when acts are considered for their disrespectful quality. Rude or insolent behavior toward a superior are examples (EDC-insolent).

There may be an invasive use of another's property or social space (RC-property). An incapacity to internalize social responsibility occurs in status segmented societies selectively. Some cannot accept a discriminatory, neglectful, or depriving authority. Being unable to identify with an alien authority prevents the assumption of any social responsibility in some minority segments of a population. They perform acts countering formal authority. Very often "delinquency" results in minority youth. The word "delinquent" in recent years refers to the behavior of youth, but delinquency also refers passively to all failures or neglects to do what duty or formal law requires.

There are expressions of excessive self-punishment over a sense of guilt (RC-hurt-s). There can be an awareness of setting a bad example (RC-example) with its negative consequences. Conversely, there are those who use their status or authority to avoid the consequences of their behavior (RC-evade).

In a religious context, and attack on authority may be regarded as a form of profanation or sacrilege (RC-sacred).

D. *Avoidance; Refusal to Internalize Social Obligations* ***RD***

RD-weak	Inability to overcome addiction or resist temptation
RD-fail	Failure to take responsibility or be responsible for other's action
RD-wrong	Avoidance, escape of consequences of wrong behavior
RD-personal	Avoidance, escape, or denial of personal obligations
RD-social	Avoidance, escape, or denial of social obligations
RD-work	Avoidance, escape, or denial of school or work duties, laziness, being (ne'er do well) deadly sin of sloth
RD-ignorant	Ignorance as destructive
RD-control	Escape from the expected obligations of an authority position demanding action influencing others
RD-environ	Escape or denial of responsibility for negative influence on social or environmental conditions

There are various forms of irresponsible behavior of a passive nature. Some narratives draw attention to a weakness of character that leads to an inability to resist temptation or overcome addition (RD-weak). There is failure to take active responsibility, or if in an authority position, to be sufficiently responsible to induce proper behavior in another (RD-fail). For example, a Japanese mother is seen as responsible for her child's proper behavior. If he or she misbehaves, it is the mother's fault.

There is avoidance or escape from the consequences of one's past wrong behavior (RD-wrong). There are a number of ways to avoid, escape, or deny personal obligations (RD-personal), or social duties (RD-social). There is escape from school duties or one's professional or other duties related to one's occupation or work (RD-work).

Simple irresponsible ignorance can have negative consequences for others (RD-ignorant). There is a responsibility to seek education or knowledge.

Some individuals escape the responsibilities attendant upon authority (RD-control). They may ignore specified obligations of either an instrumental or expressive nature, and should be double scored with the appropriate category. Many Americans have great difficulty in assuming a positive authority role because there is considerable social ambivalence about the negative meanings of control, both personal and public. This widespread lack of resolution is very evident in American projective test materials (see chapter 6, volume II). Authorities or others may avoid, escape, or deny obligations related to the amelioration of negative social or environmental conditions (RD-environ).

Guilt, Japanese Style

In this section, we discuss how emic expressions of responsibility that occur in certain narrative contexts may be interpreted etically to indicate underlying guilt in Japanese family patterns. One of the most useful findings derived from our use of the projective techniques in Japan was the revelation of underlying patterns of guilt in Japanese related to a sense of responsibility to one's family that we found consistently depicted in the TAT stories. The following is excerpted from some of our published results.[4] In this section we also illustrate how the scoring categories are assigned to these stories.

Note that it is the specific *sequence* of concerns in these stories, not the direct manifest expression of guilt, that allows us to make a subsequent interpretation of the presence of guilt. The first step is the scoring of the manifest responses. The second step is a further interpretation of a normative sequence in the telling of a narrative from which we can infer the presence of guilt.

---

[4]This section is adapted from chapter 5 in *Socialization for Achievement*, De Vos (1973).

Guilt Related to Parental Suffering: A Traditional Pattern of Responsibility

The relation of induced guilt to parental suffering is apparent in certain TAT stories in which the death of the parent follows upon the bad conduct of a child. These two events repeatedly co-occur in narratives and seem to bear an implicit relationship, as expressed in the following summaries taken from research conducted in the agricultural village of Niiike in 1954. We have underlined the sequential categories.

> (Niiike M, age 41, Card J6GF) A daughter marries for love against her father's will; she takes care of her father, but the father dies.
> [FA-love RC-pre-sex DSC-disobey NDA-family KD-death]

> (Niiike W, age 22, Card J6GF) A daughter marries against her father's opposition, but her husband dies and she becomes unhappy.
> [FA-love RC-pre-sex DSC-disobey KD-death PD-sad]

> (Niiike M, age 23, Card J18) A mother strangles to death the woman who tempted her innocent son; the mother becomes insane and dies. The son begs forgiveness.
> [FC-seduce HC-murder PA-crazed KD-death RA-apology]

In some such stories, a respondent first puts into words an act of transgression, followed by the injury or death of a beloved parent. The initial transgression could be interpreted as a wish of some kind, on the part of the informant, which is then immediately followed by the thought that self-willed transgression will injure a beloved parent. Regardless of whether one makes such a psychodynamic interpretation, it is clear that the theme of these stories is that where one seeks to follow one's own desire, it will result in injury to a beloved parent. One can also be punished by fate (K) bringing forth the death of a beloved person. Such an association governs the sequence found in several stories, especially in records obtained from a traditional farm village where we sampled in the early 1950s.

One could also interpret such behavior as objective reflections of the actual cultural tradition of inducing behavior in others by threats of self-inflicted violence. Many Japanese have practiced the emotional logic of punishing others by killing or injuring themselves. Such self-injury or suicide became an accepted pattern of behavior under the rigid feudal regime where open protest was an impossibility. Numerous works on Japanese history contain accounts of the severe limitations put on spontaneous protest. If one has decided to protest, one has decided to die.

We think that the emotional logic of this behavior requires both developmental psychological as well as cultural explanation. This "moral masochistic" tendency is inculcated first through the attitudes of parents experienced from early childhood on, especially through the behavior of a dedicated mother. The mother "suffers" whatever the child does. Being hurt constantly, she subtly assumes a never verbally expressed attitude of "look what you have done to me." The Japanese mother often gained through such devices a strong emotional control over her child, and, by increasing her overt suffering, she could punish him for disobedience or lack of seriousness of purpose. Contextualized with the knowledge of this cultural pattern, the stories given above suggest that unconsciously a mother or father is "punishing" a child by dying. Parents' dying is not only punishment, but the final possible exercise of control that breaks the child's resistance and forces obedience to the parent's moral authority.

This use of death as a final admonition lends credence to a story concerning the Japanese Manchurian forces at the close of World War II. The young officers in Manchuria had determined to fight on indefinitely, even though the home islands had surrendered. A staff general was sent by plane as an envoy of the emperor to order the troops to surrender. He could get nowhere with the officers, who were determined to fight on. Returning to his plane, he took off and circled the field, sending a radio message that this was the final directive to surrender. The plane suddenly dived straight for the landing field, killing all on board. The troops then promptly surrendered.

It is not unknown for a mother to threaten to die as a means of admonishing a child. In a therapy case discussed in a case conference in Nagoya in 1953, a psychiatrist was working with a delinquent boy. The mother at one point had threatened her son, with very serious intent, telling him that he must stop his stealing or she would take him with her to the ocean at Enoshima, and there, commit double suicide.[5] The mother reasoned that she was responsible and that such a suicide would pay for her failure as a mother, as well as relieve the world of a potentially worthless citizen. The threat worked. The boy stopped his delinquent activities, although many complex interpersonal issues remained unresolved.

For a man, receiving such a threat of further suffering on the part of a mother becomes related to the necessity to work hard in the adult occupational role; for the woman, it becomes related to working hard at being a submissive and enduring wife.

In other of the TAT stories, the death of a parent is followed by responsible reform, hard work, and success. For example, these are stories elicited by a variety of cards:

> NKW, age 16 (Card J7M) A son, scolded by his father, later, the father dies; then the son works hard and becomes successful.
>
> [DDA-scold <u>KD-death</u> <u>RA-work</u> AA-persist]

> NKM, age 39 (Card J5) A mother worries about her delinquent son, becomes sick, and dies; the son reforms himself and becomes successful.
>
> [RC-wrong RB-duty NDB-welfare <u>KD-ill-die</u> <u>RA-reform</u> AA-persist]

---

[5]Personal communication from Japanese psychiatrist Taeko Sumi.

NKM, age 54 (Card J13) A mother dies; the son changes his attitude and works hard.

[KD-death RA-reform RA-work]

NKW, age 17 (Card J6M) A father dies; his son walks out as his mother repeatedly tells him to be like the father, when he meets her again, she dies; he becomes hardworking.

[KD-death DDA-scold DSC-escape FC-split FA-mend KD-death RA-work]

NKW, age 38 (Card J9) Elder brother is going to Tokyo, leaving his sick mother; his sister is opposed to his idea; his mother dies; he will become successful.

[KD-illness FB-separate FB-accord KD-death AA-self]

NKM, age 15 (Card J6M) A son becomes more thoughtful about his mother after his father's death; he will be successful.

[KD-death RA-duty-o NDB-welfare AA-self]

Emphasis on hard work and success after the death of parents clearly suggests some expiatory meaning related to the moral masochistic attitude of the mother. The mother's moral responsibility is also suggested by other stories, such as a mother being scolded by a father when the child does something wrong, or a mother—not the father—being hurt when the child does not behave well. The feeling experienced by the child when he realizes, consciously or unconsciously, that he has hurt his mother is guilt—because guilt is generated when one hurts the object of one's love. The natural ambivalence arising from living under close parental control supplies sufficient unconscious intent to hurt to make the guilt mechanism operative.

The expiatory emphasis on hard work and achievement is also evident as a sequel in TAT stories directly expressing *hurt* of one's mother or father:

NKM, age 17 (Card J11) A child dropped his father's precious vase. The father gets angry and scolds the mother for her having allowed the child to hold it. The child will become a fine man.

[KC-break DDA-scold RD-fail RA-good]

NKM, age 53 (Card J18) A child quarreled outside; his mother is sorry that his father is dead. The child makes a great effort and gets good school records.

[HC-discord KD-death AA-persist RA-work]

NK, age 24 (Card J11) A mother is worrying about her child who has gone out to play baseball and has not yet come back. When he comes home he overhears his mother complaining about his playing baseball all the time without doing his schoolwork. He then makes up his mind not to play baseball any more and to concentrate on his studies.

[RB-duty RC-status RA-reform]

Although the realization of having hurt one's parents by bad conduct is not explicit in the following story, it is another example of the use of hard work or study—obviously as the means to achievement—*and to* expiate possible guilt:

> NKW, age 17 (Card J3F) A girl worries about the loss of her virginity, consults with someone and feels at ease. She studies hard in the future.
> [RB-regret NSA-assist RA-reform]

In the same context, if one fails to achieve, one has no way to atone. One is lost. The only thing left is to hurt oneself, to extinguish oneself—the one whose existence has been hurting one's parents and who now can do nothing for them. Suicide as an answer is shown in the following summaries:

> NKM, age 57 (Card 3BM) A girl fails an examination, kills herself.
> [CD-unable RA-injure HC-suicide]

> NKW, age 32 (Card J3F) She cannot write a research paper, commits suicide.
> [CD-unable RA-injure HC-suicide]

On the level of cultural conditioning, the traditional teaching of *on* (family obligations) enhances the feeling of guilt in the male child. For example, a son is repeatedly taught by parents, teachers, and books that his parents have undergone hardship and trouble and made many sacrifices in order to bring him up. Parents may be depicted as having suffered financial strain and ill health because of overwork for the sake of this child. Of course, the child did not ask for all this sacrifice, nor does he consciously feel that he has intentionally hurt the parents, but there seems no way out; all this suffering takes place somewhere beyond his control, and he cannot avoid the burden it imposes. Certainly the child cannot say to himself, "I did not ask my parents to get hurt; their hurt is not my business," because he knows his parents love him and are also the objects of his love. What can be done about it then? The only way open to the child is to attain the highest goal expected of him. By working hard, being virtuous, becoming successful, gaining a good reputation, and the praise of society, he brings honor to himself, to his parents, and to his *ie* (household lineage), of which he and his parents are, after all, parts. If he is virtuous in this way, the parents also receive self-satisfaction and praise from society for having fulfilled their duty to household and society by raising their children well. The pattern repeats itself; the child sacrifices himself masochistically for his own children, and on and on.

Our assumption is that among many Japanese people such a feeling of guilt very often underlies the strong achievement drive and aspiration toward success. If this hypothesis is accepted, then it can easily be understood that the death of a parent (i.e., the symbolic culmination of the parent's being hurt following some bad conduct of a child), evokes in the child a feeling of guilt strong enough to bring him or her back from delinquent behavior and to drive one with responsibility toward hard work and success, or, for a female, toward maternal dedication. This is what underlies the numerous TAT stories of parental death and the child's reform.

Marriage Relationships Related to Family Responsibility

The feeling of "*on*" obligations generated in the family situation during childhood remained a central focus in Japanese-arranged marriages in 1954. In this context, it was very pronounced in women of Niiike village at the time of our research. In a sense, a woman expressed her need for accomplishment and achievement by aiming toward the fulfillment of her roles as wife and mother within the new family she entered at marriage. A man does not face giving up his family ties in the same way. Interview data suggested that, for a Japanese woman, failure to be a dutiful bride reflected on her upbringing, and therefore any discord with her new family, even with an unreasonable mother-in-law, injures the reputation of her own parents.

Marriages that, counter to family considerations, are based on individual passion or love are particularly prone to disrupt the family structure. Such marriages are often an expression of rebellion, and any subsequent stresses of adjustment to the partner or the respective families tend to remind the participants of the rebellious tone of the marriage and to elicit guilt feelings.

The TAT stories give evidence of guilt in regard to both types of "unacceptable" behavior in marriage; they show the wife's readiness to blame herself for difficulties with her husband, and they show both men and women expressing self-blame or blame of others for having undertaken love marriages.

The Wife's Self-Blame in Difficulties with Her Husband

In several of the stories involving discord between a man and his wife, the woman feels herself to be wrong in a situation that in the United States would be interpreted as resulting from the poor behavior of the husband. There are no stories showing the reverse—a man being blamed in an even slightly equivocal situation.

Of five such stories given in Niiike village, four were given by women. The one story given by a man involves a need for reform by both partners, who are united in a love marriage and therefore conform to the guilt pattern of such marriages. In summary, the four women's stories are:

> NKW, age 26 (Card J3GF) A wife quarreled with her husband when he returned from drinking. She leaves her house to cry, feels guilty for the quarrel.
>
> [RC-abuse HC-discord RB-guilt]

> NKW, age 54 (Card J4) A husband and wife quarrel because the former criticized her cooking. The wife apologizes to him.
>
> [HC-discord DDA-scold RA-apology]

NKW, age 37 (Card J4) A husband and wife quarrel, and after it the wife apologizes to her angry husband.

[HC-discord RA-apology]

NKW, age 22 (Card J5) A husband comes home very late at night; the wife thinks it is due to her lack of affection and tries hard; he finally reforms.

[RC-duty FC-neglect RA-duty-o RA-reform]

Such attitudes seem to be reflected also in other test data, such as the "problem situations" material we described elsewhere (De Vos, 1973). It is especially interesting to note that women may attribute a husband's profligacy to the wife's failure. The husband's willfulness—like that of a male child—appears in some instances to be accepted as natural. Somehow it is not his business to control himself if he feels annoyed with his wife, but nevertheless the wife must take responsibility for her husband's conduct. In one case at the Nagoya clinic, of a psychotic reaction in a young wife,[6] the mother-in-law blamed the bride directly for her husband's extramarital activities, saying, "If you were a good and satisfying wife, he would have no need to go elsewhere."

In connection with this point it may be worth mentioning that probably on the deepest level many Japanese wives in the 1950s did not "give" themselves completely to their husbands, because the marriage had been forced on them as an arrangement between the parents in each family. Wives often might not be able to adjust their innermost feelings in the marital relationship so as to be able to love their husbands genuinely. They might sense their own emotional resistance, and believe that an evil willfulness keeps them from complete devotion as dictated by ethical ideals of womanhood. Aware in the deepest level of their minds of their lack of real affection, they became sensitive to the slightest indication of unfaithful behavior by the husbands. Feeling that their husbands were reacting to their own secret unfaithfulness in withholding, they could not blame their husbands, but threw the blame back upon themselves. When, for example, their husbands happened to be late in getting home, they might become very anxious, reflecting upon their own inadequacies and attempting to remedy them. Another possible interpretation is that Japanese women, lacking freedom to express their own impulses, identified with male misbehavior and assumed guilt as if the misbehavior were their own.

One might say, in generalization, that the ethical ideal is a woman's self-sacrifice and devotion to the family line, whether to father or elder brother before marriage, or to husband and children after marriage. This ideal carries with it internalized propensities to take blame upon oneself and to express a moral sensitivity in these family relationships that no religious or other cultural sanctions compel men to share.

---

[6]Described in personal communication by the Japanese psychiatrist Kei Hirano.

Love Marriages and Other Heterosexual Relationships

The TAT stories that depicted marriage circumstances (especially stories from Cards 6GF and 13MF obtained in Niiike in the 1950s) show that many of the men and women in Niiike, when they brought up the subject of love marriage, still did not see it in a positive light but rather saw it as a source of disruption. In certain stories, such as the following, a love marriage made in open rebellion against the parents is followed by the death of a beloved person (an implicit punishment).

> NKM, age 41 (Card J6F) They are father and his daughter. The mother has died. The daughter is sitting on a chair in her room. The father is looking in, and she is turning around to face him. He is very thoughtful of his daughter, and as she is just about of age for marriage he wants to suggest that she marry a certain man he has selected. But she has a lover and does not want to marry the man her father suggests. The father is trying to read her face, though he does know about the existence of the lover. He brought up the subject a few times before, but the daughter showed no interest in it. Today also, a smile is absent in her face. The father talks about the subject again, but he fails to persuade her. So finally he gives in and agrees to her marrying her lover. Being grateful to the father for his consent, the daughter acts very kindly to him after her marriage. The husband and the wife get along very affectionately also. But her father dies suddenly of apoplexy. The father was not her real father. He did not have children, so he adopted her, and accepted her husband as his son-in-law. But he died. He died just at the time when a baby was born to the couple.
>
> [KD-death NDA-advice DDA-free NSA-grateful RC-pre-sex FA-love <u>KD-death</u> <u>NDA-active</u>]

> NKW, age 22 (Card J6F) The parents of this girl were brought up in families strongly marked with feudal attitudes—the kind of family scarcely found in the present time—so they are very feudal and strict. The daughter cannot stand her parents. She had to meet her lover in secret. She was seeing her lover today as usual, without her parents knowing it. But by accident her father found out, and she was caught by her father on the spot. When she returned home her father rebuked her severely for it. But she could not give up her lover. In spite of her parents' strong objection, she married him. [Examiner: Future?) The couple wanted to establish a happy home when they married, but probably she will lose her husband. He will die—and she will have a miserable life.
>
> [DDB-rigid FB-accord RC-pre-sex DSA-assert <u>KD-death</u> <u>PD-suffer</u>]

There are a number of stories about unhappy events in the lives of couples married for love. Many of these are told in response to the prone figure of the woman and the man pictured with his head down on his left arm, depicted on Card J13 of the TAT.[7] Since responses to this card bring out in clear focus some basic

[7]Card J13 in the Japanese series is a slight modification of the original Murray TAT Card 13, with furniture and facial features altered.

differences between guilt over sexuality in Americans and in the Japanese, it will be well to consider them here in some detail.

Comparing Japanese and American responses to Card 13 makes it clear that while Americans never express remorse over "committing" a marriage, the Japanese, at least those of traditional Niiike, express remorse in a heterosexual situation in the context of a self-initiated love marriage. For Americans, Card 13 is apt to evoke stories of guilt related to intercourse between partners not married to each other; the woman is sometimes identified as a prostitute or sometimes as a young girl. When the figures are identified by Americans as married, the themes are usually around the subject of illness. In contrast, in the sample of forty-six stories given in response to this card in Niiike village, not one story depicts a theme of guilt over sexuality between unmarried partners. Remorse is depicted *only* when it is related to regret for having entered into a love marriage.

Most themes of Japanese stories given in response to this card fall into one of three categories: sex or violence or both (ten stories); marital discord (ten stories); and sickness or death (twenty stories). Some striking differences in themes are related to the age and sex of the subjects.

Card J13: Responses Involving Sex and/or Violence

Six stories involve themes of extramarital sexual liaison. In three, the woman is killed by the man. Five of the six stories are given by men who, with one exception, are under thirty-five, and one is given by a woman under twenty-five. In the young woman's story, a man kills a woman because she was too jealous of him. One young man sees a man killing an entertainer who rejects him. Another sees a man killing a woman who was pursuing him "too actively." Another young man tells a story of a student and a prostitute, in which the man is disturbed by the prostitute's nakedness, not by his feelings of guilt over his activity.

The man over thirty-five sees the picture as depicting disillusionment in a man who unexpectedly calls on a woman with whom he is in love, only to find her asleep in a "vulgar" fashion. As is true in the stories about marital discord told by other men over thirty-five, the man is highly censorious of the woman's position on the bed. Her arms are too loosely thrown away from her body. In the Japan of that period a woman was supposed to remain decorous—even in sleep. A too relaxed appearance was seen as reflecting a wanton or sluttish nature.

Japanese men were apt to split their relationships with women into two groups: those with the wife and those with entertainers. Other evidence supports the conclusion that, for many men, genuine affection was directed only toward maternal figures, and that little deep affection was freely available toward women perceived in a sexual role. Moreover, the Japanese male had to defend himself against any passivity in his sexual relationship, lest he fall into a dependent relationship and become emotionally tied. By maintaining a rude aloofness and by asserting male prerogatives, he protects himself from involvement.

Japanese men could resort to a violent defense if threatened too severely. Younger women especially tended to see men as potentially violent. In the stories discussed above, three women under thirty-five saw a man killing a woman, in two cases his own wife. In addition to the jealousy mentioned before, one of the motives depicted was the wife's complaint about low salary (a man must be seen as particularly sensitive about his economic prowess if such a complaint results in murder). Another expressed regret in a man for entering a love marriage. The dramatic story which follows is particularly pertinent to understanding how guilt is related not to sexuality per se but to becoming emotionally involved and losing responsibility to family.

> NKW, age 22 (Card J13) He got married for love with a woman in spite of opposition by his parents. While they were first married they lived happily, but recently he has reflected on his marriage and the manner in which he overrode his parents' opposition—and the present wife—he wishes his present wife did not exist—he attempts to push away the feeling of blame within his breast. One night on the way home he buys some insect poison and gives it to his wife to drink and she dies. What he has done weighs on his mind. He gives himself up to the police. He tells his story frankly to them. He reflects on how wicked he has been in the past. He completes his prison term and faces the future seriously.
>
> [FA-love RC-mores DSA-assert RB-guilt HC-murder RA-expiate RA-reform]

This story indirectly brings out a feeling of intense guilt for attempting to carry out a love marriage.

Card J13: Responses Involved in Marital Discord

In our experience, the flavor given stories concerning marital discord is unique to the Japanese. Seven of the twenty-one Niiike men giving stories about Card J13 mentioned marital discord. Five of these men and all three women giving such stories were between thirty-five and fifty years of age. The men tend to see the marriage as ending badly, whereas the women were more optimistic about seeing the discord resolved. Both sexes usually place the blame for the discord on the women.

As in one of the stories mentioned previously, the men took a cue for their stories from the position of the woman in the bed. They do not see the woman as ill, as do many of the women, but use the woman's posture as a basis for criticizing her. One of the chief complaints is that such a woman obviously does not take "proper care" of her man. The following stories bring out the nature of some of the feelings leading to the castigation of the wife for "looseness" and lack of wifely concern for her husband. The man, too, is castigated in some of the stories, but not with the strength of feeling that is turned toward the woman.

> NKM, age 39 (Card J13) This is also very difficult for me. What shall I say I can't tell my impressions—what shall I say—it seems to me that they do not lead a happy life. The man often comes back home late at night, I suppose. But his wife does not wait for her husband. She has decided to act independently of her own accord, I suppose—he is back home late again, and his wife is already asleep. He

thinks that it might be well to speak to her. I suppose there is always a gloomy feeling in this family. Well, if they led a peaceful life, such a scene as this would never occur. It is customary that a wife takes care of her husband, as she should when he comes home—and afterward she goes to bed. But, judging from this picture, I suppose this wife wouldn't care a bit about her husband. Such a family as this will be ruined, I think. They should change their attitude toward each other and should make a happy home. [Examiner: What about the future?] They will be divorced. It will be their end. [Examiner: Do you have anything to add?] Well, I expect a woman to be as a woman should be. A man also should think more of his family.

[RC-status NDD-neglect FB-accord FC-drift FD-split RC-status]

NKM, age 41 (Card J13) This is also—this man is a drunkard, and his wife also a sluttish woman. And the man was drunk, and when he came back his wife was already asleep—and, well—finally, they will be ruined. They have no child. They will become separated from each other. This wife will become something like a *nakai* or a procurer. The husband will be held in prison and the husband will kill himself on the railroad tracks. And—the wife will work as a *nakai*, and after contracting an infectious disease will die. The infectious disease that attacks her is dysentery. *They worked together in a company and were married for love. That is their past.* [Examiner: What does it mean that they will be ruined?] He became desperate. He became separated from his wife, so he became desperate. If a man commits a bad thing, nobody cares for him. He could not hope for any help, so he killed himself.

[FA-love RC-abuse HD-decay RC-perverse RC-mores NSD-lack KD-death HC-suicide]

NKM, age 35 (Card J13) Well, this man and woman married for love. The woman was a café waitress and married the man for love. But they have not lived happily, so the man repents the marriage very much. Well, this man used to be a very good man, but he was seduced by the waitress and lost his self-control, and at last he had a sexual relationship with her. Afterwards [after they marry], he becomes afraid and he has to think over their [impulsive] marriage. If their married life has any future at all I hope they will maintain some better stability. But if this woman doesn't want to do so, he needs to think over their marriage, I suppose.

[RC-rash FA-love PD-sad RB-regret RA-good FC-seduce RC-control FB-unmet]

The last story, especially, brings out strong feelings of guilt related to an attempt to maintain a love marriage. The story directly depicts the guilt as related to losing self-control and becoming involved with an unsuitable woman, not with sexual activity per se.

Implied, too, is the idea that any woman who would make a love marriage is not really capable of being a very worthy wife. In addition to depicting guilt for going counter to the parents in a love marriage, Card J13 is seen as indicating the potential avenue for projecting guilt onto the woman who is active enough to enter a love marriage. Such a woman's conduct obviously does not include the proper submissiveness to parental wishes and, therefore, she would probably fail in giving attention to the needs of her spouse.

This castigation of the woman is directly related to an expectation that the wife, instead of being a sexual object, should be a figure fulfilling dependency needs. The man sees his wife in a maternal role and is probably quick to complain if she renders him less care and attention than he received from his mother. Since the wife–mother image tends to be fused in Japanese men, they have little conception of companionship or of the mutual sharing of experience; moreover, the too-free sexual behavior of the wife excites in the husband aspects of sexual feelings towards the mother that were repressed in childhood. The wife–mother image cannot be conceived in gross sexual terms. It is speculated by some that some Japanese need a mistress because their sexual potency toward their wives is muted by the fused wife–mother image. Free sexual attitudes on the part of the wife would tend to change her image from mother to prostitute.

One may say that this fusion of images has a great deal to do with the conflict that often arises between the young bride and her mother-in-law. The mother-in-law's jealousy is due in part to her fear of being directly replaced in her son's affection by the bride, since their roles are essentially similar. The wife becomes more intimate with the husband after she becomes a mother, and comes to treat him essentially as the favorite child.

These attitudes were evident in the case mentioned previously in which a woman's psychotic episode was precipitated by her mother-in-law's attacks, including her interpretation that the alliance of her son with other women was proof of the wife's incompetence. It is interesting to note in connection with this case that during the wife's stay in a hospital the husband was able to express considerable feelings of concern for her. There was no doubt that he loved her. In effect, however, this feeling was more for her as a maternal surrogate than as a sexual partner. His mother knew she had more to fear from the wife in this respect than from her son's liaisons with other women, with whom he never became too greatly involved. He, on the other hand, had no manifest guilt for his sexual activities. In effect, they were approved of by his mother in her battle with the wife.

In six responses, of which five are from women, three of them teenagers, Card J13 is interpreted as a mother–son situation with the mother either sick or dead. The son is pictured specifically as working hard or studying; in one story the son steals because they are so poor. The younger girls especially seem to need to defend themselves from the sexual implications of the card by inventing a completely desexualized relationship. Unable to make the card into a marital situation, much less a more directly sexual one, some fall back on the favored theme of a sick mother and a distraught but diligent son. Emphasis on studying hard suggests the defensive use of work and study to shut out intrapersonal problems. Diligent work to care for the mother is again unconsciously used to avoid any feelings related to possible guilt. The way out is the one most easily suggested by the culture. Seeing Card 13 as a mother–son situation is rare in American records, even in aberrant cases.

Seeing Card J13 as depicting illness or death of a wife is the most characteristic response of women; fourteen women, most of them over thirty-five, gave such stories. Six men, including four of the five in the sample over age fifty, selected this theme. The middle-aged women were strongly involved in their stories about the death of a wife. Such stories were the longest of any given to the card. In sharp contrast to the derogatory stories directed toward the women by the men, the women use respectful concepts, such as *otoko-naki* ("manly tears"), in referring to the men. On certain occasions it is expected that manly tears are shed. Although a man is usually expected not to cry freely when sober, the death of a wife is an occasion on which he is expected to cry. Much emphasis is placed on the imagined love felt toward the wife by a husband, on his loneliness, and on his feeling of loss because of the absence of wifely care. Concern with potential loneliness and possible loss of such care is certainly reflected in the fact that most of the older men select similar themes. All but one of the women see the wife as dead or dying; the man is frequently seen as remarrying. Conversely, the men are more optimistic about recovery of a wife from illness and more pessimistic about remarriage if she does not recover.

One woman constructs a story of a sick wife who commits suicide so as not to be a burden to her husband. This type of story, which recalls many sentimental Japanese novels, is very moving to the Japanese, since it is supposed to reflect the degree of devotion of a wife for her husband and his goals and purposes. To the Westerner, the stories seem to be excessively masochistic and exaggerated. The Japanese ethical ideal of the self-sacrificing role of woman is here emphatically displayed.

Further Concerns with Guilt and Responsibility in Japan

The foregoing TAT material from Niiike village, 1954, with other evidence suggested to us how deeply imbued traditional attitudes were consistent with the interpretation that the potentiality for strong guilt feelings was prevalent in the Japanese of that period. Such feelings were aroused when there was failure in the performance of expected role behavior. Among the Japanese we found little pronounced guilt or otherwise negatively toned attitudes directed toward physical expression of sexuality per se. Rather, sexuality was related to guilt indirectly in the concern with possible loss of responsible control through the individual's becoming involved in a love relationship that interfered with prescribed life goals.

From a sociological standpoint, Japanese culture can be considered to manifest a particularistic or situational ethic as opposed to the more universalistic ethic built around moral absolutes as is found in Western Christian thought. This evaluation can be well documented, but it does not mean that the Japanese people evidence a relative absence of guilt. Whereas in many situations the more universalistic Western ethic may tend to transcend the family, the Japanese traditional ethic is actually an expression of rules of conduct for members of a family. Filial piety has in itself certain moral absolutes that are not completely determined situationally, though they tend to be conceptualized in particularistic terms. This difference between family-oriented morality and a more universalistic moral system is, nevertheless, a source of difficulty in the understanding of guilt in the Japanese.

Another reason for the failure of Western observers to perceive guilt in the Japanese stems from the West's customary relation of guilt to sexuality. Missionaries in particular, in assessing the Japanese from the standpoint of Protestant moral standards, were often quoted as being perplexed not only by what they considered a lack of moral feelings in regard to nonfamilial relationships, but also (and this was even worse in their eyes) by a seeming absence of any strong sense of "sin" in Japanese sexual relationships. It seems evident that the underlying emotional content of certain aspects of Christianity that requires repression and displacement of sexual and aggressive impulses has never appealed to the Japanese, in spite of their intellectual regard for the ethics of Christianity. Many modern educated Japanese recognize Christianity as advocating an advanced ethical system more in concert with modern universalized democratic ideals of man's brotherhood than are traditional Japanese ethics. As such, Christianity is favored by them over their more hierarchically oriented traditional system with its rigidly defined particularistic emphasis on prescribed social roles. For the educated Japanese, however, the concept of sin has little place in attitudes toward Christianity. This lack of interest in sin is most probably related to the absence of childhood disciplines that would make the concept important to the Japanese.

Traditional Western disciplinary methods, guided by concern with the inherent evil in man, have been based on the idea that the child must be trained as early as possible to conquer evil tendencies within. Later, one learns to resist outside pressures and maintain oneself as an individual subject to one's own conscience and to the universalistic laws of God. The traditional Western Protestant is accustomed in certain circumstances to repress inappropriate feelings. "Right" thoughts are valued highly, and one generally tries to repress unworthy motives. Justice must be impartial, and one must not be swayed by the feelings of the moment or be too flexible in regard to equity.

It is our contention that fear of punishment either by the parents, by society, or by God is not truly internalized guilt. Insofar as the punishment is perceived as *external* in source, the feeling is often fear or anxiety, as distinct from guilt.

In Japanese Buddhist thought one finds a dual concept of man as being capable of good and evil, but in Shinto thought, and in Japanese thinking about children generally, the more prevailing notion is that man's impulses are innately good. The purpose of child training is merely the channeling of these impulses into appropriate role behavior.

The definitions of proper role behavior become more and more exacting as the child grows and comes into increasing contact with others as a representative of his family. As such, one learns to be more and more diplomatic and to contain and suppress impulses and feelings that would be disruptive in social relations and that would put one at a disadvantage. One does not bring a system of moral absolutes into his relations with others any more than does a diplomat who negotiates for the advantage of one's country. The Japanese learns to be sensitive to "face" and protocol and to be equally sensitive to the feelings of others. One learns to keep personal feelings to oneself as a family representative. It would be fallacious to assume, therefore, that the Japanese is without much sense of guilt, just as it would be to assume that a career diplomat has no personal sense of guilt. The fact that so much of their conscious life is concerned with a system of social sanctions helps to disguise the underlying guilt system operative in the Japanese. This system is well disguised not only from the western observer but also from the Japanese themselves.[8] The Westerner, under the tutelage of Christianity, has learned to "universalize" aggressive and other impulses and feel guilt in regard to them in general terms. The modern Japanese is moving toward such an attitude, but he or she is affected by the traditional moral structure based on the family system, or, in expanded form, on the nation conceived of in familial terms.

Lastly, some difficulty in perceiving Japanese guilt theoretically, if not clinically, arises because psychoanalysis (the psychological system most often consulted for help in understanding the mechanisms involved in guilt) tends to be strongly influenced by Western ethical values. Psychoanalytic writers, in describing psychosexual development, tend to emphasize the superego on the one hand and concepts of personal individuation and autonomy on the other. For the Westerner, a major goal of maturation is freedom of the ego from irrational social controls as well as from excessive internalized superego demands. For an understanding of the Japanese, this emphasis is somewhat out of focus. Maturational ideals valued by the traditional Japanese society put far more emphasis on concepts of "belonging" and on adult role identity.

In studying the Japanese, it is helpful therefore to try to understand the internalization of an ego ideal that is defined in terms of social role behavior. Concern with social roles has in the past been more congenial to the sociologist or sociologically oriented anthropologist,[9] who in examining human behavior is less specifically concerned with individuation and more concerned with the patterning

---

[8]It is significant that in Japan the ceremonials for marriage and fertility and to celebrate periods in childhood are Shinto, whereas Buddhist ceremonials are used mainly to pay respect to parents—that is, in funerals or memorial services at specified times after death. It must be noted that this does not include any references to fear of punishment in an afterlife. Such references have been part of traditional Buddhism in the past, but are not much in evidence in modern Japan. Relatively few modern Japanese are concerned with life beyond death.

[9]This approach is also evident in the religious theory. Also, the recent interest in existentialist psychiatry is one attempt to bring in relevant concepts of "belonging" to the study of the human experience. See the further discussion in chapter 14, volume I, on suicide as related to a failure of belonging.

of behavior within a network of social relations. However, the sociological approach in itself does not always provide a sufficient explanation of the degrees to which individuals will invest their psychological energy in the enactment of social roles. For example, the presence of social role expectations alone does not account for the differences in the strength of the achievement motive in one person as compared with another person.

It is helpful to also use a psychodynamic framework to examine the psychological processes whereby social roles are internalized and the manner in which they influence the formation of the ego ideal and also the conscience. From the psychodynamic perspective, it is these psychic components that influence the ego mechanisms such that they direct the person's energy toward role-appropriate behavior. Erikson's (1956, 1959) idea about the development of "identity" in the process of psychosocial maturation formed a bridge between this psychodynamic perspective and the sociological analyses. In this view, the person's social identity itself is seen as a vital factor in determining behavior, yet its development proceeds through a process of psychosexual maturation in an interpersonal context.

As we too have tried to bridge these disciplines with a psycho-cultural developmental framework, we are also convinced that one must look at the relationship between the normative expectations embodied in social roles and the development of internalized evaluations that are used to produce responsible behavior. Any understanding of a person's sense of responsibility (and guilt that is produced by a failure to live up to that responsibility) must make reference to the specific kinds of demands with which the individual is attempting to comply. The extent to which these are the internalized demands of a multifaceted superego, or the direct external demands of an evaluative and punitive society, and the balance with which these are configured intrapsychically, will depend on how the specific cultural context structures psychosexual development. Additionally, with respect to superego functions, some contexts may rely more on the ego ideal and its knowledge of "propriety," whereas others may rely on the conscience and its knowledge of "sin." The analysis of narratives may be particularly useful in revealing culture-specific patterns of emic experience that are produced by this interface between social expectations and the developing self.

Illustrative Samples of Scoring in the Following Chapters

In several of the chapters of volume II we have included actual illustrations of scoring of several of the subcategories included under the [R] category. Especially notable are the verbatim responses found in chapters 1, 3, 4, 10, 11, and 12, volume II.

Notes

Bennett, Ivy Lee. 1960. *Delinquent and Neurotic Children, A Comparative Study*. New York: Basic Books.

De Vos, George A. 1960a. Psycho-Cultural Attitudes Toward Primary Relationships in Japanese Delinquents—A Study in Progress. *International Mental Health Research Newsletter*, **2**(1 and 2): 10–12 (reprinted: no. 14, 1961).

———. 1960b. The Relation of Guilt Toward Parents to Achievement and Arranged Marriage Among the Japanese. *Psychiatry*, **23**(3) 287–301. (reprinted: no. 22, 1963; no. 42, 1967; no. 85, 1974; no. 161, 1986.)

———. 1962. Deviancy and Social Change: A Psycho-Cultural Evaluation of Trends in Japanese Delinquency and Suicide. In Robert J. Smith and Richard K. Beardsley (Eds.), *Japanese Culture: Its Development and Characteristics* (pp. 153–170). Chicago: Aldine Publishing Co.

———. 1968. Suicide in Cross Cultural Perspective. In H.L.P. Resnick (Ed.), *Suicidal Behaviors: Diagnosis and Management* (pp. 105–134). Boston: Little, Brown, & Co.

———. 1970. Social Problems in Japan: The Research of American Social Scientists. In Edward Norbeck and Susan Parman (Eds.), *The Study of Japan in the Behavioral Sciences*. Houston, Tex.: William Marsh Rice University.

———. 1973. *Socialization for Achievement: Essays on the Cultural Psychology of the Japanese.* Berkeley: University of California Press.

———. 1980. Delinquency and Minority Status: A Psycho-Cultural Perspective (chapter 6). In Graeme Newman (Ed.), *Crime and Deviancy: A Comparative Perspective* (pp. 130–180). Beverly Hills: Sage Publications.

———. 1986a. Confucian Family Socialization: The Religion, Morality and Aesthetics of Propriety. In Walter H. Slote (Ed.), *The Psycho-Cultural Dynamics of the Confucian Family: Past and Present*. International Cultural Center of Korea.

———. 1986b. Religion and Family: Structural and Motivational Relationships. In George A. De Vos and Takao Sofué (Eds.), *Religion and Family in East Asia*. Berkeley: University of California Press.

———. 1992. *Social Cohesion and Alienation: Minorities in the United States and Japan.* Boulder, Colo.: Westview Press.

———. 1993a. Problems with Achievement, Alienation, and Authority in Korean Minorities in the United States and Japan. In K.K. Lee (Ed.), *Studies of Koreans Abroad* (pp. 137–194). Seoul: Society for the Study of Overseas Koreans.

———. 1993b. A Cross Cultural Perspective: The Japanese Family as a Unit in Moral Socialization. In P. Cowan, J. Filed, D. Hansen, M. Scolnick, and G. Swanson (Eds.), *Family, Self, and Society: Towards a New Agenda for Family Research.* Hillsdale, N.J.: Erlbaum Assoc.

———. 1998. Confucian Family Socialization: The Religion, Morality and Aesthetics of Propriety. In Walter Slote and George De Vos (Eds.), *Confucianism and the Family in an Interdisciplinary, Comparative Context* (pp. 329–280). Albany: State University of New York Press.

De Vos, George A. and Keiichi Mizushima. 1962. The School and Delinquency: Perspectives from Japan. *Teachers College Record*, **63**(8): 626–638.

De Vos, George A. and Hiroshi Wagatsuma. 1966. *Japan's Invisible Race: Caste in Culture and Personality.* Berkeley: University of California Press.

———. 1969. Minority Status and Delinquency in Japan. In William Caudill and Tsung-yi-Lin (Eds.), *Mental Health Research in Asia and the Pacific* (pp. 342–357). Honolulu: East-West Center Press.

Dore, Ronald Philip (Ed.). 1965. *The Legacy of Tokugawa Education*. Princeton, N.J.: Princeton University Press.

Erikson, Erik H. 1956. The Problem of Ego Identity. *Journal of the American Psychoanalytic Association*, **4**: 56–121.

———. 1959. *Identity and the Life Cycle*. New York: International Universities Press.

Fauconnet, P. 1920. La Responsabilité. *Etude de Sociologie*. Paris: Librararie Felix Alcan.

Gough, Harrison, George De Vos, and Keiichi Mizushima. 1968. A Japanese Validation of the CPI Social Maturity Index. *Psychological Reports*, **22**: 143–146.

Hermans, Philip. 1999. The Expression of Guilt by Moroccan Adolescents: Ethnocentric Interpretations by Western Teachers and Social Workers. *International Journal of Educational Research*, **31**: 303–316.

Hobbes, Thomas. 1924. *Leviathan*. London: J. M. Dent and Son, Ltd.

Lee, Changsoo and George A. De Vos. 1981. *Koreans in Japan: Ethnic Conflict and Accommodation*. Berkeley: University of California Press.

Mizushima, Keiichi and George De Vos. 1967. An Application of the California Psychological Inventory in a Study of Japanese Delinquency. *Journal of Social Psychology*, **71**: 45–51.

Piaget, Jean. 1932. *The Moral Judgment of the Child*. London: Kegan Paul, Trench, Trubner & Co. Ltd.

Power, T. and S. Manire. 1992. Child Rearing and Internalization: A Developmental Perspective. In J. Janssen and J. Gerris (Eds.), *Childrearing: Influence on Prosocial and Moral Development* (pp. 101–123). Amsterdam: Swets and Zeitlinger.

Schafer, Roy. 1968. *Aspects of Internalization*. New York: International Universities Press.

Turiel, E. 1998. The Development of Morality. In William Damon (Series Ed.) and N. Eisenberg (Vol. Ed.), *Handbook of Child Psychology: Vol 3. Social, Emotional and Personality Development* (5th edition), (pp. 863–932). New York: Wiley.

Wagatsuma, Hiroshi and George A. De Vos. 1984. *Heritage of Endurance: Family Patterns and Delinquency Formation in Urban Japan*. Berkeley: University of California Press.

Yamashita, Samuel Hideo. 1984. *Nature and Artifice in the Writings of Ogyu Sorai* (pp. 138–165). Princeton: Princeton University Press.

Chapter 12

Mutual Purpose: Patterns of Competition and Cooperation

Some mutually reciprocal (horizontal) relationships involve *cooperative* or *adversarial* activity between or among peers or adversaries in socially defined contexts. Although there may be some expressive dimensions to cooperative and adversarial activities (especially as pertain to concerns with Affiliation and Harmony) these activities can also be seen as being largely instrumental in their character. We score such concerns with the category of Mutual Purpose (M).

As is true with all the categories we are considering, *cooperation* or *competition* can be perceived both positively and negatively. In some societies competition is seen as a positive activity, in others it can be seen negatively. Individuals can hold strong implicit attitudes that define the inherent legitimacy or inappropriateness of certain forms of competitive or cooperative activities.

In their comparative work, anthropologists have been interested in how to examine the relative force of competitive and cooperative motives in societies that differ with respect to horizontally defined status relationships. In one of her earlier books Margaret Mead (1937) examined the relative presence and organizing force of competitive versus cooperative instrumental activities among such widely divergent groups as the Inuit of Greenland, Ifugao of the Philippines, the Manus and Arapesh of the New Guinea region, the Bachiga of East Africa, and several others. In all instances some forms of competition or cooperation were positively evaluated, others were not, and there were also variations in the overall saliency of competition or cooperation in the societies in question. In North American society, some instances of both competitive and cooperative instrumental behavior are also generally considered praiseworthy, but other modes of competition or cooperation can be perceived as coming into conflict with prevailing social ideology.

Generally speaking, cooperative and competitive behavior is considered to be positive and worthy of positive social sanctioning if it is performed in accord with expected standards, and if it is constructive for the total group, whatever the consequences for the immediate participants, whether losers or winners. Competitive behavior is negatively sanctioned if a competitor is considered to be "*cheating*" or otherwise active in a manner that is considered unfair. Cooperative behavior is also negatively evaluated in situations where participants act contrary to expectations, seek the achievement of personal rather than group ends, or seek to benefit from collective activity while not contributing personal effort.

Social interactions of competition and cooperation are often complex, and involve a mixture of other concerns. Both instrumental and expressive concerns can frequently be consciously described as intertwined. For example, the instrumental aspects of competition in the seeking of competitive goals (scored under the M categories of Mutual Purpose) are to be distinguished from expressive concerns with conflict or discord that are scored with the negative Harmony (H) categories. In some H responses, hostility can be expressed as an essential part of an adversarial relationship. For example, consider a prize fight wherein there is expressed hostility (HC-discord) or even contempt (EDC-contempt). In contrast, in M themes the emphasis is not on expressed hostility, but on some instrumental attempt at accomplishment, even though it be adversarial in nature. For example, consider a prize fight where the emphasis is on besting the opponent.

One can also find narrative themes that emphasize *cooperation* in goal-directed interactive behavior. The instrumental components of these M cooperative categories are distinguishable from expressive concerns noted in the F categories (Affiliation). Instrumental goals to be gained by mutual effort are to be distinguished from the expressive feelings of togetherness or separation that may also accompany such interactive activities. Themes that emphasize instrumental purpose must also be distinguished from the themes that emphasize the positive attainment of social harmony (H). Again, where narratives emphasize both instrumental purposes as well as expressive concerns, the responses must be double scored.

Clearly, instrumental and expressive concerns can frequently be intertwined in narrative descriptions of interpersonal interactions. Where instrumental and expressive concerns are so intertwined, and are so verbalized, one needs to double score such descriptions. One must caution, however, that the scoring of these concerns with should remain in accord with the "emic" attitudes of the informant, and not be a reflection of the "etic" values generally held by others, including the scorer. One cannot a priori assume that cooperation or competition are either positively or negatively perceived.

The Development of Competition and Cooperation

Competition and Hostility

From early childhood on, peer interactions provide opportunities for both cooperation and competition. Children may work together toward a common goal, hence, cooperate. Or they may vie with each other, hence, compete. Most often both cooperation and competition appear together in nursery schools, preschools, and other social settings where groups of young peers may be observed. Studies of the appearance of cooperation and competition in early childhood suggest that there is a progression from more self-focused instrumental concerns towards group-focused or social concerns.

In the development of competitive behavior, infants who are grabbing for physical objects before nine months may be relatively "impersonal" in their intentions toward the possession of objects, seeking them instead as a momentary curiosity or for immediate instrumental purpose. Between nine and thirteen months there appears observable conflict between children over the possession of play equipment (Maudry and Nekula, 1939). Such early instrumental competitive conflicts can also involve acts of aggression known as instrumental aggression. Though potentially injurious to the other, these acts may be relatively free of intentional harm, being instead focused on the instrumental effort to possess the object.

In fact, possession of an object is a central motive in aggressive acts between two-year-old children (Bronson, 1975). These acts initially involve both teasing and physical contact, but by the end of the second year increasingly involve teasing, and may also involve intentionally destructive acts directed toward the other child's possessions (Dunn, 1988).

Hartup (1974) also notes how instrumental aggressive acts developmentally precede the more intentionally injurious hostile aggression. When behavior aimed at the possession of an object is frustrated by an obstacle, the frustrated intentionality may then become linked with an internal experience of anger or rage that may be expressed as destructive power directed toward removing the obstacle. Human beings, both adult and child, will sometimes direct anger toward anything that blocks attainment of an instrumental goal. This anger can sometimes even be directed toward the desired object itself. Where the instrumental effort is socially frustrated by the actions of others, the frustration may be expressed with destructive behavior directed toward another person. In such an instance, it may be seen as "hostile aggression." By the age of three (Hartup, 1974) one sees an increase in the proportion of aggressive acts that involve apparent hostility, although they normally remain relatively few in number (Shantz, 1987).

Even where direct action is not taken, angry feelings and destructive intent can become experientially linked with the awareness of possible negative consequences. An understanding of anger's destructive potential is one basis for the experience of guilt. It is an important basis for moral awareness, and can lead to the inhibition of destructive thought and action (see chapter 11, volume I, on Responsibility).

In some instances of frustration, the instrumental purpose may have been to "possess" another person through either active control or by becoming the focus of the other's attention in a mutual recognition (see chapter 10, volume I, and Benjamin, 1988). In such situations, the object that was sought may itself be seen as the direct cause of the frustration. This may be especially problematic internally, in that the intent to injure another is particularly unacceptable when the target of destructiveness is also the source of comfort. The conflict associated with a potential hostile destruction of the attachment object may fuel the projective defenses and become manifest as a splitting of "good" and "bad" that we have discussed in chapter 10, volume I, on Control.[10]

Although frustrated instrumental intentions can be directed into hostile or destructive expressive acts they can also be directed instrumentally toward socially approved competitive behavior, or even redefined into cooperative endeavor. Either of these sorts of instrumental activity can avoid the potential feelings of guilt or anxiety that might otherwise be aroused through hostile or destructive fantasy and action. Furthermore, not all competitive behavior need be seen to involve the expression or transformation of destructive intent. Some studies have found that overt destructive aggression is not necessarily related to competitive behavior. For example, McKee and Leader (1955) observed the interactions between over a hundred three and four-year-old children, and found almost no correlation between the children's efforts to excel competitively and efforts to injure others. However, Greenberg (1932) and Leuba (1933) have noted a progressive appearance of rivalry with age. Although in the pre-school period they found that two-year-olds seemed little affected by the presence of others doing a similar task, competition became more evident among three- and four-year-olds. By that age, their efforts at task performance were somewhat distracted by the performance of others when completing a peg board task. By age five, competition could actually enhance performance in some. One must consider that during this period historically, teachers encouraged competition among the middle-class children from among whom these samples were constituted.

McKee and Leader (1955) found that competitive behavior was more intense among those of lower socioeconomic status and that boys were generally more competitive than girls in their samples, and competitiveness increased with age. The gendered nature of aggressive behavior, more generally considered, appears to be widespread. Boys appear to be more physically aggressive in many cultures (Whiting and Edwards, 1988). However, if one is careful to include a broader variety of acts in one's definition of "aggression," girls may also be seen as equally

---

[10]See also Horney's (1945) discussion of the basic conflict between the dependent and affiliative movement toward others, the hostile movement against others, and the autonomy-seeking yet isolating movement away from others.

aggressive. Aggression may take different forms in boys and girls. For example, one sees a higher incidence of acts known as "relational aggression" among girls (Crick and Grotpeter, 1995). These are attacks on social acceptability rather than being physical in nature (See chapter 6, volume I, on Esteem). Relational aggression involves the use of derogatory remarks, expressions of dislike, and explicit acts of social rejection or ostracism used in a hostile manner. The degree to which these behavioral differences are based in socialization processes or in sex differences in primate neuroendocrine function and in other inherited predispositions remains unclear, although it is clear that differential socialization and the sanctioning of role-related behavior plays at least some part in producing, maintaining, or supporting gender differences in aggressive or destructive behavior in humans.

The Socialization of Cooperative Behavior

Cooperation and Prosocial Behavior, Instrumental and Expressive Components

Obviously, not all social interactions are competitive or conflictual. In modern societies, the peer group provides opportunities for children in play and in school to learn to work together toward common goals, as well as to compete in competitive sports or in school achievement. In team sports both between-group competition and within-group cooperation are evoked at the same time. While there is within-group teamwork directed in competition with other teams, there is also, within the team, a possible rivalry for relative excellence and status. It is sometimes difficult to disentangle the complexity of instrumental motives in peer group activities. Furthermore, the instrumental behavior may also involve expressive components. The same behavior may be motivated by a variety of motives. There may be expressive motives directed within the group in disharmonious or discordant (H) intra-group rivalry or struggles for appreciation (E) and leadership status (D), while the group as a whole nevertheless cooperates in competition with another group. Or the converse might be true. What is difficult in efforts to study cooperation is to distinguish expressive affiliative interactions (F) from truly instrumental forms of cooperation, and these are confounded in some studies. For example, one early measure of cooperation explicitly included the measurement of "sympathy" (F) (Murphy, 1937; Murphy, Murphy, and Newcomb, 1937).

The scoring of expressive motives related to affiliative needs (F), or those that emphasize harmony over discord (H), or evaluative considerations of social acceptability (E), etc., should be scored with the appropriate expressive categories. It is not infrequent to double score Mutual Purpose responses with concerns from these other categories.

Developmental Contexts and Peer Interactions

As children progress from more isolated forms of play they commonly move into forms of socially interactive play (Göncü and Kessel, 1988; Parten, 1932). This does not involve a process whereby more cooperative forms simply replace the earlier forms. Instead, it is a matter of proportion and cognitive complexity, even within the categories of nonsocial or social play (Howes and Matheson, 1992). Children continue to play in an isolated manner, and by three to four years of age they are still most frequently engaged in nonsocial play. By the kindergarten age, solitary forms of play may account for a third of a child's play.

As children are encouraged to cooperate, or are given the opportunity to cooperate in play-group or preschool activities, they increasingly move from solitary or parallel play to forms of associative or interactive play that may involve working together on a task. An example of this would be the transition from playing adjacently but independently with a set of blocks (as in parallel play) to working together to construct a structure with the same blocks. As they cooperate they may discuss what the structure is going to be (as a negotiated symbolic representation for use in pretend play), what it is going to look like, how best to build it, etc. They may also struggle to come to consensus, and occasionally fail to work successfully together, such that one child may destroy the collective product (whether intentionally or through clumsiness).

The form of play that requires the form of cooperation that most resembles adult social relationships is the form of pretend play known as sociodramatic play. In this form of play, children collectively make-believe that they are enacting social roles. This form of play can involve the collective negotiation of what the group will accept as role-appropriate behavior. Children take on different roles, and will assist each other in enacting the required behavior. For example, when children play "house," one child may become the "mother," the other becomes the "baby." The "mother" may scold or be affectionate toward the "baby," while the "baby" may make infant vocalizations, suck a thumb, pretend to cry, etc. As Cole and Cole (1996) have discussed, some psychologists believe that this form of play may be very important for cognitive and social development. We are favorable to the neo-Vygotskian view that these forms of peer interaction form a zone or proximal development that supports a range of cognitive skills (Dias and Harris, 1990; Rogoff, 1990). More importantly, however, we see this form of collective activity as the initial negotiation of social role relationships, and the development of both cooperative (M) and socially harmonious (H) skills related to role enactment. These are social skills that will serve the person throughout life as he or she moves through the variety of roles in which one must partake if one is to interact cooperatively in social activity.

Madsen and colleagues have studied the cultural contexts of competitive and cooperative behavior, and have found that differential socialization affects how groups of peers from different cultures choose to collectively accomplish tasks where cooperative and competitive strategies may be relatively more or less successful. In one study, children raised in cooperation-oriented Israeli communities, known as kibbutzim, were compared with children raised in more competition-oriented middle-class urban families. The cooperatively raised children where much more successful when faced with a task that required cooperation (Shapira and

Madsen, 1969). However, not all tasks require cooperation, nor do some even allow for cooperation. One wonders how youth who are socialized to rely on peer interaction in problem-solving settings will fare when faced with the requirement of individual analytic activity.

Earlier studies of task performance under competitive or cooperative conditions of majority American children have found that efficiency of effort was consistently higher when work occurred under competition (Maller, 1929). When given the choice of working for the group in a competitive situation or working independently, boys chose to join a group effort only 26 percent of the time. Girls tended to be somewhat more cooperative than boys in these early experiments. Doob (1952) indicated that certain qualifications were necessary when considering results that demonstrate improved performance in self-oriented compared with group-oriented situations. Prizes were given to individuals, but the rewards in a group effort depended on a degree of attachment to the group and its enhancement through a collective victory. Degrees of expressively motivated affiliation help determine the efficacy of group effort, and where such affiliation was not emphasized, the competitive motives may have been prevalent. In the historical period when these experiments were conducted, the American school atmosphere certainly encouraged individual achievement over group effort.

Middle-class socialization in more traditional families has, in the past, tended toward the acquisition of more rigidified or internalized superegos. The peer group, therefore, has had less influence over the individual (Miller and Swanson, 1958; Riesman, Denney, and Glazer, 1950). In more recent decades, middle-class children have, by some appearances at least, become more group oriented than their more individualistically oriented parents. Where prevailing educational strategies emphasize cooperation and socially sensitive attitudes, such priorities may be reinforcing a peer group orientation, and deemphasizing differences in ability or judgment. As we shall presently discuss, individuals with this type of social orientation may be relatively more vulnerable to the opinions of associates. They may be more "field-dependent," where the social context itself is seen as the perceptual "field." If bolstered in their perceptions and attitudes by a peer group, they may then be more resistive to external authority figures who are seen as older or different from themselves. Conversely, the field-independent person remains more attuned to internalized standards and less sensitive to social pressure.

In American society today, we know that some minority youth groups become extremely antagonistic to any perceived authority and are susceptible or vulnerable to sanctioning only from their immediate peers. There are peer group patterns which reflect antagonism to constituted authority because exercised authority is seen by group members as alien and distant. The teacher in the school may require of the student certain deferential or compliant comportment that is out of keeping with their previous peer-focused social experiences. Peer-supported resistance to such conformity may substantially interfere with educational achievement and personal development. In contrast, however, a peer orientation can also lead to increased sensitivity to social sanctioning, and ultimately toward self-improvement, as in the case for many Japanese (see De Vos, 1992).

The fact that a peer-oriented tradition exists in a particular cultural group does not negate other evidence that the peer reference group can be psychologically compensatory in situations in which family cohesion has become weakened or broken. In such situations, the child moves out into the peer group to escape domestic disharmony and discord. We suggest that one must differentiate between a cultural pattern that exists more broadly in conditions of social stability and a "subcultural" one that exists within a pluralistic or changing society in which traditional family patterns are disrupted (see Lewis, 1966). In some instances, a peer orientation that is based in traditionally cooperative cultural patterns may be operating simultaneously with a more personal need for compensatory social affiliation to replace dysfunctional family affiliation.

Mutual Purpose and Group Identity

Comparison of Japanese and Mexican-American Samples

Very often competition or cooperation is not envisioned as individual endeavor, but part of a self-conscious consideration of self as a member of a specific group. This sense of self has a historical dimension as well as one defined by present circumstances. In this regard, there has been interest in the nature of Japanese organizations, whether in business or in the government bureaucracy. It is apparent that the Japanese as a nation have been highly successful *collectively* in competing economically with the industrial West. Their success results from various forms of internal cooperative structures that can unite individuals toward realizing collective economic and social goals. The Japanese suppress in-group forms of competition at the personal expense of the individual. On the other hand, the society encourages collective between-group competition (De Vos, 1978, 1982, 1983, 1992).

One might wonder how this is related to early socialization. Some would contend that there is correspondence between the early and later socialization practices of Japanese that emphasize various forms of deference behavior and non-confrontational social comportment. On a cognitive level, one might expect that peer-oriented socialization practices would lead to forms of thinking that use group perceptions as a basis for conceptual judgment. Yet this initial expectation has been directly contradicted by a study of high school youth in Japan and the United States (Vaughn, 1988). Vaughn demonstrated that on a cognitive level, Japanese children were more likely to make use of "field independent"[11] cognition as compared with the American sample wherein a higher incidence of "field dependence" was found.

[11]See Goodenough and Witkin's discussion of these cognitive styles (1977) and Witkin (1967).

These results suggest that Japanese youth, cognitively speaking, are relatively more independent of their perceptual context, while on a behavioral level they remain in conformity with the behavioral expectations of their immediate social group.

Child rearing that encourages more cooperative behavior and avoids the more socially disruptive individualistic motivation that has been characteristic of the achievement-oriented Protestant North American society (McClelland, 1961) is appealing to some educators. Yet one wonders whether such socialization of children also accounts for relative differences in educational and economic advancement in a society that continues to encourage individual achievement. In an effort to explain differential school performance of Mexican Americans in primary and secondary schools, some have contended that socialization toward group conformity in Mexican Americans is related to their development of cognitive "field dependence," and that this might account from some of the educational difficulties in schools that emphasized individual performance.[12] Some of this research involved comparison of Mexican American youth in school with their so-called Anglo counterparts, wherein a greater degree of field dependence was indeed found among the Mexican Americans. In what follows, we will attempt to account for these apparently contradictory findings about the effects of peer orientation found in the research on the Japanese and Mexican American samples.

Mexican American School Performance

Numerous studies in the past amply demonstrated that Mexican American children, on the average, did poorly when tested with traditional IQ and academic achievement tests. There were even some earlier studies reporting that the average IQ was going down year by year. While these results were in keeping with observed school performance, the early studies made no attempt to explicate these results within the cultural or social context of Mexican American children. Madsen (1967) took a then novel approach which considered the interpersonal styles found in traditional Mexican culture as well as cognitive performance in assessing what was going on among the minority children. It became obvious that the emphasis on individual competition that was then characteristic of the American schools was creating difficulty for many of the minority children. Individual teacher-pupil interaction was then the implicit American method of learning, each child being expected to internalize a desire to perform well and meet the expectations of the teacher. Kagan and Madsen (1972b) found that Mexican American children were consistently less rivalrous and avoided conflict more than Anglo American children. These differences tended to increase with age, in contrast to the special emphasis on rivalry found especially among Anglo American boys.

---

[12]See also Berry (1976), Kagan (1974), Kagan and Madsen (1971, 1972a, 1972b), Madsen (1967), Madsen and Shapira (1970), Ramirez and Price-Williams (1974).

For the Mexican American youth, the continued psychological use of the peer group as reference group has been related to a pattern of what psychologists have termed "field-dependence" (Witkin, 1967) found in Mexican children. Moreover, there was an avoidance of competitive confrontation among Mexican American children as a consequence of the sanctioning against such behavior by Mexican parents. The studies of Madsen and those stimulated by him emphasize the fact that middle-class Anglo American children who studied in the same schools as the Mexican Americans tend to manifest competitive attitudes in interaction with their peers, whereas Mexican American children are much less likely to do so. In contrast, both Mexican American and some lower-class urban Anglo children are more apt to be concerned with cooperative interaction with their peers rather than one to one interaction with their teachers.

From the standpoint of the need to analytically identify the social or familial contexts shared by many Mexican American youth, these research reports are somewhat lacking in any attempt to relate their findings directly to real-life situations or case histories. There are two issues that must be related here. First, one should consider how the field-dependent cognitive pattern and sensitivity to the peer group in the Mexican children might be related more generally and psychodynamically to the internalization of social norms in given families and to tensions between family expectations about school and peer group antagonism to school authorities. Second, one should consider how the field-dependent pattern might be related to observable patterns of delinquency among Mexican youth that occur in some communities but not in others. The issue is how family and community sanctions operate or fail to operate in respect to delinquent group behavior or peer group antagonism to school participation. We find there has been almost total neglect of systematic anthropological observation of the evident linkage of peer group reinforcement and resistance to learning.[13]

In comparing the behavior of mothers in six different cultures, Minturn and Lambert (1964) had previously reported that Mexican and Anglo American mothers were at the opposite extremes regarding peer group competition of an aggressive nature. The Mexican mothers severely discouraged aggressive behavior between peers. This socialization pattern may be related to an interesting contradiction one finds in contemporary Mexican American culture. There is an apparent contradiction between what is more negatively seen as socially disruptive individualistically motivated material success and the use of high-status positions in a self-serving way, on the one hand, and a more positively perceived maintenance of oneself as a peer-oriented person who does not seek special economic or personal advantage, on the other hand. In this cultural framework, instrumental self-interest is not harmoniously synthesized with expressive social needs. A person who pushes

---

[13]The current work of Marcelo and Carola Suárez-Orozco is directed toward explicitly considering the role of the peer group in the educational adaptation in youth from various minority groups. (See chapter 15, volume II.)

forward as an individual is quickly considered self-seeking and socially without virtue.

Authority problems encountered in the socialization of children may reflect this contradiction. The father, or others in positions of authority, are often depicted or experienced as a rigidly authoritarian "macho" figure. In Mexican American culture, while the concept of paternal authority can sometimes be idealized in the role of a "don," a fatherly gentleman, ordinary government officials or other authorities are seldom conceptualized as benevolent donors. This is very much in contrast with the pattern found among Japanese, as embodied in their concept of mentorship. More characteristically, traditionally Mexican officials and even family heads are distrusted. Authority, both inside and outside the family, is very often perceived as being exercised for personal benefit, not for benevolence. Individuals who attain such positions may find themselves constrained by social-structural as well as psychological demands to enact and thereby perpetuate the role expectations. Sometimes the Catholic priest as "father" is seen in a mentoring or guiding role, but he is so conceived because, by giving up competitively defined materially oriented ambition, he has stepped beyond the scope of the contradiction. He is not perceived as being the corrupt "macho" authority figure, and can therefore retain some credibility in a position of authority.

How Does Encouraging Cooperation Relate to Field Dependent Behavior? An Ideological Dilemma in Contemporary Psychology

One can distinguish in the writings of Kagan and Madsen (1972a, 1972b) some differentiation between positively perceived "competition" as a means of self-fulfillment and the more negative expressive attributes of "rivalry" (or negative Harmony H) in which rivalrous behavior is intended to maximize one's own gain at another's expense. One notes, however, that in their analysis of cooperation there is no balanced consideration distinguishing between positive cooperation, which emphasizes joint effort and mutuality in the reaching of goals, and certain non-adaptive concomitants inherent in a less differentiated, less autonomous cognitive style. According to Witkin's concept of the difference between "field-dependent" and "field-independent" cognitive approaches, a field-dependent orientation is *less developed* in cognitive maturation.

There has been controversy over the implications of Witkin's theory. In this controversy, we see confusion between what can be called psychologically *adjustive cognitive differentiation* and socially *adaptive cooperation.*[14] The field-

[14]The Japanese case (see Vaughn, 1988) demonstrates that cognitively independent youngsters can also be trained to be equally sensitive and alert to social stimuli.

dependent orientation lacks the *adjustive cognitive differentiation* that supports a capacity for internally based judgment and the exclusion of irrelevant sensory information that enable coherent inner directedness. If social cooperation is built upon individuals who lack such autonomous psychological capacities, rather than producing desired results, it instead can lead to forms of social subordination and its opposite (reflexive social diffidence) rather than leading to more constructive democratic forms of interaction and mutually considered action in which some forms of instrumental intellectual confrontation are necessary.

One can watch television talk shows and even news commentary to observe the kind of nonanalytic thought processes that pass for discussion or debate in contemporary society. Whether the discussions are between so-called pundits, or between mates who have fallen out of love, the conversation can often amount to no more than the rhetorical assertion of a popular position without reasoned justification. The often boisterous involvement of the audience in such settings, where the host may even call on the audience for their opinion, further illustrates the respect that is afforded what are often even rude expressions of peer judgment.

Field-dependent thought ultimately incapacitates members of the social group from reaching positively considered goals through mutually derived consensus based on argued rational judgment. Instead, such a group needs a leader to guide it, and without such a leader may behave more like a crowd than like a collectivity of individuals (see Le Bon, 1895/1960). Again this is illustrated in the case of some talk shows, where strong-men (bouncers) are called out to enforce the peace after the discussion has reached its peak in a collective frenzy of boisterous, angry, divisive, derisive, and even assaultive behavior. The widespread modeling of such collective behavior (as is indicated by the popularity of such shows) does not constitute a sound basis for the long-term maintenance of social cohesion in a democratic society.

In our judgment, there is an implicit bias in some of the research literature toward viewing all forms of peer cooperation positively. In such a climate, behavior that superficially appears to be cooperation is seen positively, regardless of the total context, and regardless of whether individuals are held accountable for the quality of their participation.

Conversely, all competition may sometimes be too readily seen as bad, and this may result in an ideological opposition to competitive interactions. Kagan (1974), and Kagan and Buriel (1977) have argued that field independence is correlated with learning and achievement in American schools, and hence, success in such schools is necessarily linked to patterns of socially disruptive competition. In contrast, field-dependent individuals are considered to be adaptively more alert to social stimuli, capable of achieving consensus in less time than field-independent groups, and therefore probably more skilled in the art of interpersonal accommodation and the maintenance of social cohesion. The impetus derived from that analysis has been toward changing the competitive atmosphere of schools to reinforce cooperation and thereby ultimately enable cooperative social functioning.

We think that the latter interpretation and the subsequent implementation of change in schools that it has led to is simply wrong. Some authoritative leadership may be necessary for a field-dependent group to function at all. This leadership, unchecked, can become authoritarian in nature. Contrary to the assumptions of some researchers and educators, field-independent persons may achieve democratic forms of social cohesion more readily than can field-dependent individuals. A certain amount of confrontation and disagreement and willingness to act independent of group consensus may be necessary for effective realization of mutually beneficial instrumental outcomes. We do also believe that such interactions can be optimal if the participants have the good fortune to be socially sensitive in their concerns for the viewpoint of others. Field-dependent youngsters are less able to become objective or detached in assessing the merits of a decision. Hence, one could make the argument that field-dependent individuals are less capable of carrying out democratic discussions that demand self-confidence. Internalized forms of individual, instrumentally focused judgment or integrity are necessary for arriving at satisfactory resolutions that need objective judgment. We would contend that field-independent persons may be better able to resist the influences of others where give-and-take democratic social, political, or industrial discussion are required. In contrast, the type of social accommodation that occurs among field-dependent individuals may instead result in a *subordination of self in an authoritarian structure*.

A similar dilemma is superficially apparent in collective processes in Japan. However, in that context one cannot infer that a lack of contentious discussion in a Japanese professional group is caused by a field-dependent cognitive pattern rather than by a strict social discouragement of contention in any group context. Whatever a person thinks in Japan, he or she is expected to remain silent rather than make disagreement overt. In fact, in such settings, there is input of field-independent thought from subordinates in the Japanese pattern, but it occurs in a totally different context than that found in an American hierarchical business structure. In positive instances, the Japanese manage to include well-reasoned input from subordinates without any overt display of contentious discussion. The history of success of the Honda organization, for example, is said to be due to methods of incorporating the advice of the workers working on the automobiles being produced.

We suggest that early socialization toward a cognitively stifling peer-oriented and field-dependent approach does not equip individuals for making objective decisions in a modern, nontraditional, changing social setting, whether as workers, administrators, or as public servants seeking to resolve conflicts among others. Adaptation within modern industrial and postindustrial societies necessitates more advanced, differentiated cognitive approaches. The fact that field-dependent individuals may have been well adapted to forms of authoritarian social organization does not argue for equivalence between a less developed and a more developed mode of thought. Concrete thinking, albeit quite adaptive in some societies, cannot be seen ultimately as adaptive in a variety of modern situations that frequently require abstract deductive thought. We would contend that just as there *is* a maturational-developmental progression from forms of concrete thinking toward a capacity for more abstract forms of thought, there is also a progression from the limitations of field-dependent thinking toward the capacity for field-independent cognition.[15]

Cooperative Efforts at Betterment Versus Individual Advancement: A Dilemma for Koreans in Japan

Observing trends in the United States, Daniel Bell (1975) and others (Glazer and Moynihan, 1975) have remarked that a strong reason for the resurgence of ethnicity within the United States is due to the instrumental gain to be derived; namely, that ethnic groupings have become collective interest groups, and that ethnic identity can therefore be rewarding instrumentally, given the responsiveness of government. This development may be particularly true in the United States, one would say quickly, but it does not seem to be equally true for the Koreans in Japan.

Patterned cooperative or competitive behavior has a historical dimension that differs in respect to whether those involved were of elite or subordinate background within the majority society, or of membership in some despised minority not considered properly a member of the majority society. To cite such an instance we can refer to our interviews with Koreans or Japanese in Japan conducted during several research projects (Lee and De Vos, 1981). They reveal the type of dilemma faced by members of some minority groups in which individual advancement is opposed by considerations of group loyalty.

Expressive Behavior in Korean Japanese Identity

As indicated elsewhere, on an instrumental level for noncitizen Koreans, it would seem best to "pass" and to deny one's ethnic background (see chapter 8, volume I). On the surface, the Japanese would be willing to forget origins if Koreans would manage their outer appearance in a conformist fashion, and would not attempt intermarriages that expose their background. Nonetheless, it is obvious that such "passing" is psychologically difficult for Koreans for expressive reasons. Given this

---

[15]While working as a psychological consultant in a prison for young adults, the senior author has seen reports of how the collective peer group attitudes to which Mexican American youth were subjected were influential not only in involving youths in the activities that led to their incarceration, but how Mexican peer groups in school heavily sanctioned against individual attempts at *classroom* learning. It seems evident that those who are good students had to resist strong group pressure against manifesting good school performance.

difficulty, then, we would assume that Koreans have become aware that group action is more efficacious in overcoming discrimination and more satisfying of expressive needs than the route taken by expedient individuals who pass invisibly into modern depersonalized occupations. Whether one argues simply in instrumental terms, or in respect to individual or group interest, as Daniel Bell (1975) has noted, a person's ethnicity can be used to combine instrumental interests with affective concerns. This is true also for caste-related behavior (DeVos, 1992).

It is thereby incumbent on us, using our psycho-cultural form of analysis, to reexamine and analyze in detail so-called affective group ties and their components to better understand their composition. The sources of the need for Korean ethnic identity lie within the psychological structure and inner experience of the individual. One especially notes in the discussion of expressive variables how harmony, affiliation, nurturance, and esteem—or their negative counterparts in discord, isolation, deprivation, and disparagement—are often inextricably intertwined with one another as well as with instrumental motives. We must continually return to unresolved problems of discord, deprivation, and disparagement, no matter what principal theme we pursue.

The development of modern industry in Korea is relatively recent. It is difficult at present to judge, without intensive research, how Korean organizations operate and whether they are different from or similar to those found in Japan. We know that many upper status Koreans in business and in education have been trained in Japanese settings, but we have gained the impression from some observation that patterns of interaction among minority Koreans, including the exercise of authority and the expression of loyalty by subordinates, may differ from that manifested by their Japanese counterparts.

Some cultural and historic organizational features, whatever the society, continue their influence regardless of modern exigencies imposed by industrial structures. It must be noted that culturally, Korean and Japanese organizational history is radically different in several respects. The premodern Korean administrative system was modeled on that of the Chinese bureaucracy. It was centralized around the royal court structure. Officials sent out to local regions were usually alien to the region they were sent to govern. For the most part, no patterns of intercommunication or personal loyalty were developed between local subjects and their governors. This type of organization differed markedly from that of the local feudatories of Tokugawa Japan, among whom loyalty to one's lord was espoused as a supreme virtue.

There was no Korean counterpart to the warrior class in feudal Japan. Korean officials, as with their Chinese counterparts, were totally devoid of military training or interest. As in China, the military was despised and was not trained to responsible governing. In contrast, Japan went into its modern period with a trained samurai class. Although officially abolished as a recognized group, the former samurai helped develop a modern bureaucracy, manned a system of compulsory education for all, and later, as entrepreneurs, brought forms of samurai self-discipline into modern business activities. Through samurai influence on the system of compulsory education, Confucian ideology permeated the school system in the name of national unity and defense (see chapter 8, volume I). The Confucianist hierarchy of relationships was expressed through a nationalist ideology with strong military overtones.

A second feature of the premodern Japanese social class structure also lacked a counterpart in Korea. This was the influence of a burgeoning merchant-artisan-townsman culture, with its highly elaborated hierarchical system of apprenticeships and sustaining mentorships exercised by masters over disciples. This stratum of Japanese society had its own ambiance and its own aesthetics. Korean society, in contrast, consisted of a minuscule educated upper class and a large illiterate peasantry. There was no well-established, quasi-independent townsman tradition. Although the ideology of the upper class was overtly Confucianist, it did not and could not set up vertical systems of loyalty and personal commitment of the kind constructed in Japan on both the samurai and the merchant levels. Long-range apprenticeship programs, or forms of mentorship within age-graded bureaucratic structures, were less evident.

Little wonder then, from a social structural, historical standpoint, that we do not find the same fierce sense of loyalty involved in mutual purpose, and the same intensive superior-subordinate relationship developed in contemporary minority Koreans as in the majority Japanese. Koreans are not likely to subordinate themselves to group causes with the same degree of long-range collective "altruism" we sometimes find in the Japanese. Although Koreans can work together to mutual purpose, in many respects, they seem much less cohesive in respect to social groups than the Japanese and more apt to keep to immediate family purposes. Factional disputes are frequent and can disrupt larger organizational units.

There is considerable evidence that the modern occupational structures developed in Japanese industry are of relatively recent date, and that the concept of lifelong attachment to particular companies, either by workers or management, has been strengthened since the earlier period of industrialization at the turn of the century. Whatever the merits of such arguments against direct structural continuity with the premodern past, the point is that Japanese society still had latent within it a potentially strong instrumentally focused pattern of cooperative group loyalty that could be revised and developed by Japanese industry. It is questionable whether the psychological characteristics of people comfortable in this kind of life-career pattern are to be found with equal frequency or intensity among Koreans.[16] Whatever the actuality, the Japanese for their part do not perceive those of Korean ancestry in Japan as potentially loyal subordinates who will dedicate themselves cooperatively to company enterprises. This perception may be in part a matter of

---

[16]Nevertheless it is evident that Korean society in Korea has managed to mobilize an exceptional rate of economic growth. There is a shared mutual competiveness aimed directly at rivalry with the Japanese voiced by many Koreans that sometimes ameliorates labor–management contentiousness.

prejudice, but it may also be based on the minority Koreans' sense of resistance and suspicions about acceptance within Japanese organizations, which prevents them from making emotional commitments of the type implicitly expected by Japanese. Expressively considered patterns of loyalty and interdependency are thought by Japanese as necessary for instrumental group cooperation.

It has often been reported that Japanese instrumentally oriented social behavior depends expressively on school ties and other intricate affiliative networks that are not easily broken without jeopardizing all future activities. Whereas the value of group behavior of this kind among Koreans in Korea has been reported, it is uncertain how widespread among Koreans of all classes is the application of past affiliations to present cooperative, sustained group behavior.

Japanese are age-graded vertically within organizations to avoid competition. There is a similar sense of age-grading in Koreans. Informally at least, it is also apparent in interpersonal relationships in both groups. Koreans, however, are less obviously concerned with meticulous attention to deference behavior in their relationships both outside and inside the group. They are more easily relaxed in groups of mixed status. Minority Koreans in Japan are thought to be more unpredictable. Japanese are apt to be working within institutional and personal cooperative networks so binding that the individual's behavior is supposed to be highly predictable. In this sense, Japanese can afford to trust each other in their instrumental group operations, whereas Koreans are not as bound and hence, from a Japanese point of view, not as predictable.

In contrast, there are many instances in Japan of Koreans coming together cooperatively under crisis situations of political protest. But we note that these situations are not so much examples of instrumental cooperation as they are emotional expressions of an aroused sense of group identity. It is when this sense of belonging is actualized that Koreans respond by concerted action. Japanese, in the international arena, as part of their collective identity, can apply a steady, cooperative intensity toward the long-range maintenance of economic and political relationships and thereby are very often successful in the accomplishment of mutual ends.

In summary, Koreans in Japan in many circumstances must expect to reach their own occupational goals without the available assistance of a well-established instrumental group derivative of past affiliative ties which can be reactivated in business or professional pursuits. For them, instrumental group goals are not consciously evoked as a substitute for individual accomplishment. They therefore tend to be more individualistically competitive than cooperative in their careers. Nevertheless, there is among them vehement expressive support for Korean accomplishments and pride in those of their membership who attain some prominence, especially when they do so in competition with Japanese. There is, for example, a highly developed sense of Korean competitiveness in sports vis-à-vis the Japanese and a pride in the South Korean nation's increasing competitiveness in international economic pursuits. The nationalistic collective historical sense of having been despised second class subjects within the previous Japanese empire has been a motivational goad to Korean competitive enterprise.

Politically, much can be said about the factionalism within the Korean ethnic group in Japan. Not only is there distrust of other factions, but there is distrust by members of a group of the aims and advantages taken by their own leaders. Many Koreans are suspicious that some of their leadership functions for selfish benefit. What is the ordinary individual to do in these circumstances? An individual may feel that as a Korean he should assume responsibility within some available organization, but he may not find his convictions to be well represented. There are many reasons why it is easier for Koreans in Japan to unite in expressive ad hoc protcsts than to pursue sustained, affirmative, instrumentally directed, long-range, mutually supported, instrumental programs of action.

In our volume (Lee and De Vos, 1981), we have illustrated how the main forms taken by Korean voluntary associations are both instrumentally political and economic, as well as more expressively religious or ideological. Each of these groupings is heavily concerned with how ethnic identity is maintained in an overwhelmingly Japanese cultural-economic atmosphere. The economic cooperatives are perhaps the most directly guided by simple economic motives, but they are joined almost exclusively by individuals of a similar ideological persuasion. The religious groups are even more trusted. They have a history of courageous expressive protest against Japanese domination not prompted by selfish gain.

Scoring Themes of Competition or Cooperation

We turn now to the scoring of cooperative and competitive concerns that are found in narratives.

Themes of Competition or Adversarial Conflict

*A. Positively Perceived Rivalry or Competition **MVA***

MVA-game	Regulated competition (games, contests, etc.)
MVA-work	Successful business or work competition
MVA-vie	Maneuvering for advantage or seeking to be first among peers
MVA-smart	To outwit an opponent or win an argument
MVA-regard	Seeks competitive recognition
MVA-profess	Physical, artistic, academic competitive excellence
MVA-means	Competitive success in economic ventures

MVA-gambit	Acts of giving or concession to enhance own competitive position
MVA-faction	Constructive factional in-group competition
MVA-war	Instrumental war waged against an enemy

Positive forms of competition are most often considered socially productive in sporting events or in playing games (MVA-game). Competitive business or entrepreneurial activities are sanctioned when they are considered ultimately beneficial for the group (MVA-work). Some forms of maneuvering are positively considered (MVA-vie). There may be special approbation for the wit or intelligence displayed in a competitive activity, because outwitting an opponent or winning an argument is very often seen as positive activity (MVA-smart). If social approval is explicit, it must be double scored (MVA-smart ESA-approved). Some narratives emphasize artistic, academic, competitive excellence or physical strength (CA-able). Among these there are numerous circumstances in which artistic endeavor or performance, scientific research, academic activities, or physical abilities are defined positively in competitive terms and must be double scored (CA-able MVA-profess).

Some competitive behavior seeks social recognition. When this is explicit one can double score with the Esteem category (MVA-regard ESA-approved).

There may be success in competition which involves economic benefits (MVA-means). Long-term successful competition sometimes involves intermediate forms of concession or giving, called a "gambit" in chess (MVA-gambit). In a factional struggle one may identify positively with a particular faction seeking control (MVA-faction). If questions of power are explicit it must be double scored (MVA-faction DDA-lead) or (MVA-faction DDA-group). There is implicit or explicit social approval of competitive aggressive activities, even warfare, against another group to gain some instrumental success for one's own (MVA-war). If there is emotion of a destructive intent expressed, it can be double scored with the harmony discord category.

*B. Unresolved Competitive Situations **MVB***

MVB-deal	Unresolved negotiation or deal
MVB-differ	Differ about how to compete
MVB-distrust	Distrust about fair play of competitors
MVB-envy	Envy of competitor's ability
MVB-jealousy	Jealous fear of the competence of another; fear of encroachment
MVB-anger	Anger over failure to win out or prevail
MVB-elders	Generational conflict in instrumental coping

MVB-against	Intergroup competitive emphasis (double score with other appropriate categories)

There are numerous forms of unresolved uneasiness in competitive situations. Some revolve around a business deal with unresolved negotiations (MVB-deal). There may be unresolved difference in opinion on how to compete with others (MVB-differ). The most prominent expressions elicited are those expressing a sense of distrust, especially whether a competitive situation is organized fairly (MVB-distrust). There may be some envy about an adversary's ability or situational advantage (MVB-envy), or jealousy about the increasing competence of another who is seen as encroaching on one's more advantageous competitive position (MVB-jealousy). There may be an unresolved anger about frustrated competition (MVB-anger). There are situations of generational conflict (MVB-elders). Intergroup competitive emphasis may be double scored with other categories (MVB-against).

C. Unethical or Destructive Methods ***MVC***

MVC-war	Instrumental war seen negatively
MVC-faction	Divisive factional in-group competition
MVC-cheat	Unethical business behavior; lying, trickery, cheating
MVC-slander	Calumny, slander, etc. for competitive advantage
MVC-bribe	Comparative self-enhancement or status through gift exchange or bribery
MVC-remove	Removal of an opponent even by murder
MVC-magic	Use of magic to gain unfair advantage over rival

If seen as an abusive form of competition for economic ends or enhancing power over others, war (or other extreme antagonistic behavior) against an opponent may be depicted negatively (MVC-war). There are groups that suffer internally due to divisiveness, undue internal competitiveness or factionalism (MVC-faction). There are various ways to win a contest or conduct a business unethically, through trickery, lying, or cheating (MVC-cheat). One can use calumny or slander against an opponent to blacken another's reputation (MVC-slander). Bribery can be designated as a particular form of unethical behavior in a competitive situation (MVC-bribe).

One may remove an opponent or opposition by a number of negative acts including murder (MVC-remove). One may even resort to magic to win in competition (MVC-magic).

D. Withdrawal or Victimization ***MVD***

MVD-yield	Admission of defeat or capitulation to adversary; refugee flight
MVD-quit	Withdrawal from competition
MVD-refuse	Refusal to compete
MVD-cheated	Victim of unfair competition

There are various forms of inappropriate passivity. One can capitulate too easily to an adversary (MVD-yield). One may refuse to compete strongly enough, or drop out of competition too soon or in an unwarranted manner (MVD-quit). There are instance where an individual refuses to compete when it is expected (MVD-refuse). There are victims of unfair competition (MVD-cheated).

Themes of Cooperation

A. Concerted Behavior ***MTA***

MTA-interest	Sharing common interest
MTA-task	Cooperation in a task for a goal
MTA-family	Family action for a goal, specific or not
MTA-trust	Trust in others re: tasks
MTA-union	Organizational affiliation, trade unions, etc.
MTA-contract	Contract relationship (organic solidarity)
MTA-group	Group maintenance or enhancement
MTA-allied	Intergroup cooperative emphasis (double score with other appropriate categories)
MTA-defense	Cooperation in group defense (double score with Harmony categories if necessary)
MTA-devote	Subordination or sacrifice for group goals
MTA-repay	Reciprocal behavior to facilitate common behavior (including gifts)

There are narratives about sharing mutual instrumental interests (MTA-interest). There are a number of ways, specified or not, for mutual endeavor to gain positive ends (MTA-task). There are instrumental activities performed by families (MTA-family) or other social groups to benefit all members (MTA-group). There are expressions of trust in others in cooperative relationships (MTA-trust). Some individuals function as members of a union or some other forms of voluntary organization (MTA-union). One may have some forms of mutual contract binding oneself with others (MTA-contract). There may be a narrative about group maintenance or enhancement (MTA-group). There are *inter*group alliances as well as *intra*group affiliations. Two groups may work in concert with one another (MTA-allied). There are acts defending the interests of one's own group against the attacks of competitors (MTA-defense). When these situations include an aggressive, destructive intent, double score with some form of *Discord* or *Violence*. There is the subordination of one's personal advantages to group ends, or there can be acts of personal sacrifice for common instrumental ends (MTA-devote). There are specified reciprocal acts done to one's mutual benefit (MTA-repay).

B. Inactive or Unresolved Cooperative Situations ***MTB***

MTB-worry	Worry about the success or failure of a cooperative effort
MTB-join	Doubt about desire to join group effort
MTB-differ	Disagreement not specified
MTB-means	Disagreement about the means used
MTB-ends	Disagreement about the goal
MTB-rapport	Difficulties in communicating
MTB-distrust	Mutual distrust within one's own group
MTB-secret	Secretive activity going on not defined
MTB-allied	Unresolved intergroup cooperative emphasis (double score with other appropriate categories)

There may be worry about possible success of a joint effort (MTB-worry). There can be uncertainty about joining a joint effort (MTB-join). There can be differences about accomplishing a task (MTB-differ). There may be disagreement with the means taken to accomplish mutual goals (MTB-means), or there may be disagreement about the common goal itself (MTB-ends).

There may be a sense of difficulty in mutual communication (MTB-rapport). There can mutual distrust in instrumental cooperative activities, a fear of possible unreliability, betrayal, or sabotage by a group member (MTB-distrust). There can be concern with secretive activities in which one is not included (MTB-secret). There may be unresolved intergroup cooperative problems (MTB-allied). If there are indications of envy or jealousy within one's group, one may need to double score with the affiliative (F) category.

C. Negative Group Activities ***MTC***

MTC-crime	Group criminal behavior
MTC-plot	Plotting or political conspiracy

MTC-ethic	Unethical behavior
MTC-selfish	Selfish interests stronger than group goals
MTC-false	Hypocritical, untrustworthy behavior
MTC-failure	Failure to fulfill one's part in group activities
MTC-betray	Betrayal or deception of an ally or colleague
MTC-injury	Injury to others for group ends
MTC-allied	Intergroup cooperative emphasis seen negatively (double score with other appropriate categories)

There can be depicted group criminal behavior (MTC-crime). There are forms of cooperative plotting by politicians and others that are seen as negative conspiracy (MTC-plot). There are various forms of unethical behavior practiced in cooperative ventures (MTC-ethic).

There are also negative concerns expressed about selfish interests being stronger than group purposes (MTC-selfish). In an ethnic context, for example, there can be concern about some minority individual being more concerned about individual advancement at the price of neglecting group efforts at economic gain. Instrumentally oriented individualistic "passing" can be seen as negative to group purposes.

In cooperative situations, some individuals are hypocritical and untrustworthy (MTC-false). There are various forms of failure to fulfill one's part in cooperative situations (MTC-failure). There are various forms of betrayal or deception of an ally or allies by particular individuals (MTC-betray). There are various ways that innocent outsiders can be injured as a by product of accomplishing some group end (MTC-injury). An allegiance can be seen in negative terms (e.g., an "evil axis") (MTC-allied).

D. *Betrayed or Exploited* ***MTD***

MTD-victim	Being the victim of a conspiracy
MTD-exploited	Being exploited by others
MTD-cheated	Being cheated by others
MTD-accord	Suffer lack of coordination between parts of a group
MTD-failure	A sense of failure of a group effort

Passively considered, an individual can be a victim of a conspiracy involving members of one's own group (MTD-victim). An individual can be exploited (MTD-exploited) or cheated (MTD-cheated) by others in a cooperative venture. An individual can suffer due to lack of proper intragroup coordination or communication (MTD-accord). There may be a sense of ultimate failure of a cooperative effort (MTD-failure). Double score if the reasons for failure are made explicit.

Forms of Double Scoring

There can be complex objectives in competitive concerns expressed in interpersonal behavior that need double scoring. They may be self-oriented in respect to a realization of personal potential related to achievement or to competence. For example, there is concern with competition that is an affirmation of *competence* (C). There is competition that also manifests an *achievement* need (A), involving a demonstration of excellence to the self. Competitive success may be a demonstration to others, manifesting a need to gain the *appreciation* of one's group. Competitive motives may be individual or group enhancing (E). They may enforce control (D).

Cooperation may be blended with competition. Participation in mutual efforts as distinct from individual ones toward reaching some goal is very positively considered in many contexts. Cooperation or teamwork can be necessary to ethnic group activities directed toward economic advancement of one's group with or without reference to competition with other groups.

Illustrative Examples of the Scoring of Competitive or Cooperative Responses

The set of Thematic Apperception Test (TAT) cards used in our research was not selected to evoke stories of instrumental cooperation or competition. We have obtained relatively few stories in these categories. We can, however, illustrate the scoring of a few Mutual Purpose responses by utilizing the responses given by various Brazilian groups to Card 7BM, depicting an older and younger man in some form of communication. This series can also be used to illustrate scoring of the categories of Control, Affiliation, and Nurture discussed in previous chapters.

Cooperative situations have been evoked by Card 7BM when it was given to other groups in previous research. There were also stories of Competitive or Adversarial (H) situations.

The nature of the card is such that there are very few adversarial stories in which the two figures are interpreted as of equal status. There are occasional stories of a negative relationship between a boss or father and the younger figure. On the other hand, with the exception of Asian groups that pay special heed to the relative age of the figures, the two men are more apt to be seen as of equal status in friendly or cooperative circumstances or in situations of plotting something negative together.

In the present illustrative study (see chapter 10, volume II), there were very significant differences in the responses given among the Brazilian ethnic categories—Portuguese and African-Brazilians from an urban slum (favela), and Italian and German youth from townships near Porto Alegré in southern Brazil.

First, this card evoked a different proportion of stories of an instrumental or expressive nature. Forty (40) of the 50 Japanese Brazilian stories favored an instrumental theme, contrasted with 30 of 60 youthful Brazilian subjects (5 of 16 Portuguese, 10 of 21 Afro-Brazilians, 10 of 12 Italians, and 5 of 11 Germans).

Among the 40 Japanese instrumental stories, 18 were of advice, counsel, or mentorship given by an older man, often a father, to the younger man. There was only 1 Portuguese, 1 Italian youth, and 1 German youth who gave such a story. Four more of the Italian stories were of a controlling father, 3 of the German youth were about negative features of a father's use of authority. There were stories of wrongdoing or some legal concern by the younger figure in 1 Portuguese, 1 Afro-Brazilian, 2 Italians, and 1 Japanese.

The Japanese tended to be significantly more hierarchical in their stories. Such hierarchy even appears in some stories of mutual cooperation related to family efforts. In general, however, there are many stories that show the implicit respect for the advice that can be received from the elderly. The older person expects to give counsel and advice, and in a Japanese cultural context expects compliance rather than opposition. In general, instrumental mentoring is done with an implicit, if not explicit, nurturant attitude. Patience, wisdom, and understanding comes with patriarchy. Such stories are usually scored under the D category (Control). In the Brazilian groups one must note that themes of corruption, ineptitude, or rigid exercise of authority were the most noteworthy.

Let us look at specific illustrations of the scoring of Mutual Purpose stories.

There is one adversarial story of a negotiation over the price of a house given by a Portuguese youth:

> (BPf 16) There is a man talking to his neighbor, because he won't be able to pay the price of the house. Then he asked the neighbor to lower the price a little. Then the neighbor said he would think about it.
>
> [OB-want MVB-deal KD-means]

There are positively considered competitive or adversarial instrumental situations involving two men, by an Italian and a Portuguese-Brazilian. In one Italian story positive instrumental counsel is given in an adversarial situation involving possible wrongdoing on the part of the younger figure:

> (BIm 20) A trial. lawyer is giving him an orientation so that his accuser doesn't speak any nonsense. He is instructing the young man to defend himself from the other accuser's lawyers.
>
> [MVA-smart NDA-advice]

The Japanese

There are few straightforward stories of mutual enterprise. The pattern of distrust general to Brazil is also found in the Japanese, but to a lesser degree than in the other groups. When two individuals have their heads together, questionable activities are suggested to a number of the Japanese Brazilians as well as among the samples of Brazilian youth. Even some stories that are not directly conspiratorial have an aura of danger or controversy. Cynicism is higher in the younger group. Overall, 6 of 11 younger men (55%), 6 of 14 younger women (43%), but only 5 of 18 older men (28%), and 1 of 7 women (14%), a total of 18, or 36%, saw mutual instrumental stories.

Adversarial generational differences can cause difficulties for parents trying to work toward goals with their children. Such stories are given by two Japanese Brazilians:

> (BJmy 17, 29) A father talking to his son, trying to pass on counsel. The youth is antagonistic by the expression on his face. However, it is not about a fight between the father and son, but a normal disagreement conversation with the father and son.
>
> [NDA-advice DSC-resist MVB-elders MTB-differ]

> (BJsm 8) The same as the last card (he saw Card 6BM as representing generational difficulties. . . . The direct interaction between generations is small and exists in few families. . . . The values and ways of thinking between parent and son are different. The parents raise the children and work with them but their thinking is different.)
>
> [NDA-advice MVB-elders MTB-differ DSA-free]

There a numerous situations of working on a common goal. With four exceptions these stories were given by Japanese Brazilians.

Some mutual tasks in five of these stories have no negative implications, for example:

> (BJmy 61, 24) Relationship between the father and son. They are trying to do something together and are discussing it.
>
> [MTA-family]

> (BJmy 20) Here, there are two who are commenting, whispering, talking low about a subject that interests only them. They are talking to each other and sharing their ideas with each other, or one of them is commenting on the others around them who, at this moment, are not interested in these two people. Their conversation stays within.
>
> [MTA-interest]

Another suggests controversy:

> (BJmy 11, 39) There is an exchange of ideas between the two. A conversation of a problem, a problem that is controversial.
>
> [MTB-differ]

Placed in a courtroom or in a legal situation, three stories suggest more negative situations, for example:

> (BJmy 22, 32) A father and son, commenting. They are meeting in a theater or cinema speaking of what is occurring around them. Or a jury, listening—lawyer and judge is saying something to each other—using easy words to understand whether the accused should be condemned or acquitted. It is a serious topic because the young man appears closed—stern. It is not good business.
>
> [FA-share MTC-ethic RC-wrong]

> (BJms 68, 54) He (the younger one) is having a difficult problem with the police and he is talking and discussing the issue with his lawyer.
>
> [MTC-crime RC-wrong]

Secretiveness is suggested in five stories. There is elaboration of a negative nature in some but not in others. For example:

> (BJms 7, 42) These are two men in a type of meeting between people. There exists here a confidential comment about a topic that can't be revealed to others. It is confidential. An exchange of ideas.
>
> [MTA-interest MTC-plot]

> (BJmy 4, 32) They are talking about something so that others can't hear.
>
> [MTA-interest MTC-plot]

Compared with the other samples below there is less definite negative material. Nevertheless, plots or corrupt activities are more directly suggested in four stories. The political arena is mentioned in only two records, but again suggest politicians are interested in power or money not public good:

> (BJfy 25, 27) This is a political meeting. Like the ministers here in Brazil. It is about power and its execution.
>
> [MTC-plot DDC-despot]

> (BJmy 10, 24) A problem typical of Brazil. Two politicians are intriguing to gain more money. It is only for their own benefit to strengthen their political and economic positions.
>
> [MTC-plot DDC-despot DDC-corrupt]

Only six of the eighteen stories of mutual interaction on a horizontal level are positive in content. Japanese-Brazilians go only slightly in the direction of the general Brazilian distrust of public figures or instrumental mutual activities engaged in for any purpose.

Italian and German Groups

There are three Italian stories of instrumental interaction (one German story mentioned as vertical above stressed a status difference). Their remaining stories are in categories of affective interchange.

Only one Italian story depicting public figures ends on a positive note:

(BIm 19) Two senators were discussing the problems of the Brazilian parliamentary system. Preparing themselves for a long journey of work. They go home with their families. They find a solution.

[MTA-task RA-work CA-present]

Another story deals with reestablishment of a positive instrumental relationship after previous exploitative wrong doing by a rich man:

(BIm 23) A long time ago a very rich man had got involved with a poor woman, and she got pregnant. After a long time he discovered that she had had a son of his. Then the boy became upset because his father hadn't looked for him before. The father gave him many explanations. They got along with each other and the son began to work with his father.

[KB-status RC-ex-sex HA-mend MTA-family]

The third depicts convicts working together plotting their escape.

(BIm 01) Two men at a penitentiary talking, arranging the last details of their escape. They are leaders of the penitentiary, they're the ones who decide when the escape will take place and how it will restore. They will go along with the other prisoners. Some manage, others will be arrested. When police try to prevent escaping, the older one dies and the younger one escapes.

[RD-wrong MTC-plot DDA-lead DSC-escape CD-finish]

Favela Subjects

Negative themes of mutual interaction are especially noted among both groups. Only the Portuguese see one positive cooperative story. It depicts a mutual instrumental theme very briefly:

(BPm 10) A father and son talking or thinking together.

[MTA-task FA-empathy]

Another Portuguese story of positive mutual activities between a father and son ends on a dubious note.

(BPm 5) Joel was a great young man, and he had his father by his side. Once both decided to build an ark. Then they gathered all the money they had and bought wood. Days passed by and both went on building, till one day it was ready. They took it to the sea and there they used it for the first time. As everything went all right, they decided to travel around the world. But nobody heard about them anymore. They disappeared suddenly. They were considered as definitely disappeared.

[MTA-task KD-luck]

Three Afro-Brazilian stories suggest ineptness or questionable plans, although one does not involve mutual purpose.

(BABm 20) According to their facial expression, the older man is asking the younger one to do something which has to do with economic interests, money. According to this man's facial expression, he shows not to be economically very capable, and he accepts the proposal of the other man.

[MTA-task CC-mental OA-wealth]

(BABm 2) The Mayors! This is M. Olivio Dutra, who is always increasing bus fares. He only wants to help, but he doesn't know how. For example: he could improve the vehicles, and build more plazas, houses, free places, etc. Now he is trying to turn out people who are set on green areas which don't belong to them. But these people do not have a place to go. He said he will turn out people who are squatting on the green area, and that he won't set them in a better place.

[CC-inept NDD-unable DDC-result]

(BABm 23) In a political parliament, a 38-year-old congressman and a 50-year-old one voted against a law which the government had imposed. But it didn't make difference. The law was good for the people, who had increased the hope for a better life. This law concerns the increase of the minimum wage. After the increase, the congressmen became annoyed, and decided not to take part in the next voting.

[CC-inept MVB-anger MVD-refuse]

There are six stories of a mutual conspiracy or corrupt government officials: three are given by Afro-Brazilians, two by Portuguese, one by a youth of German ancestry living in the favela, for example:

(BABf 22) They did something wrong. They are going to do another wrong thing.

[RC-illegal MTC-plot]

(BPf 2) Managers of some bank. They have to fire older workers. It is cheaper to use younger ones.

[MTC-injury MTC-plot]

The negative example of parents is a conscious theme given by one Favela youth:

(BPf 7) The lack of seriousness of these days is reaching even the heads of the families. They involve themselves with gangs, drugs, smuggling. They think it is a better way to support their families. But what kind of education are they giving to their children, who are growing up and learning how to fight against these horrible things which are occurring nowadays? Do they love their families?

[RC-duty MTC-crime AC-crime RC-example]

Corruption in government and in government figures is represented in two Afro-Brazilians and one Favela German, for example:

(BABf 27) It is a congressman, talking to his friend, who is a city father. He is talking about the wrong things he had said in the last meeting, at the assembly, in the presence of the audience.

[MTC-interest ESD-exposed]

(BGFm 38) Corruption in Government! Gesiel was a city father who had been elected in 1990, with the help of his uncle, the congressman Jarbas Vasconcellos. As time passed by, Gesiel started to see the corruption in government. He quit the post.

[MTA-family MTC-false RA-injure]

In brief, the stories of authorities or elders in a situation of mutual interchange evoke a good proportion of cynical stories by the Favela youth. Nevertheless there are also positive themes:

(BABf 34) Father and son, together they owned an industry. Face new problem together.

[OA-own MTA-task]

For one German youth, the two men may be cooperating on a mutual task, but a status difference is noted. Their use of low voice suggests conspiracy:

(BGm 23 14) Two men are planning something in a very low voice. They had made an arrangement and are going to make what they have arranged. They will succeed in carrying out the plan. the one with a mustache; he is the boss of the other one. Father and son, commenting on something. Meeting in a theater. Speaking of what is happening around. Or jury, listening. Lawyer and judge to understand whether accused be condemned or acquitted. Serious topic, stern, not good business.

[MTA-task MTC-plot EDB-evaluate DDA-author]

Illustrative Samples of Scoring in the Following Chapters

In several of the chapters of volume II we have included additional illustrations of scoring of several of the subcategories included under the [M] category. Especially notable are the verbatim responses found in chapters 3, 7, and 10, volume II.

Notes

Bell, Daniel. 1975. Ethnicity and Social Change. In Nathan Glazer and Daniel Moynihan (Eds.), *Ethnicity: Theory and Experience*. Cambridge: Harvard University Press.

Benjamin, Jessica. 1988. *The Bonds of Love: Psychoanalysis, Feminism, and the Problem of Domination*. New York: Pantheon Books.

Berry, John. 1976. *Human Ecology and Cognitive Style: Comparative Studies in Cultural and Psychological Adaptation*. Beverly Hills: Sage.

Bronson, Wanda C. 1975. Development of Behavior with Age-Mates During the Second Year of Life. In Michael Lewis and Leonard A. Rosenblum (Eds.), *Friendship and Peer Relations*. New York: Wiley.

Cole, Michael and Sheila Cole. 1996. *The Development of Children* (3rd edition). New York: W.H. Freeman.

Crick, N.R. and N. Grotpeter. 1995. Relational Aggression, Gender and Social Psychological Adjustment. *Child Development*, **66**: 710–722.

De Vos, George A. 1978. Selective Permeability and Reference Group Sanctioning: Psycho-Cultural Continuities in Role Degradation. In Milton Yinger and Stephen Cutler (Eds.), *Major Social Issues—A Multidisciplinary View* (pp. 9–24). New York: Free Press.

———. 1982. Adaptive Strategies in American Minorities. In E.E. Jones and S. Korchin (Eds.), *Minority Mental Health* (pp. 74–117). New York: Praeger.

———. 1983. Adaptive Conflict and Adjustive Coping: Psycho-Cultural Approaches to Ethnic Identity. In Theodore Sarbin and Karl E. Scheib (Eds.), *Studies in Social Identity* (pp. 204–230). New York: Praeger.

———. 1992. *Social Cohesion and Alienation: Minorities in the United States and Japan*. Boulder, Colo.: Westview Press.

Dias, M.G. and P.L. Harris. 1990. The Influence of the Imagination on Reasoning by Young Children. *British Journal of Developmental Psychology*, **8**: 305–318.

Doob, L.W. 1952. *Social Psychology*. New York: Holt.

Dunn, J. 1988. *The Beginnings of Social Understanding*. Cambridge, Mass.: Harvard University Press.

Glazer, Nathan and Patrick Moynihan. 1975. *Ethnicity: Theory and Experience*. Cambridge: Harvard University Press.

Göncü, A. and Kessel, F.S. 1988. Preschoolers' Collaborative Construction in Planning and Maintaining Imaginative Play. *International Journal of Behavioral Development*, **11**: 327–344.

Goodenough, Donald R. and Herman A. Witkin. 1977. *Origins of the Field-Dependent and Field-Independent Cognitive Styles*. Princeton, N.J.: Educational Testing Service.

Greenberg, Pearl. 1932. Competition in Children: An Experimental Study. *American Journal of Psychology*, **44**: 221–248.

Hartup, W.W. 1974. Aggression in Childhood: Developmental Perspectives. *American Psychologist*, **29**: 336–341.

Horney, Karen. 1945. *Our Inner Conflicts: A Constructive Theory of Neurosis*. New York: W.W. Norton.

Howes, C. and C.C. Matheson. 1992. Sequences in the Development of Competent Play with Peers: Social and Social Pretend Play. *Developmental Psychology*, **28**: 961–974.

Kagan, S. 1974. Field Independence and Conformity of Rural Mexican and Urban Anglo-American Children. *Child Development*, **45**: 765–771.

Kagan, S. and R. Buriel. 1977. Field Dependence-Independence and Mexican-American Culture and Education. In J. Martinez (Ed.), *Chicano Psychology*. New York: Academic Press.

Kagan, S. and M.C. Madsen. 1971. Cooperation and Competition of Mexican, Mexican-American, and Anglo-American Children of Two Ages under Four Instructional Sets. *Developmental Psychology*, **5**: 32–39.

———. 1972a. Experimental Analyses of Cooperation and Competition of Anglo-American and Mexican-American Children. *Developmental Psychology*, **6**: 49–59.

———. 1972b. Rivalry in Anglo-American and Mexican Children of Two Ages. *Journal of Personality and Social Psychology*, **24**: 214–220.

Le Bon, G. 1895/1960. *The Crowd: A Study of the Popular Mind.* New York: The Viking Press.

Lee, Changsoo and George A. De Vos. 1981. *Koreans in Japan: Ethnic Conflict and Accommodation.* Berkeley: University of California Press.

Leuba, C. 1933. An Experimental Study of Rivalry in Young Children. *Journal of Comparative Psychology,* **16**: 367–387.

Lewis, Oscar. 1966. *La Vida*. New York: Random House.

Madsen, M.C. 1967. Cooperative and Competitive Motivation of Children in Three Mexican Subcultures. *Psychological Reports*, **20**: 1307–1320.

Madsen, M.C. and A. Shapira. 1970. Cooperative and Competitive Behavior of Urban Afro-American, Anglo Americans, Mexican Americans and Mexican Village Children. *Developmental Psychology*, **3**: 16–20.

Maller, J.B. 1929. Cooperation and Competition: An Experimental Study of Motivation. *Teacher's Coll. Cont. Educ.*, No. e0384.

Maudry, Maria and Maria Nekula. 1939. Social Relations Among Children of the Same Age During the First Two Years of Life. *Journal of Genetic Psychology*, **54**: 193–215.

McClelland, David. 1961. *The Achieving Society*. Princeton, N.J.: Van Nostrand.

McKee, J. and Florence B. Leader. 1955. The Relationship of Socio-Economic Status and Aggression in the Competitive Behavior of Preschool Children. *Child Development*, **26**: 135–142.

Mead, Margaret. 1937. *Cooperation and Competition Among Primitive Peoples*. New York: McGraw-Hill.

Miller, Daniel and Guy Swanson. 1958. *The Changing American Parent*. New York: Wiley.

Minturn, Leigh and William W. Lambert. 1964. *Mothers of Six Cultures; Antecedents of Child Rearing*. New York: Wiley.

Murphy, Lois B. 1937. *Social Behavior and Child Personality*. New York: Columbia University Press.

Murphy, G., L.B. Murphy, and T.M. Newcomb. 1937. *Experimental Social Psychology*. New York: Harper.

Parten, M. 1932. Social Participation Among Preschool Children. *Journal of Abnormal and Social Psychology*, **27**: 243–269.

Ramirez, M. and D. Price-Williams. 1974. Cognitive Styles of Children of Three Ethnic Groups in the United States. *Journal of Cross-Cultural Psychology*, **5**: 212–219.

Riesman, David, Reuel Denney, and Nathan Glazer. 1950. *The Lonely Crowd: A Study in The Changing American Character*. New Haven, Conn.: Yale University Press.

Rogoff, Barbara. 1990. *Apprenticeship in Thinking. Cognitive Development in Social Context*. New York: Oxford University Press.

Shantz, C.U. 1987. Conflicts Between Children. *Child Development*, **58**: 283–305.

Shapira, A. and M.C. Madsen. 1969. Cooperative and Competitive Behavior of Kibbutz and Urban Children in Israel. *Child Development*, **4**: 609–617.

Vaughn, Curtis. 1988. *Cognitive Independence, Social Independence, and Achievement Orientation: A Comparison of Japanese and U. S. Students*. Dissertation, University of California, Berkeley.

Whiting, B. B. and C. P. Edwards. 1988. *Children of Different Worlds: The Formation of Social Behavior*. Cambridge, MA.: Harvard University Press.

Witkin, H. A. 1967. Cognitive styles across cultures. *International Journal of Psychology*, **2**: 233–250.

Chapter 13

Human Concerns with Impersonal Forces and Inanimate Objects

Our study of human concern has focused primarily on a personal and interpersonal world. However, any study of conscious experience would be incomplete without some method for addressing concerns with the impersonal world. In addition to their concern with personal and social issues, human beings hold varying attitudes toward a world that is governed by impersonal, natural, or mechanistic forces and that is filled with material, inanimate, or inert objects. People vary in their sense of involvement with this causal world, and in their desires for the possession or manipulation of objects. By and large, the Thematic Apperception Test (TAT) cards we have used were not selected nor directed toward evoking such impersonal concerns. Nevertheless, respondents will sometimes draw attention to impersonally considered situations of wealth or poverty, illness, bodily imperfection, the natural world, death, etc., depicted as impersonal occurrences. These depictions can reflect positive or negative, or unresolved attitudes about objects and fate. We use the categories of Objects (O) and Fate or Kismet (K) to cover various kinds of impersonal concerns.

As we shall consider below, concern with Objects or with Fate must very often be considered in the context of other scoring categories. The *interpersonal* context in which these concerns are mentioned is often the key to understanding their meaning. As we shall demonstrate, specific expressive or instrumental attitudes held toward objects, or toward the surrounding natural world are reflected in most of the interpersonal categories.

Concern with Objects

Under the category of Objects (O), there could be a large number of topics considered as possibly salient. However, we have limited our scoring to any direct expression of concerns about inert objects that are specifically mentioned as part of the narrative. In the category for objects, we also include objects that are mentioned as part of the surrounding world of nature, possessions mentioned concretely or abstractly and non-specifically (such as "wealth"), as well as any mention of the human body or any of its parts that are depicted in the narrative.

As Piaget has noted, objects initially exist for us as inextricable elements of sensorimotor schemes, and thus are related to the activity of our body from the beginning. Through the process of adaptive interaction with objects we come to differentiate them according to various characteristics and eventually categorize them along various conceptual dimensions. These can include perceptual characteristics such as color, shape and texture, density and weight, relative location and motion, trajectory, etc. We also recognize conceptual characteristics of objects such as their causal origination and continued existence or "permanence."

Through experience with the manipulation of objects, as well as through instruction and received knowledge, we come to see the meaning of objects in terms of their relevance to culturally constructed purposes. Objects are represented in terms of their various functional characteristics or usefulness. Our understanding of these functional properties is closely related to our sense of mastery or competence. Objects can even be seen as extensions of one's own body as they become imbued with human energy in the course of purposive activity.[1] Objects come to represent causally functioning elements, either as instruments of one's own agency or as detractors that can interfere with completion of purposive activity. Concern with *ability* in the manipulation of objects or in their creation is usually scored as a basic concern under the category of Competence (C).

Acquisition, possession, or manipulation of objects can be goals in themselves. Objects can be venerated or despised, desired or shunned, possessed or discarded, seen as useful or useless, malleable or unalterable, they can be damaged or repaired, manufactured or destroyed, ordered and disordered, lost or found, etc. Where pleasure is explicitly depicted relative to these activities, it must be double scored with the expressive Pleasure (P) category.

---

[1]Consider the experiences of driving a familiar car, whose size, shape, power, and handling characteristics are familiar, as compared with driving an unfamiliar car. The former has become familiar as an extension of one's own body, whereas the latter can require substantial accommodation or familiarization. Consider similarly the familiarity one feels with musical instruments or any kind of tool that requires repeated use. The eventual familiarity with which prosthetic devices are used is an even less ambiguous example of this capacity to adopt objects as parts of ourselves.

Seen psychodynamically, an object or its mental representation can also be used symbolically as the target of displaced or redirected purpose. Any consciously experienced attitude about an inert object can potentially reflect an underlying attitude about one's own self and body, or one's relationship with others. Among expressive concerns related to objects, the most notable are forms of evaluation. For example, objects can be appreciated in their own right, and there may be a sense of awe or reverence directed toward a particular object. They may also be related to maintaining social status where pleasure or awe are depicted in regard to objects in the natural environment, for example, one may need to double score with Pleasure (P) or Esteem (E) categories. Negatively considered, objects may be discounted or depreciated (E). They may reflect a concern with poverty or deprivation (N).

Objects (whether literal or symbolic) can provide a sense of security (NSA-secure), and fear of object loss is a frequent human concern. Where insecurity about an object or object loss is expressed, the objects may be instrumentally depicted in conscious thought, yet this may also suggest an underlying affective sense of nurturant insecurity (N) or potential threat from someone (H), that may be double scored if it is clear in the narrative.

Instrumental concerns with wealth, or the possession or use of money as an "object," are also frequent. A "job" is often mentioned as a means of gaining money. There can be expressions of happiness in the attainment of wealth. There can also be expressed a sense of pervasive insecurity or despair in relation to economic destitution. When there is an overt expression of sense of helplessness related to object possession or loss, it may sometimes be double scored with a Nurturant (N) category to note an unmet dependent need.

Concern with Impersonal Force

Our category of Fate or Kismet (K) allows us to consider the external forces of nature or human society and its history as they impinge upon the individual. There are impersonally experienced causal forces, dynamic systems, or fateful events such as accidents, injuries, illness, and death over which no human or supernatural intentionality appears to exercise intervention or control. They are what is termed in various societies as "luck," "fate," "kismet," and even "karma" (as the term is sometimes used).

Among Piaget's many accomplishments was the groundbreaking effort to describe the process by which children develop an epistemological framework for understanding causality (Piaget, 1930). According to Piaget, a major accomplishment in the child's development was a capacity to appropriately differentiate forms of "mechanical causality" from forms of causality in which "intentionality" is involved. As Piaget described it, for example, younger children in Switzerland explained the existence of the Alps as having been created by God. Older children were able to explain the existence of the Alps in geological terms.

Although older children and adults may be capable of understanding the difference between various forms of causal explanation, they may not consistently apply that knowledge. Indeed our collective representations, as applied in practice toward causal explanation, may commonly not distinguish volitional and mechanistic universes. Although Descartes' dualistic framework that described distinct realms of causality has been widely influential, there remain strong tendencies to focus either on a universe of intentional causation or on a universe of mechanical causation, while ignoring the other. Scientific explanations have tended to focus on the latter, whereas religious explanations have tended to focus on the former.

For example, as with the animism of Piaget's preoperational children, it seems difficult for many of us to not imbue the natural world with a pervasive intentional force that is sometimes directly personalized as a god. There are those who in the context of their religion continue to think of an overriding supernatural intentionality that is capable of miraculous intervention in the mechanical universe. From that view, the universe cannot be conceptualized simply as a mechanical system governed only by impersonal laws. In the East, Confucianism also envisaged a "moral" universe.[2] Conversely, modern science has tended to focus on mechanical causality and altogether remove volition from causal explanation.

As mechanistic approaches have influenced the social sciences, it has seemed inordinately difficult to consider human consciousness as a determinative force in history that is not simply mechanically patterned by cultural or institutional

---

[2]There are, however, nondualistic frameworks that do not either conflate or deny moral/volition and mechanical causation. The nondualistic Buddhist Madhyamaka tradition (see Thurman, 1984) makes reference to two realities, but they are not the realities of subject and object. Instead, one is a "relative" reality that may be seen (in modern terms) as being "culturally constructed" through the cognitive and epistemological functioning of sentient beings. The other is an "absolute" reality that reflects the underlying nature of things, distinct from our conceptualization. In this framework, the known and the knower are not distinct; there is no distinction between subject and object. Instead, that distinction is seen as an epistemological trap produced by our delusion that the objective "Me" (who I think I am) actually exists in some inherent or self-existent manner. From this view, Descartes was correct in his failure to find as an object the "I" that is at the center of our subjective experience (Thurman, 1993). Yet rather than positing the actual existence of a separate causal realm of subjective being (as Descartes did with "I think therefore I am") the very concept of the "I" is seen as an erroneous dualistic conceptual fabrication. In this nondualistic framework, there is no separation of subject and object, there is no omnipotent divine creator. There is only a simultaneous mutual or inter-dependent arising of phenomenal effects that are produced by causes (Macy, 1991), in which one's own consciousness can be a central determining force. One's own consciousness has the capacity to regulate the behavior of the body, speech, and mind such that the future can be positively or negatively affected. In this framework the seat of morality and the capacity to control one's own karma remain squarely within the individual.

systems. In such a framework, the social system as a general political or economic force can be depicted as an impersonal force that shapes events.

A person can be depicted as suffering economic fortune or destitution, or as a victim of war. Although these in fact may result from human actions, they can be experienced and depicted as impersonal phenomena, to be categorized as Fate (K). If social forces are depicted in personal rather than impersonal terms, however, they may be scored more appropriately as Control (D) or Nurturance (N) concerns.

Reference to events that are caused or controlled by impersonal forces may reflect human concerns related to a need to exercise instrumental control over a complex natural universe.[3] As we discuss in chapter 14, volume I, efforts to cope psychologically with the forces that are beyond our personal control (including the forces of nature) may benefit from beliefs in the efficacy of powerful others. The management of such relationships is at the center of many religious systems. Such beliefs sometimes appear in narratives, with reference to the activities of God or supernatural forces, where one's fate is depicted as resulting from supernatural intentionality or divine intervention (whether as punishment or succor). Where narratives refer to forces guided by intentionality, they are scored under the categories such as Control (D) or Nurturance (N). (See next chapter.)

Concerns with fate can also represent fearful uncertainty about an unknown future. There are various forms of submission or reconciliation with uncontrollable impersonal forces, even where there is no divine intervention. There can be the acceptance of negative fate, or there can be optimistic reference to the possibilities of future good fortune where the impersonal force of "luck" may help one achieve one's instrumental goals without any intervening intentionality.

There are differing normative cultural attitudes about impersonal events, accidents, good fortune or misfortune, etc. In any given cultural group one can find shared attitudes or collective representations about impersonal natural forces, or natural catastrophes, social destinies, wealth or poverty considered in impersonal terms, the vagaries of war, or the occurrence of illness as they can influence any individual. The relative saliency of such events in the thought of particular groups may depend on how these forces are understood or conceptualized. Fate intervenes in characteristic ways in different cultures.

Concerns with Objects, Possessions, and the Human Body

Manifest or explicit attention that is given in narratives to inert objects and the human body (its parts or functions) suggest some special symbolic meaning underlying the manifest narrative content. Systematic scoring of such responses enables one to further interpret possible latent or disguised symbolic meaning.

---

[3]One may argue that the Fate (K) category also reflects expressive concerns, as it appears to do in the Philippines (see chapter 13, volume II).

Some possible latent meanings are rather transparent, others are more obscure or even moot. Such interpretations are best accomplished if they include consideration of specific social and cultural patterns as they relate to underlying personality characteristics. In several chapters in this volume, we have drawn attention to possible interpretations about objects that have arisen in certain cultural groups.

In chapter 10, volume I, where we discuss the exercise of power and various forms of control and volition, we also discussed various defensive or coping strategies. One of these forms of coping (intellectualization) involves a reduction in interpersonal affect as one escapes into an intrapersonal world of ideas. Other forms of defensive control (considered psychodynamically) that may be apparent in narratives involve "depersonalization," where the focus of the narrative is shifted away from personal concerns and is focused on objects or the body depicted as an object.

A special sensitivity to possible bodily imperfections or personal appearance may be related to concerns about social acceptability (Esteem, E). For example, attention to clothes may represent a sensitivity to differences in social status, etc. In chapter 13, volume II, Robert Manlove reports on his extensive use of the TAT as part of his research in the Philippines. In the context of his overall research he illustrates how status differences related to respect are readily evoked by a special card on which two young men are wearing clothes that define their social class. Explicit attention to the clothes in the narratives bring to mind values related to what is locally termed *amor propio* (self esteem), *hiya* (shame), *pakikisama* (smooth interpersonal relations), and *utang na loob* (a debt of gratitude).

As we will discuss below, special attention to the body and explicit depiction of ill health can at one level be seen as reflecting realistic conscious concerns with health related to the occurrence of actual ill health in a particular social group. However, on a deeper level, concerns with health, or concerns with broken or imperfect objects, may indicate a more or less conscious awareness of intrapersonal or intrapsychic malfunctioning, etc. In chapter 1, volume II, Nancy Scheper-Hughes describes narratives obtained in rural western Ireland in which a broken violin was frequently depicted in responses to Card 1 of the TAT. This image was especially common in responses obtained in mental hospitals. As she contends in her chapter, these stories very likely indicate underlying uncertainties about intrapsychic integrity or mental health (see also Scheper-Hughes, 1979).

Various depictions of objects, particularly those referring to fear of theft or a need to protect objects from damage, may represent some degree of awareness of problems in social relationships or concerns about group malfunctioning, etc. In chapter 15, volume II, some migrant children can be seen to be concerned with peers who may break their violin. In the present chapter (below) we will illustrate how a concern with having one's objects stolen, or worry over broken objects appears in the TAT records of Slavey Native Americans in Canada. But first let us turn to some developmental and psychodynamic considerations.

Retentiveness

Some individuals invest more energy in possessions than they do in people. The discussion of the "anal personality" in psychoanalytic theory (e.g., Abraham, 1927) delineates how retention of objects can be related to an initial motoric control of the sphincter and anxiety about losing a part of one's body or self in defecation. Such early concerns become part of a need to maintain control in one's environment that can also be directed to the control and keeping of inert objects.

Concerns with the acquisition or loss of possessions may reflect an inherent underlying fear of loss. In Orson Welles' 1941 film, *Citizen Kane*, the main character, in amassing objects from all over the world, never assuages his initial loss of the beloved sled, "Rosebud." Furthermore, in some social settings they may become a "legitimate" source of ongoing concern about potential loss, as is evidenced in North America by the insurance industry and the use of security alarm systems to guard home and property.

Concern with anal control can also be seen as part of a stubborn maintenance of inner control vis-à-vis those who seek to control from the outside. In the psychoanalytic view, anal control is related to a subsequent intense interest in impersonal orderliness, and unresolved ambivalence about disorder. Directed toward the social sphere, this can appear as moral righteousness that serves to counter immorality, social disorder, or injustice.

Some psychoanalysts have also contended that there is symbolic equivalence between feces and money.[4] In this view, money is similar to feces in that it is commonly seen as dirty or corrupting, yet also as a source of pride. It is despised yet treasured. Like feces, one cannot hold on to money indefinitely, it is subject to an inexorable process of object loss. Money and feces are both inert de-individualized possessions in which one nevertheless remains invested.

Intellectualization and Depersonalization

In understanding the possible meaning of objects, one might also consider psychodynamic processes of "personalization" or "depersonalization." Objects can become a locus for personalized projections. In some instances they can be experienced as being animate and one may interact with them as personalized intentional beings. In childhood this may reflect normal fantasy and play. Among

---

[4] It is noteworthy that in 1960 the senior author saw this connection made explicitly by Chinese dream interpreters at a popular "Dream Temple" in Taiwan where individuals went to have their dreams interpreted after sleeping there overnight. A standard interpretation of dreams involving the appearance of feces was that such a dream was indeed propitious symbolically because it suggested an imminent acquisition of wealth.

adults in the West, only among deeply disturbed individuals are inert objects[5] generally seen as intentional.

Some forms of neurosis are marked by a defensive use of depersonalization. It can appear as forms of intellectualizing in which there is a reduction of subjective beings into inert objects to be manipulated for instrumental or intellectual purposes. More advanced forms of depersonalization may be found in some social theories. On an abstract level, most social scientists are apt to discount the interactive innovative influences of conscious individuals. By so doing, one can establish analytic theoretical systems undisturbed by considerations of untoward occurrences caused by any form of individual human motivation.

Social and economic institutions such as corporations share elements of depersonalization that can be illustrated by the game of chess. The "men" in chess are inert objects. In the game of chess it is a tactical handicap if someone has an excessive fondness for protecting bishops, or knights, in the overall strategy used in winning a game. In playing war games with humans, the generals in charge cannot think too readily of the individual experiences of those in their armed forces. They are to be moved impersonally in plotting a battle plan. Gambits in which some are lost is part of any plan. In Marxist theory, there was concern with forces of exploitation, but the untoward disturbances of irrational thought about ethnicity or religious adherence were downplayed as errant forces only causing temporary disturbance in evolutionary human progress governed by materialistic forces in the economy. In Stalin's conception of the dictatorship of the Proletariat as exercised through their Socialist State, millions of individuals could be sacrificed by the State as long as their sacrifices were directed towards the future welfare of the people as a whole in their inexorable historical movement towards a more evolved form of democratic Communism.

There is a tendency among social theorists to be disconcerted by having to deal with the effects of consciousness when formulating theoretical systems about society, whether as an anthropologist, sociologist, political scientist, economist, or behavioral psychologist. There is a mistaken notion that to be scientifically valid and "objective" one must discount the effects of intentionality or consciousness as a determiner of human behavior.

The executive's rational maximization of profit, for example, must discount disruptions in the emotional life and economic welfare of those who are "down-sized." The maximization of profits from the sale of patented drugs must discount the consequences for those who can not afford the overly expensive medicine. Economic decisions are generally considered only from a completely instrumental

[5]There are substantial cultural differences in the degree to which animistic perception in adults is normative or nonnormative. In a culture where such perception is normative, it may only sometimes represent psychopathological functioning. It may simply reflect cultural differences in the normative taxonomies by means of which objects are categorized as either animate or "inert."

point of view. Commonly there is no personal interaction of those in control with the subjects who suffer from their instrumental decisions. Counter activities by organized members of the labor force or by the electorate may not be adequately considered, although many economic institutions invest substantial resources in efforts to block union activities or to influence democratic processes through lobbyists.

The disruptive effect of rational economic decisions on community patterns, mental health, and the general welfare are commonly ignored. In recent decades, young adults receiving a professional education are being explicitly told that they should not expect job security, but instead should see their education as a means toward greater job flexibility. We presently have no knowledge as to the long-term effect of this on youth as they look forward to lives in which they can have no expectation that a commitment to any particular personal identity will endure.

The postmodernist preoccupation with multiple possible selves (including gender ambiguity) may reflect these social and economic realities. This ambivalence about commitment to an identity may reflect an inner sense of helpless impoverishment in the face of a heartless system of economic exploitation in which one must participate to survive. The phenomenon of the "yuppie" and the contemporary obsession with the acquisition of wealth toward early retirement is presently reflected in bullish equity investment patterns that generally fail to consider the social impact of industries in which investment is made.

Some individuals severely depersonalize their own role in the world. They have no hope that society can or will intervene on their behalf, and they are discouraged from participating in democratic processes or community organizing to respond to this perception. For example, many young adults have no confidence that there will continue to be a social security system by the time they retire, but they do not organize toward developing solutions. There is a sense of poverty related to the absence of helpful others or of material resources, and this is translated into a disempowered incapacity to give back to society. For some, the pursuit of money itself is emphasized in the absence of any further purpose. Jobs or careers are pursued for monetary purpose rather than for the fulfillment of a person's creative potential.

The Body as Object

What we score in the manifest content of stories sometimes suggests the underlying operation of defense mechanisms in relation to the body as "object." Hypochondriac concerns with potential or actual body malfunction appears in severely disturbed psychoneurotic personalities as well as in psychotic individuals. Psychoanalytic theory (Fenichel, 1945, 418 ff.) suggests how concern with body processes appears in those who, developmentally, have been unable with sufficient satisfaction to invest interactively in other persons in their "object" relations.[6] There can be a withdrawal from affective ties in the interpersonal world into forms of "body preoccupation" (De Vos and Boyer, 1989).[7] An underlying schizophrenic process is often marked by body preoccupation with specific organs or external body features. The individual may be experiencing actual hypochondriacal sensations.

As we have indicated in previous chapters, the discovery of the external world is made by the infant in connection with internal body experiences. There is progressive distinction of tactile sensations and internal sensations (Fenichel, 1945, 35 ff.). The body image becomes the "nucleus" of the ego experienced as "self." In some pathological conditions there is a selective lack of such sensations. Certain organs or body areas are perceived as if they did not belong to the person. There can also be alternatively, distancing without affect, or augmented self-concern.

Gift Exchange

Gift exchange is a complex social act that is primarily scored in the category of objects. When the object given or received is the central focus of the depiction, the main scoring is located under objects (OA-gift; see below). Beyond the concern with the object alone, as a social act, the giving of a gift is perhaps seen in its simplest form as an act of nurturance. Gifts can be scored under concerns with economic or material support either as donor (NDA-reward) or as recipient (NSA-reward). However, as soon as reciprocity is stressed, various instrumental concerns arise.

In the anthropological literature there are numerous descriptions of the social and personal functions of gift exchange (Befu, 1989). In numerous societies giving is used to enhance reputation and social status. The "potlatch," for example, is a highly emotional as well as instrumental competitive ceremony celebrated by the Kwakiutl of the northwest coast of North America. If positively depicted in this manner, giving may be double scored with an Esteem category (e.g., EDA-status). If it is depicted as ostentatious, it might be scored with negatively (e.g., ESC-exhibit). While the potlach is a competitive act for establishing status it may also involve negative discordant emotional states and be visualized as injurious to the recipient (H). However, gift exchange, in most cases, serves to reduce levels of possible animosity and discordance and increase possibilities of harmony within interacting groups (HA-pacify HA-rite).

---

[6]In working in a mental hospital the senior author observed how some schizophrenics can develop an intense preoccupation with some inert objects, or suddenly lose total interest.

[7]See the interpretation of anatomical material in Rorschach responses in De Vos and Boyer (1989).

Acts of distribution in some societies can be part of a causal chain of instrumental reciprocity. In this context a gift can also be an act of responsibility or induced obligatory reciprocity (RA-repay). For example, consider the necessary gifts associated in Japan with *giri* relationships. Reciprocal giving may also facilitate common purpose (MTA-repay). There are also acts of giving to enhance one's competitive position, as symbolized in certain moves in chess that may distract the opponent from an ulterior motive (MVA-gambit). Acts of giving may be used to compete unethically, as in acts of bribery (MVC-bribe).

There are instrumental forms of donation (DDA-give) to gain instrumental ends, and forms of instrumental propitiation (DSA-appease). Gifts can be used sacrificially to induce behavior in another (DDA-gambit). Such manipulation through giving can also be seen negatively, as in bribery to gain control (DDC-give).

Concern with Loss or Breakage in a Canadian Native Community[8]

Concerns with bodily integrity appear in various forms in different cultural groups. Let us take for example some of our work with a Canadian Native-American Community. In the late 1950s, the senior author worked with anthropologists June Helm and Teresa Carterette on Rorschach and TAT test materials obtained from a Slavey community of Native Americans living on the upper Mackenzie River in Canada's Northwest Territories. Many of the Slavey responses were directly concerned with fears about the loss of objects as well as fears about violence from others. We noted substantial concern with illness in the Slavey TAT records as well. By reference to this material, as well as to ethnographic evidence, we can demonstrate some of the interpretive possibilities related to the Object (O) categories.

We must also note that in chapter 12, volume II, we record in detail how the fear of violence and concern with illness appears among the Tukuna of the Amazon, a cultural group with a totally different historical experience. However, while the reality of past historical occurrences along the Amazon in which this fear appears is quite different from the recent history along the Canadian MacKenzie river, what is apparent in both instances is that the TAT is useful cross culturally in understanding differences among specific individuals, as well as determining normative trends characterizing the groups. In both instances, while the TAT is a valid, objectively scorable test instrument, the understanding or analysis of the manifest content that is scored demands the collaborative support of adequate ethnographic reporting.

---

[8]A variation of this excerpted material previously appeared as part of Helm, De Vos, and Carterette (1960).

For the study of the Slavey, we had, as initial data, the observations and interpretations of individual behavior by two ethnologists who spent fourteen continuous months in the small Slavey community of "Lynx Point." We also obtained Rorschach and TAT[9] protocols from members of the community. Personality sketches were first prepared by ethnologists Helm and Carterette. Then De Vos, in discussion with the ethnologists, brought his psychological analyses of the projective test materials to bear upon the observational sketches. The results were therefore not "blind" analyses, but considered the projective material in concert with other behavioral and ethnographic evidence.

We use this occasion to illustrate a few instances of individual interpretation, such as we have not done elsewhere in this volume. The emphasis elsewhere in this volume has been on group norms as revealed in the narrative content. However, narrative analysis of TAT responses can also be valuable in examining specific individuals in a cross-cultural context, especially in understanding the social dynamics of an intensively studied small group.

The Lynx Point Community

The Lynx Point community when contacted was a cluster of log cabins on the banks of the Mackenzie River in Canada's Northwest Territories. It comprised fifty-six individuals (twenty-two adults over twenty years of age) at the inception of the field work. They were (with four in-marrying exceptions) what were then called "bush Indians." The group consisted of unschooled people living in the sub-Arctic forest (the "bush" is a sparsely inhabited land without roads or railways). The Lynx Point people made their livelihood by trapping fur animals for sale. Only two men and a youth who had been to mission school had any extensive command of English. Most of the other men could speak some broken English. The women and children spoke very little or none. For all members, the primary language was Slavey, an Athabaskan dialect.

The Lynx Point people were members of the Roman Catholic Church or, in a few cases, the Anglican Church. The men traveled by dog-sled forty-five miles to the nearest trading post, the "Fort," about once a month during the winter to sell furs and to buy provisions. In summer, traveling by canoe and using outboard motors, some of the men might find jobs at the Fort and live there during that period. There was little interaction between Slavey and White people except in the line of business. The Slavey's main White contacts were with the fur traders, the Royal Canadian Mounted Police, the game warden, and the missionaries of the

[9]The standard Murray cards were used. Unfortunately, the TATs were administered according to the Murray procedure, certain of the "male" pictures being given to the men and certain of the "female" to the women. Thus, due to this partial difference in stimuli, the TAT results from the two sexes are not completely comparable.

Roman Catholic and Anglican churches. At the time of the research, there was little visiting between bush communities; contact with other Native Americans more commonly took place at the Fort.

Let us examine a few of the specific subjects tested as described by Helm and De Vos (Helm, De Vos, and Carterette, 1960; the identities are concealed with fictitious names). We include some scoring details gained on the Rorschach protocols for those reading this report who may be familiar with Rorschach Test analysis. It deepens our contention of the advisability of using certain projective psychological tests cross-culturally. What is evident from this Canadian Native American material is the fact that, given basic ethnographic knowledge of a community, both the Rorschach and the TAT can be interpreted readily given sufficient rapport between examiner and subjects. The material is as rich as would be found testing any western group with the same stimuli.

Cora, a Woman Who Sees the Breakage of Objects in Her TAT Responses

Observational Sketch of Cora

Marcel's wife, Cora Renard, is thirty-five years old. In her seventeen years of marriage she has had eleven pregnancies, with seven children surviving. Cora's paternal grandfather, of Cree-English descent, spent his life in the service of the Hudsons' Bay Company. Cora is by bush standards a "city girl," having been raised in the Fort and having received two or three years of schooling. Prior to her marriage, she had never followed the menstrual prohibitions of the "bush Indians" and did not know such basic feminine skills as pelt preparation.

Cora's health is poor. Her numerous pregnancies have, by doctor's report, caused her injury. Her rather delicate frame is overlaid with a flabby, unhealthy fat. She is in a continual state of discomfort or pain, and her movements are slow and fatigued. Cora is a sloppy and disorganized housekeeper. Upon her oldest daughter, thirteen-year-old Noreen, falls most of the responsibility for household matters.

Timorous, shy, gentle, and feminine are words that characterize Cora. The wind and darkness in the bush, the swiftness of the river, the unfamiliar person—all these evoke anxiety in Cora. When, after long association, Cora's shyness is dissipated, she emerges as a kindly woman who enjoys a quiet chat and mild gossip with female friends. Once rebuffed or frightened, Cora withdraws from all contact. She has not approached her next-door neighbor and sister-in-law, Thérése, for a year and a half, having received a "bad look" for some unknown reason at the time of the death of Thérése's and Marcel's mother.

Characteristically, Cora is to be found sitting or reclining on the floor of her dwelling, alternately tenderly fondling, playing with, and suckling her baby. Here lies her main pleasure in life. Her next to youngest child, replaced by the new infant, has become an unkempt gamin, running about the camp in the care of Noreen and given to frequent demands and tantrums.

Of the marital pairs of the community, Marcel is most unequivocally the dominant male, pursuing his own interests before those of his wife and children, and Cora is the subordinate partner. But Cora, although she yields before the direct pressure of a stronger will, shows a bit of iron in her soul by holding resentment and, occasionally, achieving her desires by indirection. Cora clings resolutely to the English-Anglican allegiance of her ancestors. She and Marcel were married in the Anglican Church, and she holds a grudge against Marcel because he has not, for practical monetary reasons, rejected the Roman Catholic Church and has allowed the priest to baptize their younger children in the Catholic faith. Only the three oldest children baptized Anglican are "mine," Cora says. When Marcel, ordering a new tool set from the mail-order house, refused to include an order for new clothes for their children, Cora quietly ordered the clothes on her own, on the correct assumption that, once the package arrived at the Fort, Marcel would pay for it before he realized just what had happened. But despite areas of tension and disagreement, the relation between Marcel and Cora is not an unhappy one; a strong undercurrent of affection and involvement is apparent.

Cora's Projective Test Responses

In general, we find in Cora's stories a rather mature identification with the maternal role, but considerable concern, both directly and at a symbolic level, with physical breakdown. We know that she is ill, and this may explain her both direct and underlying symbolic concern with physical dissolution. In the first TAT card Cora sees the violin as broken; a symbolic reference to concern with bodily integrity. (Note many of the stories are presented here in abbreviated form.)

> Card 1: "I think that it's broke, and how can I get another one. It fell down from the table. Try to fix it, and he fixes it all right."
>
> [OD-broken CA-repair]

> Card 3: . . . again something breaks down. A woman is washing and the machine is broken so she is crying.
>
> [OD-broken PD-sad]

> Card 13: . . . the woman dies, and the husband is crying. The woman has been sick for a long time.
>
> [KD-death KD-illness FD-death]

> Card 18: . . . a woman takes something out of the girl's ear; a spider had gotten into it.
>
> [KD-animal NDA-nurse]

In Cora's TAT stories her affiliative attitude toward a husband seems quite positive. There is again some expression of contentment with the husband. The attitude toward learning and accomplishment is positively stated:

> Card 2: They are working in the garden, and this woman thinks the husband will grow things "Just fine." The girl goes to school and wants to learn lots of things quickly.
>
> [CA-able AA-self]

> Card 4: She sees the husband angry at another man; the wife holds the husband back. They talk to each other, and he stops.
>
> [HB-anger HA-pacify]

> Card 10: There is a glad reunion of husband and wife.
>
> [FA-happen]

Other cards depict positive or integrative social relationships within the family:

> Card 7GF: A mother is teaching her daughter to pray . . .
>
> [DDA-educate DSA-prayer]

> Card 14: This card depicts the playful practical jokes of a son on his mother . . .
>
> [ESB-teased PA-play]

> Card 6GF: [This card is seen as a father-daughter card.] The girl is dressed up to go to a dance, and her father says no; she is very sad and stays home.
>
> [PA-esthetic DDA-control DSA-comply PD-sad]

Cora's Rorschach responses, with twenty-three responses, again symbolically bear out the theme of dissolution. On Rorschach Cards IV and V, old rotten trees are seen. There are also several anatomical responses—lungs and stomach—in the record. Seeing "lungs" was not unusual in this group beset by anxiety about tuberculosis, but the stomach is a little beyond the usual and suggests stronger than average bodily concerns.

Her measures of reality testing appear quite adequate as measured by good form responses on the Rorschach; but like many of the Slavey records she is very constricted in externalizing herself in relationships and is usually passively compliant and notably introversive in orientation. (On the response to Card 6GF, there is more submission and less rebellion than one sees in the story given by Thérése, Cora's sister-in-law.) All the Rorschach human responses are passive; men are seen as sleeping, sitting, or standing. There is a tendency toward stereotype in thinking and a limited range of interests beyond her immediate environment and her preoccupation with herself. (Content is limited to animals, humans, and a few botanical responses in addition to the anatomy.)

Overall, in looking at this individual record we can note that specific attention to broken objects is directly in line with other ethnographic evidence.

Thérése and Zachary Ingram and Sons (Cora's Sister-in-Law)

Ethnographic Observational Sketches

"I never had a father," Zachary says. In his early years, Zachary's maternal grandmother took over much of his care from her unmarried daughter. At six, Zachary was sent to the Anglican Residential School for eight years. He recalls that in the early period there, he was teased and bullied by the other boys, but that one of the teachers took Zachary under his wing and became a special friend to him. After leaving school, Zachary worked and lived part of the time with his grandmother and her second husband. Although his grandmother has been dead for some years, Zachary, conscious of family responsibilities, still visits and exchanges gifts with his step-grandfather. Zachary is also conscientious in visiting his mother and her present husband whenever they are at the fort. Zachary and Marcel, Cora's husband, were in their early thirties and had been good friends for several years at the time Zachary married Marcel's eighteen-year-old sister, Thérése, and moved to Lynx Point.

Zachary's facial expression is serious to the point of being glum. Even his rare smile seems to have a tinge of melancholy. Zachary's Anglican Church upbringing in the mission school "took" so well that the ethnologists came to speak of him, in joking compassion, as "The Protestant Ethic." Though he shoulders his responsibilities, he is burdened and made anxious by them. Of the bush existence he says, "It's a hard life." Zachary is a worrier. On two related points, he is very articulate. First, how can he properly provide for his family now and in the near future when life must depend upon the capricious behavior of the fur market? Furthermore, what will become of his children in later years, since he can find no way to help them escape from the economic and social circumstances in which their father and fellows are ensnared? Zachary was also very anxious about judgments being made on his character by the White anthropologists. The drunken behavior of the other Lynx Point men caused him endless worry lest he be lumped with them in the ethnologists' minds. Zachary's drinking behavior was indeed unique. Though he joined in the drinking parties, he fought the physical and emotional effects of alcohol as a "well-bred," disciplined White is supposed to, rather than joyously succumbing to and exploiting his drunken condition, as is the Slavey style. Zachary accepts certain of his perceived values and virtues of the White world namely, self-control, meeting responsibilities, the moral duty to provide a better life for one's children. But he knows that he is forever alien to that world and yet, feels apart from the ways of the bush Indians as well.

Zachary's trapping partner and most intimate companion is his brother-in-law, Daniel. When drinking, Zachary's proprietary attitude toward Daniel is noticeable;

he is likely to reprimand Daniel if the latter lapses into undignified behavior and on one occasion administered a lengthy and virtuous scolding because Daniel had ignored his advice and bought a shirt that did not wear well. Zachary's other chief social relations are with Marcel and Henri. Nevertheless, he harbors resentment toward them, because in group activities and in business activities they do not listen to the advice of "educated people," namely, Zachary.

Although Zachary feels a heavy responsibility to provide for all of his children, it is his daughter, age five, who is dearest to him. He lavishes great attention and tenderness on her and speaks of the joy he finds in her.

Thérése is a handsome woman and Zachary's junior by some ten to twelve years. At the age of eighteen she had an affair with her classificatory brother, Karl. The mothers of the two young lovers were adamant against the union, because of a parallel cousin incest prohibition. Zachary married Thérése and took on the responsibility of the coming illegitimate child. No rumors against her virtue have been circulated since her marriage.

Like her sister, Liza, Thérése gives the impression of being a strong personality, but her approach to life is different from Liza's. Although her features can be suffused by a quick warm smile, Thérése often wears a rather stern expression. Unlike Liza, Thérése appears to lean toward introversion and introspection. She knows no English but is eager to see magazines and studies each picture with frowning intensity. She has an accordion, bought with the money she earned snaring squirrels. Characteristically, she chooses to play it to herself when her husband and children are away from the house. On a couple of occasions, by means of a sullen glare, she evinced moody anger and jealousy when she felt she had been slighted by Zachary in a minor matter. As neither Liza nor Thérése spoke English, very little direct communication with the ethnologists was possible. Liza's extroverted and expressive behavior allowed for much inference. Thérése, in her dignity and constraint, remains more of an enigma.

Zachary Ingram's Projective Test Responses

Zachary's TAT is full of the expression of the values that led to the ethnologists' characterization, "The Protestant Ethic." Several of his stories correspond to those common to members of the American middle class. For example, Card 1 (the boy with the violin) is seen as an achievement picture.

> Card 1: "The little boy thinks when be grows up (he) wants to be able to play the violin and be a good one at it. And after he is able to play the violin very good and real kind of expert at it, so he could join the 'whatchamacallit,' the musician band, so he could make good money out of it later on. So later in future years he could start one, start on his own. There is a good chance he'd succeed and give himself a name."
>
> [AB-think OA-wealth <u>AA-status</u>]

In the second picture, that of a farm scene and a young girl with books, Zachary sees the daughter going to school and succeeding there, then going to college. The farmers have saved their money to send her to school, and she becomes a teacher. In Card 7, a father gives wise counsel to a delinquent son, who repents and becomes a "good working man." Card 3 is seen as a woman grieving; a comment is made at the end that it may be sickness, so "may God give her comfort to overcome her sorrows." The theme of sickness and need for Succorance or a doctor's aid is a persistent one (occurring on Cards 6, 8, and 13).

In Zachary's stories, happy endings after misunderstandings or suffering commonly result. (These may be an echo of Zachary's middle-class-oriented readings from *Reader's Digest*.)

Card 8 depicts a murky scene with a young man or boy in the foreground, and what could be seen as an operation on a prone figure in the back, with a rifle diagonally across the left foreground of the card. Sometimes it is seen as a young man dreaming of his future as a surgeon. Among the Slavey this card brings out a masochistic theme that seems to be quite prevalent and may be said to be a modal psychological characteristic of the group, that is, a fear of violence from others. [There were no known actual occurrences of any violence, or any thefts of possessions that appear repeatedly in their stories.]

On Card 8, Zachary identified first with the prone man as being attacked by a couple of "guys" who broke through the window and are going to butcher him with a knife. The boy is seen as hollering for help. [Then the narrative is changed into a nightmare.]

In contrast to American stories, where the narrator commonly identifies with the boy, in these Slavey stories the prone figure is, for two out of the four adult men, unequivocally the object of identification.

As true for both stories given by Marcel and Karl, a theme of latent homosexual interest is introduced in one of Zachary's stories. On Card 10 (an embracing couple, obviously male and female) he sees two "friends" rather than man and woman. They embrace and kiss each other after a long absence and vow never to part again. They go to "live in the same little house."

Zachary bears down more heavily on punishment than anyone else in the community as central to his narrative outcomes. Evasion of punishment is the more common theme for the group. For example: On Card 18 Zachary depicts a man is being led to the electric chair for murder—a theme of guilt and punishment. In contrast to his friend Daniel, Zachary uses a money and robbery theme only once (Card 4). However, the importance of money emerges on four Cards (1, 2, 4, 9).

Zachary's Rorschach of twenty-five responses suggests a strong reality sense with simple, constricted, and stereotyped animal responses. The record differs from that of Marcel in showing less perfectionist precision and more tendency toward obsessive defenses, diffuse anxiety, and dependent compliance. Zachary shows some difficulty in direct acceptance of human relationships by seeing human details rather than full figures. There is a childishly immature tone to his responses. Animals are seen doing human acts and some of the responses suggest a childish tone of pleasure. Strong introversive traits are present, but repression keeps them inchoate.

The overall picture Zachary presents on the Rorschach suggests a somewhat anxious, obsessive, immature person in contrast to his conscious avowals of responsibility and education. He actually is rather narrow and constricted in his interests and lacking in ability to organize and conceptualize to any degree of complexity. He shows little more than an average level of intellectual functioning.[10]

The Responses of Thérése, Zachary's Wife

Thérése's TAT shows three dominant themes: money, initiative in working, and the frustration of desires and a tendency to rebel. The money as object theme seems, in part, to be a reflection of the type of concerns entertained by her husband. Impersonal concerns with money are more evident than expressive human relationships. Rebellion and control problems (D) marked her interpersonal concerns. Let us paraphrase or give excerpts from some of her rather long stories:

On Card 1, Thérése says (via an interpreter), "Little boy? If he plays the violin very good, he is going to get paid." On Card 3, the girl is crying because, "She's got no money. She can't find job so she is crying. She has nothing to eat. She was drunk and somebody stole her money."

In Cards 9 (which depicts a group of men) and Card 10 (an embracing couple), there are stories of economic difficulties, with the wife in both cases working. These stories present activity on the woman's part, and initiative in cooperating with the husband on economic matters. In Card 4 the girl is rejected by her lover, so she gets a job instead.

On Card 6 (a man leaning over a woman), the father admonishes a girl about going to a dance and threatens to cut her hair like a boy's. The girl weeps because, "If you have your hair cut, no one will love you. She never run away from her father after that." Rebellion, flight, and sometimes subsequent punishment recur on two other cards.

Card 18 (a woman holding another figure by the throat), a girl wants to get married, but her mother doesn't want her to do so right away, so she fights with the mother. She runs away, but her father takes her back and puts her in jail for eight months. "They didn't want her to get married because she was only thirteen."

Card 8 (a figure of a woman sitting on a chair in a bemused attitude) is seen as one of four sisters, and the other sisters are jealous of her. They go to a dance and prevent her from going. The resolution is that she will go to some other place and will get married there.

---

[10]Ethnographer's comment: This is well taken, although not brought out in the observer's sketch of Zachary. Zachary's avowed adherence to certain White values are to those within a limited range—"decent" living and behavior. The intellectual challenges of Euro-American culture are lost to him.

The overall theme of these three stories is of family figures preventing the heroine's access to men. These stories suggest that Thérése's underlying rebelliousness might have been strongly operative in the previous affair she had with Karl. Now, married properly, she may have developed a reaction formation of severity and sternness. On Card 7, a mother–daughter situation, we get a glimpse of child-peer-group pressure.

> Card 7. "Every time she goes to school the kids tease her, so her mother doesn't want her to go to school. So she's sad." The father finally consults with the mother and approves of her going to school, "But mother doesn't want her to go to another school."
>
> [ESB teased DDA-control PD-sad DDA-mediate]

The twenty-seven-response Rorschach of Thérése is characterized by a pragmatic approach which has little in the way of feeling or affect directly revealed. The responses are principally in two categories: that of animals and animal heads (suggestive of obsessional trends) and landscapes. The latter are indicative of some kind of withdrawal from contact with others, or of introversion with feelings of inferiority (six of the landscapes are vista type responses seen at a distance). Note that the field observations also strongly suggest withdrawal. Only once is human movement projected into the cards (also suggesting withdrawal from direct contact with others).

Thérése's reality testing is quite strong. The responses are adequately perceived and there is some attempt to use the intellect in an organized fashion. Some responses are of a complex nature, but, inferentially her organizational abilities are not used to externalize herself in outer achievement. (She organizes details of the cards, not the entire card.) There is some affective responsiveness as witnessed by using color in formulating her responses. One of her color responses (on Card X) is "a woman's mouth with lipstick." This percept fits in with the theme of a woman acting-out sexually, as revealed in the TAT. The oppositional rebellious component in her personality found in the TAT is also apparent in reversals of figure and ground on the Rorschach using the white spaces of the card to give several responses.

The preoccupation with money in this couple's records is extreme in many respects, but it is interwoven with direct narratives suggesting fear of violence and theft which is shared by a number of other Slavey tested with the TAT. The ethnographic evidence makes it clear that such fantasies of lost possessions are not prompted by real events in the lives of the narrators.

Observational Sketches of the Ingram Boys, Jerry and Frankie

In the case of the two oldest Ingram boys, the parents have, to some extent, set them apart from the rest of Lynx Point. Their stern demeanor not only discourages the casual, frequent visiting of other children and adolescents to the home, but also limits the number of other adults who feel free to drop in to visit. Both seem as much concerned with their children as the other parents in the community—but they are very strict by Lynx Point standards. Jerry, the once illegitimate child, age eleven, and Frankie, age ten, have spent much of their lives in different surroundings; Jerry, at the Catholic mission school (the only child from the community to be sent), and Frankie, at Lynx Point with his parents.

Despite the air of bravado they assume, they give the impression of being exceptionally nervous, tense, and fearful. Attending the school sessions given by the ethnologists, Jerry and Frankie seemed to be unruly and unmanageable. At the few times when their attention was momentarily captured, neither seemed to do as well as most of the other children. Jerry, especially, appeared to suffer from anxiety which interfered with his efforts to utilize the advantage of his mission school training. These boys would often lapse into displays of aimless yelling, excitement, and bodily agitation when other children were around.

Although they are in the same age group, the two boys do not play together; and by their own reports they quarrel a great deal. Jerry tends to spend much of his time at the cabin of his biological father's bachelor brother, Ozzie, with other adolescent boys. Unlike Jerry, Frankie still retains some of the young child's demonstrativeness.

Both are required to share in the household chores so that it is not unusual to find Frankie sweeping the floor and tending his two younger siblings while his mother is out checking the rabbit snares. Though Jerry and Frankie are well clothed and fed, they are also subjected to physical punishment more often than any of the other children. So far as we could infer from such gross indications as clothing, sleeping arrangements, and toys, the parents do not show any favoritism between the two boys. However, Jerry is unquestionably dissatisfied with his lot. He described life at the mission school as a time when he has been happy and says that one of the best things that could happen to him would be to return there. Our impression is that at home the boys are generally subdued and that their transgressions are sporadic, short-lived rebellions against the inflexible parental discipline. Other adults consider them noisy and disobedient.

The overshadowing influence in the development of these boys would seem to be the restrictive and stern discipline under which they have been raised. Once beyond their parents' control they quickly become restive and wild; but the threat of punishment never quite leaves them. It is only when engrossed in group play and excitement that they relax their customary air of apprehension. There is no doubt that Jerry suffers enough from knowledge of his illegitimacy to make him different from Frankie. Of the two, he is the more distrustful of others, and his preference for the company of the adolescent boys possibly has its origin in the fact that they are too mature to torment him with references to his birth. It is not likely that his foster father is able to disguise his feelings completely about Jerry's origin. Thus, for example, although Jerry has reached an age where other boys are being initiated into trapping activities, he has never accompanied Zachary on even short visits to the trap-line. It was rumored that when Zachary is intoxicated he becomes hostile toward Jerry.

Nevertheless, in spite of Jerry's burden of bastardy and his years spent at the mission school, the similarities in the personalities of these two brothers far outweigh their differences.

The Ingram Boys: Projective Tests

Jerry. The oldest Ingram son, Jerry, was given only four TAT cards due to his complaints of a headache. The rest of the test was never given subsequently. The four cards were extremely obsessive in nature, showing feelings of inadequacy and dependence on his father.

> Card 1: "Tried to play violin but couldn't, so kind of discouraged. His father is going to play violin for him and show him how. After eating and playing ball, he's going to sleep. Practice before he goes to bed. In the morning he goes to church, after church he's going to swim. After swimming, he's going to have a little sleep. After he gets up, goes to downtown shopping. After that he's going to practice again and make some boats and play with boats, but father tells him to practice instead of playing with boats. Father went out fishing and catch fish. Guess he's going to cook. After that he's (father?) going to play violin again. After plays violin he's going to bed again."
>
> [CC-inept DDA-educate RA-work PA-play]

This obsessive recitation of routine appeared also in the other three cards. Jerry's Rorschach record of forty-five responses is an example of a rather obsessive record, with constriction and withdrawal more apparent than integrative use of energies. Only twice does he use the entire card. Like his mother he sees scenes at a great distance. The form accuracy of his responses was not as high as his parents. The majority of his responses (over half of them) were on tiny projections of various kinds, peripheral ones, indicative of an continuous, obsessional quality to his thinking. There is a series of idiosyncratic responses in this record different, from most other records obtained from his community, these are somewhat related to the use of vista responses in his mother's record. While in the latter the vista responses were landscapes with waterfalls, in Jerry's record the vista responses are of very tiny people seen at a distance, for example, climbing up a hill (all his movement responses were in such very small details). In one case, a very minute detail is picked out as two men hiding, and another tiny blob as a man looking for them.

A defensive, suspicious fear of others is implied, but also a longing for closeness in spite of actual withdrawal from contact. As in the case of many of the other children, Jerry shows some bodily preoccupation (lung responses on Cards 3 and 8). There is a great deal of diffuse anxiety in this record (looming black clouds on several cards). There are two pure color responses suggesting uncontrolled affective displays; one on Card 3, is a perception of fire, and one on Card 9, is a blue sky. Another unusual type of response is the seeing of a brooch, usually a feminine ornament, on Card 10.[11]

Frankie. Frankie, the ten-year-old, shows in his TAT material some of the themes evident in that of the parents, and in general he is very similar to his older brother. One of the themes, that of money, keeps intruding into the stories. Another theme, more pronounced in his record than in those of the rest of his family, is that of illness. Quite a few of the stories have hypochondriac feelings intermeshed in them, manifested in the illness of the principal characters. There is noteworthy ambivalence about work and an avoidance of internalizing any kind of achievement values. But more than simple avoidance, there is a feeling of being inadequate and unable to accomplish.

> Card 1: "The boy wants to play the violin but can't learn; so he doesn't want to play. Is kind of sick, doesn't feel good—is kind of worried. Doesn't feel good so he isn't going to play it."
>
> [CC-inept AD-motive KD-illness CB-worry]

> Card 3: . . . [the figure] "cries because she has nothing to eat—no money. She's a lazy woman. After she has finished crying, she is going to bed. After she gets up, she is going to try to find a job, or get something to eat."
>
> [NSD-means RC-indulge AB-inactive]

> Card 4: . . . Rich people got lots of stuff and they're happy.
>
> [OA-wealth PA-joy]

On Card 7, happiness is again equated with money. Even on Card 15 (a graveyard scene) the money theme is introduced. Card 6 (the mother-son card) is seen as two adult figures; the man is worried because he doesn't like his house, but the woman is happy because she likes the house. The man looks hungry; the woman is going to cook pretty soon.

Discord and ambivalent feelings are depicted in several other cards. In several stories men are seen as cooking meals for themselves. Frankie seems to have hit on stereotype themes throughout all his stories and repeats them with very little feeling, as is true in his Rorschach material.

In Card 8, a sado-masochistic theme is pointed in an aggressive direction, rather than a masochistic one.

> Card 8: "They got mad at him, so opening him up. The young fellow seems kind of sorry he killed him. They are cutting him up now to hide the body. There were three brothers, and the man they killed was a stranger."
>
> [HC-murder RB-regret RD-wrong]

---

[11]Observer's note: However, among the Slavey it is the men and especially the youth who wear brooches.

Frankie's Rorschach, with forty-one responses, is very similar to that of his elder brother. There are five anatomical responses, in all cases lungs (his brother had two). Evidently in these boys there is a great fear of tuberculosis, reaching hypochondriac proportions. He doesn't show stereotypy on the Rorschach in terms of percentage of animals seen, which is low, but more in terms of the obsessional preoccupation with lungs and with long narrow objects or implements such as spears (suggestive of concern with his masculinity and/or aggression). There is less diffuse anxiety shown than in his brother's record.

The preoccupation with eating found on the TAT is borne out only by one food response on the Rorschach. This response is the only one in which color is used—"It's a carrot." Ego strength as measured by the form quality of the responses is practically identical with that of his brother.

In general, there is great similarity in the approach of the two brothers to the psychological tests. The main difference is in more diffuse anxiety in the elder boy, Jerry, than is found either in father or younger brother, and more preoccupation with body in the younger one, Frankie. The vista responses, suggesting feelings of inadequacy and withdrawal, that are found in the elder brother and in their mother are lacking in the younger brother, as are any pure color responses.

As far as the TAT results are concerned, these illustrations demonstrate that fantasized concern with objects or their loss has to be interpreted in a broader context of other social relationships and may refer symbolically to affective states of anxiety rather than to real events. To extract these narratives from their personal and social context for any quick numerical comparison with another group would not allow for meaningful cross-cultural assessment.

Categories for Scoring Concern with Objects

A. Positive Use, Acquisition or Possession ***OA***

OA-body	Positive about the body
OA-clothes	Attention to clothes
OA-own	Positive about acquisition or possession of an object
OA-wealth	General concern with possessions or wealth
OA-please	Pleasurable use of objects
OA-esthetic	The aesthetic pleasure derived from object
OA-reward	Object as reward
OA-gift	Gift of an object to others or gift exchange
OA-pet	Having a pet as an object
OA-job	Job providing a sense of financial security
OA-status	Concern with status or ethnic symbols

OA-pride	Pride or attention to, beauty, or possessions
OA-guard	Protection of objects from harm; conservation
OA-create	Construction or creation of an object
OA-free	Indifference toward objects or possessions viewed as a positive attribute
OA-collect	Collection of objects
OA-order	Arranging objects, order
OA-awe	Awe or reverence toward an object
OA-magic	Magical acquisition of an object
OA-spell	Magical use of an object
OA-symbol	Object or objects symbolizing the social self
OA-alive	Object as animate (pets)

In an expressive context, positively considered emphasis may be placed on a pleasure derived from objects or the pleasure in a use to which an object is put. The body may be considered as an "object" in this respect (OA-body). Clothes may be a special concern (OA-clothes). There may be a positive expression about the possession of a specific object such as a violin (OA-own), or a positive more general feeling about acquisition of possessions or wealth (OA-wealth).

There is an overtly pleasurable use of objects that can be perceived as giving pleasure through use (OA-please). A violin or other object may be focused upon as an object of beauty (OA-esthetic). Where pleasure is depicted, the response may need to be double scored with a P category.

Objects may be considered a reward for meritorious activities (OA-reward). Objects are given or exchanged as gifts (OA-gift). One may acquire a pet as an object (OA-pet).

Having a job can represent a sense of financial security (OA-job). Objects can come to symbolize the social self or one's desired social status (OA-status). There may be a positively considered evaluative pride stated about physical appearance, clothes, or one's possessions (OA-pride). There are protective, affiliative, and evaluative attitudes held toward objects. There may be a positive sense of protecting objects from harm (OA-guard). This category may be extended to a sense of ecological conservation of the environment.

Instrumentally considered, there may be specific concern with the creation or building or construction of objects (OA-create). Indifference toward objects or possessions may be viewed as a positive attribute. There may be a positive sense of detachment or indifference toward material objects. This detachment may be seen as a religious or spiritual quality (OA-free). There may be a positive concern in the collection of objects (OA-collect). They can be ordered or arranged (OA-order). One may have a sense of awe or a sense of reverence toward objects, including objects of nature (OA-awe). Objects can be manipulated magically. In fantasy, objects can be acquired through magical means (OA-magic), or be used to perform some positive form of magic (OA-spell). Objects can symbolize. Sometimes they symbolize the social self (OA-symbol). Pets are in some respects objects. Objects may be vitalized or personalized given a sense of something interactive, with which to have a relationship (OA-alive).

B. Unresolved Concerns About Objects ***OB***

OB-think	Thinking about an object
OB-want	Desire for an object
OB-torn	Ambivalence about possession of an object
OB-body	Preoccupied with body; attention to pregnancy
OB-care	Care of body, exercise
OB-clothes	Concern with clothes
OB-money	Concern with earning money, having a job
OB-compare	Concern with relative wealth or poverty
OB-baby	Concern with pregnancy or about the baby
OB-loss	Fear of losing something
OB-theft	Fear of theft
OB-break	Fear of breakage; fear of injury or destruction of object
OB-defect	Concern with bodily defect
OB-repair	Concern with repair of object
OB-jealous	Jealous fear of losing something to another
OB-envy	Fear of having an object envied
OB-dislike	Dislike or disinterest in an object
OB-worth	Indifference toward objects or possessions
OB-nature	Story switched to attention to physical surroundings or nature
OB-depict	Deflection into card description: description of physique, etc.

There may be unresolved thinking about an object (OB-think). There may be an unsatisfied desire for an object (OB-want). On may have a basic ambivalence about an object (OB-torn). There may be a preoccupation with the body (OB-body), with its care, diet, exercise (OB-care). Any attention to sleep or the physical body (a form of somato-sensation) may represent a turn to physiological concerns as a form of avoidance of some interpersonal relationships. These expressions can be scored under (OB-body). There may be some unresolved issue in respect to clothes (OB-clothes).

There may be concern about earning money or having a job (OB-money). The concern may be with relative wealth or poverty (OB-compare). There may be an obsession about wealth or material possessions either in absolute or relative terms, comparative with others. There may be present a deep sense of relative deprivation (the latter situation should be double scored with the Nurturance category).

A frequent theme is pregnancy and concern about a baby (OB-baby). There may be an anxiety about loss of some material possession through uncontrollable circumstances (OB-loss). This anxiety may be specified as fear of theft (OB-theft). There may be a fear of injury or destruction of an object (OB-break), or possible defects or disease (OB-defect). There may be a preoccupation about repair (OB-repair).

There may be a jealous fear of losing something to another (OB-jealous), or a fear of the consequences of having objects envied by others (OB-envy). There may be an expressed dislike or disinterest in an object (OB-dislike), or have some unresolved indifference in respect to objects (OB-worth).

An avoidance type subcategory is a lack of attention to an interpersonal situation or self-consideration by expressing a preoccupation with nature and physical surroundings. Such responses are scored under its manifest content as (OB-nature). There are instances wherein objects are described in such a way one cannot determine the unexpressed ambiguous valences of the description. One may even see responses where there is no narrative, and the response is deflected into card description or a description of physical appearances portrayed in the card (OB-depict).

C. *Negative Attitudes or Activities in Respect to Objects* ***OC***

OC-display	Excessive concern with display, exhibition; physical appearance or clothes
OC-clothes	Negative appearance of other's clothes
OC-body	Negative appearance of body
OC-greed	Excessive concern with money, greed, avarice
OC-wealth	Objects or impersonal ambition (wealth) given priority over a personal relationship (double score)
OC-revere	Excessive reverence for objects; idolatry
OC-hate	Hate of an object or objects
OC-discard	Abandonment or discarding of an object
OC-debase	Depreciation of an object
OC-destroy	Hate or destruction or injury of an object or aspects of our ecosystems
OC-indulge	Destructive use of the body (e.g., gluttony or use of drugs)

OC-self-hurt	Bodily self-injury
OC-vandal	Destruction or injury of an object as a means of hurting a person or group (double score)
OC-rob	Robbery or theft
OC-control	Using objects to control people
OC-possess	Keeping an animal or person as a possession; psychic control or depersonalization of people into objects
OC-deceit	Acquisition by threat or deceit (double score)
OC-envy	Envy of the possession of others (double score)
OC-magic	Magical use of an object

Among the negatively viewed attitudes about objects there may be excessive concern with display or exhibition of either physical appearance or clothes (OC-display). A negative attitude about a body's appearance, clothes, etc. may be expressed (OC-clothes, OC-body). An individual can be depicted as driven by insatiable greed (avarice) or an excessive concern with money (OC-greed). Objects or possessions, or impersonal ambition can be expressly preferred to any positive human relationships (CO-wealth). Such stories can be double scored. There may be an excessive reverence or obsession with an object or some material possession, almost to the point of idolatry (OC-revere).

There may be an expression of hate for an object (OC-hate). There may be an abandonment or discarding of an object (OC-discard). There may be an overt depreciation of some object or the negative discounting of material possessions in a negative manner (OC-debase). (A double scoring is indicated when such depreciation occurs in the context of some social relationship.) There may be a hatred to the point of destruction or damage inflicted on one's possession or the possession of others (OC-destroy). (In some instance a double scoring is necessary with hostility under the Harmony category.)

One may be destructive toward one's own body by gluttony, drinking, use of drugs, or smoking (OC-indulge). [This is often double scored with negative responsibility (RC) categories.] One may express some deliberate self injury as an overt preoccupation (OC-self-hurt). There may be the destruction of objects as a means of attacking others indirectly (OC-vandal); robbery or theft can also be depicted (OC-rob). (Such responses should be double scored within a negative Harmony category.)

Objects or possessions may be a means of controlling others (OC-control). There may be a psychological dehumanization of a person or animal as a material possession (OC-possess). Such responses in these two categories can be double scored with the Control category. Objects can be acquired by the deceit of others (OC-deceit). These two categories can be double scored with some form of negative Affiliation. One may envy the possessions of another (OC-envy) (double score with some negative Nurture category). There may be a magical use of an object as in sorcery (OC-magic).

D. Negative Incurred Experience in Respect to Material Objects ***OD***

OD-body	Negative body image
OD-suffer	Body as object of suffering or negative depersonalized state experienced by body (including hunger)
OD-neglect	Neglectfulness toward an object or one's body as an object
OD-money	Without money
OD-loss	Loss of an object or possession
OD-robbed	Robbed
OD-broken	Suffering destruction of an object
OD-symbol	Symbolic destruction of an object
OD-taken	Being obsessed or possessed by objects
OD-used	Used as an object of kept as a possession (including slavery)
OD-psychic	Being possessed or used psychically

In a passive dimension, the body may be somehow depersonalized and viewed negatively (OD-body). The body may be viewed at a distance as a subject of suffering or negative physical states such as hunger (OD-suffer). (Double score with the Pleasure category.) There may be a neglectful attitudes toward one's possession or toward objects belonging to someone else (OD-neglect).

A person may stress being totally without money (OD-money). There are incurred losses of objects or possessions (OD-loss). One may be a victim of robbery (OD-robbed). [Note that a depiction of the victim of a robbery is distinct from a depiction of the act of robbery (OC-rob).] One may have one's object broken or destroyed by others (OD-broken). There may be a symbolized form of object loss or the destruction of an object (OD-symbol).

One may be conscious of being obsessed by objects, or possessed by them (OD-taken). There are aberrant human relationships in which an individual or a group is depersonalized and reduced to be objects. There are conditions of being so used in the condition of slavery (OD-used). One may be possessed psychically in a mentally disturbed relationship (OD-psychic). Both these scorings will usually be double scored with the Control category.

Fate: Impersonal Forces and Events

Our remaining category of "Fate" allows us to consider the external, dynamic occurrences or impersonal forces that impinge upon and shape human lives. These include natural catastrophes; social and historical changes including war; personal circumstances of inherited wealth or poverty; fateful events such as accidents, the unexpected appearance of illness, injuries and death. Events like these impinge upon every individual, regardless of culture. Yet the degree to which such events are experienced as salient, and the manner in which causation is attributed will differ across cultures. Depending on how impersonal forces are understood or conceptualized, such events may be seen as the result of what is variously termed luck, chance, accident, fate, kismet, or karma.[12]

Processes such as fate or kismet are perceived as intervening in characteristic ways in different cultures.[13] Clearly the conceptualization of occurrences of an impersonal nature differ in their conscious representation from individual to individual, and from one society to another. The relative saliency of narrative depictions of such processes, of course also depends on the stimuli that are used to elicit the narratives. By and large, The TAT cards were not designed toward this purpose. Nevertheless, in some cultural samples we have seen periodic spontaneous description of impersonal situations such as wealth or poverty, illness or death, etc. Impersonal forces are also described as governing the adversities of nature or personal destiny, and the occurrence of lucky or unlucky circumstances.

When such circumstances are depicted as resulting from an intentional force, such as the "will of God," they should instead be scored under the category *Control.* What characterizes the ICSS category of Fate, generally, is that the occurrences are depicted without reference to personal intentionality as the primary

---

[12]A common usage of the word "karma" may be relevant to a discussion of fate, but the word also refers to cause-and-effect processes that are indeed under personal control, so the word is not entirely synonymous with fate. In the Tibetan Buddhist framework, one is fully responsible for one's future karma. One's own actions produce causes that "ripen" in the future. Karma generated in the past is certain to ripen, but, like fruit from a tree that has been planted as a seed, how it ripens depends on conditions. The manner in which it ripens can be altered by purification and by attention to the conditions under which it ripens. Most importantly, in this framework, karma is, at its inception, the result of the actions of the individual. It does not arise from external impersonal causes. The concept of karma may perhaps be seen more fatalistically in a Hindu framework, wherein it also originates in actions committed in past lifetimes but is less subject to change in the present lifetime. This differential understanding of how karma ripens may be related to the historical emergence of Buddhism as a revolutionary religion that did not accept the strict social stratification of the Hindu caste system, wherein one's social status at birth was irrevocably determined by one's karma.

[13]An adequate cross-cultural examination of this topic warrants much greater consideration than can be given here. In the present chapter, we will draw on our own work with Japanese and Brazilian samples, as well as the work of other anthropologists in a variety of cultures.

cause of the situations in which individuals find themselves. One may or may not seek to personally intervene or attempt to manipulate these impersonal forces by magical means or other efficacious practices, such as warding off evil or bringing about personal benefit. Depending on how one acts relative to these potential causes, one may produce inadvertent or nonintended benefits or harm.

As with the case of the depiction of objects in narratives, when one sees reference to fateful events one's interpretations of meaning may also benefit from a consideration of psychodynamic processes. Narrative themes that refer to Fate may not always be what they seem, and may be used as a substitute for responses that would refer to either instrumental or expressive concerns.

Seen instrumentally, fatalistic causal explanation can be used in avoidance of depictions of responsibility for actions. References to fate may be either indirectly expressing or avoiding a sense of helplessness, powerlessness, inadequacy, or incompetence. Fatalistic attributions can be used as justification for an avoidance of efforts to mobilize oneself competitively in adversarial situations. Evocation of fate as an explanation can mask a general sense of alienation, suggesting that fateful forces replace any concern with internal motivation or sense of personal willpower in causing events to happen.

Expressively considered, use of fate as an explanation may be another form of resignation that can, depending on the context, prevent depression, help to tolerate depreciation, assuage loneliness, or substitute for the lack of nurture received from a non-giving world.[14] In this sense, fatalism is a depersonalization of unmanageable expressive needs. Developmentally, concerns with fate can be a continuation of an earlier adaptation to helplessness that is carried forward from childhood.

The converse to fatalism is the placing of unrealistic hope in chance or fortune. There is, in some, a magical assumption that the right attitude will bring about a positive outcome (see chapter 14, volume I). Such an optimistic attitude, when coupled with appropriate activity, may actually bring about positive results for some, although objectively only a minority of those who make the attempt will

---

[14]For five years during the late 1970s and early 1980s, the junior author lived in an isolated area of rural upper-eastern Tennessee and observed the culture of the local mountain people. Although many of the younger native residents were linked to the mainstream economy by commuting to jobs in the cities, some of their elders had substantially retained the peasant cultural heritage of the original European settlers. Some of these traditions were documented in a series of "Foxfire" books (Wigginton, 1972). The elders had seen their once thriving rural communities decimated by the Chestnut blight, by the mass exodus that occurred during and following the second World War, and by the continuing emigration of young adults to find work. Many of the elderly individuals lived in a condition that most Americans would have considered a state of extreme poverty and social isolation. In coping with their poverty and isolation, some elderly residents exhibited a resigned acceptance of their fate. In some, this resignation was suffered stoically, in others it was coupled with a warm sense of self-deprecating humor, others expressed a harsh bitterness, others suffered somatic symptoms, and others experienced clinical depression.

generally benefit from their efforts. The idea of hitting it "lucky" drives various forms of gambling. The psychology of the gambler is highly complex. A compulsive gambler himself, Dostoevsky meticulously examined the compulsive nature of such activity in his novels. Freud used Dostoevsky for his own interpretation of the ultimately self-destructive nature of the compelling excitement of gambling (Freud, 1929).

Psycho-Cultural Significance of Concern over Death and Illness[15]

Cultures differ widely in their explanations of the causes of death and illness and in the degree and nature of their preoccupation with these fateful events. Among the Japanese, illnesses or deaths of others in the family were the most frequent spontaneous concerns of a fateful nature that we found in responses to the TAT. In Brazilian samples gathered by Cicero Vaz (see chapters 8 and 12, volume II), situations of wealth or poverty or concerns with illness are represented differently depending upon the social status or ethnic background of the individual. In samples of immigrant youth from central America, Suárez-Orozco (1989) found frequent mention of the impersonal as well as personal destructiveness of war, as well as the effects of economic hardship experienced due to social inequality.

Whatever the explicit "cultural" explanation might be, social scientists have been interested in understanding the implicit psychological meaning of concerns over death and illness. We have found that where more naturalistic explanations for death or illness are lacking, malevolent sorcery or witchcraft are often seen as causes. However, psychological anthropologists such as Hallowell (1941, 1953) and Kluckhohn (1944)[16] have pointed out that the attribution of illness to sorcery or witchcraft is not due solely to an unavailability of naturalistic explanations. Such beliefs may also have a specific "function" in relation to the handling of aggressive feelings. Thus, continual concern over potential illness or death, especially when related to ideas concerning the possible evil intentions of one's avowed, or secret enemies, may serve as a *projection* of aggressive impulses.

Another type of relationship between concern over death and illness and a culturally determined mode of structuring aggression has become apparent to us in the course of work with TAT materials from Japan. Concern with death and illness for the Japanese often seems related to the *introjection* of guilt, as compared to the projection of aggression reported for the Native American groups.

---

[15]A version of this material previously appeared as part of "Psycho-Cultural Significance of Concern over Death and Illness Among Rural Japanese," by DeVos and Wagatsuma (1959).
[16]The terms *sorcery* and *witchcraft* are used interchangeably by many anthropological writers.

The fact that concern over illness is associated with belief in sorcery in some culture groups but not in others is most probably related in varying degrees to differences in the nature of the social systems, of the structuring of responsibility in adult social roles, as well as experiences in early childhood. Beatrice Whiting (1950) suggests in her study of Paiute sorcery that belief in sorcery is related to the distribution of power or control in certain features of social organization.[17] She indicated that a survey of the HRAF (Human Relations Area Files) demonstrates a statistically significant presence of sorcery in non-hierarchical societies, in comparison with its relative absence in societies with class or status difference in the distribution of power, as evidenced by superordinate justice or punishment for crimes.

The Japanese have been noted for the hierarchical nature of their society and would seem to fit Whiting's generalization. However, this explanation is somewhat unsatisfactory unless examined further in specific cases. Careful examination of the factors contributing to the developmental patterning of adult social roles would help demonstrate the way in which sorcery is functional or not functional psychologically.

The Berens River Saulteaux, as described by Hallowell, for example, live in a fairly simple non-hierarchical society. They are characterized by a lack of overt aggression in face-to-face situations. The Saulteaux appear to have placid character, patience and self-restraint. Murder and theft are rare, and there is no open expression of anger or quarrels involving physical assault. In spite of the notable lack of violence in the social behavior of their culture, the Saulteaux feel themselves constantly threatened by the hostile intentions of others. If a Saulteaux becomes ill and if ordinary medical treatment fails to produce improvement, he is bound to suspect that he has aroused another person's hostility by some action or attitudes and that, therefore, the offended person has retaliated. In fact, sick persons almost always believe that their illness is due to revenge. Hallowell concludes that their belief in sorcery provides a major outlet for aggression—that aggressive feelings are, in a sense, projected and resolved through external means.

Such belief in sorcery as an instrument of covert aggression in causing illness or death is two-edged. Whether or not the individual himself uses this means of aggression, the threat that another may be using such techniques against him constantly lurks in the background of his daily life. Thus, in spite of overtly minimizing the personal friction and hostility that periodically arise in their human relationships, the Saulteaux are dogged by anxieties and fears over possible illness or death arising from the belief that others may be prompted to covertly do them positive harm. It is not the practice of witchcraft but the prevalent belief in it that is of prime importance, because, from the standpoint of the individual who interprets his illness and misfortune as being due to sorcery, it makes little difference whether someone has gone through certain magical procedures or not.

---

[17]What Whiting calls *sorcery* is termed *witchcraft* by Kluckhohn.

Another major source of illness in Saulteaux belief is punishment from a supernatural being for what they call "bad conduct." In this society certain classes of sexual behavior (incest, homosexuality, auto-eroticism, bestiality, etc.) proscribed by the guardian spirits, may be punished by disease. It must be noted that such a fear is not generically different from the belief in sorcery. Both envision some external agent as reacting to an enraging act with destructive intent. Projection rather than introjection is operative in the Saulteaux in their fear of supernatural punishment and in their belief in sorcery. In both cases, any tendency toward what is conceived of as a transgression or an impulse toward an aggressive act is held in check by a firm belief in and fear of consequent attack by an external intentional force, be it visited on the victim in the form of illness or of some other misfortune.

In most communities in modern Japan, rural and urban, social sanctions emphasizing harmony and discouraging open antagonism are as pronounced as they are among Saulteaux studied by Hallowell or the Navaho discussed by Kluckhohn. However, in strong contrast to these Native American groups, belief in sorcery was of little or no importance in the concerns of the ordinary Japanese villager when we studied them in the 1950s. This is not to say that such a belief is entirely absent in Japanese communities. Magical practices such as sticking pins in an image can be documented, but fear of such practices has not been part of the ordinary concern of the Japanese. Illness is not generally regarded by Japanese as a punishment from an external source, yet it seems likely from the intensity of concern over possible illness noted in many Japanese that some form of displacement of affect is generally operative in these preoccupations.

Considerable concern with illness can be noted in the modern literary productions of the Japanese; such concern often appears when there is some sort of emotional crisis. In many stories there is a masochistically tinged theme of heroic suffering to attain a goal despite such difficulties as the long-term illness or death of a beloved. Only in the most ancient tales does one find much concern with the supernatural in relation to disease. One can roughly generalize that death or illness is most often seen in Japanese literary works in relation to the self-sacrificing nurturant role of women; or, when seen as related to men, illness is presented as a hindrance to one's undistracted dedication to achievement in life.

The content of fantasy productions of Japanese given to the TAT, when considered in the light of certain psychoanalytic formulations, suggests that excessive concern over either death or illness, may be related to hostility, as in the Saulteaux, but that the mechanism most operative, especially in tradition-oriented women, is an introjection of aggression. Concern over illness in many Japanese, then, seems ultimately related to unconscious internalized guilt feelings rather than to fear of projected hostility. In the Saulteaux' while possible guilt reactions may also be operative, the psychological processes involved in the use of an external agent of punishment to cope with guilt are different from those involved in the more "internalized" form of guilt in which the punitive agent is introjected and the individual in a sense punishes himself.

TAT Stories of Death and Illness as Related to Internalized Constraints

The internalization of social expectations and its relation to guilt phenomena depend largely on how these expectations are inculcated in children in the context of primary family relationships. As we have discussed in the chapter on Responsibility (R), the TAT evidence suggests the presence of a great deal of unconscious guilt in the Japanese in the 1950s and helped explain the pertinence of this to an understanding of their need for achievement and success. The Japanese virtues of self-sacrifice, persistence, and endurance toward long-range goals was learned by children from the mother, through her living example. The proper status and role behavior of the Japanese adult demanded much self-discipline. The manner in which this self-discipline is inculcated in childhood makes it impossible for the Japanese to find ready outlets for external projection of hostility or to attribute to outside causes intentional or fateful, any failure in expected performance. The effect of what may be termed the mother's moral masochism on her children makes escape from expected behavior most difficult.

Differences in the degree of internalization of the woman's role between the villages of Niiike and Sakunoshima, discussed elsewhere (De Vos, 1973) are apparent in a comparison of stories about death and illness.

The responses to the TAT pictures, analyzed quantitatively, showed in the Niiike farm women an unusually high degree of concern over problems of illness in family relationships. A comparison of the responses of farm and fishing groups to eleven TAT cards showed that approximately 20 percent of the stories given by women in the farming village were characterized by a theme involving some form of death or illness. The farm men used such themes in about 10 percent of their stories. This is still a high number in comparison with American norms, but not unusually so. The difference between men and women in Niiike was significant even at the .01 percent level.

As we demonstrated (De Vos and Wagatsuma, 1959), a specific comparison of the stories of death and illness from the two villages shows a high number of these stories from Niiike women, supporting our supposition that such stories are related to the degree of emphasis on a traditional self-sacrificing type of women's role in Niiike. The Sakunoshima women do not show a similar concern. In Sakunoshima there is no significant difference in incidence of such stories between men and women. The discrepancy between the women's groups account for most of the difference between the two villages in respect to the incidence of death and illness stories.

Analysis of the stories shows that the main difference between the two villages is the tendency for people, and especially women, in Niiike to see women as ill. The person most often specified as ill is the wife; the next is the mother. Women particularly tend to see a wife as dead, dying, or, if ill, as not recovering. This concern with a women's illness or death is an indirect reflection of a masochistic conception of her social status.

Another dimension of analysis of the TAT stories is the theme around which the death or illness is perceived. Grief, worry, and anxieties over the death or illness of a beloved are the most prevalent themes in the Niiike women's stories. Women's themes in general tend to be more pessimistic than those of men. Women seem to enjoy depicting in detail the grief of a man losing his beloved wife. Themes of anxiety usually concern the health of some individual in the family. A second theme noted in the stories given by many Niiike women and in none of the other groups considered is that of caring for a daughter who is ill. In a few stories sons are described as caring for a mother who is ill.

There is a scattering of stories from Niiike and Sakunoshima suggesting certain other Japanese ethical themes. One theme appearing in a few stories is the diligence and hard work of a son whose mother or father has died. In some of these stories in the Niiike sample there is a suggestion that the death has changed the son's attitude to one of greater diligence and application. A few stories depict illness as a result of overwork. And in another vein there is a story of suicide as an act of self-sacrifice on the part of a wife, removing herself as an obstacle to the husband's devotion to his work. In other stories, suicide is an act of dedication by a mother to a son who has died, or by a son who joins a dead father. These latter stories occur in the Niiike sample; no counterpart is found in Sakunoshima.

The number of such stories emphasizing death or illness is in marked contrast to the very few stories about being attacked or attacking with resultant injury or death.

The few stories recorded can be interpreted along psychoanalytic lines as indicating the presence of some pressing, even though unconscious, hostility. These results were in marked contrast to those obtained in our TAT study done in collaboration with Helm and Carterette on the Slavey group partly illustrated above (Helm, De Vos, and Carterette, 1960). Among the Slavey, stories of aggressive violence leading to death or injury were very much in evidence; there were many fewer stories of illness. Behaviorally, the Slavey community showed no more overt personal aggression than did the Japanese village. Nevertheless, one could see that there was more fear of personal attack, and preoccupation with the possible violent hostile feelings of others; themes of self-sacrifice were entirely lacking. This difference in emphasis on illness in TAT themes does *not* seem always related to realistic concern with illness in the communities considered. It is to be noted that the Slavey, for example, worry a great deal about actual illness; they have considerable fear of diseases, such as tuberculosis, against which their resistance is poor.

In the Japanese villages there was difference in seeing accidental death. In Niiike, the farming village, the figure seen in five of the six stories of accidental death told by men is the father or son. No such trend is evident in the Sakunoshima material. Some difference between the Sakunoshima and the Niiike men in regard to the possible unconscious hostility toward a father seen in a dominant role (as he is in the farming village) is apparent also when we look at another class of stories which are related to consequences of the absence of a parent long-since dead, usually a father. These consequences are depicted in positive and negative terms.

In Sakunoshima, the men emphasize a theme of the dead father as an inspiration to the achievement and success of the son. Memory of the father is sometimes evoked as an image inspiring the son. In contrast, in a scattering of stories, the absence of a parent is seen as leading to evil conduct, specified as being caused by lack of guidance or example. There are three stories in which a mother's conduct after the death of her husband is described as licentious, encouraging the son to learn evil ways. In Niiike there are fewer such stories, and, in contrast, certain stories emphasize expiatory themes in which a son, by reflecting upon the image of his dead father, changes his attitude toward life and reforms.

The fantasy material from Niiike includes instances in which the illness of the parent seems related to the improper behavior of a child. If such a parent becomes ill or dies, the child reforms. Introjection of guilt is strongly suggested by these stories. One's evil conduct has injured the sorrowing parent; hence, one must pay by assuming the responsibilities for hard work and diligence previously avoided. Such stories of parental illness as related to introjective guilt are particularly stimulated by the ideal cultural requirements of status and role in relation to achievement, and they also indicate a relative unavailability of aggressive outlets in traditional Japanese social relationships.

A few stories depicting mental aberration deserve special attention. Such stories given by men depict women as "hysterical" or "insane." For instance, in one story by a man, a woman is seen as "hysterical" because she "hates her husband who fools around with other women." Conversely in one story given by a woman, a young son is depicted as having gone insane. Mental deficiency or idiocy is depicted for sons in two other stories and for a daughter in yet another. Men give more stories of mental problems than do women. Men tend to see women as mentally disturbed when they act in an overly emotional manner, and, conversely, the three stories of mental deficiency or insanity in boys or men are given by women. These stories of concern with mental functioning are unique to Niiike, and no counterparts are found in Sakunoshima. This difference in sensitivity to mental malfunctioning is not readily explicable directly from the ethnographic data. It may be another reflection of differential stresses in status and role performance in the two villages. A women seen as "violent" is sometimes explained by men in the farm village as losing the ordinary ego controls that would prevent her from expressing her aggressive feelings directly to her husband. In Niiike, a boy with a weak intellect would not be considered fit to carry out ascribed adult role functions.

Further Psycho-Cultural Considerations

The generally greater concern over death and illness by women from the farming village can be interpreted as related to the greater degree to which sexual and aggressive impulses are prohibited in women in this particular village. The prohibition against outer expression of these impulses is more severe in Niiike than in Sakunoshima; hence their appearance is less tolerated in the fantasies of the farming women than in those of the women of the fishing village.

Japanese behavior raises speculation as to how introjective defense mechanisms can be related to the use of illness in various situations involving achievement drive. For some Japanese, illness may take the unconscious form of self-inflicted punishment for failure, or, if understood more deeply, for unacceptable hostility to a parent or authority figure and his expectations. It may also be used as an excuse to the self or to others for lack of accomplishment or failure to complete expected goals. Other Japanese seem to use physical illness as an unconscious mode of escape from an intolerable situation that allows no way out. Studies into the mechanisms of reaction involved in physiological and psychological stress suggested why certain Japanese were in the 1950s particularly prone to suffer a reactivation of tuberculosis, for example, when under some form of social pressure to succeed in a difficult situation, such as studying abroad.

For women, the emphasis is on the role of nurturance within the home rather than on some form of the external achievement required of men. The sacrifice of women in caring for a son after the death of a husband and her obligation to instill in him a desire for accomplishment is a favorite theme in Japanese literature generally, and such stories appeared in our TAT sample. Reik (1941) points out that if we are to understand moral masochism, we must recognize that inherent in it is the expectation of eventual triumph after perseverance. In the TAT stories, as in Japanese literature generally, the virtue most lovingly emphasized in both men and women is endurance toward the accomplishment of a goal taking lifelong dedication.

Speculating on the basis of psychoanalytic theory derived from American clinical cases, one can conceive of several possible psychological processes that could underlie such a strong concern with death and illness as that found in the TAT stories. One possibility is that with the denial of external expression there may be a turning in of affect on the body in the form of hypochondriacal concerns. This sort of mechanism could be a basic character defense in the ego controls of aggression, depending on a narcissistic withdrawal of affect from outside objects generally into an inner preoccupation. Such a process is sometimes revealed through increased concern with possible illness.

Another somewhat different possibility is that unacceptable destructive or sexual impulses are converted into excessive anxiety over the possible illness of others. Related to this sort of transmutation of feelings is what we have suggested as the moral masochistic tendencies appreciably present in Japanese. Concern over death or illness could be related to some sort of masochistic dedication to the persons of one's immediate family. Illness and death involve forms of sacrifice and suffering to be endured. The manner in which many of the illness stories are structured favors this latter type of analysis, rather than analysis in terms of hypochondriacal leanings per se.

We contend that high incidence of concern over death and illness in the TAT stories should not be related to personality defenses derived from difficulties at early developmental levels, and subsequent withdrawal of affect to an over-concern with illness in one's own body. It is more meaningful to discuss these results in the context of the effects of severely circumscribed adult social roles, especially on women. Such tendencies toward aggression as do exist are, according to inference, well transmuted by the Niiike women with masochistic identification with a traditional role in which they feel they are expected to sacrifice themselves to the care of the family. The stories often suggest themes in line with these ethical expectations. They depict women who are dutifully concerned over illness of others or women who suffer illness or death in the course of maternal or wifely devotion.

Although traditional patterns are changing, Japanese fiction still contains many stories involving a father's death that illustrate this psychological equation: mother keeps son, but mother and son both pay by maintaining diligent submission to a far-off life goal demanding endurance and self-sacrifice. In these stories the father's death is followed by the mother's aiding her son, through her sacrifice, to make a success of his life, and the implication is that for her sacrifice the son owes the mother a continued dedication to success. In these stories, the father is removed quickly so that the relationship of mother to son is an exclusive one throughout most of the telling. The mother becomes a completely desexualized figure, often ill or suffering as a consequence of her dedication to her child. Any interest in sexuality on her part would be perceived as bringing about the ruination of her son. Stories in which the theme of success is spelled out in terms of a mother's love rather than in terms of the establishment of a family are not uncommon in American literature or for that matter in American TAT stories. However, American stories point up the goal of leaving the mother and going off to marry, albeit sometimes with great reluctance. The latter stories are quite infrequent in the Japanese material. According to American standards, a son leaves the generation of the mother and takes up his own tasks in life, and his failure to do so is often attributed to some unhealthy tie to the mother.

Sacrifice and masochism are, unconsciously, forms of control. A woman's ego in the traditional Confucian ethics is encouraged to broaden itself to include her male child. She, in a sense, does not want to lose this male "principal" that is attached to her. Men, however, are often covertly perceived as weak and prone to a dependent attachment to a woman. A woman gives up the goal to direct physical fulfillment and replaces it with the subtler goal of maintaining a long-range unbroken control over the husband or the son as a masculine part of herself. The image of the terrible mother-in-law in the Japanese family, therefore, is not explicable solely as that of an older woman who is permitted displaced aggression toward a young bride as part of her status; the mother who feels a son is attached to her becomes uncontrollably hostile when someone threatens this deep attachment.

In conclusion, the basic differences hypothesized in the psycho-cultural meaning of concern over death and illness between the Japanese in our study and in the Native American groups reported on by Hallowell and others are a differential cultural emphasis on mechanisms of introjection and related masochistic defenses, on one hand, and fear of retaliation and projection of hostile impulses, on the other. In the one, guilt is internalized as a part of the ego and ego ideal; in the other, punishment or hostility is perceived as coming from the outside. Cultural conditioning is responsible for differential emphasis on the use of these mechanisms. A culture, including its socialization process, makes certain controls necessary in handling prohibited aggressive impulses, and at the same time selectively provides learning experiences in which these mechanisms are observed being used by others who are objects of future identification.

Categories for Scoring Fateful Events

*A. Good Fortune **(KA)***

KA-luck	Good fortune, good luck
KA-social	Good social circumstances
KA-wealth	Good economic circumstances
KA-status	Inherited status or propitiously received status
KA-able	Inherited aptitude
KA-hardy	Hardiness, resiliency, courage, adaptive traits
KA-know	Chance acquisition of knowledge
KA-results	Inadvertent behavior leading to good consequences for self or another
KA-recovery	Recovery
KA-dream	Recovery from a bad dream; bad circumstance but a dream
KA-accept	Recognition or acceptance of one's fate
KA-magic	Magical intervention
KA-karma	Good fortune due to karmic inheritance from the past

There can be specific spontaneous references to the good luck encountered by an individual (KA-luck). Individuals are depicted in good social circumstances (KA-social), or well-off economically (KA-wealth). Attention may be directed to inherited social status (KA-status) or to some luckily inherited aptitude (KA-able). Hardiness or resiliency are highly desired personal traits (KA-hardy). There may be some chance acquisition of useful knowledge (KA-know), or some inadvertent act leading to good consequence for the self or others (KA-results). There may be some lucky recovery from an adverse circumstance or illness (KA-recovery). One may wake up to find one is having bad circumstances in dream, not in reality (KA-dream). One may develop a positive acceptance of one's fate, whatever it might be (KA-accept). There may be some form of magical intervention toward good consequences (KA-magic). (If a personal agent is depicted this must be double score with a Nurture category.) From a Buddhist one can hear expressed that good fortune is a result of a positive karmic inheritance from a previous existence (KA-karma).

B. Unresolved Karmic Conditions: Concerns About External Events and Superstitious Fears ***(KB)***

KB-crisis	A social, environmental, or medical crisis
KB-chance	Chance situation as yet not resolved
KB-events	Concern or anxiety in reaction to external events
KB-status	Concern with relative status
KB-want	Concern or fear of economic want
KB-mishap-s	Accident or fear of accident to self
KB-mishap-o	Accident or fear of accident involving another
KB-illness	Fear of illness or aging
KB-survive	Worries about physical survival
KB-nature	Concern or fear of natural dangers darkness
KB-hurt	Fear of behavior accidentally causing or allowing negative consequences
KB-magic	Superstitious fears (including the evil eye)
KB-hope	Hope in future good fortune
KB-karma	Uncertain fortune due to karmic inheritance from the past

There are a wide variety of unresolved social or environmental situations that can be subsumed under the following subcategories. There may arise some form of social or environmental crisis (KB-crisis). There are a variety of unresolved chance situations (KB-chance). There may be worry about some specific threatening external event or events (KB-events). There may be disquiet about one's unresolved social fate or unsatisfactory social status (KB-status). There may be an unresolved fear of economic want or need to find a job (KB-want). One may worry about a possible accident injuring oneself (KB-mishap-s) or others (KB-mishap-o), or have worries about physical survival (KB-survive). There may be worry about possible illness or the effects of aging (KB-illness). There can be a fear of natural disasters or terrors of the dark (KB-nature). There may be a fear about inadvertently causing hurt to another, being the source of ill consequences (KB-hurt). There are various forms of superstitious beliefs about inadvertent behavior causing ill consequences (KB-magic). One such common belief in the Mediterranean area is belief in the "evil eye." An individual with the evil eye is personally unaware of the consequent damage done by looking at a child or the goods possessed by another. Finally, one may express a sense of still to be uncertain hope or optimism that fortune may smile in the future (KB-hope). Again, in Buddhism one can be uncertain about one's Karmic inheritance (KB-karma).

C. *Unfortunate Acts Releasing Negative Agents or Magical Consequences* ***(KC)***

KC-break	Accidental breaking of an object
KC-hurt-o	Accidentally producing negative circumstances for others
KC-hurt-s	Behavior accidentally causing fateful consequences to the self
KC-taboo	Inadvertent breaking of a proscription or taboo with negative consequences
KC-evil eye	Trait accidentally causing or allowing negative consequences for another (evil eye)
KC-karma	Ill fortune due to karmic inheritance from the past

There are some inadvertencies caused by an individual's behavior. One may accidentally break an object (KD-break). One may accidentally injure or cause the death of another (KC-hurt-o). One can accidentally cause self-injury (KC-hurt-s). There are inadvertent acts that may have negative magical consequences. The world of magic is imprecisely defined. One of the distinctions made between religion and magic in the possible absence of a personal agent in magical happenings or magical practices. Religious beliefs, by and large, involve a positive or negative supernatural intentional force as a causative agent. Magic is mechanical, religion involves a deity whose causal patterns may not be understood but whose intentional attitudes govern occurrences. Hence, religious and supernatural concerns are, by and large, found under some interpersonal category, whereas magical beliefs and practices are found more in the present category dealing impersonally with events. Among actively induced misfortunes are those related to an inadvertent breaking of a proscription or taboo (KC-taboo). One can cause ill to another by possession the evil eye (KC-evil-eye). From a Buddhist one can hear expressed that ill fortune is a result of a negative karmic inheritance from a previous existence (KC-karma).

D. *Negatively Incurred Fate* ***(KD)***

KD-luck	Bad fortune, bad luck, or failure due to unspecified external events
KD-hopeless	Hopeless or irremediable situation
KD-news	Receiving bad news, unspecified
KD-loss	Loss of someone due to inadvertent circumstances
KD-poverty	Bad conditions or consequences of bad economic conditions
KD-deprive	Depriving, ungiving environment
KD-unjust	Unjust or unfair life conditions
KD-thwart	Frustrating life situation or occupation
KD-war	War
KD-animal	Suffers animal attack
KD-mishap	Accidents; inadvertent frustration of plans by unexpected presence or absence of another
KD-ac-die	Accidents leading to death; death in war
KD-illness	Illness
KD-ill-die	Illness leading to death
KD-death	Death (natural or unspecified)
KD-age	Old age, pity about age
KD-defect	Birth defect, handicap, crippling, inherited mental or personality defect
KD-mental	Insanity or neurosis, congenital mental damage
KD-resign	Resignation or succumbing to ones fate
KD-karma	Negative destiny due to karmic inheritance from the past

One's bad luck is due to far-removed external events (KD-luck). Most misfortune is passively incurred. These are usually double scored with whatever other category or circumstance is being expressed. One may express a sense of hopeless doom or irremediable bad fate (KD-hopeless). One can receive very bad news which is not specified in the narrative (KD-news). One losses friends or loved one's due to external events or circumstance beyond one's control (KD-loss). (Such loss should be double scored with a negative Afilliative category.) One is subject to bad economic conditions (KD-poverty). There is much injustice in life (KD-unjust). One may be stuck in a frustrating life situation (KD-thwart). One suffers the ills brought on by war (KD-war). One can be attacked by an animal, where the animal is depicted as a negative circumstance of nature rather than being depicted as an intentional being (KD-animal). Accidents (KD-mishap) and fatalities (KD-ac-die) cannot be anticipated.

There are illness (KD-illness) and illnesses leading to death (KD-ill-die) as common occurrences in every society despite the advance of medicine. Death, whatever the cause (KD-death) and old age (KD-age) are inevitable. There are various other infirmities, birth injuries, defects and handicaps (KD-defect). Mental inflictions, neuroses, or psychoses (KD-mental) are incurred in every society, whatever the specific contribution of genetic inheritance or childhood circumstances.

There are attitudes expressing that the fated condition that one finds oneself in is positive, or negative, depending on the view of the teller. A passive resignation to one's fate can be viewed as negative (KD-resign), if the context is negative or positively. (KA-resign) as acceptance of one's fate with resoluteness and fortitude. In Buddhism, a negative destiny is perceived by many as due to a negative karmic inheritance from the past (KD-karma).

Illustrative Samples of Scoring in the Following Chapters

In several of the chapters of volume II we have included actual illustrations of scoring of several of the subcategories included under the [O] and [K] categories. Especially notable are the verbatim responses found in chapters 3, 8, 11, and 12, volume II.

Notes

Abraham, Karl. 1927. *Selected Papers*. London: L. & Virginia Woolf.

Befu, Harumi. 1989. A Theory of Social Exchange as Applied to Japan. In Yoshio Sugimoto and Ross E. Mouer (Eds.), *Constructs for Understanding Japan* (pp. 39–66). London: Kegan Paul International.

De Vos, George A. 1973. *Socialization for Achievement: Essays on the Cultural Psychology of the Japanese.* Berkeley: University of California Press.

De Vos, George A. and L. Bryce Boyer. 1989. *Symbolic Analysis Cross-Culturally: The Rorschach Test.* Berkeley: University of California Press.

De Vos, George A. and Hiroshi Wagatsuma. 1959. Psycho-Cultural Significance of Concern over Death and Illness Among Rural Japanese. *International Journal of Social Psychiatry*, **5**(1): 6–19.

Fenichel, Otto. 1945. *The Psychoanalytic Theory of the Neurosis*. New York: W. W. Norton.

Freud, Sigmund. 1929. *Dostoevski and Parricide.* The Realist I. London.

Hallowell, A. Irving. 1941. The Social Functions of Anxiety in a Primitive Society. *American Sociological Review*, **6**: 869–881.

———. 1953. Aggression in Saulteaux Society. In C. Kluckhohn, Henry Murray, and D. Schneider (Eds.), *Personality in Nature, Society, and Culture* (pp. 260–275). New York: Knopf.

Helm, June, George A. De Vos, and Teresa Carterette. 1960. Variations in Personality and Ego Identification Within a Slave Indian Kin-Community. National Museum of Canada Bulletin, No. 190, *Contributions to Anthropology*, Part II.

Kluckhohn, Clyde. 1944. *Navaho Witchcraft.* Boston: Beacon Press.

Macy, J. 1991. *Mutual Causality in Buddhism and General Systems Theory: The Dharma of Natural Systems.* Albany, N.Y.: State University of New York Press.

Manlove, Robert F. 1990. *Ozamiz: A Case Study in Urban Anthropology.* Unpublished Ph.D. dissertation. Department of Anthropology, Berkeley: University of California.

Piaget, Jean. 1930. *The Child's Conception of Physical Causality.* London: Kegan Paul, Trench, Trubner & Co. LTD.

Reik, Theodor. 1941. *Masochism in Modern Man.* New York: Farrar and Rinehart.

Scheper-Hughes, Nancy. 1979. *Saints, Scholars, and Schizophrenics.* Berkeley: University of California Press.

Suárez-Orozco, Marcelo. 1989. *Central American Refugees and U.S. High Schools: A Psychosocial Study of Motivation and Achievement.* Stanford, Calif.: Stanford University Press.

Thurman, R.A.F. 1984. *The Central Philosophy of Tibet: A Study and Translation of Jey Tsong Khapa's "Essence of True Eloquence."* Princeton, N.J.: Princeton University Press.

———. 1993. *A Commentary on Chandrakirti's Sevenfold Reasoning.* Talk presented at the Jewel Heart Summer Retreat, Yankee Springs Recreation Area, Mich.

Whiting, Beatrice. 1950. Paiute Sorcery. *Viking Fund Publication in Anthropology,* No. 15. New York: Viking Fund.

Wigginton, E. 1972. *The Foxfire Book.* New York: Anchor.

Chapter 14

The Existential Self: Scoring Themes Pertaining to the Supernatural or Thoughts of Suicide

Relationships with the Supernatural

In societies generally, many individuals consciously envision some interpersonal relationship with supernatural forces or supernatural entities. When Emile Durkheim (1947) considered conscious human thought to involve forms of "collective representation," he made a basic division between the interactive world of the "sacred" that included supernatural relationships with deities and with the dead, as contrasted with the relationships that comprise ordinary secular society.[1] Unfortunately, psychologists are rather hesitant to consider religious beliefs and feelings in the context of their scientific examination of human experience and expression. Nevertheless, it can sometimes be useful to consider both aspects of this sacred/secular dichotomy as they are reflected in conscious thought.

Concerns with the supernatural or sacred may be marked by ritualized collective behavior. Some also have idiosyncratic or self-oriented components as well, and may involve asocial or self-isolating behavior. In either case, the behavior nevertheless commonly involves some forms of relationship, whether with others

---

[1]There has been a quest in both anthropology and sociology to understand the evolutionary development and function of religious thought in society. In earlier anthropology there was a preoccupation with a possible evolutionary sequence to analyze the wide varieties of human religious beliefs and practices (Robertson-Smith, 1894).

or with a supernatural force or entity. Regardless of the religious faith inherited or sought after, beliefs about relationships with supernatural forces can be distinguished using the same categories that pertain to concerns with more secular relationships. Supernatural entities can be envisioned as punitive or loving, as assessors of purity and acceptability. They can be seen as the originators of the social standards that define categories of transgression, or as the enforcers of those social standards, through either direct supernatural intervention or through the more earthly acts of ordained representatives. They can also be seen as the source of absolution, obtainable through atonement and renewed adherence to divine commandments. Thus, in what follows, we shall attempt to delineate how some religious representations or thoughts about relationships with the sacred are related to the interpersonal categories we are considering in this volume.

One finds generally that humans have conceptualized some kinds of supernatural power as being related to the divine. Depending on the culture, there are notable variations in the saliency of instrumental or expressive concerns that characterize human interactions with the supernatural and the control of its power. Some religions can be distinguished as those emphasizing a centralized morality in which human authority controls the group and acts as intermediary to group interactions with the deity (Lewis, 1971). Contrastively, in some religious sects, there is no centralized control, but individualized, internalized forms of relations to the deity, and religious behavior emphasizes the absence of central control. Other societies formally seek religious control through a specialized priesthood that remains relatively distinct from secular authority.

In our cross-cultural comparisons, we find that the content of religious beliefs elicited or those given popular expression are different in emphasis not only from society to society, but also from person to person. In Japan, as elsewhere, religious belief and practices related to the supernatural comprise a complexity of experiences and motives that differ among individuals (De Vos, 1992; De Vos and Sofué, 1986; Slote and De Vos, 1998). Nevertheless, one can find definitive cultural patterns manifest as collective representations. Anthropology and Sociology have long understood the importance of these social and cultural dimensions of experience. Yet research psychologists, with their emphasis on individual behavior, cognition, or personality, have generally avoided consideration of an individual's socioculturally constituted religious beliefs or concerns. The field generally neglects to use this type of information toward a comparative understanding of the varieties of social and personal religion-based coping as well as religion-centered group-oriented interactions. A classificatory ordering such as what we present in this volume may help systematize such comparative analysis. In our own attempts to understand conscious religious thought in discussions with Japanese Buddhists and Shintoists, as well as with Christians and members of a variety of other religious groups, we have attempted to see how religious concerns are germane to the interpersonal categories considered in this volume.

Sacred communication, which is sometimes called "prayer," appears in various forms of behavior used for establishing a relationship with a supernatural force or entity. Relationships with the sacred or supernatural may at times be either instrumental or expressive in their intended function, and this may vary from individual to individual, and from time to time. A good relationship with the supernatural, achieved through prayer or supplication, for example, can be for the purpose of obtaining good fortune or material possessions. It can be for the purpose of gaining additional competence, useful for winning a competition. A supernatural relationship may be invoked to assist in attempts to resolve interpersonal difficulties with others, or in attempts to fulfill expressive needs not met in the secular social world. For example it can be used for gaining forgiveness, for the assuagement of loneliness, for seeking nurturant protection or provision, etc. It may be invoked to assist in maintaining a sense of purpose, in enforcing social regulations, in conceptualizing legitimate authority, or in enforcing social sanctions.

Collective ritual may arouse not only a sense of personal empowerment but also a sense of social harmony in the participants. Ritual participation can affirm both group solidarity and harmony with the supernatural or divine being. Additionally, the well controlled or role-structured behavior one sees in ritual performance can be seen as an effort to replicate internally (i.e., internalize) the characteristics of the supernatural or divine being (whether fierce power or beautiful quietude) with whom one is ritually communicating and communing. Examples of this "incorporation" can be seen in a variety of ritual contexts, whether one is being possessed by a demon in a trance or using mudra as part of a Vajrayana Buddhist practice. The social validation of one's internalization may also facilitate the participant's more enduring identification with those internalizations. Furthermore, a sense of aesthetic pleasure is commonly derived from these experiences, and in many instances the aesthetic experience itself may be the primary factor that keeps the ritual participants returning.

The basic differentiation between religion and magic found implicit, if not explicit, in the anthropological literature suggests that concern with magic tends to be of an instrumental nature, whereas the other religious concerns are both expressive as well as having instrumental motives. Generally the distinction we make is that magic involves the mechanical manipulation of supernatural power, whereas religion emphasizes the power of intentionality in the supernatural force or entity itself. Although this distinction is not always clear-cut, it can be a useful differentiation to assist in thinking about the thematic category of the narrative concern. Yet within the present scoring system, one finds religious as well as magical considerations in one form or other under *all* categories. Religious thought can be categorized especially in (but not limited to) the expressive categories of Nurture (N), Anger or wrath (H), and Esteem (E). The instrumental regulatory categories of Control (D) and Responsibility (R), considerations of social purpose related to Achievement (A), and the use of prayer to overcome personal inadequacy and attain greater Competence (C) can all be depicted in religious terms.

Magical Power: Instrumental and Expressive Concerns

Many societies have specialists in the use of magic. Individuals variously called witches, warlocks, sorcerers, magicians, shamans, or healers have learned to manipulate special powers, which they have acquired as specially inherited gifts, either learned from others or attained thorough undergoing special ordeals. A witch can be benevolently or malevolently motivated to use power for good or ill. He or she is variously personally empowered, or is permitted to use power, or is able to become a vehicle for some other power, through special forms of knowledge or through being possessed by a supernatural presence that is purposefully directed (Bourguignon, 1968).

What is termed "magic" is often practiced by the manipulation of the power found in use of special words or verbal formulae or special objects that emit power. When there is magical control by formulae, empowerment may or may not become personal, i.e., it may or may not exist beyond the instrumentally manipulated formula itself. Special spells, potions, or other objects can be transferred for use from one individual to another, but the power may or may not remain once the spell has been cast.

In narratives, there can be stories of the magical acquisition of an object (OA-magic). More frequent is a fantasy about some magical use of an object or a special mechanical formula possessed by someone to cast a spell (OA-spell). There are negatively tinged stories about the magical use of a formula or object (OC-magic).

Some depersonalized magical intervention can be cited as being of assistance (KA-magic). Magic is used to resolve legal problems by having some impersonal judgment or "divination" made about guilt or innocence. In some cultures there are magical means of judging truth or innocence by subjecting an individual to an ordeal. Fate may be kind in demonstrating innocence (KA-magic). There are superstitious fears of unintended or inadvertent evil influences. For example, there is such widespread belief in, and fear of the evil eye (KB-magic) throughout the Mediterranean region. There are narratives about the negative consequence of the evil eye, an inadvertently used force that is not intentionally controlled.

Magic can be related instrumentally to enhancing personal power related to competence or competition. Under narratives of competence there can occasionally appear a narrative of an individual with magical competence (CA-magic). There can be use of magic to gain unfair advantage over a rival (MVC-magic). An authority figure can wield a magical curse as punishment (DDA-curse). Magic can be used as a means of controlling others. As such it is usually seen negatively as an act of control (DDC-magic).

Use of magic may be narrated in the context of some expressive interpersonal concerns. There is some destructive negative effect visible within much witchcraft. Expressively, use of magic is very often conceptualized in situations of malevolent intent (HC-magic). An individual can be considered as injured supernaturally by being bewitched or under a spell (HD-bewitch). Sometimes in a frustrating marital or love situation, a person wishes to control a lover by magical means (FB-thwart DDC-magic). Witchcraft causes injury when it is coupled with negative feeling of destructiveness. As such it is often double scored with a negative Harmony category when it appears in occasional stories (DDC-magic HC-injure). There may be a counter use of magic as protection from the malice of another (NSA-malice).

On the positive side, there can be a benevolent succorant or protective use of magic by someone on behalf of another (NDA-magic). In fairy tales such as Cinderella, there appears a benevolent fairy godmother who uses magical means to see to her happiness. Over 50 percent of contemporary Americans believe in guardian angels. However as commonly conceptualized, their benevolent intervention does not involve "magical" means but some direct form of succor or protection (see NDA-charity).

Instrumental, Regulatory Processes in Religious Thought

A religious system may blend explanations of supernatural intentionality, magical power, and scientific understanding to give the individual some sense of regularity in experiencing the outside world, and so afford some hope for partial instrumental human control over the awesome powers of nature. Folk religious concepts often also suggest instrumental means of maintaining relationships with this awesome power, whether the power itself is conceptualized as impersonal or personal. When personalized, religious practices are, in effect, acts of submission and entreaty to sway divine will or purpose. Humiliation of the self or ascetic practices can be instrumental acts aimed toward having one's humble wishes granted.

Seen instrumentally, religious systems are regulatory or restraining and directing of behavior toward socially defined purpose (Control). They can involve a sense of personal competence or failure, which often includes some form of prayer or invocation to improve one's capacity to influence outcomes (Competence). Religious beliefs are often related to the internalization of "conscience" which governs a sense of social and personal responsibility (Responsibility). In this regard, some behavior is also defined negatively as moral transgression. Religious systems can also define patterns of legitimate cooperation among adherents (Mutual Purpose). Religious thought can be involved in or become integral with the definition of human accomplishment or alienation (Achievement).

Supernatural Power and Control

The conceptualization of power is not completely secularized in most culturally constructed explanatory systems. Some form of supernatural intentionality is frequently used to help explain why and how things happen. Human beings conceptualize deity as intentional, having purpose that must be understood by humankind so that we may comply and be regulated in accordance with some conceptualized ultimate purpose. The cognitive-representational system of causal knowledge and explanation provided within a culture may remain largely inseparable from religious thought even where some domains of explanation have come to be secularized. Scientific knowledge may provide alternative modes of causal explanation for the natural world as being totally independent of supernatural intervention. Yet explanations for problems of human intentionality, morality, and social regulation may remain addressed by religious explanatory systems.

The supernatural manifests itself most tellingly as force or power. Early "animistic" representations of power usually termed "*mana*" by anthropologists (see Firth, 1940) are found in various folk beliefs. In Japanese folk Shinto, *kami* is/are vaguely conceptualized as representations of awesome power embodied in sacred mountains, impressive trees, or other unusual manifestations of nature. In Japanese folk belief, "deity" can be represented in vague concepts of enhanced fertility, generativity, sometimes personalized and sometimes not.[2] Power also becomes represented in particularly awesome individuals who may become deified objects of worship.

In many religions the representations of deity are most concerned with the instrumental issues of power, control, regulation, and the compliant practices used to avoid wrath. Many explanatory systems include the potential of destructive or wrathful supernatural forces that cause one to seek divine protection or even submit to divine authority (De Vos and Suárez-Orozco, 1990). In some explanations, the benevolent and malevolent forces are embodied in the same deity. In others, these forces are embodied distinctly. In the Judeo-Christian tradition, it has been remarked that the concerns in the Old Testament are prevailingly concerns with a god acting not only as creator, but also as "judge" punishing transgression. This One god can be jealous or become wrathful about any wayward behavior by subjects.

An awareness of divine punitiveness can become internalized (as is also the case with the awareness of the punitive power of human authorities) and can be used to control one's own behavior without the immediate presence of an outside authority. However, in many religious representations the deity is considered to be ever present and ever observing, even all seeing and all knowing. The deity may be seen, therefore, as possessing relative degrees of both omniscience and omnipotence. There is not only self-punishment related to guilt, but always the fear of overwhelming outside power, which may be perceived as benevolent, malevolent, or both. To manage experiences of a relationship with this overwhelming outside

---

[2]It may well be that folk beliefs concerned with the supernatural are less mature forms of religious representations found supplementary to the less supernaturally concerned social orientation of Confucian beliefs and practices. In each of the societies in which Confucianism predominated, there were auxiliary folk beliefs and practices in which the supernatural intervened in human events.

power, some willingly submit to a perceived divine authority (Control, D). Some seek divine protection (Nurture, N), some use "prayer' as a means of supplication to gain supernatural help to overcome expressively considered personal unworthiness (Esteem, E) or instrumental inadequacy (Competence, C).

These various concerns are blended in religious thought, although there may be shifts in emphasis historically. In the New Testament, Judeo-Christian beliefs shifted toward greater concern with the benevolent nurturing functions of a god, ultimately expressed through the sacrifice of Jesus wherein divine suffering is experienced for the benefit of humankind. Such a self-sacrificial role is also played by many of the previous incarnations of the Buddha, as is retold in the Jataka stories. In the Christian vision, one can see an all powerful God as being saddened by humanity's failure to freely honor divine law. This sadness is represented in iconography and is developed further as the suffering of the divine mother in Western Catholicism. The Virgin Mary serves as a representation of nurturant compassion, having given birth to the world's sacrificial lamb, then suffering the loss a mother feels at the loss of a child. A similar nurturant role is also played by feminine compassionate beings (Kwan Yin or Kannon, in some popular sects of Buddhism in China and Japan, or various forms of Tara in the Tibetan traditions). Historically, one can observe how the Bodhisattva Avalokitesvara became transformed, in representative icons and in legend, from a male-gendered being to a being who manifests in female forms to more widely fulfill the goal of compassionate action.

The Scoring of Supernatural Power and Control

Seen positively, from the subordinate perspective, the deity can be experienced as exercising proper authority over a subordinate (DSA-god). There is also the possibility of punishment exercised by a wrathful god (DDA-curse). Where this is unresolved, one may be awaiting judgment (DSB-god) or absolution (DSB-pardon). One may also pray as a means of gaining forgiveness (DSA-prayer).

One may seek also to use the power of the deity to actualize individual or collective purposes, variously conceptualized or contextualized in the context of other instrumental or expressive concerns. Wherever such contexts warrant, one must double score. For example, where there is tribal or ethnic conflict or rivalry, sacrificial ritual can be used to enhance the power of a group's particular deity vis-à-vis other deities. In such cases, some categories of Mutual Purpose may be relevant (e.g., DSA-ritual, MVB-against, or MVA-war, etc.). In some pantheistic concepts of the supernatural, the deities may be in conflict or at cross-purposes, and humans must negotiate those cross-purposes to maximize the positive and avoid the negative.

Ritual supplication and prayer (DSA-ritual; DSA-prayer) involve an instrumental arousal of the deity's caring capacities in respect to the deity's exercise of power and control. Supplication can also be used expressly in respect to anticipated nurture (NSA-prayer, see below). Supplication by its nature implies autonomous intentionality on the part of the deity as opposed to magic which is a manipulation of a formula to attain one's ends. There may be use of by rites, ritual, or prayer. Human instrumental interaction with deity may also seek, by day-by-day compliant behavior (DSA-author) to avoid punishment.

Concerns with Competence

Personal Inadequacy Related to Life and Death

The most awesome fateful experiences of human life and destiny are birth and death. Concerns with life and death issues such as fertility, parenting, illness, threats to subsistence, etc. must be addressed in any representational system that aims to allay human fears and provide security (N), in the face of the unpredictable forces of nature. It is not surprising that religious systems address these realities of life. When one faces life and death issues, one is never entirely never free from a sense of individual incapacity and anxiety and a need for external assistance. Religions commonly function to bolster a sense of personal "adequacy" as well as assuaging fear of failure in the achievement of life goals. The individual often feels inadequate, and, given this sense of imperfection, seeks out means of assistance from the supernatural in reaching toward what is conceived to be the ideal level of competence (C).

Scoring Personal Competence as Related to the Supernatural

It is in the nature of human beings to recognize their comparative helplessness and incompetence in dealing with the forces of nature or the inadvertent events of a potentially hostile environment. A person recognizing helplessness in a normal state can seek to gain the instrumental assistance of supernatural intentional power. One can employ forms of prayer in seeking help (CB-prayer). In some societies empowerment is sought through embodying supernatural intentionality by ritual trance behavior (CA-trance). One can seek to literally "incorporate" the power of the deity, to be inspired, or internally empowered to overcome personal limitations through having the deity work from within for one's own benefit, or for the benefit of others.

Shamans are specialists in having divine power enter the body and transform one's capacities, sometimes magically. As discussed below, magic (CA-magic) includes forms of enhanced positive abilities that seem to have supernatural mechanical origins or assistance not involving a supernatural intentionality. Their power, however, is also conceptualized through acquiring divine intentional power (CA-trance). Shamanic behavior very often deals with problems of healing, or in divination in which knowledge of the future helps one cope with coming events, etc. Priests use prayer and ritual to gain the good will of the deity. They are not necessarily entered by its presence.

The Religious Component of Moral Regulation and Responsibility

Society, Deity, and Transgression

Although humanity has developed an increased understanding of natural causality, there remains for many the Cartesian distinction between the mechanical and dynamic operation of the world of nature on the one hand, and an intentional world of human consciousness and moral action on the other hand. In human subjective experience, causal outcomes are often related to intentional acts, and where we extend this human experience to explain natural phenomena, the natural world is also seen as the outcome of intentionality. It is this capacity for intentionality that is also the basis of moral responsibility, and this intentionality is also seen as either concordant or discordant with divine intentionality and the power of divine authority. As such, it can be seen as either contributing to or detracting from the natural and proper order of a purposeful universe.

The sense of control and security obtained through knowledge of an ordered world can also be based in secular systems of knowledge. Explanations may be progressively developed in naturalistic terms and lose their sacred or religious representations as modes of explanation. In some secular moral systems, such as that developed under Confucianism, the immediate influence of the supernatural becomes of secondary concern to more direct concern with human control and regulation. Such systems need not lose the moral and ethical imperatives, nor the sense of reverence found in religious systems. For example, Confucian thought has for the most part transcended supernatural referents in prescribing the practices of self-regulation. Instead of being occupied by a divine personal figure, the realm of the "sacred" is occupied by the family, which itself becomes a revered institution. The proper, responsible exercise of one's family role is made central to moral and ethical behavior. The family in this respect becomes a semi-sacred religious institution. In this system, there is a great deal of emphasis placed upon attaining a satisfactory level of self-control and responsibility and by so doing become more personally adequate in coping with social issues. Austerity is practiced for self-development and the enhancement of *self-esteem*, not for the propitiation of a deity. The search for knowledge as a means to competence and mastery may transcend the family, but never leaves it as the center of social responsibility.

The family is also held sacred in Shinto. In contrast, in Buddhism and Taoism, the individual may seek religious fulfillment and moral guidance apart from family considerations. One can leave the family and its obligations in order to realize personal religious salvation. Such is also true for Hindus seeking for personal religious goals.

Every social human being must ultimately confront the reality of external moral authority, whether sacred or secular. Every religious system specifies the nature and types of transgressions to be avoided, and which transgressions should produce feelings of guilt. Compliance with this external authority and the avoidance of guilt is optimally obtained through the presence of an internal sense of moral responsibility. Yet many people feel themselves incapable of becoming fully responsible as measured by compliance with moral authority, whether social or secular.

Many of concerns with transgression can be scored using various negative Responsibility (R) categories, as we have discussed in chapter 10, volume I. Among the Responsibility subcategories specifically related to religious behavior described there, RA-ritual pertains to the practice of ritual or ceremonial obligation as a personal or family responsibility, and RC-sacred pertains to sacrilegious acts.

When scoring narrative descriptions of moral transgressions or "sins" or the experience of guilt, one finds they are not all necessarily subsumed under the negative (R) category, but may be scored or double scored in a number of other instrumental and expressive categories. We have discussed the nature of guilt and transgression more extensively in chapter 10, volume I.

Scoring the "Seven Deadly Sins"

In Medieval Christianity, there was a great deal of attention paid to "The Seven Deadly Sins." These "mortal" sins, to be distinguished from less serious offenses to God, were Anger, Avarice, Envy, Gluttony, Lust, Pride, and Sloth. Where can such sins be classified? As then considered, medieval emic categories were very encompassing and covered a number of more precisely classifiable inner states or activities.

The word "anger" arises in various situations. These are sometimes not specified. Destructive, negatively aggressive urges are most readily classified under Harmony in an appropriate negative subcategory, depending whether it is an unresolved attitude (e.g., HB-anger) or an actual behavioral expression (e.g., HC-discord, HC-hostile, HC-revenge, etc.).

"Lust" was conceived of as ungoverned, possibly destructive passion, most often of a sexual nature. It can most frequently be categorized as driving some form of negative Affiliation (e.g., FC-seduce, FC-betray, etc.). When focused upon consciously as an uncontrollable inner urge directed toward another, it can be directly classified as FC-lust.

"Envy" as loosely used in the Middle Ages seems to have covered jealousy as well. Envy and Jealousy as scoring categories have already been discussed in various chapters. As noted above, Envy appears contextually in a number of different subcategories. Envy is a discordant emotion usually implying interpersonal malice (HB-envy). Envy within a family is coveting the nurturance received by another (NSB-envy). Some can express envy of the affiliative closeness of others (FB-envy). There can be envy of the regard or status afforded another (EDB-envy). Some express envy of competitor's ability (MVB-envy). There can be envy of authority exercised by another (DSB-envy). There is envy of the possessions of others (OB-envy).

"Pride" in the medieval context covered not only disdain of others in respect to negative relative status concerns (EDC-disdain), or excessive self-conceit (ESC-conceit), but hubris that challenged the position of God and the lack of sufficient humility in the face of church authority (EDC-insolent DSC-disobey).

"Gluttony" and "Sloth" seem to be deadly sins which primarily suggests lack of self control in respect to indulgence (RC-indulge), or irresponsible laziness and avoidance of duty (RD-work). In some instances, preoccupation with food can be double scored (RC-indulge, OC-self-hurt). These are the sins of insatiability or oral indulgence.

The last deadly sin, "Avarice" is a sin suggesting an insatiable retention of objects. Excessive concern with objects is scored negatively under the Objects category (OC-greed, OC-wealth).

Why these particular deadly sins were emphasized and others not suggests certain specific preoccupations found in the medieval period and its social world. For example, the then-Christian preoccupations with humility or usury have lost their salience in the moderns world, although the wisdom of that change remains to be demonstrated. Concern with transgressions related to indulgence persists, but what may be considered a social transgression has shifted to other forms of what we perceive to be immoral behavior, such as the destructiveness of our ecosystem due to heedless acts (OC-destroy) or environmental damage due to greedy self-preoccupation (OC-greed). The specified content of immoral acts changes but the sense that it is necessary to set moral strictures on behavior persists.

Achievement and a Sense of Purpose in Religious Terms

As we define Achievement, it involves a sense of purpose. The need to achieve this purpose often involves a sense of social as well as individual purpose, and these may be conceptualized in religious rather than economic or secular terms. Religious experiences may serve to resolve a lost sense of meaning. Those who are religiously oriented may achieve purpose through self-actualization in the form of dedication to or successful implementation of religious practices. Religious belief and behavioral participation in religious practices may also contribute to the achievement of social purpose. This can include the achievement of behavioral goals established in the context of religious society. Such achievement can reestablish a sense of social purpose, a renewed sense of belonging, and an internal sense of being in harmony with a social group. Seen in this context, religious leadership, or the various forms of missionary behavior, may reflect achievement motivation. Consideration of achievement-oriented behavior should include religious proselytizing and the conversion of others to what one considers properly regulated behavior.

We would contend that one primary function of any religious system is to assure a meaningful continuity of a self that is experienced as somehow immersed in a larger totality (see also further discussion under Harmony). By such assurance, a belief system opposes both personal death and social dissolution (AA-divine; see also De Vos and Romanucci-Ross, 1982 and Lifton, 1970). The obvious connection between religious thought and the explanation for what happens to the individual after death is but one dimension of this role of religion in establishing continuity.

Religious representations frame one's temporal experience and serve as regulatory means toward the realization of human purpose for the self.

A sense of continuity need not be limited to personal continuity as it is generally seen in the more individualistic Western religions. Indeed, individual continuity of one's identity or individual self may not be conceptually necessary in some religious traditions. Continuity may remain morally linked to the individual in the sense of one's personal responsibility for a continuity of causality linked to the subtle dispositions of one's individual mind-stream. Yet at the same time there may be no expectation of personal continuity in the form of an individual "identity" or individual self. This alternative pattern is found in the Hindu-Buddhist conception of reincarnation and karma.

Religious reassurances of continuity can also be focused on the persistence of one's social group[3] (or of the family, as is the case in the Confucian tradition). There may be some capacity to derive inner security from group or family survival. The group in which the person lives is interrelated with the self in so far as its members share a collective sense of past and future. Seen in biological terms, the social group in which human behavior evolved was also generally constituted of individuals with whom one substantially shared genetic information. Thus in socio-biological terms, once can see a basis for deriving satisfaction from group continuity even if it comes at the expense of individual continuity.

In Confucian society, there is continual symbolic assertion of the importance of family continuity, and this may serve both expressive and instrumental purpose. Suenari (1986) perceptively notes that relationships with the ancestors in Japan are based more on a continuity of emotional feelings than on instrumental or material enhancement of the family. In Japan, ancestors are worshipped even though secular gain is not implicitly promised. In contrast, worship of the dead can be linked to instrumental patterns, such as the distribution of goods among relatives. In an exemplary social-structural analysis Suenari (1986) describes traditional ancestor worship as it is found in a contemporary Taiwanese village. According to Suenari, in Taiwan, religious practices related to ancestor worship can be seen as forms of instrumental cooperation in service of common purpose in the lineage unit. There is economic sharing; the shares within any cooperative enterprise are carefully calculated. In effect, in Taiwan, for some there may be little difference in how a business and a religious venture are conceptualized. Although they occur in relation to sanctified purpose, these types of activities might nevertheless warrant scoring with some of the Mutual Purpose subcategories (such as MTA-interest or MTA-

---

[3]Newman and Newman (1999) see this as particularly important in old age, perhaps constituting an additional Ego crisis of very old age, seen in Eriksonian terms. They have suggested that the final crisis of adult development involves concerns about Immortality and Extinction. An excellent narrative example that illustrates both personal and social dimensions of this concern can be found in an autobiographical recounting of Black Elk's experiences as he saw the massacre of his people by Custer's troops (Neihardt, 1972, 217–234).

family, etc.). In scoring narrative content one must be alert to the degree to which sanctified behavior may serve the attainment of such instrumental purposes, whether they be Mutual Purpose or individual Achievement.

The negative aspect of personal purpose and internalized achievement is a state of alienation. As we have discussed in more detail in chapter 8, volume I, alienated or negative achievement states may be double scored, to reflect the sense of isolation and aloneness as well as a sense of a loss of purpose (AD-purpose FB-alone). We also discuss the relationship between religion and alienation in great length in the present chapter, below.

Expressive Concerns in Religious Thought

All the basic expressive human concerns are reflected in religious thought. Religion address concerns with nurture and helplessness (Nurture), with warmth and closeness, or personal isolation (Affiliation), with degrees of acceptability and unworthiness (Esteem), with peace versus violence (Harmony), and with positive or negative evaluations of pleasure-seeking and with giving meaning to suffering (Pleasure).

Nurture and Security

All religions must in some way address the initial pan-human experience of helplessness that arises with the ontogenetic dawn of human consciousness. The progressively more self-conscious human never outgrows some concern with *dependence* on an outside power for nurturance, help, or protection. A deep need of *nurturance* is reflected negatively in an existential fear of nonexistence or annihilation that some believe to be among the earliest and continuing conscious experiences. Developmentally speaking, there is a deepening awareness of how one's own *helplessness* is juxtaposed to the presence of external power, whether personal, natural, or supernatural. Some of the early childhood experiences of fearful even *malevolent* power, whether in nature (e.g., claps of thunder, the fury of fire) or the incomprehensible, unpredictable and even wrathful behavior of giant adults, remain embedded in religious representations throughout life (Spiro, 1967, 1986).

From childhood, the human consciousness begins to locate power (and providential security) as an attribute of awesome outside objects or beings. This sense of *awe* starts early and the human never completely overcomes a need to relate to such external powers as a means of assuring personal security. A belief in divine protective *benevolence* affords deep emotional security and comfort for most human beings. Note that this need for dependent security is of as strong a valence as are instrumental concerns over the exercise of power we have discussed above and in chapter 10, volume I.

For some, deity is conceived of as all-giving. Religious sentiments often foster gratitude (NSA-grateful), which may be felt toward a deity in response to various forms of physical, emotional, benevolence, and protection (NDA-nurture, NDA-comfort, NDA-secure, NDA-charity). For some, a loving god is a benevolent, caring god who protects those who worship, and who through worship express a sense of gratitude. In the Japanese case, gratitude, coupled with reverence and awe, may also be directed toward revered human beings, either mentors or parents. In the West such sentiments are more often reserved for a religious context. Most religions have some form of ritual, which is used to stimulate or awaken the benevolence or protection of deity (NDA-ritual), while simultaneously expressing awe and gratitude. (In these contexts, supplication may also be seen as an instrumental activity; see above.)

Self-sacrifice or submission to sacrifice can be seen as an ultimate form of nurturance (NDA-devote). Most sacrifices are doubled scored when there is an act of rectification or atonement at the same time as an act of benevolence for the group. The sacrifice of Jesus Christ is viewed as the ultimate nurturant act of Christendom. Depending on the emphasis, sacrifice can be double scored as an act of responsibility (RA-duty-o), or as an act of engulfed dedication to the group or self-sacrificing devotion (HA-engulf).

Affiliation: Religious Representations of Love, Warmth, and Closeness

Religious representations in some contexts take on a deeply "affiliative" meaning. They represent a search for deepening intimacy and relational understanding and act as an assurance for the individual against isolation and neglect. Individuals may find bonds of closeness enacted concretely in their religious practices as they share in the mutual worship of the supernatural. Some religious feeling is therefore associated with the sense of belonging and closeness which can happen through religious participation in a social group. The Christian Church emphasizes a sense of "brotherhood" as the meaning of "church," seen as the household of the Lord. A congregation is a group that has a sense of similarity (FA-similar). They find themselves bonded with others who are adherents of shared beliefs. There is a common sense of social belonging that unites the religious community expressively as well as instrumentally as they seek out joint purpose. Belonging and group identity is assured by common religious practice (FA-share) and can be ritually restored (FA-rite).

In East Asia, affiliative religious ceremonies take place within the family; in the West under Christianity, they are more individualistically conceived or they may be realized in a church congregation of fellow believers. In ancestor worship, the affiliative bond remains within the family. In Christianity, the so-called Christian brotherhood of the church congregation is religiously more important than individual family units. There can be a retreat into a monastic brotherhood or sisterhood. In some sects of Buddhism, monasticism is also a type of withdrawal that can come in conflict with family responsibilities and therefore must be reconciled with the Confucian family as an institution (Lancaster, 1986).

Religious conversion can be expected to assuage a deep sense of alienation and problems of loss of meaning usually associated with loss of intimate forms of human attachment. The relation of the Christian to one's God is manifestly distinct from relationships with others in one's family. An extreme sense of alienation or isolation leading to thoughts of suicide is sometimes resolved within the Christian tradition by a religious conversion experience (James, 1958). Such alienation is more likely to be resolved in an Asian tradition by a symbolic reincorporating of the individual within the family (De Vos, 1968, 1992, chapter 2).

A sense of isolation and aloneness can be experienced due to the absence of any religious belonging. Social isolation can also be experienced in some religious contexts where religious practices require personal isolation from the secular society. Such isolation from secular relationships, however, may not be experienced negatively as loneliness in that it is simultaneously an effort to become closer to the sacred. For some mystics there is an experience of closeness to the ineffable or merger with the sacred (FA-mystic) in mystic experiences of union that join the person to the supernatural. The ultimate mystical experience is the loss of the sense of selfhood that separates one from the infinite cosmos. Seen in Jungian terms, conscious experiences of mystic union may also symbolize a reintegration of formerly lost aspects of the Psyche that are rediscovered through an inner exploration that can be facilitated by periods of social isolation.

Religious Concepts of Acceptability

Purity and the State of Grace

Religions have an *evaluative* dimension by which one judges oneself emotionally in reference to individual standards of self-acceptance or self-esteem as well as in reference to standards of social or religious acceptability. There are a variety of conceptualizations that define acceptability or worthiness. Concerns with social acceptability that are scored in the appreciation Esteem (E) category include, on the positive religious side, concepts of purity and grace. On the negative side, there are concerns with unacceptability, pollution, or lack of worthiness.

In some Christian representations, there is a concept of a state of grace that conceptualizes the individual as moving "closer to God." Those who are in a "state of grace" (ESA-pure) are usually considered pure and, therefore, pleasing in the sight of God (ESA-approved). The opposite is a sense of impurity or defilement that displeases and distances one from the supernatural. "Dirty" behavior makes one unworthy of such sacred contact and may also constrain others to reject one socially, as a polluted being (ESD-impure). Individuals can thus be evaluated (and evaluate themselves) positively or negatively in terms of religious purity in much the same way one might evaluate physical cleanliness and its relationship with gustatory or olfactory acceptability. If found to be impure, through invocation of power conferred by the sacred, religious ritual, or practice can be used to purify the individual and put him/her back into a state of relative purity or "grace" (EDA-reclean) (De Vos and Wagatsuma, 1966).

Religious systems are marked by pervasive concerns with methods for addressing purity and pollution of both the individual and the group.[4] In Confucianism, for example, the individual who fails to fulfill social obligations is seen as reprehensible and, if all efforts at reform fail, worthy of social ostracism (ESD-shunned). Ostracism, "shunning," or even formal expulsion from the religious community by institutional excommunication are tools for maintaining the purity of group, free from dissension or doubt regarding dogma or common belief.

On the individual level, one can act in ways that purify the individual of sins and brings him or her closer to a possible communication with the sacred. The Christian baptism is but one example of the widespread use of ritual acts whereby sacred power is invoked to purify sins or stains (EDA-reclean). The Japanese religion, Shinto, emphasizes states of impurity and the need for cleansing. In some sects of Buddhism, karmic consequences that derive from the negative actions of previous rebirths (as well as from the present life) can be purified through the application of meditation techniques such as the "Four Opponent Powers,[5] as well as through practices wherein various forms of purification are visualized or imagined. Contemporary Judaism more than Christianity still emphasizes complex laws in regard to possible impurities and their rectification. The Mikvah or ritual bath is still used by Orthodox Jewish women to cleanse menstrual impurity. Such acts may appear simply symbolic, yet may in the emic experience of the participant be experienced quite literally as acts of real purification wherein one has actually renewed one's worthiness (ESA-worth), cleansing the stains of the unworthy past,

---

[4]This topic is considered in detail in chapter 5 of *Status Inequality* (De Vos, 1990, 164–203).

[5]In the Gelugpa tradition of Tibetan Buddhism, the Four Opponent Powers are described as follows (not always in this order): (1) the power of the basis, which is to recognize that one's negative actions have affected other sentient beings. One therefore takes refuge in the Three Jewels and develops great compassion toward sentient beings; (2) the power of regret or remorse (this can be understood by considering the attitude one would have upon discovering that one has just eaten poisoned food); (3) the power of restraint, which is to generate strong commitment to refrain from repeating the negative action; (4) the power of antidote action, which involves taking every opportunity to engage in positive action as an antidote to the accumulated legacy of negative action tendencies (see Dhargyey, 1974; Gyatso, 1993). Although the term "purification" is used to describe this process, it may also be seen as an instrumental process aimed at reducing future negative consequences by taking Responsibility (R) rather than obtaining acceptability or worthiness (E).

recommitting the individual to renewed faith and compliance with behavioral proscriptions.

"To Be Acceptable in Thine Eyes." Perhaps the deepest or most transcendent expressions of religion are found in a sense of awe and reverence directed toward the deity (EDA-awe). Such an expressive attitude can also be directed toward humans. An individual can be recognized by others as being particularly close to the sacred (EDA-holy).

The opposite of a sense of reverence occurs when those who have been considered with respect are found to be wanting. It is part of human social development to go through a sense of disillusionment with others, such as parents, who have been considered previously with awe and respect (EDB-lessen). For some people only their god remains exemplary of perfection, and free of the fallibility that is found in others. Where awareness of imperfection is turned toward the self, one experiences a sense of personal self-abasement (ESC-abase-s) or worthlessness (ESD-base).

There are situations in which both acceptability and atonement are intermingled in religious thought. However, for the purpose of scoring, a sense of unacceptability is to be distinguished from a sense of guilt over one's injurious destructive potential or one's failure to self-regulate. The expressively oriented acceptability category emphasizes a sense of personal unworthiness or shamefulness (ESB-shamed, ESB-unworthy) or a sense of being impure or defiled (ESD-impure). This is different from a sense of guilt (RB-guilt). Guilt is associated with a need for active behavioral atonement and rectification, whereas shame is associated with cleansing behavior toward restoring acceptability. Both elements may be present whenever compensatory action is taken or restitution is made.

The Regulation of Aggression and the Pursuit of Harmony

All religions regulate aggression; they regulate how or under what conditions there can be proper expression of hostility and destructiveness. Conversely, they promise the eventual attainment of forms of harmony and peace that are considered an expressive need in all societies. One sees, represented in religious beliefs, concepts of ideal harmony as well as representations of the sources of discord and unhappiness among individuals. Every religious system embodies concepts of taboos of killing or intragroup destructiveness, whereas they may condone destructiveness directed outside the group under religiously nonpolluting circumstances. The religious system gives moral justification to certain forms of aggression while proscribing others. In this sense, all religious systems regulate harmony and discord as expressive concerns as well as setting up regulations for cooperation and competition within and between societies on an instrumental level. Of course the variety of social forms that regulate aggressive impulses also include more secular processes, such as rules for athletic competition, rules of order for managing democratic meetings, as well as institutional procedures for handling grievances, etc. However, in the present context, we are most concerned with the ways in which religious rituals function to regulate aggression and preserve harmony.

Aggression is a powerful force in human behavior. It requires powerful opponents. These opponents are often depicted in religious terms as fierce or potent supernatural beings whose aim is to protect the religious practitioner from malevolent or destructive forces. Some forms of religious ritual have been designed to propitiate or otherwise develop relationship with such supernatural power.

Religious ritual itself is commonly a non-verbal process, involving role-specified enactment that includes body posture, hand gesture, facial expression, vocal inflection in incantation, etc. As such, they serve a direct regulatory function over physical and physiological processes that would otherwise support aggressive impulses. They can be seen as a form or anti-aggression training, where the aesthetic pleasure derived from the ritual enactment may serve to reduce the tension that might otherwise derive from aggressive impulses. The ritual may kinesthetically and physiologically produce a sense of inner strength or collective empowerment as well as regulating unacceptable aggressive feelings.

Through ritual one can move from untoward emotional states, towards states of tranquility or reduced anxiety. Such states of peacefulness or reduced anxiety may serve not only to reduce aggression and preserve group harmony, but may reduce a wider variety of unpleasant emotional states, a ceremonial release from pain or sorrow, loss, frustration, disappointment, etc.

As non-verbal processes, however, ritual events may not be well represented in verbal expression. We have not found that religious ritual is represented as a harmony theme in narrative responses to TAT images. In our scoring system we are usually constrained to scoring supernatural protection as a form of nurture against negative discordant destructive forces. But such protection can also be interpreted as the protection of a capacity for harmony or peace within the group or person being protected. However, such a function of protection is not usually stated explicitly in narrative discourse. So, although a narrative might describe efforts aimed at supernatural protection (NDA-god, NDA-prayer, NDA-ritual, NDA-magic), what is left implicit (and therefore unscored) is the fact that group harmony or the person's inner tranquility is a result.

A sense of religious harmony and peacefulness is the ultimate attainment gained against forces of destruction, chaos, and threatening change. Religious representations of harmony are juxtaposed in many religious systems opposing forces of destruction and discord. Some religious concepts emphasize preservation of positive harmony in eternal struggle with a destructive principle in nature or in humanity. Some rituals express this harmony (HA-rite). Other religions do not differentiate or evaluate order and chaos, light and dark, but see these in some form of fluctuating eternal balance/imbalance. There are direct expressions of god's harmony as manifest in a perfect cosmos (HA-god) and there are unresolved concerns about such harmony (HB-god). Where religious representations are of a force for harmony (HA-pacify) the emphasis should be on harmonious relationships rather than on intimacy (which would instead be scored under affiliation).

Restoratively there can be emphasis on forgiveness of enemies or of wrongs committed against oneself (HA-forgive). There may be voiced a strong sense of protective dedication, in effect a loss of self in political or religious group—becoming engulfed in a harmonious movement (HA-engulf).

In the negative direction, supernatural injury is readily perceived as various sorts of supernatural force used malevolently. These can include unresolved fears (HB-f-super, HB-f-magic), actions taken against harmony (HC-magic), or consequences incurred due to supernatural forces (HD-bedeviled, HD-bewitch). In some instance the supernatural injury should be double scored with the category of instrumental dominance and power.

Understanding and Regulating Pleasure and Pain

Both bodily pleasure and malaise can be religiously defined. Pleasure and pain are defined in social terms not simply as physiological experiences. They take on other meaning. Religions set boundaries on the legitimate use of sexual expression. This can include defining the times, occasions, and ages of maturity at which sexual practices are condoned. By defining degrees of relatedness in the family, religious beliefs can enforce incest taboos. Religions may proscribe or prescribe the use of sexual intercourse or other libidinous expressions in religious ritual or in support of sanctified institutions such as marriage. Thus, when an informant's narrative refers to negatively evaluated hedonic experiences, such evaluations may reflect religious proscriptions to which the informant subscribes. One must be cautious in scoring to avoid imposing one's own religion-based evaluations about the pursuit of hedonic experience.

Religions not only impose constraints on the individual's experience of pleasure, they also provide periodic release from regulation and psychological constraint. They can validate or elevate ecstatic or mystical experiences in which the boundaries of the self are transcended in some experience of cosmic union, sometimes with an experience of extraordinary power (PA-ecstasy). They may even provide techniques for the attainment of such states, whether through trance, ritual, or the ingestion of psychotropic substances. On a more mundane level, one may simply express a sense of happiness in one's religion, or one's sense of god (PA-god), or one may attain quietude through meditation (PA-meditate).

Religious beliefs also offer explanations for suffering, and may even provide a sense of purpose for the enduring of affliction. Thus aversive experiences may nevertheless be satisfying if seen as leading to future goals (PA-endure), and depending on the nature of the goal, one may need to double score with other categories such as Harmony, Competence, Achievement, Responsibility, etc.

There is a differential emphasis in Asian religions concerning the tolerance of emotional expression. Confucianism aims in its concepts of self-regulation and moderation toward the establishment of harmony within society (Tu, 1986) and instrumental aspects of social responsibility (de Bary, 1975). For some individuals,

Confucian practices by themselves may not offer satisfactory psychological or emotional release, nor explanations for experienced emotional states. One may note that in some societies where the Confucian traditions are practiced, Confucianism is not found without the concomitant appearance of some other forms of "folk" practices.

Shamanic practices, for example, offer alternative possibilities for those seeking ecstatic release, prevention from harm, or restitutive healing not provided within the more constraining dimensions of Confucianist ritual (Kendall, 1986). This is particularly noted in Korea where a male-centered Confucian tradition coexists with Shamanic practices primarily attended by women (Koh, 1986). Similarly, in the West one finds Christian evangelical or fundamentalist cults; in Judaism one finds Hassidic sects, in Islam one finds the Sufis. These may provide forms of emotional or hedonic experiences that are frowned upon by more staid congregations.

Buddhism, in contrast, may more directly address the ways in which concerns with pleasure and pain arise and are resolved. Indeed, as outlined in the first of Shakyamuni Buddha's "Four Noble Truths," suffering is a pervasive characteristic of sentient life. But suffering does not arise without cause, and if one could eradicate its causes, one could thereby eradicate suffering. Much of the Buddhist religious practice is specifically oriented toward identifying and eradicating the causes of suffering. From the Buddhist perspective, all forms of suffering and the afflicting emotions ultimately arise from ignorance of the nature of reality and from undue cherishing of the "self." Ignorance and self-cherishing also commonly result in negative actions that are injurious to others and costly in terms of one's own future karma. In this light, for the Buddhist, the development of an inner awareness of how emotions arise is essential in that it enables the regulation of otherwise very costly emotional expression. This is seen as an important component of the larger process of spiritual development by which one seeks to eliminate the causes of injury to others and thereby avoid the karmic causes that would ripen as future suffering (KD-karma).

The Self in Crisis: Psycho-Cultural Motives for Suicide[6]

The studies of Japanese suicide we conducted in the 1960s (De Vos, 1962, 1968, 1973, 1992) demonstrated the complexities of unconscious as well as conscious motives discussed among Japanese in considering the suicidal act. For this we drew upon psychoanalytic theory as well as the perceptive writings of Emile Durkheim. The culturally prevalent conscious emic explanations were not directly congruent with any study of the underlying unconscious psychodynamics involved in suicide.

---

[6]Adapted from De Vos (1992), chapter 2.

In the previous chapters discussing instrumental and expressive categories, we very briefly considered how narratives involving suicide can be variously classified according to the context of a story in which the act appears. When using the ICSS we must attend in scoring only to what is consciously expressed as to motive. Let us now recapitulate how the suicidal act is *consciously* described in both expressive and instrumental settings that can be categorized differently according to their specific context. Nevertheless in what follows we will also discuss at greater length some of the unconscious etically considered motives as well as the conscious emic features we have found operative in Japanese discourse on suicide.

Psycho-Cultural Motives for Suicide

The Sociological Account of Suicide

Suicide is a social as well as personal act and can be analyzed in sociological terms. Durkheim's monumental sociological analysis of Suicide (1951) examined the social atmosphere and the social meanings of suicide. He found that suicide rates vary directly with social conditions. In particular, he noted that acute disturbances of social regulatory systems produce anomic social conditions, which in turn lead to inner experiences of alienation or "anomie," which in turn foster suicidal acts.

Durkheim well understood the dangers of any attenuation of normative belief, and he found this to be central among the identifiable social conditions that precede what he termed "egoistic" suicide. Abiding social belief systems and social interaction patterns bind the individual to one or more social groups. Yet modern societies may not provide sufficient conscious experiences of closeness in family and collective community activities that express group belonging (see chapter 7, volume I). In his description of egoistic suicide, Durkheim cogently illustrated how the modernizing nineteenth-century European societies made some individuals particularly prone to a dangerous form of existential anxiety.

A Psychoanalytic Perspective

Humans remain "social" and become personally invested in normative beliefs to avoid the alternative of existential anxiety. Humans in any culture generally come to rely on some form of social participation and normative representations, and most cannot tolerate being without these. However, in our opinion, Durkheim was sometimes too prone to relate the immediate causes of a suicide directly to these crises of belonging as they are related to general anomic conditions in society. His sociological frame of analysis did not include developmental psychological formulations that could relate later adult experiences of social attenuation to childhood experiences such as early maternal separation. He tended to examine only direct societal causes as determiners of suicide.

Durkheim's basic sociological perception of society is that it constitutes a "reality existing prior to the individual." This does not, however, preclude the individual psychological processes and developmental experiences by which the individual's participation in that reality is constituted. Most importantly, society is not simply comprised of the people about us, but includes a world of symbolic meaning. Any idea, be it that of God or, as Durkheim suggested, "society" itself, or even the ideal of an "individuated self" can be seen as nothing more (nor less) than a symbolic representation. These symbolic forms are constructed through developmental experiences framed in social contexts. Such representations, whether part of culturally-constituted representational systems or whether evocative of past emotional experiences, serve as the basis of meaning in both cognitive and emotional senses. They are experienced subjectively as an overriding reality that serves as the basis for the meaning one gives to life.

To be bereft of a belief system can be likened to a reexperiencing of the overwhelming primary anxiety of the helpless infant, thrown into a world of incomprehensible causality. In the course of healthy childhood development, an individual comes to derive a personal sense of ontological validity or substantial meaning through relations with objects and persons in the world. One "cathects" or concentrates psychic energy on a particular other, on specific ideas, as well as investing energy in a generalized social world. On a social level, such derivation of "meaning" is directly related to a continuity of culturally constituted patterns of collective representations and behavior that support social cohesion. It is in this sense that Durkheim's perception of society as a "reality existing prior to the individual" seems fundamentally correct.

Developmentally, a growing sense of social belonging takes place within childhood contexts where religious or other forms of organized beliefs place the individual in a "meaningful" environment, and in which one experiences oneself to be a member of a particular society. For protection from fear, we rely on secular ideology and religious constructs that provide not only explanations but also moral expectations that structure our social relations. However impossible these ideals may be to realize in actual interpersonal relationships, they remain as illusions that fulfill expressive needs. Because these ideals may not be realized in what is afforded within existing family experiences or proximate social networks, we commonly come to experience an incongruity between our idealizations and the more unsatisfying realities of our immediate lives.

A sense of personal incompleteness is sometimes assuaged consciously, through attempts at establishing or strengthening further Affiliation through closer intimacy and Harmonious relations with others in well regulated and therefore intelligible social interactions. These interactions, whether in dyadic union, family or community participation, or in relation to a supernatural presence (as discussed above) assuage malaise. Yet given our own particular developmental vicissitudes we may never fully overcome an abiding sense of inner insufficiency and incompleteness. We may, therefore, seek out satisfaction of our dependent needs by remaining subject to the expectations of others (secular and sacred) from whom we expect Nurturance, and with whom we may also feel reciprocally interdependent. Our behavior may also be constrained so as to gain, or maintain, satisfactory social acceptability and Esteem. Should the individual become personally alienated from such social expectations and social relations, and suffer the consequences of anomic loss of self-regulation, he or she can become bereft of meaning and suffer further extreme forms of intolerable malaise, which for some, is ultimately resolved through suicide.

What is missing from the sociological analysis is the examination of why particular individuals are at particular risk for this kind of anomic experience. For explanations of how socially anomic conditions become problematic for individuals, we find that a psychodynamic approach to developmental vicissitudes can be complementary to a sociological analysis that emphasizes social cohesion. It may therefore be useful to presently shift our focus to a developmental psychodynamic analytical framework.

Failure of Attachment or Belonging: Social Attenuation

Although suicide may be influenced by social and historical forces, it generally remains an act of individual volition. To understand the suicide of a particular individual, regardless of social circumstances, one must also consider how inner experiences related to earlier problems of attachment can lead to the subsequent attenuation of a sense of meaning, or an intolerable frustration and thereby to vulnerability in some, but not in other members of a society.

Examined psychodynamically rather than socially, many suicides appear to involve some form of immature fixation or regressive withdrawal of what is termed "object cathexis." Object cathexis, generally speaking, is the investment of psychic energy in relation to specific objects or ideas. These objects can be another person, inanimate possessions, symbols and ideas (including ideas of a religious or ideological nature), or even parts of one's own body and its intellectual and physical capacities. In psychoanalytic terms, the healthy individual can flexibly or adaptively cathect (invest energy in) appropriate objects, remaining free from maladaptive fixation, and free from any inappropriate allocation of psychic energy towards objects that do not serve relevant ego functions of allowing the safe and morally acceptable discharge of psychic energy.

For mature human beings, object cathexis is largely centered on objects (including persons) found in the social and natural environment. Such energy investment can constitute an attachment of one's inner being to outside objects, whether personal or material, whether credited with autonomous subjectivity or "objectified." From one's investment of energy in relations with objects, one optimally derives satisfaction that gives life meaning and assuages a potential sense of anguished separation. In relations with others, we may avoid the experience of our being as painfully alone in a heartless world. We may thereby attempt to avoid facing the void, and the ultimate, potentially terrifying, inevitable eventuality of death.

Yet not all humans develop a sufficiently resilient self. Inadequate early relations with caregivers can produce various disorders of the self. As described by

Seinfeld (1996), Kohut (1971), and others (see Summers, 1994), the healthy development of the self requires the presence of adequately nurturant caregiver. It requires the presence of a sensitive "other" who, by being attuned to the infant's needs, serves to validate the infant's existence and form the basis of a healthy self. The caregiver becomes what Kohut has termed the "self-object." The relationship with this other person provides the basis for one's own experience of self, as one gradually internalizes the other to form the basis of one's own objectified self-representation. If the self-object responds sensitively to the infant's comfort-seeking and affiliation-seeking communications, it can become the basis for the internalization of a "good" object, thus serving as the basis of a good internalized self. This internalized self is carried within and allows the individual to retain the sense of comfort and safety that was formerly derived from the actual presence of the other, even while the other is absent.

Not all caregiver-infant relations adequately satisfy the infant's needs for nurture and consistent closeness and warmth. If the caregiver is experienced as inadequate, the infant may not be able to internalize a good self. Instead, it internalizes a self that can no more serve as a source of comfort in the absence of the other than it could while the inadequate other was actually present. If the self-object that is internalized is inadequate to serve as a basis for internal self-comforting, one may experience one's own inner being as an "empty core," from which there can be derived no comfort or security, and which also does not allow the inner generation of nurturant feelings toward others. Paradoxically, such an incapacity to rely on a healthy internalized self-object binds one to seeking security and meaning outside, while also presenting difficulties with the establishment of the very external relationships that would serve as the basis for mature interdependency. One therefore can remain not fully separated from the caregiver or from substitute objects. One is therefore also relatively less capable of autonomous yet mutual interdependency. The persistent inability to draw on inner resources that serve as the basis of one's own sense of comfort can color the individual's adult experiences, rendering him or her incapable of forming more satisfactory social attachments.

The inability to maintain for oneself a self-comforting capacity may produce a particular proneness to suicide under conditions of environmental stress or social disruption. Over the course of life there inevitably occur crises during which one must seek to establish a renewed sense of security. At those times the "empty core" may reappear as an inner void, as a fearful emptiness and lack of meaning, as a sense of incurable incompleteness and the potential for annihilation. For some, when a profound loss of social or personal meaning is so suffered, suicide may result. For those with more resilient selves, these crises can be more readily managed. They may never even be experienced as particularly threatening. Or they may be resolved through an investment of energy in socially available forms of religious or secular activity from which the individual recaptures or strengthens relational meaning.

People may resolve varying degrees of inner emptiness by attaching themselves to collectively legitimized power, religious or secular, which is held collectively as a social ideology and associated normative expectations. One can newly discover or restore social meaning through an experience of religious conversion and a renewed commitment to honor behavioral guidelines. One can newly discover or rededicate to involvement in a political or ideological purpose. Without the fear of annihilation that is based in inadequate self-development, such socially available "safety nets" might not be as compelling, nor would their absence be as existentially devastating for the individual.

Where efforts to establish an external basis for meaning fail in the face of unsustainable suffering, the last recourse may be an attempt to find meaning in terms of personalized preoccupations in which the external world becomes unimportant. Some suicidal individuals try to dedicate themselves to aesthetic refinement as a way of life, but even this fails to sustain them. One might infer that some forms of egoistic suicide represent the final outcome of failure in this attempt. Suicide becomes the final way out of misery.

As we have noted, many religious thinkers and writers have attempted to communicate the experience of a quest for ultimate meaning in those who have lost a sense of primary attachment. Either a religious conversion experience can occur, or one achieves a sudden dedication to social meaning of a political or ideological nature. A conversion experience or a sudden dedication for some provides a means to bridge the gap between the self and distant others, or, if you will, creates for the believer the illusion of love and security to be obtained beyond that afforded by immediate interpersonal relationships. One *belongs* to a church or other group and thereupon shares with others a sustaining belief in giving and receiving, nurture and affiliation. It affords a sense of guiding regulation of behavior to be rewarded or punished, internally by guilt, externally by a watchful God. In Christianity, God's "grace" heals over feelings of separation and aloneness, promising eternal closeness to God. In Buddhism, the experience of being a self that exists separate from or removed from interrelationship is acknowledged to be illusory. Instead, one's true essence is seen in continuous relationship with all life. By reframing one's perception of the self and its relationship with the world, one may symbolically heal the personal isolation and hopeless separation that may otherwise give rise to suffering. The gnawing pain of isolation and separation may be reduced if one can sustain such a phenomenological transformation.

Any idea derived from human imagination, whether it is that of "god" or "society," the "individual" or the "self," when examined in its final analysis, is only a symbol. Nevertheless, for some, the symbolic restructuring of perception through religious conversion may become of even greater sustaining importance than are the individuals with whom one relates socially, or the material objects that one possesses. Socially constructed symbols can be experienced subjectively as an overriding reality filled with meaning, so long as the individual is capable of investing psychic energy.

For others, however, no religious conversion can solve the continual corrosive enfeeblement of all forms of tenuously held object cathexis. The person becomes more and more disenchanted with the possibilities of human existence. One can infer, from a psychoanalytic standpoint, that for such individuals nothing has taken the place of the original unsatisfactory primary love object. Severe disturbances and frustrations in this original relationship has made it impossible for the individual to develop any subsequent satisfactory external affiliation with enough force to sustain and to give hope. There may be an incapacity to "feed" on new aliments of experience with satisfaction and an incapacity to draw on new expectations to maintain positive hedonic satisfaction. Nor can sustenance be gained by partaking in relationships with a spiritual power coming from the outside where there is no capacity for sustained investment in such social beliefs and associated ritual.

When Wagatsuma and De Vos examined the case histories of a series of ten famous authors who committed suicide in Japan (De Vos, 1968; De Vos, 1973, chapter 3, volume II; Wagatsuma and De Vos, 1978), they found that suicide sometimes occurred after failed attempts to find social purpose. When viewed psychobiographically, they did not find a single one of these authors who did not reveal a deep sense of personal alienation in his writings. The failures recounted included failed espousal of a revolutionary ideology, an unsatisfactory attempt at resolution through religious belief, or complete dedication to aesthetic refinement. In each instance, the authors were alienated individuals who could not accept external circumstances, and were continually compelled to look further inward, ripping apart the veils of social illusion with which others protectively cloak themselves. Such intensely introspective individuals do not accept the same levels of belief and belonging that satisfies the uncritical. They are explorers into the far reaches of the human psyche, and as such, they become far removed from the easily acceptable as too prosaic. They dare attempt to give idiosyncratic meaning to life and thereby may suffer. Through their questioning of the beliefs of others that too readily sustain the less critically perceptive, they dangerously expose themselves to the possibility of a vertiginous fall into the abyss (Mishima, 1970).

In each case of the suicidal authors, the source of profound dissatisfaction and existential anxiety could be traced to deep, abiding affilative dissatisfaction harkening back to an early separation from the mother (see Bowlby, 1952). Experiences of inadequate infant care occurred in each case, and not one of them was brought up from early childhood by his own mother! Seen in a Japanese context, this was a singular finding, for the Japanese socialization processes are heavily reliant on the mother as one's ultimate source of comfort and refuge. These authors provided clear evidence of the extent to which inadequate care in early childhood can leave a resulting incapacity to henceforth find forms of assuagement, some balm of purpose or meaning to heal the incompleteness of a damaged self.

In many instances, the psychological necessity to lose oneself in a cause or a religious commitment is necessary in order to survive a diffuse feeling of inner insufficiency. Social purpose is so intimately related to social idealism and to highly esteemed social values that is difficult to examine this subject dispassionately. If one fully understands the depth to which ideology supports the self, one can understand the difficulties or even agonies of an individual trying to break with an unfulfilled Communist ideology. A complete loss of ideology necessitates a type of internal separation experience from social ideals that many cannot countenance. In Japan during the military period, "religious" conversion of former communists took the form of a patriotic loss of a separated self in the name of the Japanese State. During this period, Tsurumi (1970) describes how it was difficult for some to comprehend how well-known radicals who had joined the Communist Party could later rededicate themselves to a belief in the emperor and the divinely ordained imperial destiny of Japan. In an enveloping act of social belonging that drowned out their own separate disquietude, by embracing *Yamato Damashi*, these men gave up their more individuated opposition to the military state. They found meaning again in becoming rededicated "Japanese."

As Durkheim saw it, when no resolution of personal alienation (religious or ideological) becomes available, one may resort to what he termed "egoistic" suicide. Such a suicide represents the last shedding of the vestiges of unsatisfactory social ties. Psychodynamically, egoistic suicide may be a final regressive movement aimed at healing the agony of separation. Through the annihilation of the self that experiences itself as separate, the act of suicide may in fact represent an attempted restoration of the lost union with the object of love. If we can but return to a state of union, then there is no continuing sense of separation of self from the larger sustaining whole. In some acute psychotic experiences, a mystical cosmic oneness may be similarly experienced. A loss of self in sacred union may also be defined in positive terms in some religious contexts, where it can even be described literally as a symbolic death, without requiring actual death.

Altruistic Suicide or Failed Attachment?

Durkheim distinguished between *egoistic* suicide (just described) and *altruistic* suicide. The latter is characterized by the willing subordination of one's self and even one's life to a social cause. Therefore, such suicide can be seen as *sacrificial* in nature. According to Durkheim, altruistic suicide is a supreme act of responsibility, a confirmation of belonging, an example of how the individual's needs are subordinated to the needs of a cohesive society. Some well-known traditional forms of Japanese suicide exemplify this notion. Such suicides include acts of self-destruction in which the individual's purpose or meaning is consciously defined so strongly in terms larger than the self that the individual's life is willingly sacrificed in the fulfillment of social role requirements. In this light, a suicidal act in the Japanese samurai tradition could be seen as an attempt to maintain a union with a purpose or force larger than the immediate self.

The Japanese have traditionally been socialized to find the deepest psychological security in belonging to a family or to a political entity, rather than in dedication to a supreme deity. A source of meaning greater than oneself might be one's place in a feudal system, or in one's family, but it might also be loyalty to an individual person, a representative, more or less, of the system.[7] A struggle between adherence to a religious power and loyalty to a temporal force rarely appears with any strength in Japanese history, in contrast to its frequent appearance in the West. There is no parallel in Japan to the Holy Roman Emperor, Henry IV, kneeling in the snow as an act of penance for his opposition to spiritual power represented in the person of the pope.[8] One could say that a quasi-religious security and a secular social belonging of the samurai were both realized in his adherence to his responsible role as a loyal subject. Such loyalty also afforded a sense of social harmony. A samurai did not seek a harmonious relationship with a deity to counterpoise a lack of harmony within the real social world as has been often the case in the Christian world.

It is not clear, from our view, that one can so readily distinguish *altruistic* suicide and its supposed opposite, *egoistic* suicide. There may often be less underlying psychological difference than is presumed between a suicide that follows one's immersion in a social role and a suicide that is derived from failed object relations. The insecure or unsatisfactory sense of belonging so directly apparent in egoistic suicide is often also present but hidden or cloaked beneath what on the surface appears to be altruistic dedication. When there is an unresolved early sense of separateness, the consequent feelings of inner insufficiency, worthlessness, and lack of satisfaction with what life has to offer are abiding core concerns that appear later in not only egoistic suicide, but in many supposedly fanatical altruistic suicides as well. Egoistic suicides include those that result when an individual ceases to pretend, to the self or others, to share in group meanings or incentives. For some so alienated, life gradually becomes empty and bereft of sustaining purpose, and the act of suicide can represent the last shedding of the vestiges of one's ties. Egoistic suicide is committed by individuals who have retreated too far from the meanings given them by their society without establishing for themselves a sustaining individualistic sense of their own purpose (De Vos, 1992, chapter 2).[9]

Altruistic suicide, which appears contrastively to be a supreme act of social or religious dedication, may in fact also be more likely occur in those whose actual relationships in day-to-day life are somehow insufficient. In some instances, an

---

[7]Upon his death, the Emperor Meiji became such a symbol of purpose for General Nogi that he committed suicide ostensibly to "follow his lord." Examined psychodynamically, the Nogi suicide was very complex. Robert Lifton (1970) did a noteworthy analysis of his character and past circumstances encountered by Nogi, explaining the personal reasoning that led to his decision to commit suicide when his Emperor died.

[8]The inner struggle over dedication to crown, barons or God in Thomas Becket as depicted by T.S. Eliot (1935) in *Murder in the Cathedral* is a paradigm western dilemma of allegiance.

[9]We have examined in detail the writings of and about three literary figures, Natsume Sõseki, Akutagawa, and Osamu Dazai in De Vos (1973).

intentional destruction of the self in a sacrificial act can be evidence of a primitive failure of belonging or an inability to maintain object cathexis, related to unresolved primary narcissism. An incapacity to invest psychic energy in external objects is an experiential malaise during which one's sense of individuality is experienced as a torment.[10] Only by gaining an overwhelming, limitless sense of belonging can one heal this sense of self-separation. Where one has successfully accomplished loyal social belonging, one may nevertheless be at risk if such belonging is threatened. The extremes of anomic and sacrificial loyalty are polar opposites, yet in some suicidal cases, one finds "egoistic" torment over loss of meaning being transmuted into attempts at a more acceptable "altruistic" loss of self by a climactic act.

Where collective representations frame altruistic sacrifices positively, they provide a convenient behavioral recourse for resolution, although this obviously does not in actuality repair the social rupture for the individual who has died. The individual who becomes an "altruistic" martyr for a cause may have nevertheless been experiencing as great a narcissistic incapacity to set limits on what can be expected from human object relations as does the individual who egoistically despairs of gaining sufficient satisfaction from human contact. In both cases the sense of belonging is ruptured, whether in life or in death. Durkheim, within his sociologistic framework, could recognize the social benefits derived from an altruistic act that engulfs in legitimized social purpose. However, he did not examine the psychodynamic motivational system that causes certain, but not all, members of a society to chose such an action out of a sense of deep unassuageable need for belonging.

When examined psychodynamically, many cases of altruistic suicide might be found to spring from psychologically primitive motives rather than from a well-developed and differentiated sense of adherence to mature human values. What requires further exploration from a psychological standpoint, is the question of under what conditions, and in what way can an altruistic loss of self in social purpose be considered a mature act rather than an infantile act.

Clearly, not all forms of altruistic death are properly considered to be suicide. There are altruistic acts that lead to one's own death yet that do not constitute an infantile self-destructive act such as we have just described. In many cases there is a conscious and socially accepted rationale for actions wherein one faces death with courage and purpose. There may realistically be causes worth dying for. For example, the soldier who dies in combat has experienced an altruistic death that is seen as contributing to the well-being of his or her social group. An act of heroism that saves the life of one's own child at the expense of one's own life can be seen as beneficial to the individual's own genetic continuity (i.e., reproductive fitness). The difficulty, from a psychodynamic perspective, is in identifying whether at any given moment an individual is acting based on consciously or even biologically

[10]In other forms of psychopathological depression, the sense of self may be that of a worthless being, incapable of giving and unworthy of receiving love (see Blatt, 1974).

justifiable motives and is regulated by healthy ego functioning, rather than acting out of a self-destructive failure to cope with unsatisfied infantile impulses.

To recapitulate, both egoistic and altruistic suicide in some cases can be related to disturbances in the establishment of object relations harking back to a disruption of the earliest formation of the separation of self from non-self, and the failed development of an autonomous yet interdependent self. Such suicides might reflect disturbances in a capacity to further relate to outside objects either because of an incapacity to invest the energy necessary for fulfillment or satisfaction, or because of an incapacity to feel satisfaction without being totally engulfed such that the separateness of the self is lost completely. In the latter context, where a sense of self is encompassed by, or fused into a larger entity, any threats to one's harmonious and responsible relationship with that entity become particularly intolerable and worthy of protection even at the cost of one's own life.

Scoring Expressive Features in Narratives About Egoistic Suicide

Some narratives scored in the Interpersonal Concerns Scoring System (ICSS) categories about suicide are definable within Durkheim's consideration of "Egoistic Suicides."

Despair Pleasure and Suffering

Sometimes a narrative will describe an individual who is considering or has acted on suicide intent without further elaboration (PC-suicide). An individual may be described as experiencing extreme despair (PD-suicide). The suicidal suffering may even be described as being physically painful (PD-suffer PD-suicide). Suicidal thoughts or actions are generally scored with the Pleasure category when mentioned as part of an individual intrapsychic dilemma with no specified social context. However, when suicidal thought or action involves a more specific interpersonal context it may be more appropriately scored relative to the other aspects of the depicted relationship.

Deprivation

Self-injurious or suicidal acts are sometimes depicted as being related to a sense of despair following deprivation or a lack of adequate emotional support (NSD-suicide). Some suicides can be also depicted as being performed for the purpose of obtaining attention or nurture (NSC-suicide).

Affiliative Failures

A failure to overcome despair about a specified aloneness after the loss of a loved one may lead to suicide (FC-suicide). Among the aged are those who have suffered the loss of a mate of long standing. For such individuals there seems in documented instances to be insufficient external emotional investment remaining to sustain interest in life. In such cases one can find "egoistic" social attenuation. Others, however, may be coping with the increasing infirmity or the pain of failing health. For such individuals there seems in documented instances to be insufficient external emotional investment remaining to sustain interest in life (FD-death).

The act of suicide may represent a symbolic restoration of affiliative loss. Some Japanese describe a desire to re-establish a lost relationship by being "united" by suicide (FC-union). In Japan, there are descriptions of suicidal pacts (FA-death) marking very complex affiliative relationships. In our Japanese materials there were several descriptions of an injurious act to self and another to create union after death. So-called "double suicides" or "love suicides," *shinju* or "true heart" suicides, were a favorite theme of premodern tragic dramas. At the heart of such a tragic drama was the insoluble conflict between one's responsibility to one's family and one's loving attachment to a socially unsuitable person (De Vos, 1968).

Frustration and Self-Destruction: Anomic and Egocentric Motives for Suicide

There is a basic difference between suicides that are an attenuation or immersion in social belonging, the Egoistic and Altruistic forms of suicide just discussed, and what Durkheim termed Anomic suicides. We (De Vos, 1973) added a category of "Egocentric" suicides not considered by Durkheim, but implicit in many psychoanalytic discussions of self destruction.

Scoring Wounded Pride, Honor, or Esteem: Anomic Suicide

Suicide can be described as an extreme form of self-destructive behavior (HC-suicide) considered under the category Harmony, in chapter 7, volume I. Such behavior is studied extensively in psychoanalytic theory as related to anger turned inward.

In making some underlying interpretations of such described behavior in Japan we found examples of how acutely experienced outbreaks of anger can result when there is an acute social rupture experienced by a "self" totally invested in a social role.[11] If the role is compromised the individual takes out rage on one's own body. The individual may be incapable of expressing rage outwardly toward the compromising circumstances. This is among the forms of suicide called "anomic" by Durkheim.

Most often the narrative description of a story focuses less on the rage turned inward (which is scored under Harmony as HC-suicide) but instead focuses more on the wounded self, on the sense of honor or self-esteem (ESC-suicide). One very consciously considered form of suicide found in Japan was the taking of one's life

---

[11]See De Vos (1973) chapter 17, Role Narcissism and the Etiology of Japanese Suicide.

after making a socially compromising mistake (ESC-suicide), or an imagined loss of status due to the mistakes of others for whom one was technically responsible (RA-buck-o ESC-suicide). Family and individual honor was a mark of the samurai.

Among the samurai taking responsibility for failed behavior could involve as a final act of responsibility, a ritual act of suicide called *seppuku* which we know by the more informal term of *hara-kiri* (ESA-restore RA-hurt-s). Notable also in contemporary Japan are published incidents wherein a mother can threaten suicide as a means of stressing her responsibility for the wayward behavior of a son. Such threats work to change errant behavior because the intent is known to be serious.

The kamikaze pilot of World War II cannot be simply classified as to actual motives. They varied in so far as they were revealed prior to death. Some were related to actual altruistic responsibility (RA-injure). Some were related to peer pressure (ESA-worth HA-engulf) and could be considered related to the collective suicidal acts of trench warfare in World War I that depended on enveloping group morale. Some few actually felt the Japanese war effort was a lost cause and immolated themselves in angry despair (HA-engulf HC-suicide). This later motive only would be a form of anomic suicide.

Recriminatory or "Egocentric" Forms of Suicide

Whereas anomic suicides are socially oriented and involve considerations of social status or social role, suicides we have categorized as "Egocentric" are only very indirectly related to external circumstances. They usually involve someone frustrated in a psychologically dependent relationship. The egocentric suicide can be readily differentiated from the egoistic suicide by an expressed or implicit sense of frustration, rather than a sense of loss or despair (see Figure 14.1).

Personal motivational factors are relatively neglected by sociologists focused on general societal determinants. One has to examine more fully why a particular culture has a tradition that discourages the suicidal type of autoplastic aggression in interpersonal involvement, and under what interpersonal conditions such occurrences arise.

Compared with egoistic and altruistic, the social-personal polarities of anomic and egocentric suicide both are related somewhat more to a sense of acute frustration of interpersonal gratification experienced at a somewhat later "egocentric" level of ego development (see Figure 14.1). At this level, the child is still narcissistically oriented. He or she is conceptually focussed on the self, but a self that is gratified by, or responded to, by others who may have their own motivations and thus may thwart wishes, or withhold the gratification demanded.

An acute sense of frustration of gratification of the self (or later on, frustration in seeking recognition of the self defined in terms of its social roles) is reacted to by an inner sense of rage. In many situations the individual may be incapable of expressing such rage outwardly toward the source of frustration (upon whom the individual is also deeply dependent). Aggression is turned inward, or is deflected into diffuse destructiveness, as can be noted in the temper tantrums of children.

Using psychoanalytic terminology, in egocentric suicide there is "object cathexis" of a dependent nature (NS) that is focused on a specific person. Any loss of response from the "other" arouses a hostile fury (H) that cannot attack its source, but is turned inward, eventuating in self-destruction. In egocentric crises, unmanageable hostility often results from a threatened permanent withdrawal of affection or care. What is deemed essential is being withheld by some specific other who is uniquely capable of gratification. In some of these situations a wife or lover who threatens to leave is killed and then suicide follows.[12] These types of murder and suicide sequences were among the most frequent forms of suicide reported in post–World War II Britain (World Health Organization, 1956).

In anomic suicide object cathexis has become more generalized and diffused into a need for outer social recognition and response (E). There is a narcissistic preoccupation with the self in respect to socially accorded status and role. The individual cannot face a perceived threat of loss of social status, even when the threatened degradation is not due to one's own mistake. Shame and chagrin can

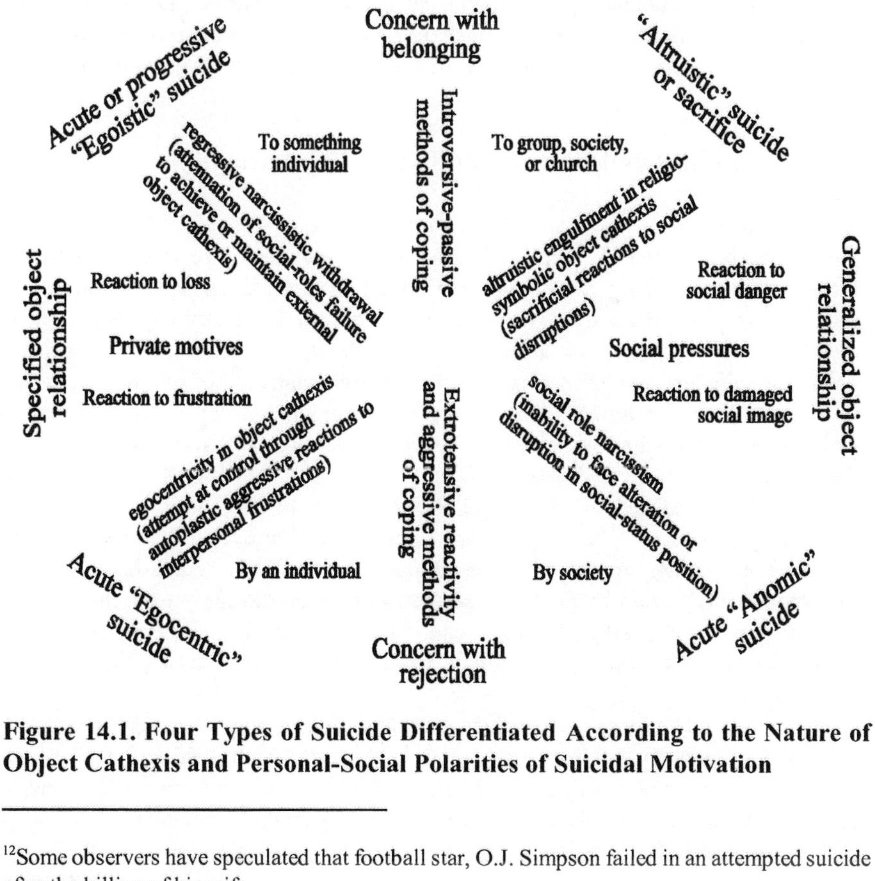

Figure 14.1. Four Types of Suicide Differentiated According to the Nature of Object Cathexis and Personal-Social Polarities of Suicidal Motivation

[12]Some observers have speculated that football star, O.J. Simpson failed in an attempted suicide after the killing of his wife.

become so extreme that the individual cannot contemplate life henceforth. Many Japanese are prone to acute anomic suicide due to the prevalence of what can be termed "role narcissism" (De Vos, 1973, chapter 17).

Whereas the acute anomic suicide is more concerned with injury to ones need for general social regard, the egocentric suicide is more concerned with receiving gratification from a specific source that threatens withdrawal. There is injury to self to evoke nurture (NSC-suicide).

The suicidal act can also be viewed as a retributive act causing pain to the frustrating agent (HC-suicide). There is an attempted evocation of pity (NSC-suicide NDB-pity) or guilt (NSC-suicide RB-guilt) in the other by injuring the self perceived as the only available mode of counterattack or recrimination. In effect, suicide can become an act of vengeance (HC-suicide HC-revenge). In some egocentric relationships the dependent person is incapable of getting beyond an egocentric perception of the other person as an extension of inner narcissistic needs. He or she, in effect, controls the other to force satisfaction. As discussed elsewhere above, "amae" in Japanese psychology is such a form of instrumental control. There is a form of emotional logic in which there is a lack of separation of self and other in close family relationships found in a number of family suicides found in Japan.

Scoring Instrumental Features of Suicidal Preoccupation

Responsibility

As noted above, various forms of self-injurious behavior are coded within the Responsibility category. Narratives can describe suicide as a supreme act of responsibility. In Japan, there were several forms of legendary sacrificial suicide described in public narrative. There were "*gisei jisatsu*," suicides of heroic spouses or family members, explicitly related to their Confucian sense of family responsibility. The traditional cultural logic of *seppuku* as punishment for a Japanese warrior included the belief that an honorable suicide as an act of responsibility preserves the status of the "*ie*" or "house" of the offender. The *ie* is thus protected from negative consequences by the atonement behavior of one of its members. By submitting positively to the regulatory demands for ritual suicide, the offender affirms both the legitimate control or authority of his superiors and his own sense of responsibility to family. He "cleanses" away his past deviation from the required code of honor and loyalty. To not do so, would eventuate his being put to death ignominiously. His family, if not killed, would also be punished by loss of status and property.

Various other forms of altruistic suicide in Japan could be seen consciously as both instrumental and expressive acts. There was both a sense of Nurturant dedication to the well-being of the family, an interest in maintaining Harmony, in addition to the more explicit sense of duty and social Responsibility. As noted before, a not infrequent theme elicited in TAT stories, gathered in 1953–1954 and in 1960 (De Vos, 1973) was that of an ailing wife who kills herself, presuming herself to be a burden interfering with her husband's career. She removes herself by suicide so as to insure his continued occupational success. A stringent enactment of a woman's responsibility to the family into whom she has married would include the ultimate thought to die to preserve and enhance the "*ie*," or house of her husband. Japanese could interpret suicide in this context positively as an edifying example of responsible dedication. In a more negative sense, some suicides by mothers have been interpreted by some Japanese to signify atonement for a past irresponsibility and failure to maintain herself properly in her role as mother.

Control and Dominance: Inducing Expected Behavior

As previously mentioned, one can use actual self-injury, or the threat of self-injury, or suicide to instrumentally force behavioral compliance (DDC-suicide). There are forms of emotional blackmail (DSC-tantrum) ranging from temper tantrums to act of actual or threatened injury to self or suicide (DSC-injury).

There is an overlap between the instrumental categories of Control and Responsibility when one examines suicide in Japan. A mother in Japan could, and does still, not infrequently threaten suicide as a deliberate means of controlling a rebellious or delinquent child (Wagatsuma and De Vos, 1984). A mother's threat of suicide may be seen positively not only as an act of extreme responsibility for guiding her children to a proper future; it can also be viewed as a threatened "advice" suicide (DDC-suicide). It can be seen as an act of both Responsibility and Control, through a reproach to a rebellious underling or underlings. Such was the behavior represented in the suicide of the emperor's emissary in front of army troops unwilling to surrender in Manchuria in 1945 (DDC-suicide RA-injure).

Many Japanese have practiced the emotional logic of punishing others by killing or injuring themselves. Such self-injury or suicide became an accepted pattern of behavior under the rigid feudal regime where open protest was an impossibility. Numerous works on Japanese history contain accounts of the severe limitations on spontaneous protest. If one has decided to protest, one has decided to dic (DSC-injury).

Loss of Purpose and Loss of Competence

Finally, to return to the primary concerns articulated by Durkhiem as pertaining to suicide, one can experience an inner loss of meaning or purpose. As Durkheim noted, there may be injury to self as apart of a total loss of meaning (AC-injury HC-suicide), and a loss of meaning for existence is not infrequently expressed before a suicidal act. One can also experience a loss of belief in one's vocational competence as a central consideration in understanding motives leading to suicide (CC-loss). Such concerns are seldom voiced as conscious considerations for suicide, but they appear as possible interpretations in some biographical or autobiographical materials (De Vos, 1992, chapter 2). A loss or diminishment of capacity or competence can also cause one to lose purpose. For some suicidal individuals the major libidinal cathexis may have been narcissistically focused on a part of the body or the mind that has ceased to function satisfactorily. For some, the most "loved" or meaningful object may be the individual's own intellectual prowess; for another, it may literally be the sexual organ and its potency or other aspects of physical capacity.

We do not yet well understand the role of our will to live, whether in recovery from illness or in coping with chronic degenerative conditions, but it appears that the loss of a vital interest can lead to death without recourse to actual suicide. In the aged, the loss of a marital companion or the final completion of some task is sometimes closely followed by a form of devitalization that results in death. This withdrawal of positive cathexis from body functions to the point of producing death is not viewed as deliberate and therefore is usually not seen as related to suicide. Nevertheless, such a loss of a will to live, whatever its origin, is an essential element in egoistic suicide.

Final Note

Many suicides leave no expressed conscious motives, nor sufficient details to allow one to speculate about unconscious motives. The difficulty in finding a sufficient motive for many suicides resides in the intimate and personal nature of what makes life worth living. For an individual, this is often a very private, verbally non-communicable feeling. It is difficult for an outsider to ascertain what sudden sense of permanent irreplaceable damage or loss another may have sustained that would lead to suicide.

Notes

Blatt, Sidney Jules. 1974. Levels of Object Representation in Anaclitic and Introjective Depression. *Psychoanalytic Study of the Child*, **29**: 107–157. New Haven: Yale University Press.

Bourguignon, Erika. 1968. World Distribution and Patterns of Possession States. In Raymond Prince (Ed.), *Trance and Possession States* (pp. 3–34). Montreal: R.M. Bucke Memorial Society.

Bowlby, John. 1952. *Maternal Care and Mental Health.* Geneva: World Health Organization.

de Bary, Wm. Theodore (Ed.). 1975. *The Unfolding of Neo-Confucianism.* New York: Columbia University Press.

De Vos, George A. 1962. Deviancy and Social Change: A Psycho-Cultural Evaluation of Trends in Japanese Delinquency and Suicide. In Robert J. Smith and Richard K. Beardsley (Eds.), *Japanese Culture: Its Development and Characteristics* (pp. 153–170). Chicago: Aldine Publishing Co.

———. 1968. Suicide in Cross Cultural Perspective. In H.L.P. Resnick (Ed.), *Suicidal Behaviors: Diagnosis and Management* (pp. 105–134). Boston: Little, Brown, & Co.

———. 1973. *Socialization for Achievement: Essays on the Cultural Psychology of the Japanese.* Berkeley: University of California Press.

———. 1990. Empathy to Alienation: Problems in Human Belonging. In David Jordan and Marc Swartz (Eds.), *Personality and the Cultural Construction of Society: Papers in Honor of Melford E. Spiro* (pp. 222–242.) Tuscaloosa, Ala.: University of Alabama Press.

———. 1992. *Social Cohesion and Alienation: Minorities in the United States and Japan.* Boulder, Colo.: Westview Press.

De Vos, George A. and Lola Romanucci-Ross (Eds.). 1982. *Ethnic Identity: Creation, Conflict, and Accommodation.* Walnut Creek, Calif.: AltaMira Press.

De Vos, George A. and Takao Sofué (Eds.). 1986. *Religion and the Family in East Asia.* Berkeley, Calif.: University of California Press. (Revised).

De Vos, George A. and Marcelo Suárez-Orozco. 1990. *Status Inequality: The Self in Culture.* Newbury Park, Calif.: Sage Publications.

De Vos, George A. and Hiroshi Wagatsuma. 1966. *Japan's Invisible Race: Caste in Culture and Personality.* Berkeley: University of California Press.

Dhargyey, Geshey Ngawang. 1974. *Tibetan Tradition of Mental Development.* Dharamsala, India: Library of Tibetan Works and Archives.

Durkheim, Emile. 1947. *The Elementary Forms of the Religious Life.* Trans. J.W. Swain. Glencoe, Ill.: The Free Press.

———. 1951. *Suicide: The Elementary Forms of the Religious Life.* Glencoe, Ill.: The Free Press.

Eliot, T.S. 1935. *Murder in the Cathedral.* New York: Harcourt, Brace and Company.

Firth, Raymond. 1940. The Analysis of Mana: An Empirical Approach. *Journal of the Polynesian Society*, **49**: 483–510.

Gyatso, Geshe Kelsang. 1993. *Universal Compassion: A Commentary to Bodhisattva Chekhawa's "Training the Mind in Seven Points,"* 2nd edition. London: Tharpa Publications.

James, William. 1958. *The Varieties of Religious Experience.* New York: New American Library.

Kendall, Laurel. 1986. Korean Shamanism: Women's Rites and a Chinese Comparison. In George De Vos and Takao Sofué (Eds.), *Religion and the Family in East Asia.* Berkeley, Calif.: University of California Press. (Revised).

Koh, Hesung Chun. 1986. Religion and Socialization of Women in Korea. In George De Vos and Takao Sofué (Eds.), *Religion and the Family in East Asia.* Berkeley, Calif.: University of California Press. (Revised).

Kohut, Heinz. 1971. *The Analysis of the Self.* New York: International Universities Press.

Lancaster, Lewis. 1986. Buddhism and Family in East Asia. In George De Vos and Takao Sofué (Eds.), *Religion and the Family in East Asia.* Berkeley, Calif.: University of California Press. (Revised).

Lewis, I.M. 1971. *Ecstatic Religion: An Anthropological Study of Spirit Possession and Shamanism.* New York: Penguin Books.

Lifton, Robert Jay. 1970. *History and Human Survival: Essays on the Young and Old Survivors and the Dead, Peace and War, and on Contemporary Psychohistory.* New York: Random House.

Mishima, Yukio. 1970. *Confessions of a Mask.* Tokyo: Tuttle.

Neihardt, John G. 1972. *Black Elk Speaks: Being the Life Story of a Holy Man of the Oglala Sioux.* New York: Pocket Books.

Newman, Barbara M. and Philip R. Newman. 1999. *Development Through Life: A Psychosocial Approach* (7th edition). Boston: Brooks/Cole.

Robertson-Smith, William. 1894. *Lectures on the Religion of the Semites*. London: Black.

Seinfeld, Jeffrey. 1996. *Containing Rage, Terror and Despair: An Object Relations Approach to Psychotherapy.* Northvale, N.J.: Jason Aronson Inc.

Slote, Walter and George De Vos (Eds.). 1998. *Confucianism and the Family in an Interdisciplinary, Comparative Context.* Albany: State University of New York Press.

Spiro, Melford. 1967. *Burmese Supernaturalism.* Englewood Cliffs, N.J.: Prentice Hall.

———. 1986. Some Reflections on Family and Religion in East Asia. In George De Vos and Takao Sofué (Eds.), *Religion and the Family in East Asia.* Berkeley, Calif.: University of California Press. (Revised).

Suenari, Michio. 1986. The "Religious Family" Among the Chinese of Central Taiwan. In George De Vos and Takao Sofué (Eds.), *Religion and the Family in East Asia*. Berkeley, Calif.: University of California Press. (Revised).

Summers, Frank. 1994. *Object Relations Theories and Psychopathology: A Comprehensive Text.* Hillsdale, N.J.: The Analytic Press.

Tsurumi, Kazuko. 1970. *Social Change and the Individual: Japan Before and After Defeat in World War II.* Princeton: Princeton University Press.

Tu, Wei Ming. 1986. On Neo-Confucianism and Human Relatedness. In George A. De Vos and Takao Sofué (Eds.), *Religion and the Family in East Asia.* Berkeley, Calif.: University of California Press. (Revised).

Wagatsuma, Hiroshi and George A. De Vos. 1978. A Koan of Sincerity: Osama Dazai. *Hartford Studies In Literature*, **10**(1, 2, 3).

———. 1984. *Heritage of Endurance: Family Patterns and Delinquency Formation in Urban Japan*. Berkeley: University of California Press.

World Health Organization. 1956. Mortality From Suicide. *Epidem. Vital Statist. Report*, **9**: 243.

Index

Appendixes

Appendix A

Basic Interpersonal Concerns, Part 1

Emotional or Expressive Behavior

Pleasure: P

Self-Oriented, Internal Emotional States [S]

Sensation, Curiosity, Elation, Serenity, Satisfaction/Pain, Boredom, Depression, Anxiety, Frustration

A. Subjective Inner States

Physical Pleasure

PA-body	Physical or sensual—food, drink, bodily functions
PA-sensual	Sensuality in sexual or other bodily functions

Curiosity; Surprise, Exploratory Excitement, Ecstasy

PA-curious	Curiosity and discovery
PA-surprise	Positive unanticipated event or discovery; new experiences, sudden waking from a dream
PA-joke	Joking or the unexpected in humor
PA-excite	A positive sense of excitement
PA-ecstasy	Ecstasy, religious state or altered consciousness

Elation; Happiness, Joy, Play

PA-joy	Emotional pleasure, happiness, joy, mirth
PA-play	Play, recreation or relaxation
PA-memory	Happy memories

Serenity—Quietude

PA-relief	Relief, relaxation, or restorative feeling after an ordeal or difficulty
PA-meditate	Meditation—peace, quietude

Satisfaction—Contentment

PA-satisfy	Pleasure in productivity accomplishment, in music or work, etc.
PA-order	Sense of order, composition or harmony
PA-vicar	Vicarious pleasure in the happiness of others
PA-purge	Activity to relieve strong feelings; catharsis
PA-endure	Satisfaction while enduring through ordeal

Mixed

PA-esthetic	Aesthetic pleasure: (a) aesthetic, (b) graphic, (c) plastic, (d) music, etc.
PA-nature	Pleasure in nature or in the environment
PA-god	Happiness in god or religion
PA-hope	Feeling of hope and optimism

B. Unresolved Concerns with Pleasure and Pain

Unresolved Physical Discomfort

PB-tired	Tired or sleeping
PB-body	Physical discomfort
PB-hunger	Hungry or thirsty
PB-rage	Inner impulse of anger not specified

Disinterest; Boredom

PB-surprise	Surprised
PB-bored	Boredom, indifference, ennui
PB-sated	To be sated or jaded

Unresolved Emotional States

PB-denial	A directly expressed denial of emotional expression

Anxious Condition

PB-trouble	Troubled or disturbed
PB-anxiety	Unspecified general anxiety
PB-exist	Existential anxiety about human mortality

Frustration; Discontent, Dissatisfaction

PB-satisfy	Lack of resolved pleasure or satisfaction
PB-dislike	Expression of dislike or discontent; dislike of situation or circumstance
PB-sulk	Sulking; in a pout
PB-work	Displeasure in relation with the work situation or occupation
PB-defer	Deferred pleasure

Mixed

PB-torn	Ambivalent or uncertain emotional state
PB-stress	Internally stressed condition

C. Negative Categories Related to Arousal

Undue Active Physical State

PC-sensual	Nonspecified undue sensuality, overindulgence of the senses
PC-lust	Out of control, nonfocused sexual experiences, a negative perception of one's lustful nature

Crazed State

PC-crazed	Crazed state caused by unusual mental reactions to external events

Negatively Judged Elation

PC-cruel	Pleasure in cruelty; sadism
PC-evil	"Sinful" or evil pleasure (to be double scored when context makes it necessary)

Agitation

PC-unrest	Continually agitated, unable to attain serenity

Frustration; Dissatisfaction

PC-anger	Diffuse unfocused experiences of anger
PC-unsated	Insatiability or overindulgence (i.e., gluttony, avarice)

Mixed

PC-pain	Self-inflicted punishment or suffering
PC-suicide	Injurious or suicidal acts or thoughts

D. Passive States of Malaise

Pain; Bodily Sensations; Physical Suffering

PD-sex	Sexual activity viewed as unpleasant
PD-suffer	Suffering
Passive State of Negative Excitement	
PD-shock	Reaction of shock to events
PD-sloth	Sense of an incapacity to mobilize effort or interest
Depression	
PD-denial	Denial of emotions, incapacity to feel (acute or chronic)
PD-sad	Sad over specified situation
PD-submit	Masochistic pleasure in submission
PD-sorrow	General or unspecified grief or sorrow (crying, etc.)
PD-depress	Depression, despair
PD-suicide	Suicidal despair
PD-witness	Witnessed or imagined present or past unpleasantness
Pervasive Anxiety	
PD-anxiety	Diffuse sense of anxiety
Frustration; Dissatisfaction	
PD-thwart	Unspecified frustration or discontent
Mixed	
PD-mad	Madness caused by possible internal personality factors
PD-disorder	A sense of disorder or disarray
PD-disgust	Disgust in contact with unaesthetic people, objects, or behavior
PD-lost	Wistful over lost innocence

Nurturance: N

Vertical, Donor-Recipient, Status Positions [V]

Care, Succor, Protection/Withholding, Deprivation

From the Donor Position (ND)

A. Positive Nurture, Succor, Protection

NDA-nurture	Love, nurture; physical care
NDA-reward	Rewards, gifts, etc.
NDA-means	Material, educational, or economic assistance
NDA-comfort	Emotional comforting
NDA-nurse	Nurturant feeding or restorative care
NDA-secure	Giving or attempting protection and security
NDA-advice	Advice, instruction, guidance
NDA-active	Helpful activities on behalf of someone or group
NDA-family	General familial (acts done for the family); adoption
NDA-social	Acts done for community, society
NDA-rescue	Rescue or saving someone
NDA-devote	To be devoted to acts of sacrifice as an act of nurturance
NDA-charity	Benevolent act (often in religious context)
NDA-god	Rewarding deity; God's help, magical protection
NDA-prayer	Prayer for another
NDA-ritual	Protective or beneficial rituals
NDA-magic	Benevolent use of magic
NDA-help-s	Self-remedial or self-helping behavior
NDA-memory	Nostalgic nurture or care for others
NDA-disown	Denial of support from undeserving recipient

B. Concerns or Worry Over Giving or Helping

NDB-pity	Sense of pity, compassion for another's need or travail
NDB-welfare	Concern with another's well-being
NDB-body	Concern with bodily problems of another
NDB-means	Concern with material problems of others
NDB-lack	Lack of another to nurture (childless)
NDB-unable	Wanting to help unresolved (presently lacking resources or knowledge to be helpful)
NDB-thwart	Frustrated or rebuffed desire to help
NDB-reject	Fear or having one's nurturant acts rejected

C. Withholding, Abandonment

NDC-hard	Hard and ungiving, stern, unapproachable
NDC-selfish	Selfish lack of concern for others' needs
NDC-deprive	To withhold materially or educationally
NDC-comfort	To withhold or deprive emotionally
NDC-succor	Refusal of help or succor
NDC-desert	Abandonment of a needy one
NDC-protect	Refusal to protect
NDC-legal	Withholding of assistance due to a legal technicality
NDC-repay	Provide something to force repayment later
NDC-indulge	Overprotection, indulge, inducing dependency

D. Omission, Inability, Ineptitude

NDD-neglect	Deprivation through neglect or omission
NDD-unable	Inept and unable to help or take care of someone
NDD-comfort	Unable to provide emotional support
NDD-means	Unable to support financially

From the Recipient or Dependent Position (NS)

A. Receiving Nurture, Succor, Protection

NSA-trust	Trust in receiving care or protection
NSA-assist	Actively seeks assistance or help
NSA-reward	Given rewards, gifts, etc.
NSA-means	Given material, educational or economic aid
NSA-comfort	Given emotional aid
NSA-nurse	Given bodily succor
NSA-secure	Given security, protection, or blessing
NSA-edified	Given advice, intellectual or educational aid
NSA-grateful	Grateful behavior or feeling
NSA-forgive	Seeks forgiveness for past action or omission
NSA-god	Being taken care of by God
NSA-prayer	Seeking for protection or care of a deity, magic
NSA-malice	Counterprotection from malevolence
NSA-s-help	Becomes independent, needs no help
NSA-memory	Memory of being taken care of

B. Insecurity, Unresolved Worry over Sustenance

NSB-help	Needs help, succor, or support
NSB-depend	Uncertain about emotional dependency
NSB-insecure	Fear of withdrawal or absence of care or protection
NSB-means	Fear of economic want
NSB-social	General uncertainty about security
NSB-other	Wants other than what given
NSB-deprive	Fear of deprivation by another
NSB-loss	Fear of losing something, or being stolen from
NSB-distrust	Distrust about receiving
NSB-envy	Unresolved envy over what another receives
NSB-jealous	Jealous and uncertain about one's dependency, related to rivalry about receiving nurture
NSB-god	Questions or distrust of God's goodness
NSB-bless	Uncertain about receiving blessing as support

C. Undue Demands, Covetousness

NSC-rivalry	Rivalrous over getting nurturance
NSC-envy	Active envy, coveting another's nurture
NSC-demand	Improperly dependent, demanding, wanting
NSC-refuse	Refusal to receive nurture, gift, etc.
NSC-injury	Injurious act to self or others' sense of deprivation
NSC-suicide	Injurious act (self or other) to force nurture

D. Passive Sense of Deprivation, Abandonment

NSD-lack	Insufficient help
NSD-comfort	Being emotionally deprived
NSD-means	Being economically or materially deprived
NSD-parent	No parents; homeless
NSD-deserted	Being or having been abandoned
NSD-no-help	No help possible
NSD-sustain	Incapacity to sustain oneself; helplessness
NSD-suicide	Despair; lack of economic and or emotional support
NSD-intake	Inability to accept assistance or help

Affiliation: F

Horizontal-Reciprocal Relationships [H]

Closeness, Reunion, Good Communication/Loss or Lack of Relationship, Poor Communication

A. Positive Contact, Communication, or Reunion

Closeness

FA-empathy	Resonance, sympathy, empathy, understanding
FA-inform	Seeking closeness through communication
FA-friend	Friendship
FA-love	Love and warmth in a relationship; physical closeness
FA-sex	Sexual relationships reviewed positively
FA-trust	Emphasis on trust in an affiliative relationship
FA-similar	Affiliation through a sense of similarity (Kinship, ethnicity, gender, class physical appearance)
FA-share	Affiliation through a sense of shared experiences or similarity in past experiences
FA-ties	Affiliation valued more than concern with objects or other activities
FA-injury	Injurious act to self or others as an act of love (includes euthanasia)

Positive Coping with Separation or Reunion

FA-distant	Contact despite distance
FA-solitude	Hermetic solitude viewed positively
FA-travel	Travel for a friendly visit
FA-console	Self-consoling, coping with separation
FA-happen	Reestablishment of contact broken due to external circumstances
FA-mend	Reestablishment of relationship broken due to discord, etc.
FA-rite	Ritual of amity or restoration of relationship
FA-death	Dyadic reunion in death
FA-mystic	Closeness to the ineffable or merger with the sacred
FA-casual	Casual relationship, nontraumatic

B. Unresolved Problems Related to Affiliation

Felt Need; Wanting Better Contact or Expressions of Warmth

FB-aware	Awareness of the sorrow or discomfort of another
FB-shy	Shyness
FB-isolate	Frustrated affiliation; inability to communicate
FB-alone	A deep sense of unresolved isolation or aloneness
FB-longing	Loneliness or longing for someone, homesick
FB-apart	Concern with possible or actual separation, temporary or not (due to circumstances)
FB-wait	Waiting for someone
FB-reach	Worry about getting close or communicating

Problematic Relationship

FB-problem	Undefined problem in relationship
FB-thwart	Thwarted in establishing a desired relation
FB-unruly	Passionately involved, helplessly in love
FB-accord	Lack of mutual understanding; unfamiliarity
FB-cry	Crying after a falling out
FB-distant	Unresolved feeling of emotional or attitudinal distance
FB-separate	Separation required by other purpose
FB-neglect	Sense of being neglected in a relationship
FB-envy	Envy of the closeness of others
FB-jealousy	Fear of being replaced; rivalry about attention or regard
FB-distrust	Distrust, anxieties about sincerity
FB-unmet	Discontent, dissatisfaction in a relation
FB-unsuited	Incompatibility in a relationship
FB-commit	Unresolved commitment
FB-split	Unresolved after attempt at split
FB-result	Negative influence of lover or peers
FB-observe	Observing without contact
FB-alien	No relationship depicted among the characters in a story
FB-identity	Problem about social identity

C. Negative Acts in an Affiliative Context

FC-split	Separation (sometimes not explained); flight from contact; withdrawal
FC-drift	Loss of feelings or closeness of another with time
FC-reveal	Reveal an uncomfortable secret
FC-neglect	Neglect of another
FC-deceit	Deception of a spouse or family member
FC-desert	Abandon friend or lover
FC-reject	Rejection and divorce
FC-triangle	Triangular relationship
FC-sex-rej	Sexual rejection of a partner
FC-betray	Deception or betrayal of a friend, lover
FC-seduce	Seduction of a sexual or nonsexual nature, also impersonal lust
FC-impose	An imposed continuance of a relationship
FC-selfish	Disregard of another, incapacity to be sensitive to another
FC-demand	Excessive demand or excessive focus (emotional or physical)
FC-affect	Inability to accept affection
FC-union	Suicide with another to create union (double score with HC-injury)
FC-injure-s	Injury to self and other due to loss of a relationship (double score with HC-injury)
FC-suicide	Injurious act to self after the hurt of a love object (Double score with HC-injury or HC-murder)
FC-pact	An affiliative pact leading to injury of both for self motives

D. Incurred Loss, Separation, or Isolation

FD-fate	Loss of love or friend due to circumstances, including death or a need to choose between loved ones
FD-death	Death following a loss of affiliation
FD-social	Loss of love due to social obedience
FD-split	Final separation (double score when necessary as due to discord, punishment)
FD-cold	Indifferent coldness or neglect of other person
FD-affect	Inability to feel affection or other feeling
FD-rejected	Loss due to rejection or divorce
FD-autonomy	Loss of love object or friendship due to another's assumption of an independent life or autonomy
FD-isolate	Experience an isolate, lonely existence
FD-no-one	No-one; homeless, bereft of companionship
FD-seduced	Seduced into a negative relationship
FD-thought	Inability to share thoughts or comprehend another
FD-shunned	A person may be shunned by one's social group
FD-retreat	Retreat from others due to feeling hurt

Esteem: E

Vertical, Horizontal, and Self-Oriented [V, H, S]

Appreciation/Denigration; Self-Respect/Shame

According Esteem or Evaluating Others (ED)

A. Positive Evaluative Attitudes

EDA-respect	According respect
EDA-awe	According awe and reverence
EDA-holy	Appreciation of another's holiness or purity (related to religion)
EDA-status	Positively perceived status
EDA-family	Appreciation of another's family or lineage
EDA-ethnic	Appreciation of another ethnic group
EDA-praise	Appreciation or praise of another
EDA-fame	Famous or recognized person
EDA-appear	Physical appreciation of another (beauty, strength, etc.)
EDA-reclean	Reestablishment of another's status after degradation or pollution

B. Unresolved Evaluative Attitudes

EDB-lessen	Disappointment in another
EDB-appear	Concern with the appearance of another
EDB-evaluate	Uncertain or undisclosed evaluation
EDB-torn	Unresolved respect toward another
EDB-envy	Envy of the regard or status afforded another
EDB-status	Concern with social status of another

C. Negative Evaluation of Others

EDC-disdain	Pride, arrogance, disdain, humiliation, degradation of another
EDC-group	Depreciation or degradation of a group
EDC-contempt	Expressing contempt despising another
EDC-sarcasm	Sarcasm, teasing; verbal dueling
EDC-insolent	Rude or insolent behavior toward a superior
EDC-brash	Brash, no respect for others' feelings or opinions
EDC-status	Defensive use of status against other/others, chauvinism, sexism, etc.
EDC-moral	Moral self righteous toward another
EDC-expect	Devaluating expectations of another
EDC-disgust	Finding another repulsive, ugly, or disgusting
EDC-slander	Slander, calumny
EDC-lessen	General disparaging of society, disillusionment

D. Ineffectual or Unseemly Evaluation

EDD-withhold	Withholding of recognition
EDD-unable	Incapable of giving recognition
EDD-awe	Excessive regard for another
EDD-praise	Excessive praise, flattery, or adulation

Esteem: E

Vertical, Horizontal, and Self-Oriented [V, H, S]

Appreciation/Denigration; Self-Respect/Shame

Subject to Evaluation of Others
or Self-Directed Concerns About Acceptance *(ES)*

A. Positive Evaluative Attitudes

ESA-status	Positively perceived social-professional status
ESA-family	Pride in one's family or lineage
ESA-ethnic	Ethnic pride as self-appreciation
ESA-worth	Self-respect, sense of worth or acceptability
ESA-praised	Appreciated
ESA-loved	Loved, popular
ESA-approved	Approval of an audience, authority
ESA-appear	Approved appearance; physical characteristic
ESA-pride	Others are proud of self
ESA-demure	Self-effacing, modest, "shy" as a virtue opposite of self-forwarding
ESA-fame	Recognition of achieved status (fame)
ESA-heroic	Recognized as heroic in deeds
ESA-awe	Receiving awe or deference
ESA-restore	Restoration of honor by sacrificial act
ESA-pure	Pure or purified, in religious terms

B. Unresolved Evaluative Attitudes

ESB-esteem	Insecure self-respect or self-esteem
ESB-praised	Worry about being appreciated
ESB-shamed	Worry about negative evaluation of others; embarrassment
ESB-appear	Worry about appearance
ESB-accepted	Worry about being accepted
ESB-regard	Unresolved regard or recognition of peers
ESB-ignored	Worry about being ignored
ESB-teased	Concerned with being teased
ESB-unworthy	Concern about unworthiness
ESB-status	Doubt about social acceptance or status
ESB-expose	Worry about compromising exposure

C. Negative Active Evaluation Related to Self

ESC-conceit	Narcissistic preoccupation or pride
ESC-exhibit	"Showing off" unduly exhibitionistic
ESC-lessen	Disappointment someone loses others' esteem
ESC-detract-s	Self-depreciation (general)
ESC-group	Self-depreciation related to one's group
ESC-appear-s	Active self-depreciative sense of ugliness
ESC-hate-*s*	Sense of active self-hatred
ESC-abase-s	Self-abasement before others
ESC-disgrace	Behavior brings disgrace on family or group
ESC-injury	Hurt to self or others due to loss of status
ESC-suicide	Suicide due to loss of social regard
ESC-honor	Vengeance related to personal or family honor (Double score with HD-revenge)

D. Negatively Incurred Evaluations

ESD-unfair	Unfairly unappreciated
ESD-shamed	Feeling of being shamed, humiliated, mortified
ESD-shunned	Being shunned for one's behavior
ESD-disgraced	Family or group shamed by another member
ESD-exposed	Exposed or revealed for bad behavior
ESD-infamy	Considered notorious or infamous
ESD-base	Sense of worthlessness
ESD-impure	Sense of impurity or defilement
ESD-illusory	Disillusionment with the self

Harmony: H

Vertical and Horizontal [V, H]

Harmoniousness, Conciliation/Discord, Destruction (Hostility)

A. Positive Harmony, Cohesion, Reconciliation; Group Maintenance or Protection

Internal Harmony

HA-depict	Descriptive appropriate role behavior
HA-family	Expressions of harmonious family relationships
HA-group	Harmonious interaction or group concordance
HA-conform	Conformity to preserve group harmony
HA-agree	Agreeable, congenial, good-natured disarming role behavior
HA-pacify	Attempted mollification, mediation, or conciliation of discord
HA-forgive	Forgiveness to reestablish group or mutual togetherness
HA-mend	Reestablishment of harmony
HA-reunite	Group reunion occasioned by death, usually a family member
HA-symbol	Symbolic peace
HA-rite	Group ceremony or ritual; religious activity, attendance
HA-god	Belief in the harmony of God's world or in a divinely or perfectly ordered cosmos

Positive Defensive Postures

HA-courage	Courage enabling one to face personal adversaries or opponents
HA-secure	A sense of harmonious within-group security
HA-combat	Righteous combativeness or defense aggression, or protest to preserve group
HA-engulf	Dedication, loss of self in political or religious group; engulfed in a movement as an expression of role dedication toward group maintenance, including self-sacrifice

B. Unresolved or Potential Discord; Fear of Malice

Unresolved Anger

HB-dislike	Unresolved dislike
HB-anger	Anger (sometimes nonspecified)
HB-inhibit	Repressed, inhibited physical violence
HB-revenge	Desire for vengeance
HB-envy	Envy
HB-jealous	Jealous of one's love
HB-hurt	Hurt feelings
HB-resent	Unresolved resentment, real or imagined deception, or injury
HB-family	Concern about family cohesion
HB-group	Concern about group cohesion
HB-unrest	Condition of social unrest
HB-split	Concern about potential removal from family
HB-control	Unresolved anger, irritation over being pressured or controlled
HB-torn	Ambivalence about expected social role participation
HB-break	"Fed up" with a social or personal situation; desire to break ties
HB-role	Possible conflict between role expectations
HB-deceit	Deceit to avoid anger or preserve harmony

Impending Fears

HB-fright	Frightened, not specified as to source
HB-f-attack	Feared attack (animal or human)
HB-f-anger	Feared anger of another
HB-f-fury	Fear of potential violence
HB-f-repay	Fear of possible vengeance
HB-f-envy	Fear of envious behavior
HB-f-super	Fear of malevolent supernatural
HB-f-magic	Fear of magic
HB-god	Questions about religious harmony

C. Negative Active Discord, Destruction, Violence

HC-discord	Anger, quarrel, or discord
HC-hostile	Some form of specified or nonspecified hostility toward others to make them suffer
HC-verbal	Abusive verbal attack; Excessive nagging
HC-beat	Physical expression of violence, beating
HC-injure	Physical injury of another
HC-cruel	Cruelty, sadism, inflicting psychological trauma
HC-rape	Rape; force used in sexual situation
HC-murder	Homicide
HC-elder	Generational animosity
HC-triangle	Discord in triangular relationship
HC-faction	Factional behavior; also excluding a group member
HC-selfish	Inconsiderate behavior causes hurt
HC-revenge	Revenge (when with physical violence double score)
HC-control	Dominance as a gratification of power at the expense of another (double score with DDC)
HC-contempt	Expression of repugnancy or contempt causing hurt (double score with EDC-contempt)
HC-vandal	Vandalism, arson, wanton destruction
HC-rake	Dissolute or self-destructive behavior
HC-suicide	Suicide, anger directed toward self
HC-magic	Malevolent magic

D. Passively Incurred Discord or Dissolution

HD-hurt	To feel hurt by another or others
HD-injured	To be physically injured by others, to be made ill
HD-crime	Victim of an assaultive crime
HD-death	To incur the violent death of someone
HD-withheld	To feel hurt by destructively intended withdrawal or withholding (double score)
HD-maligned	Victim of malice, or being maligned
HD-vilified	To be hurt by derogation or disparagement, or social injury (double score)
HD-decay	Dissolution, decay, or decomposition of an individual, group, family, or society
HD-paranoia	Delusions of persecution
HD-bedeviled	Taken or captured by supernatural being
HD-bewitched	Bewitched, or injured supernaturally

Basic Interpersonal Concerns, Part 2

Instrumental, Purposeful, Regulatory Behavior

Achievement: A
Self-Oriented [S]

Purpose/Anomy, Alienation

A. Positive Active Achievement or Purpose

AA-self	Self-initiated activities toward the attainment of a goal
AA-persist	Persistence toward a goal, hard work-endurance
AA-inspire	Inspired by person or idealized achievement (including religious thought)
AA-counter	Compensatory achievement; overcoming the past, or avoiding future negative circumstances
AA-else	Alternative goal
AA-status	Achievement for status
AA-duty	Achievement as responsibility or duty
AA-nurture	Achievement to nurture others
AA-repay	Achievement as repayment for past nurture, etc.
AA-parent	Parent- or mentor-initiated activities toward the attainment of a goal
AA-peer	Peer group–initiated activities toward the attainment of a goal
AA-moral	Moralistic statement about achievement
AA-purpose	Existential meaning; self-defined positive purpose of life
AA-divine	A sense of divine purpose inspiring or guiding behavior

B. Passive Inactive or Unresolved Commitment

AB-inactive	Inactivity but interested in a task
AB-dream	Daydreaming about achievement (unrealistic ambition)
AB-think	Thinking about the future
AB-decide	Undecided future goal or contradiction or ambivalence about alternative goals
AB-torn	Alternative goal as possibility unresolved
AB-waver	Vacillation or inability to arrive at a commitment
AB-endure	Questions about endurance or frustration tolerance toward the realization of a goal
AB-purpose	Worry over possible loss of purpose or meaning of life

C. Anomic or Lawless Behavior

AC-illicit	Achieving through questionable activities
AC-crime	Direct criminal-oriented activity toward a goal
AC-chance	Looking for opportunity for negative behavior
AC-bribe	Bribery to achieve
AC-plot	Plotting to achieve goal
AC-theft	Thefts and crime against property
AC-gang	Organized illegal activities
AC-motive	Dysfunctional activity due to insufficient motivation
AC-hurry	Impatience leading to abandonment of a proper long-range goal
AC-asocial	Success at the expense of relationships with others
AC-injury	Injurious action to self or others due to alienation

D. Alienation; Social Withdrawal or Lack of Purpose

AD-motive	Lack of motivation
AD-mediocre	Mediocre attainment due to lack of strong purpose
AD-lack	Give up ambition due to lack of funds, proper education, opportunity
AD-bias	Give up ambition due to discrimination, unfair treatment
AD-refuse	Refusal of proffered opportunity
AD-withdraw	An alienated withdrawal from a task or goal
AD-purpose	Expressed alienated sense of lack of social purpose
AD-endure	Incapacity to endure or tolerate frustration necessary toward attainment of a goal
AD-dream	Escapist daydreaming (so seen by the storyteller)
AD-irony	Ironic form of distancing from social goals
AD-meaning	Attenuation of social meaning
AD-regress	Psychological withdrawal can result in a regressive psychotic state

Competence: C

Self-Oriented Internalized Judgment of Performance [S]

Mastery/Failure, Incapacity

A. Realization of Mastery and Adequacy in Problem-Solving Behavior

CA-present	Expression of present mastery, capacity, ability, or adequacy, including awareness of aging
CA-past	Expression of past mastery, capacity, ability, or adequacy
CA-future	Expression of future mastery, capacity, ability, or adequacy
CA-test	Demonstration of competence (passing a test or ordeal)
CA-endure	Capacity to endure or survive tribulations or difficulties in life
CA-body	Reference to one's capable body
CA-defect	Overcoming a handicap
CA-comic	Success despite inadequacy (the comic-comedy)
CA-repair	Capacity to repair
CA-improve	Self-improvement through persistence or hard work; mastery
CA-open	Open-minded and adaptive to circumstance
CA-expert	Capacity through experience
CA-able	Positive actualization of one's own occupation or destined role
CA-create	Positive sense of capacity to be creative
CA-model	Copy or use model to emulate, learn, or gain proficiency
CA-aware	Scientific causality and awareness to solve problems
CA-help-s	Self-help, self-improvement by internal reordering (meditation)
CA-relief	Internally achieved confidence as a relief from anxiety
CA-affirm	Affirmation of an achieved status
CA-know-s	Knowledge, perception (insight) into oneself
CA-know-o	Knowledge, perception (insight) into others
CA-magic	Supernatural or magical ability
CA-trance	Empowerment through a supernatural entity by entering a trance state

B. Unresolved Issues of Personal Ability

CB-help	Needs help to solve problem—outside assistance
CB-worry	General or unspecified worry, doubt, or anxiety
CB-arduous	Difficulty with a task, or emergency situation; need to solve a problem or enigma
CB-able	Worry, doubt about capacity, ability
CB-blind	Innocence or ignorance preventing adequate behavior
CB-age	Concern about diminishing ability with aging
CB-inferior	Worry, doubt about inferiority
CB-decide	Vacillation in a decision; making a decision with great difficulty
CB-chafing	Impatient, chafing, to complete task
CB-else	Secondary or compensatory goal of which one is capable rather than primary objective
CB-hope	Hope for the future capacity of another
CB-defect	Difficulty in repairing or overcoming a defect
CB-status	Worry about the capacity to realize a desired social status
CB-delay	Procrastination, put off starting
CB-weak	Concern about weakness in self-assertion
CB-prayer	Seeks supernatural assistance in a task

C. Ineptitude in Attempted Performance

CC-inept	Ineptitude in proper performance of a task
CC-fake	Fraudulent or faked competence
CC-mental	Frustrated or bungled action due to internal factors of an intellectual order (lack of intelligence, or knowledge)
CC-body	Frustrated or bungled action due to internal factors of a physical order
CC-artist	Frustrated or bungled action due to lack of artistic capacity
CC-tragic	Failed action due to tragic flaw; tragedy
CC-loss	Injurious action to self or others due to failing professional, mental, physical, or sexual capacity
CC-break	Inept inadvertent breakage
CC-grand	Grandiosity

D. Withdrawal from Tasks Due to Ineptitude or Sense of Inner Incapacity

CD-inept	Judged to be inept by others or by self
CD-mediocre	Mediocre attainment due to inability, not lack of purpose
CD-unable	Inability to initiate or do task
CD-finish	Inability to realize a task that has been started
CD-weak	Feelings of weakness, powerlessness, helplessness
CD-inferior	Sense of inferiority in relation to others
CD-sex	Sexual incapacity or ineptitude
CD-chagrin	Chagrin or a sense of mortification over one's incapacity or lack of mastery
CD-aide	A helpless incapacity to aid or ameliorate the conditions of others
CD-psycho	Psychotic withdrawal due to incapacity to solve problems
CD-belief	Inability to perform or protect due to countering beliefs or convictions
CD-age	Loss of ability due to age

Control: D

Vertical, Superordinate-Subordinate Status Positions [V]

Influence, Power, Domination/Autonomy, Rebellion, Submission

From the Superordinate or Influential Position (DD)

A. Positive Control, Compliance, or Autonomy

DDA-control	Legitimate power, authority including family control
DDA-scold	Parental scolding, disapproval, censure
DDA-punish	Parental punishment
DDA-reject	Rejection of family membership as punishment
DDA-group	Group or peer pressure
DDA-lead	Lead or seek to influence peers (score with MVA)
DDA-educate	Educational directives, or supervisory control
DDA-advice	Advice or persuasion (either peer or authority); mentorship
DDA-author	Exercise of proper civil authority or interdiction
DDA-police	Punitive community authority or surveillance
DDA-censure	Censure or disapproval from authorities
DDA-pardon	Pardon, absolution tolerance, or approval
DDA-mediate	Intervention or mediation in an authority context
DDA-trust	Put trust in or delegate to a subordinate
DDA-patient	Be patient or understanding with a subordinate
DDA-give	Instrumental giving used positively
DDA-free	Permission for another to assume autonomy
DDA-gambit	Instrumental sacrifice to induce behavior
DDA-curse	Supernatural punishment by legitimate authority
DDA-create	Creative act used to influence others
DDA-model	Influence others by serving as role model

B. Unresolved Legitimacy or Uncertainty about Authority

DDB-result	Doubting consequences of authority to others
DDB-torn	Ambivalent about assuming authority
DDB-worry	Worry about how to exercise authority
DDB-rigid	Uncertain about rigidity in enforcing regulations
DDB-free	Uncertain or insecure over autonomy of another
DDB-licit	Ambiguity of the legitimacy of one's actions
DDB-order	Fear of chaos or disorder, a need for social control
DDB-jealousy	Jealous about one's authority
DDB-example	Fear of influence of one's past or present behavior as negative example
DDB-patient	Unresolved patience or understanding with subordinate

C. Negative or Illicit Control or Resistance

DDC-unfair	Unfairness or discriminatory authority
DDC-press	Undue pressure or punishment
DDC-rigid	Undue inflexibility or rigidity in enforcing control
DDC-despot	Undue dominance or the exercise of power for its own sake (political or religious)
DDC-exploit	Exploitation of vulnerability
DDC-corrupt	Corrupt authorities
DDC-punish	Overexertion of punishment or destructiveness
DDC-result	Negative consequence to others (may be due to poor judgment)
DDC-capture	Capture of another person
DDC-manage	Manipulative control
DDC-give	Manipulative giving or reward-inducing behavior
DDC-provoke	Provocative teasing
DDC-suicide	Threat or act of injury, suicide against subordinate
DDC-watch	Undue surveillance spying (police, etc.)
DDC-magic	Exercise magical control over another

D. Excessive Passivity in Exercising Control

DDD-lax	Lax and too indulgent in training role; lack of proper supervision
DDD-neglect	Irresponsibility or neglect
DDD-inept	Inept or ineffective exercise of power
DDD-weak	Failure to punish others when expected
DDD-helpless	Failure to respond to rebellion, or a sense of helplessness about attack by subordinates
DDD-deluded	Paranoid delusions in respect to subordinates

From the Subordinate or Autonomous Position (DS)

A. Positive Compliance or Exertion of Autonomy

DSA-permit	Asks permission of authority
DSA-assert	Autonomy or self-assertion from authority, family, peer pressure
DSA-mutiny	Overthrow of despotic authority
DSA-free	Escape from a status discrimination or from wrong scolding or punishment (family or authority)
DSA-free-s	Self-liberation; freeing self from excessive self-control or super-ego
DSA-comply	Proper compliance to family authority
DSA-author	Compliance conform with legitimate authority
DSA-trust	Trust in authority or superior
DSA-soothe	Supplication acts to please another
DSA-forgive	Supplicating forgiveness
DSA-appease	Instrumental donation or propitiation
DSA-persuade	Induced positive action by authority due to subordinate's persuasion or instigation
DSA-disobey	Disobedience as ultimate respect for authority
DSA-god	Belief in being subject to divine control
DSA-ritual	Ritual of supplication of the supernatural
DSA-prayer	Use of prayer

B. Unresolved Legitimacy or Uncertainty about Authority

DSB-punish	Fear of punishment by authority
DSB-torn	Ambivalent about legitimacy of authority
DSB-rebel	Concern with legitimacy of rebellion
DSB-obey	Reluctant obedience
DSB-ignore	Ignore or disregard authority
DSB-control	Uncertain of how to overcome dominance
DSB-advice	Uncertain about advice or guidance
DSB-envy	Envy of the greater influence of another
DSB-pardon	Concerns with pardon or absolution
DSB-approve	Need for approval
DSB-god	Awaiting God's judgment

C. Illicit Resistance or Manipulation

DSC-accuse	False accusations against a superior or authority
DSC-disobey	Defiant, self-willed, lacking proper humility
DSC-family	Resistance or rebel against family authority
DSC-resist	Resist or rebel against tutoring or social authority
DSC-escape	Escape from family, jail; violation of interdiction
DSC-rude	Rude, disrespectful behavior
DSC-tantrum	Emotional blackmail (temper tantrums)
DSC-seduce	Seductive or "Amaeru" behavior to influence others
DSC-manage	Manipulative to avoid any control
DSC-amaeru	Submissive to either gain instrumental goals or gain expressive gratification
DSC-give	Manipulative giving to please controller
DSC-injury	Injury to self to induce action of a superior

D. Excessive Passivity or Submissiveness

DSD-family	Excessive submission to family control
DSD-submit	Excessive submission to social authority
DSD-peer	Excessive submission to peer group
DSD-captive	Remain captive to a person or to a system of external or ideological control
DSD-fawning	Excessive fawning, obsequiousness, to gain instrumental ends

Responsibility: R

Self-Oriented Internalized Social Status and Self-Judgment [S]

Duty, Role, Fulfillment/Dereliction, Transgression (Guilt)

A. Active, Responsible Behavior

RA-work	Work; daily tasks as a responsibility
RA-good	A "good" person; responsible products or activities or unspecified as to nature of "goodness"
RA-example	Behavior as an example for guidance or training of others
RA-duty-s	Assumption of self-oriented or self-defined obligations or duties
RA-duty-o	Assumption of externally or socially defined obligations or duties
RA-order	Proper exercise of propriety, regularity, a positive sense of order
RA-control	Self-control in order to accomplish goals or duties
RA-stoic	Stoic reactions to adversity
RA-sex	Responsible in sexual behavior
RA-reform	Taking responsibility for previous behavior by reform, or reparation, resolution of guilt
RA-apology	Taking responsibility by apology, confession
RA-expiate	To give oneself up for punishment as a means of expiation
RA-hurt-s	Self-punishment or injurious behavior as an act of taking responsibility for negative behavior
RA-buck-o	Taking responsibility for the behavior of another, e.g., family members, subordinates, etc.
RA-injure	Injurious behavior to self or others in taking responsibility for the negative behavior of others
RA-repay	Obligatory reciprocity; necessary gifts (Japanese "giri" relationships)
RA-ritual	Ritual or ceremonial obligations
RA-suicide	Suicide as an act of duty or responsibility

B. Inner Concerns About Responsibility (Feelings Rather Than Actions)

RB-guilt	Guilt; unresolved repentance for present or past acts
RB-regret	Regret; ruefulness
RB-omit	To experience guilt or negative feelings for not having done something; guilt of omission
RB-duty	Unresolved duty or uncertain about how to be responsible
RB-resign	Unresolved resignation to the role behavior expected by others
RB-torn	Ambivalence about accepting responsibility
RB-role	Conflict between role responsibilities
RB-ideals	Internal conflict over social values or ideals
RB-legit	Ambivalent activities; questions of legitimacy

C. Excessive Irresponsible or Forbidden Behavior

RC-wrong	Wrongdoing unspecified; a "bad" person, unspecified
RC-group	Irresponsible group activities
RC-duty	To violate one's duty; corrupt authority
RC-rigid	Excessively rigid and inflexible
RC-control	Loss or lack of self-control
RC-indulge	General or unspecified acts of indulgence; sins of gluttony, laziness (sloth), lust with prostitutes, etc.
RC-messy	Messy or disorderly behavior; lack of inner or outer regularity, impropriety
RC-abuse	Self-indulgence, substance abuse (drink, narcotics, etc.)
RC-waste	Wasteful with money (gambling, etc.)
RC-rash	Rash, heedless, irresponsible acts
RC-illegal	Illicit or illegal acts
RC-ex-sex	Extramarital or prohibited sexual behavior (violating rights of legitimate partner)
RC-pre-sex	Premarital or nonmarital sexual behavior (with socially prohibited partner)
RC-perverse	Acts perceived as socially perverse; homosexuality, incest, fetishes, etc.
RC-mores	Violation of norms or customs, e.g., gossip, impoliteness, and improprieties of behavior
RC-status	Status violation, such as wife or husband neglect duties; children behave badly against family expectations; rowdiness; etc.
RC-property	Irresponsible or invasive use of another's property or social space
RC-hurt-s	Excessive self-punishment due to guilt
RC-example	Setting a bad example for others
RC-evade	Use of role or authority for evasion of responsibility
RC-sacred	Religious sacrilege

D. Avoidance; Refusal to Internalize Social Obligations

RD-weak	Inability to overcome addiction or resist temptation
RD-fail	Failure to take responsibility or be responsible for other's action
RD-wrong	Avoidance, escape of consequences of wrong behavior
RD-personal	Avoidance, escape or denial of personal obligations
RD-social	Avoidance, escape or denial of social obligations
RD-work	Avoidance, escape or denial of school or work duties, laziness, being (ne'er do well) deadly sin of sloth
RD-ignorant	Ignorance as destructive
RD-control	Escape from the expected obligations of an authority position demanding action influencing others
RD-environ	Escape or denial of responsibility for negative influence on social or environmental conditions

Mutual Purpose: M

Horizontal Reciprocal or Peer Relationships [H]

Competition/Cheating; Cooperation/Defection

Competition or Adversarial Conflict (Versus-MV)

A. Positively Perceived Rivalry or Competition

MVA-game	Regulated competition (games, contests, etc.)
MVA-work	Successful business or work competition
MVA-vie	Maneuvering for advantage or first among peers
MVA-smart	To outwit an opponent or win an argument
MVA-regard	Seeks competitive recognition
MVA-profess	Physical, artistic, academic competitive excellence
MVA-means	Competitive success in economic ventures
MVA-gambit	Acts of giving or concession to enhance, own competitive position
MVA-faction	Constructive factional in-group competition
MVA-war	Instrumental war waged against an enemy

B. Unresolved Competitive Situations

MVB-deal	Unresolved negotiation or deal
MVB-differ	Differ about how to compete
MVB-distrust	Distrust about fair play of competitors
MVB-envy	Envy of competitor's ability
MVB-jealousy	Jealous fear of the competence of another; fear of encroachment
MVB-anger	Anger over failure to win out or prevail
MVB-elders	Generational conflict in instrumental coping
MVB-against	Intergroup competitive emphasis (double score with other appropriate categories)

C. Unethical or Destructive Methods

MVC-war	Instrumental war seen negatively
MVC-faction	Divisive factional in-group competition
MVC-cheat	Unethical business behavior; lying, trickery, cheating
MVC-slander	Calumny, slander, etc. for competitive advantage
MVC-bribe	Comparative self-enhancement or status through gift exchange or bribery
MVC-remove	Removal of an opponent even by murder
MVC-magic	Use of magic to gain unfair advantage over rival

D. Withdrawal or Victimization

MVD-yield	Admission of defeat or capitulation to adversary; refugee flight
MVD-quit	Withdrawal from competition
MVD-refuse	Refusal to compete
MVD-cheated	Victim of unfair competition

Cooperation (Together-MT)

A. Concerted Behavior

MTA-interest	Sharing common interest
MTA-task	Cooperation in a task for a goal
MTA-family	Family action for a goal, specific or not
MTA-trust	Trust in others regarding tasks
MTA-union	Organizational affiliation trade unions, etc.
MTA-contract	Contract relationship (organic solidarity)
MTA-group	Group maintenance or enhancement
MTA-allied	Intergroup cooperative emphasis (double score with other appropriate categories)
MTA-defense	Cooperation in group defense (double score with Harmony categories if necessary)
MTA-devote	Subordination or sacrifice for group goals
MTA-repay	Reciprocal behavior to facilitate common behavior (including gifts)

B. Inactive or Unresolved Cooperative Situations

MTB-worry	Worry about the success or failure of a cooperative effort
MTB-join	Doubt about desire to join group effort
MTB-differ	Disagreement not specified
MTB-means	Disagreement about the means used
MTB-ends	Disagreement about the goal
MTB-rapport	Difficulties in communicating
MTB-distrust	Mutual distrust within one's own group
MTB-secret	Secretive activity going on not defined
MTB-allied	Unresolved intergroup cooperative emphasis (double score with other appropriate categories)

C. Negative Group Activities

MTC-crime	Group criminal behavior
MTC-plot	Plotting or political conspiracy
MTC-ethic	Unethical behavior
MTC-selfish	Selfish interests stronger than group's goals
MTC-false	Hypocritical, untrustworthy behavior
MTC-failure	Failure to fulfill one's part in group activities
MTC-betray	Betrayal or deception of an ally or colleague
MTC-injury	Injury to others for group ends
MTC-allied	Intergroup cooperative emphasis seen negatively (double score with other appropriate categories)

D. Betrayed or Exploited

MTD-victim	Being the victim of a conspiracy
MTD-exploited	Being exploited by others
MTD-cheated	Being cheated by others
MTD-accord	Suffer lack of coordination between parts of a group
MTD-failure	A sense of failure of a group effort

Basic Interpersonal Concerns

Objects and Fate

Objects: O

Attention to Objects, Possessions, the Environment, or the Body

A. Positive Use, Acquisition, or Possession

OA-body	Positive about the body
OA-clothes	Attention to clothes
OA-own	Positive about acquisition or possession of an object
OA-wealth	General concern with possessions or wealth
OA-please	Pleasurable use of objects
OA-esthetic	The aesthetic pleasure derived from object
OA-reward	Object as reward
OA-gift	Gift of an object to others or gift exchange
OA-pet	Having a pet as an object
OA-job	Job providing a sense of financial security
OA-status	Concern with status or ethnic symbols
OA-pride	Pride, or attention to beauty or possessions
OA-guard	Protection of objects from harm; conservation
OA-create	Construction or creation of an object
OA-free	Indifference toward objects or possessions, viewed as a positive attribute
OA-collect	Collection of objects
OA-order	Arranging objects, order
OA-awe	Awe or reverence toward an object
OA-magic	Magical acquisition of an object
OA-spell	Magical use of an object
OA-symbol	Object or objects symbolizing the social self
OA-alive	Object as animate (pets)

B. Unresolved Concerns About Objects

OB-think	Thinking about an object
OB-want	Desire for an object
OB-torn	Ambivalence about possession of an object
OB-body	Preoccupied with body; attention to pregnancy
OB-care	Care of body, exercise
OB-clothes	Concern with clothes
OB-money	Concern with earning money, having a job
OB-compare	Concern with relative wealth or poverty
OB-baby	Concern with pregnancy or about the baby
OB-loss	Fear of losing something
OB-theft	Fear of theft
OB-break	Fear of breakage; fear of injury or destruction of object
OB-defect	Concern with bodily defect
OB-repair	Concern with repair of object
OB-jealous	Jealous fear of losing something to another
OB-envy	Fear of having an object envied
OB-dislike	Dislike or disinterest in an object
OB-worth	Indifference toward objects or possessions
OB-nature	Story switched to attention to physical surroundings or nature
OB-depict	Deflection into card description; description of physique, etc.

C. Negative Attitudes or Activities in Respect to Objects

OC-display	Excessive concern with display, exhibition; physical appearance or clothes
OC-clothes	Negative appearance of other's clothes
OC-body	Negative appearance of body
OC-greed	Excessive concern with money; greed; avarice
OC-wealth	Objects or impersonal ambition (wealth) given priority over a personal relationship (double score)
OC-revere	Excessive reverence for objects; idolatry
OC-hate	Hate of an object or objects
OC-discard	Abandonment or discarding of an object
OC-debase	Depreciation of an object
OC-destroy	Hate or destruction or injury of an object or aspects of our ecosystem
OC-indulge	Destructive use of the body (e.g., gluttony, or use of drugs)
OC-self-hurt	Bodily self-injury
OC-vandal	Destruction or injury of an object as a means of hurting a person or group (double score)
OC-rob	Robbery or theft
OC-control	Using objects to control people
OC-possess	Keeping an animal or person as a possession; psychic control or depersonalization of people into objects
OC-deceit	Acquisition by threat or deceit (double score)
OC-envy	Envy of the possession of others (double score)
OC-magic	Magical use of an object

D. Negative Incurred Experience in Respect to Material Objects

OD-body	Negative body image
OD-suffer	Body as object of suffering or negative depersonalized state experienced by body (including hunger)
OD-neglect	Neglectfulness toward an object or one's body as an object
OD-money	Without money
OD-loss	Loss of an object or possession
OD-robbed	Robbed
OD-broken	Suffering destruction of an object
OD-symbol	Symbolic destruction of an object
OD-taken	Being obsessed or possessed by objects
OD-used	Used as an object or kept as a possession (including slavery)
OD-psychic	Being possessed or used psychically

Kismet, Fate: K

Fortune, Fate, Circumstances, Inadvertencies, Accidents

A. Good Fortune

KA-luck	Good fortune, good luck
KA-social	Good social circumstances
KA-wealth	Good economic circumstances
KA-status	Inherited status or propitiously received status
KA-able	Inherited aptitude
KA-hardy	Hardiness, resiliency, courage, adaptive traits
KA-know	Chance acquisition of knowledge
KA-results	Inadvertent behavior leading to good consequences for self or another
KA-recovery	Recovery
KA-dream	Recovery from a bad dream; bad circumstance but a dream
KA-accept	Recognition or acceptance of one's fate
KA-magic	Magical intervention
KA-karma	Good fortune due to karmic inheritance from the past

B. Unresolved Karmic Conditions: Concerns About External Events and Superstitious Fears

KB-crisis	A social, environmental, or medical crisis
KB-chance	Chance situation as yet not resolved
KB-events	Concern or anxiety in reaction to external events
KB-status	Concern with relative status
KB-want	Concern or fear of economic want
KB-mishap-s	Accident or fear of accident to self
KB-mishap-o	Accident or fear of accident involving another
KB-illness	Fear of illness or aging
KB-survive	Worries about physical survival
KB-nature	Concern or fear of natural dangers, darkness
KB-hurt	Fear of behavior accidentally causing or allowing negative consequences
KB-magic	Superstitious fears (including the evil eye)
KB-hope	Hope in future good fortune
KB-karma	Uncertain fortune due to karmic inheritance from the past

C. Unfortunate Acts Releasing Negative Agents or Magical Consequences

KC-break	Accidental breaking of an object
KC-hurt-o	Accidentally producing negative circumstances for others
KC-hurt-s	Behavior accidentally causing fateful consequences to the self
KC-taboo	Inadvertent breaking of a proscription or taboo with negative consequences
KC-evil eye	Trait accidentally causing or allowing negative consequences for another (evil eye)
KC-karma	Ill fortune due to karmic inheritance from the past

D. Negatively Incurred Fate

KD-luck	Bad fortune, bad luck, or failure due to unspecified external events
KD-hopeless	Hopeless or irremediable situation
KD-news	Receiving bad news, unspecified
KD-loss	Loss of someone due to inadvertent circumstances
KD-poverty	Bad conditions or consequences of bad economic conditions
KD-deprive	Depriving, ungiving environment
KD-unjust	Unjust or unfair life conditions
KD-thwart	Frustrating life situation or occupation
KD-war	War
KD-animal	Suffers animal attack
KD-mishap	Accidents; inadvertent frustration of plans by unexpected presence or absence of another
KD-ac-die	Accidents leading to death; death in war
KD-illness	Illness
KD-ill-die	Illness leading to death
KD-death	Death (natural or unspecified)
KD-age	Old age, pity about age
KD-defect	Birth defect, handicap, crippling, inherited mental or personality defect
KD-mental	Insanity or neurosis, congenital mental damage
KD-resign	Resignation or succumbing to one's fate
KD-karma	Negative destiny due to karmic inheritance from the past

Appendix B

Japanese Cards

J-1: Boy with violin

J-2: Farm scene

J 6BM: Mother-Son

J-7BM: Mentor

J-8BM: Surgery

Japanese Cards

J-9: Family crisis

J-12F: Mother-in-law

J-13MF: Sex scene

J-18GF: Hand on neck

J-22: Family dispute

Kenyan and Filipino Cards

K-1: Boy with violin

P-1: Boy with violin

K-2: Farm scene

P-2: Farm scene

K-17BM: Man on rope

P-17BM: Man on rope

Additional Examples from Filipino Set

P-4: Man and woman

P-12: Two men

P-13B: Boy in doorway

P-19: In a store

About the Authors

George A. De Vos is both a psychologist and an anthropologist. He was trained at The University of Chicago and is now emeritus professor of anthropology at the University of California, Berkeley. His integrative social-sciences perspective is reflected in more than fifty years of field research in the United States, East Asia, and Western Europe. His twenty books and 180 articles have addressed topics such as delinquency, status inequality, ethnic identity, and the use of psychological tests in cross-cultural research.

Eric De Vos earned his doctorate in psychology at The University of Chicago's Committee on Human Development. He is currently professor of psychology at Saginaw Valley State University. His interests include thematic analysis of narratives as a cultural psychology methodology; the development of "self," self-regulation, and moral responsibility in cultural contexts; psychosocial factors in pregnancy outcome and infant development; Tibetan culture and Tibetan Buddhist psychology; and philosophical and psychological perspectives on consciousness and causality.